Think Critically

To students and teachers everywhere,
may developing critical thinking help you
stay forever young.

Think Critically

Third Edition

Peter Facione

Carol Ann Gittens

PEARSON

Boston   Columbus   Hoboken   Indianapolis   New York   San Francisco
Amsterdam   Cape Town   Dubai   London   Madrid   Milan   Munich   Paris   Montréal   Toronto
Delhi   Mexico City   São Paulo   Sydney   Hong Kong   Seoul   Singapore   Taipei   Tokyo

Vice-President/Director/Product Development: Dickson Musslewhite
Product Data and Operations: Craig Campanella
Senior Acquisitions Editor: Debbie Coniglio
Editorial Assistant: Veronica Grupico
Director of Product Marketing: Maggie Moylan
Team Lead Program Management: Amber Mackey
Program Manager: Nicole Conforti
Team Lead Project Management: Melissa Feimer
Project Manager: Richard DeLorenzo
Operations Specialist: Mary Ann Gloriande
Senior Art Director: Blair Brown
Cover Art Director: Maria Lange
Director of Digital Media: Sacha Laustsen
Digital Product Manager: Claudine Bellanton
Digital Media Project Manager: Amanda Smith
Full-Service Project Management and Composition: Lumina Datamatics, Inc./Melissa Sacco
Printer/Binder: Manufactured in the United States by LSC Communications
Cover Printer: Manufactured in the United States by LSC Communications

Library of Congress Cataloging-in-Publication Data

Facione, Peter A.
    Think critically / Peter Facione, Carol Ann Gittens. — Third edition.
        pages cm
    Includes index.
    ISBN 978-0-13-390966-1 — ISBN 0-13-390966-2
    1. Critical thinking—Textbooks.   I. Gittens, Carol Ann.   II. Title.
    B809.2.F33 2014
    160—dc23
                                                    2014040474

7   17

Student Edition:
ISBN 10:   0-13-390966-2
ISBN 13: 978-0-13-390966-1

Instructor's Review Copy:
ISBN 10:   0-13-391412-7
ISBN 13: 978-0-13-391412-2

A la Carte:
ISBN 10:   0-13-391413-5
ISBN 13: 978-0-13-391413-9

PEARSON

Brief Contents

Contents

Acknowledgments

Just as teaching and learning critical thinking is a collaboration, so is putting together all the words, images, exercises, video clips, page layouts, and digital materials for *THINK Critically*. This project could not have happened were it not for the wonderful participation, support, and guidance of a great many people.

The biggest thank you of all goes to my co-author, Carol Gittens, Associate Dean of the College of Arts and Sciences at Santa Clara University. Every chapter benefits from her hard work, her humane sensitivity, her insights, and her attention to the finer points of authoring for learning. Dr. Gittens authored the Instructor's Manual, a wonderful resource that offers strategies on teaching *for* thinking.

This third edition benefited from Benjamin Hamby's insightful, positive, and helpfully detailed review of the second edition and from many follow-up conversations during the drafting of this edition. You may download Dr. Hamby's review of *Think Critically* from **academia.edu**.

It was again a pleasure be working with the people at Pearson Education. Carol and I are grateful to everyone, including the publisher, the marketing director, the permissions and images people, the designers, the copyeditors, and many more. Our project directors, Melissa Sacco, Richard DeLorenzo, and Veronica Grupico deserve special thanks. We thank our senior editor, Debbie Coniglio, for her singular drive and vision, and for bringing a plethora of digital assets and resources to *Think Critically*.

Co-author Peter writes, "Good ideas come from thinking and discussing things with other people. Great ideas come when that other person happens to be brilliant and wise. The ideas in this book come from a lifetime of those kinds of experiences, but mostly from talking and thinking with the one brilliant and amazing person who has shared that lifetime with me. Through her words and ideas, she contributed inestimably to this book, to other books, to a myriad of projects both professional and domestic, and to every other part of my life. No 'thank you' can do justice to all that I owe to her. But let me say it anyway. Thank you, Noreen."

Co-author Carol Gittens writes, "When Pete asked me to join him as a main author of the second and subsequent editions, I jumped at the opportunity to add my voice to a text that is designed to nurture students' critical thinking skills and habits of minds, not only to promote success in the academic arena, but to promote success in life. I would like to express my gratitude to my long-time research colleague and professional mentor Peter Facione and by extension his wife and fellow colleague, Noreen, for extending our scholarly partnership to include this project. Even more importantly, I want to acknowledge and thank my wonderful husband William who supported me unconditionally even when my efforts on this book required more of my attention than he or our children would have wished to share."

Preface

In "Forever Young" songwriter Bob Dylan expressed our hopes for all who learn with and teach with *THINK Critically*. What more could we wish for one another than we all should seek to know the truth, walk in the light of well-trained reason, be courageous, have the intellectual integrity to stand strong, and that, no matter what our chronological age, that we should stay mentally forever young?

This book aims to strengthen critical thinking skills and nurture the courageous desire to seek truth by following reasons and evidence wherever they lead. We all may have different beliefs, values, perspectives, and experiences influencing our problem solving and decision making. But we share the human capacity to be reflective, analytical, open-minded, and systematic about thinking through our problems and choices, so that we can make the best judgments possible about what to believe or what to do. That process of well-reasoned, reflective judgment is critical thinking. Exercising our critical thinking helps our minds become stronger, healthier, and more youthful.

Our approach, proven successful by us and by others, is simple, practical, and focused. To strengthen critical thinking skills, we have to use them. To build positive critical thinking habits of mind, we have to see critical thinking as the optimal approach for solving real-world problems and making important decisions. Every chapter of this book builds critical thinking skills and engages critical thinking habits of mind in every way possible. Why? Because we believe with every fiber of our beings that critical thinking is all about real life, and so the very best way to build strong critical thinking is to use engaging material from the widest possible range of real-life situations.

"Knowing about" is not the same as "using." It is more important that a person *learn how to use* critical thinking to make the best judgments possible than that the person memorize gobs of technical vocabulary and theory about critical thinking. Yes, learning about critical thinking certainly can expedite things. But engaging in critical thinking is the payoff. That is why there are hundreds of exercises of many different kinds woven into the written text and each chapter's digital learning support assets. There is no substitute for learning by doing. So, here's a plan:

Chapters 1 and 2 explain what critical thinking is, why it is so vitally important to all of us, and how critical thinking connects to our academic studies and to our personal, professional, and civic lives. Chapter 3 builds immediately on the theme of the practical value of critical thinking by describing the IDEAS approach to problem solving and then applying that approach to the kinds of problems typically encountered by college students of all ages.

Chapters 4–9 are building block chapters, each addressing one or another of the core critical thinking skills in the context of real-world applications. Chapters 4 and 5 focus on the skills of interpretation and analysis; when we can understand what people are saying, we can articulate the reasons being advanced on behalf of a particular claim or choice. Without these vital critical thinking skills we wander in a cloud of confusion, not really knowing what things might mean or why people, including ourselves, think what they think. Chapters 6, 7, 8, and 9 focus on the skill of evaluation as applied to the truthfulness of claims, the trustworthiness of so-called experts, and the quality of arguments.

Chapters 10 and 11 connect critical thinking to contemporary understandings of human decision making. Illustrating the risks and the benefits of our heuristically driven snap judgments and releasing ourselves from the grip that our past decisions can have on our current thinking are the two purposes of Chapter 10. Chapter 11, by contrast, provides multiple strategies for approaching decision making reflectively. Together these two chapters emphasize the essential critical thinking skills of self-monitoring and self-correction, along with the habits foresight, open-mindedness, and truth seeking

The three most important chapters of this book are 12, 13, and 14. Why? Because comparative reasoning, ideological reasoning, and empirical reasoning are the three most widely used methods human beings have for supplying reasons on behalf of their beliefs and ideas. With real-world examples, some that are disturbing in fact, these three chapters focus on the core critical thinking skills of inference and explanation, because drawing conclusions and explaining one's reasons, even to one's self, in real life are products of our comparative, ideological, and empirical reasoning.

Chapters 15 through 19 are joyful explorations of the diverse applications of critical thinking—in writing, in ethical decision making, in logic, in the social sciences, and in the natural sciences. Thinking like professionals, instead of simply studying about them or trying to memorize what they may have said, is way more fun, and much more effective learning.

We authors offer all who encounter *THINK Critically* this Dylanesque blessing: That you should have a strong foundation, even in the shifting winds of change, that joy should fill your heart and learning guide your life, and, of course, that by using your mind to reflect on what to believe and what to do, that you should make good decisions and stay forever young.

Instructor Resources

Additional resources found in the Instructor Resource Center include the following:

- Critical Thinking in the Social Sciences
- Critical Thinking in the Natural Sciences
- PowerPoint Presentations
- Test Bank
- Chapter Opener Videos
- Chapter Review Videos
- Writing Space Essay Prompts
- Simulations
- Explorer Activities

What's New to This Edition

- Newly developed tools—videos, argument maps, simulations, data explorations, truth tables, and graphics—that are woven with the core narrative
- Both new and updated examples and exercises connect critical thinking to substantive, real-world concerns

- Emphasis on critical thinking across the curriculum and on problem solving for student success
- New chapters on Ethical Decision Making and on Declarative Logic
- Expanded individual and group writing opportunities, more emphasis on student diversity, and updated treatment of argument, deduction, and induction
- STEM supplement chapter on critical thinking in the natural and social sciences

REVEL™

Educational technology designed for the way today's students read, think, and learn

When students are engaged deeply, they learn more effectively and perform better in their courses. This simple fact inspired the creation of REVEL: an immersive learning experience designed for the way today's students read, think, and learn. Built in collaboration with educators and students nationwide, REVEL is the newest, fully digital way to deliver respected Pearson content.

REVEL enlivens course content with media interactives and assessments—integrated directly within the authors' narrative—that provide opportunities for students to read about and practice course material in tandem. This immersive educational technology boosts student engagement, which leads to better understanding of concepts and improved performance throughout the course.

Learn more about REVEL: www.pearsonhighered.com/REVEL

About the Authors

Peter A. Facione, PhD, has dedicated himself to helping people build their critical thinking to become better problem solvers and decisions makers. He does this work not only to help individuals and groups achieve their own goals, but also for the sake of our freedom and democracy. Facione draws on experi-  ence as a teacher, consultant, business entrepreneur, university dean, grandfather, husband, musician, and sports enthusiast. Now he is taking his message about the importance of critical thinking directly to students through *THINK Critically*.

"I've paid very close attention to the way people make decisions since I was 13 years old," says Facione. "Some people were good at solving problems and making decisions; others were not. I have always felt driven to figure out how to tell which were which." He says that this led him as an undergraduate and later as a professor to study psychology, philosophy, logic, statistics, and information systems as he searched for how our beliefs, values, thinking skills, and habits of mind connect with the decisions we make, particularly in contexts of risk and uncertainty.

A native Midwesterner, Facione earned his PhD in Philosophy from Michigan State University and his BA in Philosophy from Sacred Heart College in Detroit. He says, "Critical thinking has helped me be a better parent, citizen, leader, consultant, teacher, writer, coach, husband, and friend. It even helps a little when playing point guard!" In academia, Facione served as provost of Loyola University–Chicago, dean of the College of Arts and Sciences at Santa Clara University, and dean of the School of Human Development and Community Service at California State University–Fullerton. "As a dean and provost, I could easily see that critical thinking was alive and well in every professional field and academic discipline."

Facione spearheaded the international study to define critical thinking, sponsored by the American Philosophical Association. His research formed the basis for numerous government policy studies about critical thinking in the workplace, including research sponsored by the U.S. Department of Education. Published by Insight Assessment, his tools for assessing reasoning are used around the world in educational, business, legal, military, and health sciences. Today, Peter operates his own business, *Measured Reasons*. He is senior level consultant, speaker, writer, workshop presenter. His work focuses on strategic planning and leadership decision making, in addition to teaching and assessing critical thinking. With his wife, who is also his closest research colleague and co-author of many books and assessment tools, he now lives in sunny Los Angeles, which he says, "suits [him] just fine." You can reach him at **pfacione@measuredreasons.com**.

Carol Ann Gittens, PhD, is an Associate Dean in the College of Arts & Sciences at Santa Clara University (SCU). She is an associate professor with tenure in the Liberal Studies Program and directs SCU's under-  graduate pre-teaching advising program and the interdisciplinary minor in urban education designed for students interested in pursuing careers in PreK-12 education.

Gittens was the founding Director of Santa Clara University's Office of Assessment from 2007 to 2012. As assessment director, she performed key activities related to institutional re-accreditation, educated academic and cocurricular programs in the assessment of student learning, and designed and oversaw an innovative multiyear, rubric-based assessment plan for a new core curriculum. She is an educational assessment mentor and accreditation evaluator for the Western Association of Schools and Colleges (WASC) as well as Board of Institutional Reviewers member of the California Commission on Teacher Credentialing (CTC), and a senior research associate with Insight Assessment, LLC.

The central focus of Gittens' research is on the interface of critical thinking, motivation, mathematical reasoning, and academic achievement of adolescents and young adults from diverse cultural and ethnic backgrounds. Dr. Gittens is an author or co-author of numerous articles and assessment tools focusing on critical thinking skills, numeracy, and dispositions in children and adults. As of this writing, her forthcoming paper is "Assessing Numeracy in the Upper Elementary and Middle School Years."

Gittens' consulting activities include working with college faculty, staff and administrators, PreK-12 educators, as well as business executives, managers, and employees. Dr. Gittens' areas of expertise include assessment of institutional effectiveness and student learning outcomes, institutional and professional accreditation planning, translating strategic vision into measureable objectives, designing sustainable assessment systems at all levels of the institution, critical thinking pedagogy and assessment, integrating critical thinking and information literacy across the curriculum and in cocurricular programs, as well as statistics and assessment design for individuals and institutions.

Gittens earned her PhD in Social and Personality Psychology from the University of California at Riverside. She received her BA in Psychology and Women's Studies from the University of California at Davis. Prior to her appointment at Santa Clara University she taught at California State University, San Bernardino and at Mills College in Oakland, California. Gittens and her husband live in California's Silicon Valley with their teenaged daughter and son, and their 4-year-old daughter. She is an active parent volunteer in her children's school, and is involved with K-12 schools in the local community, offering teacher training workshops on nurturing and assessing students' critical thinking.

Chapter 1
The Power of Critical Thinking

When students study together, both teach and both learn.

WHY is critical thinking important?

WHAT does "critical thinking" mean?

HOW can we evaluate our critical thinking?

 ## Learning Outcomes

1.1 Explain why critical thinking is important in a world filled with risk and uncertainty by supplying reasons and examples that relate to you own life, to the well-being of your community, and to the preservation of a free and open society.

1.2 Explain why a strong critical thinker's healthy sense of skepticism is not the same as negativity and cynicism. From your own experience supply examples showing the unfortunate results of a failure of critical thinking as here defined.

1.3 Using the "Holistic Critical Thinking Scoring Rubric" as your tool for evaluation, evaluate the quality of the critical thinking evident in samples of written material and explain which elements in the written material led you evaluate it as you did.

Walking down 10th Street in Hermosa Beach the other day, I saw a helmetless young man skillfully slalom his skateboard downhill toward the beach. Ignoring the stop sign at Hermosa Boulevard, he flashed across all four lanes of traffic and coasted on down the hill. My immediate reaction was "Whew! Lucky that that guy wasn't killed!" because I had often seen cars on Hermosa roll through that particular stop sign. Whatever was occupying his attention, the skateboarder did not appear to have self-preservation on his mind that day!

Whether he reflected on it or not, the skater *decided* to run the stop sign. Similarly, we all make decisions all the time, with some of our choices made more thoughtfully than others. We've all underestimated obstacles, overlooked reasonable options, and failed to anticipate likely consequences. Life will continue to present us with our full share of problems, and when we err, we often think about the better decisions we could have made if we'd given it a little more thought.

Critical thinking is the process of reasoned judgment. That is, judgment that is both purposeful and reflective. Because this book is about that process, it is about *how to go about deciding* what to believe or what to do. This is not a book about what we should believe or do. The purpose of the book is to assist you in strengthening your own critical thinking skills and habits of mind so you solve problems and make decisions more thoughtfully for yourself.

1.1 Risk and Uncertainty Abound

We might not skateboard through an intersection, but none of us can escape life's risks and uncertainties. Uncertainties apply to potentially good things, too. For example, each of us might be uncertain when choosing a major, taking a part-time job, making a new friend, or responding to a disaster stricken nation's call for volunteers. You never know what new friendships you will make, what new skills you will acquire, what new opportunities might emerge for you, how your efforts will benefit other people, or how much satisfaction you may feel. Whatever the choice being contemplated or the problem being addressed, to maximize our chances for welcome outcomes and to minimize our chances for undesirable outcomes, we need to employ purposeful, reflective judgment. Sure, winning is great, but it's just not a good idea to play poker unless we can afford to lose. We need to think ahead, to plan, and to problem solve. This means we need **critical thinking**.

Often, what seems like an exclusively personal decision ends up having consequences that go far beyond just ourselves. Everyone knows that driving while wasted can lead

"Dude! What are you thinking?"

to tragic results for passengers, other drivers and pedestrians. That one is obvious. And DUI is illegal. But even choices that seem to be perfectly innocent can have unexpected impacts on other people. Think, for example, about deciding to go back to college as an adult. You try to anticipate what it will cost, how much time it will take, whether you can manage being a college student along with all the other responsibilities in your life. Suppose you consider the risks and the uncertainties, and the pros and cons as best you can anticipate them, and end up deciding to take on all those challenges. In due time you graduate. With your new qualifications you get offered a better job, one that requires moving to a new neighborhood or new city. That means living further from your old friends. But, it also means a new home, better pay, and new friends. You think, although I tried to anticipate all the consequences, I really could not have known all the ways my decision would affect all the people I will be leaving, and all the people I will meet.

Critical Thinking and a Free Society

We are fortunate in a society that values self-reliance, economic competition, and individual initiative. The stronger our critical thinking skills and habits of mind, the greater our prospects for success, whatever the endeavor. Given the pace of innovation and the fierceness of the competition, and the unpredictability of world events, today more than at any time in the past 70 years businesses are concerned to find workers who can solve problems, make good decisions, learn new things, and adapt to an uncertain future. To succeed in a global high-tech world, a corporation will have to hire workers with strong critical thinking and cultivate a corporate culture that fosters

JOURNAL

How Would You Describe Your CT Skills?

Employers consistently report that they prioritize skills in critical thinking and communication when evaluating job applicants. Employers want to hire people who can solve customers' problems and make good business decisions. And the employers want people who represent the company well and communicate clearly, understand directions, and carry out assignments.

How would you describe to a prospective employer your critical thinking skills and communication skills? Use examples.

strong critical thinking.[1] In a 2013 survey of 318 employers 93% agreed that a job candidate's "demonstrated capacity to think critically, communicate clearly, and solve complex problems is more important than their undergraduate major."[2]

But if information is power, then controlling the flow of information is wielding power. Any government, any agency, any group of whatever kind that can withhold information or distort it to fit official orthodoxy is in a much better position to suppress dissenters and maintain its position of control. As we have seen recently in Syria, Egypt, Yemen, Libya, China, the Central African Republic, North Korea, Lebanon, Iraq, Ukraine, Thailand, Kenya, Afghanistan, and elsewhere, cutting off Internet access, expelling foreign journalists, disabling cell phone relays, and attempting in every way to block messages on social media have become standard tactics for suppressing protests and maintaining power. All done to curtail the free flow of accurate information.

We who live in the United States are also fortunate because of the high value we place on freedom—including the freedom to think for ourselves. In a free society education is about learning how to think for yourself, learning how to seek the information you need, learning how to correct mistaken assumptions, how to evaluate the claims people make, how to reason well, and how to detect and resist fallacious reasoning. In a free society the power of government is used to protect the right to free and open inquiry, the right to share what we learn, and the right to collaborate with others to make better decisions and to learn more about the world. Watch "Why Critical Thinking." Find this short video and more by searching "Peter Facione" on YouTube.

A closed society does not permit the freedom to think, it fears and it suppresses learning. A closed society, whether it is a government, a corporation, a religion or whatever, stifles independent critical thinkers, punishes those who do not adhere to the party line, denies access to full and accurate information, and buries scientific findings and policy recommendations that run counter to interests of those in power. The worst of these closed societies equate education with memorized orthodoxy, label dissenters as traitors, and, if need be, use ridicule, bullying, disinformation, deceit, character assassination, and in the worst cases physical assassination—whatever it takes, including creating martyrs for the cause, faking enemy threats, lying to the media, destroying document and so on—to achieve its goals.[3]

Positive Examples of Critical Thinking

- A person trying to interpret an angry friend's needs, expressed through a rush of emotion and snide comments, to give that friend some help and support

- A manager trying to be as objective as possible when settling a dispute by summarizing the alternatives, with fairness to all sides to a disagreement

- A team of scientists working with great precision through a complex experiment in an effort to gather and analyze data

- A creative writer organizing ideas for the plot of a story and attending to the complex motivations and personalities of the fictional characters

- A person running a small business trying to anticipate the possible economic and human consequences of various ways to increase sales or reduce costs

- A master sergeant and a captain working out the tactical plans for a dangerous military mission.

- A soccer coach working during halftime on new tactics for attacking the weaknesses of the other team when the match resumes

- A student confidently and correctly explaining exactly to his or her peers the methodology used to reach a particular conclusion, or why and how a certain methodology or standard of proof was applied

- An educator using clever questioning to guide a student to new insights

- Police detectives, crime scene analysts, lawyers, judges, and juries systematically investigating, interrogating, examining, and evaluating the evidence as they seek justice

- A policy analyst reviewing alternative drafts of product safety legislation while determining how to frame the law to benefit the most people at the least cost

- An applicant preparing for a job interview thinking about how to explain his or her particular skills and experiences in a way that will be relevant and of value to the prospective employer

- Parents anticipating the costs of sending their young child to college, analyzing the family's projected income, and budgeting projected household expenses in an effort to put aside some money for that child's future education

Films like *The Insider, Promised Land, Cry Freedom, Syriana, Wag the Dog, Body of Lies, Seeds of Death,* and *The Panama Deception* give us insights into how it is possible for corporate and government greed, orthodoxy, and lust for power to crush freedom, distort the truth, and destroy lives. Some films in this genre are well researched, fair, and accurate; others are fictional exaggerations or fabrications. Either way, they all illustrate the dire consequences of passivity, apathy, and indifference toward matters of public policy. Given the possibilities, strong critical thinking suggests vigilant readiness to ask tough questions about what is being done in our name.

> "Our whole constitutional heritage rebels at the thought of giving government the power to control men's minds."
>
> Thurgood Marshall, Former U.S. Supreme Court Justice[4]

Why is American higher education internationally admired and yet feared? One reason is that our colleges have the potential to teach critical thinking. The upside is great progress in learning, wealth and culture, and hence huge benefits for society. Problem solvers using critical thinking have achieved massive breakthroughs in science, technology, engineering, commerce, and the arts. But, at the same time, leaders around the world know that when the people are given a good education and begin thinking for themselves, things get harder for would-be tyrants. People who are thinking for themselves are more apt to disagree, policy issues become more complicated to resolve, public discourse more confusing, the "old ways" are questioned, and decision making takes more time.

Strong critical thinking demands a healthy skepticism wherever entrenched organizational power is concerned. Strong critical thinkers know that defending the freedom to think demands vigilance. Passivity and indifference toward thinking and learning weaken not only our bodies but our minds as well. None of us want to wake up one fine day groggy, cross-eyed, and hung over from Fantasy Football, nonstop Grand Theft Auto, double cheese and bacon burgers, vacuous Hollywood gossip, online hoarding sprees, and stale beer, only to discover that while we were otherwise occupied our rights and freedoms were quietly, yet systematically, stripped away. We believe that one way to protect our cherished and hard-won freedoms is by using our critical thinking to assure open scientific inquiry, access to complete and accurate information, and the right to ask challenging questions, and follow the reasons and the evidence wherever they may lead.

But we do not need to rely only on films and novels to illustrate our point. Recent history shows what happens when people are not vigilant defenders of open, objective, and independent inquiry. We saw the results to a greater or lesser extent in Hitler's Germany, Stalin's Russia, Mao Tse Tung's China, and, sadly, in the twenty-first century.

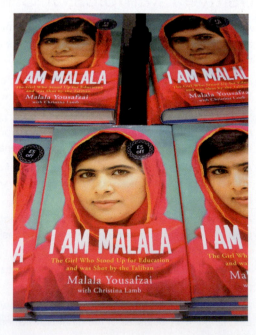

What would you have done if religious extremists attacked you or your daughter for seeking an education?

See, for example, the autobiography *And Then They Came for Me*, by Maziar Bahari, 2011, and then Google the phrase "and then they came for me" for several even more recent examples of similar incidents around the world. Or consider how her co-religionists punished young Malala Yousafzai, a female, just for wanting the freedom to learn. In 2014 the systematic suppression of the freedom to learn, critical thinking, and science was the purpose of school curriculum changes imposed under threat of physical punishment by extremists in territories controlled by the group known as the "Islamic State."[5] Where critical thinking, science, and open inquiry by men or by women are crimies, a society cannot call itself "free."

If he were alive today, American folk song legend, Pete Seeger, might sing, "Where have all the waters gone?"

The One and the Many

Individual decisions can seem isolated and yet when they accumulate, they can have a far-reaching impact. For instance, in China the one-child policy has been in force for about 30 years. Culturally, there has always been a strong preference for male children; and if families could only have one child, most wanted a boy. In household after household, family after family made the choice to do whatever seemed necessary, including infanticide, to ensure a male heir. The collective impact of those millions of individual decisions now burdens that nation. In some villages, the ratio of unmarried men to unmarried women is 20 to 1. Today brides fetch payments as high as five years of family income.[6] Those parents who decided to raise their first-born daughters sure look smart now.

Around seven billion members of our species, give or take, share a planet in which economic, cultural, political, and environmental forces are so interconnected that the decisions of a few can impact the lives of many. Short-sighted and self-interested decisions made by corporate executives, bankers, stock traders, borrowers, and government regulatory agencies plunged the world into a global economic depression, which has cost trillions of dollars, devastated honest and well-run companies, bankrupted pension plans, destroyed families, and put tens of millions of people out of work. What were the decision makers thinking? What blinded all of us to the foreseeable consequences of our choices? Did we think that there wouldn't be adverse consequences if we all ran our credit card and mortgage debts to levels that were beyond our capacity to repay those debts? For some insights into the poor critical thinking that contributed to this global economic meltdown watch the HBO film *Too Big to Fail*.

The historical evidence suggests that civilizations rise and fall, that economies flourish and flounder, that the arts are encouraged and suppressed, that advances in learning are made and then forgotten. As a species we have very few advantages, other than our oversized brain and the critical thinking it can generate. We would be unwise not to use what little we have. Often catastrophic events, like the plagues that decimated Europe in the fifth and twelfth centuries, are beyond the ability of the science of the time to predict or to control. The same goes for the prolonged drought that triggered the dust bowl of the 1930s, the climate-changing drought suspected of driving the Anasazi out of North American Southwest.[7] But what about droughts that we can predict? What about the water crisis we have made for ourselves today in the North American Southwest? We know that we foolishly over-use our water resources, waste water on silly things like trying to have green lawns in desert lands. We know that unless something changes, the Columbia River and the Sierra Nevada watershed cannot support the tens of millions of people, and the homes, farms, businesses, fisheries, forests, wildlife, pets, resorts, fountains, golf courses, schools, hospitals, and fire departments. Strong critical thinking tells us that we need to reform water policy and change our ways of using that essential resource. But change is so slow in coming. We cannot kick the empty water can any further down the dusty road. What are we thinking?

> "Very few really seek knowledge in this world. Mortal or immortal, few really ask. On the contrary, they try to wring from the unknown the answers they have already shaped in their own minds—justification, explanations, forms of consolation without which they can't go on. To really ask is to open the door to the whirlwind. The answer may annihilate the question and the questioner."
>
> Anne Rice's character, the vampire Marius in *The Vampire Lestat*.[8]

Why farms vs. cities if everyone knows Water = Jobs & Food & Survival?

1.2 What Do We Mean by "Critical Thinking"?

At this point you might be saying, "OK, I get it. Critical thinking is important. But what *is* critical thinking, exactly?" To answer that question precisely, an international group of 46 recognized experts in critical thinking research collaborated. The men and women in this group were drawn from many different academic disciplines, including philosophy, psychology, economics, computer science, education, physics, and zoology.

Expert Consensus Conceptualization

For more than a year and a half, from February 1988 through September 1989, the group engaged in a consensus-oriented research process developed by the Rand Corporation and known as the "Delphi" method.[9] The challenge put to the experts was to come up with a working consensus about the meaning of "critical thinking," which could serve instructional and assessment purposes from K–12 through graduate school, and across the full range of academic disciplines and professional fields. They also asked themselves questions that relate to Chapter 2, namely,: "What are the core critical thinking skills and subskills? How can we strengthen those skills in students? Who are the best critical thinkers we know, and what habits of mind do they have that lead us to consider them the best?"

Long story short, the expert consensus defined "*critical thinking*" as "*the process of purposeful, self-regulatory judgment.*"[10] The purpose is straightforward: to form a well-reasoned and fair-minded judgment regarding what to believe or what to do. The "self-regulatory" part refers

to our capacity to reflect on our own thinking process. We can monitor our own thinking, spot mistakes, and make needed corrections to our own problem solving and decision making.[11]

Strong critical thinking—making well-reasoned judgments about what to believe and what to do—is essential to consistently successful decision making. For many years we authors have consulted with various branches of the U.S. military, including Special Ops, with senior business executives and mid-level managers, and with educators, policy makers, health care professionals, scientists, jurists, and engineers. Time and again we learn that strong critical thinking can contribute to achieving goals and that poor critical thinking contributes to mission failure. Strong critical thinking is essential wherever the quality of one's decisions and the accuracy of one's beliefs make a difference.

Critical thinking is not the *only* vital element, don't get us wrong. Knowledge, dedication, training, and ethical courage also factor into the formula for success. We often learn more from our failures than from our successes; when we examine unsuccessful operations we often find that individuals or groups have failed, somewhere along the line, to make well-reasoned judgments. Failures of critical thinking can result in some truly unfortunate outcomes, as the examples in the figure indicate. Can you think of any such instances in your own experience?

Failures of critical thinking contribute to...

patient deaths / lost revenue / ineffective law enforcement / job loss / gullible voters / garbled communications / imprisonment /combat casualties / upside down mortgages / vehicular homicide / bad decisions / unplanned pregnancies / financial mismanagement / heart disease / family violence / repeated suicide attempts / divorce / drug addiction / academic failure / ... / ... /

WHAT WERE WE THINKING?

Failures of critical thinking often contribute to some of the saddest and most unfortunate accidents. In 2009, for example, 288 people died in the crash of an Air France jetliner. Investigators who examined the crash and its causes indicated that the pilots might have had enough time to prevent the disaster had they realized that the plane was stalling, instead of climbing to a safe altitude. But they appear to have misinterpreted the warning signals and wrongly analyzed their problem, which led them to make the wrong inferences about what they should do.[12] Asiana Air Flight 214 crash-landed at SFO in 2013 because of the decision to permit an inexperienced pilot to practice landing a jetliner full of passengers.[13]

Occasionally we see in the news that some poor individual has had a tragic lapse in good judgment. Like the three young people who stepped passed the guard rails to take pictures at Yosemite Park's Vernal Falls. Other park visitors called to them, urging them to get back to safety, but they did not. Then suddenly one fell, the other two tried to help, and all three were swept over the falls to their deaths.[14] Sad as it was, we have to ask ourselves, what were they thinking? If they had thoughtfully considered the risks and benefits, we doubt that they would have made the tragic decision to ignore the posted warnings.

Realizing that strong critical thinking often results in positive outcomes, but failures of critical thinking could lead to major problems, the experts who were asked to define critical thinking determined that it was best to focus on the *process of judgment*. What they wanted to capture was that strong critical thinking was reflective, well-reasoned, and focused on a specific purpose, such as what to do or what to believe. "Should we ignore the posted warnings?"

Given the expert consensus definition of critical thinking as purposeful reflective judgment, one of the first things the experts realized was that critical thinking was a "pervasive human phenomenon." Critical thinking is occurring whenever an individual or a group of people makes a reasoned and reflective judgment about what to believe or what to do. They also realized that strong critical thinking was thoughtful and informed, not impulsive nor knee-jerk reactive.

How important did the experts think critical thinking was? They put their answer to that question this way: "Critical thinking is essential as a tool of inquiry. As such, critical thinking is a liberating force in education and a powerful resource in one's personal and civic life. While not synonymous with good thinking, critical thinking is a pervasive and self-rectifying human phenomenon."

So long as people have problems to solve and decisions to make, so long as they have things to learn and issues to resolve, there will be ample opportunities to use our critical thinking skills and habits of mind.

"Critical Thinking" Does Not Mean "Negative Thinking"

Critical thinking is not about bashing what people believe just to show how clever we are. Nor is critical thinking about using our skills to defend beliefs that we know are untrue or decisions we know are poor. Critical thinking is skeptical without being cynical. It is open-minded without being wishy-washy. It is analytical without being nitpicky. Critical thinking can be decisive without being stubborn, evaluative without being judgmental, and forceful without being opinionated.

Critical thinking skills enable us to seek truth (small "t") with intellectual energy and with integrity. Respect for one another and civil discourse goes hand in hand with strong critical thinking. We can thoughtfully and fair-mindedly reject an idea without ridiculing or embarrassing the person who proposed it. And we can accept an idea from any source so long as the idea is well-supported with good reasons and solid evidence. The results of applying the critical thinking process speak for themselves by virtue of the quality of the analyses, inferences, and explanations involved. So there is no reason, and very frequently no advantage either, in being aggressive, strident or hostile in how one presents those results.

Strong critical thinking can be independent, it can lead us to diverge from the norm, and it can impel us to challenge cherished beliefs. And, as a result, applying critical thinking skills to a question or issue can be disquieting if not disturbing to ourselves and others. Critical thinking can also be insightful, collaborative, and constructive. And, as in the case of good

"I saw the man's eyes when he went over the falls. That was devastating," says witness.

THINKING CRITICALLY

Risk and Respect

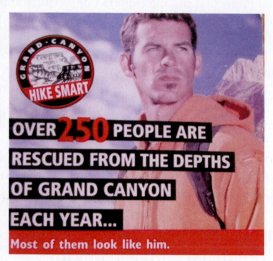

Why do so many vacationers and sightseers foolishly risk their lives each year that our government must post warnings against even the most obvious dangers?

1. According to the National Park Service, over 250 people need to be rescued each year after they have tried to hike down into the Grand Canyon to reach the Colorado River and back up to the rim all in one day. More interestingly, these people tend to be young, healthy males. Why might this be? Is there something the research literature can tell us about the decision making of young healthy males that leads them, more than any other demographic, to take the kinds of risks that result in their needing to be rescued?

2. Group Discussion: Not all risks are unreasonable. Parents worry all of the time about keeping their children safe, but what is the role of risk taking in childhood and adolescence? Are their "healthy risks" parents should encourage timid children to take? Should children be encouraged to climb trees? Rather than taking one side or the other, as in a debate, try instead to identify and elaborate on the best reasons for both sides of that question. A web search will reveal some interesting posts relating to risk and parenting.

3. Group Discussion: Given our advice about being respectful rather than hostile when applying critical thinking, does that mean that some topics are off limits? Is it even possible to have a respectful reasoned, evidence-based, and fair-minded analysis and evaluation of the truth, our moral, religious, or political opinions? What if people take offense because something they were raised to believe is called into question by seriously applying critical thinking skills to that idea?

science, critical thinking brings deeper and richer understandings. And too, as in the case of good leadership, critical thinking results in more successful outcomes. The only real mistake is to go forward with beliefs or choices that we know, because of strong critical thinking, are false or foolish.

Improvement Takes Practice

Think for a moment about learning to play a musical instrument or learning to play a sport. In both, improvement comes from practicing the requisite skills and strengthening our resolve to keep at it until we begin to see improvements. As we experience success at the skills part, enjoyment increases, and our disposition to keep applying ourselves grows. And, having an ever more positive attitude about striving to improve, we tend to enjoy more success as we seek to refine our skills. Each aspect feeds the other. To be a success the player must become not only able but willing, not just skillful but disposed to use those skills.

We learn to play a musical instrument so we can enjoy making music. We learn a sport to enjoy playing the game. We work on our skills and mental dispositions not for their own sake, but for the sake of making music or playing the game. This is true with critical thinking, too. The defining purpose of critical thinking is to make reflective judgments about what to believe or what to do. We will work on both the skill part and the dispositional part as we move through this book Our purpose as authors is to enable you to become more effective in using critical thinking when you are deciding what to do or what to believe.

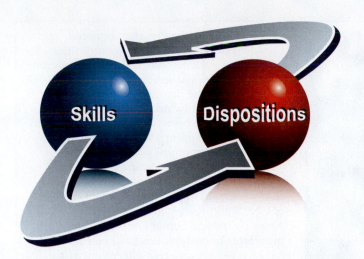

Critical Thinking - Willing and Able

There is convincing scientific evidence that students can improve their critical thinking.[15] As with any skills based activity, the key is guided practice. To guide you we loaded this book with exercises, examples, explanations, and topics to really think about. Each represents an opportunity. And, yes, here and there we have included topics/and questions some may find unsettling, maybe even jarring. Why? Because thinking about difficult topics and troubling questions often makes us stronger critical thinkers. Just like with sports or music, those who skip practice should not expect to perform at their best when it really matters. Those who are so closed-minded that they cannot entertain hypotheticals that diverge from their own opinions will find progress in critical thinking difficult. But the rest of us can expect many interesting and enjoyable opportunities to exercise each of our critical thinking skills and to strengthen our critical thinking habits of mind.

1.3 Evaluating Critical Thinking

Even when we are first learning a musical instrument or a sport, we can tell that some of our peers are better at the instrument or the sport than others. We all make progress, and soon we are all doing much better than when we first started. We do not have to be experts to begin to see qualitative differences and to make reasonable evaluations. This, too, is true of critical thinking. There are some readily available ways to begin to make reasonable judgments concerning stronger or weaker uses of critical thinking. The following example illustrates some of these methods.

THE STUDENTS' ASSIGNMENT—KENNEDY ACT

Imagine a professor has assigned a group of four students to comment on the Edward M. Kennedy Serve America Act, signed into law on April 21, 2009. The group has access to the information about the bill at the website for the Corporation for National & Community Service. The bill:

- Dramatically increases intensive service opportunities by setting AmeriCorps on a path from 75,000 positions annually to 250,000 by 2017, and focusing that service on education, health, clean energy, veterans, economic opportunity, and other national priorities.

- Enables millions of working Americans to serve by establishing a nationwide Call to Service Campaign and observing September 11 as the National Day of Service and Remembrance.

- Improves service options for experienced Americans by expanding age and income eligibility for Foster Grandparents and Senior Companions, authorizing a Silver Scholars program, under which individuals 55 and older who perform 350 hours of service receive a $1,000 education award, which they can transfer award to a child or grandchild.

- Provides for a summer program for students from sixth through twelfth grade to earn a $500 education award for helping in their neighborhoods.

- Authorizes a Civic Health Assessment comprised of indicators relating to volunteering, voting, charitable giving, and interest in public service to evaluate and compare the civic health of communities.

For more information search "**americorps.gov**" "**nationalservice.gov**" and "**serve.gov**".

THE STUDENTS' STATEMENTS—KENNEDY ACT

STUDENT #1: "My take on it is that this bill requires national service. It's like a churchy service sorta thing. But, u know, like run by the government and all. We all have to sign up and do our bit before we can go to college. That's great. Think about it, how could anyone b against this legislation? I mean, unless they r either lazy or selfish. What excuse could a person possibly have not to serve r country? The president is right, we need to bring back the draft so that r Army has enough soldiers, and we need to fix Wall Street and Social Security and immigration. I don't want to pay into a system all my working life only to find out that there's no money left when I get my chance to retire."

At today's event, the President honored President George H.W. Bush's contributions to service and volunteerism, including his signing of the 1990 national service legislation and his creation of the Points of Light movement and its signature award. The Daily Point of Light Award has been presented 5,000 times to individuals and groups who find innovative ways to meet community needs.

"Volunteer service is and always has been a fundamental part of the American character," said Wendy Spencer, CEO of CNCS, the agency that administers AmeriCorps and Senior Corps. For decades, presidents of both parties have embraced national service as a cost-effective way to tap the ingenuity and can-do spirit of the American people to get things done.

Source: "President Obama Expands National Service Opportunities for Americans," National Service news release, July 15, 2013.

STUDENT #2: "Well I think this bill is a stupid idea. Who's going to agree to work for a lousy $12,000 a year? That's nuts. I can earn more working at Target or by enlisting in the Navy. This legislation is just more foolish liberal nonsense that takes our nation one step closer to socialism. Socialism is when the government tries to control too many things. And now the president is trying to control volunteer service. Maybe you want to build houses for poor people or clean up after hurricanes, but I don't see how any of that is going to help me pass physics or get me a better job after college."

STUDENT #3: "I think there are problems with the legislation, too. But you're wrong about people not wanting to volunteer. The number of hits on the AmeriCorps Web site keeps going up and up each month. Retired people, students, and people who just want to make a difference go there and to Serve.gov to see what opportunities might exist near where they live. On the other hand, I do have issues with the government being the organizing force in this. Volunteerism was alive and well in America before Big Brother got involved. I don't see why we need to spend billions of dollars getting people to do what they were already going to do anyway. We shouldn't pay people to be volunteers."

STUDENT #4: "That's the point, some of them wanted to do volunteer service but they need a small incentive. Nobody is going to get rich on the stipends the government is offering. But the new grant competitions for nonprofits, schools, and universities to create programs for at-risk youth in low-income communities and academic and service program for all young people is a way of directing government funds toward proven effective organizations that need money to keep doing good things for kids, teens, and families especially in these tough economic times. I think that people who want to keep government at arm's length are going to have problems with this bill. They are right that it is another way that government is worming itself into every facet of our lives. But a lot of people feel that way about religion, too; that's why they do not want to volunteer in programs sponsored by religious groups, because they don't want to be seen as agreeing with all the beliefs of that group. The real question for me is the effect that this legislation might have on the future politics of our nation. All these volunteers could become, in effect, people the administration can call on in the next election. Organizing tens of thousands Americans who basically agree with the idea of public service at public expense is like lining up the Democratic voters who will want to be sure these policies are not reversed by the Republicans. I'm not talking about a vague idea like "socialism," I'm talking about clever politics, positioning the Democratic Party for success in the next election. I'm not sure what I think about that yet. But we need to understand that this legislation will result in more than just a lot of wonderful work by a large number of generous Americans who are willing to give of their time to help others."

Having reviewed the information about this legislation and read the statements by each of the four students, how would you evaluate those statements in terms of the critical thinking each displays? Remember, base your evaluation on what the statements reveal about the quality of the reasoning, not on whether you agree or disagree with their conclusion. We'll offer our evaluative comments on these four statements in the paragraphs below. But before you read on, first make a preliminary assessment. Which of the four student statements would you rate right now as showing strong critical thinking and which do you regard at this point as showing weak critical thinking?

The Holistic Critical Thinking Scoring Rubric

Every day we all make decisions about what to believe or what to do. When we are being reflective and fair-minded about doing so, we are using our critical thinking skills. The idea behind a critical thinking course is to help us strengthen these skills and fortify our intentions to use them when the occasion arises.

If that is true, then there probably is room for improvement—just as with other things we do that we may not have formally studied. But we are not starting from zero. We have critical thinking skills, even if we have not yet refined them to their maximum potential. We know what it means to be open-minded and to take a systematic and objective look at an issue. We are familiar with the ordinary English meanings of common words for talking about thinking such as *interpret, analyze, infer, explain, reason, conclusion, fallacy,* and *argument.* And, in a broad sense, a lot of the time we can tell the difference between strong reasoning and weak reasoning, even if we do not yet know all the details or terminology.

So, given that none of us are novices at critical thinking, we should be able to make a reasonable first stab at an evaluation of the thinking portrayed by the four students in the example. Just using our experience and common sense we can agree that #4 and #3 are stronger than #2 and #1.

A tool designed to help us with this process of evaluation relies on the ordinary meanings of common terms used to talk about thinking. Called "The Holistic Critical Thinking Scoring Rubric" (HCTSR), this tool can aid us in evaluating real-life examples of critical thinking because it requires us only to consider the four evaluative descriptions: "strong," "acceptable," "unacceptable," and "weak" and see which of the four fits best. At this point, before we have worked through any of the other chapters of the book, this simple tool/approach is sufficient to get us started evaluating critical thinking. Naturally, as we learn more about critical thinking, we will become better at applying the rubric and more facile at using the terminology it contains. Our evaluative judgments will improve, and our ability to explain our judgments will improve as well. In this way, the rubric actually helps us to improve our critical thinking. Where we may disagree with one another at first about the evaluative levels that best fit, in time as we work with the rubric and with others on applying it, we will begin to form clearer ideas of the differences not only between the extreme examples, but between examples that fall between the extremes.

To apply the HCTSR, take each student's statement and see *which level of the Rubric offers the best description of the reasoning evident in that statement.* You will see that they line up rather well with the four levels of the HCTSR. Statement #4 is a good example of the top level, "strong"; student statement #3 is "acceptable"; student statement #2 is "unacceptable" because it displays the problems listed in the HCTSR in category 2; and statement #1 is so far off base that it qualifies as "weak."

Now that you have the HCTSR available to evaluate examples of real-life critical thinking, let's try it again with another set of four essays. As you read each essay response, compare what you are reading to the language on the HCTSR to determine which of the four descriptions, "strong," "acceptable," "unacceptable," and "weak" fits the best.

THE STUDENTS' ASSIGNMENT—HAITI

This time imagine a professor has asked her students to respond to the following essay question "Did the international community abandon Haiti or not?–give reasons and evidence to support your claim." The group has access to the information about the earthquake in Haiti reproduced here and on the Internet.

- On January 10, 2010, Haiti experienced its most deadly earthquake in the country's history. The quake left the capital city of Port-au-Prince flattened and the country devastated.

- The death toll is estimated to be upward of 250,000 individuals, with 300,000 others being injured.

- The estimated cost of damage due to the earthquake is between 8 and 14 billion dollars.

- As of January 2014, *Time* reported that billions of dollars in promised aid have not yet been dispersed.

- *Time* also reported that 70% of Haitians lack access to electricity, 600,000 are food-insecure and 23% of children are out of primary schools. At least 172,000 people remain in 306 displacement camps.[17]

THE STUDENTS' STATEMENTS—HAITI

STUDENT #1: "I wouldn't say that the international community has abandoned Haiti as much as I would say that the international community has done nothing but make matters worse! That impoverished country had an earthquake that killed nearly 250,000 people and injured 300,000 more. I saw on Facebook that

The Holistic Critical Thinking Scoring Rubric[16]

A Tool for Developing and Evaluating Critical Thinking

Peter A. Facione, Ph.D., and Noreen C. Facione, Ph.D.

Strong 4. Consistently does all or almost all of the following:

- Accurately interprets evidence, statements, graphics, questions, etc.
- Identifies the salient arguments' (reasons and claims) pros and cons.
- Thoughtfully analyzes and evaluates major alternative points of view.
- Draws warranted, judicious, non-fallacious conclusions.
- Justifies key results and procedures, explains assumptions and reasons.
- Fair-mindedly follows where evidence and reasons lead.

Acceptable 3. Does most or many of the following:

- Accurately interprets evidence, statements, graphics, questions, etc.
- Identifies relevant arguments' (reasons and claims) pros and cons.
- Offers analyses and evaluations of obvious alternative points of view.
- Draws warranted, non-fallacious conclusions.
- Justifies some results or procedures, explains reasons.
- Fair-mindedly follows where evidence and reasons lead.

Unacceptable 2. Does most or many of the following:

- Misinterprets evidence, statements, graphics, questions, etc.
- Fails to identify strong, relevant counterarguments.
- Ignores or superficially evaluates obvious alternative points of view.
- Draws unwarranted or fallacious conclusions.
- Justifies few results or procedures, seldom explains reasons.
- Regardless of the evidence or reasons, maintains or defends views based on self-interest or preconceptions.

Weak 1. Consistently does all or almost all of the following:

- Offers biased interpretations of evidence, statements, graphics, questions, information, or the points of view of others.
- Fails to identify or hastily dismisses strong, relevant counterarguments.
- Ignores or superficially evaluates obvious alternative points of view.
- Argues using fallacious or irrelevant reasons and unwarranted claims.
- Does not justify results or procedures, nor explain reasons.
- Regardless of the evidence or reasons, maintains or defends views based on self-interest or preconceptions.
- Exhibits close-mindedness or hostility to reason.

---

the cholera epidemic was caused by a Red Cross volunteer. That means that someone from the outside world caused a deadly disease to run rampant through the country. Everyone knows that developed countries only help out when there is something in it for them—like oil or bananas. Why else would the relief effort be run by a former U.S. president? What's his political motivation? One could say that the Haitian government or lack thereof is the main reason why Bill Clinton's commission has to run the recovery efforts and coordinate the funds for reconstruction, but I heard somewhere that Clinton's commission collected a ton of money for Haiti relief but hasn't spent even half of it yet. I don't get why not. You can be sure, however, that when the commission does spend the money it will only harm the Haitian economy. Clinton will probably give it all away like some kind of welfare program. The international community should abandon efforts so that no further harm is done."

STUDENT #2: "I don't think the international community abandoned Haiti after the devastating earthquake. Even a year later you could still find news coverage

What Are Scoring Rubrics?

Rubrics articulate the criteria used for judging different levels of performance. If you were the instructor of this course how might you use a rubric like the HCTSR to help your students learn? As a student, how might you use this rubric to develop your peers' critical thinking? How about your own?

of Haiti pretty much every day on the Internet. That means that Haiti has not been forgotten. Though the number of people who are still homeless is high, there are organizations over there that are rebuilding camps and schools. *60 Minutes* even showed a story about a guy who was rebuilding a soccer field. They say that thousands of people have been able to go home and kids are able to attend the schools that have been reopened. I know the United States is not the only country that is helping in Haiti because the United Nations has sent money and workers—this means it is an international effort. Given that Haiti is not the only country needing our help, like Japan who had the tsunami, not to mention the hurricanes and tornados right here in America, the fact is that everyone is doing all that they can to help Haiti. What more can we possibly expect? I mean, we all have our problems. The biggest challenge is the cholera epidemic, which is slowing down efforts to rebuild the country. Nobody knew what to do about that. But now that the president has been elected it should be possible to move forward with getting medicines to that country."

STUDENT #3: "Haiti was abandoned by the international community. How else might we explain why numerous countries all over the world would have promised billions of dollars but then reneged on payment? Yes, lots of money and hundreds of emergency aid workers have been sent to that impoverished country, along with food, medicine, water, temporary shelters, and heavy machinery to clear the collapsed buildings that once were homes, schools, and businesses. But at the end of the day (or year in this case!) there is still so much left to be done. Several thousands of people are still living in camps, and those who are able to go home are afraid to live inside because they don't trust that their houses won't still collapse. At first there were no major issues related to diseases that typically follow a major natural disaster, and this was touted as a successful part of the relief effort, but now we see the country stricken with a cholera epidemic. The international community has made big promises to the people of Haiti but those promises have not yet been fulfilled. I support the people who are asking for

an explanation of what is being done with the money that has been collected from the international community. If there is a reason to hold back on distributing the funds then that should be stated so that everyone knows the short- and long-term plan to achieve recovery and so that the people of Haiti know that the world still cares about them. And if we find no good reasons for holding back the money, then we should be told why it was not used sooner."

STUDENT #4: "This is a really difficult question, but I'd have to say that the international community has not abandoned Haiti. This is not to say that the relief effort has been smooth, or that the country has been totally rebuilt in the years since the deadly earthquake leveled Port-au-Prince. Nevertheless, an important distinction needs to be made between relief and recovery. Immediately following the earthquake monies and aid workers including doctors were rushed to Haiti. These monies and humanitarian aid were contributed by almost 40 different countries around the world, and involved organizations such as the United Nations, American Red Cross, and NGOs that are still hard at work in Haiti. These funds and workers were able to provide food, shelter, water and medicine to the survivors who were left homeless. Yes, many countries have pledged billions to help Haiti, and not all of the money has been spent. This has angered some—particularly the Haitian people and individuals directly involved in the organizations who are on the ground in Haiti trying to make the recovery effort move more quickly. It has got to be frustrating to know that monies have been pledged or collected but remain unspent, but the turmoil over the contested presidential elections has to be considered—an unstable government is a liability when it comes to a wise and efficient use of public funds, even in the best of times. Finally, though it was once thought that the prevention of looting and disease in the immediate aftermath of the quake was evidence of the relief effort working, we should consider the cholera epidemic as evidence that the international community has forsaken Haiti. The cholera was entirely predictable when thousands are living in unsanitary camps. On the other hand, some international humanitarian organizations have stepped up their efforts to curtail the spread of cholera by providing medicine, sanitation, and fresh water which has effectively lessened the number of people who are dying from the outbreak. For these reasons I feel that the world has not given up on helping Haiti."

As with the first set of student essays, we can apply the HCTSR to determine which level of the Rubric offers

THINKING CRITICALLY

Who's Supposed to Help?

If you lost your home in a natural disaster, how many months and years would you and your family be willing to live in a temporary tent city? What if your government was unwilling or unable to provide more suitable housing, food, water, and loans to rebuild your home and business? Perhaps it is not the government's responsibility to offer those kinds of assistance.

If not, is it any organization's responsibility? Perhaps a church, a university, or a charity? Or should the hurt and homeless after a natural disaster simply be left to fend for themselves? Whatever your view, articulate your reasons and then evaluate your reasoning using the HCTSR.

the best description of the reasoning evident in that statement. When reading these four student essays on Haiti in order we find that each displays stronger critical thinking than the one before. Statement #4 is a good example of the top level, "strong"; student statement, #3 is "acceptable"; student statement #2 is "unacceptable" because it displays the problems listed in category 2 on the HCTSR; and statement #1 has many errors in thinking thereby qualifying it as "weak."

At this early stage in our discussion of critical thinking you only need to begin to differentiate among the four essays in terms of the quality of the critical thinking they displayed. As we go through the chapters in this book the more technical explanations for their relative strengths and weaknesses will become much clearer. In the meantime, what is important is that you are able to recognize that the critical thinking generally improves as you go from the initial essay in the series on through to the fourth essay. As in real life, none of these four is absolutely dreadful and none is superbly stellar. But they do differ in the quality of the critical thinking displayed. Their differences will come

into better focus as you get deeper into this book and progress in developing your own critical thinking.

The HCTSR is a great tool to use to evaluate the quality of the critical thinking evident in lots of different situations: classroom discussions, papers, essays, panel presentations, commercials, blog posts, Yelp reviews, editorials, letters to editors, news conferences, infomercials, commentator's remarks, speeches, jury deliberations, planning sessions, meetings, debates, or your own private thoughts. Keep the focus on the reasoning. The key thing is that people have to express some kind of a reason or basis for whatever it is that

A Healthy Sense of Skepticism

Critical thinking is **skeptical without being cynical**. It is open-minded without being wishy-washy. It is **analytical without being nitpicky**. Critical thinking can be decisive without being stubborn, evaluative without being judgmental, and **forceful without being opinionated**.

they are saying. It is tough to apply the HCTSR to tweets, slogans, gestures, signs, billboards, and epithets because reasons are seldom given in those cases.

Do not let the fact that you may agree or disagree with the particular conclusions being advocated sway you. Do not worry if you feel unsure of yourself, having used the HCTSR only a couple of times so far. There will be plenty of additional opportunities for you to practice with it in the exercises in this chapter and in future chapters. Like a new pair of shoes, the use of the tool will feel more comfortable with time. Think of it this way: The more you use the HCTSR, and the more adept you become at sorting out why something represents stronger or weaker critical thinking, the more you will improve your own critical thinking.

When people first begin using a rubric like the HCTSR, it is important they calibrate their scoring with one another. Some individuals might initially rate something higher and others rate it lower. However, through mutual discussion, it is possible to help one another come to a reasonable consensus on a score. Identify two editorials and two letters to the editor that appear in your campus newspaper. Here is a good way to begin. Working with two or three other classmates, individually rate those letters and editorials with the HCTSR. After each of you have rated them, compare the scores everyone in your group initially assigned. Where the scores differ, discuss the critical thinking evident in the editorials or letters, and come to consensus on a score. With practice and with what you will learn as you go through this book you will strengthen your critical thinking skills, including you're ability to analyze, interpret and evaluate the claims people make, and the arguments they present.

Summing up this chapter,

critical thinking is the process of purposeful, reflective judgment focused on deciding what to believe or what to do. Neither negative nor cynical, but thoughtful and fair-minded, critical thinking is essential for learning, is a liberating force in education, and a precondition for a free and democratic society. Strong critical thinking is a tremendous asset in one's personal, professional, and civic life. We all have some level of skill in critical thinking and we all have the capacity to improve those skills. In the next Chapter we will examine more deeply the specific skills and habits of mind that are central to critical thinking.

Key Concept

Critical thinking is the process of purposeful, reflective judgment. Critical thinking manifests itself in giving reasoned and fair-minded consideration to evidence, conceptualizations, methods, contexts, and standards to decide what to believe or what to do.

Applications

Reflective Log

What did you decide? Think back over today and yesterday. Describe a problem you faced or a decision which you considered. Who was involved, and what was the issue? Describe how you thought about that problem or decision—not so much what you decided or what solution you picked, but the process you used. Were you open-minded about various options, systematic in your approach, courageous enough to ask yourself tough questions, bold enough to follow the reasons and evidence wherever they led, inquisitive and eager to learn more before making a judgment, nuanced enough to see shades of gray rather than only stark black and white? Did you check your interpretations and analyses? Did you draw your inferences carefully? Were you as objective and fair-minded as you might have been? Explain your decision in your log with enough detail that would permit you to go back a week or two from now and evaluate your decision for the quality of the critical thinking it demonstrates.

Individual Exercises

Explain the mistake. One sign that we understand concepts well is our ability to explain the mistake or mistakes when they are used incorrectly. Here are 23 mistaken statements related to critical thinking and its value. Briefly describe the mistake in each. Use examples from your own experience if those help clarify your explanation.

1. Critical thinking has no application in day-to-day life.

2. If critical thinking is purposeful judgment, then if I do not agree with your judgment, that means I'm not thinking critically."

3. "Critical thinking" means being critical. That's too much constant hostility. We should all just relax and agree.

4. Democracies get along just fine even if people do not think for themselves.

5. Decisions about how I want to live my life do not affect other people.

6. Reflective decision making requires little or no effort.

7. I'm always disagreeing with authority figures, so I must be a great critical thinker.

8. If we disagree on something, then one of us is not using critical thinking.

9. Every time I make a judgment, I am engaged in critical thinking.

10. Teaching young people to think critically will only result in their losing friends.

11. Reasons are irrelevant; having the right opinion is the only thing that matters.

12. Some people achieve popularity, wealth, and power without appearing to be strong critical thinkers, but you're saying that this can't happen to me.

13. We cannot be responsible for what we were taught to believe when we were children. We can try to apply critical thinking to those beliefs, but we can never change our minds about them.

14. I'm already very confident in my critical thinking ability, so there is no reason for me to go any further in this book.

15. If critical thinking is a mental process, then it will not help me learn the informational content of my other college courses.

16. You only are going to make trouble for yourself by rocking the boat with challenging questions and demands for reasons and evidence. Hey, you got to go along to get along.

17. I like many of the things that my city, county, state, and national governments do, so I must be a weak critical thinker.

18. It is fine to apply critical thinking in education, business, science, law enforcement, and international problems, but there is no place for critical thinking in religious matters.

19. Looking at the HCTSR, I find that my family and friends do not seem to be very good critical thinkers, so I don't have much of a chance to become one either.

20. People should not be taught critical thinking because it will only undermine their faith in their leaders.

21. If you are a strong critical thinker you will automatically be an ethical person.

22. Every government wants its citizens to be strong critical thinkers.

23. Once you become adept at engaging problems and making decisions using strong critical thinking, it is easy to quit.

Don't think! Critical thinking takes effort! Why work so hard? Imagine what it would be like to live in a community where critical thinking was illegal. What might the risks and benefits of such a life be? How would the people living in that community redress grievances, solve problems, plan for the future, evaluate options, and pursue their individual and joint purposes? Now imagine what it would be like to live in a community where critical thinking was unnecessary. Can there be such a place, except perhaps as human specimens in some other species' zoo?

SHARED RESPONSE

Positive Critical Thinking

From your own experience, share one recent positive example of critical thinking, like the 10 we described near the beginning of Chapter 1. Explain why your example shows strong critical thinking. Be sure to provide your reason(s), not just your opinion. And comment respectfully on the examples others offer.

Group Exercises

The words or the message? A master of irony, the late comedian George Carlin said critical thinking can be "Dangerous!" Just search "Carlin critical thinking" on the Internet. Carlin said some are so worried about the risks to their own power and position that they do not see the benefits to their organization's core purposes if employees or members are strong critical thinkers. Unscrupulous mega-corporations and Machiavellian leaders might well ponder the question of how to distract, divert, or derail other people's critical thinking so that they can maintain their own power and control. Carlin warned us not to swallow the mental junk food being served up by those whose only purpose is to maintain their own personal and corporate power and control. Carlin used a lot of vulgarity and potentially offensive language in his routines, which is unfortunate since people can be put off by the words and not hear the message. The questions for group discussion are: "Can strong critical thinkers identify the good ideas and claims a person may be making in spite of the person's off-putting way of expressing himself?" And, "Does the use of vile, vulgar, or offensive language exempt others from the obligation to think about the good ideas that may be contained in what the person is saying?"

Be hard on your opinions: Comedian and philosopher Tim Minchin offers nine stunningly simple yet powerful pieces of advice to the graduating class of his alma mater, the University of Western Australia. A romantic at heart, he urges each of us to embrace our chance existence and to fill our lives with learning, compassion, sharing, enthusiasm, exercise, love and more. Minchin notes the importance of critical thinking when he recommends that we should be hard on our own opinions. This bit, point five, comes 6:17 into his talk. Search for the video of his twelve minute address on the Internet. By searching "Minchin commencement address 2013" we found a video of Minchin's September 2013 address posted on several websites including **upworthy.com**. List his nine points, and consider specifically point five. Is there a good reason to wait until you graduate before considering whether there is value for you in what Minchin has to say? In other words, are any of his nine points relevant for college students, or only for graduates? Give reasons for your opinions about the relevance or non-relevance of each of the nine.

What are we thinking? If we learn best from our mistakes, then what can the international community learn about how best to assist a nation in recovering from catastrophic events given the experiences like Hurricane Katrina in 2005, the 2010 earthquake in Haiti, the 2011 tsunami that hit Japan, or the sustained subzero temperatures, floods, and winter ice storms in the Northern Hemisphere during the winter of 2014? Discuss these catastrophes, respond to the question concerning what can be learned, and provide reasons and evidence in support of your group's response to the question.

Chapter 2
Critical Thinking Mindset and Skills

In *Apollo 13*, Tom Hanks and Kevin Bacon portray astronauts working together using critical thinking to identify the exact problem threatening their mission and their lives.

HOW can I cultivate positive critical thinking habits of mind?

WHAT questions can I ask to engage my critical thinking skills?

HOW will this book help me to develop my critical thinking?

 Learning Outcomes

2.1 Contrast the positive vs. the negative critical thinking mindset. Describe four specific ways a person can continuously cultivate a positive critical thinking mindset.

2.2 Write a set of investigative questions about a current event or topic of broad interest such that the questions engage each of the six core critical thinking skills.

2.3 Take charge of your own learning: Analyze the organization of this book focusing on which skills or parts of the critical thinking process are emphasized in each chapter. Describe how you anticipate applying those skills, including the art of asking good questions, to the other courses you are taking now or expect to be taking soon.

After training for every conceivable contingency, the unexpected happened. Initially, the challenge was simply to figure out what the problem was. If it could be correctly identified, then there might be some slim chance of survival. If not, the outcome could be tragic. Ron Howard's award-winning documentary, *Apollo 13*, is a dramatic reenactment of the breathtaking voyage that had the whole nation rooting for the three astronauts whose lives hung in the balance. The actors, music, camera angles, staging, props, and lighting all contribute to our overall experience. That said, this portrayal of individual and group problem solving is so highly consistent with the research on human cognition and decision making that it just might be the best depiction of group critical thinking ever filmed.[1] The problem is simple, yet vitally important. *What could the problem be?* If the crew and the ground control personnel apply their reasoning skills to the best of their ability, perhaps they will identify the problem before the crew's electricity and breathable air run out. The situation is dire. More than their thinking skills only, it is the mental habits of being analytical, focused, and systematic that empower the technicians, engineers, and astronauts to apply those skills well during the crisis. Locate *Apollo 13* and watch the memorable scene described below.

2.1 Positive Critical Thinking Habits of Mind

The *Apollo 13* sequence opens with the staff at Mission Control in Houston and the three-person crew of *Apollo 13* well into the boredom of routine housekeeping. Suddenly, the crew of *Apollo 13* hears a loud banging noise and their small, fragile craft starts gyrating wildly. The startled look on Tom Hanks's face in the video reenactment is priceless. A full 15 seconds elapses before he speaks. During that time his critical thinking is in overdrive. He is trying to interpret what has just happened. His mind has to make sense of the entirely unexpected and unfamiliar experience. He neither dismisses nor ignores the new information that presents itself. His attention moves between checking the craft's instrument panel and attending to the sounds and motions of the spacecraft itself. He focuses his mind, forms a cautious but accurate interpretation, and with the disciplined self-control we expect of a well-trained professional, he informs Mission Control in Houston, Texas, that they most definitely have a problem![2]

At first, the astronauts in the spacecraft and the technicians at Mission Control call out information

from their desk monitors and the spacecraft's instrument displays. They crave information from all sources. They know they must share what they are learning with each other as quickly as they can in the hope that someone will be able to make sense out of things. They do not yet know which piece of information may be the clue to their life-or-death problem, but they have the discipline of mind to want to know everything that might be relevant. They have the confidence in their collective critical thinking skills to believe that this approach offers their best hope to identify the true problem.

One member of the ground crew calls out that O_2 Tank Two is not showing any readings. That vital bit of information swooshes by unnoticed in the torrents of data. Soon a number of people begin proposing explanations: Perhaps the spacecraft had been struck by a meteor. Perhaps its radio antenna is broken. Perhaps the issue is instrumentation, rather than something more serious, like a loss of power.

The vital critical thinking skill of self-regulation is personified in the film by the character played by Ed Harris. His job is to monitor everything that is going on and to correct the process if he judges that it is getting off track. Harris's character makes the claim that the problem cannot simply be instrumentation. The reason for that claim is clear and reasonable. The astronauts are reporting hearing loud bangs and feeling their spacecraft jolt and shimmy. The unspoken assumption, one every

pilot and technician understands in this context is that these physical manifestations—the noises and the shaking—would not be occurring if the problem were instrumentation. The conclusion Harris's character expressed has the effect of directing everyone's energy and attention toward one set of possibilities, those that would be considered real problems rather than toward the other set of possibilities. Had he categorized the problem as instrumentation, then everyone's efforts would have been directed toward checking and verifying that the gauges and computers were functioning properly.

There is an important critical thinking lesson in what we see Ed Harris doing. Judging correctly what kind of problem we are facing is essential. If we are mistaken about what the problem is, we are likely to consume time, energy, and resources exploring the wrong kinds of solutions. By the time we figure out that we took the wrong road, the situation could have become much worse than when we started. The *Apollo 13* situation is a perfect example. In real life, had the people at Mission Control in Houston classified the problem as instrumentation, they would have used up what little oxygen there was left aboard the spacecraft while the ground crew spent time validating their instrument readouts.

Back on the spacecraft, Tom Hanks, who personifies the critical thinking skills of interpretation and inference, is struggling to regain navigational control. He articulates the inference by saying that had they been hit by a meteor, they would all be dead already. A few moments later he glances out the spacecraft's side window. Something in the rearview mirror catches his attention. Again, his inquisitive mind will not ignore what he's seeing. A few seconds pass as he tries to interpret what it might be. He offers his first observation that the craft is venting something into space. The mental focus and stress of the entire Houston ground crew are etched on their faces. Their expressions reveal the question in their minds: What could he possibly be seeing? Seconds pass with agonizing slowness. Using his interpretive skills, Tom Hanks categorizes with caution and then, adding greater precision, he infers that the venting must be some kind of a gas. He pauses to try to figure out what the gas might be and realizes that it must surely be the oxygen. Kevin Bacon looks immediately to the oxygen tank gauge on the instrument panel for information that might confirm or disconfirm whether it really is the oxygen. It is.

Being by habit inclined to anticipate consequences, everyone silently contemplates the potential tragedy implied by the loss of oxygen. As truth-seekers, they must accept the finding. They cannot fathom denying it or hiding from it. Their somber response comes in the form of Mission Control's grim but objective acknowledgment that the spacecraft is venting.

OK, now we have the truth. What are we going to do about it? The characters depicted in this movie are driven by a powerful orientation toward using critical thinking to resolve whatever problems they encounter. The room erupts with noise as each person refocuses on their little piece of the problem. People are moving quickly, talking fast, pulling headset wires out of sockets in their haste. The chaos and cacophony in the room reveal that the group is not yet taking a systematic, organized approach. Monitoring this, Ed Harris's character interjects another self-correction into the group's critical thinking. He may not yet know how this problem of the oxygen supply is going to be solved or even whether this problem can be solved, but he is going to be sure that the ground crew addresses it with all the skill and all the mental power it can muster. He directs everyone to locate whomever they may need to assist them in their work, and to focus themselves and those others immediately on working the problem.

As depicted in this excerpt, the combined ground crew and spacecraft crew, as a group, would earn a top score on "Holistic Critical Thinking Scoring Rubric." The emotions and stresses of the situation are unmistakable. The group's powerfully strong critical thinking habits of mind enable the group to use that energy productively. It gives urgency to the efforts. Thus, the message about our thinking processes that emerges is that emotion need not be the antithesis to reason; emotion can be the impetus to reason.

> *"To repeat what others have said requires education, to challenge it requires brains."*
>
> Mary Pettiborn Poole, Author[3]

The Spirit of a Strong Critical Thinker

In the film skillful actors displayed the behaviors and responses of strong critical thinkers engaged in problem solving during a crisis. Authors of screenplays and novels often endow their protagonists with strongly positive critical thinking skills and dispositions. Sir Arthur Conan Doyle's brilliantly analytical Sherlock Holmes, played in this century by Jonny Lee Miller in the CBS series *Elementary*, by Benedict Cumberbatch in the PBS series *Sherlock*, and in the movies by Robert Downey Jr., comes to mind. Matthew McConaughey's dark, driven, and keenly observant character on HBO's series *True Detective* is another rich example. A key difference, of course, is that fictional detectives solve the mysteries, while, as we all know, in the real world there is no guarantee. Critical thinking is about *how* we approach problems, decisions, questions, and issues even if ultimate success eludes us.

Having the mindset that disposes us to engage our skills as best we can is the "eager" part of "skilled and eager." First we will examine the "eager" part, beginning with taking a closer look at the overall critical thinking mindset. Later in this chapter we will examine the "skilled" part, the core critical thinking skills.

> "It is an old maxim of mine that when you have excluded the impossible, whatever remains, however improbable, must be the truth."
>
> Sir Arthur Conan Doyle, Author[4]

Positive vs. Negative Habits of Mind

A person with a strong *disposition* toward critical thinking has the *consistent internal motivation* to engage problems and make decisions by using critical thinking.[5] Operationally this means three things: The person consistently *values* critical thinking, *believes* that using critical thinking skills offers the greatest promise for reaching good judgments, and *intends* to approach problems and decisions by applying critical thinking skills as best as he or she can. This combination of values, beliefs, and intentions forms the habits of mind that dispose the person toward critical thinking.[6]

Someone strongly disposed toward critical thinking would probably agree with the following statements:

- "I hate talk shows where people shout their opinions but never give any reasons at all."
- "Figuring out what people really mean by what they say is important to me."
- "I always do better in jobs where I'm expected to think things out for myself."
- "I hold off making decisions until I have thought through my options."
- "Rather than relying on someone else's notes, I prefer to read the material myself."
- "I try to see the merit in another's opinion, even if I reject it later."
- "Even if a problem is tougher than I expected, I will keep working on it."
- "Making intelligent decisions is more important than winning arguments."

Persons who display a strong positive disposition toward critical thinking are described in the literature as "having a critical spirit," or as people who are "mindful," "reflective," and "meta-cognitive." These expressions give a person credit for consistently applying their critical thinking skills to whatever problem, question, or issue is at hand. People with a critical spirit tend to ask good questions, probe deeply for the truth, inquire fully into matters, and strive to anticipate the consequences of various options. In real life our skills may or may not be strong enough, our knowledge may or may not be adequate to the task at hand. The problem may or may not be too difficult for us. Forces beyond our control might or might not determine the actual outcome. None of that cancels out the positive critical thinking habits of mind with which strong critical thinkers strive to approach the problems life sends their way.

A person with weak critical thinking dispositions might disagree with the previous statements and be more likely to agree with these:

- "I prefer jobs where the supervisor says exactly what to do and exactly how to do it."
- "No matter how complex the problem, you can bet there will be a simple solution."
- "I don't waste time looking things up."
- "I hate when teachers discuss problems instead of just giving the answers."
- "If my belief is truly sincere, evidence to the contrary is irrelevant."
- "Selling an idea is like selling cars; you say whatever works."
- "Why go to the library when you can use made-up quotes and phony references?"
- "I take a lot on faith because questioning the fundamentals frightens me."
- "There is no point in trying to understand what terrorists are thinking."

When it comes to approaching specific questions, issues, decisions or problems, people with a weak or negative critical thinking disposition are apt to be impulsive, reactive, muddle-headed, disorganized, overly simplistic, spotty about getting relevant information, likely to apply unreasonable criteria, easily distracted, ready to give up at the least hint of difficulty, intent on a solution that is more detailed than is possible, or too readily satisfied with some uselessly vague response.

Preliminary Self-Assessment

It is only natural to wonder about our own disposition. The "Critical Thinking Mindset Self-Rating Form" offers us a way of reflecting on our own values, beliefs, and intentions about the use of critical thinking. As noted on the form itself, "This tool offers only a rough approximation with regard to a brief moment in time."

We invite you to take a moment and complete the self-assessment. Keep in mind as you interpret the results that this measure does not assess critical thinking skills. Rather, this tool permits one to reflect on whether, over the past two days, the disposition manifested in behavior was positive, ambivalent, or averse toward engaging in thoughtful, reflective, and fair-minded judgments about what to believe or what to do.

Research on the Positive Critical Thinking Mindset

The broad understanding of being disposed toward using critical thinking, or disposed away from using critical thinking, has been the object of empirical research in the cognitive sciences since the early 1990s. This research has given greater precision to the analysis and measurement of the dispositional dimension of critical thinking.

SEVEN POSITIVE CRITICAL THINKING HABITS OF MIND One research approach to identifying the elements in a positive critical thinking mindset involved asking thousands of people to indicate the extent to which they agreed or disagreed with a long list of statements, not unlike those in the two short lists presented above. Using statistical analysis, these researchers identified seven measurable aspects within the overall disposition toward critical thinking. We can think of these as the seven positive

---

Critical Thinking Mindset Self-Rating Form

Answer yes or no to each. Can I *name any specific instances over the past two* days when I:

1. _____ was courageous enough to ask tough questions about some of my longest held and most cherished beliefs?

2. _____ backed away from questions that might undercut some of my longest held and most cherished beliefs?

3. _____ showed tolerance toward the beliefs, ideas, or opinions of someone with whom I disagreed?

4. _____ tried to find information to build up my side of an argument but not the other side?

5. _____ tried to think ahead and anticipate the consequences of various options?

6. _____ laughed at what other people said and made fun of their beliefs, values, opinion, or points of views?

7. _____ made a serious effort to be analytical about the foreseeable outcomes of my decisions?

8. _____ manipulated information to suit my own purposes?

9. _____ encouraged peers not to dismiss out of hand the opinions and ideas other people offered?

10. _____ acted with disregard for the possible adverse consequences of my choices?

11. _____ organized for myself a thoughtfully systematic approach to a question or issue?

12. _____ jumped in and tried to solve a problem without first thinking about how to approach it?

13. _____ approached a challenging problem with confidence that I could think it through?

14. _____ instead of working through a question for myself, took the easy way out and asked someone else for the answer?

15. _____ read a report, newspaper, or book chapter or watched the world news or a documentary just to learn something new?

16. _____ put zero effort into learning something new until I saw the immediate utility in doing so?

17. _____ showed how strong I was by being willing to honestly reconsider a decision?

18. _____ showed how strong I was by refusing to change my mind?

19. _____ attended to variations in circumstances, contexts, and situations in coming to a decision?

20. _____ refused to reconsider my position on an issue in light of differences in context, situations, or circumstances?

If you have described yourself honestly, this self-rating form can offer a rough estimate of what you think your overall disposition toward critical thinking has been in the past two days.

Give yourself 5 points for every "Yes" on odd numbered items and for every "No" on even numbered items. If your total is 70 or above, you are rating your disposition toward critical thinking over the past two days as generally positive. Scores of 50 or lower indicate a self-rating that is averse or hostile toward critical thinking over the past two days. Scores between 50 and 70 show that you would rate yourself as displaying an ambivalent or mixed overall disposition toward critical thinking over the past two days.

Interpret results on this tool cautiously. At best this tool offers only a rough approximation with regard to a brief moment in time. Other tools are more refined, such as the *California Critical Thinking Disposition Inventory*, which gives results for each of the seven critical thinking habits of mind.

The Disposition toward Critical Thinking

- **Inquisitive**—meaning that the person habitually strives to be well informed, wants to know how things work, and seeks to learn new things about a wide range of topics, even if the immediate utility of knowing those things is not directly evident. The inquisitive person has a strong sense of intellectual curiosity.

- **Judicious**—meaning that the person approaches problems with a sense that some are ill structured and some can have more than one plausible solution. The judicious person has the cognitive maturity to realize that many questions and issues are not black and white and that, at times, judgments must be made in contexts of uncertainty.

critical thinking habits of mind.[7] Based on this research, we can describe someone who has all seven positive critical thinking habits of mind as a person who is:

- **Truth-seeking**—meaning that the person has intellectual integrity and a courageous desire to actively strive for the best possible knowledge in any given situation. A truth-seeker asks probing questions and follows reasons and evidence wherever they lead, even if the results go against his or her cherished beliefs.

- **Open-minded**—meaning that the person is tolerant of divergent views and sensitive to the possibility of his or her own possible biases. An open-minded person respects the right of others to have different opinions.

- **Analytical**—meaning that the person is habitually alert to potential problems and vigilant in anticipating consequences and trying to foresee short-term and long-term outcomes of events, decisions, and actions. Another word to describe this habit of mind might be "foresightful."

- **Systematic**—meaning that the person consistently endeavors to take an organized and thorough approach to identifying and resolving problems. The systematic person is orderly, focused, persistent, and diligent in his or her approach to problem solving, learning, and inquiry.

- **Confident in reasoning**—meaning that the person is trustful of his or her own reasoning skills to yield good judgments. A person's or a group's confidence in their own critical thinking may or may not be warranted, which is another matter.

NEGATIVE HABITS OF MIND After the measurement tools were refined and validated for use in data gathering, the results of repeated samplings showed that some people are strongly positive on one or more of the seven positive mindset attributes. Some people are ambivalent or negatively disposed on one or more of the seven.

We can associate a name to the negative end of the scale for each of the seven, just as we associated a name with the positive end of each scale. The "Critical Thinking Habits of Mind" chart lists the names, for both positive and negative attributes. A person's individual dispositional portrait emerges from the seven, for a person may be positive, ambivalent, or negative on each.

Critical Thinking Habits of Mind	
Positive	**Negative**
Truth-seeking	Intellectually Dishonest
Open-minded	Intolerant
Analytical	Heedless of Consequences
Systematic	Disorganized
Confident in Reasoning	Hostile toward Reason
Inquisitive	Indifferent
Judicious	Imprudent

In the award-winning film *Philadelphia*, Denzel Washington plays a personal liability litigator who is not above increasing the amount a client seeks for "pain and suffering" by hinting to the client that he may have more medical problems than the client had at first noticed. Locate the film and watch the scene where a new potential client, played by Tom Hanks, visits Washington's office seeking representation. The scene starts out with Denzel Washington talking to a different client—a man who wants to sue the city over a foolish accident that the man brought upon himself. The scene establishes that Washington is a hungry lawyer who will take almost any case. Tom Hanks comes into the office and says that he wants to sue his former employer, believing that he was wrongly fired from his job because he has AIDS. You would think that Washington would jump at this opportunity. There is a lot of money to be made if he can win the case. Truth-seeking demands that the real reason for the firing be brought to light. But at this point in the story, Washington declines to take the case.

Notice what the filmmakers do with the camera angles to show what Washington is thinking as he considers what to do. His eyes focus on the picture of his wife and child, on the skin lesion on Hanks's head, and on the cigars and other things Hanks touches. The story takes place during the early years when the general public did not understand AIDS well at all. It was a time when prejudices, homophobia, and misinformation surrounded the disease. Washington's character portrays the uncertainty and misplaced fears of the U.S. public at that time. Not understanding AIDS or being misinformed, Washington's character is frightened for himself and for his family. Notice how he stands in the very far corner of his office, as physically far away from Hanks's character as possible. He wipes his hand against his trousers after shaking hands. The nonverbal thinking cues are so well done by the filmmakers that we are not surprised when Washington, having thought things through, refuses to take the case.

There is no question that critical thinking is wonderfully powerful. Yet, by itself it is incomplete. We need knowledge, values, and sensitivities to guide our thinking. Washington's character is sensitive to what he thinks are the dangers of the disease

> ### Some Habits Are Desirable, Others Are Not
>
> The expressions *mental disciplines* and *mental virtues* can be used to refer to *habits of mind* as well. The word *disciplines* in a military context and the word *virtues* in an ethical context both suggest something positive. We use *habits of mind*, or at times *personal attributes*, or *mindset elements*, because these expressions are neutral. Some habits of mind, personal attributes, or mindset elements are positive, others not. A habit of mind like truth-seeking is positive. Other habits of mind, like indifference or intellectual dishonesty, are negative.

and what he believes (wrongly) about the ways it might be transmitted. His character uses his critical thinking skills, which turn out to be quite formidable as the film progresses. But his beliefs about AIDS are simply wrong. He makes a judgment at the time not to represent Hanks's character. It is not the same judgment he will make later in the film, after he becomes better informed. Fortunately, he has the open-mindedness to entertain the possibility of representing Hanks's character, that perhaps Hanks's character does have a winnable case, and that perhaps the risks associated with AIDS are not as great as he had at first imagined. He has the inquisitiveness and the truth-seeking skills to gather more accurate information. And

In *Philadelphia*, the plaintiff, played by Tom Hanks, and his lawyer, played by Denzel Washington, wade through a crowd of reporters. How does Denzel Washington's character use critical thinking throughout the course of the film?

he has the judiciousness to reconsider and to change his mind.

> "If we were compelled to make a choice between these personal attributes [of a thoughtful person] and knowledge about the principles of logical reasoning together with some degree of technical skill manipulating special logical processes, we should decide for the former."
>
> John Dewey, *How We Think*[8]

Is a Good Critical Thinker Automatically a Good Person?

To get a clearer sense of the colossal problems that result from our collective failures to anticipate consequences, watch the documentary film *The Unforeseen* (2007, directed by Laura Dunn). It is the remarkable story of the loss of quality of life and environmental degradation associated with real estate development in Austin, Texas, over the past 50 years. What if the city planners or the developers, when undertaking their due diligence, actually became aware from the evidence that they were setting the stage for serious future environmental problems? And what if, knowing that, they decided to move ahead anyway with the project? Thinking about these hypothetical questions makes us wonder about the ethics of the decision makers involved. Similarly, thinking about Denzel Washington's character in *Philadelphia*, raises the question: "Does having strong critical thinking skills make a person ethical?"

We have been using the expression "strong critical thinker" instead of "good critical thinker" because of the ambiguity of the word *good*. We want to praise the person's critical thinking without necessarily making a judgment about the person's ethics. For example, a person can be adept at developing cogent arguments and adroit at finding the flaws in other people's reasoning, but that same person can use these skills unethically to mislead and exploit a gullible person, perpetrate a fraud, or deliberately confuse, confound, and frustrate a project.

A person can be *strong* at critical thinking, meaning that the person can have the appropriate dispositions, and be adept using his or her critical thinking skill, but still not be an ethical critical thinker. Take, for example, the remarkably deceitful Congressman Francis Underwood played by Kevin Spacey and his equally manipulative wife Claire Underwood played by Robin Wright from the Netflix series *House of Cards*. Or, consider the Machiavellian pope, Alexander VI, AKA Rodrigo Borgia, played by Jeremy Irons from the Showtime series *The Borgias*. These film characters use strong critical thinking to exploit, mislead, manipulate, and coerce whomever it takes to achieve their interests. Compelling examples however are not limited to the big screen. There have been people with superior thinking skills who, unfortunately, have used their talents for ruthless, horrific, and unethical purposes. It would be great if critical thinking and ethical virtue were one and the same. But they are not.

At times people make a public confession of the shameless efforts to figure out how to deceive others. Consider, for example, the revelations that Victor Crawford, a tobacco lobbyist, made in his *60 Minutes* interview with Leslie Stahl. For excerpts search the Internet for "Victor Crawford Leslie Stahl." Crawford admits that he deliberately mislead and manipulated legislators and the general public to advance the interests of the tobacco industry. He says, "Was I lying? Yes, yes. . . Yes, yes. . . Of course. My job was to win. . . . Even if you're going out lying about a product that's gonna hurt kids."[9] Ms. Stahl calls him out, saying that he was unethical and despicable to act that way. For years Crawford used his critical thinking skills to confuse and deceive consumers so that his corporate masters could sell a product known to be addictive and deadly. Now, all these years later, he regrets having done that. The interview is part of his effort to make amends for his lies and the harm they may have caused to others.

Francis and Claire remind us in every episode that some strong critical thinkers are criminally unethical.

THINKING CRITICALLY

How Does TV Portray Critical Thinking?

You can do this exercise by yourself or with a classmate. This exercise requires watching TV for two hours. Begin with a clean piece of paper and draw a vertical line down the middle of the page. Mark one side + and the other –. With pencil and paper in hand, watch CBS, NBC, or ABC, or a major cable network that shows commercials along with its regular programming. Pay close attention to the commercials, not the regular programming. Note each of the people who appear on screen. If you judge that a person is portrayed as a strong critical thinker, note it (e.g., Woman in car commercial +). If you think a person is portrayed as a weak critical thinker, note that (e.g., Three guys in beer commercial - - -). If you cannot tell (e.g., in the car commercial there were two kids riding in the back seat but they were not doing or saying anything), do not make any notation. After watching only the commercials during one hour of programming, total up the plusses and the minuses. Now repeat the same activity for another hour, but this time pay attention only to the regular programming, not the commercials. Again note every character who appears and indicate on the paper if the person is generally portrayed as a strong critical thinker (e.g., evil bad guy +, clever detective +) or a weak critical thinker (e.g., victim who foolishly walked into the dark alley alone –). Tally up the plusses and minuses. Based on your observations, is there a tendency or pattern that might be evident regarding the critical thinking strengths or weaknesses of children, adolescents, young adults, middle-aged people, and senior citizens?

Alternative: Or do the exercise with old episodes of *Breaking Bad*, *Dexter*, *Mad Men*, and *Law and Order SVU*.

Critical thinking is very useful in ethical decision making, but like any tool or process, it can be applied to unworthy and shameful purposes as well.

> They spend billions of dollars every year lobbying . . . lobbying, to get what they want. . . . Well, we know what they want. They want more for themselves and less for everybody else, but I'll tell you what they don't want . . . they don't want a population of citizens capable of critical thinking. They don't want well informed, well educated people capable of critical thinking. They're not interested in that . . . that doesn't help them. That's against their interests.
>
> George Carlin, Comedian[10]

Cultivate a Positive Critical Thinking Mindset

Critical thinking skills can be strengthened by exercising them, which is what the examples and the exercises in this book are intended to help you do. Critical thinking habits of mind can be nurtured by internalizing the values that they embody and by reaffirming the intention each day to live by those values.[11] Here are four specific suggestions about how to go about this.

1. **Value Critical Thinking.** If we value critical thinking, we desire to be ever more truth-seeking, open-minded, mindful of consequences, systematic, inquisitive, confident in our critical thinking, and mature in our judgment. We will expect to manifest that desire in what we do and in what we say. We will seek to improve our critical thinking skills.

2. **Take Stock.** It is always good to know where we are in our journey. The "Critical Thinking Disposition Self-Rating Form," presented earlier in this chapter (page 22), will give us a rough idea. If we have general positive critical thinking habits of mind, that should show up in the score we give ourselves using this self-rating form.

3. **Be Alert for Opportunities.** Each day we should be alert for opportunities to make decisions and solve problems reflectively. Rather than just reacting, take some time each day to be as reflective and thoughtful as possible in addressing at least one of the many problems or decisions of the day.

4. **Forgive and Persist.** Forgive yourself if you happen to backslide. Pick yourself up and get right back on the path. These are *ideals* we are striving to achieve. We each need discipline, determination, and persistence. There will be missteps along the way, but do not let them deter you. Working with a friend, mentor, or role model might make it easier to be successful, but it is really about what you want for your own thinking process.

Putting the Positive Critical Thinking Mindset into Practice

Here are a few suggestions about ways to translate each of the seven positive attributes into action.

Truth-seeking – Ask courageous and probing questions. Think deeply about the reasons and evidence for and against a given decision you must make. Pick one or two of your own most cherished beliefs, and ask yourself what reasons and what evidence there are for and against those beliefs.

Open-mindedness – Listen patiently to someone who is offering opinions with which you do not agree. As you listen, show respect and tolerance toward the person offering the ideas. Show that you understand (not the same as "agree with") the opinions being presented.

Analyticity – Identify an opportunity to consciously pause to ask yourself about all the foreseeable and likely consequences of a decision you are making. Ask yourself what that choice, whether it is large or small, will mean for your future life and behavior.

Systematicity – Focus on getting more organized. Make lists of your most urgent work, family and educational responsibilities, and your assignments. Make lists of the most important priorities and obligations as well. Compare the urgent with the important. Budget your time to take a systematic and methodical approach to fulfilling obligations.

Critical Thinking Confidence – Commit to resolve a challenging problem by reasoning it through. Embrace a question, problem, or issue that calls for a reasoned decision, and begin working on it yourself or in collaboration with others.

Inquisitiveness – Learn something new. Go out and seek information about any topic of interest, but not one that you must learn about for school or work, and let the world surprise you with its variety and complexity.

Judiciousness – Revisit a decision you made recently and consider whether it is still the right decision. See if any relevant new information has come to light. Ask if the results that had been anticipated are being realized. If warranted, revise the decision to better suit your new understanding of the state of affairs.

2.2 Core Critical Thinking Skills

We have talked about the "eager" in the phrase "skilled and eager" to think critically. Now let's explore the "skilled" part by examining those mental skills that are at the core of purposeful reflective judgment.

Interpreting and Analyzing the Consensus Statement

When thinking about the meaning and importance of the term "critical thinking" in Chapter 1, we referred to an expert consensus. That consensus identified certain cognitive skills as being central to critical thinking. Their research findings are shown below.[12] Let's unpack their quote. The experts identify six skills:

- **Interpretation**
- **Analysis**
- **Evaluation**
- **Inference**
- **Explanation**
- **Self-Regulation**

As the Delphi definition of the critical thinking process indicates,[13] we apply these six skills to:

- **Evidence**   (facts, experiences, statements)
- **Conceptualizations** (ideas, theories, ways of seeing the world)
- **Methods**   (strategies, techniques, approaches)
- **Criteria**   (standards, benchmarks, expectations)
- **Context**   (situations, conditions, circumstances)

We are expected to ask a lot of tough questions about all five areas. For example, How good is the evidence? Do these concepts apply? Were the methods appropriate? Are there better methods for investigating this question? What standard of proof should we be using? How rigorous should we be? What circumstantial factors might lead us to revise our opinions? Good critical thinkers are ever-vigilant, monitoring and correcting their own thinking.

Delphi Definition of Critical Thinking

"We understand critical thinking to be purposeful, self-regulatory judgment which results in interpretation, analysis, **evaluation**, and inference, as well as explanation of the evidential, **conceptual**, **methodological**, **criteriological**, or **contextual** considerations upon which that judgment is based."

— *The Delphi Report*, American Philosophical Association

The Jury Is Deliberating

In *12 Angry Men* by Reginald Rose a jury deliberates the guilt or innocence of a young man accused of murder.[14] The jury room is hot, the hour is late, and tempers are short. Ten of the twelve jurors have voted to convict when we join the story. In the classic American film version of Rose's play, one of the two jurors who are still uncertain is Henry Fonda's character.[15] That character first *analyzes* the testimony of a pair of witnesses, putting what each said side by side. Using all his critical thinking skills, he tries to reconcile their conflicting testimony. He asks how the old man could possibly have heard the accused man threaten the victim with the El Train roaring by the open window. From the facts of the situation, Fonda's character has inferred that the old man could not have been telling the truth. Fonda then *explains* that inference to the other jurors with a flawless argument. But the other jurors still want to know why an old man with apparently nothing to gain would not tell the truth. One of the other jurors, an old man himself, *interprets* that witness's behavior for his colleagues. The conversation then turns to the question of how to *interpret* the expression "I'm going kill you!" that the accused is alleged to have shouted. One juror wants to take it literally as a statement of intent. Another argues that context matters, that words and phrases cannot always be taken literally. Someone asks why the defense attorney did not bring up these same arguments during his cross-examination of the witness. In their *evaluation*, the jury does seem to agree on the quality of the defense—namely, that it was poor. One juror draws the conclusion that this means the lawyer thought his own client was guilty. But is that so? Could there be some other explanation or interpretation for the half-hearted defense?

The jury has the authority to question the quality of the *evidence*, to dispute the competing *theories* of the case that are presented by the prosecution and the defense, to find fault with the investigatory *methods* of the police, to dispute whether the doubts some members may have meet the *criterion* of "reasonable doubt" or not, and to take into consideration all the *contextual* and *circumstantial* elements that may be relevant. In other words, a good jury is the embodiment of good critical thinking that a group of people practice. The stronger their collective skills, the greater the justice that will be done. To more fully appreciate the mix of emotion and interpersonal strife within which a group of people must make a life altering decision, locate and watch *12 Angry Men*. There are many great scenes in the classic release, particularly the El Train Scene.

> "Pretending to know everything closes the door to what's really there."
>
> Neil deGrasse Tyson, Scientist[16]

Critical Thinking Skills Fire in Many Combinations

One way to present critical thinking skills is in the form of a list. But lists typically suggest that we move from one item to another in a predetermined step-by-step progression, similar to pilots methodically working down the mandatory list of preflight safety checks. Critical thinking is not rote or scripted in the way that a list of skills might suggest.

Critical thinking is not the set of skills the experts identified, but rather *it is using those skills in the process of making a reflective, purposeful judgment*. Imagine for a moment what it is like looking for an address while driving on a busy and unfamiliar street. To do this, we must simultaneously be coordinating the use of many skills, but fundamentally our focus is on the driving and not on the individual skills. We are concentrating on street signs and address numbers while also interpreting traffic signals such as stoplights, and controlling the car's speed, direction, and location relative to other vehicles. Driving requires coordinating physical skills such as how hard to press the gas or tap the brakes and mental skills such as analyzing the movement of our

The old man could not possibly have heard the threat.

Core Critical Thinking Skills Interact

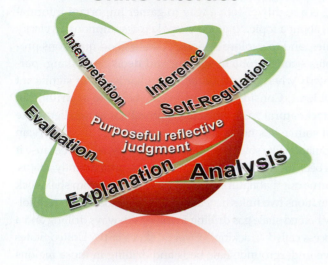

vehicle relative to those around ours to avoid accidents. In the end, however, we say that we drove the car to the destination. We do not list all the skills, and we certainly do not practice them one by one in a serial order. Rather, we use them all in concert. Critical thinking has certain important features in common with looking for an address while driving on a busy and unfamiliar street. The key similarity to notice here is that critical thinking requires using all the skills in concert, not one at a time or sequentially.

The intricate interaction of critical thinking skills in real-life problem solving and decision making may begin with an analysis, an interpretation, an inference, or an evaluation. Then, using self-regulation, we may go back and check ourselves for accuracy. On other occasions, we may first draw an inference based on an interpretation and then evaluate our own inference. We may be explaining our reasoning to someone and realize, because we are monitoring our own thinking, that our reasoning is not adequate. And this may lead us to recheck our analyses or our inferences to see where we may need to refine our thinking. That was what the jury, considered as a whole, was doing in *12 Angry Men*—going back and forth among interpretation, analysis, inference, and evaluation, with Henry Fonda's character as the person who called for more careful self-monitoring and self-correction. The jury's deliberation demanded reflection, and an orderly analysis and evaluation of the facts, but deliberation is not constrained by adherence to a predetermined list or sequencing of mental events. Nor is critical thinking.

No, it would be an unfortunate and misleading oversimplification to reduce critical thinking to a list of skills, such as the recipe on the lid of dehydrated soup: first

analyze, then infer, then explain, then close the lid, and wait five minutes. To avoid the misimpressions that a list might engender, we need some other way of displaying the names of the skills.

We[17] have always found it helpful when talking with college students and faculty around the world about critical thinking skills to use the metaphor of a sphere with the names of the skills displayed randomly over its surface.[18] Why a sphere? Three reasons.

- First, organizing the names of the skills on a sphere is truer to our lived experience of engaging in reflective judgment, as indicated above. We have all experienced those moments when, in the mental space of a few seconds, our minds fly from interpretation to analysis to inference and evaluation as we try to sort out our thoughts before we commit ourselves to a particular decision. We may go back and forth interpreting what we are seeing, analyzing ideas and drawing tentative inferences, trying to be sure that we have things right before we make a judgment.

- Second, a sphere does not presume any given order of events, which, for the present, is truer to the current state of the science. Maybe brain research will lead to refinements in our understanding of the biochemical basis and sequencing of higher order reasoning. But for the present, maturity of judgment suggests that we should not jump to conclusions.

- Third, a sphere reminds us about another important characteristic of critical thinking skills, namely, that each can be applied to the other and to themselves.[19] We can analyze our inferences. We can analyze our analyses. We can explain our interpretations. We can evaluate our explanations. We can monitor those processes and correct any mistakes we might see ourselves making. In this way, *the core critical thinking skills can be said to interact.*

Strengthening Our Core Critical Thinking Skills

Musicians, salespeople, athletes, nurses, teachers, and soldiers strive to improve their likelihood of success by strengthening the skills needed in their respective professions. Even as they train in one skill or another, working people must not lose sight of how those skills come together in their professional work. The quality of the concert, the number of sales made, the games won, the health care outcomes achieved, the learning accomplished, and the success of the mission—these are the outcomes that count. The same holds for critical thinkers. Success consists of making well-reasoned, reflective judgments to solve problems, and to make decisions effectively. Critical thinking skills are the tools we use to accomplish those purposes. In the driving example, our attention was on the challenges associated with reaching the intended street address. In real-world critical thinking, our attention will be on the challenges associated with solving the problem or making the decision at hand.

> I cannot teach anybody anything,
> I can only make them think.
>
> Socrates (469—399 BCE), Philosopher[20]

The Art of the Good Question

There are many familiar questions that invite people to use their critical thinking skills. We can associate certain questions with certain skills. The table below gives some examples.[21] Often, our best critical thinking comes when we ask the right questions.[22]

Asking good questions, ones that promote critical thinking, is a highly effective way to gather important information about a topic, to probe unspoken assumptions, to clarify issues, and to explore options. Asking good questions promotes strong problem solving and decision making, particularly when we encounter unfamiliar issues or significant problems. Consider for a moment the topic of drilling to extract natural gas from shale. Natural gas as an alternative fuel source has not enjoyed the attention of the American population like solar energy or wind energy, mostly because it has been thought to be in short supply—until recently, that is. It turns out that natural gas can be harvested from shale rock formations two miles beneath the Earth's surface. The technology behind shale gas drilling involves sideways drilling and a process called "fracking." Over 30 states in the United States have underground shale beds and drilling in those regions

The Experts Worried That Schooling Might Be Harmful!

The critical thinking expert panel we talked about in Chapter 1 was absolutely convinced that critical thinking is a pervasive and purposeful human phenomenon. They insisted that strong critical thinkers should be characterized not merely by the cognitive skills they may have, but also by how they approach life and living in general.

This was a bold claim. At that time schooling in most of the world was characterized by the memorization of received truths. At that time in the USA, the 1980s "back to basics" mantra echoed the pre-1960s Eisenhower era, when so much of schooling was focused on producing "interchangeable human parts" for an industrial manufacturing economy. Critical thinking that frees the mind to ask any question and evaluate any assumption naturally goes far beyond what the typical classroom was delivering. In fact, many of the experts feared that some of the things people experience in our schools could actually be harmful to the development and cultivation of strong critical thinking.

Critical thinking came before formal schooling was invented. It lies at the very roots of civilization. The experts saw critical thinking as a driving force in the human journey from ignorance, superstition, and savagery toward global understanding. Consider what life would be like without the things on this list, and you will appreciate why they had such confidence in strong critical thinking. The approaches to life and living, which the experts said characterized the strong critical thinker included:

- inquisitiveness and a desire to remain well-informed with regard to a wide range of topics,
- trust in the processes of reasoned inquiry,
- self-confidence in one's own abilities to reason,

- open-mindedness regarding divergent world views,
- flexibility in considering alternatives and opinions,
- understanding of the opinions of other people,
- fair-mindedness in appraising reasoning,
- honesty in facing one's own biases, prejudices, stereotypes, or egocentric tendencies,
- prudence in suspending, making, or altering judgments,
- willingness to reconsider and revise views where honest reflection suggests that change is warranted,
- alertness to opportunities to use critical thinking.

The experts went beyond approaches to life and living in general to emphasize how strong critical thinkers approach specific issues, questions, or problems. The experts said we would find strong critical thinkers striving for:

- clarity in stating the question or concern,
- orderliness in working with complexity,
- diligence in seeking relevant information,
- reasonableness in selecting and applying criteria,
- care in focusing attention on the concern at hand,
- persistence though difficulties are encountered,
- precision to the degree permitted by the subject and the circumstances.

Table 5, page 25. American Philosophical Association. 1990, *Critical Thinking: An Source: Expert Consensus Statement for Purposes of Educational Assessment and Instruction.* Used with permission from Insight Assessment-Measuring thinking worldwide. www.insightassessment.com.

Questions to Fire Up Our Critical Thinking Skills	
Interpretation	• What does this mean? • What's happening? • How should we understand that (e.g., what he or she just said)? • What is the best way to characterize/categorize/classify this? • In this context, what was intended by saying/doing that? • How can we make sense out of this (experience, feeling, statement)?
Analysis	• Please tell us again your reasons for making that claim. • What is your conclusion/What is it that you are claiming? • Why do you think that? • What are the arguments pro and con? • What assumptions must we make to accept that conclusion? • What is your basis for saying that?
Inference	• Given what we know so far, what conclusions can we draw? • Given what we know so far, what can we rule out? • What does this evidence imply? • If we abandoned/accepted that assumption, how would things change? • What additional information do we need to resolve this question? • If we believed these things, what would they imply for us going forward? • What are the consequences of doing things that way? • What are some alternatives we haven't yet explored? • Let's consider each option and see where it takes us. • Are there any undesirable consequences that we can and should foresee?
Evaluation	• How credible is that claim? • Why do we think we can trust what this person claims? • How strong are those arguments? • Do we have our facts right? • How confident can we be in our conclusion, given what we now know?
Explanation	• What were the specific findings/results of the investigation? • Please tell us how you conducted that analysis. • How did you come to that interpretation? • Please take us through your reasoning one more time. • Why do you think that (was the right answer/was the solution)? • How would you explain why this particular decision was made?
Self-Regulation	• Our position on this issue is still too vague; can we be more precise? • How good was our methodology, and how well did we follow it? • Is there a way we can reconcile these two apparently conflicting conclusions? • How good is our evidence? • OK, before we commit, what are we missing? • I'm finding some of our definitions a little confusing; can we revisit what we mean by certain things before making any final decisions?

Source: © 2009, 2011, 2014 User Manual for the *California Critical Thinking Skills Test*, published by Insight Assessment. Used with permission.

has made some homeowners into overnight millionaires. The drilling has given a boost to the local economies in terms of jobs and retail sales. But, as reported in 2011 by Lesley Stahl on *60 Minutes*, and many more times by other news outlets in recent years, accidents and other safety concerns have people who live in drilling communities concerned. Those living near shale gas drill sites are questioning the contamination of the drinking water by the chemicals involved in the fracking process. In 2014 Lesley Stahl followed up with a piece on the myth of the clean tech crash. Search "60 Minutes fracking Stahl" to locate her reports. Notice how she uses her critical thinking skills to investigate and ask good questions.

Before forming an opinion for or against fracking under residential real estate in your community, as a strong critical thinker you first would want to know more about this natural gas extraction method. Let's try to think of good critical thinking questions to ask. You might ask "What is known about the environmental risks of the chemicals involved in the fracking processes?" or "What exactly is involved in establishing a new drill site in my community?" to promote **interpretation**. You could also ask "What are the statistics on the frequency and severity of the accidents and safety violations associated with shale gas drilling?" to promote **inference**. Perhaps we would ask "If our community were to permit fracking, what would be the economic impact of that decision, and for whom, and how long would we have to wait before seeing those benefits?" to promote **evaluation**. Or you could ask "Do

Leslie Stahl, Investigative Reporter, interviews Valerie Jarrett, Senior Advisor to President Obama and Presidential Assistant for Public Engagement and Intergovernmental Affairs.

JOURNAL

Engaging Critical Thinking Skills?

In June of 2014 the U.S. Supreme Court ruled that if a family owns a corporation that corporation is exempted from one of the provisions of Obamacare. Specifically, the corporation does not have to pay for contraceptive options which the family objects to on the basis of their religious beliefs. Some people see this ruling as an affirmation of religious freedom, others see this ruling as restriction on the rights of women employees.*

What questions could you ask to engage your critical thinking skills of analysis, inference, and evaluation regarding what this ruling means, its potential implications, and the positive or negative practical impact of this ruling on the everyday lives of people?

*Supreme Court of the United States, "Burwell, Secretary of HHS et. al. v Hobby Lobby Stores, Inc." (Search suggestion "Hobby Lobby Scotus")

---

the expert consensus research discussed earlier.[23] The experts provided this more refined level of analysis of the concept of "critical thinking skills" to assist students and teachers in finding examples and exercises that could help strengthen these skills. But, remember that "critical thinking" does not refer to a package of skills. Rather, critical thinking is what we do with the skills—which is making purposeful reflective judgments about what to believe or what to do.

If you have access to an iPad, download the free Insight Assessment sample critical thinking test app. Search "critical thinking" at the App Store. The app offers a five-question critical thinking skills test and short critical thinking mindset survey.

2.3 Looking Ahead

"Wait! If critical thinking is a process, why haven't you authors given us the steps in that process? In fact, what you did say was that nobody knew the order in which the different critical thinking skills fire. So, if the process of critical thinking is not applying the skills one after another, then what is the process?"

You are correct, critical thinking as a process needs to be explained and illustrated. **Throughout the first two chapters we equated the critical thinking process with thoughtful problem solving and fair-minded decision making.** Every discipline from music composition to biochemistry and every professional field from military leadership to counseling psychology has its experts talking about how people working in those domains engage in problem solving and decision making. Our question was this: Is there a more general way to describe the process, one that has applications across all the academic disciplines and professional fields, and beyond. And, as decades of research by ourselves and others[24] indicates, the answer, affirmed by the Delphi Panel, is a resounding Yes! Revealing, detailing, and guiding the correct application of that process, including each of the core skills, is what the rest of this book is about.

In Chapter 3 is an overview of the critical thinking process. There we present a basic five-step critical thinking process for problem solving. Then later in the book, when the timing is right, we refine that process in a chapter

---

my past statements in support of alternative energy policies, or my financial interests in residential real estate, or my fears for the health and safety of myself and my family bias my review of the information about shale gas drilling?" to exercise our judiciousness habit of mind and our **self-regulation** skills.

Skills and Subskills Defined

The six core critical thinking skills each has related subskills, as shown in the table Core Critical Thinking Skills. The descriptions in the table of each core skill come from

THINKING CRITICALLY

Ask Good Critical Thinking Questions

Using the discussion about shale gas drilling as an example, practice formulating good critical thinking questions about the topics listed below. Look too at the table entitled "Questions to Fire Up Our Critical Thinking Skills" to get ideas about how to target specific critical thinking skills with your questions. Write at least four good critical thinking questions about each of the topics below. Instead of making them all analytical or inferential, spread the questions over at least three core critical thinking skills. Before you write the questions, go online to review relevant recent news stories about the topic.

1. Sagarika Ghose, a former CNN news anchor and writer for a leading newspaper in India, has over 175,000 followers on Twitter. Ms. Ghose regularly receives cyber threats of gang rape and stripping. Assume you are a reporter for an American TV network that does balanced and fair stories on serious topics, and assume you have the opportunity for a Skype interview with Ms. Ghose. Write four good critical thinking interview questions. Before you write the questions, do some background research. Start by searching "Sagarika Ghose rape threats."

2. Boko Haram is a militant organization violently opposed to Western culture. In the past two years the group has killed more than 1,000 people with suicide bombers, and vicious raids on churches, schools, and villages. (Search "Boko Haram Nigeria BBC News.") The group's opposition to Western education is so strong that it has threatened, kidnapped, and killed female students and their teachers. And yet, many parents still seek opportunities for Western education for their daughters and those young women continue to go to schools that teach dangerous subjects, like history and science, and use Western educational methods, like critical thinking. Assume you have the opportunity to interview a teacher at a school that offers a Western education to girls in a region where Boko Haram kidnappings and attacks have occurred. Frame four good critical

Abubakar Shekau, Boko Haram leader. From a video calling for more attacks on schools to protect Islam from the threat of Western education.

Source: AFP/Getty Images

thinking questions to ask the teacher. Search "Boko Haram kidnaps school girls" to begin your background research.

3. Perhaps with more foresight strong critical thinkers might have anticipated this problem. But when the one-child policy was put in place, China was also beginning to experience a phenomenon that has continued for many decades, namely, the migration of young people into urban areas in search of better jobs and a lifestyle different from what is available "back on the farm." In 2013 China passed a law requiring children to visit their elderly parents who lived in the countryside. Search "China requires visit parents" to get the details. Then formulate good critical thinking questions about this policy and its potential benefits and difficulties.

4. Recently a study of 86,000 women who gave birth and 9,000 women who had abortions reported that 40 percent of all pregnancies in the United States were unwanted. The study appeared online in the journal *Perspectives on Sexual and Reproductive Health*. Review the study and the news coverage that report on the study and offer editorial comments. Then write four good critical thinking questions about this phenomenon.

5. The plant called quinoa offers "an exceptional balance of amino acids; quinoa, they declared, is virtually unrivaled in the plant or animal kingdom for its life-sustaining nutrients," according to a *New York Times* story about the problems of too much success. As global demand skyrockets, quinoa producers and other Bolivians may not be receiving either the nutritional or the economic benefits of this crop. Learn more about quinoa and the problems of its success by searching "quinoa economic impact." A 2013 story in the *Huffington Post* should be one of your search results. Then formulate four good critical thinking questions about this issue. Let one of the questions be about the importance of having foresight.

6. The Buddhist nation of Bhutan has a Gross National Happiness Commission, and the head of that commission has a problem: Domestic violence appears to be rampant among a population whose religion abhors any kind of violence. Search "Bhutan domestic violence Commission for Gross National Happiness" and then formulate a related series of four good critical thinking questions from the perspective of the head of the Gross National Happiness Commission.

7. Search "survey seven social classes in UK" and you will see a BBC report on a scientific survey that suggests that the familiar grouping of social classes in to just three, "upper, middle, and poverty" no longer effectively describes social stratification in the United Kingdom. Review the BBC story and related stories, and write four good critical thinking questions about that report. Some questions can focus on understanding the report and its implications, others could focus on whether or not a similar finding would result if the study had focused on the social class structure of some other industrialized country, for example, the United States.

Core Critical Thinking Skills		
Skill	**Experts' Consensus Description**	**Subskill**
Interpretation	"To comprehend and express the meaning or significance of a wide variety of experiences, situations, data, events, judgments, conventions, beliefs, rules, procedures, or criteria"	Categorize Decode significance Clarify meaning
Analysis	"To identify the intended and actual inferential relationships among statements, questions, concepts, descriptions, or other forms of representation intended to express belief, judgment, experiences, reasons, information, or opinions"	Examine ideas Identify arguments Identify reasons and claims
Inference	"To identify and secure elements needed to draw reasonable conclusions; to form conjectures and hypotheses; to consider relevant information and to reduce the consequences flowing from data, statements, principles, evidence, judgments, beliefs, opinions, concepts, descriptions, questions, or other forms of representation"	Query evidence Conjecture alternatives Draw conclusions using inductive or deductive reasoning
Evaluation	"To assess the credibility of statements or other representations that are accounts or descriptions of a person's perception, experience, situation, judgment, belief, or opinion; and to assess the logical strength of the actual or intended inferential relationships among statements, descriptions, questions, or other forms of representation"	Assess credibility of claims Assess quality of arguments that were made using inductive or deductive reasoning
Explanation	"To state and to justify that reasoning in terms of the evidential, conceptual, methodological, criteriological, and contextual considerations upon which one's results were based; and to present one's reasoning in the form of cogent arguments"	State results Justify procedures Present arguments
Self-Regulation	"Self-consciously to monitor one's cognitive activities, the elements used in those activities, and the results educed, particularly by applying skills in analysis, and evaluation to one's own inferential judgments with a view toward questioning, confirming, validating, or correcting either one's reasoning or one's results"	Self-monitor Self-correct

Source: From Peter A. Facione, American Philosophical Association, *Critical Thinking: A Statement of Expert Consensus for Purpose of Educational Assessment & Instruction,* (also known as The Delphi Report). Copyright © 1990, The California Academic Press, 217 La Cruz Ave., Millbrae, CA 94030. All Rights Reserved. Reprinted by permission.

devoted specifically to more sophisticated strategies for reflective decision making. In both chapters we point out how all the steps and strategies call for positive critical thinking habits of mind and rely on multiple critical thinking skills. To supplement these broader overview chapters, five chapters at the end of the book take the critical thinking process into several different areas of inquiry.

We used the phrase "when the timing is right" in the last paragraph because learning things in the right order is very important. Like coaches working with very promising artists or athletes, we have a plan for when and how each critical thinking skill can be developed. We begin with *interpretation* and *analysis* in Chapters 4 and 5. There we examine strategies for clarifying the meanings of individual claims and ways to visually display the reasoning people use to support claims and conclusions. In Chapters 6 through 9 we work on *evaluation*, looking first at how to assess the credibility of individual claims and then at how

THINK CRITICALLY

What Are Your Professors and Textbooks Asking of You?

1. A good education includes learning content knowledge and learning skills. Because there is so much to learn, it is understandable that many instructors focus a lot of attention on helping students get the content knowledge right. These profs often call on students in class to answer questions that show that they know the meanings of technical terms or have learned the material from a previous lesson. Sprinkled in among those questions from time to time are critical thinking skills questions, like those listed in the "Questions to Fire Up Our Critical Thinking Skills" table. Here is your challenge: In each of your classes over the next two class days, keep a list of the questions that the instructors ask students. Then, take the complete list and evaluate each question to see which were intended to evoke the use of critical thinking skills. Which skills were most often evoked?

2. Some textbooks include exercises at the end of each chapter. Those exercises can address content knowledge to be sure it is well understood. They can also invite students to apply their critical thinking skills to that knowledge—for example to interpret some data, to analyze arguments, to draw out the consequences of certain principles or facts, or to explain the right methods to apply. Take the textbooks for your other subjects and review the exercises at the end of the unit or chapter you are on. Identify those questions, if any, that are intended to evoke critical thinking skills. In the case of each textbook, write five additional "exercise questions" that evoke critical thinking about the content of the chapter.

to evaluate the quality of arguments. Strengthening our *self-regulation* skill is the emphasis in Chapters 10 and 11 as we take a closer look at what science tells us about our real-life decision making. The advantages and disadvantages of snap judgments and reflective decision making are the topics for these two chapters. Chapters 10 and 11 are of particular importance to people pursuing careers in professional fields like business, health care, education, communication, counseling, law, social work, or engineering because effective decision making is so valuable in professional practice disciplines.

We draw all the bits and pieces together in Chapters 12, 13, and 14. This trilogy of chapters emphasizes *inference* and *explanation*. At one level they explore the benefits, uses, strengths, and weaknesses of the three most powerful forms of argument making: comparative ("this is like that") reasoning, ideological ("top down") reasoning, and empirical ("bottom up"). But for us they are more than just chapters in a text book.

Do not miss Chapters 12, 13, and 14. They are the heart of the matter. These three set up the most powerful contrasts between how the members of our species think. These chapters illustrate why we humans so often are unable to come to reasoned accord, even when we are giving it our best effort. It turns out that many of our personal doubts and much of the discord in the world have more to do with how we think than what we think. Chapter 12 explains how powerful analogies and pattern recognition strategies shape our thinking, color our expectations, and persuade us using a minimum of evidence. It turns out that even poor analogies and fumbling metaphors can be wildly effective, amazingly so. We also use top down ideological reasoning, as Chapter 13 explains, to hammer home our prejudices and preconceptions. Ideological reasoning can often generate unwarranted metaphysical and moral certitude. And these are the seeds of war. And at the same time, as Chapter 14 explains, we use hypotheses and evidence to creep ever so slowly toward a truer and truer

scientific understanding of this marvelously complex universe, always knowing that certitude is beyond our grasp and that the next generation will overturn what truths we feel we have so confidently articulated. These three divergent ways of reasoning often create as many conflicts within our own minds as they create between ourselves and other people. Given how we human beings think, it is clear that strong critical thinking skills and habits of mind are needed if we are to negotiate livable paths not just to our own individual well-being but to the truth about how our universe works, to mutual respect, and to harmony in the world community.

As we said earlier, the final chapters take the critical thinking problem solving process into several quite different but important domains. Because *effective writing* and critical thinking are connected in the classroom, in every professional field, and all throughout our lives, Chapter 15 shows how to write sound and effective arguments. Because we all have to deal with vexing ethical problems at many points in our lives, Chapter 16 connects critical thinking with *ethical decision making*. Chapter 17, on the *logic of declarative statements*, builds on the ideas first presented in the Chapter 8 on valid inferences People interested in accounting, technology, engineering, and mathematics will see connections with their disciplines and the effort to connect logic, symbolic notation and natural language. Strong critical thinkers engage in *social science* inquiry into human behavior and apply social science findings to problems in professional fields like education and communication. Critical thinking is manifested in systematic *natural science* inquiry into the causal explanations for the observed patterns, structures, and functions of natural phenomena from the subatomic to the galactic in scope.

Strong critical thinking skills and a positive critical thinking mindset are integrally connected to success in each of these important domains of life and learning. Use these final chapters to connect the process of critical thinking to what interests you.

Like athletes or artists, we practice the skills so we can integrate them smoothly when the time comes to perform and to compete.

Summing up this chapter,

the critical thinking process applies cognitive skills of interpretation, analysis, inference, evaluation, explanation, and self-regulation in an effort to judge what to believe or what to do. That is the "able" part of being "eager and able" to think. The "eager" part is being strongly disposed toward using critical thinking to solve problems and to make decisions. People exhibit the positive critical thinking mindset when they are truth-seeking, open-minded, analytical, systematic, confident in reasoning, inquisitive, and judicious in their application of critical thinking. Strong critical thinking does not make a person automatically ethical or unethical. But critical thinking skills are valuable for decision making of all kinds, including ethical decision making. A major asset in critical thinking is the capacity to ask good questions.

Key Concepts

truth-seeking means that a person has intellectual integrity and a courageous desire to actively strive for the best possible knowledge in any given situation. A truth-seeker asks probing questions and follows reasons and evidence wherever they lead, even if the results go against his or her cherished beliefs.

open-minded means that a person is tolerant of divergent views and sensitive to the possibility of his or her own possible biases. An open-minded person respects the right of others to have different opinions.

analytical means that a person is habitually alert to potential problems and vigilant in anticipating consequences and trying to foresee short-term and long-term outcomes of events, decisions, and actions. "Foresightful" is another word for what "analytical" means here.

systematic means that a person consistently endeavors to take an organized and thorough approach to identifying and resolving problems. A systematic person is orderly, focused, persistent, and diligent in his or her approach to problem solving, learning, and inquiry.

confident in reasoning means that a person is trustful of his or her own reasoning skills to yield good judgments. A person's or a group's confidence in their own critical thinking may or may not be warranted, which is another matter.

inquisitive means that a person habitually strives to be well-informed, wants to know how things work, and seeks to learn new things about a wide range of topics, even if the immediate utility of knowing those things is not directly evident. An inquisitive person has a strong sense of intellectual curiosity.

judicious means that a person approaches problems with a sense that some are ill-structured and some can have more than one plausible solution. A judicious person has the cognitive maturity to realize that many questions and issues are not black and white, and that, at times, judgments must be made in contexts of uncertainty.

interpretation is an expression of the meaning or significance of a wide variety of experiences, situations, data, events, judgments, conventions, beliefs, rules, procedures, or criteria.

inference identifies and secures elements needed to draw reasonable conclusions; it forms conjectures and hypotheses, it considers relevant information, and it reduces or draws out the consequences flowing from data, statements, principles, evidence, judgments, beliefs, opinions, concepts, descriptions, questions, or other forms of representation.

evaluation assesses the credibility of statements or other representations that are accounts or descriptions of a person's perception, experience, situation, judgment, belief, or opinion; also assesses the logical strength of the actual or intended inferential relationships among statements, descriptions, questions, or other forms of representation.

self-regulation is a process in which one monitors one's cognitive activities, the elements used in those activities, and the results educed, particularly by applying skills in analysis, and evaluation to one's own inferential judgments with a view toward questioning, confirming, validating, or correcting either one's reasoning or one's results.

analysis identifies the intended and actual inferential relationships among statements, questions, concepts, descriptions, or other forms of representation intended to express belief, judgment, experiences, reasons, information, or opinions.

explanation states and justifies reasoning in terms of the evidential, conceptual, methodological, criteriological, and contextual considerations upon which one's results were based; also presents one's reasoning in the form of cogent arguments.

Applications

Reflective Log

Schooling and Critical Thinking – This is a three-part interviewing and writing exercise: **Part 1:** Mark Twain is reported to have said, "I have never let my schooling interfere with my education."[25] Connect that sentiment with the information in the box, "The Experts Worried That School Might Be Harmful!" What is your reasoned opinion on the matter? If you were critical of schooling, what would you recommend be done to improve it? What evidence do you have that your suggestions would actually work in the real world? Now ask someone who is 10 years younger than you what Mark Twain meant. Note the response in your log. Then ask someone who is at least 20 years older than you what Twain's saying might mean. Log the response. Compare the three opinions: yours, the younger person's, and the older person's opinions. End this notation in your log by reflecting on these this question: Should K–12 schooling be designed to prevent students from learning to think critically for themselves? Why or why not? **Part 2:** You were specifically asked not to "defend," "evaluate," or to "argue for" one side or the other in the previous items. Here's your new challenge:

Keeping an open mind and maybe stirring up a bit of courage, too, interview two professors and two students not in your critical thinking class. Present them with the same two claims, but invite them to agree or disagree with each one and to give their reasons. Note their reasons respectfully, and ask follow-up questions aimed at evoking more critical thinking. You should be able to base your follow-up questions on the group work you did earlier when you developed the best arguments for and against each claim. Then, in your reflective log, record the conversations and highlight some of the places where the people you interviewed did, in fact, engage in some deeper critical thinking about the topic. **Part 3:** Using the "Holistic Critical Thinking Scoring Rubric" from Chapter 1, how would you evaluate the critical thinking displayed by each of the four people you interviewed? Quote some of the things each side said that led you to evaluate them in the way that you did. [We know you caught it, but just in case you didn't, that was another critical thinking skills question. This one asked you to explain the evidence you used for your evaluation.]

Individual Exercises

Explain the mistake. Here are six misconceptions about critical thinking habits of mind or critical thinking skills. Write a brief explanation of why each is wrong.

1. Calling on people to be systematic means that everyone must think the same way.

2. Critical thinking habits of mind are always positive.

3. People with a strong desire to be analytical have the skill to foresee the consequences of options and events.

4. People who have not taken a course in critical thinking cannot have strong critical thinking skills.

5. Critical thinking is applying the six critical thinking skills in their proper order one after the other.

6. Self-monitoring and self-correcting are unnecessary skills when your ideas are right in the first place.

Apollo 13 – There is a memorable scene in *Apollo 13* when engineers are put in a room and tasked with designing something that will reduce the toxicity of the air in the spacecraft. Their challenge is that the device must be something the astronauts can fabricate (a) as quickly as possible because time is running out, (b) using only materials and tools the astronauts have at their disposal in the spacecraft, and (c) using methods the astronauts can perform inside the spacecraft's cramped environment. Locate that scene online and watch it two or

three times. The second or third time through, focus on trying to identify evidence of the critical thinking skills and habits of mind. Listen to what the characters say and watch their body language. It helps to take notes when watching. Prepare a brief description of the scene, like the description that begins this chapter. In your description emphasize the critical thinking skills and habits of mind you noticed the characters displaying either individually or as a group. Hint: to emphasize the critical thinking in your description use verb forms of the critical thinking skill names, (like "analyze" and "evaluate") and adjective forms of the positive habits of mind, (like "open-minded" and "systematic").

"Truthiness" – In October of 2005 Stephen Colbert, a master of humor and irony, offered "truthiness" as his word of the day. In 2006 *Merriam-Webster Online* made "truthiness" the word of the year for 2006. That dictionary defines it two ways:[26] 1. truthiness (noun) "truth that comes from the gut, not books" (Stephen Colbert, Comedy Central's *The Colbert Report*, October 2005); 2. "the quality of preferring concepts or facts one wishes to be true, rather than concepts or facts known to be true" (American Dialect Society, January 2006). How does "truthiness," in either of its two definitions, relate to "truth-seeking" as we have defined it in this chapter. Oh, BTW, you can still find a clip of Colbert's October 2005 episode online if you search.

Pros-and-cons video project – Consider this claim: "*Effective writing and critical thinking are the two most important things to learn in college.*" Do not take a position on that claim; instead present the strongest possible arguments pro and con. One way to gather information about this is to ask other people their views and the reasons they have for those views. Ask at least three teachers or professors, ask three successful people in business and three in other professions, and ask three people who graduated at least 20 years ago what they think. Get their reasons, not just their opinions. Then formulate the arguments pro and con. Make and post a Web video that shows both sides.

Evaluate the critical thinking in editorials – Look at the descriptions of each of the four levels of the "Holistic Critical Thinking Scoring Rubric" in Chapter 1. In each, underline the elements that call out positive or negative critical thinking habits of mind. Then go online and locate two editorials from this week's *New York Times, Washington Post, Huffington Post, San Jose Mercury News,* or *BBC News*. Select any issue or topic you wish. But find something that is controversial enough that you can find at least one pro and one con editorial. Approach the two editorials with an open mind. Resist forming a judgment about the issue at least until you have read and considered both carefully. Evaluate both using the "Holistic Critical Thinking Scoring Rubric." Explain in detail the reasons for the score you assigned.

Ask two friends to rate you – If you feel comfortable with the idea, ask two of your friends to rate you using the "Critical Thinking Mindset Self-Rating Form." To do this your friend would replace the word "*I*" and the word "*my*" with references to yourself. This assessment could provide valuable information about how your critical thinking disposition manifests itself to others.

SHARED RESPONSE
Cultivating a Positive CT Mindset

How can you cultivate positive critical thinking habits of mind in your everyday life? Give examples. Comment respectfully on the examples others offer.

Group Exercises

What would it be like? Our habitual attitudes affect our behavior and the way that we interact with one another. People who are habitually intellectually dishonest, intolerant, or indifferent act differently in household and workplace settings than those who have opposite, positive habits. This discussion exercise invites you to draw on your experience and your imagination, your foresight, and your inference skills to describe to others what it would be like to interact regularly with a person with negative critical thinking habits of mind. **Scenario #1.** You have a brother, close to your age, who is habitually intellectually dishonest, intolerant, and imprudent in making decisions. He has been like this since junior high school, and he recently enrolled at your college. Now he wants to share your apartment, borrow your car, and get you to help him with his academic assignments. What is it like to have this person as your family member? Given that you have the power to say "no" to his requests, what are your plans with regard to his requests? **Scenario #2.** You have a part-time job in a department store as a clerk. Your old manager used to let your group solve a lot of the store's own problems, like who is going to cover a shift if someone can't work on a given day. But now you have a new manager. This person makes scheduling decisions arbitrarily, and is disorganized, and this means that your group always seems to be rushing to meet deadlines. She also habitually does not think about the consequences of her actions. What is it like to work for this supervisor? Given that you have the right to complain to management about your new supervisor, is that an option you will pursue? What other plans might you make to help you cope with the approach taken by this new supervisor?

Textbooks – Consider this claim: "If textbooks used more critical thinking exercises, students would learn the material better." What are the best arguments for and against that claim? Do not take a position on this. Rather, through group discussion and analysis, work to develop the strongest arguments possible for both sides. What additional information would you need to investigate, to ground each side's arguments in solid facts? What assumptions about learning and schooling are required to make each side's arguments as strong as possible? Again, do not evaluate (yet).

Professors – Consider this claim: "Professors should ask content questions, not critical thinking questions. It's the responsibility of the professor to lay out the content, but it's the job of the student to think critically about the subject matter." Through discussion develop the best arguments for and against that claim. As with the previous discussion topic, avoid taking a position on this. Rather, work to develop the strongest arguments possible for both sides. What additional information is needed to ground each side's arguments in solid facts? What assumptions about learning and schooling are required to make each side's arguments as strong as possible? Again, do not evaluate (yet).

Chapter 3
Solve Problems and Succeed in College

Every combination of decisions and circumstances is perfectly designed to produce exactly the results we are getting. If we do not like the results, we need to change the decisions or the circumstances.

WHAT are the five steps of the "IDEAS" critical thinking process for problem solving and decision making?

HOW can we use the IDEAS critical thinking process to navigate the day-to-day challenges of being a college student?

Learning Outcomes

3.1 Identify the five steps of the IDEAS Critical Thinking General Problem Solving Process.

3.2 Explain how to use the IDEAS critical thinking process to solve problems that

occur in the day-to-day lives of college students.

3.3 Recognize the potential application of the IDEAS process to any problem-solving situation in college or beyond.

A door down the hall slammed and John's eyes popped open. Immediately he blinked them shut. What time is it? He opened one eye to peer at the huge yellow-faced clock his roommate, Trent, had put on the wall. Almost noon!

John sat up in bed and groaned as he realized he was still wearing his jeans and jacket from yesterday, and even his shoes. He wondered how he had made it back to the dorm. But somehow he had. I need a shower, bad, he thought. He struggled to his feet and looked for some clean clothes. Nothing. Maybe he could borrow a shirt from Trent? He pulled open the drawer where Trent kept his T-shirts and socks and saw a piece of paper with his name on it.

"John, No. Don't touch my things. Get a new roommate. Get some help. Stay away from my things. Trent." John pulled open a couple of other drawers and saw copies of the same message.

John's phone was dead, so he plugged it into the charger. When it beeped back to life he saw four unopened messages from the last couple of days. John recognized that one was from his Math Prof who used Blackboard to message the whole class with a one-liner. "Midterm exam is Thursday." Aw, no. John knew that it was too late. One more math exam missed! John wondered what the deadline was for dropping the course.

The next message was from his Dad. "Hi, John. It's official, your mother and I are getting divorced. I'm moving to Dallas. After I get settled maybe you could visit. Keep in touch. Oh, and let me know if you want me to call the Business School Dean about getting into the Finance program. Dad."

Aw, man. Dad's back on that B-School thing. I told him that I wanted to be a cop. If I had gone to Oakland Community College maybe I'd be in the law enforcement program right now. But noooo. He and mom insisted I go to a four-year school. Finance?! What, and end up like dad—an overweight, stressed-out banker? I don't think so.

There was a day old message from some guy named Rodney who wrote, "John, what are you doing? We need your section for the group paper. We're meeting tonight at Samira's apartment. She's going to cut and paste all our pieces together. Tomorrow we proof it. It's due Friday. We need your section now!"

OK, so today the group's proofreading. Maybe I can pull a couple of pages from Wikipedia or something, thought John. What was the goofy topic anyway, ah . . . , something about retired Baby Boomers taking part-time jobs. . . . Who picked that topic anyway? Ugh.

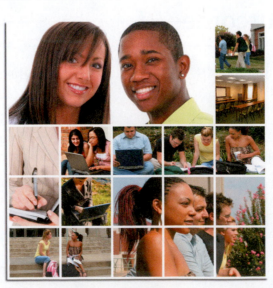

There is no one stereotypic kind of college student.

Three text messages chimed into John's phone. He was about to open the first one when he noticed the date on the phone's display. There was something wrong. It wasn't Thursday at all. It was Friday. Ah, no.

The Soc class met at 10:00 AM. It was almost noon!

He saw a text from Rodney. "Handed in group paper. Your name left off. See e-mail."

John looked back at his e-mail. There was another, more recent message from Rodney. "We talked with the Prof about you. She said we should turn in the paper without including your name. She said it would be academic dishonesty to put you as an author. You're busted, man."

Noon, Friday! He had just enough time to get to his 12:30 Philosophy course. John wondered how he'd ended up in a senior honors seminar on nineteenth-century European ideologists anyway. He hefted the 2-inch-thick book of readings off the shelf to put it into his backpack. John hated the philosophy readings. Did these guys get paid by the word or what? But the Prof was funny, the class discussions were lively, and, although they were seniors and never talked to him, the girls looked good.

His phone rang. John let it go to voice. A moment later the message came and John listened to it.

"Hey, dude! How you doing, man? You were really messed up the other night. Thought you were going to puke in the stairwell or something, man. Zach and I literally poured you into bed. It was like three in the morning and your roommate was pissed that we woke him up. Hey, like I need the thirty dollars you owe me from earlier this week, man. OK. So, text me or something when you get this. It's Friday, man. Weekend! Dude. Parrrrrtaaaayyy."

John groaned. He looked out the window at the November gray Michigan sky. His head throbbed. This was not how college was supposed to be! I'm screwed. Maybe his roommate was right, he thought. "Get some help." But, how? Who?

Obviously, John's life is in disarray. He is beset with problems of many kinds: social, vocational, academic, physical, emotional, and spiritual. He does not appear to know where or how to begin to resolve them. You may know someone like John, who seems to pile one problem on himself after another. John's story illustrates the downside of not having the critical thinking skills and the positive critical thinking habits of mind associated with successful problem solving. In this chapter we present a step by step critical thinking general problem solving process. The process utilizes those core critical thinking skills and is supported by the positive critical thinking habits of mind. In later chapters we will dissect the skills individually. But first, since critical thinking is a process, we need to understand that process. And what better way than by using as our examples the kinds of problems that college students may encounter.

Differences and Similarities

There is no one stereotypic kind of college student. Some college students are younger people, recently graduated from high school, who are attending full-time and living on campus. Others are working adults with family responsibilities who enroll in only one or two courses at a time. Some college students attend nationally known research universities, some attend regional colleges and universities, some attend community colleges or liberal arts colleges. Some students have disabilities, some are military veterans, some are going back to college after years of raising families. Some college students are deeply religious, some are politically active, some enjoy music more than sports, some enjoy video games more than music, some play chess. Some college students are fortunate enough to have plenty of money, some are scraping it together with loans and part-time jobs. Some live at home with parents and siblings, some live alone, some live in apartments with friends, some on military bases around the world. Some take all their courses online, some take all their courses on campus, some take courses that are hybrids of both. Some students are enthusiastic about their chosen major, and some are totally undecided about a major.

About the only thing we can say about "all college students" is that from time to time they all have problems that are social, academic, physical, emotional, vocational, or spiritual. Not in all those domains all the time, and certainly not, we hope, all the same problems. Oh, and one other thing, those college students who have an effective process of problem solving stand a greater chance of successfully earning a degree, achieving their other goals, realizing what it means to have the right and the skills to think for themselves.

> "Students must have initiative; they should not be mere imitators. They must learn to think and act for themselves—and be free."
>
> Caesar Chavez, Farm Worker and Human Rights Activist[1]

No guarantees, mind you. This is the real world. External factors beyond our control, like accidents, illness, natural disasters, social upheavals, and economic downturns can delay our progress toward our goals and, occasionally, lead us to change our minds about those goals entirely. I'm reminded of a college student I knew, a real one—not a fictional one like the John in the opening story—who enrolled as a full-time student, living on campus, and majoring in English Literature. She soon met someone, fell in love, married, and had a child. So the student dropped out of college and, together with her husband, began raising their family. A few years later, with three small children, she decided that she wanted to return to get her degree. Instead of going back as an English Lit major she chose health sciences, because it seemed more practical to her as a young mother. She went to school part-time for many years and sure enough, 11 years after first enrolling, she graduated with her baccalaureate degree. She often used the critical thinking problem-solving process developed in this chapter to work though the many expected and unexpected problems and obstacles that came along during those years.

> "Education delivers a variety of benefits. Higher educational attainment is associated with better labor market outcomes including higher earnings, lower poverty, and lower unemployment. In addition, education is linked to various other benefits including higher job satisfaction, better fringe benefits, and better health."
>
> Women in America: Indicators of Social and Economic Wellbeing[2]

And, of course, I know another college student who came to college, her mind firmly set on becoming a high school science teacher. She dedicated herself to her studies, majored in Biology and in Secondary Education, and graduated in four years.

Your situation may be like these folks or it may be different.

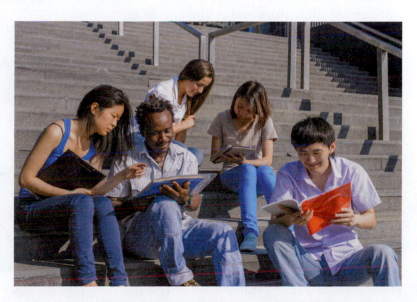

Again, there is no one stereotypic kind of college student.

Your success in college depends, for the most part, on you.

Other people's stories about their college days are *their* stories. How those stories turned out does not determine how your story will turn out.

"Hold up a mirror and ask yourself what you are capable of doing, and what you really care about. Then take the initiative—don't wait for someone else to ask you to act."

Sylvia Earle, Oceanographer and 1998 *Time* "Hero of the Planet"[3]

In addition to the abstract goal of describing a critical thinking process of problem solving which can be very widely applied, this chapter has a very practical goal. Namely, assisting you to be successful as a college student. That starts with a basic question: What does being successful as a college student mean *to you*?

3.1 IDEAS: A 5-Step Critical Thinking General Problem-Solving Process

Each of us must learn how to seize the initiative and solve our own problems—in other words, to take responsibility for our own lives. In my own life I found that there was quite a difference between saying that I was ready to take full responsibility for myself and actually being ready. I had to learn a lot about myself, my friendships, and, most importantly, about how to think through the difficulties and challenges in my life. What really turned out to help me was a critical thinking process I could rely upon whenever a major problem arose. Calling my parents all the time made me feel more dependent than independent, and I knew what advice they were going to give anyway.

And that's the heart of this chapter—the process of using critical thinking to make reflective decisions about how to handle our own problems. There's no way this chapter can cover every possible problem or fit exactly every person's individual unique situation. That is why the critical thinking problem-solving process is so valuable. The process can be applied no matter what kind of problem is at hand—social, vocational, academic, physical, emotional, or spiritual. So even if the specific examples in this chapter don't exactly fit your

particular situation, there's plenty in each chapter that a good critical thinker will easily be able to adapt. One other note: Resolving a problem does not mean that it will never come back. Often the resolutions to our difficulties are sufficient only for a time, or only if conditions do not change.

For the sake of clarity, we define **problem solving** as moving from the point at which we initially realize that we have a difficulty that requires our attention to that point where we regard the difficulty as being sufficiently resolved for the current time and circumstances. There are five steps to reflective, well-reasoned problem solving about what to believe or what to do—that is, to engage in good critical thinking as we work through the problems and challenges in our lives. The process is universally applicable, but in this chapter the examples are the kinds of concerns that are more likely to occur in the lives of college students.

We have named the process *IDEAS*. IDEAS is a 5-step critical thinking problem-solving process that is comparable to the critical thinking used in many professional settings, including health care, legal analysis, arbitration and negotiation, scientific research, engineering and architectural design, financial planning, marketing and advertising, agricultural advancement, and criminological investigations. It is highly valuable in real-life situations such as buying a car, dealing with a difficult boss or co-worker, making a career change, ending a bad relationship, investing, starting or operating a small business, or selecting a candidate in the upcoming election.

JOURNAL

What Does "Success in College" Mean to You?

Write down your personal concept of what it means for you to be successful in college.

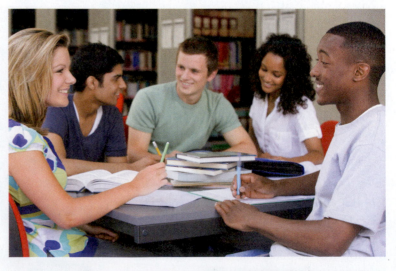

What's the secret to success? Answer: Show up, do your part, repeat again, and again.

THINKING CRITICALLY

Institutional Programs and Measures of Students' Success

Each individual student has a concept of what it means for him or her to be successful in college. And the colleges have an idea as well of how they seek to define and to measure student success. Colleges, accreditation agencies, and the media often think of student success in terms of graduation. At the undergraduate level the metric most often used is the "6-year graduation rate," which refers to the percentage of entering freshmen who complete a baccalaureate degree within six academic years. That metric, however, often fails to capture the successes of some important groups of students. Specifically that metric often misses successful degree-completing students who may have transferred from one institution to another, or who may have taken more than six years because they could not attend full-time or to attend continuously due to family, job, health, military service, or financial reasons. Each year *U.S. News & World Report* puts out its *Best Colleges* edition. One metric the editors use is a comparison between an institution's actual graduation rate and the rate that it might be predicted to have based on its financial resources and on its students' entry test scores. The aim was to reward institutions that succeed in graduating at-risk students.

Another metric used by *U.S. News & World Report* and by many higher education leaders and researchers to gauge the quality of an institution is the percentage of last year's full-time freshmen that the institution is able to retain into their sophomore year. Unfortunately some institutions are revolving doors, taking in large freshmen classes only to fail to retain them as sophomores. But institutions committed to the academic success of their students work hard to assist them make a successful transition to college life. Learning communities, first-year experience courses, internships, study abroad programs, undergraduate research opportunities, creative and collaborative projects, writing in the disciplines, service learning programs, strong academic advising services and student success service centers, faculty committed to the enterprise of teaching, welcoming and helpful staff, good physical facilities, a campus culture of learning, institutional pride, and a positive school spirit are all elements that contribute to higher student retention rates.

Woody Allen, movie producer and philosopher, suggests that four-fifths of the recipe for success is simply showing up. And while that hardly tells the whole story, there is a kernel of wisdom there. If you are a freshman, showing up as a sophomore next year is a very important part of graduating some time, if not on time.

Visit the *U.S. News & World Report* Web site, or get a copy of its latest issue of *Best Colleges*, and look up your institution. Then look up 10 or a dozen institutions like yours. Compare their stats on freshmen retention and graduation rates. What programs does your institution offer that are specifically designed to help ensure undergraduate student success? Are you participating in one or more of those programs?

With our research team we have studied problem solving in business, education, health sciences, the military, law, and a number of other fields and in all of these domains critical thinking and problem solving comes down to the same five things. The 5-step IDEAS critical thinking process is simple to understand and to apply and yet powerful enough to work with problems of significant complexity. The steps are straightforward. And yet, in response to the demands of the problem at hand, each step in the process can involve substantial analysis, inference, and evaluation. The IDEAS process calls for good critical thinkers to take the time to make well-reasoned, reflective and yet timely decisions about how to resolve their problems. We need to be patient enough to apply the process well, and yet savvy enough to avoid "paralysis by analysis" because in fact a judgment must at some point be made. The name of the process, IDEAS, is a mnemonic, which simply means that it is a device to help us to remember more easily these five steps:

- Step 1, represented by the "I" is **Identify Problems and Set Priorities**. The first step in problem solving is to realize that we have a difficulty that needs our attention. Knowing our priorities helps us identify situations, which are or could become problems for us. In turn, examining the characteristics of the problem helps us clarify our priorities.

- Step 2, represented by the "D" is **Determine Relevant Information and Deepen Understanding**. Deciding what information is relevant, gathering that information and deepening our understanding of the problem ensures that we know all that we should know to move ahead in the problem solving process.

- Step 3, represented by the "E" is **Enumerate Options and Anticipate Consequences**. Enumerating genuine options helps us focus on those consequences that have a greater likelihood of occurring, rather than fantasizing about extreme and remote possibilities. In turn, anticipating consequences helps us discard the infeasible options quickly, thus saving energy and time so we can address the more realistic and practical options.

- Step 4, represented by the "A" is **Assess the Situation and Make a Preliminary Decision**. Assessing our situation thoughtfully helps us make an initial tentative decision about what steps we are going to take to resolve the problem. In turn, making a preliminary decision helps us clarify our expectations so we can better assess what level of resolution will be good enough, given the current circumstances, for us to consider the problem to be resolved at least for the present.

- Step 5, represented by the "S" is **Scrutinize the Process and Self-Correct as Needed**. Scrutinizing the whole process enables us to see possible flaws and gaps in our thinking so that we can correct ourselves before we make a mistake. In turn, self-correcting can lead us to necessary reconsiderations of any aspect of our problem-solving process: We may realize that we should reassess the nature of the problem, rework our priorities, gather more information, identify a new option, more carefully anticipate likely consequences, reassess our situation, reevaluate our expectations, and, in the end, make a better decision. This final step is our assurance that the problem has been resolved sufficiently for the current time and circumstances.

A person can improve the problem solving at any point along the IDEAS process. Although IDEAS is presented as five steps, we do not have to go all the way through Step 5 before we correct our own thinking. The IDEAS process can fold back on itself whenever a thoughtful person realizes adjustments need to be made. For example, if the relevant information we developed in Step 2 indicates that we have been mistaken in identifying the problem, then we can go back to Step 1 and fix that before moving on. Or, if the options and consequences enumerated in Step 3 all are problematic, a person can go back and reconsider his or her priorities from Step 1 or revisit Step 2 to determine whether additional information might be available to assist in expanding the options. IDEAS is a thoughtful and reflective process, not rigidly linear. We never have to wait for Step 5

to correct mistakes or make improvements on the work of earlier steps.

Using the IDEAS process well takes practice and that is what we are going to do in this chapter.[4] So here's our plan: To develop an understanding of this process and how to apply it to real problems in our lives we will explore each of the five steps, emphasizing how the step applies to actual problems faced by a wide range of college students. In the second part of this chapter we present six mini case study scenarios. The mini cases illustrate problems that typify the kinds of issues that arise in six different domains of college life: social, vocational, academic, physical, emotional, and spiritual. We will use the first five scenarios to explore each of the five IDEAS steps individually, emphasizing a different step with each scenario. Then in the final section of the chapter we'll put the five IDEAS steps back together. Every problem worth solving requires that we apply all five steps of the IDEAS process.

3.2 Educating the Whole Person

Armed with IDEAS, let's attack a few problems. In this section of the chapter we will explore the kinds of problems that college students often face. With each scenario we will take another step into the IDEAS process to illustrate how to apply strong critical thinking skills and positive critical thinking habits of mind to the problem or issue at hand. There are individual and group exercises suggested along the way because the best way to strengthen critical thinking is to engage those skills and habits of mind to solve problems.

Research about college students of all different ages and backgrounds often focuses on how the experience of attending college impacts and shapes their lives. Our development as human beings continues throughout our lives. But the decade or so from late adolescence through young adulthood is particularly important because during these years we are

- developing the competencies we will need to make a living in a complex society,

- learning to manage our emotions,

- moving through autonomy toward interdependence,

- developing mature interpersonal relationships,

- establishing our personal identity,

- developing and refining our sense of purpose,

- developing a greater integration of who we are with what we say and do in all circumstances.[5]

IDEAS

A 5-Step Critical Thinking General Problem Solving Process

I = IDENTIFY the Problem and Set Priorities

D = DETERMINE Relevant Information and Deepen Understanding

E = ENUMERATE Options and Anticipate Consequence

A = ASSESS the Situation and Make a Preliminary Decision

S = SCRUTINIZE the Process and Self-Correct as Needed

Although the domains into which problems might fall remain pretty much constant throughout the arc of our lives as human beings, the particular issues and concerns college students experience are not the same as those expressed by children or as those expressed later in midlife. Our success in college, as in life, depends on our ability to address these concerns and issues, as these are manifested in the problems of our day-to-day lives.

Figure 3.2 illustrates some of the issues and concerns typically experienced and expressed by college students. Again, we are all different. You may not have personally wrestled with each of these issues or concerns. Don't worry if the problems, which hound your life in these different domains do not happen to be listed here. The important thing is to realize that we all experience problems and challenges, and that there is a sensible process for working through them. So, let's begin.

Social Relationships

Social relationships are complex. The meanings that we attach to what others say or do can differ vastly. What one person might see as an apology, another might interpret as sarcasm. What one person thinks of as a harmless prank, another might experience as a deeply hurtful personal assault. What one person intends as respectful silence, another sees as unwitting acquiescence or as cold indifference. Seeing ourselves as others see us is not an easy thing. But throughout our lives those rare moments when we are able to see ourselves as others see us often yield valuable insights for personal reflection and growth.

Consider Haley's situation in this story: There was a huge party at a nearby dance club last Saturday night after the football team's victory. Haley and her roommate went to the party, and Haley drank a few too many. A cute guy from her Communication class was there and he was buying Haley and her roommate a fresh drink every time they finished the ones they had. The next day Haley learned from her roommate that something made Haley get into a shouting match with another female partygoer. In a fit of anger Haley screamed, cursed, and called the other girl several nasty and unflattering names. Ultimately, Haley was subdued and escorted out of the club by the bouncer. This verbal display was in front of a big crowd at the party. Or at least Haley thought it was only the partygoers. She quickly learned that someone at the party had posted a video of her performance. Haley's younger sister, a high school junior, had already sent Haley a frantic text because she had seen the video. Haley wondered who posted the video to the Web, who else had seen her act this way, and what was going to happen to her as a result. This was bad, really bad, Haley thought.

How would Haley's roommate interpret what happened? Did Haley lose respect in her eyes? How about in the eyes of the young man, whom she'll be seeing in her Comm class? And what about Haley's sister, the high school junior? What might she be thinking about her older sister and about college life in general, having seen the video? Haley's mother is on Facebook a lot. She is sure to find out about the video. What will she think?

Circle of Well-Being

Domain	Example Issues and Concerns of College Students
Social	How do I build lasting friendships and relate in a positive way to other people? What responsibilities do I have as a member of a community? What can I expect of others, what contributions do they have the right to expect of me?
Vocational	What major or career field shall I choose? What knowledge, skills, and experiences do I need to be successful in that career? How do I get started in that field?
Academic	How do I study, when and where? How do I prepare for tests? How can I improve my writing skills? How can I connect what I'm learning in one course with what I'm learning in another?
Physical	What should I eat or not eat? How can I stay fit? I know I'm free to do anything I want, but what kinds of risks with my health and safety are worth taking, and which are just too stupid?
Emotional	How do I cope with the stress and pressure of grades and the expectations that parents and others put on me? How do I cope with being alone, away from my family and the friends I grew up with? How do I get out of bed in the morning when I feel so depressed?
Spiritual	What are my true values? What do I really care about? What do I hope to achieve in my life? What about God, religion, patriotism, democracy, and all those things I used to believe without question?

STEP 1: IDENTIFY the Problem and Set Priorities

Haley regards what happened as "bad, really bad." But there are no do-overs.

If Haley really wants to repair some of the damage, she's first going to have to identify the problem as accurately as she can, or in this case, problems that she's created for herself by her drunken indiscretion.

In some cases, the problem will be relatively straightforward, meaning that you can state your problem directly and simply. This doesn't mean that your problem is simple! It means, however, that you have clarity on what exactly the problem is that you need to think critically about. For example, "I'm going to see that guy in class and I have to think about what I'm going to say."

Other times your problem may be part of a constellation of related problems and your task in this first step is to clarify and prioritize the problems at hand so that you can systematically address the main or most pressing problem. For example, "I know that my sister saw the video and probably Mom will have seen the video. I'm going to want to apologize and make it clear to them all that nothing like that is going to happen ever again. But should I talk to my sister and my Mom together, or separately? And if separately, which one first?"

You may have experienced a situation where you spent a great deal of time thinking about a problem and coming up with a solution only to find out later that the thing that you *thought* was the problem turned out to be not really what you needed to work on. You were solving the wrong problem! What questions might we ask ourselves to be sure we have accurately identified the problem? For example, what might Haley ask herself to help her clarify the *main problem(s)* in this situation and to establish her priorities going forward?

- What aspects of last Saturday cause me the most concern or embarrassment?
- Should I be concerned about my drinking?
- Should I make it a priority to address the drinking issue?
- Has a verbal rage like this happened before and is it a pattern?
- Am I excessively vulnerable to peer pressure?
- Are my friends worthy of my trust?
- How badly have I hurt my relationship with my sister and my family?
- Have I jeopardized my enrollment at this university?
- What should I do first to repair my relationships with others?

Let's assume that Haley prioritizes mending her relationships with others. There are four more steps to the IDEAS process before Haley will have made a fully reflective and thoughtful decision about what to do to repair her

damaged relationships. Before going on in this chapter, as an exercise, work though those four steps as if you were Haley and your first priority was to repair your relationship with your sister. You can do this exercise yourself as a personal reflection, or as a group discussion.

> "If you don't know where you are going, you might wind up somewhere else."
>
> Yogi Berra,
> Hall of Fame Baseball Player and Manager[6]

Vocation

The word *vocation* means "calling," and it is associated with the kind of work for which one is most suited or "called to do." One's vocation is intimately associated with one's identity. People often describe themselves in terms of the professions they have pursued or the work they have done throughout their careers. "I'm an apprentice carpenter." "I'm a physical therapist at the Med Center." "I'm a teller at Chase." "I'm in marketing." etc. A combination of temperament, knowledge, skill, and desire goes into forging one's sense of what one "ought to become"—that is, the career one ought to pursue. But the reality for college students often is that the jobs they happen to have during college do not represent the careers to which they aspire nor the majors they are pursuing. Rather, the forging of one's future identity as a contributing member of society through the vocation one will pursue is, for college students, focused in the selection of one's major. Many factors go into the selection of a major, and one's sense of one's potential career or vocation is certainly one of the central factors in that mix. But it is not the only factor. And whenever many different forces are at play, some can converge to make a decision easier, but others can diverge or even conflict, making the choice more difficult. We have all felt these pushes and pulls.

Consider this scenario: Deshan was sitting in the college library pouring over the university catalog and clicking through the campus Web site. Staring at the multitude of departmental Web pages, each featuring pictures of smiling, successful students, had made Deshan frustrated that he didn't have a major yet. Even though he had just started college, he felt pressure from his family to have his career plans all laid out. His parents had made it very clear that college was expensive. Unless he picked a major he felt like he was wasting time and money. He agonized over which major would be the best. Which would fit his interests and talents? Which would be the most enjoyable? Which might lead to the most exciting and lucrative career? And which would honor his parents' sense of worthy respectability and also their wishes

Major in what you love. Become what you most want to be.

because, not yet having clearly established his priorities, he does not know what information is the most relevant to his particular situation. What is Deshan's problem, really? Is it that he must choose a major? No, that's a solution to some other problem. Clearly Deshan has a substantial wish list: He believes that he must declare a major to be happy like the students on the campus Web site. He wants to make his parents proud. He wants to graduate on time. He wants to have a good job when he is out of school. He wants a major that fits his interests and skills, to be enjoyable, and to fit his parents' sense of what is worthy and respectable.

Part of Deshan's problem is that he is trying to satisfy too many demands at once. Treating each demand as equal only pulls him apart. First he needs to figure out if selecting a major is vital at this very moment in his college career. It might be, if he is interested in a major that requires a large number of units. But it might not be if he is enrolled in courses that will count toward his graduation requirements no matter which of several majors he might select. He needs more information about this because it can be a mistake to make a decision that does not yet have to be made.

> "All that is required to become an optimist is to have the goal and to practice it."
>
> Sonja Lyubomirsky, Professor of
> Psychology, UC Riverside.[7]

Deshan also needs to set some priorities. For example, is fulfilling his parents' expectations the top priority or not? Is it more important to select a major one's parents find worthy or one that fits your interests and talents? In the chapter on the positive critical thinking habits of mind, we identified courageous truth-seeking, which plays an

that he get through college and out into the work world as quickly as possible? There were so many possibilities! Deshan wanted to yell out loud with frustration. He did not know where to begin!

Your first reaction to Deshan's situation may be this, "Since when did having a lot of good choices become a problem?" Think back to a situation when you felt overwhelmed by your choices. The 5-step IDEAS problem-solving process can help counter the feelings of being overwhelmed by a challenging decision, like this one, which appears to have such momentous consequences. For Deshan, the first step would be to analyze the situation to identify the main problem and set his priorities. From there he could focus on determining what information he needs to deepen his understanding of the realistic option. Not of every option, but rather of those options that were most relevant to his priorities.

STEP 1: IDENTIFY the Problem and Set Priorities
Deshan is in the library gathering information about all the academic majors his college offers. But his efforts are less than effective

DAVE GRANLUND © www.davegranlund.com

important role in clarifying priorities. In this case Deshan will need to muster the courage to ask himself some tough questions, like whether or not he wants to spend his college years preparing for a career that does not interest him. His parents may want him to become a lawyer, scientist, business executive, or physician. But Deshan may have other interests.

After reflecting on what is most important to him, let's assume that Deshan has determined that his primary problem is how to identify a major that will motivate him the most because it fits with his skills and interests. The more passion and motivation he has for the major, the more likely he is to enjoy his studies and do well. Even with his priorities in mind, Deshan might imagine that this major or that major is going to be the right one for him, but to continue to make progress on solving his problem he now needs to gather more information.

STEP 2: DETERMINE Relevant Information and Deepen Understanding

After the main problem has been identified, Deshan would be ready to systematically gather the relevant information needed to inform his choice(s) of major. Other positive critical thinking habits of mind discussed in Chapter 2 alongside of truth-seeking include systematic inquiry and inquisitiveness. These are valuable habits during information gathering. Deshan would be wise to organize his inquiry the same way he would if this were an important academic assignment. He might begin by listing several questions related to the problem at hand so that he could understand the problem better and so that he could focus his information-gathering efforts. Here are a few examples:

- What do I know about myself in terms of my knowledge, skills, and values?
- What topics do I find most interesting?
- In which academic subjects do I excel?
- What careers am I most interested in pursuing?
- What kinds of problems do I find most compelling?
- What can I learn from talking to other people?
- What might my academic advisor be able to do to help me?
- What could my professors this term do to help me?
- What might my friends who are juniors and seniors be able to tell me about picking a major?
- What could I learn from talking to people who work in careers that I think are interesting?
- What can I learn by consulting other available resources?
- What resources exist on campus to help students pick a major or pick a career?

- What could I look for on the Internet to learn more about career options?
- Where do I look to find out what careers are possible with what majors?
- If I can narrow it down to two or three best options, are there any experiences, maybe internships or site visits that might help me learn more?
- Does it really matter what major I choose, or could I get into the career field I want with any of several different majors?

"Success is not the key to happiness. Happiness is the key to success. If you love what you are doing, you will be successful."

Albert Schweitzer, Physician and Humanitarian[8]

Part of deepening our understanding of a problem is gathering information that is *relevant*. Determining what information is relevant involves the critical thinking skills of *interpretation and analysis*, which are discussed in Chapters 4 and 6, on clarifying ideas and evaluating the credibility of sources of information. This is a two-way process. As we gather more information we deepen our understanding of the problem. Developing our understanding helps us see what additional relevant information might still be needed.

Deshan's decision will not be well made until he works through the three remaining steps in the IDEAS process. But let's assume that he has narrowed his choices to these three possible majors: Political Science (to become a Foreign Service Officer), Forensic Chemistry (to become a Criminologist or Crime Scene Investigator), and Psychology (with a view toward attending Law School to become a Criminal Defense Attorney). As an individual exercise or as a group project, find out what programs your institution offers that most closely fit with these vocational choices. Investigate the next steps, beyond graduation from your institution with an Associate of Arts Degree or a Baccalaureate Degree that a person would have to pursue to actually prepare for one or more of those careers. And then play out the conversation between Deshan and his parents, assuming they had been hoping he would become a physician or an engineer, as he explains to them that he has decided to dedicate his efforts during college to preparing for one of these three professional careers instead. Having worked your way through these steps in detail, what are the lessons that you might now bring to your own efforts to solidify your long-term career and vocational decisions?

"All I'm saying is that you're an adult now . . . And the tough thing about adulthood is that it starts before you even know it starts, when you're already a dozen decisions into it. . . .The decisions you make now are yours and yours alone from here until the end."

Robert Redford's character, Professor Stephen Malley, to promising young student, played by Andrew Garfield. *Lions and Lambs*, 2007[9]

Academics

Effective preparation for exams and assignments in college is not the brute memorization that many find works well enough in high school. College assignments and exams often require the application of critical thinking skills, like analysis, explanation, evaluation, interpretation, and inference. For years we have given "open book and neighbor" tests, allowing students to collaborate with one another and to look things up online or in their textbooks. But success on exams like that is never only about getting the informational content correct. They always demand a deeper understanding borne of reflective analysis, thoughtful interpretation, warranted inferences, and clear explanation based on reasons and evidence. And good exams often require, in addition to knowledge, thoughtful application, and informed analysis, a measure of skill at effective writing. What's the point of a college course otherwise? Today, information—some of it reliable and some not—is as abundant as sand on an LA beach. If a college education were no more than a game of *Jeopardy*, then everyone with a smartphone would have a doctorate.

Consider Maria's situation. In high school, where memorization was the main cognitive skill needed, Maria had always considered herself a good student. Maria earned excellent grades in high school and was in the Advanced Placement or Honors classes in most subjects. So, when Maria got her first test back in college—it was in an Introduction to Cultural Anthropology course—she was shocked to see the big, red "F" at the top of her exam. In fact, it was one of only three Fs in a class of 45 students. And a bunch of people got Bs and As. What the heck happened? She thought she knew the material! She had memorized the terminology and read the chapters,

THINKING CRITICALLY

How Can We Use Our Study Time Most Effectively?

Given how busy college students are these days, it is important to get everything possible out of every minute we can devote to studying and preparing for exams. It is better to study with highly focused intensity for 30 solid minutes, and then to take a mental break, than it is to waste an hour or two on a distracted, disengaged, disjointed, and half-hearted effort. Successful studying at the college level means becoming intimately, actively, and at times even passionately engaged with the material. Some students find it useful to make outlines of chapters, to write sample test questions, to make lists or tables or charts, or to create line drawings and diagrams showing interrelationships and linkages. A casual read is not enough—it might be a mile-wide overview but it will end up being only inch-deep understanding. On the other hand, if you can simulate teaching each section and each paragraph to yourself—or better, actually teach the material to someone else—you will have significantly magnified your comprehension and your chances of earning high marks on tests. Memorizing definitions, facts, and theories is not enough. Beyond just being able to find or to recite the facts a successful student is able to interpret them in a sensible and meaningful way and to apply them correctly when drawing inferences and giving explanations. Simply being able to identify names, events, objects, and dates is not the same as being able to

One way to study is to explain to each other why the wrong answers are wrong.

analyze those objects and to explain the key relationships among those objects. Reading through a set of exercises does not pay half the dividends that actually working the exercises provides. And, figuring out exactly why a mistaken answer is an error can be more valuable for deeper learning than happening to get the answer right but not being sure why.

Training is learning the material; education is learning to learn.

THE FIRST TWO IDEAS STEPS IN MARIA'S CASE

STEP 1: What is Maria's problem and what is her priority? The "F" grade is not the problem. It is the result. The problem, in retrospect, became very clear to Maria: She quickly realized that she was not sufficiently prepared to take the kind of exam that the college professor gave. Her priority is to reverse that situation. Like going into an important game without appreciating how much it would take to be successful, she had no idea how much critical thinking, as compared with information recall, the professor expected. And now she intends never to put herself in that disadvantageous situation again. Okay, but how? That brings us to the second step.

highlighting almost every sentence it seemed. She was definitely confused because she had come to college thinking she was pretty smart. Maria was right about that, too; she was a very smart woman. But the demands of college work clearly were not going to be the same as high school. Maria knew she had to do something different if she was going to pass this class.

What should someone in Maria's shoes ask themselves? Following the 5-step IDEAS process in this situation, the first two steps would be to analyze the situation to identify the problem and set priorities and then systematically gather the relevant information needed to deepen understanding of the problem and change future behavior.

STEP 2: How can Maria determine what information is relevant and gather that information? What questions could a student ask to learn what the professor expects? The question, "Is this going to be on the exam?" is not one of them. In college everything and anything might turn out to be on the exam. A more helpful question might be "Can you give us an example or two of the kinds of questions we might expect on the exam?" The purpose of that question is not to find out if the questions are essay, short answer, or multiple choice, but to find out, no matter what the

---

THINKING CRITICALLY

What If Art or Ideas Make Us Uncomfortable?

Some students at Wellesley College were disturbed by Tony Matelli's statue of a man sleepwalking in his underpants. The statue, part of an exhibit, was located outdoors in a busy part of campus. It was a "source of apprehension, fear, and triggered thoughts regarding sexual assault," said a petition seeking its removal. To which Wellesley's president, H. Kim Bottomly, is reported to have responded, "The very best works of art have the power to stimulate deeply personal emotions and to provoke unexpected new ideas, and this sculpture is no exception." The college's President went on to praise the consequences flowing from the placement of the statue because it "started an impassioned conversation about art, gender, sexuality and individual experience, both on campus and in the social media." (Associated Press, February 8, 2014, "Mass college man-in-undies sculpture causes stir.")

If President Bottomly is correct in saying that art that evokes unsettling and disturbing ideas has an educational value, what about ideas? What if professors or other students raise questions about beliefs that we have been taught from childhood? Or, what if other students or professors challenge our traditional community practices? No doubt art and ideas that strike at deeply held beliefs and personal feelings can be very troubling and maybe even hurtful, although perhaps no disrespect was ever intended. But should college students be subjected to this kind of cognitive assault? Is that even ethical to do? Don't students have the right to be protected from art and ideas that they might find personally offensive?

If you say No, you may be opening the door to the whirlwind. Every idea and every work art will be permitted. But, if you say Yes, then you are agreeing that professors and students do not have the right to challenge practices you may abhor, like honor killing, hazing, or gay bashing.

format, whether the questions demand interpretation, analysis, inference, evaluation, or explanation. What other questions would you ask? How about, "Can you share with us some examples of really strong papers or exams from the last time you taught this course?" If yes, then the professor is providing you with benchmarks and paradigms of the kinds of performances on assignments and tests that this professor hopes to see.

> ## "The definition of success: fall down seven times, stand up eight times."
>
> Japanese Proverb

STEP 3: ENUMERATE Options and Anticipate Consequences The twin goals of this third step in the 5-step IDEAS process are to generate potential choices and to reflect on their ramifications. One way to think about this is to visualize yourself standing in the center of an intersection, with paths heading in multiple directions around you. The first thing to do is to imagine as many options, or potential paths, as you can. This sounds easy, but it can be difficult to see all the options because of our natural human tendency to lock into a one possible solution or option prematurely, without giving due consider to the other options. Chapter 11, "Reflective Decision Making," offers a great many suggestions on how to avoid the common mistake of locking into an inferior option before having seriously considered some better possibilities.

There are almost always more options than we first might think.

Suppose you were worried or disappointed, or downright embarrassed, about your poor academic performance. Each of these questions could generate options for future behavior.

- Are my study habits effective, and if not, how can I change them?
- What could I ask my professor that would improve my performance in each class?
- How might I engage with my classmates to help us all do better on the next test or assignment?
- How could I utilize the textbook, online resources, or class sessions to help my learning? The section about introductory college courses and language communities in Chapter 4 on clarifying ideas can be helpful. The same for the three important chapters (12–14) on comparative, ideological, and empirical reasoning, because those chapters explain the kinds of thinking, which characterize knowledge acquisition in different academic domains of inquiry.
- What distracts me or takes me away from my studies? Can I eliminate, contain, or control these factors?
- How might my family or friends help me improve as a student?
- What campus resources are available to students who are trying to bring up their grades? Most student success centers at colleges these days are intended to help average students become good students and to help good students become superior students.

The second part of this step is to consider what is likely to happen if you choose a particular option and, obviously, to be able to explain to yourself why that is the likely outcome. The positive critical thinking habit of mind of striving to anticipate consequences as objectively as possible is particularly valuable to cultivate. There are some helpful tips on how to do this in Chapter 2's section on critical thinking habits of mind. Some of us overestimate our capacity to control events, and others of us underestimate our potential. But the wise person is one who thinks ahead when considering choices, and tries to figure out what is likely to happen or not happen if a given choice is made. The more we can understand ourselves and the reasons we make certain choices, the more likely we are able to capitalize on opportunities and avoid negative or disappointing results. As explained in Chapter 10 on heuristic thinking and snap judgments, pausing to consider first the potential consequences of our decisions will make us wiser, more reflective decision makers. It certainly helps us eliminate the kinds of impulsive, reactive, shoot-from-the-hip choices that so often lead to unexpected problems.

Let's practice anticipating the consequences of some potential actions in response to getting a less than fully satisfying grade on an academic assignment or test. Considering your own personal situation, how would you fill in the blanks?

- If I spend twice as much *time* studying as compared to last time, it is likely that _____ because _____ .

- If I spend the same amount of time or less time, but studied more intensely and more frequently than last time it is likely that _____ because _____ .

- If my attendance in class stays the same that will likely result in _____ because _____ .

- If I participated more in class discussion this will likely _____ because _____ .

- If I go to my professor during office hours, or send an e-mail asking for some help with a particularly confusing or difficult concept, the professor will likely tell me that _____ because _____ .

- If I study with one of my classmates we will likely _____ because _____ .

- If I looked for a campus office that is designed to assist students I will likely find _____ because _____ .

- If I increased the amount of sleep I get at night that would likely result in _____ because _____ .

- If I continue to eat the way I have been eating, this will likely _____ because _____ .

We suggest you go through these fill-ins a couple of times each, just to practice anticipating multiple possible consequences for yourself.

One more hypothetical situation for you to consider: Suppose that Maria, who likes to e-mail and text her mother every day, told her mother about the failing grade on that Cultural Anthropology exam. And suppose that, without informing Maria of her intentions, Maria's mother decided to phone the academic dean or the Anthropology Department chairperson to complain about the professor's "impossibly unfair tests" and to ask the dean to void that exam score or transfer Maria to a section of the course taught by some other professor. What do you think will happen in such a case? Apart from guessing or speculating about what the dean or the department chairperson might do, how can you find out for sure what is likely to happen at your institution if this kind of a situation should arise? Once you know what is likely to happen, would you want your partner, parent, or best friend making such a call on your behalf unbeknownst to you? Explain why or why not?

Health and Physical Well-being

Attributed to the Roman poet Juvenal, the popular saying *"Mens sana in corpore sano"* ("A sound mind in a sound body") suggests that human happiness is intimately connected with one's emotional and physical well-being. That Latin phrase, which has become the motto of many educational institutions, sports clubs and products, and military organizations, has echoed through the centuries in the writings of poets, presidents, and educational philosophers. Today, attending to physical health and well-being covers a lot of territory: diet and dietary supplements, fatty fast foods, fitness products, exercise regimens, drugs and alcohol usage, safe and risky sexual activity, and so on. And, when we care about others, we often find ourselves worried about their physical well-being, not just our own.

Consider this scenario: Leah could not believe how much she was agonizing over whether or not to say something to her roommate Stephanie. It was the beginning of the semester, and she had been with Stephanie in the cafeteria talking with two other girlfriends about their summer breaks. Stephanie had clearly surprised her friends when she told them how she was still seeing Brett and that they spend most every night together these days. One friend at the table blurted out "I hope he at least uses a condom!" and Stephanie replied 'Nah, he got so mad when I asked him to wear one . . . he says he HATES those things. Anyway, I am on the pill and I know he is a good guy so we're good." Leah had been stunned by Stephanie's reply, but her friends seemed not to be. Without missing a beat their conversation immediately moved to a discussion of the lunch entrées they were eating. Three days later Leah was still trying to decide if she should talk to Stephanie about her relationship with Brett. Brett was pressuring Stephanie to gamble with her health and Stephanie was dismissing it. This concerned Leah greatly. She cared about Stephanie a lot and wanted to see their friendship grow. But Leah was still getting to know her roommate, and she was not sure how Stephanie would react if she seemed to be criticizing Stephanie's love life.

THE FIRST THREE STEPS IN LEAH'S CASE   Suppose Leah had been introduced to the 5-step IDEAS process. What might her thinking have been as she worked through the first three steps in the process? Here's one possibility.

STEP 1: Identify the problem and set priorities. Leah would first analyze the situation to clarify her priorities and determine the main problem. Clearly one of her objectives is to develop her friendship with Stephanie. That Stephanie has unprotected sex seems unnecessarily risky to Leah, and Leah is concerned that perhaps Stephanie perceives herself to be invulnerable for one reason or another. Getting to be a better friend to Stephanie becomes Leah's paramount objective. But being a person's friend means acting in their best interests. So Leah's problem is to find a way to be honest with Stephanie about her concerns, even if acting in such an honest way puts their relationship at risk. For if the relationship is to blossom into a lasting friendship, then that level of honesty is mandatory. Friends do not lie to each other or withhold their concerns.

STEP 2: Determine Relevant Information and Deepen Understanding. The goal of Step 2 is to clarify the parameters of the situation, illuminate the relevant perspectives, and bring whatever needs to be known to the table. In this situation, Leah thought about how she didn't know Stephanie well enough to simply begin a conversation by telling her that she was foolish for taking such risks. Leah decided to ask the other two women who were at the table that day what they thought she should do. Their responses were mixed; one said Leah should definitely talk to Stephanie because that would show her that someone cared (even if Leah was a relative stranger). The other told Leah that Stephanie seemed like a smart person and that Leah shouldn't feel like she had to say anything. In fact, maybe, she said, what Stephanie did was none of Leah's business. It looked like the outcome of this step in the IDEAS process for Leah was going to be ambiguous. And then Leah asked herself how the idea of having unprotected sex based on a guy's opposition to

THINKING CRITICALLY

How Can We Protect Ourselves from Ourselves?

Scientifically we know a lot about the relationships between dietary habits and health. A generation ago colleges worried about anorexia and bulimia, still problems today, but not about the opposite—obesity and the long-term health problems associated with excessive weight. The evidence is mounting to associate obesity with diabetes, heart disease, orthopedic difficulties (hips, knees, ankles, and back), birth defects, and higher-risk pregnancies. Oh, and premature death. We sure hope that this isn't the government's plan for fixing the Social Security budget!

Our question is this: Why, when we know that a given behavior has harmful long-term effects, do we engage in that behavior anyway? Smoking is another obvious example. Alcohol abuse is as well. Over-eating, not just occasionally, but consistently to the point of gaining significant poundage, going more than 20 percent above one's ideal weight, taking into consideration height and sex, is an interesting puzzle. There is nothing necessarily wrong with eating. Food, unlike cigarette smoking, does not necessarily introduce anything harmful into a person's body. And, unlike alcohol, eating a lot all at once does not cause intoxication. But consistently eating too much does ruin a person in the long run. Just like consistently eating too little can ruin a person.

Perhaps the answer to this dilemma can in part be found in the arguments used to support "sin" taxes. A sin tax is a government tax on various products or activities that can cause us harm. Taxes on alcohol and tobacco products, and on gambling, for example, can be called sin taxes. According to Harvard Economics Professor N. Gregory Mankiw, the best argument for "sin" taxes is that "taxes on items with short-run benefits and long-run costs tell our current selves to take into account the welfare of our future selves." Another good argument is that the costs of which the professor speaks are not paid only by the sinner. Often there are costs to the rest of the society—namely other taxpayers—too, for example for

"But it seemed so right at the time."

medical expenses to treat people who suffer from the chronic diseases and debilitating effects of their own unwise behavior.

Professor Mankiw's remarks were published in an opinion piece he wrote on the topic of taxing soda. His question is "Is a soda tax a good idea?" You can find his article and commentary about it on the Internet by searching "Mankiw soda tax". Consider his perspective, consider the various options and their consequences, and then formulate one of your own and explain your point of view using good reasons and solid evidence.

wearing a condom fit with her own sense of being a smart person. To Leah those two ideas didn't go together in her mind at all.

STEP 3: Identifying Options and Anticipating Consequences. When Leah imagined bringing the subject up with Stephanie she could see her reacting in many different ways—appreciation, anger, embarrassment, defensiveness, helplessness, happiness, and so on. Leah realized she didn't know Stephanie well enough to predict which of these would actually happen. But when she imagined her other option, not approaching Stephanie, Leah envisioned a variety of futures. Stephanie might continue to take risks with her sexual health, or she might insist on using a condom from here on out. She might be told one day by a doctor that she has contracted a sexually transmitted disease. Or she might realize that she had been lucky in her relationship with Brett, even though no one said anything to her. But to Leah, the risks for Stephanie were rather large, and the benefits of not bringing up the issue were almost zero, particularly since Leah wanted to cultivate a deeper friendship with Stephanie. On the other hand, there were risks associated with bringing up the topic. If Stephanie reacted with anger or hostility, that could prevent the friendship from ever happening. As with many difficult problems, it was not easy for Leah to infer what would be the better option. She knows that she needs to think carefully about these options and that she needs to make a choice.

Leah realized that procrastinating or failing to make any decision in a case like this is the same for all practical purposes as explicitly deciding to do nothing. Ignoring the problem is not the same as resolving it. Leah realized that a timely decision was essential. And so she moved on to Step 4.

STEP 4: ASSESS The Situation and Make a Preliminary Decision. The goal of Step 4 is to evaluate the relevant information, use it to inform your understanding of the problem at hand, and to come to a tentative initial decision about what to believe or what to do. Even in contexts of uncertainty and risk it is often necessary to find the courage to make a decision and stick with it. Chapters 10 and 11 on human decision making focus on the differences between reactive and reflective decisions, warn us about typical human decision-making errors, and provide helpful guidance on how to make timely and well-reasoned decisions without being locked prematurely into a less than optimal choice. The box "Critical Thinking Problem-Solving and Decision Making Strategies" includes many

of those recommendations. Each of these derives not only from research about how humans can make better decisions, but from the practical school of hard knocks. Some of the best decision makers are people and organizations that debrief their past decisions looking for why they may have been wise or unwise. From as impartial an analysis as possible, they derive for themselves some "lessons learned" to help with future decision making.

What questions could Leah ask herself in this specific situation to reflect on her options and come to a decision of what to do about her concern for Stephanie? Here are three. Can you think of others she might ask?

- Will I be able to live with myself if I don't approach Stephanie with my concerns for her health and well-being?

- Am I confident that approaching Stephanie and risking a negative response on her part is worth it, because showing my concern is the right thing to do?

- Will I be able to handle the rejection if she doesn't want to talk to me about something so intimate?

In the end one question Leah asked herself seemed to make all the difference. She asked herself this: "If Stephanie and I were real friends and the situation were reversed, what would I want or expect Stephanie to do to help me?" And her answer then became clear to her: "I would want her to tell me about her concerns, even if she thought that it would be difficult to raise the issue with me." And so Leah's tentative decision was to find an appropriate opportunity in the very near future to have a friend-to-friend conversation with Stephanie about how much it worried her that Stephanie took the risk of having unprotected sex with Brett and how troubling it was that he seemed to reject the idea of doing everything possible to keep them both healthy.

If the situation were reversed, what would I want my friend to say to me?

There is one more step to the IDEAS process, and we will focus on it with the next scenario. But first, this question for you: "When you last had a conversation with a good friend about a health risk behavior—such as abusing alcohol or drugs, or overeating or not exercising, or not sleeping enough, or bulimia, or whatever worried you— how did that conversation go? Specifically, did having that conversation hurt your friendship, help it, or not affect it at all? How do you know?"

3.3 Problems in College and Beyond

We are going to extend the application of the IDEAS process to problems relating to emotional well-being and spiritual development momentarily. But, as we are sure you have already noticed, the kinds of problems, which impact us during our days as college students can impact our lives at other times as well. Physical, social, and vocational problems certainly can be challenges any time in life. Academic problems, less so, but even here we can find that our skillset or knowledge base is not well-suited to our aspirations for a new job, or to coping well with an unexpected problem. And when that happens, we realize the need for continued learning.

Anticipating consequences, like the other steps in the 5-step IDEAS critical thinking general problem-solving process, applies to big decisions as well as small ones. Consider the big decision of whether or not to go to college and graduate. A look at the correlations between income and education suggests that the decision to graduate may have very different financial impacts on future earnings potential. While the numbers, as you will see, are impressive, noted economist Daniel Kahneman cautions against confusing correlations with causality.[10]

Emotional Well-Being

The decision we reach in Step 4 is called "preliminary" or "tentative" because it is not the end of the problem-solving process. Yes, that preliminary decision is our best candidate for what often becomes our final decision. But before we embrace it and consider our problem to have been resolved, we must first double-check how we got where we are. Step 5 challenges us to scrutinize our own decision-making process with as much rigor and objectivity as we can muster, and then to correct any lapses or errors we might find. As psychologically challenging as being our own tough critic might be, this step is vital, if we hope to be consistently successful at problem solving and decision making.

Consider, for example, Angelica's situation: Angelica walked into the student lounge and flopped down on the couch across from her classmates Shawna and Bree. The three of them had a formidable group project deadline looming. There was a lot of work to do before the end of the week. But, before they could start talking about their group project tears started to well up in Angelica's eyes. Her grades were slipping, and today that was weighing heavy on her mind. Nevertheless, what Angelica didn't anticipate was getting emotional in front of her classmates. She hated the weakness she felt in herself and she did not want to be telling her classmates about all of the things that were stressing her out. But it just all started pouring out. She had so many responsibilities; in addition to carrying a full load of units this term Angelica was working nights and weekends waiting tables. And since her parents both had multiple jobs, she was expected to be at home with her little brothers and sisters when she wasn't in class or working. She was also expected to contribute some of her tip money each week to cover the family's expenses. Angelica didn't resent the responsibility because she loved her family, but she was in college now and she wondered how she was going to get it all done without failing out of school. By the time she was done talking she was obviously distraught.

In this scenario we have three participants, Angelica, Shawna, and Bree, and they all could apply our 5-step IDEAS process. But would they all focus on the same problem (Step 1)? Maybe not. Bree may determine that the main problem they are facing right now is how to successfully finish the group project. Shawna may determine that the main problem is to help her classmate with her troubles. Meanwhile Angelica can't focus on the group project because she is distraught about keeping her grades up.

Critical Thinking, Problem-Solving, and Decision -Making Strategies

First of all, be sure you have correctly identified "the problem."

Specify which factors and priorities are most critical.

Gather relevant information from multiple reliable sources.

Identify and clearly differentiate viable options.

Be clear about why each option is in or out.

Evaluate viable options with disciplined impartiality.

Listen to both sides first—hear the pros and cons before evaluating them.

If new critical factors or priorities emerge use those as well.

Evaluate options in terms of all the critical factors and priorities, not just a subset.

Treat all the viable options equally—don't focus only on the advantages of the one you like and the flaws of the ones you don't like.

Have the courage to follow the reasons and evidence wherever they lead and to ask all the hard questions before making a final decision.

Seek advice from independent, informed, and unbiased sources

Decide when it is time to decide, and then make the decision in a timely way.

Check to see that the process you used has been reflective, complete, and fair-minded.

Check to see that the outcomes anticipated are the outcomes being attained. If not, make mid-course corrections to get back on track.

Have the maturity of judgment to stick with a decision if it is well made, but to change direction if there is good reason to reconsider and revise the decision.

What Is the Relationship between Education and Income?

Anticipating consequences, like the other steps in the 5-step IDEAS critical thinking problem-solving process, applies to big decisions as well as small ones. Consider the big decision of whether or not to go to college and graduate. The options appear to have different financial impacts on future earnings potential. Sure, there are always stories about someone who made it big financially but never went to college. Just like there are stories about people who smoked for decades but never contracted heart disease, lung cancer, or emphysema. But, statistically speaking, those celebrated examples are the rare exceptions. Like winning a fortune in a casino, it can happen; but the smart money says don't bet your life on it.

In its May 8, 2010, issue, when the public mood was growing severely impatient with the continuing U.S. economic problems, *The Economist* published a graphic "Richer by degrees" (page 33) based on data from the Brookings Institution. The graphic describes the relationship between academic attainment, gender, and income. As a critical thinking exercise, how would you interpret what this graphic is telling us about the changes in real hourly earnings by sex and educational attainment? What do you suppose explains the generally better numbers for women at every educational level? Do you believe that the next 30 years will be different than the previous 30 with regard to earnings by educational level? What are the reasons and the evidence for your view?

An analysis focusing on the supercharged Silicon Valley economy appeared in the February 7, 2014, *Silicon Valley Business Journal* (page 8). The story there includes information on the jobless rates, and income differences by sex, race, and shifts of income by household.

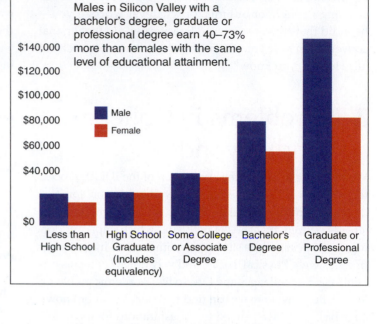

INCOME BY GENDER, EDUCATION

Males in Silicon Valley with a bachelor's degree, graduate or professional degree earn 40–73% more than females with the same level of educational attainment.

Here are data presentations from the Brookings Institution, the U.S. Census Bureau, and the *Silicon Valley Business Journal*. Applying you critical thinking skills of analysis, interpretation and inference, what do the data indicate to you? What questions do you have about the data?

Mean Earnings by Highest Degree Earned, $: 2009 (SAUS, table 232)	
Education level	Mean Earnings
Doctorate	103,000
Professional	128,000
Master's	74,000
Bachelor's	57,000
Associate's	40,000
Some college, no degree	32,000
High school graduate only	31,000
Not a high school graduate	20,000
All	42,000

Statistical Analyses of the United States Table 276. U.S. Census Bureau,

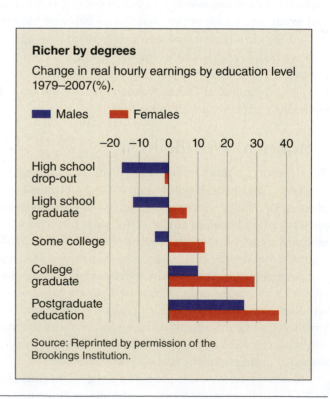

Richer by degrees

Change in real hourly earnings by education level 1979–2007(%).

Source: Reprinted by permission of the Brookings Institution.

THINKING CRITICALLY

Lifestyles of the Wealthy and Renown

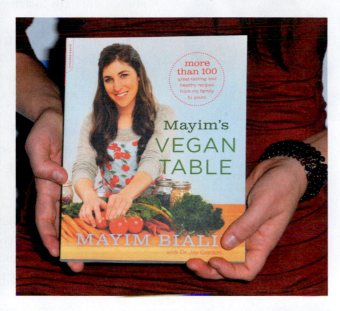

Consider the conversation between Garrett and his easily excited suitemate, Taylor, who has just burst into their shared living room:

"Garrett! Garrett! Look at this!! That Big Bang Theory chick wrote a cookbook! I've decided to become a total Vegan. And I'm going to sell all my stuff, give all my money to the Red Cross, get to a zero carbon footprint and dedicate my life to finding that Blue Zone everyone is talking about!" Without taking a breath, Taylor shoves the tablet version of Mayim Bialik's latest book, *The Vegan Table*, into Garrett's hands.

"Okay... Taylor... hey!...Calm down," says Garrett. But Taylor keeps roiling on.

"You know, Mayim Bialik! She's Amy Farrah Fowler on Big Bang. Was Blossom Russo on "Blossom" back in the day, and she did a movie called "Beaches" when she was a kid. But did you know that she has a PhD in neuroscience from UCLA in real life? If someone as smart as her is a vegan, then, really, why not me too?

Knowing there is no cause that Taylor does not embrace, nothing on Facebook Taylor does not "like," and no cute kitty video that Taylor does not watch 10 times, Garrett wonders what he can say or do. He is worried about Taylor. And his initial reaction is to talk Taylor down from this infatuation with profound eco-poverty and extreme veganism.

But, on second thought, maybe it wouldn't hurt, thinks Garrett, to take this vegan thing a little more seriously. Garrett knows exactly who Bialik is, and he's heard about her cookbook too. He knows the book is not a radical vegan manifesto. It contains some sensible ideas.

If you were Garrett what would you do to help your friend, Taylor? Explain why.

> "I don't think of myself as a poor deprived ghetto girl who made good. I think of myself as somebody who from an early age knew I was responsible for myself, and I had to make good."
>
> Oprah Winfrey, Entertainer and Philanthropist[11]

Let's take Bree's version of the problem at hand. As Bree navigates the remaining steps in the process, she will seek to clarify the situation, analyze the available options, evaluate the likelihood of success from choosing a particular option, and then after reflection, choose a course of action. To accomplish this, Bree may want to review the assignment with her two classmates, and go over what they had decided to do separately and together over the next day or two before the due date. She may ask the group to think about whether the plan is still realistic. Specifically she may ask Angelica whether she will have the time to complete her part of the project. She may also ask Shawna whether she can take on some additional work to assist Angelica. Bree would reflect on her own ability to assist Angelica.

STEP 5: SCRUTINIZE Processes and Self-Correct as Needed. Let's assume that Angelica regained her composure and promised Shawna and Bree that she will get her parts of the project done on time. In light of this new information, Bree would need to consider the ramifications of trusting Angelica (Step 4). Bree would also want to ask questions that would help her anticipate the consequences of accepting Angelica's promise (Step 3). Ultimately, Bree accepts Angelica's promise and is confident about this decision. Does this mean that Bree's critical thinking about this situation is done? Actually no. The final step in the 5-step IDEAS process includes ongoing monitoring, analyzing, and evaluating the consequences of our chosen actions or beliefs. Mid-course corrections may always be necessary, no matter what the decision.

Only gods and fools never reconsider!

Anonymous

Step 5 directs us to be deliberately mindful of our decisions and whether or not they are leading to our desired outcomes. Sometimes when we move forward with a decision we are rewarded with things going as we had envisioned them. But as often as not, our planning is imperfect or the unexpected happens. Or, if there are competitors in the mix, they respond to our moves by making tactical adjustments that counteract or nullify our own efforts. The situation changes, people do not fulfill their responsibilities, or events beyond anyone's control intervene. Things go awry. Bad stuff happens!

Monitoring progress toward important goals and successfully achieving intermediary benchmarks and objectives are very much a part of thoughtful and effective problem solving. And, when we see things beginning to slip, revising our assumptions, reviewing our options, investigating why, and self-correcting are essential. This applies as much to beliefs—as the Chapters 12, 13, and 14 on comparative, ideological, and empirical reasoning explain—as it does to actions.

Here are some questions to help when reviewing and revising a decision:

- What is actually happening as a result of my decision, and is it what I thought would happen?

- If my decision was related to a short-term goal, was the goal achieved? Why or why not?

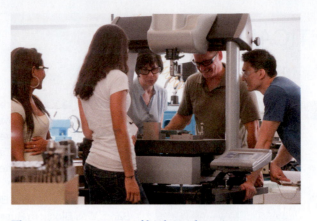

The primary purpose of higher education may not be the same as the goals each of us has for attending college. Is this a problem?

- If my decision was related to a mid-range or long-term goal, what evidence can I collect to gauge whether I am still on the path to achieve my goal?

- Whom might I consult to get feedback on my decision and the ramifications of my chosen action (or belief)?

- If my decision impacts the actions of another person, what can I do to support this relationship?

- If I need to make a self-correction, where should I start? Do I have the problem and the priorities right? Is there new information to consider? Are some options looking better now than before? Was I mistaken about the consequences? Did I act prematurely or delay too long on some aspect of this?

- If the situation did not turn out as I had anticipated, how might I rethink this problem, minimize the damage my error may have caused, and make the best out of the position I now find myself in?

- Are there some questions that I should have asked, some techniques or methods for information gathering I should have used, some assumptions or expectations that I made which were unfounded, some

THINKING CRITICALLY

What Is the Primary Purpose of Higher Education?

In the "Measures of Students' Success" box earlier the purpose of higher education was associated with student success. But "student success" was not defined except perhaps by whatever metrics influential media, like *US News*, might be using. And, if success in those rankings means that a college is achieving the primary purpose of higher education, then perhaps we need to take a step back and ask the question a different way. If you had to rank the many purposes higher education serves, for example, if it became necessary to make budget cuts or to decide between competing priorities, which purpose would come out on top?

Would the primary purpose of higher education be to maximize each student's life time income, as the box on the "Relationship between Education and Income" might be interpreted as suggesting? Or, is the primary purpose to train people for a particular job or to prepare them for a given professional field, even if that job or profession is not one of the most lucrative? Many universities market themselves with that

promise. Or, moving beyond the individual's good and looking to the nation's needs, perhaps the purpose of higher education is to be an engine of future economic growth by producing scientists, engineers, entrepreneurs, and innovators. Many countries have based their funding of higher education on its potential to benefit the economy over the long haul. Or perhaps the primary purpose of education is to reinforce the beliefs and practices of a given religion so as to ensure that the religion will continue into the future unchanged. This is the case in many countries as well.

Obviously some of the candidates for "the primary purpose of higher education" require stronger critical thinking on the part of students than do other candidates. OK, so let's put some skin in the game. Education is not free, and it cannot serve all purposes equally well. Ask yourself, what is and what should be the primary purpose of higher education? How would you adjust your answer if it applied only to public higher education or only to private higher education?

standards of performance or quality that I failed to apply, and some contextual factors, which I failed to take into consideration?

Bree saw "the problem" as the looming deadline. But what if Angelica's or Shawna's way of seeing the problem were more reasonable? How would "the problem" be best handled if it were interpreted in those ways?

Spiritual Development

In the previous sections we emphasized first one then another step in the IDEAS process. Along the way we have seen examples of problems in five of the six domains listed in the section on educating the whole person: social, vocational, academic, physical health, and emotional well-being. The one remaining domain is called the "spiritual" domain. *Spiritual* can be a troubling word for some of us; so if it helps to think of this domain as the province of one's core values, ethical principles, and deep commitments, that is fine as well.

Here's the situation: Max had been feeling ambivalent about the community service project he got sucked into over spring break. A group from his residence hall had signed up to spend the week building houses with Habitat for Humanity. His friends had coaxed him to join in by pointing out that Max's father was in construction so Max would be a natural asset. Max knew that his friends were mostly joking about his being "an asset" and that they just wanted more hands working on the project so they would finish faster. What they didn't know is that Max's father was constantly telling Max that a college education would be his "ticket out of Pop's blue collar life, and don't look back." Max always found that statement puzzling, but he knew that Pop was thrilled when Max announced that he was majoring in Engineering Management. Max never saw the curveball coming, but his life was irrevocably changed by his experience during spring break. Max had never witnessed poverty like that before, nor the tearful gratitude from the families who were receiving the new houses. Ever since, Max can't stop thinking about how his own family actually has it pretty good. Max finds himself asking hard questions about privilege, social justice, and what is fair in the world. He's not only wondering what happened, he's wondering now about the advice his Pop gave and about a lot of societal and political values and beliefs that he had never before questioned.

The central themes linked with the category we are calling "Spiritual Development" pertain to nurturing a positive and enthusiastic outlook on life and the future, setting goals for oneself, and achieving those aspirations—by cultivating open-mindedness, forming a personal value system and appreciating others' value systems, establishing a sense of ethics and ethical behavior, and engaging existential questions about life and the world around us.

Throughout this chapter we have highlighted the important factors that shape our college experience: social relationships, vocational direction, academics, physical health, and emotional well-being. These are not discrete domains; the life decisions we make during college inevitably touch on and are influenced by many of these factors in complex ways. The 5-Step IDEAS Critical Thinking Problem-Solving Process works well for the practical, day-to-day problems that vex and at times torment us. Now, we end this chapter by acknowledging and celebrating the "big questions" that are likely to be raised by the experiences you'll have while in college. In fact, the big questions are likely to be ones that we come back to more than once throughout our lifetime. It seems that every stage of life holds its share of experiences that can cause a person or a community to revisit core values, principles, and commitments. Let's take a brief look at how the five IDEAS steps might apply.

We make our lives meaningful by embracing purposes larger than ourselves.

> "I really wanted to do something positive on the Internet. I wanted to try to get young people talking about, thinking about, life's big questions—make it cool and OK to wonder about the heart, the soul and free will and God and death and big topics like that, big human topics."
>
> Rainn Wilson, Actor[12]

Max is grappling with the big question of "Who am I in this world?" Reflecting thoughtfully about one's identity is a hallmark of the college experience. Erik Erikson and other developmental psychologists remind us that

THINKING CRITICALLY

Religious Practices and Beliefs—What *Do* We Know?

Whether it is through a religious tradition or a personally defined spiritualism, faith in a higher power, for many students, is a recognizable expression of their value system. How important is religion in your life—very important, somewhat important, not too important, or not at all important?

And how important is religion to the other students in your classes? Do you practice your religion at least once a week? Do other students practice theirs? Given the diversity of religious views, practices, and traditions among college students, perhaps a more fundamental question is how much do we really know about the practices and beliefs of those other religions . . . or even of our own?

According to a recent Religious Knowledge Survey conducted by the Pew Research Center nearly 60 percent of U.S. adults said religion is "very important" to them. And 40 percent of adults said they regularly (at least once a week) attend religious services. Nevertheless, a large number of Americans could not correctly identify the tenets, practices, history, and leading figures of *their own faith tradition,* let alone those of other major world religions.

The strongest predictor of religious knowledge was not having a religious upbringing, but it was a *person's years of schooling.* Other important factors included a person's religious affiliation, overall levels of religious commitment and frequency of reading religious materials, their gender and ethnicity, and where in the country a person resides.

Initial questions: Review the survey findings at Report of survey results. Search "Pew U.S. Religious Knowledge Survey". How can we explain the relationship between education and religious knowledge? Search "Pew U.S. Religious Knowledge Quiz." How well do you know the Bible and Christianity, world religions, or the constitutional restrictions on religion in the public schools? Take the Pew Research Center's Religious Knowledge Quiz for yourself:"

Obvious follow up questions: How does knowing a religion relate to practicing a religion? In the preface of *The God Delusion*, Richard Dawkins describes coming to the consciousness raising realization that adults can give themselves permission to question the religious beliefs taught to them in childhood. If you have not done so already, in the spirit of Dawkins' "But I didn't knew I could,"[14] give yourself permission to explore potential differences between what you were taught as a child and what you have learned as a more mature and better informed adult?

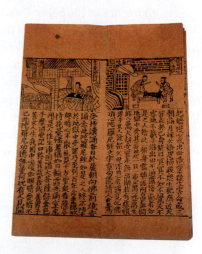

many of the elements of the college environment—academic, co-curricular, administrative, and community-based—facilitate college students' identity formation and social development.[13] The table "Levels of Thinking and Knowing" in Chapter 6 describes a progression from the naïvely trusting ways children deal with ideas all the way to the subtle and complex ways that "truth-seekers" and "sages" think. Critical thinking, and the cultivation of a healthy skepticism, can aid our cognitive development and help us not to be trapped in any one stage along the way. Max finds that he can no longer accept his father's views about society and about work without questioning. Max's experiences during the service learning project reveal a troubling disconnect between what he had believed before and what he has learned since about relative wealth and poverty, and the conditions under which people live. Max is not so naïve as to think that he can go out and "save the world." But neither is he so insensitive as to think that "none of this is about me."

> "Faith consists in being vitally concerned with that ultimate reality to which I give the symbolic name of God. Whoever reflects earnestly on the meaning of life is on the verge of an act of faith."
>
> Paul Tillich, Theologian[15]

Applying the 5-step IDEAS process can help counteract the feeling of being overwhelmed by the magnitude of big questions, such as those with which Max is wrestling. Forming a clear, solid, and durable sense of self takes time. Max is not going to have this all figured out in a day or two. But he does have the courage to face his question. He wants to know who the man is that he is going to become. And he knows that choices along the way are going to affect how he reacts each morning when he looks at the face of the man in the mirror. Rather than doing anything drastic that might impact his future options, Max is not going to drop out of college to take up missionary work in the inner city. Although that is one option that some might pursue. Nor is Max going to turn his back on his Habitat for Humanity experiences, trying to pretend that they never happened. Again, that is an option some others might pursue. Max is probably going to end up agreeing with his father that a college degree is essential, but that will be an inference Max draws for his own reasons, and not simply because his father may or may not have said so. Max will see the value of a college degree for the work he wants to do in life. Max may or may not decide to stick with his Engineering Management major. Either way, again, this decision will be for his own reasons, and whether it pleases or displeases his father will be of secondary consideration. Probably Max will gather data information about Engineering Management careers that have the potential to combine employment and service to the greater good. It is highly unlikely that Max would take a job that fulfilled only one of those two compatible objectives. Max may then decide to seek summer internships with firms that appear to offer those kinds of job opportunities after graduation. Not only would taking those kinds of internships help Max review and validate or amend his thinking about the man he will become, but internships can position him to be a stronger job candidate in those firms, if it turns out that the experiences affirm the direction he thinks he wants to take in his life.

Max's case reminds us that the 5-step IDEAS process can work over an extended period of time when applied to larger problems and dynamic circumstances, just as it can work with smaller, more well-defined problems. The key thing is that good problem solving and decision making during our college experience, and for all the rest of one's life, demands purposeful reflective judgment—that is, critical thinking.

Summing up this chapter,

the process of reflective judgment known as critical thinking can be described as a widely applicable 5-step general method of problem solving and decision making. For ease of remembering the steps, use "I D E A S." Identify the problem and set priorities. Determine relevant information and deepen understanding. Enumerate options and anticipate consequences. Assess the situation and make a preliminary decision. Scrutinize the process and self-correct as needed. To illustrate how the process works, we applied it to the many different kinds of day-to-day challenges and difficulties college students encounter. In Chapter 4 we begin focusing on specific critical thinking skills, the tools used in multiple steps of the critical thinking process.

Key Concept

problem solving is moving from the point at which we initially realize that we have a difficulty, which requires our attention to that point where we regard the difficulty as being sufficiently resolved for the current time and circumstances.

Applications

Reflective Log

What's on my list? No doubt every one of us has small problems, if not big problems, which can aptly be classified as social, vocational, academic, physical, emotional, or spiritual concerns. Take a moment to jot down some of your issues, questions, and problems in each of these areas. When you have done that, reflect for a moment on which of the ones you've listed appears to you to be the most challenging.

Having done that, now ask yourself what constructive steps are you taking to address that/those issues, questions, and concerns? How are those approaches working out for you? If not as well as you had hoped or expected, what might you do differently? Remember what Albert Einstein said, "Insanity is doing the same thing over and over again and expecting a different result."

Individual Exercise

Believing our own press releases: Hundreds of millions of us use social media to post pictures and share personal information for friends, family, contacts and all the world to see. And that includes everyone and anyone who is just surfing, snooping, or stalking cyberspace. The *Craig's List* murderer, phishing schemes by identity thefts, and feature films like *Headline*, *Her*, *The Social Network*, and *Catfish* dramatize the complexity of online relationships. They bring home the need to evaluate how trustworthy the information might be that someone posts about themselves. And that includes how honest we are about what we say about ourselves. Have we applied the right degree of healthy

skepticism to what we say about ourselves? Or, do we fall prey to the problem of believing our own press releases? Do a picture-by-picture and line-by-line analysis of your own postings about yourself. Are there exaggerations, strategic omissions, or misleading descriptions there? Is the impression we are trying to give people about ourselves an honest one? Not that we should post all of our flaws and fears for the whole world to see, but we might ask: To what extent might some degree of depth, substance, and sincerity actually present a truer picture? And if we know we are not being fully honest ourselves, then how can we trust what others are saying about themselves?

SHARED RESPONSE

Give IDEAS a Try

Describe how you could use the five-step IDEAS critical thinking process to work through a current problem that you may be dealing with, or that is fairly typical for college students like yourself. Comment respectfully on the problems and IDEAS solution strategies offered by others.

Group Exercise

Investigate, classify, and rank the purposes of college: Students have their reasons for attending college, parents and family members have their hopes and expectations, governments and foundations have their reasons for funding colleges, religious communities have purposes in mind for starting and sustaining colleges, and the colleges themselves have mission statements and Web sites proclaiming all the worthy things they expect all their graduates to have learned. Compare those lists. What are the commonalities of purpose, if any? Which are the most worthy and reasonable, even if they are not the most common?

Which do the faculty, staff, alumni, and financial supporters of your college most value and spend the most effort to achieve? Which do you prize most and focus your greatest efforts on achieving? Which define the college and you as a success? Suggestion, begin with web searches for mission statements, government policy statements, and political statements about the value or worth of a college education. Interview some faculty and people from other walks of life. In other words, determine the relevant information and deepen understanding before responding to the evaluation questions in this exercise.

Chapter 4
Clarify Ideas and Concepts

In one of the most dramatic moments of the Academy Award–winning film version of *Inherit the Wind* two of the great actors of the previous century confront one another. Spencer Tracy, playing Harry Drummond, cross-examines Fredric March, playing Harrison Brady, on this point: How shall we interpret the biblical meaning of *day*? Watch this wonderful film, the scene is near the end. It is such a famous scene that you may be able to locate it on YouTube or elsewhere online.

HOW do context and purpose affect the quality of an interpretation?

WHEN are vagueness and ambiguity problematic?

HOW can I resolve problematic vagueness and ambiguity?

WHAT are language communities and in which do I hold membership?

 ## Learning Outcomes

4.1 Explain how context and purpose affect the quality of an interpretation.

4.2 Explain the conditions under which vagueness and ambiguity become problematic, clarify your explanation with examples.

4.3 Apply five strategies to effectively resolve problematic vagueness and ambiguity.

4.4 Explain why strong critical thinking, particularly judicious interpretation, is helpful when encountering a new language community.

You interpret! The verbal gauntlet is hurled at the over-confident prosecution witness, Harrison Brady, by defense attorney Harry Drummond in *Inherit the Wind*.[1] Drummond is defending a schoolteacher fired for teaching evolution. Brady maintains that evolution is demonstrably false, given the creation story presented in *Genesis*, the opening book of the Bible. The Harrison Brady character is a staunch advocate of reading every word and verse in the Bible as the exact historical truth in all respects. But, thinks Drummond, if Brady is offering an interpretation, then Brady has strayed from his strictly literal reading of the sacred text. An interpretive analysis would be a crack in Brady's mental armor, a weakness that Drummond, like any good attorney, vigorously exploits. Drummond challenges Brady's thinking with questions about how to make sense of the word *day* as that word is used in Genesis. How long is a day to the eternal Creator, particularly if the Sun had not yet been created? There would be no way to measure a day, there would be no sundown to sundown, for example. So, is a "day" necessarily a 24-hour day; or might a day have been longer (or shorter) than 24 hours? Might it have perhaps been a year, hundreds of years, thousands of years, or, who knows, maybe millions of years?

Scientific advances over recent centuries have reshaped our understanding of ourselves, our world, our solar system, and our universe. Without diminishing the value of the biblical book of Genesis for other purposes, to offer the book as a historical record of actual events occurring within the specific time frames stated there is to invite precisely the kind of exposure that *Inherit the Wind* delivers. On a literal level, Genesis's obvious contradictions (e.g., daylight on earth being created before the Sun) and vast inconsistencies between that text and all that we have learned scientifically pose too great an intellectual obstacle for reason to vault. For a visually beautiful and personally inspirational scientific recap of the age of our planet, watch episode 7, "The Clean Room," of the celebrated FOX Television 2014 series *Cosmos: A Space Time Odyssey*."

But, planetary history aside, what if the authors and editors of Genesis had entirely different purposes in mind as they told their marvelous and meaningful stories around the campfires of their nomadic kinsmen? What other interpretations might those authors and editors have intended?

This chapter is about interpreting the meanings of ideas as they are conveyed in language. Our goal, in the exercise of our critical thinking skill of interpretation, is to achieve as much accuracy and precision as may be required or as may be possible for the purposes and the context at hand.

4.1 Interpretation, Context, and Purpose

The authors and editors of Genesis meant to communicate their faith perspective. By telling of the powerful and awe-inspiring Yahweh, the authors of Genesis wanted to reassure the Israelites that Yahweh was far superior to the pagan gods. The tales of fearsome divine reprisals for straying from the teachings of Yahweh (e.g., death for those who went with the Moabite women to ceremonies honoring the god Baal) were meant to reinforce compliance. Genesis is meant to bind the Israelites as a group by giving them a common religious heritage and identity. To do this, the authors and editors of Genesis used some of the most memorable stories known to man.[2]

We do not expect a scientific publication to be a musical score. And we do not defend it or criticize it using the standards that are meant to be applied to music. The purposes and context of the material determines how it should be interpreted and used. Take the book of Genesis, for example—to interpret it as a scientific work would be a mistake. First, as indicated earlier, it is very probably not an accurate understanding of the purposes of the authors. Second, the historical, social, and cultural context within which the work was produced was pre-scientific. The investigatory methodology we know as science was foreign to the authors and the audience of Genesis. Thus, it would be equally wrongheaded either to criticize or to defend that collection of religious stories as if it were astronomical, biological, or geophysical science. In fact, the whole question of the Bible's historical context and purpose is fascinating. And given the political, moral, religious, and social significance of the Bible in today's world, it is a question well worth examining carefully.[3] As we shall see throughout this chapter, a grasp of context and purpose forms the starting point for interpretation.

Meaning Matters

How best to interpret Genesis is a significant concern for a great many people. But it is only one of many disputes where everything depends on interpretation. For example, the words "father" and "sibling" in the context of MTV's reality series *Generation Cryo*. Is it reasonable to call a sperm donor a father? Is it reasonable to think of another person fathered by that same sperm donor as a sibling? If two children adopted into the same family are siblings, and they do not have any ancestors in common, why wouldn't two children from the same sperm donor be siblings, even if raised in different homes? Does it make a difference? Yes,

Does sperm donorship = fatherhood?

that day the meaning of the term "parent," with all of its psychological, social, legal, ethical, and financial implications will again become more ambiguous.

Talking about the impact on people, what exactly is the definition of "person"? In the landmark case "Citizens United vs. the Federal Election Commission," the U.S. Supreme Court ruled that corporations are persons too. The issue originally focused on whether the protections of the First Amendment right of free speech extended to political positions expressed by corporations. The Supreme Court said as persons that right is protected. So, "We the people ..." includes Wal-Mart Stores, Exxon Mobil, General Motors, Bank of America, Boeing, and others. And if free speech is protected, it seems logical that the other First Amendment rights are protected too, including the right to the free exercise of religion. Which leaves us with the mental puzzle, what religion does a Fortune 500 public corporation practice? Is it the religion of its founder, the religion agreed upon by majority vote of the stock holders, or what? But, more importantly for the biologically based people involved, does a large, public, for-profit corporation, for example, Hobby Lobby with over 20,000 employees, have the right to refuse to provide its female employees with certain health care benefits on the basis of the religious beliefs of its founder? Does a corporation upon which millions depend, for example, Cardinal Health Systems or Comcast, have the right not to provide services to customers on Sunday because the Board of Directors believes for religious reasons its employees should be attending worship services with their families on Sundays? Until the courts clarify its precise meaning, at this point in time "the free exercise of religion" as applied to corporate persons is unhelpfully vague. Meaning matters.

especially if love, identity, opportunity, or money come into the picture. There was a legal battle in Michigan over whether a genetic child can receive Social Security survivor benefits if the sperm donor father dies.[4] The key words here, "father" and "child," are ambiguous. Meaning matters.

Or, to take another current example, one that rose to the level of a U.S. Supreme Court case, consider the meaning of "family" and "mother" within the context of twenty-first century technology. A child born today can have a birth mother, a genetic (egg donor) mother, and female parent (mother) who adopts and raises that child. In Florida a birth mother took her nine year old child from the home of the woman who was the genetic mother and who had raised the child. Sounds terrible, but the issue is complicated. The genetic mother's egg was fertilized in vitro by a donor sperm, then implanted in the birth mother. But, because the genetic mother was in a lesbian relationship, and because Florida does not recognize same sex marriage, and the genetic mother could not legally adopt her daughter.[5] The legal outcome of this custody battle will impact this child and many others. Meaning matters. And as soon as we can replace one female's nuclear DNA in an ovum with another female's nuclear DNA so that it can interact with the mitochondrial DNA that is outside of the nucleus, we will be able to have a three-genetic-parent child. And on

But, Clear Enough for What?

How clear must the meaning of an expression be before we can say that we understand? Not surprisingly, that depends almost entirely on purpose and context of the communication. Interpretation, along with the habit of judiciousness, is the primary critical thinking skill for determining the meaning and significance of what is being communicated. *The first rule of fair-minded interpretation is to be sensitive to context and purpose.*

Strong critical thinkers use four interpretive questions to reveal context and purpose. These questions apply to written and oral communications. But not just to those two ways of communicating. The four interpretive questions apply also to nonverbal ways of communicating, including using music, dance, gestures, signs, posters, pictures, icons, maps, data charts, dashboard displays, and so on.

Christianity's iconography is rich with meanings. This stained glass window shows the four evangelists, Matthew, Mark, Luke, and John, each holding a book representing the gospel attributed to his authorship. The figure in the middle represents Jesus, whom we are intended to recognize because the figure is holding a lamb.

Icons have historically been used as non-verbal ways of communicating. In our current technology-rich culture, almost everyone knows that the colorful little icons on the home screens of mobile devices signify the app that they also enable the user to open. Carved into the pavement of the streets near the port of the ancient Roman city of Pompeii, are phallic icons intended to guide visiting sailors to houses of prostitution. But, like the gods of ancient civilizations, the icons which signified so much to people living in other times and places often are of little significance for us today. Search "Mayan icons" or "Aztec icons" to see examples. Unfamiliar with context and purpose, today we have difficulty figuring out what they mean or meant. Some icons are meaningful today only to people who are members of particular communities, and that is because the members of that community know their purpose and context of use. Outsiders often do not. For example, can you identify the cultural context and meaning of the two sets of icons pictured here? Hint, one set is intended to celebrate five individuals. The other set is advice to visitors to a public beach.

And most importantly, to mixed communication modalities, including video that combines words, music, images, gestures, and iconic symbols.

1. What values, beliefs, events, or issues were important enough to motivate the author to initiate communication?

2. Who was the author's intended audience?

3. What did the author intend to communicate?

4. Given the context and the intended audience, what did the author believe that audience already knew?

For example, assume that someone texts this message: "Torch in boot." At first this message appears nonsensical. Here is some context: The message was sent in response to a question, "Do we have a torch?" A Liverpool teenage driver sent this message at night to her dad. The dad's purpose in sending "Torch in boot" was to respond to his daughter's question. OK, now we can make a reasonably accurate interpretation of the message. It means, "Yes, we do have a torch (flashlight). You'll find it in the boot (trunk) of the car you are driving."

Knowing that not every visitor to Morrow Bay Harbor can read English, the Harbor Patrol informs visitors about the laws and warns them about dangers using icons.

Worth 1000 Words

Some messages are better communicated in images than in text. But even so, the four interpretive questions apply. Consider, for example, the two Herblock editorial cartoons shown here. Within the context of U.S. politics and the influence the K Street lobbyists have in drafting legislation that serves the interests of their corporate clients, we can understand exactly what the cartoonist is saying. What surprised us about these two cartoons was their publication dates. Fifty years apart and the message is still meaningful.

Suppose an author's purpose is to assist eligible people to understand how much subsidy in tax credits they could receive from the government as a way of reducing their health insurance premiums under the Affordable Healthcare Act. Knowing that millions of eligible individuals may have poor reading skills, instead of quoting the regulations, the author might try using a graphic like this one. But, without understanding that the context is health insurance premium savings, it would be difficult to know what this chart is intended to communicate since it does not mention insurance anywhere.

It would take a page or more of formidably dense text to describe the range and distribution of critical thinking skills test scores for 2768 undergraduates. Or, if the audience can be assumed to understand simple numerical charts and descriptive statistics, we can communicate more effectively simply by using one image of a bar chart. The bar chart, which statisticians would refer to as a "Histogram," includes an abundant amount

"IT'S STILL A REPRESENTATIVE FORM OF GOVERNMENT—THEY REPRESENT US"

©2000 HERBLOCK

of information. But, to access that information a person needs to understand what the community of statisticians means by odd sounding words like "Quartile" or by abbreviations like "N". Like anything else, once we know how words and symbols are used by the people who form a given community of language users (in this case statisticians), it is very easy to interpret all that is being said. As a kind of personal mini-initiation into that community, watch the short video "Interpreting Group Score Report Histograms". Search for it on YouTube by name, or by adding "Facione" or "Insight Assessment" to your search.[6]

"What Do You Figure This One Would Cost?"

Under the Affordable Care Act, you qualify for savings in 2013 depending on the size of your family and the income you make. Find the size of your family to see what the upper limit on income is for you to qualify for government supported savings.

Family Size	Max Income to Qualify
😀	Qualify $ 45,960
😀😀	$ 62,040
😀😀😀	$ 78,120
😀😀😀😀	$ 94,200
😀😀😀😀😀	$ 110,280
😀😀😀😀😀😀	$ 126,360
😀😀😀😀😀😀😀	$ 142,440
😀😀😀😀😀😀😀😀	$ 158,520

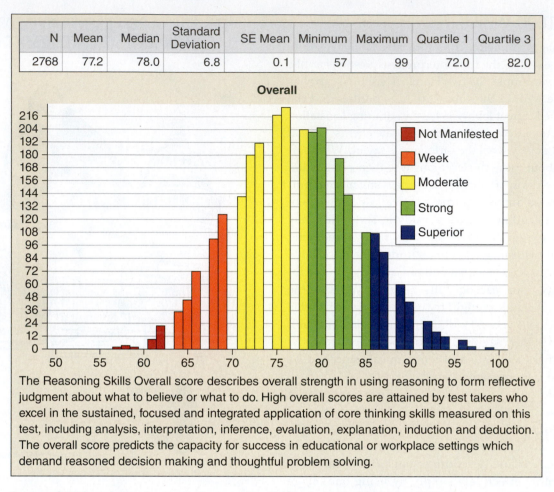

N	Mean	Median	Standard Deviation	SE Mean	Minimum	Maximum	Quartile 1	Quartile 3
2768	77.2	78.0	6.8	0.1	57	99	72.0	82.0

Overall

Legend:
- Not Manifested
- Week
- Moderate
- Strong
- Superior

The Reasoning Skills Overall score describes overall strength in using reasoning to form reflective judgment about what to believe or what to do. High overall scores are attained by test takers who excel in the sustained, focused and integrated application of core thinking skills measured on this test, including analysis, interpretation, inference, evaluation, explanation, induction and deduction. The overall score predicts the capacity for success in educational or workplace settings which demand reasoned decision making and thoughtful problem solving.

Scores of 2768 undergraduate students on the *California Critical Thinking Skills Test*

Communication, Language, and Thought

Our complex ways of communicating, our uses of language, and our thinking are so closely connected that most of us think in our native language. As children, years before formal schooling, we begin to learn how to express our ideas in words and sentences. As we grow and learn more, our vocabulary expands, as does our ability to express ourselves with greater precision. If we try to learn a new language as an adult, we often find ourselves translating from the new language into English (if English is our native language) and then back into the target language.

Some anthropologists maintain that the capacity to use language gave the young species *Homo sapiens* great advantages over the other hominids, such as Neanderthals, who had greater numbers and greater physical strength.[7] Using language, early human beings were able to coordinate efforts in combat and refine strategies for acquiring the resources our species needed to survive. Early human language may have included, along with words and pictographs, sounds like clicks and whistles, which we do not use in English. Because communication was almost always face-to-face in the centuries before writing, gestures, and movements were also used to facilitate communication. Taken in its broadest sense, language in the earliest millennia of our species was a rich and varied system of gesticulations, sounds, pictures, and symbols.

As human society became more complex and agreements and ideas became so important that they had to be passed down to future generations, written language evolved to capture those ideas and agreements. Whether it was the location of the family plot of land in a river delta that flooded each spring, or the dictates of the monarch, some things needed to be remembered. Written language became our means of commemorating important things like these.

Written communications are poor messengers as compared to face-to-face conversations. In the presence of the other person facial expressions, gestures, and body language add so much. When immediate face-to-face communication is reduced to texts or voice recordings, we increase the risk that vagueness or ambiguity will make accurate interpretation more difficult. But, we gain a huge benefit, namely that reliance on written communication relieves us from needing to memorize everything. Most often we

December 26, 1987

Dear Susan, Bill, and Karl,

You probably never thought you'd see our last will and testament, but here it is. We know that you are all over 40, but Pop and I still think of you as our kids. We're getting old and we've been thinking a lot lately about passing our belongings on to the three of you. We have no plans to do this in the near or foreseeable future. But, you never know. We have our aches and pains, and we are getting to that point when it is important to be sure that our ideas are known before it gets to be too late.

So, here's what we want. We want all our money to go to each of you equally. Bill, we want you to have our business, which is no prize because it takes a lot of work. But we love it, and it has been good to Pop and me over all these years. Each year it provides us with a little profit, so we can't complain. And you are the only one who ever really took an interest in it. Susan, we want you to have our house in Milwaukee. We had some fun times there when you kids were growing up. Maybe you can sell it if the economy improves. Karl, we want you to have the house here in Lakeland we're living in now. The real estate market is the pits right now. And the house needs a new roof and the plumbing is a mess. But you know all that because you're living here now. So, Karl, it's yours.

Divide up our furniture, pictures, books, and personal things, and give everything you don't want to Goodwill.

The main thing is for you three to divide everything equally. Including whatever might be left in our 401K. Please respect our wishes about not squabbling over what little there will be in our estate.

We love you.

Oh, and Karl, you get our dog, Lobo Loco. Lucky you.

interpret textual or recorded communications correctly when we know the person with whom we are communicating. If we know that person, then we often are able to infer his or her purpose and the context of their communication correctly. If we do not know the person who is sending the text, e-mail, or voice message, we are at risk of misunderstanding, or worse, of being duped or conned. A strong critical thinker will always ask "Who sent me this, and why?"

Occasionally even longer and more carefully prepared messages can be difficult to interpret. Consider the example of the December 26, 1987, letter shown here. It was written by an older couple to their adult children. Suppose the day has come when the three adult children pull out their parents' letter and try to figure out how to honor what it tells them. Imagine the three of them, Susan, Bill, and Karl, discussing their parents' letter:

- **Susan:** "Our parents said that their whole idea was to divide everything equally. But the house in Milwaukee is worth only 70 percent of what the house in Lakeland, Florida, is worth. So, how is that equal?"

- **Bill:** "The business was making money back in the day when Mom and Pop were more active, but the last few years it has been a struggle to break even. These days, it is nothing but headaches. Even if I sold the business I would have almost nothing left after I paid off the loans they needed just to keep operating these past couple of years. How is that equal to a house in Milwaukee or a house in Lakeland?"

- **Karl:** "Look, they didn't want us to fight over things like this. So, why don't we put a value on each house and on the business, then sell everything, and divide the proceeds equally?"

- **Susan:** "Well, that makes financial sense. But would it really be what they wanted? After all, they were very specific about which one of us would receive each of the houses and the business."

As we review the parents' letter, we can see the problems that the three siblings are having. The parents thought that their instructions were clear and precise. But, as it turned out, they were wrong. The instruction to "divide everything equally," is problematic in two ways. First the word *everything* is vague. Did the parents intend that "everything" should include the two houses and the business, or does it apply to all their money and possessions other than the real estate and the business? The siblings need to clarify what's in and what's out so that they can fulfill their parents' intent and divide "everything" equally. The letter is vague. Arguments could be made for both interpretations.

The second problem has to do with the instruction to divide everything "equally." Should the siblings interpret that to mean "financially exactly the same dollar value," or should they interpret "equally" to mean each gets one major asset, each gets one third of the books, furniture, and personal possessions, and each gets one third of the dollar value remaining in the parents' 401K? In this second sense of "equally," the result may not be that each person would receive the exact same total dollar value, but each would have been given an equal share of each category of objects in the parents' estate. The letter is ambiguous. Arguments could be made for both interpretations. In this context and for this purpose the term "equally" is unhelpfully ambiguous. And, although the parents did not want their heirs to squabble, since meaning matters, it would not surprise us if one or more of them hired lawyers or if the process of dividing the parents' estate caused hard feelings.

4.2 When Vagueness or Ambiguity Cause Misunderstandings

Since meaning matters, we need to examine vagueness and ambiguity. Our aim is to identify the strategies strong critical thinkers can use to analyze or clarify the context and purpose of a communication to more accurately interpret what it means.

Vagueness: "Does the Meaning Include This Case or Not?"

Common sense tells us that we should not bring animals to the airport. Cows, chickens, cats, goldfish, snakes, and monkeys are not welcome there. Although we all can agree with the general principle, it would still be reasonable to ask, "What about companion animals and assistance

Does "No dogs allowed" apply to companion animals if prescribed by a doctor for a person's health and well-being? Is the animal's care an allowable medical expense for tax return purposes?

animals?" And as soon as the question is asked, we realize that our common sense understanding, while generally correct, is not precise enough for practical purposes.

A guide dog is an assistance animal, which we would not *intend* to prohibit from the airport. We can address the uncertainty about whether the term "animal" *in this context* is meant to refer to guide dogs or not by adding a qualification or exception to our initial statement. We could say, as they do in Tampa, "No animals are allowed in the airport terminal except assistance animals."

OK, but now what about "companion animals"? For example, for reasons of psychological health, in some states elderly people and others are permitted to legally register certain animals as "companion animals." Often this registration permits the owner of the companion animal to be granted exceptions to restrictions that generally apply to pets. So, we might want to make a further amendment to our dictate about no animals at airports to permit another exception. In this case, for "registered companion animals." Again, the uncertainty about whether the word *animals* applies *in this context* to companion animals needs to be resolved. Our intent is to permit them to be brought to the airport. So, for our current purposes, a dog that is either an assistance animal or a companion animal is permitted. In real-life situations, we think about our purposes and about the context to decide how to resolve uncertainties just like these.

Notice that we did not ask whether human beings were excluded from airports because human beings were animals. In terms of the purpose and context, it simply was not a reasonable question. But in other contexts or for other purposes, it could be, as for example in the question of whether or not a viral strain, say avian flu, can jump animal species. In that situation, human beings are animals, rather than plants.

Consider this question: Given the purposes for not permitting animals at airports, how would you resolve the vagueness in the word *airport* if a child were to ask, "Is it OK if we bring our pet dog with us in the car when we take Grandma to the airport? Please, we are only going to drop Grandma off." Does "airport" in this context and for these purposes include or not include the interior of vehicles that use the departure street outside the terminal building?

Problematic vagueness is the characteristic of a word or expression having an *imprecise meaning or unclear boundaries in a given context or for a given purpose*. However, as the "animal" and "airport" examples illustrate, vagueness is best considered *not as an absolute feature, but as being relative to the context within which and purposes for which the term is being used*.

Problematic Vagueness

Imagine you work in the marketing department at H&M, and you receive the following memo from corporate for the next campaign: "We want to go after a young adult demographic." Does that mean the tech-savvy, e-money using, social networking, style conscious Gen-Y Echo Boomers or the more skeptical, "what's in it for me?" yet brand-loyal, credit card carrying, urban Gen-Xers?[8] In the sentence "We have to find those who were responsible for causing this terrible car accident," does the expression "those who were responsible" include only the drivers who were involved, or does it also include any or all of these other persons: the manufacturers of the vehicles involved in the accident, the engineers who designed the street, the city officials who refused to install a stoplight, the people living along the street who never trimmed or pruned their shrubs and trees

(which grow so thick that the vision of the drivers was limited), or the business owner who put up the huge, distracting billboard?

The H&M example does not pose major problems. If Gen-Xers want to buy H&M clothing, the corporation will happily agree to make the sales, even if the marketing campaign was targeted for the younger and much larger population of Gen-Yers. However, the corporation does care whether the campaign is reaching those who are clearly members of the target audience. Marketing campaigns are expensive. But they're also like shotgun blasts. As long as the campaign hits its main target, it is not a problem if some of the pellets spray raggedly around the edges. The boundary between Gen-Y and Gen-X is not sharp and bright, at least for the purpose of selling youthfully styled clothes. So, resolving the question of whether "young adults" does or does not overlap Gen-X and Gen-Y a bit is probably not a major problem for the corporation.

The car accident example is different. There the vagueness of the expression "those who were responsible" could become the object of highly contentious legal battles. If it is proven that vehicle manufacturers knew of some defect in the braking system of one of the cars but did not recall the vehicle for repairs, then a jury may decide to hold the manufacturer partially responsible for the accident. Similarly, it might be argued that the others listed each knew something, did something, or failed to do something that contributed to the accident. The vagueness of the term *responsible* as it applies to the car accident needs to be resolved for the purposes of determining criminal and financial responsibility. This matter is so problematic and yet so important that our society

Do you think this ad hits the "young adult" market? Will this ad appeal to any other markets as well?

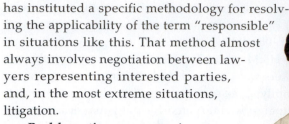

has instituted a specific methodology for resolving the applicability of the term "responsible" in situations like this. That method almost always involves negotiation between lawyers representing interested parties, and, in the most extreme situations, litigation.

Problematic vagueness is the characteristic of a word or expression having an imprecise meaning or unclear boundaries such that uncertainty about precisely what is included in that meaning or excluded from that meaning results in troublesome miscommunications in a given context or for a given purpose.

Ambiguity: "Which Meaning Are We Using?"

In the hilarious comedy *My Cousin Vinny*,[9] Ralph Macchio's character has been brought in by an Alabama sheriff for questioning about a crime. Did he do it, or not? Listen carefully to the exact words Macchio uses when he confesses to the sheriff. Macchio's character is referring to his having walked out of a convenience store with a can of tuna fish in his jacket pocket. He forgot it was there and so left without paying for it. He is trying to confess to inadvertent shoplifting. The sheriff, on the other hand, is investigating the killing of the cashier at that same convenience store. The sheriff interprets Macchio as having said, "I killed the cashier" when Macchio apologizes for having left the store stupidly forgetting to pay for the can of tuna. The ambiguity triggers a chain of events that includes Macchio and his traveling companion, played by Mitchell Whitfield, being charged with murder.

When a word, expression, or statement has more than one meaning, we call it ambiguous. A quick look at the dictionary shows that a great many words have more than one meaning. Why, then, are we not confused on an almost constant basis? Because, again, knowing the context of the conversation and the purpose of the speaker, we can readily pick out the speaker's intended meaning. "Heads up!" shouted at the people sitting behind first base at a baseball game is not a command to look toward the sky; it is a warning to duck because the batter has just fouled off a pitch. "30–love," at a tennis match is intended to reveal the score, not the number of someone's amorous relationships. "That's sick!" is slang for "That's terrific." And, "Baby, you're the greatest!" is Hollywood hyperbole for "On your best day you're no better than average."

Problematic Ambiguity

Macchio's ambiguous confession is problematic because the misunderstanding results in his arrest. Were it not for the stunning defense put on by Joe Pesci, Macchio's character could easily have been convicted of murder and sentenced to the electric chair. The ambiguity of *"equally"* in the parents' letter about dividing up their estate was problematic because the multiple meanings of that expression left the three siblings uncertain how to fulfill their parents' wishes.

Problematic ambiguity is the characteristic of a word or expression, which can have multiple meanings such that uncertainty about exactly which meaning applies in a given context for a given purpose results in troublesome misunderstandings.

4.3 Resolving Problematic Vagueness and Ambiguity

Resolving problematic vagueness and problematic ambiguity requires the application of critical thinking skills and habits of mind. We need to analyze the communication to draw reasonable inferences about the context and purpose. We need to explain why we are interpreting the message in a given way and not in some other way. And we have to be reflective enough to search for and to correct any mistakes we might have made, rather than plunging ahead as if there could be no way we could have misinterpreted anything. In the case of problematic vagueness, our critical thinking problem is to determine where the borderlines of the term are to be located. In the case of problematic ambiguity our critical thinking decision relates to determining which one of the possible meanings the author intended.

Strong critical thinkers address problematic vagueness or problematic ambiguity using five strategies:

- Contextualizing
- Clarifying intent
- Negotiating
- Qualifying
- Stipulating

Contextualizing

AAA can refer to the American Automobile Association, the American Anthropological Association, the American Accounting Association, the American Academy of

Audiology, the Amateur Astronomers Association, the American Association of Anatomists, the American Ambulance Association, the Aikido Association of America, and the Arkansas Activities Association, just to name a few. So, if a person were to say, "I'm joining the AAA," we might find the ambiguity in that statement to be problematic.

Contextualizing resolves problematic ambiguity by reminding us of the topic being discussed or the circumstances within which a statement was made. In the "I'm joining the AAA" example, simply noting that the person was an undergraduate physics major talking about her interest in astronomy would clarify which AAA she meant.

Consider another example. "We need to find some more offensive people," can mean one thing in the context of sports and quite another thing spoken as irony after someone has made a particularly rude remark during a meeting. In the first context, the discussion is about building up the team's capacity to score more points by improving its offense. In the second context, the speaker probably intends to express a negative opinion about the behavior of one of the other people at the meeting.

To establish context we ask questions like these:

- Who said it to whom?
- When and where was it said?
- What was the topic of the conversation?
- What information, events or issues, public or personal, may the speaker have assumed that the intended audience knew about?
- Was the expression meant to be ironic, hyperbolic, misleading, or deceptive, rather than taken literally?
- Were technical terms, abbreviations, symbols, slang, code words, double entendre, euphemisms, or acronyms used?

That final question is important because often knowing that the conversation took place among members of a particular interest group or professional group helps us immediately recognize that a given word or expression is used with the special meaning that the given group attaches to that expression. We will talk more about this in Language Communities later in the chapter.

Words taken out of context can be misleading. Consider, for example, "I smoked 50 years . . . today I can run a marathon." We might interpret this to be a reasonably unambiguous statement suggesting that smoking is not always physically detrimental. The only clue that there may be more to the story is the three-dot ellipsis. What were the words that the author omitted? The out of context quotation was sliced from this, "I smoked 50 years ago, when I was in high school. But only a few cigarettes just to see what it was like. It was cross-country season, and my coach told me that I was one of the best in the state. He said that if I started smoking, I could kiss the state

championship good-bye. So, I quit smoking before I ever really got started and stayed away from cancer sticks ever since. Because I quit smoking and because I've worked out several days a week all of my life, today I can run a marathon. That and go to the funerals of my classmates who did smoke." Seeing the author's words in context, our interpretation becomes the opposite of what it was at first. Now we know that the author is advising people not to smoke, instead of saying that it might not be a problem.

Putting an author's words in context not only permits us to make an accurate interpretation, it helps us not be misled by unscrupulous individuals. Intellectual integrity and a strong habit of truth-seeking are needed when we summarize and de-contextualize the words and ideas of others. Accuracy is important, but so is a truthful preservation of the author's original intent. Unfortunately these days the disturbing practice of taking an opponent's words out of context in a political message, talk show, or public debate has been raised to an art form. Oh yes, the quote was technically accurate. But, still it was intentionally untruthful. Misleading by taking words out of context is only a step short of its cousin, the abysmal practice of intentionally misconstruing an opponent's remarks to confuse other people about what the opponent meant.

Clarifying Original Intent

Because problematic vagueness and ambiguity emerge when we are trying to interpret what someone means, one reasonable way to resolve the vagueness is simply to ask for clarification. Let's go back to the marketing department at H&M. One of the first things we will want to do is clarify the target audience that the executives have in mind for the campaign.

We would not want to put all our effort into designing the marketing approach until we were clear whom corporate H&M wants to reach. And our best method for doing this would be to ask the executives, "Can you clarify for us exactly which demographic you have in mind when you say 'young adults'?" We might hear back that we should target single men and women between the ages of 22 and 29 who are college graduates and employed at jobs that pay $35,000 to $70,000 per year. If so, that would add a lot of useful clarification, and we might be able to apply our critical thinking to the question of how best to reach that market segment.

On the other hand, we might hear back from our client that "young adults" is as clear as the client can be at this time about the target audience. In this case, we would probably try to help clarify that problematic vagueness. Given our experience and expertise in producing marketing campaigns, we might explain that the approach we would take to reach a single person who is a college graduate and has a good job is not the same as the approach we would use to market a product to someone who is the same age but married with children, or the same age but not a college graduate, or the same age but not currently employed.

Clarifying the speaker's intent becomes more challenging when multiple alternative wordings are possible and it is not possible to ask the author for clarification. For example, suppose our job was to resolve problematic phrases such as "unreasonable search and seizure," "the right to bear arms," or "freedom of assembly." The framers of the U.S. Constitution and the Bill of Rights are not available, and times and conditions have changed over the centuries. Although not the only way to interpret the U.S. Constitution, endeavoring to discern the framers' intent is one recognized approach.[10] And, although we do not have benefit of access to the original authors, we have letters they wrote and other documents they authored, we have their official votes and rulings on legal matters relating to issues in the Constitution, and we do have a large number of previous court rulings that established important precedents. In fact, endeavoring to discern intent is part of the process of interpreting the law in general. It is essential to our criminal justice system.[11]

Anyone can download a copy of the Constitution of the United States of America, with analytical and

Not Automatically a Problem

There is nothing inherently wrong with vagueness or ambiguity unless they introduce problems in a given real-life context or for a given purpose. The priority humans give to efficient communication should give way to concerns about problematic vagueness and problematic ambiguity only if miscommunications have occurred or are likely to occur.

interpretive information citing court rulings and historical documents, from the Government Printing Office. Historically one of the most contested clauses in the First Amendment is this one, "Congress shall make no law respecting an establishment of religion, or prohibiting the free expression thereof...." People on both sides of issues relating to the "separation of Church and State" often claim to know what the framers of the Constitution intended. And, with regard to James Madison and Thomas

Framers of the U.S. Constitution and the Bill of Rights were intentionally vague so future generations could interpret these documents to fit changing times and national circumstances, which the framers themselves wisely knew they could not anticipate.

Jefferson that is not difficult because of the historical record showing positions they took on other legislation, documents or letters they wrote. But, that said, an appeal to the intent of the framers goes nowhere if "the intent, insofar as there was one, of the others in the Congress who voted for the language and those in the States who voted to ratify is subject to speculation."[12]

Perhaps the problematic vagueness was intentional. The framers of the U.S. Constitution and the Bill of Rights were wise enough to realize that times and conditions would change and that therefore it would be prudent to write in ways that left room for future generations of Americans to interpret these fundamental documents to fit their times and circumstances. Wise judgment is a very good thing. We want to cultivate that in ourselves and leave room for it to be exercised by others, too, because it is impossible for any individual or any group to anticipate every kind of problem and every set of circumstances. The habit of judiciousness, which we talked about in Chapter 2, inclines us toward wisdom and prudence in making judgments. It is precisely this virtue that the framers of the Constitution trusted that future generations of Americans would need and would have if the young Republic were going to survive and flourish.

On the other hand, at times intentional vagueness can be frustrating when precise, practical answers are what people desire. Imagine the blustery Senatorial candidate who pounds the electorate with bromides like these: "I will bring transparency and fiscal accountability to Congress!" "Our educational system is such a mess that we need a war on ignorance." "When I'm in

office, our nation will never again negotiate from weakness." "Too many hard-working Americans are fed up with Washington politicians who take a business-as-usual approach." As voters, we might do well to demand greater clarity and operational precision, rather than accepting platitudes like those.

Negotiating the Meaning

Suppose you decide to hire me and we come to a handshake agreement that you will pay me a fair wage. As it turns out, we then discover that you regard a "fair wage" to be $25 per hour. But, I think a "fair wage" for the work you want me to do is $30 per hour. Because we both want the working relationship to start out being friendly, we decide to try to negotiate away the problematic vagueness by trying to reach a compromise between our two divergent positions. So, for our purposes in this context we can negotiate the mutual agreement that "fair wage" means $27.50 per hour.

The assumption that "negotiating" means "finding a mutually tolerable compromise" leads us to split the difference. But strong critical thinkers reflect on their own thinking process and often discover that their assumptions may have been mistaken. As it turns out, our assumption about the meaning of "negotiation" is mistaken because that word is ambiguous. Yes, it can refer to bargaining or haggling until a compromise is reached. But it can also refer to a process known as "interest based negotiation."[13]

The word "Compromising" suggests settling for less. Your position was that "fair wage" for the work you hired me to perform meant $25 per hour. My position was that "fair wage" meant $30. So we compromised. That form of negotiating is known as "position-based negotiating." Each side has its opening position and negotiation means chipping away at those positions. Position-based negotiation can result in a resentment, disrespect, and hostility toward the people on the other side of the table. They are the adversaries and we must never give them everything they want or they will have won! Some people believe that the only successful compromise is one that leaves both sides dissatisfied.

But those implications do not follow when we use "negotiating" in its other meaning. Interest-based negotiation begins with trying to figure out each party's interests. Apart from saving money, why is it in your interest to limit the pay to $25 per hour? And, apart from wanting more money, why am I so determined to get $30 per hour? Once we

To negotiate successfully, it is more important to know your interests (your needs) than your position (your wants).

each understand the other person's interests we can seek some way to achieve the interests of both sides. We are not adversaries in interest-based negotiation. We are collaborators. We are sitting on the same side of the table because neither side is trying to force the other side to abandon any of its interests. Our initial ideas about the solution we believe will work best are less important because during the search for how to achieve our interests both sides will probably see that some other solution will work better.

Using the interest-based negotiation method, we might reach a different and far more amiable result. We ask each other to talk first about our interests. You say that the reason why you want to limit the hourly pay to $25 is because you cannot afford the precedent of paying more per hour. I would not be your only employee, and it is not fair to pay me more than the others who do the same work. You further explain that you have an independent external benchmark that you used when you first set that rate of pay. That benchmark is an industry study showing the average hourly wage for the kind of work I will be doing for you is actually $23.65. But you pay me $25.00 per hour, just like you pay your other employees.

For my part, it is not the dollars per hour that concerns me. Rather, my interest is in the total number of dollars I will make in a week. And my other concern is the number of hours I have to be away from my mother because I am her primary caregiver. I explain that I need to make $1,200 per week because I am expecting to pay $250 per week ($50 per day) for her dependent care expenses if I must commute to work five days a week. And I am not happy about the long commute, almost 90 minutes each way. With the commute time added in, I was expecting that my workdays would require me to be away from home for 11 hours each day of the workweek. And I was worried about what that would mean in terms of my mother's care.

Knowing each other's interests, we can mutually explore creative resolutions. We might discover, for example, that I would accept $1,100 per week if you would permit me to telecommute from home two days a week. Working at home those two days saves me six hours of commuting time per week and $100 of dependent care expenses per week. In return, I guarantee you that I will give you 44 hours of work each week. This agreement permits you to preserve your $25-per-hour pay policy, which is fine with me.

Notice too that we have now expanded the meaning of "fair wage" beyond simply dollars per hour. Now it can include telecommuting and a variable number of work hours per week. Our negotiation resolved our problem without promoting greater conflict. In fact, neither of us feels dismayed, disrespected, or dissatisfied with the process or the result.

Remember when we defined the critical thinking process and said that the process can reflect back on the evidence, concepts, methods, context, and criteria used. Right here is a good example. We questioned the meaning of "negotiating" and noticed it referred to two different methodologies. So we applied the alternative method and came up with a different, and better, result. Let's ask about the criteria too. The idea that success means that both sides are dissatisfied does not fit with interest-based negotiation. In fact, the correct criterion now is the opposite: both sides should come out very pleased because the interests of both sides were met.

Now that we have agreed that I will work for you, I ask you if there is a dress code of some kind that I should know about. You say, "Why, yes. Glad you asked. We expect everyone who works in our office to wear a shirt with a collar. No T-shirts, tank tops, or V-necks."

I think, "What if we don't mean the same thing by 'shirt with a collar'?" I imagine a golf shirt with a soft collar, a loud Hawaiian shirt with a big collar, and a conservative dress shirt with a button-down collar. The expression "shirt with a collar" is causing problematic ambiguity. So, I ask you to be more specific and you say, "Oh, I meant a dress shirt. You don't have to wear a tie, but we expect everyone to wear a dress shirt to work."

Still some vagueness, I'm thinking. What about colors? Or will only white shirts count as what you mean by "dress

Interest-based negotiation can replace the resentment of compromise with the connection of collaboration.

shirt"? But I decide not to ask about that because I can just keep my eyes open the first couple of days on the job to see if anyone wears a dress shirt that isn't pure white. I do want to ask one more question—kind of a mini-negotiation. "What about Fridays? Do you have casual Fridays?" And happily you respond, "Of course, we do. You'll see a lot of golf shirts on Fridays at our office." "Shirt with a collar" as a problematic ambiguity—gone!—for our purposes in this context.

When negotiating meanings, strong critical thinkers realize that they must not end up with a definition that renders the term useless. If a word can mean anything any person might want, then the word has marginal value for communication. Richard Dawkins gives us this example, "Some people have views of God that are so broad and flexible that it is inevitable that they will find God wherever they look. One hears it said that 'God is the ultimate' or 'God is our better nature' or 'God is the universe.'... If you want to say 'God is energy' then you can find God in a lump of coal.... If the word "God" is not to become completely useless, it should be used in the way people have generally understood it: to denote a supernatural creator that is appropriate for us to worship."[14]

THINKING CRITICALLY

Negotiating a Job on Campus

Most colleges hire large numbers of students part-time. They work as assistants in academic and non-academic departmental offices all over campus, or they work in the library, food services, recreation, and residence life. Colleges often have rigid pay structures that do not permit room for negotiating the hourly wage. It is in the student's interest simply to secure a job, given that pay often cannot be a negotiating point. But the person doing the hiring has other interests: They want to hire students who are flexible about how many hours of work they will do per week and flexible about which hours and which days they will work. They also want students who are friendly, professional, fast learners, and who show initiative.

So, if it is in your interest to get a job that you might be able to count on for some part-time income not only this year but in future years, and if it is in your interest that the job be close to where you live and go to class (e.g., on campus),

then you would want to show that you are willing to be flexible about your work schedule. When you interview you might say that you know how important it is that the supervisor should be able to find students who are flexible about scheduling. Showing you understand the other person's interests is as pleasant for the person who is hiring you as it is for you when that person shows that he or she understands your interests.

The negotiation does not begin after you are offered the job, it begins when you walk in the door to ask for a job. Put yourself in the mind of the person doing the hiring. Ask yourself, if I were that person, what would be most important to me? And, once you do get an interview, ask the person directly, "As you make this hire, what are the most important considerations?" Just asking that question will show the person that you are trying to understand and respond to their interests, not just your own.

There are hundreds of part-time staff jobs on most college campuses. How can critical thinking help you get one?

Using Qualifications, Exceptions, or Exclusions

One of the most practical ways of resolving problematic vagueness and ambiguity is to introduce qualifications that clarify which cases are included or excluded. Here are some examples of using qualifying expressions to introduce a measure of clarity.

Why are some terms regarded as "swear words" or "expletives" by some groups, but not by others? Can the same sound be a forbidden expletive in one language and a perfectly acceptable word in another? Should "clean language" directed at someone in anger be regarded as more or less offensive than "dirty words" used for the sake of humor? Give reasons and examples to support your opinion. And take a moment to search "Lewis Black bad language" for the comedian's social commentary on this controversial topic.

As the examples above suggest, we can clarify expressions a lot or a little, depending on our purposes, by using descriptive phrases, contrasts, technical

veteran	→	person with prior experience, as contrasted with beginner
veteran athlete	→	player who was with the team last season, as contrasted with rookie
military veteran	→	soldier who has been honorably discharged from service
military veteran	→	soldier who served in combat
cold weather	→	chilly enough to need a scarf and jacket
cold weather	→	outdoor air temperatures lower than 40 degrees Fahrenheit
cold weather	→	chill factor less than 20 degrees Fahrenheit
bad language	→	curse, a solemn invocation of misfortune to be visited upon some person, group or object
bad language	→	blasphemy, an expression that is contemptuous of a religiously significant person, object, custom, or belief
bad language	→	vulgarity, an expression that is crude, unseemly, not in good taste
bad language	→	obscenity, an expression that is lewd, licentious, or indecent
bad language	→	indecent expression, one that is improper with respect to prevailing social standards especially in sexual matters
bad language	→	profanity, an expression that is irreverent or contemptuous of what is considered sacred
bad language	→	offensive expression, one that inflicts or is intended to inflict emotional pain such as ridicule, abuse, mockery, or hate speech
bad language	→	expletive or swear word, a grammatical term classified as profane, indecent, vulgar, or obscene by a given language community

terminology, and thorough examples. In the "animals at the airport" example, we clarified the problematic vagueness by making exceptions for two kinds of animals. Our exception allowed us to make a statement that actually appears self-contradictory. "Companion animals are not animals as far as airport policy is concerned." But, in fact, the statement makes good sense given the purpose and context.

If you are getting the sense that critical thinking in real-life contexts requires refining our skill at making good judgments relative to the circumstances and situations at hand, you are correct. The judicious habit of mind impels us to strive to make judgments about what to believe or what to do that are as precise as the subject matter, context, and purposes permit. But no more precise than that. In fact, it would be unwise to strive to be more precise than that. Real-life judgments are often made in contexts in which absolute certitude is not attainable.

> "Everyone in a complex system has a slightly different interpretation. The more interpretations we gather, the easier it becomes to gain a sense of the whole."
>
> Margaret Wheatley, Management Consultant[15]

Stipulating the Meaning

When the determination of the exact meaning of a term has major consequences for one or more of the parties involved, then adding qualifications or noting exceptions and exclusions may not be sufficient. This often happens in financial and legal matters, when a word's meaning must be circumscribed as precisely and completely as possible.

We would not want the legal definition of "driving under the influence" to be left to each individual police officer, judge, or prosecuting attorney to define in any way he or she might wish. There would be too much variability in practice. One person might show favoritism to locals, but eagerly arrest folks from out of town. Another person might rely on a person's answer to the question "How many drinks have you had?" Still another might believe that being drunk meant that the driver slurred his words or could not walk a straight line.

It is in the interest of justice and public safety to use a uniform definition of the term "driving under the influence." Ideally, the definition would provide for some objective way of telling which drivers it applied to and which it did not. Knowing exactly how many drinks a

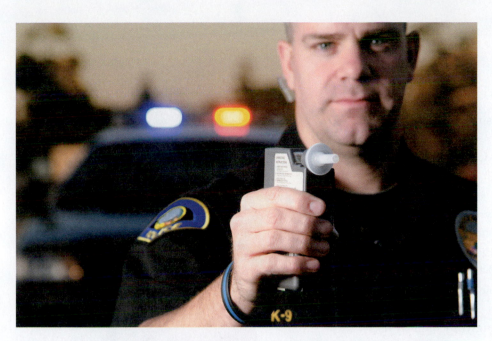

they are penetrable. Ordinary taxpayers, for example, are expected to understand the basic rules that apply to filing their tax returns. One of the basics is determining whether or not you can claim a person as your dependent on your tax return. If you can, then this will, in most circumstances, reduce your taxes. The term *dependent* in the sentence, "Are you dependent on your parents?" can be interpreted to mean "needy" or "reliant" as contrasted with "independent." But for purposes of filing federal income tax, the term "dependent" has a far more precise meaning that is stipulated in the tax code.

Which is better, stipulating an objectively measurable meaning for "DUI" or leaving it up to each police officer to make his or her own decision about what "DUI" means?

person had, for example, will not work. Some drinks have a higher alcohol content than others, some people weigh more than others, and some metabolize alcohol at different rates than others.

As in other states, California lawmakers stipulated the meaning of the expression "driving under the influence." Stipulating meaning is intended to remove problematic vagueness and problematic ambiguity by establishing what a term shall mean for a specific set of purposes. In this case, for legal purposes within the state of California the term "driving under the influence" means exactly what Section 23152 of the state's motor vehicle code says it means. No more. No less.

The rules and regulations, which specify the legal meanings of common terms are often complex, but

Donkey Cart Words Signal Twisted Meanings

It is one thing to knowingly negotiate or to stipulate a term's meaning when the term is problematically vague or problematically ambiguous. It is quite another to be tricked into accepting a twisted meaning for a perfectly good term. Donkey cart words are words, typically adjectives, which are used to distort or twist the meanings of other perfectly good words.

The signal that a word's meaning is about to be twisted is the appearance constructions like these:

- "True _____,"
- "Real _____,"
- "Genuine _____,"

Driving Under Influence of Alcohol or Drugs

California Vehicle Code 23152 states:

(a) It is unlawful for any person who is under the influence of any alcoholic beverage or drug, or under the combined influence of any alcoholic beverage and drug, to drive a vehicle.

(b) It is unlawful for any person who has 0.08 percent or more, by weight, of alcohol in his or her blood to drive a vehicle.

For purposes of this article and Section 34501.16, percent, by weight, of alcohol in a person's blood is based upon grams of alcohol per 100 milliliters of blood or grams of alcohol per 210 liters of breath.

In any prosecution under this subdivision, it is a rebuttable presumption that the person had 0.08 percent or more, by weight, of alcohol in his or her blood at the time of driving the vehicle if the person had 0.08 percent or more, by weight, of alcohol in his or her blood at the time of the performance of a chemical test within three hours after the driving.

Source: California Department of Motor Vehicles, August 25, 2009 <**http://www.dmv.ca.gov/pubs/vctop/d11/vc23152.htm**>.

- **"Authentic _____"**
- **"Natural _____"**
- **"Pure _____"**

For example:

- *"True freedom* means not choosing to do what you know you cannot do."
- *"True faith* embraces that which is known to be unknowable."
- *"Real men* drink till they puke."
- "The *real victim* here is not the young man who was killed, it is the poor fellow who shot him."
- *"Genuine power* rests only with those who rule by the unchallenged power of their will."
- *"Authentic human beings* ride their emotions, relishing the lows as well as the highs."
- *"Authentic love* requires emptying your identity as a gift for the other."
- *"Natural water* is better for you than water out of a tap."
- "This sports drink is made with all *natural ingredients.*"
- "The *natural leader* is he who has the audacity to speak when all others are silent."
- *"Pure* courage ignores all risk to self."
- "He who has a *pure heart* is he who hears and responds."

Although each may seem like a pearl of wisdom, they are in fact donkey droppings. Seriously, we just now made up those examples. They are nothing more than thinly disguised stipulations that twist meanings just enough that counter-evidence to refute them is difficult, if not impossible, to find. And, we offered the examples without providing any rationale or evidence for their truth. There is none. They are stipulations.

In each case we twisted the meaning of the word that rides in the donkey cart—that is, the word that follows behind *true, real, genuine, authentic, natural,* or *pure.* And we tossed in a couple of profound sounding, but vacuous, "he-who's" just for fun. "He-who" sounds a little like our donkey's "He-Haw!"

Charlatans love donkey cart words. Why? Because using them enables the charlatan to sound wise and knowledgeable. By beguiling the listener the charlatan hopes to exert control. If you can control what people think, you can control what they do. And, by using donkey cart words effectively, the charlatan can gain control without being burdened with providing proof or evidence. Instead of stepping away from twisted meanings toward more conventional definitions, if confronted the charlatan is more apt to bully or ridicule the critic. "Oh, how unfortunate, the ignorant uninitiated one does not know what we know, and that is the word's true meaning!"

Resorting to the use of donkey cart words is not a sign of wisdom, it is a signal that someone is trying to mislead

"It isn't true hazing if it's voluntary," said the bully, as if his donkey cart expression worked to excuse his abusive excesses.

and possibly exploit gullible individuals by twisting language. Zealots and hustlers of all kinds rely on donkey cart words to impose on their gullible disciples a way of talking and thinking that immunizes them against evidence-based criticisms. Talking "our special way" forms us into our own community and isolates us too. We know what we mean and that's all that is important. But because we use words in our own special (twisted) way, communicating successfully with the rest of the world is much more difficult. And the evidence others might use to show that we are mistaken simply does not apply, because we meant something else. You see, "We know the true meanings of the words we are using."

The clanging bell that should be our warning signal is the speaker's use of one of the six precursor words in front of a noun. Or the solemn gonging of the classic "he-who." We hear those expressions and we know the speaker is inviting us to depart from the community of those who use words as they are defined. The speaker wants us to follow that donkey cart into a dark mythic forest where words no longer mean what they are supposed to mean. If we follow that cart, well then we shall need to be careful where we step.

Nothing Speaks for Itself

The first rule of fair-minded interpretation is to be sensitive to context and purpose.

THINKING CRITICALLY

It Means What We Can Measure

One way of stipulating the meaning of a problematically vague term is to create an index to measure it. Take "slavery" for example. Suppose we wanted to know how prevalent slavery is today, and which countries were the biggest offenders when it came to permitting or tolerating slavery. We would need some way to measure slavery, a way of deciding if a person is or is not being kept as a slave. Not in a metaphorical sense, as in "I'm a slave to my computer," but in the sense that the person's only recourse would be to risk punishment or death trying to escape to freedom. In 2013 the Walk Free Foundation estimated that there were 29.8 million human beings worldwide who lived in slavery. They used the Global Slavery Index to give "slavery" an operational definition, meaning that they made the term "slavery" measurable. The definition includes people in debt bondage, people in forced marriages, and people who are sold as commodities in human trafficking. (Source "New global index exposes 'modern slavery' worldwide," BBC World News, October 17, 2013).

Some people take great pride in being able to render problematically vague terms measurable. Having trouble with a vague term like "better team?" No problem, the better team is the team that wins the game. One objection to defining an abstract concept using an operational measure is that we are apt to lose some of the richness of the term by thinking it means no more than what we can easily count. Happiness is more than money. The value of the work is more than the wage received. Greatness in a movie is more than ticket sales. On the other hand, if happiness, or the value of work, or cinematic greatness mean "something more" and if we cannot possibly measure that something more, then what is it? How would you define "happiness," the "value of work," "great movie," and "slavery?"

4.4 Language Communities

One way to identify communities is by attending to how they use particular words, symbols, and expressions. We can often move seamlessly among these communities if we understand what they mean by common words. For example, consider the word "defensive." The word's meaning morphs depending on which community is using it. For psychologists talking about a "defensive response" it means one thing. For military equipment engineers talking about "defensive weapon" it means something else. And for coaches and athletes "defensive specialist" has yet a slightly different meaning. Speaking about sports, "punter" means one thing to the community of people who enjoy American football, and quite a different thing to the vice squad of the London police force.

National and Global Language Communities

Over the millennia our species developed many languages to facilitate effective communication between people living in various regions of the world. Sounds became words and took on different meanings within the communities. To preserve ideas, various systems of writing were invented that used symbols, words, and icons that meant specific things to the people of a given tribe, region, or nation. People who shared an understanding of the meanings of the words and icons can be thought of as a community defined in part by its shared language, or a **language community**. For example, we mentioned the language community of statisticians earlier in the chapter.

The meanings of the words that form a given language are conventional. The words mean what they mean in a given language by virtue of the tacit mutual agreement of the people who speak that language. Those tens of millions of us who speak English never voted what each English word should mean. We learned our shared language by learning the conventions for how words are used by the English-speaking language community. Dictionaries were invented to record a language community's conventions for what its words shall mean. But, as Mark Twain Prize winner George Carlin illustrates in his comedic bit "I'm a Modern Man," English is a very dynamic language. You can find this comic routine several places on the Internet. New words are invented, and old words take on new meanings. Dictionaries need updates.

At the national and global levels the expression *language community* refers to the community of people who can communicate in a given language (e.g., Thai-speaking people, Polish-speaking people, and English-speaking people form three language communities). A given person may be a member of one or more of these communities, or none of them, being instead a member of some other language community, such as those who speak Italian, or those who speak Arabic, Bahasa, Dutch, Farsi, Tagalog, Turkish, or Yoruban.

Even when people in different parts of the world happen to be talking about the same thing, they may use expressions that are emblematic of their own language community. For example, when talking about something as universal as bribes, people speaking Farsi will say "money for tea." In Brazil, however, a bribe is "a little coffee," in China a bribe is "little token of gratitude," and in Mexico "a bite."[16]

Language Communities Formed of People with Like Interests

Today the idea of a language community has taken on even richer meaning. Those who understand and use the technical vocabulary of a more specialized field of human endeavor can also be called a "language community." For example, there are language communities of musicians, mathematicians, electrical engineers, military officers, bankers, biochemists, health professionals, and model train hobbyists. The words and symbols used within these communities have conventional meanings that are known and used by the members of the community. Look at the "Symbols, Terms, and Expressions Used by Different Language Communities" chart to see examples of sets of symbols that are well known to those who are members of specific language communities, but not well known to other people.

A speaker seeking to communicate with a listener whom he or she knows to be a member of the same language community will use the special language and symbols of that community. For example, a hobo wanting to warn other hobos to beware of the local authorities will use a particular symbol that to the members of the hobo language community has that particular conventional meaning. *To make a correct interpretation, we need to know how words and symbols are used by the members of the language community.*

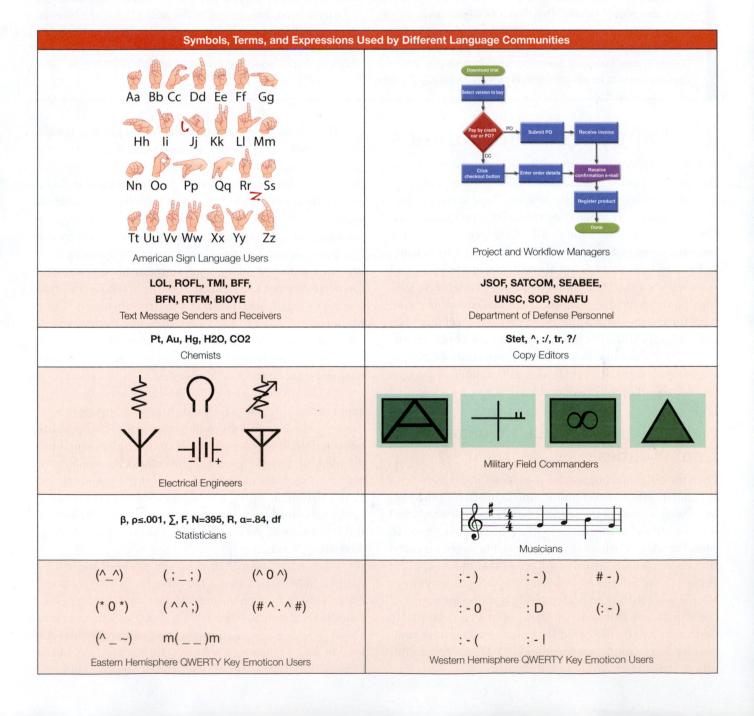

Symbols, Terms, and Expressions Used by Different Language Communities

American Sign Language Users

Project and Workflow Managers

LOL, ROFL, TMI, BFF,
BFN, RTFM, BIOYE
Text Message Senders and Receivers

JSOF, SATCOM, SEABEE,
UNSC, SOP, SNAFU
Department of Defense Personnel

Pt, Au, Hg, H2O, CO2
Chemists

Stet, ^, :/, tr, ?/
Copy Editors

Electrical Engineers

Military Field Commanders

β, ρ≤.001, Σ, F, N=395, R, α=.84, df
Statisticians

Musicians

(^_^)   (;_;)   (^0^)

(*0*)   (^^;)   (#^.^#)

(^_~)   m(__)m

Eastern Hemisphere QWERTY Key Emoticon Users

;-)   :-)   #-)

:-0   :D   (:-)

:-(:-|

Western Hemisphere QWERTY Key Emoticon Users

Academic Disciplines as Language Communities

When we are novices relative to a given area of human endeavor—for example, the subject fields represented by the academic departments of a college or university—we may feel somewhat intimidated by those language communities. We know those who have already been initiated into that community—for example the faculty, graduate students, and undergraduate majors—know vocabulary we do not know. They are able to speak with one another about that subject field in ways that we cannot yet comprehend.

As newcomers to those language communities, we may not fully understand the textbooks or lectures senior members of that community have prepared for us. One reason is that the terminology differs from one discipline to another. *Freedom*, for example, has different meanings depending on whether the discipline is political science, mathematics, economics, philosophy, statistics, or chemistry.

Another reason understanding what is being said can be difficult for novices is because there are different conventions within the different disciplines for how one conducts inquiry and communicates findings. As we shall see in the chapter on empirical reasoning, science proceeds by seeking evidence to disconfirm hypotheses. In science the professional papers that present research findings follow a specific outline in which methods, findings, and results are described separately; data are displayed in charts and graphs; and often statistical analyses are used to establish that the data are not simply the result of random chance.

In contrast, in the humanities, scholars work to refine the meanings of terms and provide textual analyses based on the author's intentions, cultural context, word choice, and historical time and place. We illustrated this briefly at the beginning of this chapter in the Genesis example. Charts and graphs displaying experimental data are almost never found in the humanities, although its scholars take due note of evidence, such as historical and cultural facts. Their work is presented in papers that often begin by stating a problem and then proceed by introducing important distinctions and parsing out alternative meanings.

Historians, musicians, accountants, political scientists, poets, nurses, civil engineers, journalists, physicists, social

THINKING CRITICALLY

"How Are We As We Are?"

Different academic fields and disciplines interpret the question "How are we as we are?" in different ways or from different perspectives. To some extent noting how scholars and practitioners from different areas respond to this question helps us understand how the various academic language communities differ from one another. It gives us an insight into what each regards as "important" and "interesting." From the practical perspective, knowing this helps a person do better in his or her courses and it invites adventurous minds to explore the wonderful and varied landscape of human learning.

For example, biologists and physical scientists see this as a question about how our species and our world evolved, how all the parts interact at every physical level from the galactic to the subatomic, and in particular how human beings function as complex organisms with biological, chemical, and physical characteristics. Psychologists and behavioral scientists interpret this as a question about our human-to-human interactions, how we think about ourselves and how we relate to others in socially complex and culturally distinct communities.

Humanities and arts disciplines seek ways of expressing answers to "How are we as we are?" using creative and narrative means, such as poems, novels, dances, drawings, sculptures, songs, and plays. History responds by recounting the complex and often unpredictable or unexpected sequence of events that brought us individually and as different communities to this juncture in the human story.

The health professions respond by diagnosis of how we are as we are, if we are not as we might hope to be physically or mentally. These disciplines go on to proposing treatments that might be useful in moving us to our own levels of optimal health and functioning. Educators do the same with regard to the skills, knowledge, attitudes, and values that may be seen as needed or underdeveloped. Business-oriented fields see this question in terms of our economic interactions and our needs for organization, leadership, and teamwork. Engineers see the question as a call for equipment, infrastructure, tools, and devices that would enable us to do what we otherwise could not do, since we are as we are.

Philosophers respond to "How are we as we are?" by trying to fathom and to articulate the fundamental characteristics of the human condition, and they occasionally ask how we ought to behave if we were to desire to be at our best. And theologians explore the question of how we are as we are by considering the extent to which forces revealed only through the mysteries of a faith perspective offer possible glimpses into the supernatural forces which may shape human destiny in general and personal lives in particular.

One way to think about your own academic major, or about choosing a major, is to ask yourself which way of interpreting this question resonates most with you.

workers, lawyers, and all the other academic language communities at a university each follow the standards of their professional or academic field for how to conduct inquiry and communicate findings.

Critical Thinking and College Introductory Courses

There is a strong connection between critical thinking in general and critical thinking in specific fields of study. Often college freshmen and sophomore general studies requirements are intended to introduce students to the array of different academic language communities. To help us understand how a given academic discipline functions, the typical introductory course is designed to explain

- The kinds of questions that the discipline seeks to address

- The evidence the discipline understands to be relevant to resolving its questions

- The concepts, terminology, and basic theories of the discipline

- The methods and techniques of inquiry used in the discipline

- The criteria the discipline applies when evaluating the quality of work produced

- The contexts within which the discipline conducts its work

Notice how well this list matches the list presented by the expert consensus researchers as they described critical thinking, cited in the opening chapters of this book: "We understand critical thinking to be purposeful, self-regulatory judgment that results in interpretation, analysis, evaluation, and inference, as well as explanation of the *evidential, conceptual, methodological, criteriological,* or *contextual* considerations upon which that judgment is based."

JOURNAL
My Language Communities?
What language communities am I a member of? What language communities would I like to be a member of, and why?

Critical thinking within a disciplinary language community is like critical thinking within any language community. Different language communities, and in particular different academic disciplines, focus on the specific evidence, concepts, methods, criteria, and context. But the critical thinking skills and habits of mind apply across all language communities. As a result, strengthening our critical thinking skills and habits of mind helps us when we venture into different academic language communities.

Through steady effort, practice, and attention to the language conventions of the different communities, we gain warranted confidence in our own ability to speak effectively and interpret accurately. In our introductory college courses, our challenge is to learn the terminology and the way that the discipline conducts its work—its questions, evidence, concepts, methods, criteria, and context of inquiry. By applying our critical thinking skills, and in particular the skill of interpretation, we can begin to take a few successful steps along the path toward fuller membership in these different academic language communities.

"The world is a complex place, and the influence of the media in its representation and its power of communication and interpretation is a remarkable amplifier of emotions, and of illusions."

Tariq Ramadan, Professor[17]

Summing up this chapter,

knowing the context within which a word or expression is used and the intent of the speaker in using that word or expression is essential to making an accurate interpretation. Vagueness and ambiguity are not problems if context and purpose make the speaker's meaning clear to the listener. But vagueness and ambiguity can be problematic in those contexts in which multiple plausible interpretations are possible. We can work to resolve problematic ambiguity and vagueness by asking probing questions. Our critical thinking skills give us the tools to clarify meaning. We can interpret by contextualizing, clarifying intent, negotiating the meaning, establishing exceptions and inclusions,

and stipulating the meaning for a given purpose. Even so, at times we may still be uncertain about how to interpret an expression, word, or sign because it is being used in a special way by a particular language community. Academic language communities, also known as professional fields or academic disciplines, are defined not only by their terminology, but by the sets of questions, kinds of evidence, conceptualizations, methods, and standards of proof that they accept. Thoughtful interpretation enables us to understand what words and symbols mean in a given context and, therefore, what the members of these different language communities are saying.

Key Concepts

problematic vagueness is the characteristic of a word or expression having an imprecise meaning or unclear boundaries such that uncertainty about precisely what is included in that meaning or excluded from that meaning results in troublesome miscommunications in a given context or for a given purpose.

problematic ambiguity is the characteristic of a word or expression, which can have multiple meanings such that uncertainty about exactly which meaning applies in a given context for a given purpose results in troublesome misunderstandings.

language community is a community in which people share an understanding of the meanings of words and icons. Dictionaries were invented to record a language community's conventions for what its words *shall* mean.

Applications

Reflective Log

Interpreting verse: Song lyrics and poetry often contain references to emotions, ideas, issues, persons, or events well known to the members of the language community for whom the song was written. Select a song you particularly enjoy. Write out the lyrics. Research the song and the composer or author to learn what you can about the purpose and context of that work. Restate what is being said to explain what the composer or poet is trying to communicate with each verse.

Locate and listen to Bob Dylan's original version of "Forever Young," then listen to Rod Stewart's 1988 version. Compare those interpretations to each other and to Will.i.am's rap rendition, which was used in the 2009 Pepsi Super Bowl commercial. Use your critical thinking skills to explain how each artist's interpretation slightly modifies what the song is intended to mean.

Apply your interpretive skills now to this verse from the poem "Today I Will Be," by the undergraduate poet JJF[18] quoted here with the poet's permission.

Today I will be the strings that I strum;
Gently thundering by the will of my thumb,
Constantly changing the rhythm and tone,
Based on my finger—No—based on my bone.

Individual Exercises

Resolve problematic vagueness and ambiguity: Each of the *italicized terms in the statements below introduces a degree of troublesome vagueness*. The underlined terms are ambiguous. Use qualifications, exceptions, exclusions, or stipulations to rewrite each statement with sufficient precision to resolve the problematic vagueness or ambiguity.

1. America is *overeating*. [Hint, people eat, countries do not.]

2. *Successful people* should *give back*.

3. "We may be living in *the most peaceable era* in human history." [Hint: Pinker, S., "The Better Angels of Our Nature."][19]

4. She had the *good judgment* to dump the *creep*.

5. The *tennis star* had to forfeit the match due to *unsportsmanlike conduct*. [Hint, the thing people use to light candles?]

6. Kate Winslet was riveting in her portrayal of a *desperate* housewife in "Revolutionary Road."

7. The high schools in our state are a *mess*. [Hint, private college prep schools too? Hint: terrible janitorial services?]

8. We do not negotiate with *terrorists*.

9. The measure of our *greatness* is our ability to *change*.

10. I want to live a meaningful life.

11. Every living breathing *person* has rights.

12. We need to talk *tomorrow*?

13. We never had sex.

14. I was shocked when *she left*.

15. *Usher's lyrics* move me.

16. Direct *inquires* to the front desk.

17. Kathleen Madigan is hysterical.

18. It's defensive. [Hint: Soccer vs. Military vs. Psychology]

19. *The crowd* carried signs that said "*Free* Republic"

20. Workers carried signs *downtown* that read "Free *Health Care*."

21. In a nonviolent protest, five hundred off-duty firefighters carried signs outside the mayor's office that read "Free Education for *Low-Income Families*."

22. *Everything and everyone* <u>has a cause</u>. [Hint: Physics vs. Philanthropy]

23. *Nobody* <u>under 6</u> is permitted in the ER or the ICU. [Hint: Hospitals]

24.

1	2	1
2	3	0

[Hint: Hockey vs. Baseball]

25. *For you,* <u>connection</u> *with all who came before cannot be helped.* [Hint: Horoscope]

Interpreting claims: Reword each of the following to expose the problematic ambiguity or vagueness, if any, that each statement contains. Add context as needed. Remember that a given statement might be both ambiguous in some respects and vague in other respects. Mark as "OK AS IS" any that are crystal clear and entirely unproblematic no matter what the context or purpose.

1. This is a land of opportunity.

2. If you can't afford food, then you're not free.

3. I love my brother and my wife, but not in the same way.

4. God is love.

5. When in doubt, whistle.

6. Organic foods are healthier.

7. Clean coal is a green business!

8. *Hamlet* contains timeless truths.

9. Music soothes the savage beast in all of us.

10. Ignoring lazy thinking is like snoozing on a railroad crossing—not a problem until it's too late.

Interpreting data: The Pew Research Center's "Science and Technology Knowledge Quiz" asks 13 questions. Men and women, young and old, with differing levels of education have taken the quiz. Different groups scored higher or lower on each question. The patterns are quite interesting. Take the quiz first, it is quick. Then go to the Results table and analyze the data presented there. How would you interpret those data? For example, what does it suggest about differences between men and women, and to what might any differences evident in those data be attributed? Search "Pew Science and Technology Quiz."

SHARED RESPONSE

Context, Purpose & Quality

How do context and purpose affect the quality of an interpretation? Give one good example and explain how the example makes your point. Comment respectfully on the examples and explanations offered by others. Do they work? Why or why not?

Group Exercises

Interpreting "science" and "pseudoscience": For many years the National Science Foundation (NSF) has conducted surveys of the public attitudes and understanding about science and scientific knowledge. The results inform policy development, legislation, and funding for scientific research and science education in the nation. NSF reports: "In 2002 the survey showed that belief in pseudoscience was relatively widespread. . . . For example 25% of the public believed in astrology . . . , at least half the people believe in the existence of extrasensory perception, . . . 30% believe that some of the UFOs are really space vehicles from other civilizations, . . . half believe in haunted houses and ghosts, faith healing, communication with the dead, and lucky numbers." Form a small working group with one or two others in your class. Do steps 1, 2, and 5 as a group. Divide the work among yourselves for steps 3 and 4.

1. Review the public information on the NSF Web site, particularly the public understanding of science and technology part of the NSF's most "Science and Engineering Indicators" report.

2. Define the words *pseudoscience* and *science* in a fair-minded and reasoned way.

3. Survey 10 of your friends and family members about their views on astrology, extrasensory perception, and ghosts. In each case invite them to use their critical thinking skills and explain why they believe what they believe.

4. Objectively summarize the reasons pro and con for each of the three topics.

5. Using the Holistic Critical Thinking Scoring Rubric in Chapter 1, evaluate the quality of the thinking pros and cons for each of the three topics. Explain your evaluation.

Meaning matters and meaning mutates: A great many public policy issues turn on our understanding of words that evoke strong emotional responses, either positive or negative. But *before taking a stand* for or against something, strong critical thinkers will step back to be sure that they understand what is being said. This exercise challenges you to use contextualization, clarification of intent, negotiation, qualification, or stipulation to clarify the underlined term(s) in each passage. *This is not an exercise aimed at evaluating the claims being made in these passages.* Rather the goal of the exercise is to achieve as clear an understanding of the key term(s) as possible. Correct analysis and interpretation comes before thoughtful evaluation. Otherwise, like a slimy eel, poorly defined terms make it difficult to get a grip on exactly what is being argued.

1. "Sorry, Mr. Miller, your dead." The Ohio judge did not have the authority to void the legal declaration of death, even though Mr. Miller was standing there in good health. It might not matter, except that his widow had collected death benefits from Social Security. And now, if her husband was "undead" then Mrs. Miller would have to return that money.[20] What should the legal definition of "death" be? Should it be brain dead, heart-stopped dead, missing-for-seven-years dead, or what? Think about the implications for health care and end of life care in particular.

2. "In today's world truthfulness is at risk. To quote what Dr. House is often heard saying on the TV drama *House MD*, 'People lie'." [Hint, lying includes more than trying to mislead a person by telling them something the speaker believes to be untrue.]

3. Are the winners of the annual League of Legends tournament cyber athletes? Is playing League of Legends a competitive sport? Is preparing for the tournament a form of athletic training? Where exactly are the boundaries of terms like "sport," "athlete," and "training"?

4. "Misrepresentation by deceptive naming has become an art form. Today pollsters, political pundits, and populist politicians attach misleading names to ballot propositions, Web sites, and campaign contribution mailers. Often the public is not deceived. But occasionally a name creeps into common usage. Take

for example "Clean Energy." What exactly is that?" [Suggestion: Begin with the interview with Noble Award–winning physicist, Steven Chu, and watch "Power Surge" and other recent shows available for free Web viewing from NOVA]

5. What do you think of when you hear about a cultural exchange program for young people to promote "mutual understanding" and "cultural exchange" Search "corporate abuse of J-1 visa" to see how these terms can be twisted. How might you stipulate the meanings of cultural exchange program to prevent these abuses?

6. "I worry about the pornographic, vulgar, and lewd commercials and television shows that pour forth from the cable and satellite TV vendors today. Even the big networks are producing programming that would have been considered indecent only a generation ago. Yes, I realize that in July of 2010 the U.S. Court of Appeals dealt a serious blow to the American Family when it struck down the TV indecency rules that the FCC and the Congress had put in place. Which is partly why I'm so upset—we have to do something to protect the children."

7. "My grandfather said that he did not want the doctors to use extraordinary measures to prolong his life. I never expected to have his medical power-of-attorney. But that's how things in our family have worked out. So, now that I find myself legally responsible for his medical decision making, I'm really wondering what he meant."

8. In what ways was it both fair and yet unfair for Bill Maher to define religious faith as "the purposeful suspension of critical thinking" when he interviewed Ralph Reed of the Faith and Freedom Coalition. Don't jump to conclusions. Instead, before answering this question, search and watch the interview. It comes after the opening monologue and just before the panel discussion segment of episode 320 of the HBO show *Real Time with Bill Maher*, June 6, 2014.

Chapter 5
Analyze Arguments and Diagram Decisions

Preschoolers learn to ask why-questions early and often. Adults reinforce this behavior by responding with explanations and reasons. For a three-year-old, asking why may only be a way to get attention. But by the time children start school they have come to expect that there are reasons and explanations for events, decisions, and beliefs.

HOW can we use our analytical skills to discover the reasons people advance on behalf of the claims they are making?

HOW can we use mapping to represent the relationships between reasons and claims?

HOW do unspoken assumptions, context, irony, sarcasm, wit, and humor factor into making complete and accurate argument maps?

HOW can we extend mapping techniques to represent complex pro-and-con decision making?

 ## Learning Outcomes

5.1 Identify the reason or reasons, explicit or implicit, a person is using to argue that a given claim is true or very probably true.

5.2 Display the analyses of arguments using argument maps, showing where appropriate the final conclusion, various lines of reasoning used, implicit but unspoken reasons.

5.3 Given more complex conversations containing multiple arguments, pro and con, made in a given context, analyze

and map those arguments including the divergent conclusions being advocated and the counter-arguments presented to the reasons advanced by one side or another.

5.4 Apply argument-mapping techniques to display analyses of decision making by individuals or groups, include statements that indicate that a decision is needed, lines of reasoning that abandoned, options which were considered but not accepted.

Making arguments and giving reasons to communicate the basis for our beliefs and decisions are universal in our species. There is a way to ask "Why?" in every language. For example, if we ask the National Shooting Sports Foundation (NSSF) why it supports the sale of guns made for children, like the Cricket, a spokesperson may reply, "Because we are trying to develop the next generation of gun users." And if we pursue that response a bit further, the representative may explain, "The NSSF is a trade association for the American fire arms industry." To the question "Why did you order a moratorium on Illinois death penalty executions in January 2000?" former Illinois governor George Ryan might have responded, "Because our state's criminal justice system has made mistakes, and innocent people have been wrongly executed. There is no way to undo that kind of a mistake." In episode 19 of season 10 of the *Law and Order Special Victims Unit*, detectives go after a mother who refused to have her son vaccinated. In her own defense the mother says it was her right to make that decision about her own child's health. She asserts that she is not accountable for the consequences of her decision. And she says that for her child the outcome was exactly as she had hoped. Without incurring the risk she associated with a vaccination, her son got sick with measles and then recovered. In the final analysis, her reason is this: "Measles vaccinations have dangerous side effects. Those risks worry me a lot." Apart from the TV drama, we know that those risks are exceedingly rare and that the disease itself is a far greater risk to her child and to other children.[1] And so, although we can identify with a mother's concern for the welfare of her child, we may want to evaluate this decision negatively, particularly because in the TV drama her child infected other children and one died.

Whether we agree with NSSF, or with Governor Ryan, or with the mother whose decision resulted in the death of another mother's child, will become important later, when we work on the skill of evaluation. For the present, however, our goal is to analyze exactly what people's claims are and the reasons they use to establish them as worthy of acceptance. In some ways applying our core critical thinking skill of analysis can be more difficult than offering an evaluative opinion. Analysis, like interpretation, is about understanding at a deep level. Often we are too quick to react positively or negatively to someone's decision, only to discover later that we did not even understand the person's decision or their reasons for it.

The goal of this chapter is to strengthen our analytical skills. We will use a technique called *mapping* to help clarify how a person's reasoning flows from initial statements taken as true to the conclusion or decision the person regards as being supported by those statements. Like a Google map showing how to get from point A to point B, the maps we will draw show how people reason from their beliefs and assumptions to reach a particular opinion or decision. The criteria for successful analyses are accuracy, completeness, and fair-minded objectivity.

5.1 Analyzing Reasons and Claims

Consistent with common usage, we will use the expression **make an argument** to refer to the process of giving one or more reasons in support of a claim.[2] Here are some examples of arguments:

1. [Reason] Student journalists should have the same rights as professional journalists. [Claim it is intended to support] So, laws that shield professional journalists from imprisonment will apply to student journalists, too.

2. [Reason] Confidential sources of information would be in danger if they were publicly identified. To legally require journalists to reveal confidential sources to the police will have the effect of publicly identifying those confidential sources. [Claim] Therefore, the law should not require journalists to reveal their confidential sources.

3. [Claim] Encephalitis (swelling of the brain) cannot be said to be a side effect of measles vaccination. [Reason] Here's why: "This happens so rarely—less than once in a million shots—that experts can't be sure whether the vaccine is the cause or not."[3]

4a. [Claim] I need to get a better job! [Reasons] My boss is an unappreciative moron. And my commute is brutal.

4b. [Reasons] My commute is brutal and I work for an unappreciative moron. [Claim] Man, do I need to get a better job or what?

The term **claim** refers to the statement that the maker of the argument is seeking to show to be true or probably true. We will often refer to an argument's claim as the argument's **conclusion**. The other sentences in the argument, namely those that are used to show that the conclusion is true or that it is probably true, constitute the **reason** or **reasons**. Remaining faithful to the variety of ways we have of talking about thinking in everyday language, we can refer to reasons using synonyms, like **considerations** or **rationale**. We can use the term **argument** to refer to the combination of a person's claim and the reason or reasons a person presents in support of that claim. To argue, in this sense, is to invite others to draw the inference from the reason(s) offered to the conclusion intended.[4]

Accuracy Depends on Context and Purpose

In conversation people may give more than one reason in support of the same conclusion. Example #4a and #4b illustrate that practice. Without knowing more about the speaker and about the context, we cannot determine whether the person thinks of the brutal commute, the boss' moronic behavior, and the boss' lack of appreciation as three independent reasons each of them sufficient to lead the speaker to look for a better job. Or, if the speaker thinks of the three reasons as small in themselves, when linked together as being enough to tip the balance in favor of looking for a new job. Why does that matter? Because if the three considerations are separate reasons in the mind of the speaker, then showing that two of them are mistaken will still leave one reason standing. If tomorrow the boss was replaced with a wonderfully appreciative, sophisticated and brilliant new boss, the brutal commute would still be an independent reason why the speaker would want to find a new job. However, if the speaker regards the three reasons as mutually reinforcing, then the arrival of the new boss might lead the speaker to tolerate the commute to stick with the job and the new boss. To be fair to the speaker and to make a full and accurate analysis, we would want to ask the speaker to explain those reasons more fully. We might ask, "What if the commute problem went away because your boss allowed you to work from home? Would you still want to find a new job?"

The takeaway from this example is that context and purpose will again be vitally important as we apply our analytical and interpretive skills to arguments and decisions. The more we know about the events and circumstances within which the argument is made, and the more we know about the people involved, the more likely we are to develop an objective, complete, and accurate analysis. As analysts, just going from the words on a page only, we are at a huge disadvantage.

Let's practice with another short scenario: Joel says to his friend Mike, "Hey, let's get a pizza." Mike says, "Great, what kind." Joel replies, "Thin crust. Costs less and tastes better." In this example, is Joel giving two independent reasons or are the two considerations he offers (cost and taste) linked in his mind? If Joel intends the two considerations to be separate reasons, then Joel is making two independent arguments. And, if he can be persuaded that thin crust pizza does not always taste better, he will still hold on to the cost argument. Or, vice versa, if we tell him he does not have to pay for the pizza, he will still hold out for thin crust because of the taste argument.

5a. [Reason] Thin crust pizza costs less. [Claim/Conclusion] We should buy thin crust.

5b. [Reason] Thin crust pizza tastes better. [Claim/Conclusion] We should buy thin crust.

But, if in Joel's mind the two reasons are mutually reinforcing such that taken together they tip the balance in favor of thin crust, then, to be fair to Joel, our analysis should reflect that he is making one argument, not two. And, if he discovers that either of the two mutually supporting reasons should be mistaken, he might decide that the pizza does not have to be thin crust.

6. [Reason] "Thin crust pizzas are less expensive and better tasting. [Claim/Conclusion] We should by thin crust.

The accuracy of our analysis depends on knowing which is which. And, from the words in the dialogue so far, we cannot tell. So let's supply more context. Mike says, "What? Remember the last time we had thin crust? You called it cardboard." Joel replies, "Yeah, I remember. But I didn't say 'cardboard' I said it tasted like sunbaked Wyoming roadkill." "Okay," says Mike, "Then I'm going to order us a Chicago style deep dish." "Go for it," says Joel. If the conversation ended as described here, then we would analyze Joel's two considerations (taste and cost) as constituting a set of mutually reinforcing reasons. Our evidence is that, in context, when Mike defeated one of the considerations (taste), Joel agreed with the conclusion to order deep dish instead. So, from the context we can infer that Joel probably intended to be making one argument. Not two.

We need to do our best to make accurate analyses; it will pay off in deepening our understanding of what other people are saying. And it will pay off when the time comes to evaluate or to make cogent counterarguments.

For the purposes of making an accurate, objective and complete analysis, we can use this rule of thumb: *The number of arguments depends on the number of independent reasons the argument maker intends.* But, if the context or circumstances of the communication do not reveal what the speaker intends, what should we do? We have had two examples of this earlier in the book. One was a will left by parents to their three children, the other was the question of the intentions of the authors of the U.S. Constitution. When it is important to interpret reasons and conclusions in circumstances where the intent of the author is difficult or impossible to determine, it is reasonable to interpret those arguments in ways that are consistent with the general pattern of the author's words and deeds.

Over-Simplification Masks Reality

Our analytical and interpretive work would be easier if speakers would always be clear about their reasons, if speakers always knew their own minds, and if people never withheld their reasons, lied, or concealed their reasons behind political correctness. But that is not the way the world is. And critical thinking, if it is of any value at all, must be applicable to the world as it is, and not as we might wish it were.

In reality, the rationale people offer for what they believe or what they decide is often murky, even in their own minds. As we will see in Chapter 10 "Snap Judgments," we humans are not always fully reflective and thoughtful when we make decisions. One of the major benefits of asking why, and of pursuing that question beyond the first or second quick response, is to open up the structure of the reasoning behind a given claim or decision. Obviously, asking why helps us with our analysis. But there is another benefit too. Asking "why" can help the speaker. Being pushed to explain our thinking leads truth-seeking critical thinkers to a clearer understanding of their own beliefs and decisions.

Ask "why." And then ask for clarification. Analysis is an active skill. Analysis includes digging below what people first say. We should not be afraid of asking ourselves or others why we think what we think. Like good investigators, analytical people probe. Getting people to explain their own reasons provides the analyst with the material necessary for a fair-minded, complete and accurate analysis. Guessing at another person's reasons, or worse mistaking our own reasons for the other person's reasons, only leads to misunderstanding. Guesswork and misattribution are marks of weak critical thinking.

TWO CONFUSIONS TO AVOID There are a couple of confusions to avoid. First, by using the word *argument*, we do not mean "quarrel" or "disagreement." The discussions that result when making arguments and giving reasons can be civil, constructive, respectful, and collaborative. And, yes, they can also be emotionally charged, but yet rational. Remember too that when people argue, in the sense of quarrel, they may be name-calling or worse, but they can also be giving reasons. So, again, good judgment is needed. Our focus in this chapter is on the claims people make and the reasons they give in support of those claims, even if the context is a quarrel. It is always a good practice to interpret another person's arguments charitably. Give the other person the benefit of the doubt, and interpret what they are saying in a reasonable and plausible way. Not only is that the more respectful approach, but it is often the smart approach. Although the temptation may be great, it is almost always a mistake to underestimate the thinking of people with whom we disagree.

Second, when using the word *conclusion*, we do not mean to suggest that the person's conclusion must come at the end. Examples #3 and #4a above demonstrate that the conclusion—that is, the claim that the speaker intends to support—can be the first statement in the speaker's argument. In everyday discourse, it often is. Often a speaker will start a conversation with their conclusion and not give any reason, unless asked. The speaker may assume that the person they are talking too agrees, or that the person already knows the reasons, or at least knows the speaker's reasons. If we remain silent in that situation, then the speaker and others may interpret our silence as agreement or consent. When the issue is important, and if we do not agree, then one reasonable response is to probe for the speaker's rationale before the speaker pushes ahead, believing that we are totally onboard with what they said.

"Reason" and "Premise"

In example arguments #1, #4a, #5a, and #5b above, the reason is expressed in a single statement. In #2 two statements are used together to express the reason. In #3, grammatically only one sentence is used. But when we analyze what that sentence tells us, we see that it expresses two statements[5]:

- For every 1 million measles vaccinations administered, 1 case of encephalitis occurs.
- The rate of 1 in 1 million is so rare that experts cannot be sure if the vaccine was the cause or not.

By contrast, in examples #4a and #4b the expression "I work for an unappreciative moron" contains two potentially separate considerations: one is that the boss is unappreciative, the other is that the boss is a moron.

The take away from these looks at grammatical structure by itself is that our interpretation can be guided by grammatical structure, but grammar is not the whole story. Context and purpose must be considered as well if we are to make a correct analysis. Again, analysis is not an easy skill to execute correctly. Oversimplification, for example, trying to reduce everything to grammatical structure in this case, will lead to mistakes.

Because we know many of you know the term "premise," we want to clarify one point. A single reason may have component parts, to which we can apply that word, "premise." For example, look at argument #2. There one reason is given. But that reason has two component premises. By extension, we can speak of the two premises seen there as "premises of the argument." Like a bicycle, tricycle, or car requires two, three or four wheels to be complete, some reasons require two, three or four (or more) premises to be complete.

In normal everyday conversations, if we give a reason at all, we seldom articulate every premise. The context and our shared understanding of the topic enable us to communicate much more efficiently. We put into words only what we believe is needed to communicate our thinking.[6] Here are two examples. In their proper contexts, the makers of these arguments correctly believe that they can afford to leave a premise unexpressed.

7. Optimus Prime and Bumblebee are Transformers. So, obviously they are made of metal.

8. Salerno is south of Napoli. So, it is south of Roma.

The premise missing from #7 is "All Transformers are metal," which is a true statement within the fictional universe of the many Transformers action adventure movies. If you know that fictional universe, then it is unnecessary, redundant, and even a little insulting to remind you of such an obvious fact. But if you do not know that fictional universe, argument #7, like a bicycle with only one wheel, may not even make sense. Too much information is missing. The implicit premise of #8 is about the relative location of two cities in Italy. Specifically, "Napoli (Naples) is south of Roma (Rome)." It is unnecessary to remind anyone who knows Italy about the location of Naples. But, if the speaker thought that he or she was making argument #8 to someone who did not know the locations of major cities in Italy, then the speaker would be wise to voice the unspoken premise about Naples being south of Rome.[7] Do not be concerned if the distinction between a reason and its component premises is not clear to you yet. We will reintroduce the term "premise" in Chapter 7. For now it is only important to know that reasons often have components which are implicit when making arguments or justifying decisions within a given context.

DISTINGUISHING REASONS FROM CONCLUSIONS
Our language is rich with words we can use to communicate our intentions when it comes to expressing arguments. Some words signal our conclusion, and others signal our reason. The table lists some of the most common words and phrases used when we want to be sure people know we are making an argument. Naturally, it would be an error to think that we always are so clear and obvious about our argument making. Grammar and vocabulary are important, but not the whole story. Even when we know the context and the purpose, miscommunication can happen. Ask "What is the conclusion that the speaker is trying

to establish as true?" Or, "What is the decision that the speaker is trying to explain or justify?" And ask "What considerations does the speaker present to establish the truth of that claim or the basis of that decision?"

Words That Signal Conclusions	Words That Signal Reasons
So . . .	Since . . .
Thus . . .	Given that . . .
Therefore . . .	Whereas . . .
Hence . . .	Because . . .
We can now infer . . .	For the reason that . . .
It follows that . . .	Suppose . . .
This means that . . .	Assume . . .
This implies . . .	Let us take it that . . .
These facts indicate . . .	Let us begin agreeing that . . .
The evidence shows . . .	The evidence is as follows . . .
Let us infer that . . .	We all know that . . .
So it would seem that . . .	In the first place . . .
And so probably . . .	Is supported by . . .
We can deduce . . .	Is implied by . . .
This supports the view that . . .	Is derived from the fact that . . .
You see, therefore, that . . .	Is justified because . . .
This justifies our decision that . . .	Is understandable when you consider . . .

About Technical Vocabulary

In general, specialized terminology is valuable because it improves communication among the members of a specific language community. Professional fields, businesses, government agencies, religions, social organizations, clubs, and societies of all kinds inevitably generate specialized vocabulary—words that have special definitions for the members of that language community, definitions that differ from what those words might mean when used by the rest of the people who are not members of that language community. There are many important reasons to generate specialized terminology; often the reasons relate to the activities the language community is engaged in together and the nuanced understandings those activities require. For example, the social media community has introduced new verb forms of familiar words "friend," "text," and "like." And that community has created new terms, such as "unfriend." To become a participating member of one of these language communities, we must learn to use words with their specialized community meanings.

Along with the benefit of clarifying the precise meanings of key terms for the members of the language community there is a risk. The risk is that that the members of the community will find it more difficult to communicate effectively with people

who are not privy to the specialized meanings they attach to those words. The more a language community generates specialized terminology and technical definitions, the less people who are not members of that language community can understand what is being said, even if the words are familiar and have been in everyday use for centuries.

In Chapter 4 on clarifying ideas, we suggest that to make progress in an academic discipline that is new to you, it is vital to discover how to communicate using the specialized language of that discipline. Learning technical terminology means acquiring the facility to use words that have specialized meanings the same way that the other members of the disciplinary language community use those words when conversing with one another.

Specialized vocabulary poses major problems for talking with people about their critical thinking. Critical thinking is a pervasive human phenomenon. It is evident everywhere, in all academic disciplines, in every professional field, in all language communities. So, the more we want to talk with people about how to analyze, evaluate, or explain reasoned judgments about what to believe or what to do, the more important it is for us *not* to create a specialized vocabulary.

Instead, to be able to talk to everyone about critical thinking we need to use the vocabulary of human thinking in ways that are consistent with the ordinary, everyday meanings of words. We need to be able to talk about these things with people no matter what discipline, profession, political party, religion, business, club, or other language community they may be a member of. If we attach special meanings to common words like *reason, claim, analysis, open-mindedness*, and so on, we only limit the utility of those words to communicate across the greatest possible span of people, topics, and real-life situations. The language community for critical thinking includes everybody. So, the words have to be used in ways that can be understood by everyone . . . even if they were not fortunate enough to have attended college or to have read this or any other book about critical thinking.

Another reason not to go overboard about creating technical terms to talk about critical thinking is to avoid the "to name it is to tame it" delusion that Stewart Firestein warns about in the wonderfully insightful book *This Will Make You Smarter*. (Ed. Brochman J., Harper Perennial: New York, 2012, p. 62) In his essay, "The Name Game," Firestein points out that students are often misled into thinking they understand something just because they have memorized the technical terminology. But to know what "analysis" means is not the same as having strong analytical skills. And in the case of critical thinking, it is strong skills that matter most.

5.2 Mapping Claims and the Reasons for Them

When we are trying to be precise in our analysis of an argument, especially a complex argument or a conversation in which several arguments pro and con are made, many of us find it useful to represent the reasoning visually. In effect, we try to map the arguments. Using familiar shapes and connecting lines, we express how we understand the ideas to be related. As analysts, our main responsibility is to develop as accurate an understanding as possible of what the person expressing the argument had in mind. Like crime scene investigators, we analyze the evidence and map out our findings. Our aim is to show how that person intended to support the claims being made by the reasons that were used.

Let's map a few simple examples to get started. We will use a *rectangle* to represent the argument's conclusion. Let's use an *oval* to represent the reason. And we will simply draw an *arrow* from the reason to the conclusion to show that the person who made the argument intends to support that claim with that reason. Remember, just because the speaker intends that a given reason should support a given claim, it does not follow that the reason actually does support that claim. Some reasons fail. But, evaluation comes later. For now focus on analyzing the arguments, that is digging out the elements (reasons and claims) and figuring out how those elements relate to each other.

Map 1 illustrates the most basic case: A person gives one reason in support of a conclusion. The conclusion in Map 1 is "Pot should be legalized." The reason, according to Map 1, is "The state can get sales tax when people buy pot, just like with alcohol." The maker of this argument is making a simple comparison of pot to alcohol.

Let's put the argument illustrated by Map 1 in context. A local news reporter is asking a friend of yours, Karen, for her views on the decriminalization of marijuana. Karen says, "I think pot should be legalized because, just like alcohol, the state could get sales tax revenues, and because people over 21 could buy pot legally. Oh, and another thing, then we could regulate pot to ensure consumers get consistent quality." The argument in Map 2 shows Karen as having offered three separate reasons in support of her claim that pot should be legalized.

When the topic of an argument is important to us we may be tempted to "repair," "reword," or "supplement" what the original argument maker is saying For example, we might want to build an argument concerning legalizing pot by using public opinion polls or the outcomes of recent ballot initiatives.[8] Or we may want to editorialize about the economic impact of farming the cash crop, cannabis.[9] Or we may be tempted to polish the speaker's argument just a bit by pointing to examples of where pot is legal. But,

Map 1

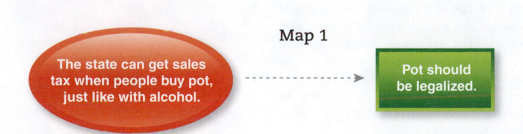

fixing arguments is not the analyst's job. We must resist the temptation to improve, to diminish, or to editorialize. As analysts our responsibility is to unearth and to describe the speaker's arguments, not to bolster or to undercut them. Intellectually honesty demands we be rigorously objective about *the speaker's* claims, reasons, and unspoken assumptions. Our aim is to display with accuracy *the arguments as the speaker made them.*

MAPPING A LINE OF REASONING There are times when a claim becomes a reason for another claim, thus forming a *chain of reasoning*. For example, say a person named Sara was to share her reasoning for having rented an apartment on State Street this way: "I wanted a place near the library because I love to study there. It was the closest rental available." Were we to ask Sara why she loves to study in the library, she might give as her reason, "Because it's quiet there." And if we push her to say why quiet is important to her, especially in a world where background music seems to assault us all the time, she might say, "I like music, but I need quiet when I study. Music, or anything that disturbs the quiet, distracts me from my work." The analysis of Sara's reasoning would map out this way:

Sara's line of reasoning begins with a fundamental thing she knows about herself ("anything that disturbs the quiet causes me to be distracted") and concludes with the idea that she should rent an apartment on State Street. If she learns that any of the links along that chain of reasoning is not well connected, then she may well decide to reconsider and rent someplace else.

A diagram like Map 3, which shows a chain of reasoning, suggests that we might want to reserve the word *conclusion* for that claim that the speaker is ultimately trying to establish. The other claims along the way are intermediate relative to the conclusion. OK, we could do that. But, on the other hand, every additional tweak or restriction on how we will use any given word raises the question: Why? Can't we make ourselves understood to more people without that rule?

MAPPING IMPLICIT IDEAS In natural conversational contexts when people give their reasons for a claim, they typically offer a specific fact, opinion, observation, or belief. "Thin crust pizza costs less." "It's quiet in the library." "The state can get sales tax." "Optimus Prime and Bumblebee are Transformers." The speaker typically believes that he or she has said enough, given the context, the purpose of

Map 2

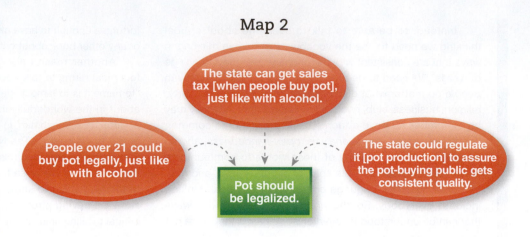

the communication, and the understandings shared with the others in the conversation. That is, unless someone asks for a clarification. In the case of argument #7 about the Transformers, if we did not know the movie reference, we might well ask how the person jumped all the way to "So, Optimus Prime and Bumblebee are made of metal." The response would be to articulate the implicit but unspoken premise, "All transformers are made of metal." But for the most part, most days, in most contexts, we get it. Argument making and reason giving are highly efficient processes.

So, cutting to the chase, how should we map argument #7 if we want to show both the expressed premise and the

Map 3

Map 4

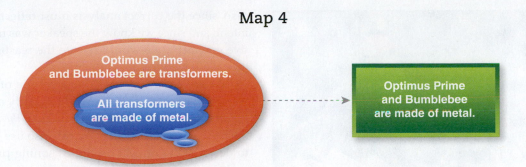

implied premise? We can simply put both statements in the oval. To note that the speaker implicitly relied on an idea, but did not actually express that thought, we can use a *cloud shape*, like in a comic strip. The cloud shape is one of the devices we can use to keep track of things we have added to the analysis beyond what the speaker actually said. Looking at the cloud shapes, we will know exactly which ideas we have attributed to the speaker, and we can double-check to see whether our interpretations are reasonable or need to be refined. Map 4 describes argument #7 about the two Transformers characters.

Interpreting Unspoken Reasons and Claims in Context

Teammates are talking about next Saturday's softball game. One says, "Look, we shut out State last week, and the week before that State buried Western. So, Saturday should be easy." Before we can map this argument, we need to interpret it so that the reasoning is more fully expressed, and we may have to restate it for the sake of clarity.

- Our team defeated State's team last week.
- State's team defeated Western's team the week before that.

- [Our team is scheduled to play Western's team on Saturday.]
- [So, our team will probably defeat Western's team on Saturday.]

How many reasons does the speaker use to support the claim? Only one. The context permitted the speaker to communicate successfully by offering only two facts. Our interpretation of what she said revealed that the team's shared knowledge of their game schedule enabled the speaker to omit the third fact. Map 5 shows that this argument includes both of the elements not spoken in the original: a premise and the conclusion itself.

When we give reasons, we naturally assume that the others in our conversation understand us. Much is left unsaid because it very often does not need to be said, given factors like context, shared experiences, common knowledge, and similarities of cultural backgrounds. But, obviously, what we leave unspoken can cause problems. From time to time, we all have experienced such a situation. Either we get someone else's unspoken assumptions wrong, or they are mistaken about our unspoken assumptions. Fortunately, these problems are easy to spot and easy to fix. Going back to the pot example, clarification could go like this: "Karen, are you saying that the state should raise

Map 5

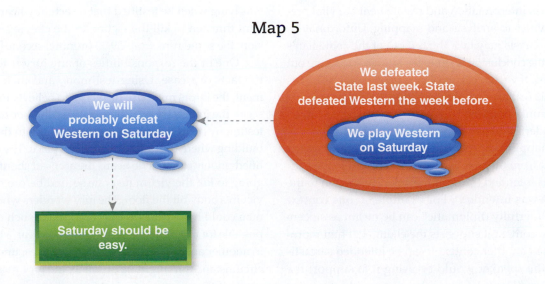

We beat State. State beat Western. Saturday should be easy.

the sales tax?" "No, I'm saying that an entirely new source of revenue, namely a tax on the sale of pot, will be beneficial to the state budget."

Interpreting the Use of Irony, Humor, Sarcasm, and More

It would be a naïve to always take what people say literally. If we were unable to interpret irony, wit, humor, and sarcasm, then Stephen Colbert, Sarah Silverman, Dennis Miller, Seth Meyers, Jimmy Fallon, Amy Schuler, and most other comedians would be out of work. Unlike computers, we humans enjoy spicing up our conversations with smack talk, innuendo, double entendre, exaggerations, understatement, slang, imagery, emotion, provocation, and much more. These language tools can give an expression many different meanings. For example, the words "Nice tat!" can mean that a person thinks your tattoo is awesome, thinks your tattoo is silly, thinks your tattoo should not be showing, thinks your tattoo makes a poignant statement, and so on. As we did with the softball team example above, interpretation and restatement are vital preliminary activities to analysis and mapping. Unfortunately, our explicit analysis may take the fun out of the comedian's shtick. Often the conclusion is left to the audience to figure out and then enjoy. If we have to explain a joke, it isn't nearly as funny. But this realization only reinforces the realization that human communication, and particularly the reasoning woven into it, is wonderfully, and often joyfully, complex.

Before mapping an ironic or sarcastic comment, switch the statement from the positive that was spoken to the negative that was intended (or from the negative spoken to the positive that was intended). For example, in one context "He was wonderfully diplomatic" can be meant as sincere praise. In this context it supports the claim "Let him represent us." But in another context it can be intended sarcastically. There the speaker would be using it to support the opposite claim: "Don't let him represent us." In the latter

case, since the correct analysis must reflect the speaker's intent, and since we know the speaker was making a negative comment, we would restate the reason as, "He was [not at all] wonderfully diplomatic."

As we have already done a couple of times above, we can use words in *[brackets]* to clarify a statement so that it can be read in the argument map *the way the speaker intended it to be understood*. We can also use bracketed text to describe the impact on the reasoning process of nonverbal cues. For example, people frown, scoff, cross their arms, or roll their eyes to show that they disagree. Such nonverbal cues can be represented in an argument map in this way: "[Arms are crossed and he's shaking his head—John strongly disagrees with Karen about legalizing pot.]"

5.3 Analyzing Arguments in Context

Asking someone about their reasons and having them share their thinking honestly and fully are complex human social interactions. A gesture, a look, a facial expression, the past history between people, unspoken assumptions, and all kinds of other things can enter into how we interpret what people really mean. As we mature, we gain the skills, knowledge, and experience to understand others and to express ourselves better. As our skills advance, we can handle more challenging arguments.

The El Train Argument

The famous El Train scene from *12 Angry Men* offers examples of sarcasm, irony, expressive body language, and raw emotion, all of which may or may not be influencing the thinking of the various members of the jury as they deliberate.[10] Let's apply our argument-mapping techniques to the argument offered in support of the claim that the old man was lying when he testified that he actually heard the defendant threaten to kill the victim. In the classic 1957 film version, the scene runs from 39:30 [minute: second] to 43:00.

One of the responsibilities of any jury is to determine the facts of a case. Using testimony and their good judgment, the jurors must decide whom to believe. In the El Train scene the jury is trying to determine whether to believe the testimony of an older gentleman who lives in the apartment building where the murder had taken place. The old man testified under oath that he heard the accused shout that he was going to kill the victim just one second before he heard the victim's body hit the floor. The jury wonders whether the old man could have heard the accused make such a threat. Is it possible for a person in one apartment to hear what someone in another apartment is shouting? Well, yes, under ordinary circumstances it might be possible, the jury reasons, particularly if the apartment windows are open. And they were open, according to the witnesses. So perhaps the old man heard the threat through his open window. The jury has vital information about the moments during which the threat was supposed to have been heard. Another witness has testified that the murder occurred just as a noisy elevated train went shrieking past the window of the apartment where the victim was killed. Several members of the jury comment about how incredibly noisy an elevated train can be, and this train passed so close to the side of the apartment building that the clatter of its passing might have been unbearably loud. So the question becomes: Could the old man have heard the killer shout a threat over the racket made by the passing train? The jury determines that it took the train roughly ten seconds to pass the apartment window. According to the testimony of the other witness the killing happened just as the last part of the train passed by the window. Putting the testimony of the old man together with what the other witness said implies that the threat was shouted while the train was roaring past the window. Not possible, reasons the jury. We have a major conflict in the testimony of these two witnesses. Either we believe the eyewitness who said that the murder occurred just as the train went past the window, or we believe that the old man could hear the threat being shouted over the roar of a passing train. No, the jury decides, the old man's testimony is not credible. Because of the noise of the train the old man could not possibly have heard anything people in another apartment were saying, even if they were shouting threats.

The summary of the scene we have provided here leaves out things that the playwright has the characters doing while the argument was unfolding. For example, two of them start playing tic-tac-toe instead of paying attention. The summary also omits the snide comments and exasperation some of the jurors express, which also interrupts the flow of the reasoning. But even with these distractions not present in our summary, many of us would still have a difficult time following the twists and turns of a complicated argument like this one when all we have is a long paragraph of text. We need some way to organize the ideas, to diagram the flow of the reasoning, to clarify and to display for ourselves and others our analyses of relationships between reasons and claims. Argument maps provide the solution. And, because the reasoning is presented using simple shapes and

Map 6

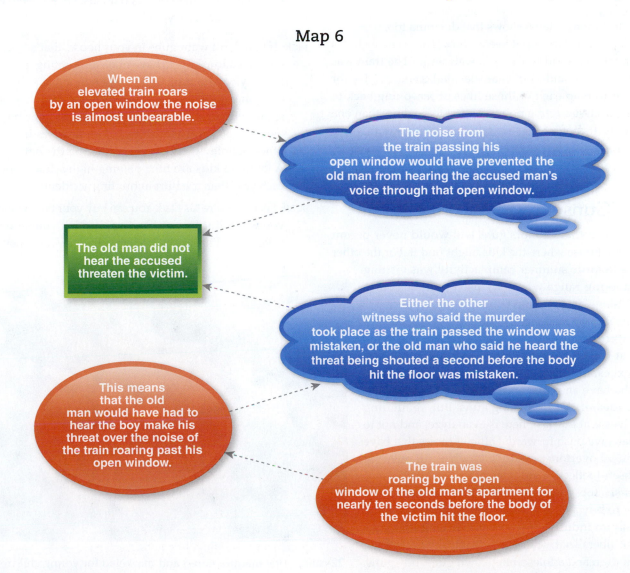

arrows, the flow of the thinking quickly becomes apparent. It is easier to collaborate on the analysis of complicated arguments using visuals, which can spread across a page in all directions, versus a text-based approach, which can only move from left to right and from top to bottom line by line.

Of course, to appreciate the advantages of visual mapping when analyzing more complicated passages, one must understand the mapping process. Practice. That's the ticket. So, how about we try to map an argument for not believing the testimony of the old man from our summary of the El Train scene?

Here are a few tips. It often works best to begin an argument map by identifying the speaker's final conclusion. In this case, it is easy because the whole scene builds up to the claim the old man did not hear the accused make the threatening statement. Let's put that down first, and then, working backward from that conclusion, let's add the two strands of reasoning, which collide at the point where the old man's testimony about what he says he heard conflicts with the fact of how noisy it is when an El Train roars by. The dilemma for the jury is that they either have to reject the facts about noisy trains or reject the old man's testimony. Map 6 shows that dilemma too.

Map 6 is a start, but it needs work. The scene includes arguments that lead to the two ovals with "The train was roaring by . . ." and "When an elevated train . . ." Try for yourself to map each of those lines of reasoning back to their respective starting points. Expect to do more than one or two drafts before you are satisfied with your analysis. Mapping is like writing. The key to quality comes from drafting and redrafting.

The "Guns for Kids" Conversation

One of us authors abhors guns and would never permit one in the house where the kids might find it. For the other of us a favorite summer camp activity was visiting the shooting range where we used bolt lock rifles and .22-long ammunition to bang away at the paper targets. But we campers did not own the guns; and there were always adults supervising our use of the rifles at the range. We share this with you because the next example is as difficult for us as it is for others who have an initial positive or negative reaction to the idea of children using guns. But, reminding ourselves that our task here is to analyze, and not to evaluate, we push forward. Difficult topics that have emotional overtones are exactly what call most for purposeful reflective judgment.

Is six too young to own a gun? Is eleven too young to buy a gun? In state houses throughout the nation gun industry lobbyists are urging that state laws be liberalized. They argue that it should be legal for children and adolescents to own guns, buy guns, and participate in shooting sports provided there is adult supervision and that the child has completed a course in gun safety. The National Shooting Sports Foundation is one of the driving forces behind the concerted effort to put more guns in the hands of America's children. An Internet search of "guns for children" produces ads for firearms designed and marketed to appeal to children and news stories about the issue of guns for kids run by CNN, ABC News, NBC News, and other media. *Real Sports with Bryant Gumbel* (HBO) presented a 15-minute segment illustrating the strongly held views on all sides of the guns for children issue. (Search for episode #203, February 25, 2014.)

Imagine the following conversation between two friends, Josh and Nick. They are sitting in the stands watching their twelve year old sons play Little League baseball. Nick has just told Josh that he is buying his son a hunting rifle for his next birthday.

JOSH: Why on earth would you give your boy a gun? Think of the risks. An accident and, God forbid, the boy hurts himself or another kid. Look, these days we parents do everything we can to protect our kids. I don't get it. Why do you want to give your boy a gun?

NICK: If you don't want guns in your house, that's fine. But the laws allow kids to have guns for hunting. I want to take my boy hunting and I want him to have the right equipment. Really, it's not so different than any other sport, when you think of it. You bought your boy his own aluminum baseball bat. If he misuses it to hurt other people, well that would not be the bat's fault. A lot more kids are hurt playing high school football each year than are hurt in hunting accidents.

JOSH: I get it, you're his Dad. You can buy your boy whatever you want. But I don't like the idea that your son will have a gun. I'm sure he'll tell the other boys and they will

.22-caliber rifle manufactured and marketed for young children

want guns too. Next thing you know some messed up middle school kid skateboards off to a gun show to buy an AR-15. That's legal, you know. We have laws against minors buying beer, cigarettes, pornography, and lottery tickets. But any kid can buy a gun! That's crazy. Guns are no different, they are dangerous. The law should protect kids from buying dangerous products including guns.

NICK: No argument there. Selling guns to kids should be illegal.

JOSH: So, we agree on that. But what about a thirteen year old possessing an AR-15? You're not going to tell me an AR-15 is designed for hunting rabbits. It's a military assault weapon. In fact, isn't an AR-15 the kind of gun that boy used to kill all those children in Newtown, Connecticut?

NICK: That guy was 20 years old.

JOSH: Yeah, and he was around guns all his life.

NICK: He was unstable. And that incident, tragic as it was, is the exception, not the rule.

JOSH: Our country is averaging one incident a month where some child takes a gun to school to shoot other kids. Where are the so-called responsible adults? What happened to all that wonderful gun safety training?

NICK: Look, Josh, I know you don't like guns. But there are nearly 2 million kids ages six to fifteen years old who

Using battle and assault imagery, ads for for AR-15-style semi-automatic rifles tend to tout their speed, size, accuracy, and durability, but omit mentioning accident risks or criminal violence.

have hunting rifles and use them safely. Look at the numbers.

JOSH: No, you look at the numbers. Two million is terrifying. It only takes one troubled kid with a gun to kill my son! And I wish I could give you more stats on suicides, sibling killings, and the other terrible things that easy access to guns causes. But the NRA lobbied Congress in 1996 to prevent the CDC from funding research on gun violence and public health.

NICK: Those laws were changed.

JOSH: But there is no funding yet to gather the kinds of numbers that will put this in perspective.

Map 7

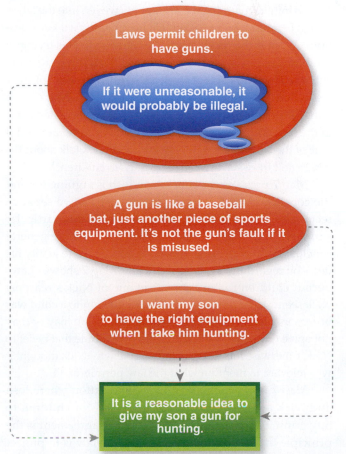

NICK: Look, what exactly is your point? Are you opposed to kids having guns, or buying guns, or guns in general, or what?

JOSH: I don't have problems with gun ownership. In fact, I own one myself. But kids should not own guns and the manufacturers should be barred from targeting kids, just like cigarette companies are barred from advertising to children.

NICK: Wait a minute. Guns are legal to manufacture and to sell. It's legal for kids of have guns. Every business has the right to explore new markets.

JOSH: I do not know if it is insane or just immoral to market weapons to children.

NICK: Neither, Josh. Look, I was brought up in a family where we all hunted. There were hunting rifles in our house and all of us children were taught how to handle them safely. Learning to hunt was as natural as learning to ride a bike. So, again, what's the problem here?

JOSH: Look, the problem is ownership. Ownership implies control over when and how the gun is used. Kids just are not mature enough to be given that kind of control. The whole thing just puts the kid, the family and the community at greater risk unnecessarily. You mix the emotional ups and downs of a middle school or high school kid with easy access to a lethal weapon and you are just begging for something tragic to happen.

To initiate mapping the arguments woven into the fabric of this complex conversation, we begin with two key questions: What is the fundamental conclusion Josh is trying to establish, and what is the conclusion Nick is arguing for? What reasons do each of them present in support of their respective conclusions? Map 7 illustrates our analysis of each father's basic position. These positions are articulated early in the conversation. After Map 7, we will explore the second part of the conversation, where Josh and Nick talk about the AR-15 and the issue of marketing guns to children.

Map 7 presents the conclusion Josh is arguing for and the conclusion Nick is trying to establish as two separate rectangles. Note that both could be true in this particular situation. Josh presents two reasons for his more general conclusion. Nick presents three considerations to justify his decision regarding his son specifically. Map 7 shows "Laws permit children to have guns" as one of Nick's reasons. Nick seems to be thinking that if giving a gun to a child was unreasonable, it would probably be illegal. We may or may not agree with that. But it seems fair to attribute that belief to Nick, otherwise it is difficult to imagine why Nick thought it was relevant to mention what the law permits at all.

Map 7 omits the part of the conversation where Josh and Nick agree that it should be illegal for children to buy guns. The rationale for that point of agreement is the principle that one of the purposes of the law is to protect

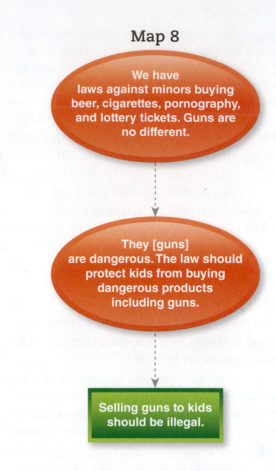

Map 8

We have laws against minors buying beer, cigarettes, pornography, and lottery tickets. Guns are no different.

They [guns] are dangerous. The law should protect kids from buying dangerous products including guns.

Selling guns to kids should be illegal.

children from harming themselves with dangerous, but otherwise legal, products like cigarettes, alcoholic beverages, gambling, and pornography. Josh and Nick appear to agree that guns fall into the category of dangerous products. Map 8 captures this moment of agreement.

As often happens in a conversation, a word or mental image triggers another idea by association. The mental image of the troubled boy on a skateboard with an AR-15, and the simple mention of the AR-15 prompted two thoughts in Josh. One was the realization that an AR-15 was not designed as a sport hunting rifle, and the second was a vivid memory of the tragic shooting in Newtown, CT where so many innocent young children died. These ideas are relevant to Josh's main conclusion. The image of killing defenseless children with an AR-15 is repulsive. Josh evokes that image as part of his effort to persuade Nick that it is not a good idea to give a gun to a child. To further bolster his position Josh notes the rate of school shooting incidents that do involve children. Our analysis of Josh's position requires that we represent these three considerations in our map. It appears from the context that Josh intends that this particular set of reasons should function as mutually supporting considerations, rather than as entirely independent.

Nick reminds Josh that the shooter in the Newtown tragedy was an adult, not a child, and that he was an unstable individual. Nick does not dispute the characterization of the AR-15 as an assault weapon. But Nick does challenge the numbers. In contrast to the two million

Map 9

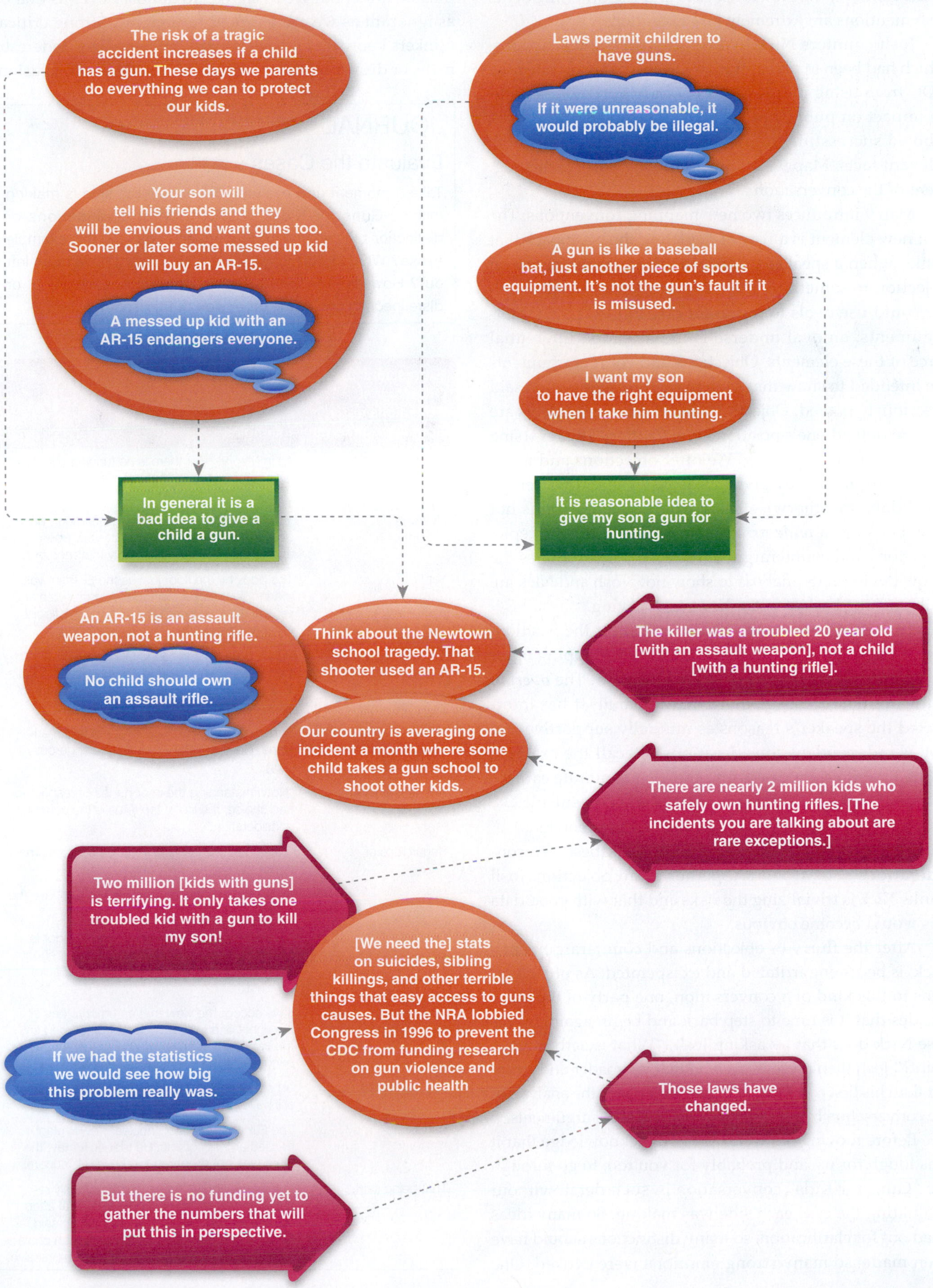

The risk of a tragic accident increases if a child has a gun. These days we parents do everything we can to protect our kids.

Your son will tell his friends and they will be envious and want guns too. Sooner or later some messed up kid will buy an AR-15.

A messed up kid with an AR-15 endangers everyone.

Laws permit children to have guns.

If it were unreasonable, it would probably be illegal.

A gun is like a baseball bat, just another piece of sports equipment. It's not the gun's fault if it is misused.

I want my son to have the right equipment when I take him hunting.

In general it is a bad idea to give a child a gun.

It is reasonable idea to give my son a gun for hunting.

An AR-15 is an assault weapon, not a hunting rifle.

No child should own an assault rifle.

Think about the Newtown school tragedy. That shooter used an AR-15.

The killer was a troubled 20 year old [with an assault weapon], not a child [with a hunting rifle].

Our country is averaging one incident a month where some child takes a gun school to shoot other kids.

There are nearly 2 million kids who safely own hunting rifles. [The incidents you are talking about are rare exceptions.]

Two million [kids with guns] is terrifying. It only takes one troubled kid with a gun to kill my son!

[We need the] stats on suicides, sibling killings, and other terrible things that easy access to guns causes. But the NRA lobbied Congress in 1996 to prevent the CDC from funding research on gun violence and public health

If we had the statistics we would see how big this problem really was.

Those laws have changed.

But there is no funding yet to gather the numbers that will put this in perspective.

children who have guns but do not take them to school to do violence, the Newtown case and the other incidents Josh mentions are extremely rare exceptions.

Josh counters Nick by bringing up the restrictions, which had been in place for many years that prohibited the CDC from using public funds to study gun violence and its impact on public health. Josh's point is that the NRA lobbied successfully to prevent us from knowing all the relevant facts. Map 9 expands Map 7 by adding this segment of the conversation.

Map 9 introduces two new mapping conventions. The first new element is a way of depicting the push back that comes when a speaker presents a counterargument or an objection to something the other speaker said. Although we could use ovals to represent objections and counterarguments, an oval undersells the intended inferential force of these elements. Objections and counterarguments are intended to show that something the other person said is seriously flawed. Objections and counterarguments are used to defend one's position by metaphorically reversing the flow of the reasoning. We offer objections and make counterarguments by giving reasons to disprove, refute, invalidate, or otherwise show that a given claim is not true. Let's use a *wide arrow* with words inside to depict objections and counterarguments. Map 9 incorporates the arrow device in its analysis to show how Josh and Nick are both pushing back at what the other is saying.

The second new mapping convention is the positioning of the shapes. Map 9 shows ovals overlapping other ovals and an oval overlapping a wide arrow. The *overlap* convention suggests visually that the analyst has interpreted the speaker's reasons as mutually supportive and not as independent considerations. (Recall the example of the unappreciative boss and the long commute earlier.) The oval that begins "[We need the] stats on suicide...." overlaps the wide arrow that begins "Two million kids...." We are interpreting Josh as intending that these two considerations should work together as an objection. Josh thinks Nick is trivializing the risks and that with good data this would become obvious.

After the flurry of objections and counterarguments, Nick, is becoming irritated and exasperated. As often happens in this kind of a conversation, one party of the other decides that it is time to step back and begin again. In this case Nick does that by asking Josh, "What exactly is your point?" Josh then presents a claim that is broader and stronger than his first conclusion. Map 10 completes the analysis of the conversation by representing the final set of arguments.

Before moving on, we do want to acknowledge that it was tough for us, and probably for you too, to go through the "Guns for Kids" conversation in such detail without evaluating the case each side was making. So many ideas cried out for clarification, so many distinctions should have been made, so many strong emotions were evoked. One lesson, reinforced again and again over the years, is that those with whom we disagree are almost never as evil or as ignorant as we are tempted to imagine. Strong critical thinkers know that it is never wise to demonize, underestimate, or disrespect those arguing for a different conclusion.

JOURNAL

Evaluate the Cases

Take a moment and evaluate the case each side is making in the "Guns for Kids" example. What clarifications or distinctions would you add? What emotions did this example evoke? What important considerations might have been left out? How did you avoid demonizing, underestimating, or disrespecting one or the other side of this issue?

Expressions that Often Signal Objections or Counterarguments	Examples
But	As in Map 9, "But there is no funding yet to gather the numbers that will put this problem in perspective"
However	You say you heard the body hit the floor, however the El Train was roaring by your open apartment window at precisely that moment.
Yet	The body hit the floor just as the El Train was roaring by the open window. All that noise and yet the old man heard the body hit the floor? No, I don't think so.
On the other hand	Public polls do support legalizing medical marijuana. On the other hand the majority of people in our state do not support total legalization of all uses of pot.
Nevertheless	Public polls support legalizing medical marijuana. Nevertheless it remains a dangerous drug.
Notwithstanding	"Notwithstanding the importance of respect for free choice, the life of the fetus is the central consideration."
Regardless of	"Regardless of the risks to other children, I have to put the safety of my children first."
Still	As in Map 13, "No he doesn't. We still have the problem about . . ."
Despite	"Despite what the esteemed ambassador is saying, according to reports from independent journalists the facts on the ground are quite different."
If we were to accept the view that . . . , then . . .	If we accept the view that an embryo has all the rights of a fully developed human person, then abortion at any time during a pregnancy is unethical.
. . . , all the same . . .	An option may be unethical, all the same it can still be legal.
Be that as it may . . .	The Fukushima Daiichi nuclear power plant passed all inspections. Be that as it may, the plant was not prepared for the 2011 tsunami.
That being said, . . .	The international community generously responded with millions of dollars in relief after the Haiti hurricane disaster. That being said, the international response to the Haitian cholera epidemic that followed was far from impressive.

Map 10

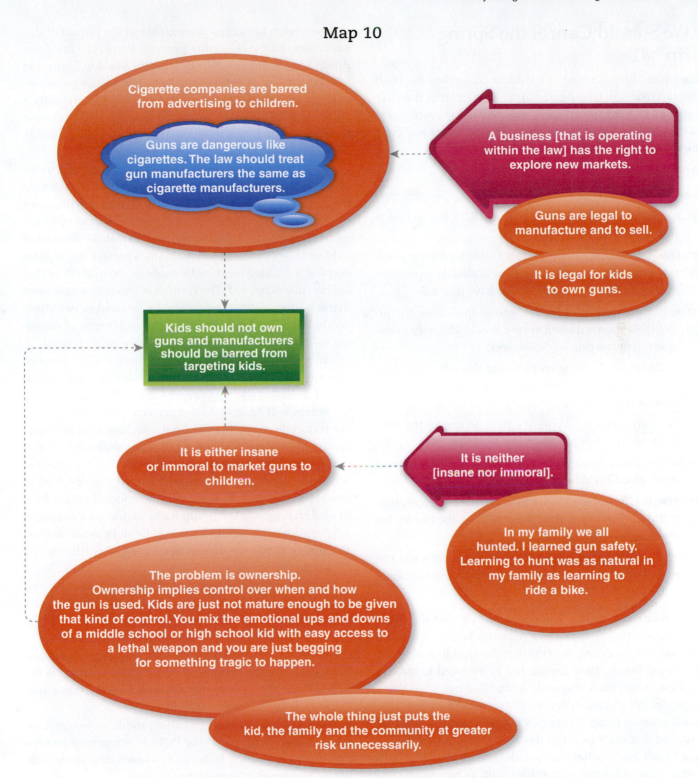

5.4 Analyzing and Mapping Decisions

When people are interviewed about difficult decisions they have made, they often talk about how they considered various options and, for various reasons, came to select one rather than any of the others.[11] In effect, they are describing a series of arguments. *A decision map depicts all the arguments, pro or con, which are used in the decision-making process during the consideration of various options and the selection of the final choice.* Decision maps can be thought of as argument maps used to analyze and depict the deliberations involved in individual or group decision making. To show how to build decision maps, and for more practice mapping critical thinking, consider the following extended example about a spring trip.

"We Should Cancel the Spring Trip" #1

The planning committee of a student club called the High Sierra Hikers is talking about a camping trip the club hopes to take during spring break. Eve is the chairperson of the group, Melissa is the treasurer, and James and Felix are the trip coordinators.

MEETING TRANSCRIPT:

EVE: How are the plans coming for the spring camping trip?

FELIX: Bad news. The room rates at the Base Camp Lodge have doubled since last year.

MELISSA: Yes, and the money we've set aside for the trip won't cover the difference. Our budget is already a problem because of the all other events we have planned.

FELIX: Even if we could get the money, the Lodge has no available rooms during spring break. The only available rooms are during finals week.

JAMES: But wait. We've been planning this trip for almost a year. People are all excited about going. It's going to be a lot of fun.

EVE: So, Felix, you're saying we have to cancel the trip. What about other places we can stay?

FELIX: Yes, I am. There aren't enough rooms in any one other place. We'd have to split up our group.

MELISSA: It would be a hassle to organize transportation from different sites. And we could use the money for the other events this year.

EVE: OK, we'll cancel. I agree with Melissa, let's use the money we would've spent on the camping trip some other way.

An analysis of this transcript reveals that the planning committee is making a decision between canceling and not canceling the trip that the club had planned for spring break. They are alerted to the need to make a decision when Felix responds with, "Bad news" to Eve's question. We can interpret the expression "Bad news" in this context to mean, "There's a problem about our spring trip." At this early point in the conversation, though, we would not know what that problem might be. We could use an oval to represent that idea. But, as before, an oval does not seem to suggest enough about the impact of this realization on the reasoning process. Recall the line from *Apollo 13* when the pilot calls down to Mission Control in Houston to say there is a problem. The rather commonplace assertion that there was a problem was actually a stunning realization. That declaration alerted everyone that they needed to be thinking about what could possibly be happening.

To capture the sense that some assertions put us on notice that we have to start thinking—although we may not yet know which direction our thinking will go, or what the nature of the problem really is—we can opt for a more dramatic shape than the humble oval. As illustrated in Map 11, we can use a *diamond* to represent the realization that a decision needs to be made or the realization that deliberation is needed. The content is typically a statement that is *neutral relative to the various options* and draws attention to the opportunity, need, or appropriateness of engaging in decision making with regard to the issue at hand.

In the final map of a decision there will be lines of reasoning flowing toward each of the options considered. One of them will end up being the choice that is made, and the others will be options not selected. We already have the rectangle shape for the final conclusion of an argument map, so let's continue to use that shape for each of the options. This gives us the fundamental structure of the decision at hand. Since we know that the group decided to cancel the trip, we can represent the rejected option by a *shaded rectangle*. If the group had considered a couple of other options, we would have put them in as rectangles. The only one we would not have shaded would be the option that the group actually chose.

After we have this, we can add the argument for and against the options. When the reasoning to be mapped is more complex, as it is here, it takes a couple of drafts to design an effective decision map. Redrafting helps refine the analysis and clarify exactly what is being said. Redrafting also lets you move the shapes around on the page so that the flow of the reasoning, as you have analyzed it, can be seen more readily.

Decision Map 12 emerged after producing two or three earlier versions. Same for the El Train scene map and the maps of the guns and kids issue; in each case there were two or three preliminary drafts.

Map 11

Map 12

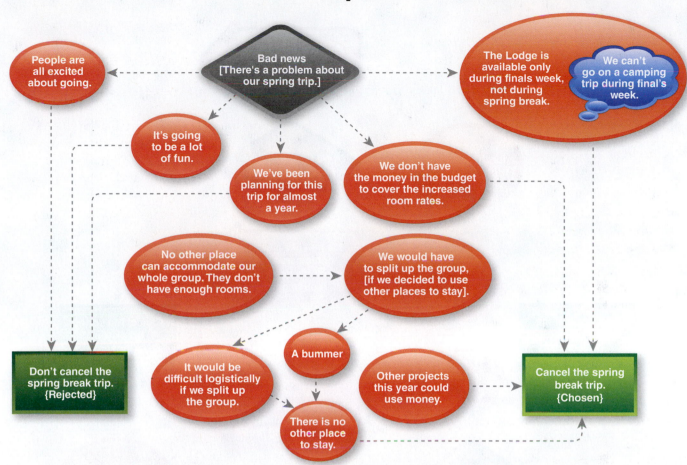

People are all excited about going.

Bad news [There's a problem about our spring trip.]

The Lodge is available only during finals week, not during spring break.

We can't go on a camping trip during final's week.

It's going to be a lot of fun.

We've been planning for this trip for almost a year.

We don't have the money in the budget to cover the increased room rates.

No other place can accommodate our whole group. They don't have enough rooms.

We would have to split up the group, [if we decided to use other places to stay].

Don't cancel the spring break trip. {Rejected}

It would be difficult logistically if we split up the group.

A bummer

Other projects this year could use money.

Cancel the spring break trip. {Chosen}

There is no other place to stay.

"We Should Cancel the Spring Trip" #2

Surely, we could make a plausible case not to cancel the trip. Maybe the logistical problems could be overcome, and it might not be so bad if the whole group wasn't able to be in the same hotel. Perhaps some money could be shifted from those other events toward this spring trip. But, as decision analysts, it's not our job to solve the problems, but rather to uncover the reasoning process behind them.

Suppose that James, still wanting to go, pushes the group to reconsider.

MEETING TRANSCRIPT CONTINUED:

JAMES: I know we have to think about the budget. But we could pay for this year's trip using next year's funds.

MELISSA: That would be great. Let's just raid the coffers for next year.

FELIX: Spoken like a true graduating senior, James!

EVE: Calm down, you guys. Maybe James has a point.

FELIX: No, Eve, he doesn't. We can't take the trip during finals week. And we still have problems with where to stay if we go during spring break. It just doesn't make sense.

JAMES: Forget it.

James begins by acknowledging there's a budget problem. From this point of consensus, arguments could flow in either direction, so we can treat it as another invitation to the group to engage in deliberation. We will use the diamond shape for this when we map the group's decision-making process. It opens up the possibility that a new decision can be made. But James's invitation to reconsider is immediately met with a flurry of objections and counterarguments. From the context we can interpret Melissa's "That would be great" as something not meant to be taken literally. Using irony and the slanted and emotionally charged word *raid*, she rejects James' proposal. Felix joins in with his contemptuous "graduating senior" remark. Felix is implying that James doesn't care about what future problems he might be making for the club because he will have graduated and left. Eve tries to keep things civil and to reopen the deliberation with a respectfully neutral observation, "Maybe James has a point." But Felix counters by reminding everyone about the issues James's proposal simply ignored. In the end James abandons the effort to salvage the trip. He's so frustrated he says, "Forget it."

How should we map that remark? "Forget it" is a powerful signal that James is abandoning the effort to salvage the trip. Discontinuing a line of reasoning can be a very important turning point in the decision-making

Map 13

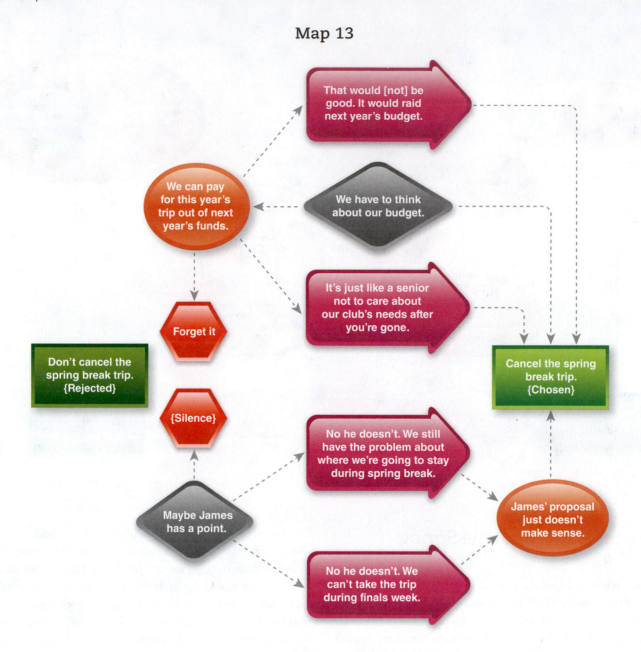

process. We could map it with an oval, but that would not fully convey the force of this element in the group's critical thinking about the trip. Another shape would be better. We will use a *hexagon* to convey that a line of reasoning has been abandoned. A hexagon marks an ending point of a line of reasoning that otherwise would have eventually connected to a conclusion. See Map 13.[12] Be sure to position the red hexagons indicating abandoned lines of reasoning near the shaded rectangle that represents the conclusion not chosen. The best maps, when viewed holistically, show immediately which lines of reasoning were abandoned before they reached their potential conclusion.

To separate any notes or interpretive comments added by the analyst from what the speakers themselves said, simply put the analyst's notations inside *{braces}*. The hexagon with the word *silence* inside the braces is the analyst's way of showing that the group abandoned the possibility

of moving in that direction, toward not canceling the trip, after Eve's suggestion that James might have a point.

Looking for more example maps? There are several in the Appendix that display real decisions people have made about important personal and public issues. This Appendix also illustrates some creative ways to use and to extend the basic argument and decision-making system presented in this chapter.

The map of a human decision can display the realization that a decision or deliberation is needed. It can show the lines of reasoning pursued, the implicit but unspoken ideas relied upon, the choice selected and those not selected, the objections or counterarguments advanced, and lines of reasoning that may have been abandoned. Thus, by providing good analyses, argument and decision maps position us individually and working collaboratively to make informed and comprehensive evaluations.

[green rectangle]	RECTANGLE	CONCLUSION OR DECISION
[shaded rectangle]	SHADED RECTANGLE	CHOICE NOT SELECTED
[orange oval]	OVAL	REASON SUPPORTING A CLAIM
- - - - - →	CONNECTING LINES WITH ARROWHEADS	INTENDED FLOW OF REASONING FROM REASON TO CLAIM
[....]	BRACKETS	CLARIFICATION OF SPEAKER'S INTENDED MEANING
[cloud]	CLOUD	IMPLICIT BUT UNSPOKEN ELEMENT
[wide arrow]	WIDE ARROW	OBJECTION OR COUNTERARGUMENT
[diamond]	DIAMOND	RECOGNITION OF THE NEED TO DECIDE INVITATION TO DELIBERATE
[hexagon]	HEXAGON	ABANDONMENT OF A LINE OF REASONING
{....}	BRACES	ANALYST'S NOTE OR INTERPRETIVE COMMENT
[oval overlap shapes]	OVAL OVERLAP	MUTUALLY REINFORCING REASONS

MAPPING CONVENTIONS[13]

Summing up this chapter,

an argument is a claim and the reason or reasons offered in support of the truth of that claim. We make arguments and offer reasons to justify our decisions and to explain the basis for our opinions. Offering arguments is like inviting others to consider the inferences we have drawn. Because human communication is highly expeditious, in a given context, people will express aloud some, but not all, of the elements of their arguments. We must take context and purpose into account when interpreting and analyzing arguments that occur in conversations because so much is implicit and understood by the people with whom one is conversing. To respectfully and correctly interpret what people mean and to analyze their arguments in an objective, complete, and fair-minded way, we must make explicit all the premises contained in a person's reason and all the unspoken assumptions that the person relies upon to support a given conclusion.

Mapping is a technique for analyzing and displaying the reasoning used when making arguments and decisions. In mapping reasons and claims are made explicit and accessible. The map shows the flow of the inferences from reasons through intermediate claims to the final conclusion. Argument mapping offers many advantages simply reading or listening to arguments. Making the maps aids us in our interpretation and analysis of a person's thinking or a group's thinking. Map making can be collaborative. Working with others refines and strengthens our core critical thinking skills of interpretation and analysis.

Key Concepts

make an argument refers to the process of giving one or more reasons in support of a claim.

claim refers to the statement that the maker of the argument is seeking to show to be true or probably true.

conclusion is another way of referring to an argument's claim.

reason those sentences in the argument that are used to show that the conclusion is true or that it is probably true,

considerations or rationale are other terms used to refer to reasons.

argument refers to the combination of a person's claim and the reason or reasons a person presents in support of that claim.

Applications

Reflective Log

In regard to a choice a friend has made, ask, "Why do you decide to do that?" After the friend gives his or her initial response, ask that she or he elaborates so that you can understand his or her thinking. In your log, explain why you decided to ask that friend about that particular decision, describe the context within which your conversation occurred, and write down the questions you used to get a full and accurate understanding of your friend's reasoning. Then write your friend's response as fully as possible. Capture not only the option chosen, but the other options considered and the reasons leading to rejecting those options and selecting the option chosen. Carefully analyze what your friend said, but do not evaluate. In your log, map the decision your friend made, showing the reasoning process as objectively and fair-mindedly as possible, whether you agree or disagree with it. In fact, go out of your way *not* to reveal your evaluation of your friend's decision.

Share a draft of the map with your friend and explain to your friend how to interpret it. Listen to your friend's comments about the accuracy of your analysis as it is revealed in the draft decision map you made. Note in your log all the amendments or revisions your friend wants to offer. Make another draft of the decision map in your log and compare the two side by side. Reflect on what you learned by allowing your friend to view and comment on your analysis. Did your friend change his or her story, add more reasons in favor of the selected choice, add more reasons opposed to rejected choices, ask you to remove argument strands that looked like weak reasons, or ask you to bolster argument strands that looked flimsy?

Using the Holistic Critical Thinking Scoring Rubric from Section 1, add a final part to your reflective log in, which you permit yourself a few evaluative comments on your friend's decision making.

Individual Exercises

Analyze and map the arguments in these quotes:

1. "Swimming is a great workout. When you swim you use all your muscles."

2. "If it weren't for how much it costs and how big it is, I'd buy that TV for our bedroom."

3. Why did *Billboard* stop listing older albums on its "Billboard 200" web page? Simple—it's about money. The recording companies make money selling the most popular new albums. There is no money for them in the old releases people can download from iTunes.

4. "Michael Jackson was truly the 'king of pop.' Just look at all that he achieved. He was a pop sensation by the time he was 11 years old. His album, *Thriller*, was the best-selling album of all time. He started out in show business when he was only 5, and he performed for more than 40 years. And he had millions of fans all over the world."

5. "People believe that small class sizes are essential for better learning. I'm not convinced. I say that a good teacher with a large group can be just as effective as a lousy teacher with a small group."

6. "A study in the San Mateo County schools of second grade students' reading and math skills shows that students from classes averaging 15 to 20 students scored significantly higher than students from classes averaging 25 to 35 students. A second study looking at the same test scores for fourth and fifth grade students in the Fresno County schools showed the same results. Kids from the schools with average class sizes around 30 had significantly lower scores, on average, than did kids coming from schools with class sizes around 17. Three other studies, all of them conducted several years ago in Los Angeles, San Diego, and Anaheim, reported similar findings. So, it is reasonable to conclude that average class size makes a difference when it comes to elementary school students' test score results in math and reading."

7. "Everyone knows that if we ever needed change in Washington DC, it is now. And, everyone believes that change is possible. So, elect me! I can bring the change we need in Washington DC."

8. "The university's anti-bias policy goes too far. I agree that campus clubs should be open to anyone. But the part of the anti-bias policy that says that leadership positions in those clubs must be open to anyone is the problem. What about religious clubs. Should a Palestinian be permitted to hold a

leadership position in the campus club for Jewish students? If a conservative Christian fellowship club wants to ban gays from leadership positions, it should have the right to do so without being kicked-off campus."[14]

9. "Nobody really believes in climate change. You can tell that by how people act. Political leaders don't pass the legislation needed to change our nation's dependence on carbon-based fuels. Cities do not require solar heating in all new construction. We keep building condos along the ocean in places that will flood as the sea levels rise. We pave over our farms to build suburbs. Instead of wearing a sweater, we keep the thermostat too high in the winter. Instead of taking off our suit jackets, we keep office buildings too cold in the summer."

10. "Many families who have pet dogs also have children. Julio and Teresa have a cute pet dog named Bowser. I know because Teresa was talking about Bowser and how he loves to put his paws on the windowsill and bark at the passing cars. I overheard her telling Arnold about Bowser and the cars last week. So, long story short, Julio and Teresa probably have a couple of kids, too."

11. "I need a break! It's been nothing but nonstop work since last Thursday. I didn't even get a weekend. My parents visited unexpectedly, and that was majorly stressful."

12. "So, let me get this right. You're Harvey's sister's husband. And you're saying that Harvey is actually my uncle. So, this makes his sister my aunt. And, I guess that makes you my uncle, too. Wow."

13. "A 2014 study in the *Journal of Urban Health* linked Missouri's 2007 repeal of gun permit background checks to an increase of 60 murders per year statewide. During the same years homicide rates nationally decreased. Homicide rates involving guns remained steady in neighboring states where laws were not changed. Other possible explanations for the increase in gun related homicides in Missouri, such as incarceration rates, were ruled out statistically. Therefore, gun control regulations save lives.[15]

14. The new store manager called the staff together and said, "Looking at our marketing, I think we need to make some changes. First, the display in the store window looks like something out of the 1980s. It's dated and shabby looking. Second, our in-store signage isn't colorful. There are no pictures of happy people. The signs are so small they are hard to read. And they are positioned in places that make them unnecessarily hard for our customers to find. Third, we have to do something about our Web site.

When was the last time it was updated—2008? It is clunky, confusing, wordy, and has lots of out-of-date information. Our phone number on the Web site is wrong, for heaven's sake! Finally, our newspaper ads are a total waste of money. Why are we paying graphic designers and printers to produce things nobody pays any attention to? We keep printing 10 percent coupons in those newspaper ads but we have not had any customers bring in a coupon from one of those ads in over three months."

15. "Everyone has two biological parents. Each of them in turn had two biological parents. So, it must be true that in our grandparents' day there were four times as many people as there are today!"

16. "I was about to register online for music updates, but decided not to. The thing was that if you registered they gave you an e-mail account. You couldn't use any of your existing e-mail accounts. And the last thing I wanted was one more e-mail account. It takes too much of my day to check the three I already have."

17. *Frontline*, the PBS documentary series, describes how for-profit colleges are changing how Americans think about higher education. The PBS website highlights the May 4, 2010 *Frontline* broadcast, "College Inc." with "The business of higher education is booming. It's a $400 billion industry fueled by taxpayer money." Analyze and map the arguments and counterarguments as presented in that PBS documentary for the claim that the for-profit college business is booming and that its boom is being fueled by taxpayer money.

18. The 2012 historical film *Lincoln*, includes a scene where President Lincoln explains why he wants the Thirteenth Amendment passed by Congress before the end of the Civil War. If you can get access to the film, which is enjoyable in its own right, locate that scene and write down the arguments pro and con that the characters articulate. Then map those arguments.

19. The long-running Showtime series *Penn & Teller: Bullshit!* examines the arguments for some of the most cherished urban myths, popular misconceptions, and "Internet Truisms" in our culture. The show is definitely not PG. There is always a dollop of vulgarity and sexual explicitness to these broadcasts. But each show does make an argument, not necessarily a strong argument, but an argument nevertheless. In the case of show 10 of season 8, "Vaccinations" (August 28, 2010), Penn and Teller argue that the anti-vaccination movement is, well, not to put too fine a point on it, thoroughly mistaken.

Analyze and map their arguments as objectively as possible. You can access this show and many episodes directly from the Showtime website.

Explain the mistake. Here are five misconceptions about argument analysis and mapping. Write a brief explanation of why each is wrong.

1. A good analyst will fix the obvious mistakes in a person's argument.

2. Every line of reasoning in a map eventually connects to a conclusion.

3. Unless people actually say what's on their minds, we can't tell what they are thinking.

4. Every sentence in an argument gets represented by an oval.

5. Argument maps differ from decision maps because argument maps are used when an individual's reasoning is being displayed, but decision maps are used when a group's reasoning is being displayed.

But what does Fox and MSNBC say? Every election year offers strong critical thinkers plenty of delicious arguments. They are made by proponents and opponents of both sides of every ballot initiative and the supporters and detractors of every major candidate. Radio and television entertainers/commentators on Comedy Central, Fox, HBO, MSNBC, and CNN comment extravagantly, provocatively, and convincingly (to some). Pick an issue or a candidate. Locate an editorial/discussion/debate as presented on one or more of the networks listed, and map the arguments presented. This exercise may challenge not only your analytical skills but also your ability to remain objective and "above the fray" as you dig out the reasons, counterarguments, intermediary claims, and, most importantly, the unspoken assumptions.

SHARED RESPONSE

Irony and Sarcasm in Arguments

Give an example of the use of irony and sarcasm to make an argument. You might want to find something by writers like Tina Fey, Lewis C.K., Lady Roz G., Ellen DeGeneres, Kevin Hart, John Oliver, Steven Colbert, or Ariana Huffington. Analyze your example showing how the argument is constructed. And, comment respectfully on the examples others offer.

Group Exercises

Three-person group: Working in a team with two other students, identify an issue in this week's campus newspaper. Then, go to the office of the faculty members or administrators involved and respectfully ask for 15 or 20 minutes to talk about the issue. Bring a tape recorder or a phone with voice recording capability and ask permission to record the person's comments. Be open about this; never secretly record conversations. Explain that the purpose is so that you can be accurate in your portrayal of the person's point of view. Then interview the person with particular emphasis on questions such as:

- Why did you think that?
- Why did you do that?
- Why is that a problem?
- Why is that a good way to resolve the issue?

After the interview, transcribe the things the person said and number each sentence or statement made so you can refer to that statement more easily in your analysis. Then make a map of the person's reasoning. If the interview transcript is too long, focus instead on shorter segments, as we did in the "Guns for Kids" example.

Analyze and map the decision making decision to join ROTC:

ANA: Hey, girl! Guess what? I just came from the recruitment office. I think I should join ROTC. I have always been interested in the Army.

CAROLINE: It's just . . .

ANA: What?

CAROLINE: I don't know. There is still a war going on, even if our troops are not in combat. You could be sent. Isn't that, like, dangerous?

ANA: This is the best time to join—when I can make a difference.

CAROLINE: I could so totally see you in fatigues, looking cute.

ANA: Be serious.

CAROLINE: I am being serious, at least about the danger part. I'd be afraid.

ANA: ROTC is a way to pay for my education. By the time I graduate, the war will be over anyway.

CAROLINE: Whatever. It's not for me. But you'd be great, Lieutenant!

Decision to buy a gun: A young woman who lives alone hears that a neighbor's apartment was broken into. She knows that neighbor. The woman is just like her—single, full-time job, pet cat, and part-time student. Not one of those old-white-guy-NRA-gun-nuts by any means. It's terrifying to think that somebody is breaking into apartments in the neighborhood. What does the person want, money? What if it's a rapist? So, the young woman decides to purchase a gun and keep it, loaded, in the top drawer of her nightstand. She thought about moving, but that would have cost her a lot of money, and it would have been really disruptive and time consuming. She thought about getting a watch dog, but then she would have all the responsibilities that go along with having another pet. Dogs are more trouble than cats by a lot. She thought about trying to find a roommate, but she wasn't sure she could find anyone whom she really would want to share her apartment with. And finding someone would take a lot of time and effort, too. Forget that, the burglar-rapist-whatever-jerk is in the neighborhood right now. And she thought about just doing nothing; after all she has a deadbolt on the door and she's on the third floor so sleeping with a window open isn't that much of a risk.

Decision not to have heart valve surgery: An elderly widower sits alone in his silent house. He is short of breath, and sleeping is difficult because aortic heart valve stenosis has caused fluid to accumulate in his chest. The cardiologist he saw earlier in the week recommended surgery. Yes, he knows he must decide whether to have the operation before it is too late. The doctor said in a year or so without an operation his heart will fail completely, and he will die. His children, now all middle-aged and living far away, have phoned to urge him to have the surgery. He knows they are worried about him and that they are trying to talk some sense into him. Ah, but they are young. Is it really worth all the pain and bother of heart surgery just so that afterward he can return to his current life? He'll still be alone most days. He'll still be struggling with the problems of old age. He might not survive the surgery. He thinks not.

Decisions to donate a live kidney to a friend: "Ah, well, I found that, um, I saw a very dear friend of mine in trouble and, ah . . . I didn't like the uh, the uh, prospects for him if he didn't get a live donor. I didn't like the idea of him being on dialysis or waiting for a kidney for several years. And I love him and I love his wife and his baby daughter. And I felt that I've got two kidneys, I don't need both and it was, it was a decision that I made in about 60 seconds or so. Yeah. . . . So, as soon as I found out from him, . . . He said, "And it looks like I'm going to need a transplant," I thought about it for maybe 60 seconds and said, "Well, count me in as a possible donor if you want to have a test done on me."[16]

Decision to buy the 2013 model instead of the 2016: "You see, I need a car to get to work and school. And I plan to keep it a long time; I'll probably drive it till the wheels come off or I get to 250,000 miles. Beside durability, I'm big on safety. So I visited **www.SaferCar.gov** to see which models had 5-star ratings, and a Honda Civic seemed the best way to go. It was affordable—which is big—and reliable; and it had good safety ratings too. Then I went to **www.Cars.com**, **www.Edmunds.com**, and **www.AutoTrader.com** to find out more about the Civic and a few other makes and models, just to compare prices. I even went to the home pages of Honda, Acura, Nissan, Mazda, Subaru, Ford, Hyundai, Chevrolet, Dodge, and Chrysler. That took a lot of time! I used the "build your own" feature, which they all have, to see what it would cost to get exactly what I was looking for. Long story short, it turns out I'm back looking at Civics. The other makes and models each had some good features, but none that I could find were able to combine price, reliability, trade-in value, safety, size, style, and fuel efficiency the way the Civic did. So I settled on looking at Civics. I liked the Si Coupe, which is very sporty. I found I could get a 2015 for about $31,500, including leather seats and 6-speed manual transmission. That is very fun to drive! There were a few very basic 2016 models available, but the prices were about the same as the 2015 Si Coupe. Then I found this great-looking racing-blue 2013 Civic Si. It's a four door, not a coupe, but that's not a problem. The dealer had used it as a demo model and it was fully loaded with all the accessories. The car had only 100 miles on it, too, which is as good as new as far as mileage goes. The price was $25,500 out the door, and that includes taxes, fees, and destination charges. I figured I could save $6,000 and get a machine that was in every way identical to the 2016. And in a color I like a lot better! So that's how I decided to buy the 2013 for $25,500."

[*Hint:* This passage includes a description of a process of fact finding and a series of arguments whereby the speaker narrows the choices until eventually deciding on one in particular. Your challenge is to sort through the passage and find the reasons, the intermediary claims, and the connecting points that show why the one option was selected and all others rejected. This is a challenging passage and your map will probably go through three or four revisions. Although not an easy decision to map, it is authentic. It comes from an interview with a person who spent several days learning the facts and reflecting on options. To that person it was effort well spent because of how much money the car would cost and because of how long the person expected to have the car.]

Video and analyze: We all know people with whom we disagree. For this exercise identify one such person in your life. Perhaps it's a friend, classmate, sibling, whomever. The two conditions are that the person has to be articulate enough to make arguments that you do not accept and that the person has to agree to help you with this exercise. With the person's knowledge, permission, and consent, video the person and yourself discussing a topic about which you disagree. Your job in the videotape is to interview the person. Explain to the person that you will be asking the person to give reasons for their point of view on the topic. But you will not be debating the person. Instead you will be asking questions aimed at eliciting the person's assumptions and premises and the person's counterarguments to the most obvious objections. But, again, remind the person that you are not bringing up the objections to make the opposite argument. Only to make explicit the fullness of the person's own position. Then, after the video session, and after the person agrees that indeed it does capture his or her thinking, map out the person's arguments for his or her claim. Save the videotape because you may well want to review the tape to practice your argument evaluation skills.

Chapter 6
Evaluate the Credibility of Claims and Sources

World War II Women Air Force Service Pilot (WASP) Elizabeth L. Gardner from Rockford, Illinois, before takeoff in the cockpit of her plane at Harlingen Air Field, Texas.-Photo, undated (c. 1944).

WHICH sources should I trust?

WHICH claims should I believe?

HOW can I evaluate a claim's truth or falsity for myself?

 ## Learning Outcomes

6.1 List the characteristics that qualify a person or source who is making claims about a given topic as trustworthy.

6.2 Explain how to decide which claims standing on their own, absent reasons or

a credible source, should be believed and which should not.

6.3 Explain how to evaluate the plausibility of a claim independently.

"1976: USAF admits first female to pilot training." With that claim the Air Force signaled a major policy. In keeping with society's demands for equal employment rights for women, the Air Force would train women to fly military aircraft. It was difficult to move up the officer ranks in the Air Force if a person had not been a pilot. But to become a pilot, a person had to be male, or at least that had been the Air Force's policy until 1976.[1]

But, wait a minute. Is it true that the Air Force did not have any women pilots before 1976? Well, actually, no. In 1942 the US Air Force formed a unit of highly skilled and experienced women pilots known as the Women's Auxiliary Ferrying Squadron (WAFS). The WAFS became the Women's Airforce Service Pilots (WASPs) in 1943. Before it was disbanded over 1000 women flyers served in the WASPs. During World War II the women flew every kind of military aircraft, including an experimental jet fighter.[2] The unit was disbanded in December of 1944 and the records were sealed until 1977.[3] The historical wrong was not set right until 1977, when the WASPs were finally recognized by Congress as military veterans. In 2009 the unit was awarded the Congressional Gold Medal.

Fortunately in this case we have documentary evidence in the form of photographs taken by the Air Force itself, and we have the testimony of the women who served as WASPs to set the record straight. But more often than not claims are presented without any reasons or background information given at all. As critical thinkers, how can we evaluate claims like these? Answering this question is the focus of this chapter.

Madge Moore showing the Daedalian Fighter Flight (Nellis AFB, NV) WASP Congressional Gold Medal she was presented in Washington, D.C. in 2009.

6.1 Assessing the Source: Whom Should I Trust?

As critical thinkers, we are inquisitive truth-seekers with a healthy sense of skepticism. Positive critical thinking habits of mind incline us not to accept naively every claim someone may happen to make. Like a store clerk examining a twenty dollar bill to be sure it is not counterfeit, strong critical thinkers use their knowledge and skills to assess the *credibility of the source* and the *plausibility of the claim* itself.

Claims without Reasons

In Chapter 5 on analyzing arguments, we defined the term *argument* as the combination of a claim plus the reason or reasons given to support that claim. But what if the speaker simply makes the claim and does not give any reasons? An announcement, a headline, a tweet, a sound bite, a poster, a passing comment, a billboard, a rumor—there are so many situations when people make claims without giving their reasons. Here are some examples:

1. Salesclerk to customer trying on a sports jacket: "That looks great on you."

2. Political commentator speaking about a member of the opposition party: "So-and-so's proposal will cripple the economy."

3. Person under arrest to police investigator after hearing that if he implicates others he will receive a lighter sentence: "Well, now that I think of it. There was this guy. He calls himself 'B-Lucky.' The whole thing was his idea in the first place."

4a. Witness #1: "I remember exactly what the defendant shouted as he rushed the victim waving a huge hunting knife."

4b. Witness #2: "I saw the defendant sitting quietly waiting for the bus when the victim charged at him from behind."

5. Posting on Yelp: "This place sucks."

6. Best friend: "You really need to do something about how much you drink at parties."

7. Parent to daughter in the eighth grade: "No, it is not a good idea to go out with a high school junior."

8. Co-worker to new employee: "Everybody here plays fantasy football using their office computer."

9. Roommate: "The apartment manager was looking for you this morning."

10. Doctor to patient: "The lab test came back positive."

The question that comes to mind for critical thinkers when they hear a claim made but no reason given is, "Can I trust this person to be telling me the truth or even to know the truth?" Looking back over those ten examples, we can think of reasons why we probably can or probably cannot trust the speaker in each case. For example, in #1 maybe the salesclerk's compliment is nothing more than an insincere sales tactic used to get the customer to buy the jacket. Maybe the salesclerk would have said the same thing if the jacket looked dreadful. In #2, unfortunate as it may be, the criticism that a political commentator representing one party hurls at a member of the other party is occasionally exaggerated, inaccurate, and alarmist. In #3, the person who was arrested might say anything that the police would find credible to reduce his sentence. So, in the first three examples we might be inclined to discount the claims because each of the speakers has an ulterior motive: to make a sale, to prevent you from voting for or supporting the other party, to receive a lesser punishment.

It is becoming apparent from the research on memory and eye witness testimony that when two people disagree the difference in recollection of the event can be explained by the fact that we as humans tend to be influenced by our prior beliefs and therefore focus on different bits of evidence. In other words, we are primed to remember evidence that fits with our beliefs or strong emotions than evidence that doesn't fit as well. Our memory can be influenced by heightened states of emotion.[4] The witness in #4a might have been so frightened by seeing the knife that his memory of the defendant's exact words could be mistaken. But witness #4b reports remembering events very differently. Memories are vulnerable to influence and distortion because of our prior beliefs, emotions, and even information that is learned after the event such as details that appear in a news story or are shared between a group of people who all had varying levels of engagement with an event. All of these factors and evidence that well-intentioned people who are recounting an event can vividly remember things that never actually happened has made many rethink the emphasis placed on eyewitness testimony during legal proceedings.[5]

"Yelp admits that a quarter of submitted reviews could be fake."[6] "The court said anonymous users were not protected by the First Amendment … if the review was based on a false statement [such as if the posting was by someone who was never a customer]."[7]

Virginia Court of Appeals

On the other hand, in #7 why shouldn't the daughter trust her parent's judgment in that case? She may not like the advice at all. And she may ignore it. But there is no obvious reason in normal circumstances to think that the parent has some ulterior motive that makes the parent untrustworthy. In fact, the opposite. Typically a parent has the child's best interests at heart, even if the child does not like the guidance the parent is offering and even if the parent can anticipate an unpleasant confrontation will ensue. In #10, the doctor example, we would also expect that the doctor has no ulterior motive. In normal circumstances, why would the patient not trust the doctor about the lab results? Yes, we can imagine a scenario or two in which a child should not trust her parent and a patient should not trust the doctor. But more likely than not, such scenarios would be implausible—interesting as movie scripts, but not likely to happen to most people in real life. When we do not know if a claim is true or false, and if we cannot independently evaluate it, then the question becomes one of trust. We ask ourselves *how can we use our critical*

The sales clerk's compliment may be disingenuously intended only to make the sale and thereby only to earn herself a commission. But the physician earns her salary whether or not the patient likes what the doctor has to say.

thinking skills to evaluate the credibility of the source of the claim? Whom should we trust? Whom should we not trust?

Cognitive Development and Healthy Skepticism

The issue of trust, and in particular, trust of authorities, is connected to our maturation. The table "Levels of Thinking and Knowing" describes seven stages of maturation.[8] For children in those early stages, trust in authority figures—primarily their parents and teachers—is a major factor in shaping what young minds believe. Karen Kitchener and Patricia King, on whose work the "Levels of Thinking and Knowing" table is primarily based on, report that most students entering college are in stage 3 or stage 4, what we are calling "Feelers" and "Collectors." Many college students become "Relativists" as their studies progress. And there is still room for growth. Even the "Truth-Seeker" stage, which critical thinkers greatly value, is not the highest we can achieve.

Strong critical thinkers cultivate a healthy sense of skepticism. They do not trust the word of authority figures in the same uncritical way that those in the early stages of their cognitive development might. Nor are strong critical thinkers satisfied merely to collect information, even though it is important to be well informed.

While valuing context and perspective, strong critical thinkers understand that some reasons, perspectives, and theories are actually superior to others. Strong critical thinking habits of mind—such as truth seeking, inquisitiveness, and judiciousness—impel us to try to apply our critical thinking skills to the question of trustworthiness. We know that there are many reasons why we should not always trust everything that anyone might tell us. Some people lie, some speak of things about which they have no expertise, some say things under duress that are not true, and some may have been deceived themselves and pass on misinformation unwittingly. We can be skeptical without being cynical. And certainly one good time to keep this in mind is when it comes to evaluating the credibility of sources.

Authority and Expertise

We have been using the word *authority* to refer to a person who is potentially a trustworthy source of information and good advice. In the context of cognitive development, the typical examples of authorities for children would be parents, grandparents, teachers, ministers, and police officers. But that is where "authority," as we have been using it, begins to reveal its problematic ambiguity and problematic vagueness.

Levels of Thinking and Knowing

(7) **"Sages"**—We can seek and discover many truths and we can address ill-structured problems with greater or lesser levels of success. But even what we call "knowledge" inevitably contains elements of uncertainty, for as we build from the known toward the unknown, new ways of organizing knowledge often yield unforeseen conceptual revolutions. Even well-informed opinion is subject to interpretation and reasoned revision. Yet, justifiable claims about the relative merits of alternative arguments can be made. We can assert with justifiable confidence that some judgments are rightly to be regarded as more reasonable, more warranted, more justifiable, more sensible, or wiser than others. We solve problems the way a truth-seeker does, but we realize that judgments must often be made in contexts of risk and uncertainty, that some issues admit greater precision than others, that at times we must reconsider our judgments and revise them, and that at other times we must hold firm in our judgments. Wisdom comes as we learn which are which.

(6) **"Truth-Seekers"**—Some claims are true and some are not; some evaluations or approaches are not as good as others. Some reasons, perspectives, and theories are actually superior to others. Information is essential, uncertainty is real, and context is important. But not everything is context bound. We can reasonably and rationally compare evidence, opinions, theories, and arguments across contexts. We solve problems by following the reasons and the evidence with courage wherever they lead, by asking the tough questions, by being inquisitive, by being open-minded and tolerant about a wide range of ideas and possible explanations, by being persistent and systematic in our inquiry, and by not fearing what this process will turn up as possible answers.

(5) **"Relativists"**—Facts exist, but always and only in context. Everything is relative. There are no absolutes. Ill-structured problems abound. Every theory and every perspective is as good as every other theory or perspective. Proof and evidence are entirely context dependent. Disagreements about basic theories and fundamental principles cannot be resolved by any rational means because the criteria themselves are perpetually contested.

(4) **"Collectors"**—All knowledge is idiosyncratic—a collection of isolated facts to be memorized for later retrieval if needed. There are many separate databases—for example, scientific, business, political, and religious. They are not combinable. Information in one of them may or may not be consistent with information in another one of them. Uncertainty is real; external validation is impossible. So-called authorities and experts are just as limited as everyone else. To solve any problem, look for all the information you can find about that topic.

(3) **"Feelers"**—Authorities know everything that can be known now, but the evidence is incomplete, even to the authorities. Some things may never be known because of the limitations of the human mind. Uncertainty is real, so we need to be cautious or we are apt to stray and make mistakes. The best policy is to stick with beliefs that feel right to us because they are familiar, comfortable, and conform to what everyone else in our peer group thinks.

(2) **"Trusters"**—Truth is knowable. We have absolute confidence in the authorities who share the truth with us. All problems have solutions, and all questions have answers. What we do not know today will someday be known by somebody. Anyone who disagrees with the truth as presented by our authorities must be wrong. To question any element of the truth is to abandon all of it. We must learn to defend ourselves from any person or idea that threatens the truth.

(1) **"Touchers"**—To touch is to know. Knowledge is nothing but direct personal experience. Facts are absolute, concrete, and readily available. There are no lenses on experience; things are exactly as they appear to be.

"Authority" can also mean "a person with the rightful power to control the behavior of another." Parents and teachers have authority, in that sense of the word, over children. But as we mature, we realize that a police officer, our boss at work, our landlord, or even a teacher or parent may have the rightful power to control our behavior, but that does not necessarily make the person more knowledgeable than we are on a given topic.

The sense of the word *authority* we are looking for is "person with expertise." To a child, parents, ministers, teachers, and police officers are authorities in both senses of the term; children perceive them to be experts with the power to control behavior. Okay. But we are not children anymore. The authorities we may wish to trust are those with *expertise*.

As a starting point, *Wikipedia* offers a discussion of expertise, including this characterization:

An expert is a person with extensive knowledge or ability in a particular area of study. Experts are called in for advice on their respective subject, but they do not always agree on the particulars of a field of study. An expert can be, by virtue of training, education, profession, publication or experience, believed to have special knowledge of a subject beyond that of the average person, sufficient that others may officially (and legally) rely upon the individual's opinion. Historically, an expert was referred to as a sage. The individual was usually a profound thinker distinguished for wisdom and sound judgment. . . . An expert is someone widely recognized as a reliable source of technique or skill whose faculty for judging or deciding rightly, justly, or wisely is accorded authority and status by professional peers or the public in a specific well distinguished domain. . . . Experts have a prolonged or intense experience through practice and education in a particular field.[9]

LEARNED AND EXPERIENCED Being learned with regard to a given topic and having significant relevant experience with the application of that knowledge are the two conditions a person must establish to be recognized as an expert on a given topic. The first condition, being learned, can be accomplished through formal education or through training under the guidance of good mentors and coaches. The second condition, having relevant experience, means that the person is not a novice or a beginner when it comes to the activities and practices associated with that topic.

We will use the word **expert** to refer to someone who is both experienced and learned in a given subject matter area or field of professional practice. Establishing that a person is both learned and experienced is important in the legal context, because that person's expert testimony on matters within the domain of his or her expertise can be relied upon by juries when they deliberate the guilt or innocence of a person accused of a crime. We all have seen courtroom dramas where a pathologist, a fingerprint expert, or a psychiatrist is put on the witness stand to provide expert opinion with regard to the cause of death, the match of the fingerprints found at the scene of the crime and the fingerprints of the accused, or the mental state of the accused at the time of the crime. In standard examples, the people whom the defense or the prosecution attorneys

THINKING CRITICALLY

Wikipedia! OMG!

The bitter irony of citing *Wikipedia* in a discussion about the trustworthiness of sources screams out. Why should we trust *Wikipedia*, you may well wonder. *Wikipedia* is not a source; it's a vehicle. Anyone can edit a *Wikipedia* entry. How can we know if what it says is actually true? It might be plagiarized, it might be wrong in some important but subtle ways. Hey, it might be outright fiction! In fact, that's the same problem we have for everything we see on the Internet or in print: Who wrote that, and can we trust that person (or that government agency, corporation, or organization)? These days there is so much untruth, disinformation, misdirection, propaganda, and outright deceit on the Internet that we dare not believe it simply because we see it in Wikipedia or anywhere else on the Internet or in a tweet, text message, or TV infomercial.

Your challenge in this exercise is to fact-check the *Wikipedia* entry for "expertise" for its accuracy. We suggest you use three different ways to do this: (1) Go to the entry itself and see if you can tell who wrote it and what references are used. Fact-check those references and Google the authors using *Google Scholar* to see if they are credible authorities on the topic of expertise. (2) Seek independent confirmation by looking up "expertise" in other, more trusted sources, including dictionaries, encyclopedias, and books on expertise. (3) Show the *Wikipedia* characterization of "expertise" to people who have expertise in their various fields, like your professors, and ask them if they would agree with the *Wikipedia* interpretation. If all three ways point to the accuracy of the entry, then good, we'll go with it. If the three ways diverge or contradict each other, we have problems. Use your analytical and interpretive skills to articulate an accurate understanding of "expertise" if the one in *Wikipedia* is defective.

Marisa Tomei takes the stand as an expert witness in *My Cousin Vinny*.

introduce as expert witnesses are considered to be qualified due to their many years of professional experience, formal education, and relevant state licenses.

As the movie *My Cousin Vinny* so aptly and humorously illustrates, on-the-job training and many years of practical experience can qualify a person as an expert in certain domains. Marisa Tomei, who plays a hairdresser and the fiancée of the defense attorney, played by Joe Pesci, is put on the witness stand as an expert in automobiles. The prosecuting attorney tries to discredit her as an expert, but fails. The judge accepts her as an expert on automobiles. We're told that this clip might be on Netflix, YouTube, Hulu, or other online sources.

Determining that a person qualifies as an expert witness is a matter of serious concern for strong critical thinkers because the person's expertise, if established, gives us a good reason to consider putting our trust in what the person has to say regarding the area of his or her expertise.

Assuming that a person qualifies as an expert on X by virtue of prolonged, relevant experience, training, or education, what else could go wrong that would lead us not to find the person credible? Lots of things!

- The expert on X may be speaking about some other, unrelated topic.
- The expert, having qualified long ago, may have failed to stay current on X.
- The expert on X may not be able to articulate exactly how X is done.
- The expert may be biased.
- The expert may lie or intentionally mislead.
- The expert may have a conflicting personal interest.
- The expert may knowingly give advice that is not in the best interest of his or her client.

- The expert may be under duress, threatened, or constrained in some way.
- The expert may be uniformed or misinformed about the facts of the specific situation.
- The expert may have become mentally unstable.

ON-TOPIC, UP-TO-DATE, AND CAPABLE OF EXPLAINING   Expertise with regard to a topic, X, implies that the expert is knowledgeable about X. But suppose that someone—say, an accomplished musical virtuoso—makes the claim, "The best way to eliminate pesky aphids from a rose garden is by spraying on a mix of water, mineral oil, and Murphy's soap." That concoction might work. But wait—gardening is not the virtuoso's area of expertise. Whatever measure of trust we would reasonably extend to the expert, were she or he speaking about music, does not carry over to claims the expert may make that are off-topic. Regarding gardening, the musical virtuoso is no more or less of an expert than any other person. To be credible, the expert must be speaking on-topic.

A good friend of ours was an accomplished physician. She retired about 15 years ago and moved to Sarasota to enjoy her retirement playing golf and bridge. One of her friends asked her the other day about a cancer treatment that another physician had recommended. Unlike traditional chemotherapy, the treatment was one of the newer pharmacological approaches that targets the protein receptors on the cancer cells. Our friend rightly declined to offer an expert opinion about the new treatment method. Why? Because she knew that she had not kept up-to-date about advances in cancer treatment since her retirement. Although as a doctor she had the credentials to provide an expert opinion about cancer treatment in general, as a responsible expert she knew that it would be wrong for her friend to rely on her expertise in this case.

> "In government institutions and in teaching, you need to inspire confidence. To achieve credibility, you have to very clearly explain what you are doing and why. The same principles apply to businesses."
>
> Janet Yellen, Chair of the Federal Reserve[10]

We trust experts when they speak within their areas of expertise in part because we assume that, were they challenged, they could explain exactly why their claim is true or their advice is good. The capacity to explain why is a critical component of expertise. The second half of the *My Cousin*

Does earning an advanced degree, a professional license, or a certification of advanced training mean that one is an expert?

Vinny video clip illustrates this. Marisa Tomei offers the expert opinion that the defense's theory of the crime does not hold water. So the defense attorney, Joe Pesci, who had called her as a defense witness, demands that she explain exactly why she thinks that. She draws upon her extensive knowledge and experience as an expert to provide a factual, precise, and cogent explanation. And, in the process, the explanation she offers exonerates the defendants as well.

What if the expert cannot articulate the explanation? For example, a superstar athlete fails as a head coach and we learn afterward that the star was not able to teach others all that he or she knew about the game. The successful head coach turns out, instead, to be a former athlete who was good but not great. Unlike the person blessed with extraordinary natural ability, this person had to think constantly as a player about how to maximize his or her own talents to compete effectively against other, more skilled players. And those years of reflective practice translate later into the ability to teach and coach others.

As the Nobel Laureate, Daniel Kahneman, reminds us, there are many reasons why experts may fail to provide adequate explanations.[11] Because Kahneman's insights are important to strong critical thinking, not just for experts but for all of us, in the chapter on snap judgments we will explore the kinds of mistakes we humans are apt to make. But, for the moment, here are a five ways that experts in particular can err:

- Some may never have developed the practice of reflecting on their experiences to explain to themselves why events occurred as they did.
- Lacking the critical thinking habit of being foresightful, they may have failed to anticipate the likely effects of decisions and actions.

- Lacking the critical thinking habit of inquisitiveness, they may have failed to examine the implications of new information for their field of expertise.
- Experts who have weak skills in self-monitoring and self-correcting may not take the time to be sure that they can explain their current beliefs to themselves.
- Being unreflective, they may describe their own thinking using expressions like "I go with my gut" or "I just instinctively knew what I had to do." Unfortunately, statements like those explain nothing and teach nothing.[12]

It is difficult to place trust in experts when they cannot explain why they believe what they believe or why they do what they do. For the same reason, it is challenging to learn from these experts. Although we may be able to copy what they are doing, and it may even work, what we most need for learning is to know *why* it works. And these experts have a difficult time communicating that.

Consider this example: Suppose it is the first day of class and your Biology professor says, "This course will require more time than most other courses. So if you haven't got a job, don't bother getting one. If you thought you could work and study Biology in my class, think again." Suppose that someone asks the professor to explain the basis for that advice. Here are two possible responses:

Professor #1 offered nothing more than a statement of his or her own past practice and a veiled threat. Professor #2 explained why the course would demand a lot of time and why taking on outside responsibilities could become a problem for a student enrolled in this course.

We now have five conditions to check when we are deciding whether or not a source is credible when that source makes a claim about topic X: Is the source experienced, learned, on-topic, up-to-date, and capable of explaining why his or her opinion on the matter is right?

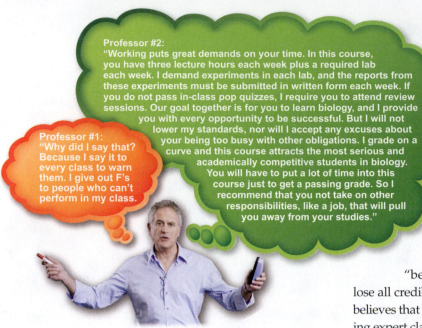

Professor #2:
"Working puts great demands on your time. In this course, you have three lecture hours each week plus a required lab each week. I demand experiments in each lab, and the reports from these experiments must be submitted in written form each week. If you do not pass in-class pop quizzes, I require you to attend review sessions. Our goal together is for you to learn biology, and I provide you with every opportunity to be successful. But I will not lower my standards, nor will I accept any excuses about your being too busy with other obligations. I grade on a curve and this course attracts the most serious and academically competitive students in biology. You will have to put a lot of time into this course just to get a passing grade. So I recommend that you not take on other responsibilities, like a job, that will pull you away from your studies."

Professor #1:
"Why did I say that? Because I say it to every class to warn them. I give out F's to people who can't perform in my class."

UNBIASED AND TRUTHFUL Experts are human beings and, like the rest of us, they may have biases. Olympic gymnastics and figure skating judges, each an expert in the sport, are often accused of showing favoritism toward more experienced athletes and being tougher when evaluating the performances of athletes who may be newer to that high level of competition. Ask anyone who has tried to umpire a baseball game or referee a high school basketball game, and they will tell you that accusations of bias are a regular feature of officiating.

If an expert is called as a witness in a trial and that expert happens to be biased in favor of or against defendants of a certain race or age or socioeconomic status, that fact alone should be enough to cause the jury not to trust that expert's testimony. Expert claims are supposed to be grounded in learning and experience, not in prejudices, biases, or favoritism of any kind.

But even unbiased experts may elect not to speak the truth. Recall that great scene in the 1992 film *A Few Good Men* where Jack Nicholson tells Tom Cruise that he couldn't handle the truth. Nicholson's character, a senior military officer and clearly an expert by training and experience, loses his temper. In his outburst, he explains why Tom Cruise, like so many of his complacent countrymen, does not want to know the truth about what, in Nicholson's opinion, the military must do to keep this nation safe and free. In other words, Nicholson's character is condoning our nation's defense experts' practice of misdirecting and lying to the American people.

We can interpret Nicholson's character as practicing the "Noble Lie," as proposed by Plato in *The Republic*.[13] In Plato's opinion, most people do not recognize their own best interests, nor can they fully comprehend what is in society's best interests. Plato's recommendation was that well-informed leaders who know the whole truth should guide the rest of us by using, when necessary, the "Noble Lie." That is, Plato proposes that the leaders should flat out lie to the people, if they are impelled by the most beneficent and purest of motives. In other words, the Noble Lie is a lie our leaders tell us because the lie is in our best interests. Not knowing the truth, we would be passive, content, and compliant. Social harmony would be preserved, unrest and discontent prevented. Of course, when the lie is discovered, the people may become more than a little disenchanted with their "benevolent" leaders. The leaders would surely lose all credibility. We should not trust an expert source who believes that lying and misdirecting are acceptable when making expert claims and offering expert opinions.

Edward Snowden, Tim Berners-Lee, and WikiLeaks notwithstanding, there are a great many things that corporations, governments, and individual people have good reason not to make public—for example, the plans for developing and marketing new products, military battle strategies and contingency plans, the vulnerabilities of public buildings, the answers to the final exam, personal medical information, bank account PIN numbers. But hold on for a moment! The Noble Lie! My, how convenient for totalitarian leaders who are intent above all on maintaining power for themselves. Surely they would be able to rationalize just about any propaganda they wished to put out as being "in the best interests of the people." A little healthy skepticism would be very useful about here!

FREE OF CONFLICTS OF INTEREST, AND ACTING IN THE CLIENT'S INTEREST If an expert's personal interests diverge from the interests of the person he or she is

An angry Jack Nicholson on the witness stand in *A Few Good Men*.

advising, then there is good reason not to trust what that expert may have to say. Suppose you are interested in applying for a job and you know someone who already works for that company. So you ask that person what it is like working for that company and you ask too if the person knows about the job opening. Suppose the person says good things about working for that company, but discourages you from applying for the job by saying that you do not have the kind of work experience needed for that position. So, you decide not to apply, but you thank the person for the advice. And then, later you discover that the person's intention was to keep you from applying for the job so that some friend of that person would have a better chance to get the job. The person's advice was not intended to be in your interest. In fact, it was intended to be in someone else's. Now take that same scenario and assume instead that the person to whom you go for advice wants to apply for that same job. So, again, the person advises you not apply. Again, the advice is not in your interest, but rather in the interest of the person who is giving the advice. That person wants the job too!

Experts, being human, have interests. Perhaps they want something for themselves, or perhaps they want something for a friend or family member or business associate. There is nothing wrong in having interests. We all have interests. The problem comes in when an expert, while appearing to be giving you information or advice so that you can advance your own interests, is in fact misleading you so that the expert's interests are served instead. For the most part, we know to be cautious when seeking help. We know there are people who will pretend to be our friends and pretend to be acting on our behalf or in our interest, when actually they are not.

But what about situations, which call for very specialized expertise? Situations, for example, involving legal issues, buying or selling cars or houses, or medical situations? That is where the law steps in to protect us from unscrupulous experts who might give us bad advice. There are laws that require that health care professionals, real estate professionals, bankers, lawyers, high-level executives, government officials, and members of boards of directors act in the interests of their clients or in the interests of their organizations. Under the law, this obligation is called their *fiduciary responsibility*. The president of the university has a fiduciary responsibility as the institution's chief executive officer to make decisions that are in the best interests of the university. A doctor has a fiduciary responsibility to make medical decisions and offer medical advice that is in the best interests of the patient.

If the university president makes decisions that are not in the university's best interests, but rather are in the best interest of some other organization (e.g., the city, the employees of the institution, the department of athletics, or to some other organization to showcase his own reputation) to the detriment of the university as a whole, then the president has failed to fulfill his or her legal obligations. Having broken trust with the institution by that decision, the president might be fired. If a doctor gives medical advice that is in the best interest of a scientific experiment but not in the best interest of the patient, then the doctor has broken trust. If a lawyer reveals confidential information about a client, the lawyer can be disbarred and may do jail time. In cases where the expert makes claims or offers opinions that are not in the best interest of the person or organization to which the expert owes a fiduciary responsibility, the expert cannot be trusted as a reliable source of truthful information or sound advice.

> "Inconsistency on the part of pastors and the faithful between what they say and what they do, between word and manner of life, is undermining the Church's credibility."
>
> Pope Francis[14]

Money Subverts Objectivity: Objectivity suffers when experts become hired guns. Today corporations with economic goals and individuals with political ambitions fund specialized organizations to advance those corporate or personal interests. Whether they are called political action committees, think-tanks, foundations, alliances, or industry institutes, many organizations today exist simply to promote the interests of their benefactors. Their strategy is to influence public opinion, to promote legislation that is favorable to the moneyed interests, and to derail government regulations that threaten profits. These organizations lobby legislators, blog and issue press releases, publish "white papers" and "newsletters" (advertisements), host "conferences" (sales events), and make "speakers" (salespeople) available.

The Hartland Institute just might be an example of such an organization. Its primary funders, before they were concealed behind an intermediary foundation that is not obligated by law to list its sources of money, were known to be large multinational petroleum corporations and people, like the Koch brothers, with billion dollar interests in fossil fuel industries. James Taylor, an attorney, works for the Hartland Institute. Mr. Taylor, the editor of the Hartland Institute's *Environmental and Climate News*, describes himself as an expert who is skeptical about the science behind wind and solar energy. The Hartland Institute pays Mr. Taylor to travel from state legislature to state legislature sharing his doubts, just like agents for tobacco companies did years ago when their employers did not want the public to trust the science that said smoking caused health problems. Tobacco companies, like Phillip Morris, knew that public doubt

THINKING CRITICALLY

Who Checks What the Experts Claim?

We tend to think of our elected leaders and those who comment regularly on Washington issues as people with expertise and experience. But because of conflicts of interest, we have reason to be skeptical. After all, aren't the first three rules of politics "Get Elected, Get Re-elected, and Get Re-Re-elected?" And aren't the first three values in broadcasting "Ratings, Ratings, and Ratings?" So when we hear claims like these, what can we do to check the facts?

- Under current policies "we're going to reduce the overall debt of the United States by $3 trillion over the next 10 years." –Senator Richard Durbin, D-IL.

- "About 47 percent of able-bodied people in the state of Maine don't work." –Gov. Paul LePage.

- "In Oregon, students are skipping math class to learn about the Bible." – Hemant Mehta.

- "Mitch McConnell voted with Harry Reid to infringe on our gun rights." –Matt Bevin, R-KY.

- "No doctors who went to an American medical school will be accepting Obamacare." –Ann Coulter.

- "What we said was, you can keep (your plan) if it hasn't changed since the law passed." –President Obama.

- "Obamacare will question your sex life." –Betsy McCaughey.

- The United States has seen "a net loss of people with health insurance" because of Obamacare. –Rep. John Boehner, R-OH.

- "Millions of Americans are paying more and getting less under Obamacare." –Americans for Prosperity.

- The Keystone Pipeline will create 39,000 jobs. –US State Department.

- The Keystone Pipeline will create 50 jobs. –Opponents of the project.

- The Keystone Pipeline will create 120,000 jobs. –Supporters of the project.

To see which of the above statements were "Barely True" and which were "Pants on Fire False," visit the Web site of the *Tampa Bay Times'* Pulitzer Prize–winning **politifact.com**, or visit **FactCheck.org**, which is a project of the Annenberg Public Policy Center. When you are visiting these sites notice the quality of the evidence that is presented in order to back up their evaluations. Those sites pull together documentation and statistical evidence to support its assessment about the truth or falsity of the claims being made—far more work than any of us individually could undertake on our own, but necessary to the democracy so we voters can make informed decisions.

We were talking with a political observer the other day who cynically suggested that one or both of the major political parties might intentionally dissuade young people and independents from voting. Here is what that person said:

> By repeatedly making outlandish claims, one of the parties, or maybe both, is trying to turn off independents and young voters. That party wants these two groups to become so cynical about Washington politics that they decide not to support any candidate. Because this party (or these parties) believes that young voters and independents will not support their party's slate, they just want those voters out of the mix entirely. "If they will not vote for us, let's be sure that they don't vote for the other guys either" seems to be the strategy. "So let's turn them off and tune them out." The tactic is to make Washington politics so scummy and fraudulent that young people and independents will not want to be contaminated by the rot and the stench. "It's not important that what we say is true, it's only important that we get media attention, excite our base to go out and vote for us, and to repel independent thinkers and young people from voting at all."

What do you think? Are the two major U.S. political parties (the Democratic Party and the Republican Party, including the Tea Party) trying to drive young people and independents away from the national political process? Or, the opposite? Is one or both trying to appeal to those groups? Since opinions without reasons are thin soup at best, how might you investigate this question and get some hard evidence upon which to base an informed opinion?

---

alone was enough to stall or derail regulatory action. Yes, we could predict that regulatory delay would result in more tobacco related illnesses and deaths. But, we could also predict that delay would result in greater tobacco industry quarterly and annual profits. Question: Should Mr. Taylor be regarded as a credible expert on alternative energy sources? Search and watch episode 6, "Winds of Change," of the Showtime series *Years of Dangerously*. In that episode America Ferrera profiles Mr. Taylor and uses strong critical thinking to investigate his credibility. For the other side, search "Hartland Institute James Taylor." After watching the episode, and after checking out Mr. Taylor's credentials at the Hartland Institute's website, ask yourself if you think Mr. Taylor should be trusted as a credible source of expert information given in the best interests of the public, or if Mr. Taylor is simply promoting the economic interests of natural gas and oil industry giants.

Very important to remember, nothing here is illegal. Lobbying is not illegal. It is not illegal for corporations or individuals to get their points of view out to the general public. There is nothing illegal about seeking to advance one's own interests. Free speech as an incredibly valuable Constitutional right, one that we definitely do not want to lose or to compromise. *And so, it is clearly our responsibility to evaluate the credibility of sources.*

JOURNAL

A Disinterested Party - or Not?

A "disinterested party" is an individual or a group that does not stand to benefit from the resolution of a dispute. Three examples would be: an expert witness who gives information, a referee who is paid for officiating regardless of which team wins, or a good friend who offers advice genuinely and exclusively concerned to help without any expectation of personal gain.

How can you tell if an expert who is offering you information or advice is a disinterested party? Write an example of when a person had represented themselves as a disinterested party, but on closer review turned out to have a vested interest in the outcome.

UNCONSTRAINED, INFORMED ABOUT THE CASE AT HAND, AND MENTALLY STABLE

Constrained: When being tortured, people say whatever their tormentor wants to hear to stop the pain. Intelligence services, knowing this, have devised other tactics to extract accurate and useful information. Torture is one form of constraint that can cause an expert to make claims that are not reliable. Also, an expert may be legally constrained from offering advice or information on a given topic. For example, the expert may have signed an agreement with a former employer that prohibits the expert from revealing proprietary business secrets that are the property of the former employer for a certain period of time, typically a year or two. In this case, even if the expert goes to work for a new employer, the expert cannot legally violate the agreement with the previous employer. Under this constraint, the expert's claims will not rely on the expert's full range of knowledge. Legal or physical constraint is a reason not to fully trust what the expert has to say.

Informed about the Case at Hand: A friend of ours is a personal trainer with great expertise. People he happens to meet often ask him casually for advice. They want to know which exercises to do to gain greater strength, speed, or endurance. He could give them broad general answers, but he declines. Why? Because in these casual encounters, he does not have the opportunity to fully evaluate the person's physical status, so he worries that any advice he may offer or any claims he may make might be wrong for this particular person. As an expert, he realizes that knowing a lot about exercise in general is not always enough

to give this particular person the right advice. The expert must also become informed about this particular person's individual circumstances and condition. To use another example, general advice about how to prepare for a job interview may or may not be the right advice to give one particular person who is preparing for one specific interview for one specific job. An expert's claims and advice gain credibility if the expert has taken the time to inform himself or herself about the specific case at hand.

Mentally Stable: We have come quite a long way in developing our list of things to think about when evaluating the credibility of a source. And there is only one more issue to add, and that is that the expert is mentally competent, unimpaired, and, to use a layman's term, "stable." Drugs and alcohol can impair judgment, including expert judgment. Psychosis, severe clinical depression, and recent traumatic experiences can cause people who may ordinarily have good judgment to make mistakes. Senile dementia can render an expert unfit any longer to be providing credible guidance. And, as research with health care providers and pilots shows, long hours in stressful situations and sleep deprivation are associated with increased risk of errors. An expert who is not mentally stable cannot be trusted to provide reliable information or advice.

TWELVE CHARACTERISTICS OF A TRUSTWORTHY SOURCE In summary, when evaluating a **trusted source** on topic X, it would be reasonable for us to trust a person (or the words of a person) who fulfills all 12 of the criteria below.

1. Learned in topic X
2. Experienced in topic X
3. Speaking about X
4. Up-to-date about X
5. Capable of explaining the basis for their claim or their advice about X
6. Unbiased
7. Truthful
8. Free of conflicts of interest
9. Acting in accord with our interests
10. Unconstrained
11. Informed about the specifics of the case at hand
12. Mentally stable

This may seem like a formidable list, but asking people who have a healthy skepticism to take a person's claims and advice on faith is a sizable request. So it is reasonable that we should have high standards when it comes to establishing and maintaining trust. You may already have noted many of these positive characteristics in people whose advice you trust.

An Expert on Hate in America

"*They* are dirty, promiscuous, lazy, ignorant, immoral, impulsively violent, and sexually deviant. *They* are destroying our way of life! We must protect ourselves. *They* must be stopped!"

At one time or another throughout history frightening claims like these have been used to dehumanize every ethnic, religious, racial, and national group. Fear and hate undercut our sense that we all should treat others as we would wish to be treated ourselves. Why? Because "They" are not people—at least, not people like "Us." History shows repeatedly that when hate and fear dominate, beatings, killings, rapes, mob violence, reprisals, revenge, lawlessness, war, and even genocide too often follow. The gruesome reports from the Central African Republic are one bloody example of that pattern. But we have plenty of bitter examples of hate induced violence right here at home in the U.S. The Pew Research Center reported that there were 293,790 reported hate crimes in the U.S. in 2012. 28% of these were rooted in religious bias, 26% in gender bias, and 51% in ethnic bias (defined as relating to the victim's "ancestral, cultural, social or national affiliation").

Who keeps track of hate groups in America? Who has the courage to call them out for spreading their poison?

There may be no one organization monitoring every hate group in the world, but at least one organization is not afraid to identify the hate groups in America. The Southern Poverty Law Center (SPLC) is "a nonprofit civil rights organization dedicated to fighting hatred and bigotry, and to seeking justice for the most vulnerable members of society. Founded by civil rights lawyers Morris Dees and Joseph Levin, Jr. in 1971, the SPLC is internationally known for tracking and exposing the activities of hate groups." In recent years it has focused its legal efforts on overturning anti-LGBT and Jim-Crow policies and practices.

To promote tolerance and respect in our nation's schools, "the Center produces and distributes documentary films, books, lesson plans and other materials free of charge." The disturbing but engaging 2011 documentary film, *Erasing Hate*, "chronicles the redemptive story of a violent, racist skinhead" who risks his life to renounce the white power movement. Over a period of almost two years "he undergoes an excruciating series of laser treatments to remove the racist tattoos that covered his face and hands."

In 2014 the SPLC identified 939 active hate groups in the United States, among them the groups affiliated with the Ku Klux Klan, New-Nazi, White Nationalist, Racist Skinhead, Christian Identity, New-Confederate, and Black Separatist organizations. The SPLC defines a hate group as an organization that has "beliefs or practices that attack or malign an entire class of people, typically for their immutable characteristics." The Center compiled its 2014 list "using hate group publications and Web sites, citizen and law enforcement reports, field sources and news reports." According to the SPLC, "hate group activities can include criminal acts, marches, rallies, speeches, meetings, leafleting or publishing." Appearing on the SPLC list "does not imply a group advocates or engages in violence or other criminal activity."

The number of "Patriot" movement groups identified in 2014 was 1096. These are self-described armed militias, "sovereign citizens," and other conspiracy-minded organizations that regard the government, and in particular the federal government, as an enemy. While over 2000 groups were identified, the SPLC list does not attempt to represent everyone engaged in spewing hateful or violent messages. The SPLC notes "Web sites appearing to be merely the work of a single individual, rather than the publication of a group, are not included in this list."

Citations are from the Pew Research Center report on hate crimes February 21, 2014, the *SPLC Report*, Spring 2014 edition, and from the Southern Poverty Law Center Web site: **http://www.splcenter.org**. See also, "The Invisible Hate Crime: How to combat hate crimes against people with disabilities," Jack Levin, *Miller-McCune,* March-April 2011, page 50.

Dr. Facione, the lead author of *Think Critically*, a financial supporter of the SPLC for decades, has arranged for the Center's founder, Morris Dees, to speak on college campuses and to national organizations of academic leaders. Knowing where you can learn more about the SPLC for yourself, and knowing about Dr. Facione's endorsement and support of the Center's work, independently evaluate this claim made by Dr. Facione: **"The SPLC is an expert on hate in America."**

For more than forty years Morris Dees and the SPLC have provided *pro bono* (free) legal services to victims of hate crimes.

6.2 Assessing the Substance—What Should I Believe?

In the previous section, we focused on assessing the *credibility of the person* who makes an assertion without supplying reasons. Here we ask how strong critical thinking can help us evaluate the *credibility of a claim when it stands alone*. It might be posted on the Internet, cut from an e-mail and forwarded, printed in a poster, scrawling across the TV screen, included in an ad paid for by some political PAC, whispered as a rumor. Whatever, its source is unknown, and no reasons are supplied. Here are a few examples:

1. "Rumor has it that the dean is going to resign."
2. "I heard that she was so angry with her boyfriend that she keyed his new car."
3. "An unnamed source close to the police investigation told us that murder indictments were going to be handed down soon for as many as 35 gang members."
4. "According to a high-ranking administration official, the President is not happy with the leadership of his own party."
5. "Wind power generation of electricity will cost so much to implement that reliance on coal is financially a better option."
6. A global ebola epidemic could kill half of the human beings on the planet.
7. "The nursing staff knows that what happened today in room 314 was assisted suicide."
8. "The patient in 314 was dying of cancer and had less than a week to live."
9. "Doctors recommend getting your annual flu shot early this year."
10. "A huge killer anaconda lives in the utility tunnels under the main campus quad."

In this section, we will look at ways of evaluating the truth or falsity of assertions in the absence of supporting reasons and in the absence of identifiable sources.

Personal Muck and Gunk Monitor

Except for two rare situations that we will take up momentarily, there is no reliable way of telling that a claim, standing alone, is true or false. We may have some initial impressions or some common-sense notions—for example, that a claim like #10, about a killer anaconda, is highly unlikely and that a claim like #9, about getting a flu shot early, seems plausible. But initial impressions are not proof, and so-called common sense is not something that a person with a healthy sense of skepticism is going to rely upon. In fact, a healthy sense of skepticism (which is the alternative name for our "Personal Muck and Gunk Monitor") turns out to be our best defense against being deceived by false or misleading claims.

A strong critical thinker with a healthy sense of skepticism would probably respond to the 10 numbered claims by asking probing questions. Here are some examples. Note that some questions focus on trying to identify the source of the claim and that others focus on the plausibility of the claim itself.

1. Who said that about the dean and how would that person know?
2. Who told you that? Did the person actually see her key the car? Are we sure that the car was keyed? If so, might it not have been someone else who vandalized his car?

3. Why would the police leak information like that to anyone? Revealing their plans for a major bust would only cause the suspects to flee, if they knew that they were going to be arrested.

4. Did anyone else in the President's administration confirm that rumor? Isn't the President the leader of his political party, so you're saying he's unhappy with himself?

5. Can you show me the financial projections that support this?

6. Perhaps, but doesn't that assume that guarantees will fail, that the virus will continue to be virulent, that we will not have found a vaccine, and that known methods of caring for ebola victims effectively will have been abandoned? And, if so, why only half the population? What will stop the epidemic from killing even more people than that?

7. Oh, and how do you know that?

8. Did someone on the hospital staff share information about that patient's diagnosis with you?

9. Which doctors, the ones working for the pharmaceutical company, doctors with independent practices, or doctors working in the CDC? Why do they recommend getting a flu shot? And, who should get flu shots? Everyone? What does "early" mean? September? December?

10. Right. And it devours what food? Freshmen spelunking those tunnels?

Self-Contradictions and Tautologies

We said that there were two rare situations where we actually could know that a given claim was false or was true just by what it says. The first situation is when the claim is self-contradictory, as in these examples:

- No point on the circumference of a circle is the same distance from the center of the circle as any other point on the circumference of the circle.

- The moon orbits the earth and does not orbit the earth.

- Everyone in our club despises our club president, and only a couple of club members still admire her.

A **self-contradictory statement** cannot be true. The self-contradiction comes about because of the meanings of the words used to form the claim. For example, the definition of the word *circle* is not consistent with the notion that the circumference is variable distances from the center. Conveniently, self-contradictions, when you stop and think carefully about them, do not make sense. As they stand, they are un-interpretable. In real life, if someone happens to make a self-contradictory claim, strong critical thinkers use their question-asking skills to seek clarification from the speaker.

- If you are talking about a circle, then by definition every point on the circumference is the same distance from the center. Or else you are not talking about a circle. Which is it?

- Which is it, does the moon orbit the earth or not? Pick one. Both can't be true.

- That does not make any sense. You can't say that everyone despises the president but some do not. How can you despise a person and admire the person at the same time? What are you trying to say?

Some may worry that they will not always be able to identify self-contradictions in real life. But as a practical matter, what is important is that we recognize that a person's claim is not making sense to us for whatever reason. As we saw in Chapter 4 on clarifying and interpreting ideas, whenever we are trying to interpret a claim correctly, we should be prepared to ask the author respectful but challenging questions about what the author intends to communicate, by making the claim that we find to be confusing or self-contradictory.

Just as some claims cannot be true by virtue of what their words mean, other claims cannot be false by virtue of what their words mean. Here are examples:

- Every student enrolled in this university is a student enrolled in this university.

- Two straight lines on a plane that are not parallel to each other intersect at one and only one point.

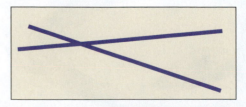

- If God is all-powerful, then there is nothing that God cannot do.

The first example almost sounds as redundant as "if a student is enrolled, then a student is enrolled." The second is a truth of plane geometry. The third is equivalent to saying "If God is all-powerful, then God is all-powerful" except that a definition for "all-powerful" is used in the predicate. In each of these cases, the statements must be true based simply on what the words mean.

A statement that is true entirely because of the meanings of the words it contains is called a **tautology**. Here's one more example:

- You gotta do what you gotta do.

Imagine the late James Gandolfini playing his famous character, Tony Soprano, saying something like this to one of his HBO series Mafia lieutenants. Yes, technically he is speaking a tautology. But we might ask ourselves, "Why?" In context, people use statements like these for purposes other than to communicate informational content. Here, the Mafia don may be giving a murderous assignment to that underling, saying, in effect, "This decision to act is absolutely necessary." From the point of view of critical thinking and to make a full and accurate interpretation, we must always consider context and purpose, as was emphasized in Chapter 4, rather than only the literal meaning of a claim.

A more serious threat to good judgment is generated by speakers whose claims appear to be information culled from careful observation, but in reality turn out instead to be empty tautologies. I listened to a professional motivational speaker recently during a conference for upward-climbing corporate junior managers. They were looking for ideas about how to get ahead in their careers. The speaker had made a name for himself advising business audiences just like this one. As the next speaker on the program, I had the opportunity to listen to what he was telling our audience and to watch their reactions. I wrote down some of the claims he made. Here are three: "Every job pays exactly what it is worth in terms of its contribution to society." "There is no skill you cannot learn." "We all start off equal in life."

Whoa, I thought. Those claims are not true. A teacher is worth far more to society than what he or she is paid, and, arguably, a Wall Street financier who trades in junk bonds and mortgage derivatives is worth far less to society than the salary and bonus taken home. Given that the context is not just fumbling through a skill like a beginner, but becoming professionally competent at the skill, then his second claim is false. No, not everyone can play basketball at the level of a college or professional athlete, not everyone can write a best seller novel, and not everyone can perform a concert-quality violin sonata. And, in terms of the third claim, a child born in a peaceful and prosperous community with nurturing parents and to a household that enjoys a modest but adequate income starts off life in a far better position than a child born in a

war-ravaged land, orphaned at birth, and struggling each day to scrounge for food while at the same time trying not to be maimed, raped, or killed.

The speaker, it seemed to me, was either an idiot or a charlatan. He was no idiot. And yet the more than 300 people in the audience seemed to be eating up every word. Why? I wondered. Why do they not see that either his claims are objectively false, or if true, they are nothing more than empty tautologies? If he meant to say that a teacher is worth no more nor less than she is paid when we factor her value into the mathematical formula for calculating the gross national product (GNP), then okay, I can understand that. It is only one small piece of how economists calculate GNP. But his way of saying it was a gross disservice to underpaid teachers. And absurd to advise corporate executives to equate their value to society with their take home pay. People are not awarded the Medal of Honor or the Nobel Prize based on their salary.

If the speaker meant to say that something is not a skill unless it can be learned, then thanks, but that's an empty tautology. Or, if he is only telling the audience that they can learn to be more effective negotiators or better at doing their current jobs, sure. That's probably true. But that will not guarantee you the senior VP job. If the speaker meant that each individual's economic contributions at birth is equal, that is zero, then, as the dolphins said in the *Restaurant at the End of the Universe*, "Good bye and thanks for all the fish."

By the way, not a one of those listening to that motivational speaker stack up the donkey excrement raised a hand to challenge his economic gospel. I felt sad for them—they seemed so innocent and gullible. That speaker appeared to want everyone in his audience to believe that he or she could become the corporate CEO by working hard and acquiring the requisite skills. Do the numbers people! That's nuts. Even if you do work hard and build all the skills, there are 300 of you in this audience, and only one senior VP over all of you. And only a handful of senior VPs all of whom report to only one CEO.

We absolutely agree with working hard and improving your skills. But, for realistic reasons. Earning your pay and keeping your job are good reasons to put in a decent effort. A fair day's work for a fair day's pay is a matter of justice. And, as jobs become more complex, you have to work at your skills to continue to be effective. And, for many of us, striving for excellence in what we do is, quite simply, motivation enough.

The speaker did motivate me to do something! That was to include this warning in *Think Critically*: Be vigilant! Do not let yourself be misled by empty tautologies masquerading as informative facts. *A strong critical thinker maintains a healthy skepticism.* Do not be afraid to ask, "What exactly do you mean when you say . . . ?" If you have ever found yourself arguing with someone only to discover that what she or he is saying is, in that person's view, true by definition then you understand the problem.

Marketing, Spin, Disinformation, and Propaganda

Claims without supporting reasons are the stock and trade of people who have ulterior motives. A marketer, wanting us to purchase something, makes claims about the virtues of the product. Extremist organizations eager to discredit someone make claims about the opponent's position on controversial issues. Sports promoters trying to generate press coverage and audience interest for a forthcoming game exaggerate the rivalry between the competing teams and over-interpret the significance of the game. Typical examples:

- Over 75 percent of the cars we make are still on the road.
- Supreme Court Justice Sonia Sotomayor supports Puerto Rican terrorists.

Really? Your pizza is all these things? You must be joking!

- This week's grudge match between the Bears and the Lions could determine which team will make it to the Super Bowl.

Those with a healthy sense of skepticism are ever on the alert for the donkey excrement being distributed by people with ulterior motives. Whether they wrap it in humor, sincerity, or vitriolic rhetoric, it comes to the same thing: They are unsubstantiated claims made specifically for the purpose of getting us to do something that we otherwise would not do—such as to buy something we do not need, to vote for something we don't believe in, or to support a cause we might not otherwise support. Or, perhaps it is simply a way of responding to the desire some have to be the center of everyone's attention.

Skepticism is not cynicism. We need to remember that open-mindedness is a positive critical thinking habit of mind. So, when we evaluate the plausibility or implausibility of claims, we must discipline ourselves to be open-minded. Fortum, a Scandinavian energy company, won a Clio Award for its ad that features that claim that Fortum...

- fills its brand with positive energy by activating its customers rather than only sending them bills.

Is this only a clever marketing gimmick, or might there be something more to the idea? Before you propose an evaluation, you will need to understand how to interpret Fortum's curious claim. We suggest you begin by watching the ad yourself. If you search Fortum and Clio Award you probably will find it. Given that consumers can become jaded and skeptical, marketers often try to separate us from our money using humor and entertainment, rather than with extravagant claims. This is particularly true if the product being marketed is something familiar, rather than a new program as in the Fortum example. Many Clio Award–quality commercials employ entertainment value and humor. We easily found many great examples by visiting YouTube and searching "Clio Award Commercials." The Guinness "tipping point" ad, Dr. Pepper's take-off on the "Hunchback of Notre Dame," and the Skittles "touch" commercial were some of our favorites. Does it make sense that we should be more inclined to purchase a product after seeing a funny and entertaining ad? And if so, why? It often takes imagination, good critical thinking, a team of professionals, and millions of dollars to produce commercials of this quality. What does it take not to be drawn in by them?

Slanted Language and Loaded Expressions

It can be difficult to evaluate claims that use language that carries a positive or negative emotional charge. Some expressions are so loaded down with social and cultural baggage that the very use of them excites strong positive or negative reactions. Here are sets of three statements each. The first in each set is intended to elicit a generally positive response to the topic, the second is neutrally factual, and the third is slanted negatively.

- John is a true American hero.
- John is a New York City firefighter.
- John is just another overpaid municipal employee working in public safety.
- Basketball combines finesse, grace, power, and skill.
- Basketball combines passing, dribbling, shooting, and defense.
- Basketball combines sweat, aggression, cunning, and brute force.
- Love is you and me together happily forever in each other's arms.
- Love is a strong emotional attachment to another.
- Love is that stupefying feeling you had before you really knew the bastard.

Slanted language and loaded expressions are not always easy to recognize. The problem for all of us is that if we happen to agree with what is being said, we have great difficulties seeing anything particularly unfair, loaded, or egregious with the claims being made. Everyone likes to think of himself or herself as objective and able to see all sides of an issue. But the psychological fact is that most of us have a very difficult time putting ourselves in the minds of people with whom we disagree. Rather, we tend

to prefer to make an idiot out of our opposition in our own minds, underestimating the merits of what the person may be saying and overestimating the clarity and strength of our own views. We saw a little of this in the "Guns for Kids" debate in Chapter 5 and we will learn more about the psychology behind this common human propensity in the chapter on snap judgments. That said, evaluating claims that tug at our emotions, either positively or negatively, by virtue of the language those claims employ must be done with care. A strong truth-seeking habit of mind can dispose us to approach this evaluation more objectively.

Political attack ads are particularly offensive because they often combine emotional messages with misleading claims. Speaking for their generation and all that have followed, the rock band The Who captured our disgust and our vulnerability with lyrics warning us not to be fooled again. We could provide wagonloads of examples of marketing half-truths and political assault ads, like the ad in the 2014 Michigan primary where a strongly anti-abortion candidate was accused by a political rival of supporting "gender-election abortions."[15] But we knew you could find plenty of examples of this just by watching the barrage of mean-spirited, attack ads that precede every election. The 2012 comedy, *The Campaign*, with Will Farrell and Zach Galifianakis is a humorous, but not entirely untrue, reminder of how ambition trumps truth when votes are on the line.

The outrageously false claims, accusations, and innuendos in some political attack ads are so pernicious and incendiary that they approach hate speech. By dividing us one from another, these slanders and falsehoods rip away at the very fabric of our pluralistic democracy. So outrageous are the claims made by the religious, ethic, nationalistic, racial and political fear merchants and hatemongers, so thick is their muck and gunk that thankfully the great majority of us recognize them for the lies that they are. Most of us are not swayed by the vitriolic "Us-vs-Them" rhetoric. But, sadly, some believe those claims. And too often, when that happens, violence follows. One filmmaker, Rachel Lyon, has taken on the challenge of examining hate crimes in America and the role of the media in exploiting our fears and prejudices with exaggerated claims and inflammatory reporting. Her 2014 documentary "Hate Crimes in the Heartland." tells the story of two tragic events that occurred in Tulsa, Oklahoma, but over 90 years apart.

To sum up, we need a healthy skepticism when trying to evaluate claims that stand alone, without their authors and without reasons. Except for self-contradictions and tautologies, it is almost impossible to evaluate the claims by themselves as either true or false. Through tough questioning, we may find some claims more plausible and others less plausible. But even then, other factors, including the ulterior motives of the people who are making the claims and the emotion-laden language that is often used, make it difficult, if not impossible, to evaluate a claim standing alone.

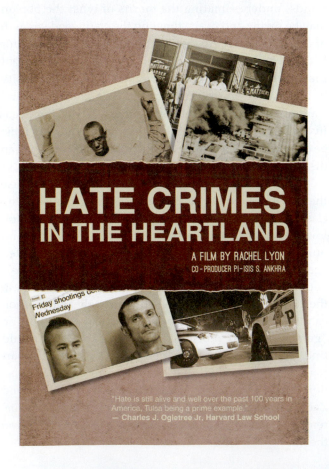

HATE CRIMES IN THE HEARTLAND

A FILM BY RACHEL LYON
CO-PRODUCER PI-ISIS S. ANKHRA

"Hate is still alive and well over the past 100 years in America, Tulsa being a prime example."
— Charles J. Ogletree Jr. Harvard Law School

Almost, but not entirely impossible. There is one other quite excellent strategy, and that is to take upon ourselves to investigate the claim independently.

6.3   Independent Verification

Suppose we encounter a claim on the Internet and we hear it repeated by friends and talked about in the media. Assume that on its face the claim appears plausible, yet we are skeptical. We know no claim is true simply because it is widely believed and frequently repeated. What can we do if we need to make a decision and this particular claim, if true, would lead us to make one decision, but, if false, would lead us to make a different decision? Is there any other way to figure out if we should believe the claim or not? Yes. One way to do this is to ask if the claim can be confirmed. The other is to ask if it can be disconfirmed. Let's look briefly at both.

The best, and funniest, example how one might independently attempt to verify or to disconfirm an apparently incredible claim is John Oliver's look at the claim: "The Miss America Pageant is one of the world's largest providers of scholarship assistance for young women." The claim appears on the Miss America organization website. It was repeated many times in news stories and by by talk show personalities during the week of the annual pageant. They all appeared to have swallowed the claim as given, without checking it out first. But Oliver was skeptical. Watch the September 21, 2014 episode of HBO's *This Week Tonight*. Oliver and his staff do just about everything one can imagine in their effort to confirm or to disconfirm that claim.

Can the Claim Be Confirmed?

A claim becomes more plausible if we can find confirmatory information or information that is consistent with the claim. For example, suppose someone claims:

- Mother's Day is the most popular holiday celebrated in the United States.

How might we go about finding confirmation for this? First, we would need a measure of "popularity" as applied to holidays. For example, we could use the number of greeting cards sold per holiday, the money spent sending flowers per holiday, restaurant revenues per holiday, telephone calls made per holiday, or an opinion survey with an appropriately structured sample.

Another approach when attempting to confirm a claim is to ask ourselves if the claim in question is consistent with other things we may know. If it is, then the claim takes on more plausibility in our minds. Consider this claim:

- Samuel was the last person to leave this morning, and he forgot to lock the apartment door.

To confirm this claim, we might begin by asking how many people live in Samuel's apartment, and then we might ask each of those people what time he or she left the apartment this morning and whether he or she noticed who was still there when he or she left. But suppose that this line of questioning results in uncertainty because people can't recall the exact time they left or because they are not sure if others may or may not have been in the apartment when they left. Then we would go to things we know about Samuel, looking for something that may be consistent with the claim being evaluated. For example, we may learn that Samuel is often the last one to leave in the morning because he does not have any early classes. We may learn that in the recent past Samuel admitted to having forgotten to lock the apartment door when he left. And we may learn that Samuel is a generally irresponsible and unreliable person, often neglecting his responsibilities and not keeping his promises. If things should turn out this way upon investigation, then we would have reason to evaluate the claim as highly plausible.

One difficulty with seeking confirmation is that, even if we find it, the claim might still not be true. We can say that the claim is consistent with the facts as we know them. But, there may be more facts, or the way that the facts were measured was less than adequate. For example, judging only form the money spent, Christmas is the most popular holiday in the Unites States. But there are plenty of people who will tell you, if asked, that they really do not like Christmas all that much. It is a lot of work, for one. And too often the cost of the gifts is not commensurate with the affection felt. Rather some gifts are given more out of a feeling of obligation than of love. Or, consider the other example, about Samuel. It is highly plausible that he left the door unlocked. But what if we learn that one of the other people who live there suddenly remembers needing to come back to the apartment after Samuel had already gone. Then, in a hurry, the person confesses that he rushed out again and forgot to lock the door.

Finding confirmatory evidence is great. It is certainly a lot better than deciding if something is true or false based on no independent information at all. But is there something better than confirmation? Yes. The strategy scientists use: devising ways to gather evidence, which would disconfirm the claim.

Can the Claim Be Disconfirmed?

An alternative to trying to confirm that the claim is true is setting about trying to establish that it is false. Consider these two claims:

- You are the person who murdered Mrs. X on Sunday at noon in her home in Boston.
- President Obama does not have a valid U.S. birth certificate.

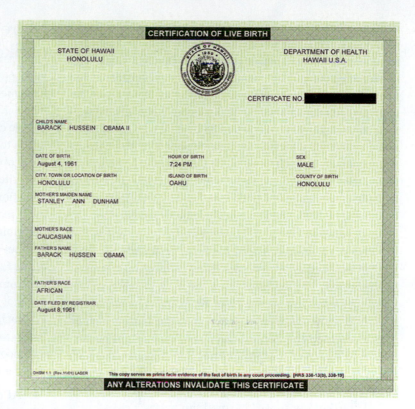

In the first case, to disconfirm the accusation, the accused would have to establish a solid alibi. For example, "No, sir, I did not kill Mrs. X. I was onstage in Orlando, making a speech to 2000 people exactly on the date and time that the murder occurred in Boston. My proof is the videotape of the speech, which is date-stamped, and the testimony of the audience members and technical support staff who were present at the time."

Some claims, like the second example about the President Obama's birth certificate, are more challenging to disconfirm for reasons that go beyond the substance of the claim itself. All that would appear to be required to disconfirm that claim would be presenting the President's birth certificate for public inspection. Although we may not personally be able to access the president's birth records, presumably the President or his attorney can. "Public inspection" in a case like this would then be the responsibility of the news media, or some trustworthy and unbiased expert panel.

Prior to the general election in November 2008, the *Chicago Tribune*'s Washington Bureau did post a story confirming that both presidential candidates were natural-born U.S. citizens, Mr. Obama having been born in the state of Hawaii and Mr. McCain at a naval hospital in the then U.S.-controlled Panama Canal Zone.[16] And settled the matter at least for all legal purposes relating to their eligibility to run for president.

But if your purposes are different, then let the games begin, or should we say "continue." In the summer of 2009 a U.S. Army reserve soldier named Stefan Cook, a "Birther," refused to be deployed to Afghanistan on the grounds that he was being sent by a commander-in-chief who was not eligible to be president because he was not a native-born U.S. citizen. It turned out that Mr. Cook was misleading the public, for he had in fact volunteered for the military assignment in Afghanistan. And when he changed his mind about volunteering for military service in that country, his orders to deploy to Afghanistan were revoked, which is standard policy in the case of volunteers.[17] But with the media attention to the initial story, these subsequent facts went relatively unnoticed and the rumors about Mr. Obama's birth certificate lived on. Then, in 2011, the celebrity publicity seeker, Donald Trump, jumped on the Birthers bandwagon. But when the President again released his birth certificate, the teapot tempest settled down. Mr. Trump almost hurt himself by vigorously patting himself on the back in self-congratulations for having sorted all of that out on behalf of the nation. If someone were to claim that the Trump-Birther episode helped the Republican Party, they might be surprised to discover that influential Republicans like Karl Rove, Colin Powel, and Jeb Bush repeatedly expressed concern in 2011 and for years afterward that what they called "birther nonsense" harmed the party.[18]

The durability of claims like the one about Mr. Obama and his birth certificate is fascinating in its own right. Some claims—call them "urban legends"—seem to endure no matter what investigative findings reveal. Even when the claim has been plausibly refuted, there are those who will not accept the evidence. Alex Koppelman offers an interesting analysis of why "conspiracy theorists" will never be satisfied about the validity of the birth certificate or the eligibility of Mr. Obama to be president.[19]

But with due respect to the conspiracy theorists of every stripe, there is a major difference between healthy skepticism and stubborn refusal to abandon a discredited position. The skeptic is asserting uncertainty about the truth of the matter. The skeptic will continue to be uncertain until the question is suitably investigated. But then the skeptic will be able to determine which side of the issue has more credibility. The conspiracy theorist, on the other hand, is making a very bold claim. And it is often a claim that can be neither confirmed nor disconfirmed. The conspiracy theorist is saying that a certain version of events is the truth *and* that all other versions are false. This puts an enormous burden of proof on the conspiracy theorist, not the skeptic. The conspiracy theorist must do much more than discredit *all* other known, plausible, or possible versions of events. The conspiracy theorist must confirm the truth of the one version of events he or she is putting forward. This work is seldom done. Too often the conspiracy theorist picks and pecks at some of the more plausible versions as a way of making space for the version he or she wants everyone to believe, but never gets around to providing solid confirmation for that version.

More than a Healthy Sense of Skepticism Only

Web pages and blogs can be posted by reliable and informed experts and by unscrupulous people bent on fraud, hate, or mischief. Truths and falsehoods spread as people cite other Web pages as their sources, as they e-mail URLs to friends, and as they post, blog, tweet, and comment about things they have seen on the Web. Blogs and Web sites can provide pros and cons for almost any idea. Question: In addition to healthy skepticism, what are the most reasonable, most reliable, and smartest strategies to determine what on the Web can and cannot be trusted?

Let's practice those strategies you've identified. Each of the following claims may be true. But as they stand, cut off from any of the reasons their sources may have supplied, it is difficult to know whether they are true or false. For each claim, write four questions that, if answered, are likely to yield information that would tend to confirm or to disconfirm the claim and thus aid you to evaluate the claim's plausibility or implausibility.

1. At the present time electric cars are not, on balance, environmentally sound.[20]

2. "As a society, we [in the US] live and breathe the idea of religious freedom and religious tolerance."[21]

3. "The USA is not the best country in the world"— Spoken by Jeff Daniels playing news anchor Will McAvoy on the HBO series *The Newsroom*.[22]

4. "The health risks of obesity have been underestimated."[23]

5. Your presence will be powerfully felt by your loved ones if you eliminate that which does not add value to your life.

6. Subscriptions to online pornography Internet sites are more prevalent in states "where surveys indicate conservative positions on religion, gender roles, and sexuality."[24]

7. "Forgiveness liberates the soul. It removes fear."— Spoken by Morgan Freeman playing Nelson Mandela in the 2010 film about South Africa, *Invictus*.

8. As the nurse in rural Michigan kissed the dying patient's forehead, the patient's Muslim family in Iran, watching this simple act of compassion on a laptop, wept. Later, at the funeral an Episcopal priest read Muslim prayers.[25]

9. Unlike the protests for justice, dignity and equality by San Jose State University student-athletes, Tommie Smith and John Carlos, at the Mexico City 1968 Olympic Games, not a single athlete at the Sochi Russia 2014 Olympic Games protested for gay rights.

10. If you exhume my father's grave and move his casket to another location, he will never rest in peace again.

11. The vulnerable workers in Zimbabwe's diamond fields are protected from external violence and lawlessness by the presence of Zimbabwe's military, which has restored order in the Marange district.

12. More children between the ages of 13 and 17 have been killed playing football in the past 60 years than have been killed by other children with firearms.

13. Teen virginity pledges are effective in reducing the percentage of teens who have sex and in reducing the number of unwanted pregnancies among teenagers.

14. Unaware of how long they have to live and not knowing how chemotherapy will affect their lives, more than 20 percent of Medicare patients who have advanced cancer start a new chemotherapy regimen two weeks before they die.

15. Seamus Hogan of Rathkeale, County Limerick, Ireland claims that the tree stump with the image of the

Blessed Virgin Mary brings people of all ages, races, and religions together in prayer. Seamus adds that as far as he can tell it is doing no harm.[26]

16. When choosing colors for your favorite room, remember that "the antidote to fog is color. . . . A warmer color temperature in a room is a really good approach, so you don't feel like you're living on a glacier."[27]

17. Permanently restore your hair with Bosley.

18. Playing a musical instrument improves kids' brains.[28]

19. Iraqi rights groups protest legislation, which would permit girls as young as nine to be married.

20. For-profit colleges blocked legislation that would have penalized colleges if their graduates are not able to find jobs that pay well enough to enable those graduates to pay off student loans.

We have been learning about the importance of conducting our own independent investigations to see if we can confirm or disconfirm claims evoke strong emotional responses. But what about others, including our friends? How can we guide them to use their critical thinking skills to be less reactive and more reflective about the claims they encounter.

Independent Investigation and the Q-Ray Bracelet Case

The case of the Q-Ray bracelet offers us an excellent example of the value of independent investigation into the veracity of the claims people make to promote products and reap profits at the expense of gullible consumers. Perhaps you have seen the ads for the Q-Ray bracelet. Millions of Q-Ray bracelets have been marketed and sold, at prices ranging from $50.00 to $250.00, to people seeking relief from chronic pain caused by a variety of illnesses and medical conditions, including pain from chemotherapy. Its inventor, an infomercial entrepreneur, formed a company, QT Inc., to manufacture and sell the Q-Ray bracelets. Initially, the bracelets had been described as having been made from special metals that offer natural and effective pain relief. The fundamental claim made in the promotional infomercials and on the Q-Ray Web site between the years 2000 and 2003 was that an "activated" Q-Ray bracelet relieves pain. Whether or not the Q-Ray works or not turned out to be a multimillion-dollar question because of lawsuits charging that the product was ineffective. In 2002, the Mayo Clinic conducted an independent investigation into the effectiveness of the "ionized" Q-Ray bracelet as to whether it did or did not relieve pain.[29]

The independent Mayo Clinic researchers set up a clinical trial like the ones used to test the effectiveness of pharmaceuticals and medical devices. Subjects (people with chronic pain) were randomly assigned to two

Q-Ray promoters were guilty of false advertising.[30] Did this put an end to the sale of Q-Ray bracelets? Hardly. To see for yourself what new claims are being made search "Q-Ray Wellness Bracelet."

Why use metal when rubber bands are cheaper? Remember "Power Bracelets?" On November 21, 2011 the company that produced athletic power bracelets filed for bankruptcy. The founders admitted that claims that the rubber wristbands improved flexibility, balance, and strength were unsubstantiated. The bankruptcy meant that celebrities, like LA Laker star Kobe Bryant who had $400,000 endorsement deal, would not be paid their fees. Customers could apply for refunds. Good luck with that. Our question is not "What went wrong?" but instead, "How could we be so gullible?" Really, a rubber band on the wrist is the secret to athletic success! What about human decision making that enables such obvious nonsense to separate people from their hard earned money so easily?[31]

different groups. The first group of subjects was given authentic activated Q-Ray bracelets to wear. The other group was given non-active replicas of Q-Ray bracelets to wear. At the end of the trial, 75 percent of the people in the first group reported experiencing pain relief. None of the subjects knew whether he or she had an "activated" or "non-active" bracelet.

What do you suppose was the percentage of people in the group with the non-active replicas that reported experiencing pain relief? It turned out to be the same: 75 percent! This investigation established that the Q-Ray bracelet has a placebo effect only. It is the equivalent of taking a sugar pill instead of taking medication that has been demonstrated to be effective. Based on the research at the Mayo Clinic, the judge dealing with the lawsuits ruled that the

Suspending Judgment

Judgments in contexts of uncertainty are unavoidable, given the human condition. The critical thinking habit of judiciousness disposes us toward prudence and caution when deciding what to believe or what to do. Our healthy sense of skepticism tells us that if we can neither confirm nor disconfirm a claim through independent investigation, then the wisest course would be to suspend judgment with regard to that claim. The best judgment about the plausibility or implausibility of some claims may be to make no judgment at all.

Summing up this chapter,

strong critical thinkers with a healthy sense of skepticism have three options when presented with a claim absent any reasons. One is to evaluate the credibility of the person or source of the claim. Is the person an expert whom we can trust? We established a dozen considerations to guide us when considering the credibility of the person or source of the claim. Or, second, we can examine the claim itself, interrogating its plausibility by inquiring into the context within which the claim is positioned and

the possible ulterior motives behind the use of the claim. The second option can present difficulties because so much is unknown and because "common sense," "everyone agrees," and "feels right" are notoriously unreliable guides. The third option, which is often the best option, is to investigate the claim independently, seeing if we can lend it some plausibility by confirming it, or seeing if we can establish that it is very likely untrue by disconfirming it.

Key Concepts

expert refers to someone who is both experienced and learned in a given subject matter area or professional practice field.

trusted source on topic X is a person (or the words of a person) who is learned in X, experienced in X, speaking about X, up-to-date about X, capable of explaining the basis for their claim or their advice about X, unbiased, truthful, free of conflicts of interest, acting in accord with our interests, unconstrained, informed about the specifics of the case at hand, and mentally stable.

self-contradictory statement is a sentence that is false entirely because of the grammatical construction and the meanings of the words used to form the sentence.

tautology is a statement that is necessarily true because of the meanings of the words.

Applications

Reflective Log

Your favorite nutritional supplement[32] The ads and testimonials for nutritional supplements are among the most effective marketing tools ever, as is supported by the unprecedented growth in the sales of energy drinks, dietary supplements, vitamin beverages, and stimulants. Select for this exercise one of these products you are already purchasing for your own use or any product of this kind that interests you. Use information provided on the product label and from the product's Web site as needed to respond to these questions in your log:

1. What claims are made about the benefits of the product?

2. What research is cited or what evidence is supplied to support the truth of these claims?

3. Who are the people who have provided testimonials in support of the product?

4. What level of expertise do these individuals have with regard to human nutrition?

5. Were any of these individuals paid to provide their endorsement?

6. What warnings, risks, or potentially harmful side effects are presented?

7. What ingredients does the supplement contain?

8. Biologically and nutritionally, what does each ingredient do? In other words, what is its function?

9. Is the supplement "specially formulated" in any way that is purported to enhance its efficacy?

10. Who are the target consumers of the supplement? Who should use it?

11. What have you been told about the supplement by friends, coaches, and salespeople?

12. Who produces/manufactures the supplement? What is that producer's reputation?

13. Is the supplement approved as "safe and effective" by the federal Food and Drug Administration?

14. In terms of the nutritional benefits and risks, how does the supplement compare to the items on this list: orange juice, milk, coffee, standard multivitamin tablets, carrots, apples, broccoli, ordinary yogurt, cottage cheese, peanut butter, tuna fish, baked turkey breast, and wheat bread?

15. Reflect on your answers to questions #2–14 and then evaluate the claims you wrote down in #1. Are they true, plausible, implausible, or untrue, or should you suspend judgment about those claims?

Individual Exercises

What's wrong here? For each of the following, explain the mistake that makes it untrue.

1. A statement is a tautology if it is true.

2. A statement that is self-contradictory is seldom true.

3. We can tell if a claim is true or false by looking at what it means.

4. If a claim cannot be confirmed by an independent investigation, then it must be false.

5. If an independent investigation produces evidence that is consistent with a given claim, then the claim must be true.

6. Experts have the rightful authority to impose their beliefs on other people.

7. Relativism is the highest stage of cognitive development college students can achieve.

8. To doubt the truthfulness of a rightful authority means that a person is being disrespectful.

9. If a celebrity endorses a product, you can be sure that the product is of high quality.

10. If we do not believe that a claim is true, then we must believe that the claim is false.

11. No one can evaluate emotionally charged claims.

12. Critical thinking forces people to be cynical.

Your best and worst commercials: We see or hear dozens of ads and commercials each day on TV, on the radio, on Web pages, in the newspaper, on T-shirts, on billboards, etc. (Have you ever asked yourself why we pay for clothing that sports a logo or promotes a brand name, instead of demanding that the corporation pay us to wear that clothing?) Mark the time. For the next 24 hours, keep track of the ads and commercials you see or hear. Focus on the ones you think are the very best and the ones that are the very worst. Keep two lists and refine the lists by crossing off and adding candidates as you hear or see another that is better or worse. After 24 hours, analyze your top three and your bottom three. What makes them the "best" and the "worst" in your mind? Were they funny, informative, creative, and effective in influencing you to want the product they were promoting? Or were they boring, stupid, confusing, and ineffective?

Selling risk with the Evening News: Watch the national news on CBS, NBC, or ABC. Focus on the commercials and make a list of each one and what it is advertising. In each case, the product can benefit people, and yet each comes with a measure of risk. The job of the commercial is to lead us to desire the product in spite of its inherent risks. When a commercial for a drug or medical device comes on, listen very carefully to the list of side effects and cautions. Write down as many as you can for each drug or medical device that is advertised. When a car commercial comes on, note what the manufacturer is using to sell the car (e.g., sex, power, prestige, popularity, comfort, fuel economy, safety, or resale value). When a banking or investment commercial comes on, record the disclaimers, cautions, and exceptions, like "not a guarantee," "read the prospectus carefully before investing," and "rates and conditions subject to change without notice." After the news broadcast is over, review your lists. Which of the commercials, in your judgment, was the most misleading with regard to the risks associated with the product? Why? Which company provided the least substantive guarantees with regards to the product's expected benefits in its commercial? Explain your choices.

In whom do *you* trust? When you think about it, you have known a great many people now and throughout the years, such as family, friends, teachers, co-workers, and classmates. Identify two people you trust. Then review the list of 12 criteria of a credible and trustworthy source and see how many of them are fulfilled by each of the people on your list. Did either of those people do things or say things that lead you to evaluate them highly on one or more of the 12 criteria? Did either ever do anything that would disqualify them from being trusted by you because they missed on one or another of the 12 items? Next, think of two people you do not trust. Has either done something or said something relating to one or more of the 12 criteria that leads you to regard him or her as untrustworthy? What did he or she do and how did you connect that to being untrustworthy? Do you notice that it takes much effort to build trust and little effort to lose it?

Pacific Northwest tree octopus endangered! "The Pacific Northwest tree octopus (*Octopus paxarbolis*) can be found in the temperate rainforests of the Olympic Peninsula on the west coast of North America. Their habitat lies on the Eastern side of the Olympic mountain range, adjacent to Hood Canal. These solitary cephalopods reach an average size (measured from arm-tip to mantle-tip,) of 12–13 in. (30–33 cm). Unlike most other cephalopods, tree octopuses are amphibious, spending only their early life and the period of their mating season in their ancestral aquatic environment. Because of the moistness of the rainforests and specialized skin adaptations, they are able to keep from becoming desiccated for prolonged periods of time, but given the chance they would prefer resting in pooled water." For remarkable pictures and background info on this problem search "Pacific Northwest Tree Octopus." Seriously, why did the tree octopus problem cause such a stir among teachers?

SHARED RESPONSE

Two Better Than One?

Evaluate the claim "It is better for children to be raised in a two-parent household." Be sure to provide your reason(s), not just your opinion. And, comment respectfully on the reasons others offer.

Group Exercises

Claims cost money and cause pain #1: Occasionally reputable sources present apparently divergent claims. But strong critical thinkers can still sort through the divergent claims and assess them by looking for the reasons and evidence upon which they are based. Many reputable investigators have looked into the health claims for the dietary supplement ginkgo biloba. It is said to improve cognitive functioning, assist memory, and help focus attention. Google "Ginkgo biloba health study" and review the research published in respected sources over the past four years. Focus on Web sites that provide information to the educated public, but which are not simply promoting particular products or medical services. You will find some serious research studies, some excellent summaries of multiple studies, and some detailed criticisms about the methods or the analyses of other studies. As strong critical thinkers, work through those reports and make a well-reasoned and thoughtful evaluation of the claim, "Ginkgo biloba supplements are beneficial for human cognitive functioning."

Claims cost money and cause pain #2: Autism is a heartbreaking diagnosis and a growing medical problem. How do the 12 characteristics of a trustworthy source factor into a parent's decision about seeking care for an autistic child? In its January 14–21, 2011 issue, the *San Francisco Business Times* ran a story, "In Autism's Storm," about a wealthy CEO and philanthropist, Zach Nelson, and his wife, who are advocates for families with autistic children. The Nelsons support the work of British physician, Andrew Wakefield, who claims, contrary to what many physicians and medical researchers believe, that autism originates from digestive problems and can be cured. Dr. Wakefield has written a book, *Callous Disregard: Autism and Vaccines—The Truth Behind the Tragedy*, and the Nelsons, along with filmmaker Elizabeth Horn, have produced a film, setup a Web site, and raised money in support of his work. Meanwhile, the *British Medical Journal* published an editorial denouncing Wakefield, and Wakefield has been stripped of his license to practice medicine by the British medical authorities. Search the article by its title and apply the 12 characteristics to evaluate the trustworthiness of claims made by the Nelsons, Ms. Horn, and Dr. Wakefield.

Claims cost money and cause pain #3: Dr. Mark Geier of Maryland developed a drug called Lupron for the treatment of autism and he is marketing the "Lupron Protocol" across the country by opening clinics in several states. Dr. Geier's theory is that autism is caused by a harmful link between testosterone and mercury, according to a story that appeared in the *Los Angeles Times* on May 24, 2009. Leading pediatric endocrinologists say that the Lupron Protocol is baseless. Experts warn that the protocol can have harmful effects on young children, "disrupt

normal development, interfering with natural puberty and potentially putting children's hearts and bones at risk." But the protocol is FDA approved, albeit for the treatment of an extremely rare condition that has little if anything to do with autism. Like Dr. Wakefield, defenders of Dr. Geier claim that mainstream medicine condemns his work because he has been vocal about his criticism of "pediatricians, health officials, and drug companies" for "covering up the link between vaccines and autism." What is a desperate parent to do? Who should a parent believe? How can parents who love their autistic child and want only the best, decide whether or not to try the Lupron Protocol? Research the Lupron Protocol and Dr. Geier on the Internet, and apply the 12 characteristics of a trustworthy source to Dr. Geier's claims.

The most popular holiday on campus: Suppose you see a claim in the campus paper, published on February 10 that says "Valentine's Day is the most popular holiday on this campus." Develop a strategy by which you can determine which holiday is the most popular among the students enrolled in your university or college. Write up your recommended procedure in draft form. Work with up to two other students to combine the best ideas from your approach and their approaches. Then, develop a final recommendation for how to conduct the investigation. The critical thinking involved in this strategy includes the question, "What sorts of evidence should we be able to find if we assume that the claim is true?" And our answer to that question in the Mother's Day example was evidence about cards, flowers, phone calls, etc., which would reflect that if people valued this holiday, they would show that in their behavior. The strategy is a good one if cards, flowers, phone calls, etc., are part of other holidays too. As you discovered in doing the exercise, another aspect of attempting to confirm or disconfirm a claim is to be sure exactly what the claim means. Interpreting the expression "most popular" required finding a way to measure popularity. Interpreting "holiday on this campus" required coming up with a list of holidays, some of which might have been unique to your specific campus (e.g., a "Founders Day" holiday or a religious holiday not celebrated at other colleges or universities).

Chapter 7
Evaluate Arguments: Four Basic Tests

Every worthwhile activity has its own standards for success. What makes an argument successful?

WHAT presumptions are we making when we offer one another reasons to support our claims?

WHAT four tests must an argument pass to be worthy of acceptance?

HOW can we recognize common reasoning mistakes more readily?

Learning Outcomes

7.1 Explain the four presumptions about argument making we all rely upon when offering one another reasons to support our claims.

7.2 Evaluate the worthiness of arguments by applying the four tests: Truthfulness of the

Premises, Logical Strength, Relevance, and Non-Circularity.

7.3 Recognize common reasoning mistakes known as fallacies of relevance.

"**I don't get why** you want to quit," said Malcolm. "You came here to play volleyball. Volleyball is all you ever want to talk about! Now suddenly you want to quit?"

Caitlin looked at Malcolm. He couldn't possibly be this dense. "Look, I explained it all to you already."

"You said that you didn't like Coach Williams. So what? She's your head coach. Nobody likes a head coach. I don't like the marching band director, but you don't see me quitting the band," said Malcolm.

"Coach was screaming at everyone again. She's so negative, always screaming at the players, and that doesn't motivate me to try harder. I just hate all her yelling! Anyway, it's the setter, Jenny; she kept putting the ball too far from the net. It messes up everybody. But coach kept yelling at the rest of us, when it was all Jenny's fault."

"So," said Malcolm, "you're quitting because the coach yells at you? Williams has been a screamer since she took over as head coach two seasons ago. Her yelling never bothered you before. Or is it something else?"

"Yes! No. I don't know," replied Caitlin in exasperation. "Who cares? It's not like I have a future in volleyball after college."

"What does that have to do with anything? You knew a spot on the Olympic team or the AVP beach volleyball pro tour was like a near-impossible long shot before you came here. And another thing: Don't tell me you don't get motivated when the coach is fired up. I've seen you in games. You're angry because you know you can play Jenny's position better than she can. But the coach doesn't let you. So, you're pissed at the coach. It's not about the yelling."

"You're right. Jenny's terrible. I don't understand how she ever made the team."

"But, Caitlin, nobody can spike and defend at the net like you. Coach knows that, and so does everyone else on the team. So, you're going to play the front line. Which is great. I'll bet that Jenny wishes she could play where you play."

"Well, I don't care about any of that anymore. I'm quitting and therefore I'm quitting. End of story. Let's talk about something else. . . . Tell me how your marching band practice was today."

"Fine, I hear you. You're going to quit. And, yes, we can change the subject. But let me just say for the record that I still don't think you're really being honest about why you're leaving the team and the sport you love. And just saying over and over again that you plan to quit does not explain why you plan to quit."

In the scene that just played out, Caitlin explains her decision to quit the college volleyball team. Her stated reason is that she is not motivated to play harder by the coach's constant criticism. Ergo, she's going to quit the team. That may be a reasonably logical argument, if we also assume that Caitlin is the kind of athlete who does

not respond well to that coaching style. But her friend Malcolm knows better. He does not accept her argument because he has seen her respond positively to the coach's style in game situations. The truth is that Caitlin does get motivated to play harder when the coach is fired up. Although Malcolm does not make the point, we might observe that the word *yelling* is negatively slanted. It fits Caitlin's current negative attitude toward the coach. But "yelling" is probably not the best word to use when talking about those times when the coach is successful in motivating Caitlin.

Caitlin offers another argument, saying that she has no future in volleyball. Malcolm points out the irrelevance of that consideration, and then he suggests that her real reason for being upset with her coach has to do with which position she wants to play. Caitlin ends the conversation about volleyball with a definitive and somewhat defensive, "I'm quitting and so I'm quitting." Malcolm makes it clear that her final statement forcefully affirms her intention, but it is not an acceptable answer to the question "Why?"

Throughout their conversation Malcolm has been evaluating his friend Caitlin's arguments. This chapter focuses on building argument evaluation skills. It presents a comprehensive and straightforward evaluative process that we can apply in everyday situations, much in the way that Malcolm did in the opening conversation with Caitlin. The process includes four specific tests. An argument must pass all four tests to be considered worthy of acceptance as proof that its conclusion is true or very probably true. Each of these four criteria is rooted in the natural and universal human practice of making arguments and giving reasons. Because critical thinking requires skill at evaluating arguments in real-life contexts, we begin with the expectations and responsibilities associated with giving reasons and making arguments.

7.1 Giving Reasons and Making Arguments

The dynamic conversational practice of explaining to one another the reasons for our claims—that is of making arguments—is part of every human civilization and culture. Every natural human language includes terminology and social conventions for making arguments as well as for evaluating them. But argument making is sensible only because of a set of presumptions we all implicitly rely upon to engage in this practice successfully. These presumptions are operative wherever and whenever people engage in a sincere effort to make arguments to one another regarding a decision about something of serious mutual concern. These presumptions form the basis for the expectations the listener has—and the responsibilities

All of us make arguments when explaining the reasons for our decisions or beliefs.

the argument maker has—when offering reasons to explain why the argument's claim is worthy of acceptance as true or very probably true.

Truthfulness

The practice of argument making rests in part on the presumption upon which so much of human discourse depends, namely that the speaker is telling the truth. In other words, when making arguments we expect that the statements offered as part of any reason are, in fact, true. As a rule, people collaborating with one another to think something through do not intentionally use erroneous information or lie to one another. If a disagreement about the truth of any statement that is part of a reason should arise, then the people involved have two options. They can make an effort to find out if that statement is true, or they can qualify the force with which they assert and maintain any claims in the line of reasoning that relies on that statement. Of course, people do lie on occasion. And so this presumption often goes unfulfilled.

In Chapter 5 we used the familiar term *premise* to refer to a statement, either explicit or implicit, that is a component of a reason. Another way to express the truthfulness presumption is like this: In a conversation that involves making arguments, we expect that *all the premises offered are in fact true.*[1]

The assumption that premises are true provides a reasonable basis for moving to consider whether those premises imply that the conclusion is true or very probably true. But without first really considering the truthfulness of the premises, it becomes only a conceptual exercise, rather than a matter of practical significance, to consider the argument's logical strength. Here are two arguments with true premises.

- Chicago is north of St. Louis. St. Louis is north of New Orleans. Therefore, Chicago is north of New Orleans.

- There are 325 children registered in grades 1 through 6 at the Carver Elementary School. We have tested 40 percent of these children for reading skills. We also have taken a number of physiological measurements of each of those same children. Our data show that there is a strong positive statistical correlation between the size of a child's feet and the child's reading skill level.

Not sure if the premises in the first example are true? No problem. We can check a map or pull up Google Earth and find the relative position of the three cities mentioned. Regarding the second example, one obvious question is whether the measurements mentioned in the third sentence included foot size. If not, we may want to call into question the truthfulness of what the speaker is saying. If the speaker does not have any information about the children's foot sizes, then the speaker's argument falls apart.

Logical Strength

Consider the following example. In this case, *were we to take the premises to be true*, then its conclusion would have to be taken as true as well.

- We have been keeping track of how often the weekday 6:56 AM Caltrain from San Francisco arrives late at the Millbrae station. We conducted three 6-week surveys over the past 12 months. In each survey the weekday train arrived at the Millbrae station late 24 out of 30 times. Therefore, there is an 80 percent probability that the weekday 6:56 AM Caltrain will arrive late at the Millbrae station.

In this next example let's assume that what the speaker is saying about John is true and let's assume that we agree with the speaker about the pattern of behavior that is the precursor to a breakup. If so, then it seems reasonable to conclude that the relationship with John will not endure.

Physical development and reading level—how are they related?

- This is not the first time someone has broken up with me. I recognize the pattern. First the person is too busy to do things together. Then the person doesn't return texts or phone calls. Then the person "forgets" that we had plans. And then comes the "we can still be friends" conversation. John has progressed to the "too busy" phase. As much as I don't want to believe it, my relationship with John is probably heading for a break up.

Assume, for this next example, that there was a comet one night and that the next day the king took ill. So the premises are true. But the reasoning is an unacceptable leap from those observations to a claimed causal relationship. The premises of this argument do not logically justify accepting conclusion as true.

- I saw a strange light streak across the midnight sky last night. And, look, this morning the king became deathly ill. This can only mean that the strange light in the night sky caused our king's sickness.

When someone offers an argument, the speaker's reason is supposed to be the logical basis for the speaker's claim. The point of giving reasons for our claims is that the reasons support the claims. The second presupposition of the practice of argument making is that the speaker's reason, if true, is the logical basis for the speaker's claim. Notice that this is hypothetical. *Were we to assume that the reason a person gives for his or her claim is true*, that assumption would then imply that the person's claim is probably or necessarily true as well. In the language of logic, this presupposition is expressed this way: The assumed truth of the premises of an argument justifies or implies that the conclusion of the argument also be taken as true.

> Most people would sooner die than think; in fact, they do so.
>
> Bertrand Russell, Author,
> Mathematician, & Philosopher[2]

Relevance

It happens that a conclusion might be true *independent of* whether the premises are true or whether the premises logically support the conclusion; because this is so, when we make arguments we also presume that the truth of the reason is *relevant* to the claim. This presumption might be called the "So What?" presumption. Consider this

---

THINKING CRITICALLY

It's All Thanks to the Ionians!

Where did our persistent practice of trying to resolve problems by making arguments and giving reasons originate? Today the practical "pro-and-con" approach is applied to problems of every kind by people throughout the globe. Human beings have tried other ways of deciding what to believe during the long history of civilization, like accepting as true whatever the king, high priest, or soothsayer declared. Today in many places around the world people are less inclined to accept an authority figure's declarations on blind faith. The public give-and-take of making arguments and offering reasons to try to solve practical problems, while not unknown in more ancient times, is a three-thousand-year-old cultural legacy of the Ionians. Locate and watch the fascinating video "The Way We Are," for an entertaining historical account of the rise and the impact of this approach to resolving practical problems. Search for episode 1 of the series *The Day the Universe Changed* hosted by James Burke.

Questions: How would we decide, individually or as a community, what to believe or what to do if we did not have the practice of reason giving and argument making? Would we go back to the servile trust of our rulers? Or would we perhaps try to invent some other method for discovering truth? And, now, in the twenty-first century, given all that we know about using science to understand, explain, predict and control so many things, why do so many of us still rely on non-scientific or even anti-scientific sources for our beliefs?

Anyone ever say something circular like this to you at school, home, or work?

example, where the premises are true and the conclusion is true, but the reason is not relevant to the claim.

- To many around the world, the Statue of Liberty symbolizes the welcome our nation extends to all freedom-loving people. So, as the great Yogi Berra says, "You can observe a lot just by watching."

This argument is so odd that it would get a squawk out of the Aflac duck. The reason given has no relevance to the truth of the claim. Their only connection is that Yogi Berra happened to have been a player for the New York Yankees, and the Statue of Liberty happens to be in New York. That happenstance is not sufficient to say that the one is relevant to the other. If anyone were to seriously present this reason as the basis for the truth of the conclusion we would say, "So what? That's not relevant!" And this reveals our third presupposition: *the listener takes the reason given by the speaker to be relevant in believing the speaker's claim.*

There is no point to giving reasons if the listener is not going to rely on those reasons in deciding what to believe with regard to the claim. Recall that in our opening example, Caitlin changed her story about why she wanted to quit the volleyball team. At first she talked about how the coach's yelling and berating players was her issue. But then she gave a different reason, saying that she was going to quit because she did not anticipate a future as a professional volleyball player. Malcolm challenged her on that, noting that it was not even relevant, in his view. A future in professional volleyball was never her reason for joining the college team, and the absence of that opportunity is not relevant to why Caitlin now wants to quit the team. Everyone, including Caitlin, may believe that Caitlin wants to quit the volleyball team. But nobody, not even Caitlin, believes that whether or not she has a future in professional volleyball has anything to do with her wanting to quit at this point in time.

Non-Circularity

Our fourth precondition when we give reasons for our claims is that *the claim must not be part of the basis for believing in the truth of the reason.* Argument making in real life is essentially a one-way street: The reasons are used to establish the acceptability of the claim. But we do not use the claim to explain the reason. We use the premises of the argument to support the conclusion, not the conclusion to support the premises. In other words, there is directionality to argument making. The flow of reasoning is from reason toward claim, not the other way around. All the examples of mapped arguments in Chapter 5 show this, because in mapping arguments we used the arrow convention to display the intended directionality of the argument maker's reasoning.

In the Dilbert's cartoon strip the boss criticizes Dilbert's presentation for being full of technical words and way too long. We naturally think that the boss came to those conclusions about the presentation by having seen it and evaluated it. But no. The boss then turns around and uses those same two claims as his reasons for not seeing or evaluating the presentation. It makes no sense to give a reason as the basis for one's claim and then to use that claim as the basis for one's reason. In a comic strip, circular reasoning is funny, and in real life it can be infuriating.

7.2 The Four Tests for Evaluating Arguments

The four presumptions about argument making as an interpersonal human activity form the bases for the four evaluative criteria applicable to all arguments. In other words, it would be reasonable to accept a person's argument if it met all four of the conditions implied by those presumptions. Given a reason offered in support of a claim, these are the four conditions that must be met:

1. To the best of our knowledge and understanding, the *reason is true.*

2. The *logical relationship* between the reason and claim is such that the reason implies, entails, strongly warrants or strongly supports the claim, such that the claim must be true or very probably true if the reason is assumed to be true.

3. The *relevance* of the reason to the claim is such that the truth of the claim actually depends on the truth of the reason.

4. The *flow of the reasoning* is such that truth of reason must not depend on the truth of the claim.

An argument that satisfies all four conditions is worthy of our acceptance as a proof that its claim is true or very probably true. We will apply the adjectives *good* and

Like a commuter train moving only in one direction and stopping at each local station along the track, the four tests must be applied in a specific order.

worthy to those arguments. A **good argument** or a **worthy argument** is an argument that merits being accepted as a proof that its conclusion is true or very probably true. The four conditions listed to define four tests to apply when evaluating arguments are to be applied in the order given. As soon as an argument fails to meet one of the four, it is no longer eligible to be considered a good or worthy argument. Let's see how to apply each of these four to determine whether or not an argument is worthy of acceptance.

Test #1: Truthfulness of the Premises

In everyday situations, the truth or falsity of premises is our first concern. If one or more of the premises of an argument is not true, then, for all practical purposes, there is little point in moving forward to evaluate other aspects of the argument. Our first job is to get our information straight. The critical thinking habits of truth-seeking and inquisitiveness demand that we courageously endeavor to learn what we can before moving forward with claims and arguments based on incomplete knowledge.

The Test of the Truthfulness of the Premises is a favorite in police dramas. We have all seen the scene in which detectives interrogate someone who gives a lame alibi like this one: "My friends and I were at a movie the night the crime took place." The detectives check the story and discover it is a lie. Having

exposed his lack of truthfulness, the detectives no longer accept the person's alibi and may even make the liar their prime suspect.

Test #2: Logical Strength

One practical way to apply the Test for Logical Strength is to challenge yourself to imagine a situation, if possible, in which all the premises of an argument are true, but the conclusion is false. If there is no possible scenario in which all the premises of an argument can be true while at the same time its conclusion is false, or if such a scenario is extremely improbable, then the argument passes the Test of Logical Strength.[3] However, to the extent that such a scenario is possible, plausible, likely, or actually true, the argument fails this test.[4] If there is a possible scenario, but it is remote and implausible, perhaps as unlikely as 1 chance in 20 or 1 chance in a 1,000, then we can maintain a comparable degree of confidence in the argument's logical strength. Logicians call an argument with true premises that has also passed the Test of Logical Strength a **sound argument**.[5] *Sound* is used here in the sense of "healthy," meaning that such an argument ordinarily is rather robust and deserves our attention as we deliberate what to do or what to believe.

What if there is more than one independent reason given to support a claim? Does discovering that one reason has a false premise make the claim unacceptable? Consider this example; here a claim is supported by two reasons, which the speaker wants the listener to take as independent considerations.

- "I'm not an alcoholic. First of all, I only drink beer. And, second, I've never been drunk in my life."

Map #1 shows the two reasons as independently supporting the claim.

Suppose we discover that the speaker is telling the truth when he says that he only drinks beer. However, the implicit but unspoken premise ("Someone who only drinks beer

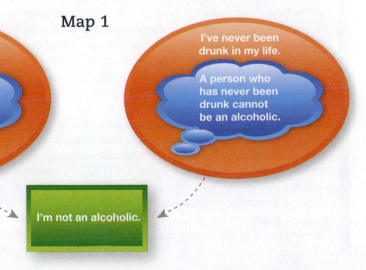

Map 1

I only drink beer.

Someone who only drinks beer cannot be an alcoholic.

I've never been drunk in my life.

A person who has never been drunk cannot be an alcoholic.

I'm not an alcoholic.

cannot be an alcoholic") is false. So, the first argument fails the Test of the Truthfulness of the Premises. Suppose we then discover that the speaker is also being truthful when he says that he has never been drunk in his life. This, along with the generally accepted truth of the implicit, but unspoken, premise "A person who has never been drunk cannot be an alcoholic," indicates that his second argument passes the Test of Truthfulness of the Premises.

The Test of Logical Strength comes next, and the second argument also passes that test. It is difficult to imagine a case where a person who has never been drunk is an alcoholic, although it is not impossible to imagine such a case. So, it would seem reasonable to accept that our speaker is not an alcoholic, even though one of his reasons (that he only drinks beer) was poor. His second argument, based on the other reason (he has never been drunk in his life), which is independent of the first, was sound.

People often provide multiple independent reasons for a given claim and some of those reasons may turn out to be false. One may be inclined to dismiss the claim itself, having heard the speaker present one unsound argument.

Dismissing an otherwise-worthy claim simply because one or more of the arguments made on its behalf contains false reasons is one of the most common human reasoning errors. Before determining that a claim should be rejected, a strong critical thinker would first need to find problems with the soundness of *all* the arguments being advanced.

Because there are so many important varieties of arguments, which require special attention when testing for logical strength, we will suspend this discussion at this point but return to it again in the coming chapters. We will devote Chapters 8 and 9 to the evaluation of inferences. And then later we will look more closely at inferences based on pattern recognition, ideological reasoning, and empirical reasoning. For the moment, let's complete our review of the four basic tests of an argument's worthiness to be accepted.

Test #3: Relevance

The Test of Relevance requires making a reasoned judgment that the truth of the conclusion *depends upon* the truth of the reason given. If an argument passes the first two

---

THINKING CRITICALLY

Logical Strength and *The Name of the Rose*

Consider an example from Umberto Eco's renowned play *The Name of the Rose.* The feature film by the same name stars Sean Connery, Christian Slater, and F. Murray Abraham. Early in the story the abbot in charge of a fourteenth-century monastery comes to a visiting Franciscan scholar-detective, played by Sean Connery, to explain why he believes that a recent death was caused by the devil. The abbot's attribution of the cause of death to a supernatural intervention occurs about 9 minutes and 15 seconds into the film version.

Using your critical thinking problem solving skills, Google search and locate the play or the video, find the relevant scene, and then consider carefully the abbot's argument. The abbot begins by describing how the monks were shocked and terrified when they discovered the body of their dead brother after a violent hailstorm. The abbot's argument is only a few lines. Transcribe it so that you can have the language in front of you. Map it and then evaluate it for logical strength by asking yourself if you can think of how the monk might have died other than at the hand of the devil given what little other information you have at that point in the story. Is there a set of circumstances such that all the premises of the abbot's argument could remain true but the claim still be false? How plausible or implausible are those circumstances? For example, if someone were to answer, "Yes, an alien from another galaxy could have transported into the closed room and killed the monk," we probably would regard that as highly implausible.

As you watch the film, new information is presented. But the key piece of information is supplied visually, not verbally.

The director gives us a shot looking up a steep ravine at the monastery, which wraps around the crest of the hills above the ravine. There appear to be two towers. Sean Connery's character and the viewer can use that information to show the logical flaw in the abbot's argument about the death being caused by the devil. Connery as he completes his alternative explanation to his young apprentice, played by Christian Slater, says that there's no need of the devil to explain this death. The death was from far more natural causes. Go 6 minutes and 29 seconds further into the movie and view this short scene. Transcribe Connery's alternative explanation. Map his argument and evaluate it for logical strength.

What is Connery's argument for the claim that there is no need for the devil?

tests, then The Test of Relevance is the next one to apply. Recall that the presumption we are seeking to fulfill is that the author's reason is, in fact, the basis for believing the claim. And the listener must judge if accepting the claim as true depends on support derived from that reason. For example, the following example passes the Test of Relevance.

- A study from the Harvard Center of Risk Analysis estimates that cell phone use while driving contributes to 6 percent of crashes, which equates to 636,000 crashes, 330,000 injuries, 12,000 serious injuries, and 2,600 deaths each year. The study also put the annual financial toll of cell phone–related crashes at $43 billion. The research investigated whether or not a hands-free device was less dangerous. The statistical evidence suggests not. It appears from the data that the fact that the driver was distracted by the conversation was a greater factor than was the type of cell phone technology, hands-free or not, that was being used. The researchers concluded that using cell phone technology of any kind while driving was associated with a greater risk of automobile accidents.[6]

By contrast, the next argument fails the Test of Relevance.

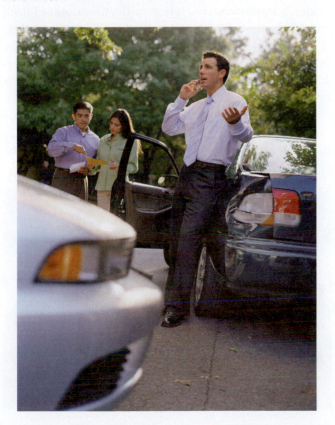

Is it reasonable or ethical for another driver to expose you to greater risk just so he or she can text a friend?

So, how does a person connect San Francisco's Golden Gate Park with a trip to the Botoli Garden in Florence, Italy? Find out about the influence that unreflective associational thinking has on human decision making in Chapter 10.

- Yeah, I'm looking forward to visiting Italy, you know, Old Europe. Why is too obvious. See, I've been working part-time at the Golden Gate Park in San Francisco. It's incredible there. Beautiful, open, free. There's this one garden there that kind of reminds me of pictures I've seen of Italy. I love being outside in the spring, the flowers and the fresh air, the smell of fresh-cut grass. And all that makes me think how great it would be to just live slow and relaxed, like they do in Europe, taking life as it comes. You know what I mean?

That the research on car accidents and cell phone usage is relevant to the conclusion in the first example is obvious in the first example. The connection between visiting Italy and working part-time in Golden Gate Park in the second example seems to be tenuous at best, more based on the person's free association of ideas than on any actual evidence. Even if the speaker imagines a connection, the listener can judge that the reason given, even if true, is not a basis for believing that the speaker wants to visit Italy. In fact, if the speaker had simply said, "I want to visit Italy," that might have been more credible than his having come up with the far-fetched and irrelevant dissertation about the glories of a part-time job in a city park—even if it is one of the greatest public parks in this nation.

Applying the Test of Relevance is substantially easier for people with knowledge and experience appropriate to the context and issues under discussion. For example, U.S. laws prohibiting using gender as the basis for workplace promotions express American society's judgment that a person's gender is not a relevant consideration when deciding whether the person merits a promotion. In another country with a different set of cultural mores, gender-based promotion decisions might be considered both legal and reasonable. The Test of Relevance is important because people often make the argument that they should be excused from

THINKING CRITICALLY

Pythagoras and the Shape of Immortal Perfection

Pythagoras, the controversial Greek metaphysician (570 to ca. 490 BCE) and his followers, the Pythagoreans, have had a significant influence on Western thinking. They were among the first to suggest that human beings possessed immortal souls, that the heavens moved with harmonious mathematical precision, and that unchanging stability was a characteristic of divine perfection. The Pythagoreans took a special interest in mathematical relationships (e.g., the Pythagorean Theorem) and often attributed moral characteristics to them. They noted that certain two-dimensional shapes could be converted into three-dimensional solids: a circle into a sphere, a triangle with three equal sides into a three-sided pyramid, a square into a box. Noting these relationships, the Pythagoreans considered the circle, triangle, and square to be "Perfect" shapes. And, because perfection was evident in the universe, it made sense to them to infer that the only possible source of such perfection had to be divine. Hence what Carl Sagan called the "God-Hypothesis" in the first episode of the original 1980 *Cosmos* series. Today we might take issue with a leap from geometric observations to theology. We would question the relevance of the one to the other. Likewise, we might question the leap from "unchanging" to "incorruptible" to "immortal" and on to

"perfect." We would perhaps challenge an unspoken assumption by asking, "Why would the attribute of being unchanging be considered relevant to the concept of perfection?" What do you think? Might there be reason to think that adaptability is a superior quality?

For more on this extremely influential and fascinating, even if illogical, progression of ideas from geometric shapes to divine perfection, search, locate and watch the episode 1 of the original 1980 *Cosmos* where Carl Sagan is talking about the influence of the ancient Greek philosophers on modern thinking. (The 2014 Neil deGrasse Tyson FOX Network remake of *Cosmos* is terrific too. We reference it in other chapters.)

responsibility for certain actions. However, as a people, having heard these arguments before, we have come to the judgment that certain reasons are not going to be accepted as relevant. For example:

- Claiming that one was following the direct orders of one's superior is not a relevant defense against charges of war crimes.

- Claiming that one's judgment was impaired by drugs or alcohol is not a relevant defense against charges of vehicular manslaughter resulting from driving while under the influence.

- Claiming that one must protect his or her GPA because one plans to become a doctor is not a relevant defense against charges of academic dishonesty in any course, including general education elective courses.

Test #4: Non-Circularity

The fourth and final test of an argument's acceptability is the Test of Non-Circularity. This test requires that a claim is not being relied upon either implicitly or explicitly as part of a chain of reasoning used to support its own reason. If such a chain looping back on itself is found, then the argument maker is reasoning in a circle. An argument is like a river that flows in one direction, from reasons and

evidence toward the conclusion. A river cannot feed itself and still be described as a river; rather, it becomes a stagnant moat. So it is with good arguments: Claims cannot be the bases for their own reasons. If they were, then the reasoning would simply be stagnant and self-justifying in the most unflattering sense.

The final argument Caitlin made about quitting the volleyball team was "I'm quitting and therefore I'm quitting." Here the circle is so tight that the reason and the

Circular reasoning, like a noxious moat around a castle, is stagnant thinking.

Map 2

I'm quitting

I'm quitting

Map 3

We can make this marriage work.

We're talking through our problems.

We still care for each other.

claim are identical. The map of her circular argument would look something like Map 2.

We can interpret this way of speaking as a way of emphasizing one's claim, but not as a way of proving one's claim. It is like saying "I'm quitting" real loud. But volume is not proof.

Reasoning in a circle results most frequently from the use of multiple arguments in combination with each other. At times people lose track of the reasons for their beliefs, forgetting, for example, that their basis for believing one idea, X, was because they accepted another idea, Y, and that their reason for accepting Y had been their belief in X. The result is that the person has high confidence, although misplaced, in both ideas. However, because their support for X is Y and their support for Y is X, the reasonable thing would be to have no confidence in either. For example, consider the pair of arguments in this passage:

• I'm sure we can make this marriage work. That's why we're talking through our problems, which shows that we still care for each other. And that's why I'm sure we can make this marriage work.

The speaker's reason for the claim that the marriage is salvageable is the belief that both parties still care for each other. And the basis for believing that goes back to the idea that the marriage can be saved. If we were to map

these arguments, it would look like Map 3. This reasoning is as fragile as a house of cards; touch it in the least with an analytical finger and it collapses upon itself.

Argument Making Contexts

There is nothing about argument making that demands that the format be a debate. There is nothing about argument making that requires that it be an adversarial confrontation either. In fact, it does a great disservice to decision making and collaborative effort to imagine the process must be oppositional or confrontational. In an adversarial context, it is too easy to forgo truth-seeking in the false belief that argument making is simply the search for facts that support one's preconceptions. Too often, the courageous desire for best knowledge is trumped by the competitive need to vanquish the opposition. In that case, the honest pursuit of reasons and evidence, wherever they may lead, even if the reasons and evidence go against one's preconceptions or interests, is abandoned because intellectual honesty and integrity are not always suitable virtues for warriors who must bring home the victory for their side. Just like winning a legal action does not guarantee that justice has been done, winning an argument does not guarantee that we have made the best decision or that we have discovered the truth. Taking a page from the best practices of scientists and criminal investigators, optimal decision

Four Tests of an Argument's Worthiness		
Test Name	**Order of Application**	**Test Condition**
Test of Truthfulness of the Premises	First	The reason is true in each of its premises, explicit and implicit.
Test of Logical Strength	Second	If the reason were true, it would imply, entail, strongly warrant, or strongly support the conclusion making the conclusion (claim) true or very probably true.
Test of Relevance	Third	The truth of the claim depends on the truth of the reason.
Test of Non-Circularity	Fourth	The truth of the reason does not depend on the truth of the claim.

Evaluative Adjectives for Arguments and Their Elements		
PREMISES	POSITIVE	True, Possible, Probable, Verifiable, Believable, Precise, Clear, Accurate, Factual, etc.
	NEGATIVE	False, Improbable, Self-Contradictory, Fanciful, Fabricated, Vague, Ambiguous, Unknowable, etc.
REASONS	POSITIVE	Certain, True, Probable, Verifiable, Relevant, Wise, Sensible, Well-Applied, Plausible, Believable, etc.
	NEGATIVE	False, Irrelevant, Improbable, Self-Contradictory, Poorly Applied, Foolish, Irrational, Fanciful, Unknowable, Vague, Equivocal, Ill-Conceived, etc.
CLAIMS/ CONCLUSIONS	POSITIVE	Well-Documented, Strongly Supported, Well-Argued, Certain, True, Reasonable, Plausible, Probable, etc.
	NEGATIVE	Improbable, Poorly Supported, Unfounded, Self-Contradictory, Uncertain, False, Biased, Preposterous, Implausible, etc.
ARGUMENTS	POSITIVE	Worthy, Good, Acceptable, Sound, Valid, Warranted, Logical, Strong, Persuasive, Reasonable, etc.
	NEGATIVE	Unworthy, Poor, Unacceptable, Unsound, Fallacious, Illogical, Incomplete, Unreasonable, Bad, Circular, etc.

making and problem solving are more likely to occur when we are fully invested, focused, and yet objective about our argument making.

Good arguments—subtle and yet effective as solid proofs that their claims are worthy of being accepted as true—can be expressed in so many ways that listing them all may be impossible. In natural language contexts argument making can take the form of a personable and convivial conversation between friends as they explore options and consider ideas. Good argument making can occur in front of juries and judges in the push and pull of a legal dispute. Managers seeking budget approvals present arguments for more funding. Fundraisers seeking donations offer reasons that tug at our minds and our hearts for why we should contribute to their charities. Researchers present complex and detailed arguments when reporting their findings in professional journals. Good argument making can be embedded in warnings, ironic commentary, allegorical dramas, one-line counterexamples, recommendations, policy statement preambles, public addresses, conversations, group meetings, negotiations, comic monologues, serious pro-and-con debates, meandering reflections, and even the lyrics of songs.[7]

The vocabulary we use to evaluate arguments must be as flexible as our understanding of the wide variety of contexts within which argument making can be found. A conversation with a colleague about an impending decision can be helpful, even if we would not think about calling it *valid*, or *persuasive*. Natural language offers such richness in its evaluative repertoire that it seems wise, at least at this early point, not to close our options by prematurely stipulating a set of evaluative categories. Thus, with the understanding that the terms listed in the table "Evaluative Adjectives for Arguments and Their Elements" are not meant to be interpreted rigidly or in some special technical way, let us simply go forward with our evaluation of arguments using common language. The table offers suggestions regarding the range of evaluative adjectives that might reasonably be applied when evaluating the different elements of major concern, data, warrants, claims, and arguments.

7.3 Common Reasoning Errors

Humans learn from their mistakes. We can capitalize on that truism to strengthen our skill in evaluating arguments by studying those errors of reasoning that have over the centuries earned themselves a reputation as alluringly deceptive and misleading. As a group they are called "fallacies." **Fallacies** are deceptive arguments that appear logical and seem at times to be persuasive, but, upon closer analysis, fail to demonstrate their conclusions. Many types of fallacies have their own name, as we shall see.

Learning to recognize common fallacies and learning how to explain in ordinary, non-technical terms the mistaken reasoning they contain is a great aid to evaluating arguments. The seven fallacies of relevance described in this chapter are types of arguments that will fail the Test of Relevance. In Chapters 8 and 9, to help with the application of the Test of Logical Strength, we will expand the list of fallacies to include several more.[8] Skill in recognizing when someone is making a fallacious argument is a strong defense against being misled about what to believe or what to do.

Fallacies of Relevance

Like alerts warning of bad weather, for centuries logicians have supplied lists of the kinds of deceptive arguments that tend to mislead people.[9] When it comes to being deceived by the rhetoric of gifted speakers, eloquent writers, or clever advertisements, many of us are no wiser or more sophisticated than people were in Aristotle's time. Yet in our effort to make an honest argument to another person about what to believe or what to do, we are asking that person to accept the truth of the claim *because of the reason given*. This expectation of relevance at times goes unfilled. Instead we provide a reason that is not relevant. Creative questioning is a powerful tool for uncovering the false assumptions that lie at the core of fallacies of relevance. Whatever the specific application of the question, the fundamental issue is "What does that reason actually have to do with that claim?" From this fundamental concern we can derive a number of more specific queries.

It is impossible to list all the ways that the reason given might be irrelevant to the claim being made. There are too many ways to be irrelevant. Some arguments appeal to tradition, others, particularly in marketing, try to sell us something simply because it is new. Some use emotions such as fear to move us to accept the claim being made. Others try flattery, praise, trust, or affection to move us to accept a claim that we otherwise would not believe. Some challenge our ability to quickly come up with an alternative. Or they toss in an irrelevant cliché. Others barrage us with true but irrelevant statements anticipating we will accept the conclusion sooner or later out of sheer mental fatigue.

- Nice idea, but it's not for us. We don't change horses in midstream.

- Try the mushroom, jalapeño, mango margarita. It's new!

- It would be a grave mistake to think that there is no Hell. In fact, an eternal error.

- Hey, trust me. Would I lie to you, baby?

- Absolutely she was the one who told that lie about you. Who else would have done that?

Many kinds of irrelevant appeal fallacies are so notorious that they have earned their own name. The name can be helpful to remembering the type of mistaken assumption being made.

APPEALS TO IGNORANCE   It is false to assume that the mere absence of a reason for (or against) an idea should itself count as a reason against (or for) the idea. Consider these examples:

- We know we have a corporate spy someplace in the organization, probably on the management team itself. There is no evidence that it is Francesca. In fact, she's too clean, if you know what I mean. We should fire Francesca; she's got to be the spy.

- Someone here took my computer and I need it back. Who was it, John? Was it you? No, you say. Well prove it! Aha, you have no proof to offer. Well then, John, it was you. And I want it back now!

- Impressionism, and especially French Impressionism, is the best form of art. You don't believe me? Then name some other form that has been proven to be more beautiful. You can't, can you? So, I'm right.

APPEALS TO THE MOB   It is false to assume that because a large group of people believes something or does something that their opinion or their behavior is necessarily correct or appropriate. Here are two examples of the Fallacy of Appeal to the Mob, also known as the *Bandwagon Fallacy*. This seems like such an obvious mistake that it may be hard to imagine that people can be so gullible as to think

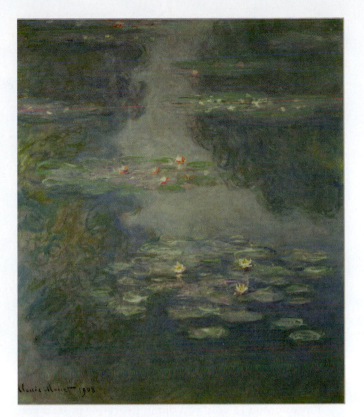

If you cannot name a superior art form, does that imply that French Impressionism is the best art form?

something is true just because everyone believes it. That is, right up until you remember the power that mythology and superstition still have in this world.

- Everyone knows that a black quarterback will not be able to lead an all-white team. So we will not put Doug Williams at the quarterback position.[10]

- All the kids at school are getting tattoos. Every one of my friends has one, and some have two. I see adult men and women with tattoos. So, I'm thinking that it's about time that I get a tattoo.

- A lot of people like Michigan State to win the Big 10 Championship this year. So I guess I've got to go with the Spartans as my pick too.

- Everyone believes Martha might be practicing witchcraft, so be careful how you act when she's around.

APPEALS TO EMOTION   It is false to assume that our initial emotional response to an idea, event, story, person, image, or proposal is necessarily the best guide for forming reflective fair-minded judgments. Chapter 10 discusses this in greater detail, because the relationship between our emotional responses and our decisions about what to believe and what to do are complex. Because gut reaction and reasoned reflection are both real factors in human decision making, strong critical thinkers learn to draw on both of those resources. But, at times, people offer fallacious arguments that provide nothing more by way of a reason than an appeal to one's unreflective emotional response. Here are some examples of the Appeal to Emotion fallacy, which tends to rely on emotionally loaded words and expressions.

- I love you like the son I never had, and so I believe you. No, I must believe you. Love leaves no other option.

- He's a lousy, rotten terrorist. One of those people. So, there's no question but that he deserves to die.

- Watch out—the political right is populated by a dangerous pack of hate-mongering jackals. They will destroy this nation because they have no respect for the truth or common decency. You can't believe anything they say.

- Watch out—the political left is a goose-stepping gaggle of dangerous tax-and-spend activists. They will destroy this nation with their bloated, ineffective social programs that we hardworking taxpayers can't afford. You can't believe anything they say.

- I know you have your heart set on going to Stanford; it's something you talked about since you were in the ninth grade. You kept up your grades, aced the SATs and did everything you could to be admitted. And, I'm so proud of you, you did it. Everyone is. And you know what, I don't care what it takes or what the family has to do, we'll mortgage the house, get another

job, anything. But somehow, some way, whatever it takes and whatever the consequences for me or for your younger brothers and sisters, we are going to find the money so you can go to Stanford. I've made up my mind. That's what we'll do!

AD HOMINEM ATTACKS   It is false to assume that because the person making the argument is deficient in some real or imagined way, the person's argument, work product, or views should not be accepted on their own merits. *Ad hominem* is Latin for "against the person" and it expresses the error this fallacy makes, which is to claim that a person's ideas must be tainted because the person has some vice or flaw. The opposite would be equally fallacious, which is to assume that because the person making the argument is virtuous the argument must be good, too. Strong critical thinking no more obliges us to reject every argument a convicted felon makes than to accept every argument the Dalai Lama might make. Arguments are to be judged on their own merits, not on the merits of their producers. The *Ad hominem* fallacy is a favorite verbal assault weapon in the arsenal of talk-radio hosts.

- I don't trust you because of what you did last week at the party. Don't bother trying to explain yourself. As far as I'm concerned, anything you say is a lie.

THINKING CRITICALLY

Is Competitive Cheerleading a Sport?

Many activities that are recognized as sports include artistic and musical components—for example, synchronized swimming and figure skating. With hundreds of thousands of junior high school, high school, and college students participating in cheerleading, why is cheerleading, at least in its competitive format, not a recognized varsity sport? Cheerleading is as physically demanding as many varsity sports (more than some, such as golf) and certainly every bit as dangerous as football and hockey in terms of the number of serious injuries each year. Is it tradition, gender politics, pressure by the companies that make money off of cheerleading competitions, what?

Research the arguments for and against recognizing cheerleading as a high school and college sport. Map and evaluate the arguments on both sides of this issue. Be on the lookout for the fallacies discussed in this section, you should spot a few. You might begin with

"Cheerleading: Controversy and Competition" from the ESPN series, *Outside the Lines.* Search "cheerleading as a sport debate" for multiple resources and references.

- The guy's a lazy, rich moron, and an egomaniac. He'll never be elected. So why are you bothering to try to understand his proposals on tax reform and immigration? They have to be total garbage.

- I'll grant you that President's nominee is a widely respected Harvard educated physician. And that he is known for his many years of working to improve medical services for the poor. But a few years ago he once tweeted that hand guns were an urban health hazard. So as far as I'm concerned, that comment alone shows he is not qualified to be Surgeon General.

The Claim Might Still Be True!

Dismissing an otherwise-worthy claim simply because one or more of the arguments made on its behalf contains false reasons is one of the most common human reasoning errors.

- The Senator was spotted drunk in a Bangkok bordello. There are pictures on the Web already. So we can't believe anything he says about environmental problems or clean energy solutions.

- You have nothing of value to contribute to this conversation about minority race relations. You're not black, Latino, Asian, Native American, or anything. You're white.

- I'm sorry, but I don't find his income and expense projections credible. I don't see how he could have done those numbers correctly. After all, we know he's looking for another job. He has no company loyalty.

STRAW MAN FALLACY This fallacy relies on the false assumption that, by refuting a weaker argument among several independent reasons given in support of a claim, one has successfully refuted all the reasons for that claim. For example:

- Look, we can't approve your request for additional advertising funds. You said that one of the four marketing options you were reviewing was Web page design. But we have a policy not to support any further Web-based development.

- You said that legalizing pot was a good idea, because then pot could be regulated for quality and taxed. And you said it would permit us to shift law enforcement resources toward preventing other more harmful criminal behaviors. But I'm opposed to new taxes of any kind. So, I cannot agree with you about legalizing pot.

A variation on the theme, also called the Straw Man Fallacy, is the pernicious practice of attributing to the opposition an argument that is not theirs, and then demolishing that argument. The misattribution may be mistaken, or worse, intentional. From this the person committing the fallacy misleadingly then argues that he or she has destroyed the opposition's position entirely. Besides being intellectually dishonest and inconsistent with the critical thinking virtue of truth-seeking, this practice violates the values of objectivity and fair-mindedness.

Adopting the strategy of trying to make an idiot out of your opposition can be risky. To use straw men and misrepresentations when presenting the opposition's arguments can lead one's listeners, and at times one's self, to the

	Use Creative Questioning to Challenge the Relevance of Reason to Claim	
	Here are six examples of arguments we might hear in everyday situations. In every case the reason given is not relevant to the claim asserted. By asking "What does the reason actually have to do with the claim?" we can focus the issue of relevance in each case.	
1	Claudia, a beautiful model for Victoria's Secret, endorses Brand XYZ motor oil. So, Brand XYZ motor oil is an excellent product.	What about being a successful lingerie model makes one an expert on motor oil?
2	Students are always saying how much they enjoy Professor Smith's classes. She's really popular. So, Professor Smith must do an excellent job getting her students to learn the material.	What about being popular implies that a professor is effective in getting students to learn? What if the professor was just an easy grader or funny or likable, but actually a lousy teacher?
3	I can't think of any practical alternatives to gasoline as a vehicle fuel. So, there is no practical alternative automotive fuel.	Are the limits of the possibilities for alternative fuels to be equated with the limits of my imagination?
4	Yesterday in class when we were working on our project, you didn't say a word. So, you must not know anything about the topic.	Could there not have been many reasons, other than ignorance of the topic, why a person does not speak up during group project time in class?
5	If we look around us, we see that people everywhere value human life. So, it is right that we should defend this value over all others.	Why does the fact that many people value something make it imperative that it be regarded as the highest of all possible values? Would we say the same for other things people everywhere value, such as a true friend, a respectful and appreciative supervisor, or satisfying dinner followed by delightful entertainment and a good night's sleep?
6	We chose to go to the moon not because it is easy, but because it is hard.	Just because something is difficult, should we now choose to do that thing? Yes it was difficult, but that was not the basis for our decision to choose to go to the moon.

mistaken belief that there is little or no merit to the opposition's view. In the vicious health care reform debates during the summer of 2009, those opposed to "death panels" demonized the proposed legislation for a provision that, as it turned out, was already part of existing Medicare law. The actual provision to which they objected provided for reimbursement to health care providers if patients voluntarily sought end-of-life counseling about such matters as living wills, power of attorney, do not resuscitate (DNR) orders, or hospice care. When the dust settled, even some who had raised the specter of government death panels backed away from that overly dramatic straw man criticism. Others, however, continued to believe wrongly that the proposed legislation would mandate euthanasia.

Underestimating one's opponent in a debate or dispute can backfire. One reason is that listeners can be alienated when they realize that we have not been fair or objective. A second reason is that we may become overconfident. Strong critical thinkers try not to mislead themselves. They school themselves to follow the political adage, "Never believe your own press releases." In so doing, strong critical thinkers try not to confuse defeating

a straw man argument with giving due consideration to the opposition's array of worthy arguments.

PLAYING WITH WORDS FALLACY Vagueness and ambiguity can be problematic in certain contexts. The Playing with Words Fallacy exploits problematic vagueness, problematic ambiguity, donkey cart expressions, stereotyping, and slanted language in attempting to support a claim. Because Playing with Words Fallacies are so varied and so vexing, we devoted Chapter 4 to learning how to apply our critical thinking skills to resolve those problems. Here are three more quick examples of arguments that are fallacious because they exploit problematic uses of key terminology.

- Everyone who is in prison can still be free, for true freedom is the knowledge of one's situation. The more one knows about one's self, the more one is truly free.
- I'm selfish, you're selfish. When you really look at it, everybody tries to meet their own needs. So, we are wrong to be so harsh on a guy just because he spends all his money on nice clothes and fine food for

THINKING CRITICALLY

Bluster, Bark, Badger, and Whine

Strong critical thinkers lament the incivility, degradation, and degeneration of today's political discussions in the media. Too often the best-known political commentators engage in fallacious argumentation. They can be recognized by their reckless and irresponsible rhetorical tactics: Instead of carefully presenting the best arguments for both sides of an important issue, these commentators stridently, if not also irrationally, defend one side and verbally assault the other. Their opinions are laced with ridicule and *ad hominem* attacks. They dismiss out of hand any evidentiary facts, which the opposition might present, and often they insist their own untrue "facts" instead. They opine loudly. Redefine terminology. Interrupt often. They rudely talk over any representative of the other side who might be present. They whine about being victimized by the other side and yet they complain that the other side whines about being victimized. They scoff at divergent opinions. And they disrespect anyone and everyone who disagrees. To see examples of these abusive and misleading tactics in action Google "Top 10 political commentators." If you wish to insert adjectives like "crazy," "opinionated" or "hated" in front of "political," of course, you may.

In episode 203 (February 18, 2011) of *Real Time*, the political commentator Bill Maher takes on Liberals for their wishy-washy relativism in regard to the rights of women in the Middle East. Search "Episode 203 Real Time Bill Maher."

Watch his commentary after the "New Rules" segment that comes toward the end. As a challenge exercise, map and evaluate Maher's arguments. While you have episode 203 cued up, look for elements of bluster, badger, interrupt, whine, and scoff in that episode. One of the biggest risks to effectively analyzing and evaluating the strength of the other side's perspectives is to regard those who disagree as either "evil" or "stupid." Does Bill Maher or any of his guests in Episode 203 make this mistake? State your argument by providing reasons and evidence.

himself while letting his children run around hungry and in rags.

- We cannot know that others experience the world as we do. To truly know is to be inside the minds of others. And that is simply not possible.

MISUSE OF AUTHORITY FALLACY   One version of the Misuse of Authority Fallacy relies on the false assumption that if a powerful or popular person makes a claim, then the claim must be true. In addition to this error, there are other ways that expertise can be misrepresented and misused. We talked about the many characteristics of an authority whose word should, in all probability, be accepted. Because reliance on the word of another is such an important part of how people decide what to do or what to believe, critical thinkers are alert to the fallacies of Misuse of Authority. Here are a couple more quick examples:

- When asked why the curriculum had been changed, the Superintendent of Schools replied that the city's Chamber of Commerce had advised that the students in the Junior High School would be educationally better served if all teachers used more class time to prepare students to take standardized math tests and less time on American History, Creative Writing, Social Studies, Art, Leisure Reading, or Health Education.[11]

- In the annual NCAA March Madness office pool, the boss picked North Carolina State to win it all. I'm going to pick the same team she picked. After all, she's the boss.

The written historical record shows that the question of how to evaluate arguments goes back at least 2,500 years to the birth of the field study today known as logic. Logic, with its historical roots in rhetoric and argumentation, explores the question of how to decide whether or not the claims based on various kinds of arguments should be accepted. More specifically, it focuses on one of the four presumptions of the practice of argument making: If the premises of an argument are taken to be true, that implies that the argument's conclusion is probably or necessarily true as well.[12]

The wisdom and intellectual treasures of many of the world's great cultures and civilizations are evident in the rich history of logic. Fortunately, there are many important and enduring lessons that critical thinking can draw from the study of logic with regard to testing the logical strength of different kinds of arguments, recognizing common fallacies, and understanding the conditions for using various methods of reasoning correctly. Drawing on those enduring lessons, we have begun to assemble our tool kit for evaluating arguments in this chapter. Later, we will add some precision tools for the evaluation of arguments.

JOURNAL

Weak Thinking

Give an example of an argument someone recently offered to you that fails one or more of the four tests for evaluating arguments. State the argument and explain which test or tests it failed and why.

Better than Memorizing—Analyze, Internalize, and Explain

Here and in the next two chapters we introduce a great many names traditionally used to categorize reliable argument patterns and unreliable fallacious varieties of arguments. The terminology of logicians and other scholars who study arguments is valuable to the extent that it helps us remember the underlying ideas. But the key to learning is to practice and internalize the process of interpreting people's words correctly so that we can understand exactly what their arguments are, and then evaluating those arguments fair-mindedly. People with strong critical thinking skills are good at evaluating arguments because they can recognize logically correct forms of arguments as well as common mistakes that make an argument invalid, unwarranted, or fallacious. And, they can explain in their own words why one form is reliable and

another is fallacious. All around the planet, there are people who are skilled at evaluating arguments, but who may never have learned the academic terminology to classify arguments. Unfortunately, there are others who can recite the textbook definitions of the rules and terms from memory but yet, in practice, lack skill at evaluating arguments.

Being able to explain why an argument is unworthy of acceptance is a stronger demonstration of one's critical thinking skills than being able to remember the names of the different types of fallacies. Exercising one's skills in analysis and explanation leads to stronger critical thinking and better communication of one's thinking in daily life. Rote memorization, which is valuable for other things, is not a critical thinking skill.

Summing up this chapter,

the universal human practice of reasoning with a friend or colleague to seek the truth reveals how, in argument making and reason giving, four important presumptions support the expectations and responsibilities that make that practice work in real life. The reasons we give should be true. The arguments we use should be logical. The reason given should be a relevant basis for accepting the truth of the conclusion. And the conclusion should not be used to lend support or credence to the reason. These four conditions ground the application of four straightforward tests to determine whether an argument is worthy of being accepted. The four are the Test of Truthfulness, the Test of Logical Strength, the Test of Relevance, and the Test of Non-Circularity. The tests, which are to be applied in a particular order, must all be passed if an argument is to be worthy of acceptance as a demonstration that its conclusion is true or is very probably true. To help with the application of the Test of Relevance, we examined seven common fallacies of relevance. Arguments that manifest these notoriously fallacious approaches to presenting reasons and claims often beguile and mislead us.

Key Concepts

good argument/worthy argument is an argument that merits being accepted as a proof that its conclusion is true or very probably true.

sound argument is an argument with true premises that also passes the Test of Logical Strength.

fallacies are deceptive arguments that appear logical, but upon closer analysis, fail to demonstrate their conclusions.

Applications

Reflective Log

The ethics of fallacious argumentation: What if we discovered that we could manipulate the voting public more effectively by the use of fallacious arguments than by the use of worthy arguments? Consider the political impact of the "death panels" issue described under the Straw Man Fallacy. The entire episode generated more heat than light. And, yet, it may have achieved its political purpose. Many who heard and believed that the proposed legislation envisioned a eugenics program akin to that advanced by Nazi Germany showed up at town meetings to vent their anger and voice their objections. If the goal was to delay or derail the Democratic legislative agenda, then the strategy succeeded. This is only one example of using one's skills at argument making to achieve one's goals. Defense attorneys who get juries to acquit criminals is another, as are prosecuting attorneys who get juries to convict innocent people accused of crimes. The ethical question for all critical thinkers is: To what purposes ought I to put my powerful critical thinking skills? This question is analogous to the question: To what purposes ought I to put my college education? These are, in part, ethical questions and, in part, questions about one's sense of how to make the meaning of one's life. And what are your answers? Why?

Individual Exercises

Evaluate argument worthiness and explain—Tests 2, 3, and 4: Assume that all the premises that are asserted are true. Apply the remaining three tests to evaluate each argument to see if it is worthy of acceptance. Remember, if the argument fails a test, you do not have to apply any further tests because at that point the argument is not worthy to be accepted. In each case, give a detailed explanation to support your evaluation. State in your own words why the argument is worthy of acceptance, or why it is not a good argument.

1. When I stop at a traffic light, I hear this funny rattling sound coming from under my car. It is sort of in the middle or maybe toward the back, but definitely not

toward the front. I only hear it when the car is idling, not when I'm driving along at a reasonable speed. My dad said once that the metal baffles inside a muffler can loosen up if the muffler is old and rusty. He said that a loose baffle makes a rattling sound when it vibrates, like when the engine is idling or when the tires are out of alignment. My muffler is at least nine years old. So, I'm thinking that probably the rattling sound is coming from the muffler.

2. In a perfect world, the government should investigate whether any laws were broken relating to the treatment of wartime detainees. But this is not a perfect world. So, it would be a mistake for the government to engage in such an investigation.

3. Having turned up some new information, a cold case homicide detective interviewed the victim's husband some years after his wife's death. The distraught husband said, "I have been praying all these years, asking God to send us something. My wife's murder could not have been simply a random accident. God would not permit that."[13]

4. If God intended marriage for the sole purpose of human reproduction, and if same-sex couples are entirely incapable of human reproduction, then it follows that God did not intend marriage for same-sex couples.

5. As you all know, there has been a successful Chinese experiment that used a single cell from a laboratory rat to generate a living chimera of that rat. In the chimera, which lived to adulthood, 95 percent of its genetic material was identical to the donor rat. Noted cell biologist Dr. Kastenzakis believes tinkering with nature is just what scientists do. Therefore the Chinese experiment raises no ethical questions and poses no ethical risks.

6. In the past whenever the TV news programs in Chicago ran headline stories featuring a sketch artist's drawing of a fugitive, the Chicago Police Department (CPD) hotline received over 200 phone calls from people all over the city who said that they spotted the person. Tonight the Chicago TV news programs are going to feature a sketch artist's drawing of a fugitive whom the police are trying to locate. This will probably yield hundreds of calls on the CPD hotline.

7. Suppose we imagine electricity flowing through wires in the way that water flows through pipes. With this analogy in mind, it would be reasonable to infer that wires that are larger in circumference should be capable of carrying greater electrical loads.

8. Former NFL quarterback James Harris tells a story about how he committed to throwing footballs until his arm hurt. Knowing that the NFL regarded the down-and-out pass pattern as one of the more difficult passes for the quarterback, Harris visited the local park and, while nobody watched, he tested himself. He targeted a tree and threw at it blindfolded. He knew that if he missed, he would have to walk a long way downfield to pick up the football. And he did miss the first time. So he wondered whether it was a good idea to even try again. But he did try. And when he heard the ball hit the tree that sound gave Harris a ton of confidence.[14]

9. My client did not intend to use the weapon, and so he is not guilty of armed robbery. Yes, we agree with the prosecution that he committed the robbery. And, yes, we agree that he was carrying a weapon and that he brandished the weapon to intimidate the store clerk and the customers. We agree that the law reads, "Anyone who carries a weapon in the commission of a robbery shall be guilty of armed robbery." And, yes we admit that he shouted, "Everyone down on the floor or I'll shoot." But, and here is the key fact, the weapon was not loaded. He did not have ammunition anyplace on his person or in his possessions. He never intended to use that weapon. And, therefore, the crime that he is guilty of is robbery, but not armed robbery.

10. Look, officer, you can't arrest me on felony rape charges just because she's 17 and I'm 21. Yes we had sex. But it was consensual. And anyway, in two weeks she's going to be 18, and we plan to get married.

11. I like the President's approach to trade with China, and I haven't heard anyone give any evidence that his approach is not going to be effective. So, it must be the right thing for our country to do at this time.

12. Not every argument is of equal quality. Therefore, at least one argument is better than at least one other argument.

Using all four tests, evaluate argument worthiness and explain: Evaluate the following arguments using all four tests, applied in their proper sequence. In each case, give a detailed explanation to support your evaluation. State in your own words why the argument is worthy of acceptance, or why it is not a good argument.

1. Being a sports writer offers challenges that writing standard news stories do not. Here's why. Unlike with standard news stories where the writer is telling the reader something that the reader does not yet know, most of the time the reader knows who won the game before reading your article. Readers probably watched the game on TV. This means a sports writer has to find some angle or some clever and captivating way of telling the story.

2. The *Seattle Post-Intelligencer* and *Denver Rocky Mountain News* are going to close unless they find a buyer. Same for the *San Francisco Chronicle* and the *Miami Herald*. The *Minneapolis Star-Tribune* may file for bankruptcy. The *Los Angeles Times* Sunday edition has shrunk to half its former size. And the list of newspapers in financial trouble goes on and on. I think it is safe to say that the newspaper business may be dying.

3. Torturing prisoners of war often results in poor-quality intelligence. Experience has shown that people in pain will say anything to get the pain to stop. The pain can be either physical or psychological—it does not matter. People crack under the pressure of an experienced interrogator using torture methods. So, we cannot trust the information that comes from that source.

4. Torturing prisoners is against the Geneva Conventions, but it can be a useful means of gathering potentially valuable intelligence. There have been cases where the information given to us by prisoners who have been repeatedly waterboarded, for example, has turned out to be correct. Therefore, we are justified in using torture on prisoners even if our laws explicitly prohibit such methods.

5. More than transferring genes from one organism to another, biologists have successfully engineered synthetic chromosomes into yeast, replacing 16 original chromosomes.[15] Our species now knows how to alter the DNA of living cells using synthetically manufactured chromosomes. Synthetic bio-engineering makes possible new biofuels, new medicines, and other genetic improvements.

Therefore this landmark scientific achievement is a very good thing.

6. More than transferring genes from one organism to another, biologists have successfully engineered synthetic chromosomes into yeast, replacing 16 original chromosomes. Our species now knows how to alter the DNA of living cells using synthetically manufactured chromosomes. Synthetic bio-engineering is tampering with nature in a way that goes beyond all previous methods. Nobody knows what damage might be done to our species and to other animals and plants. Therefore this landmark scientific recklessness is a very bad thing.

Should DUI homicide be prosecuted as murder? What do you think? A prosecuting attorney in New York is bringing charges of murder against individuals who have killed other people while driving under the influence. The attorney argues that everyone understands that driving while under the influence poses risks for the driver and for other people, including the risk of a fatal accident. The statutes provide for charges of "depraved indifference" when one's behavior results in the unintended but foreseeable death of another human being. Defense attorneys argue, among other things, that the laws pertaining to murder were never intended to be applied in this way. The debate was captured by CBS's *60 Minutes* in a segment that aired on August 2, 2009. Search "Should DUI Homicide be Prosecuted as Murder 60 Minutes" to locate and watch that segment. Map out the reasoning for both sides of this debate. Evaluate the reasoning using the four tests for evaluating arguments. After completing your evaluation, present your own reasoned views on the matter.

SHARED RESPONSE

Not So Cool Any More

Joseph P. Allen, a psychology professor at the University of Virginia, makes the argument that pseudo mature behavior observed in early teen years is positively correlated with relationship troubles, substance abuse and other social problems for those children when they reach their early twenties. Such outcomes were remarkably likely among the sample of 184 children from ages 13 to 23 who were followed in this study. You can find news about this study on the web by searching "Cool at 13, Adrift at 23." The exact reference is Allen, J.P., et. al., "Whatever happened to the 'Cool' kids? – Long-term sequelae of early adolescent pseudomature behavior," *Child Development*, 2014 DOI: 10.1111/CDEV.12250.

Does one counter-example of a "cool" kid who turned out just fine invalidate the professor's argument? Link your answer to the four tests for evaluating arguments. Comment respectfully on the examples and reasons given by others.

Group Exercises

Should DUI homicide be prosecuted as murder? What do others think? This exercise works best with a five person group. Each member of the group, having seen the *60 Minutes* video and worked on the individual exercise will have thoroughly considered the issue of homicidal DUI as murder. But for this project, you must first set aside your individual opinions on this matter. This project involves interviewing people for whom this issue is much more than a textbook's abstraction. So you and the other members of your group need to focus on what you hear in the interviews without letting your personal opinions get in the way.

Your group will conduct four sets of interviews. You must always have at least two members of your group participate in each interview. This is so that you can help each other remember what the person being interviewed said.

First set of interviews: Locate at least one person—two or three if possible—who has been arrested for driving while under the influence of alcohol or drugs even if not for homicide. Find out what that person or those people think. Listen to their arguments, and then write them down and evaluate those arguments. Be objective and fair-minded in your evaluation, regardless of whether you agree or disagree with the person's position.

Second set of interviews: Locate at least one person—two or three if possible—who is a former drinker. Interview that person the same way. Get his or her views on the matter, write down the person's arguments, and evaluate those arguments objectively and fair-mindedly.

Next, contact Mothers Against Drunk Driving (MADD) or some other volunteer organization that is known for its stance on issues relating to drunk driving. Follow the same drill. Get that organization's arguments down and evaluate them.

Finally, contact the office of your local prosecuting attorney, or the state police and, again, conduct your interview and evaluate the arguments you hear.

Having talked directly with people who are close to this issue, your group must now assemble all the arguments that came forward in the various interviews. In light of these perspectives, take a stance individually and as a group on whether or not homicide by DUI should be prosecuted as murder. Write out the group's opinion and give the reasons. Write out your individual opinion, if you disagree, and give your reasons. Whatever you finally decide, use strong critical thinking and sound reasons.

Assisted suicide: Assisted suicide is legal in Oregon and in Sweden, but not in many other places. There are arguments pro and con. Begin this exercise by familiarizing yourself with those arguments. Map and evaluate the most common arguments on both sides. Then interview two or more people over the age of 60, two or more people between the ages of 18 and 30. With their permission, record the interviews so that you can check the accuracy of your analysis and interpretation of their perspectives. Ask each person to consider whether or not they would agree with a law that permitted a competent adult to seek and to receive suicide assistance from a licensed health care professional, if that adult knew with a very high level of confidence that she or he had a medical condition that would result in painful death in less than three months. Map and evaluate, using the four tests of the worthiness of arguments presented in this chapter, the set of arguments you collect from the eight people. Is there a pattern?

Chapter 8
Valid Inferences

The dilemma that opens this chapter illustrates how facts and logic can lead us to have certainty in our conclusions even when we might want very much not to face the results of our reasoning process.

HOW do we evaluate the logical strength of inferences offered as if their conclusions are certain?

HOW can we recognize common fallacies related to these inferences?

 ## Learning Outcomes

8.1 Evaluate the logical strength of inferences presented to imply or entail that their conclusions must certainly be true if we take all their premises to be true.

8.2 Recognize reasoning fallacies masquerading as valid inferences.

You need a liver lobe now! Imagine that you, like 78,000 other Americans each year, overdose on acetaminophen, the active ingredient in Tylenol. Imagine you are one of the 33,000 whose overdose is so severe that you are rushed to the hospital.[1] You go into acute liver failure. Fortunately you survive. Your liver, however, does not. You need an organ transplant. Specifically, you need a liver lobe. You have three and only three options: You must get on the waiting list here in the United States and hope that you do not die before a donor liver is found for you. Your second option is to travel overseas where you can be assured of receiving a liver transplant. Your third option is to die. But, let's assume that you cannot be put on the waiting list for a liver here in the United States because you have other medical issues. Disqualified from the waiting list option, that door is closed. And let's assume that you do not want to die. So Door #3 is closed. The only possible conclusion from this set of assumptions is that you have but one option: travel overseas where you can be assured of receiving a liver transplant. Apart from changing the premises, there is no logical way of escaping that conclusion. Of course, that conclusion implies an ethically repugnant result, which is that you must now become a buyer in the international marketplace for human organs. The liver lobes sold in that marketplace are harvested from healthy but desperate people living in abject poverty who sell their body parts to feed their families. (To learn more, search and watch "Tales from the Organ Trade," an HBO documentary.[2])

In this chapter and the next, we will be refining our argument evaluation skills. Here our attention will be on arguments that are structured in such a way that their premises guarantee the truth of the conclusion. In everyday language we would say that *the premises imply the conclusion or entail the conclusion,* meaning that there is no possibility that all the premises could be true and the conclusion false. The opening scenario is structured so that you have exactly three possible options. But two of them

Deductive Reasoning

To learn to think well we must accept the challenge of digging deeply into core ideas and key questions.

The core idea in Chapter 8 is this: An important group of inferences logically require that their conclusion must be true if their premises are all true. The key critical thinking question is how to recognize and evaluate those inferences.

Logicians, mathematicians, computer engineers, and many others mean to convey that core idea by using words like "imply" and "entail." The core idea is captured in technical vocabulary too. Traditionally the term "deduction" named this class of inferences. Without deductive reasoning our species would not have sequenced DNA, traveled to the Moon, spanned the Golden Gate, or built shining towers into the sky.

Like Chapter 8, Chapter 13 "Ideological Reasoning" and Chapter 17 "The Logic of Declarative Statements" are about deduction. Why, you might ask, is the topic of deduction spread over three non-sequential chapters? If our purpose had been to cover the topic of deduction like an encyclopedia, then, yes, we would have grouped the three chapters together. And we may have added a fourth or fifth taking you further into formal logic.

But our purpose is different. The goal is the development of your critical thinking skills and habits of mind.

The evidence from testing hundreds of thousands of college students with the *California Critical Thinking Skills Test* tells us that evaluation is initially their strongest skill area. Good teachers and coaches know it is important to build on a person's strengths. So, beginning in Chapter 1 and continuing in the early exercises we used an evaluation rubric. We started focusing on other skills in Chapter 4. By Chapter 7 it was time to expand your argument evaluation skills with the four tests. In this chapter and the next, we work on applying the Test of Logical Strength.

This chapter offers a sampling of deductive inferences. But, like cross training athletes, critical thinkers develop stronger inference skills by exercising across the full range of inferences. Deductive inferences are only one kind of inference. Chapters 9 through 12 introduce other kinds. Chapters 10 and 11 connect inference and the other critical thinking skills to decision making. This sets the stage for the bigger real world (game time) issues addressed in Chapters 13 and 14.

How do we understand deductive reasoning? Here is what we wrote after decades of research: "Decision making in precisely defined contexts where rules, operating conditions, core beliefs, values, policies, principles, procedures, and terminology completely determine the outcome depends on strong deductive reasoning skills. Deductive reasoning moves with exacting precision from the assumed truth of a set of beliefs to a conclusion which cannot be false if those beliefs are true. Deductive validity is rigorously logical and clear-cut. Deductive validity leaves no room for uncertainty, unless one alters the meanings of words or the grammar of the language."

Source: *California Critical Thinking Skills Test User Manual,* San Jose, CA: Insight Assessment. 2014. Page 22. Used with permission from Insight Assessment-Measuring thinking worldwide. www.insightassessment.com.

turn out to be closed to you. Therefore we can infer with certainty that your one and only choice is to go overseas for the organ transplant. The situation is structured like this: There are only three doors: #1, #2, and #3. You must select one of the three doors. Door #1 is nailed shut and so is Door #2. Therefore Door #3 is your only option.

If the assumption that all the premises are true makes it impossible for the conclusion to be false, that is, if the premises entail or imply that conclusion, we will evaluate that argument or inference as **valid**.[3] Needless to say, a valid argument passes the Test of Logical Strength. In this chapter we will learn how to recognize valid arguments by the way the inference is structured and we will consider a group of common fallacies that masquerade as valid inferences.

8.1 The Structure of the Reasoning

One important distinguishing feature of valid arguments is that if the conclusion is false, then one or more of the premises must also have been false.

Consider MAP #1, which shows the structure of the organ transplant scenario. Trace the reasoning backward, against the flow of the arrows. What can we infer if we assume that the claim "I must go overseas for a transplant," is false? That may mean that you decided to accept your fate and embrace death. If so, then the premise "I want to live" has turned out to be false. Or perhaps you were invited to join a clinical trial for a newly invented synthetic liver. If so, then the premise "A transplant is my only option" is false. Or maybe you received the unexpected news that the US organ donor policies had been changed so that you could now be put on the waiting list. If so, then the premise "I am not eligible for a transplant in the United States" is false. Or maybe your physician calls to say that your liver function has unexpectedly improved to a level that you no longer require an immediate transplant. In that case the starting point assertion "I need a

liver lobe now" is false. This is an example of the principle that if the conclusion of a valid argument turns out to be false, then one or more of its premises must be false too.

As they say in the TV infomercials, "But wait! There's more." Suppose you are so distressed about needing to go overseas for a liver transplant that you cannot sleep. Late one night you see a commercial that promises a "miracle cure." For only $19.95 plus shipping you can buy "liver seeds." The hawker, dressed in a white lab coat, says "these seeds take root in your body and grow into a healthy new liver." The hawker goes on, "Yes, this is the first truly surgery free transplant!" Wow, have we found something that makes the conclusion false but permits all the premises to still be true. No. Even this ridiculousness makes the premise "A transplant is my only option" false. Remember donkey cart words from another chapter? The bogus "truly surgery free transplant" is not a transplant in the standard medical definition of that term. What changed is the structure of the argument. Adding the "miracle cure" is like adding the clinical trial option, it alters the structure of the reasoning by creating Door #4.

Inferences Offered as Certain

"Aristarchus deduced that the Sun was much larger than the Earth," explains Carl Sagan in the 1980 Cosmos series.[4] We often attribute the idea that the Earth is a planet revolving around the Sun to the fifteenth-century Polish astronomer–priest named Copernicus. But, in fact, the first scientist known to have reasoned with certainty to a Sun-centered view of the solar system was the Greek astronomer–mathematician Aristarchus (310–230 BCE). More than two millennia earlier than Copernicus, and using no telescope, but only his own eyes and the then newly invented mathematics we call Geometry, Aristarchus considered the size of the Earth's shadow on the Moon during a lunar eclipse. He then concluded that the only possible explanation for the size of the shadow of the Earth on the Moon during a lunar eclipse was that the source of light shining toward the Earth and the Moon from a very great distance away

Map #1: My Liver Lobe Transplant Options

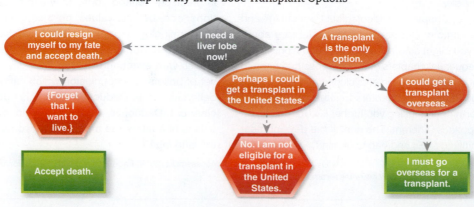

Moon crater Aristarchus

must itself be of immense size. Must be. We are not talking high degrees of probability here. This was certitude. If you assume that light travels in a straight line, and if you know anything about shadows, then you must infer with certitude that the Sun is gigantic as compared to the Earth and that it is very much further from the Earth than is our Moon.

There are times, perhaps not many, when a person makes an argument believing that truth of the premises completely guarantees the truth of the conclusion.[5] The Sagan quote in the Aristarchus example is one such instance. Sagan meant that there was no other possible explanation, no other inference Aristarchus could draw except that the Sun was very large and very far away. One important caution, however. Thoughtful and fair-minded interpretation is important. People do not always speak with the logical precision Sagan used. So we need to keep in mind the context and the intention of the argument maker. Strong critical thinking requires that we not attribute more than the argument maker intends. A friend of ours uses the expression "that must be what happened" when he means only "that is probably what happened."

Although at times we all have wished otherwise, none of us can suspend the laws of nature or the laws of logic. In business, a company that is losing money may have absolutely no choice but to lay off good employees. In a medical emergency, health care professionals have to decide which of the victims to treat first, knowing that they cannot get to everyone in need. Military leaders have to send brave soldiers into combat knowing with certainty that there will be casualties. Regardless of our feelings in the matter, there are times in our lives when the facts and

the logic of a given situation force us to entertain options we had hoped never to face. In those situations we cannot afford to be wrong about the facts or about the logical strength of our reasoning.

In this chapter we will assume that the examples are inferences and arguments presented to show that their conclusions must be certain, given the premises. From the perspective of building critical thinking skills, the important question is *how to evaluate the logical strength of an inference or argument offered as certain*. Because the argument maker is asserting that there is no possibility whatsoever that the premises could all be true and yet the conclusion turns out to be false, our evaluative task is clear. *If we can come up with a counterexample, namely a scenario in which all the premises are true but the conclusion is false, then the argument is not valid.* It is not logically certain! Given that counterexample, we know that the premises do not imply the conclusion.

Because this chapter focuses on the Test of Logical Strength only, we will assume that the examples used here have already passed the Test of the Truthfulness of the Premises. This will be a lot to swallow, because some of the premises are patently false. But, for the educational purpose of focusing on the logic strength of the example arguments, let us entertain the fiction within the context of this chapter.

> It is the mark of an educated mind to be able to entertain a thought without accepting it.[6]
>
> Aristotle, Philosopher, Physicist, & Zoologist (384–322 BCE)

Reasoning with Declarative Statements

The first group of valid argument templates[7] we will consider include those that derive their valid structures from the way simple statements interact grammatically when we use prepositions or adverbs that have logical force. These include the words *and*, *or*, *not*, and *if . . . then. . .*

DENYING THE CONSEQUENT[8] One valid argument template we rely on regularly produces arguments structured like this:

Premise #1:	If **A**, then **B**.
Premise #2:	Not **B**,
Conclusion:	Therefore, not **A**.[9]

The argument template uses the capital letters *A* and *B* to stand for simple positive declarative statements, like **A = "The city has a reliable public transportation system."** And **B = "I will use the city's public transportation**

system." Substituting those two statements in the template for **A** and for **B** produces this argument:

- Premise #1: **If the city has a reliable public transportation system**, then **I will use the city's public transportation system**.

- Premise #2: It is not the case **I will use the city's public transportation system**.

- Conclusion: Therefore it is not the case that **the city has a reliable public transportation system**.

In each of the examples below, **the blue statement** is **A** and **the orange statement** is **B**. Here are three more examples of valid arguments built by substituting declarative statements into the Denying the Consequent argument template.

- **If Richard graduated with honors**, then **Richard maintained a GPA of 3.2 or higher**.
  It is not the case that **Richard maintained a GPA of 3.2 or higher**.
  Therefore, **Richard did** not **graduate with honors**.

- If **you have been promoted to the rank of captain**, then **you have served for at least a year**.
  You have not **served for at least a year**.
  It follows then that **you have** not **been promoted to the rank of captain**.

- If **the sun shines on the far side of the moon**, then **red roses grow inside the barns in Iowa**.
  It is not true that **red roses grow inside the barns in Iowa**.
  So, it is not true that **the sun shines on the far side of the moon**.

This last example is curious because it is structurally valid, but in fact we would not rely on it as a proof that the sun does not shine on the far side of the moon. The argument is not acceptable because even if it were true that no red roses grew in any Iowa barns, the first premise is not true. This example is a quick reminder that logical strength, while essential, is not the only consideration that strong critical thinkers have in mind when evaluating arguments in real life. Again, in all the examples here and to follow we are maintaining our focus on the logic while assuming that all the premises are true. Yes, it can be challenging to assume that the premises are true, but that is why we separated the Test of the Truthfulness of the Premises from the Test of Logical Strength. Facts and logic are two different things.

Using short declarative statements fill in the argument template to create two valid Denying the Consequent examples of your own.

If _____, then _____ .
It is not the case that _____ .

Therefore it is not the case that _____ .
If _____, then _____ .
It is not the case that _____ .
Therefore it is not the case that _____ .

AFFIRMING THE ANTECEDENT[10] A second very commonly used argument template also relies on the meaning and grammatical power of "if…, then…" expressions. In this case, however, the second premise affirms that the "if" part is true.

Premise #1:   If **A**, then **B**.
Premise #2:   **A**.
Conclusion: Therefore, **B**.

Here are three arguments that are valid on the basis of affirming the antecedent argument template.

- If **the price quote from College Insignias is lower than the price quote from University Logos**, then **we will get the T-shirts for our ACS Relay for Life team printed at College Insignias**.
  The price quote from College Insignias is lower than the price quote from University Logos.

Relay for Life team marching to support American Cancer Society.

Therefore, **we will get the T-shirts for our ACS Relay for Lifeteam printed at College Insignias**.

- If **you are eligible to graduate with honors**, then **you will receive notification from the Registrar**.
  You are eligible to graduate with honors.
  So, it follows that **you will receive notification from the Registrar**.

- If **the sun shines on the far side of the moon**, then **carrier pigeons get high in Denver**.
  The sun shines on the far side of the moon.
  So, **carrier pigeons get high in Denver**.

As with pre-algebra, we are substituting values for the variables in the formula. In pre-algebra the result was an equation; here the result is a valid argument. Using short declarative statements, fill in the Affirming the Antecedent argument template to create two valid examples of your own.

- If _____, then _____.
  _____.
  Therefore, _____.

- If _____, then _____.
  _____.
  Therefore, _____.

DISJUNCTIVE SYLLOGISM When we are presented with various alternatives and then learn that one or more of those alternatives will not work, it is logical to reduce our options. The argument template for this valid structure produces arguments with this pattern:

Premise #1:   Either **A** or **B**.
Premise #2:   Not **A**.
Conclusion: Therefore, **B**.

Here are two examples of arguments that are valid by virtue of the Disjunctive Syllogism argument template.

- Either **we'll go to Miami for spring break**, or **we will go to Myrtle Beach**.
  We are not **going to Miami for spring break**.
  So, **we will go to Myrtle Beach**.

- Either **I'll take organic chemistry over the summer**, or **I'll register for that course next fall**.
  No way **will I take organic chemistry over the summer**.
  So, **I'll register for that course next fall**.

The next example is a variation on the second. Instead of the first alternative being eliminated so that the second emerges as the only remaining option, in this case the second alternative was eliminated so that the first emerged logically as the only remaining option. The template for this is:

Premise #1:   Either **A** or **B**.
Premise #2:   Not **B**.
Conclusion: Therefore, **A**.

- Either **I'll take organic chemistry over the summer**, or **I'll take that course next fall**.
  There's no way **I can take that course next fall**.
  So, **I'll take organic chemistry over the summer**.

In context "that course" refers to organic chemistry. In actual practice, when we make arguments, we seldom repeat statements verbatim. Instead, we use internal references that are contextually unproblematic.

The chapter "The Logic of Declarative Statements," extends the discussion above into the discipline of Logic. That chapter presents a method for expressing the key logical relationships between simple declarative sentences using symbols. And it provides a surefire way of evaluating the validity of arguments expressed in that symbolic notation.

Reasoning about Classes of Objects

Other arguments derive their valid structures from the meanings of words in the language used to show the interaction of groups of objects. Words like *some* and *all* are used to express our ideas about how individual objects and groups of objects relate.

Grammatically Equivalent Structures			
These pairs of logically equivalent grammatical structures . . .		. . . give us two ways to say the same thing.	
A unless B	A or B	The dishwasher is still full unless you emptied it.	Either the dishwasher is still full or you emptied it.
Not A unless B	If A then B	The table is not set unless Grandma set it.	If the table is set, then Grandma set it.
A only if B	If A then B	It is time to eat only if Dad is done grilling the steaks.	If it is time to eat then Dad is done grilling the steaks.
If A then B	Either A or not B	If it is time to clear the table then we are done eating our meal.	Either it is time to clear the table or we are not done eating our meal.
Neither A nor B	Not A and not B	Neither Bill nor Sue likes singing.	Bill does not like singing and Sue does not like singing.
Not both A and B	Either not A or not B	We cannot buy both a car and a boat.	Either we cannot buy a car or we cannot buy a boat.
A if and only if B	If A then B, and if B then A	We will rent a cottage if and only if our vacations coincide.	If we will rent a cottage, then our vacations coincide, and if our vacations coincide we will rent a cottage.
If A then not B	If B then not A	If the rent is due then we cannot afford to go out to dinner.	If we can afford to go out to dinner, then the rent is not due.

THINKING CRITICALLY

Neither, Unless, and *Only*

There are other terms that, when used correctly, can be used in valid argument templates. Create five arguments by first filling in the templates using the three declarative statements provided. If you are not sure whether a given argument in this group of five is valid, then first check the table "Grammatically Equivalent Structures" to be sure you are interpreting the words correctly. And, if you are, then describe a scenario such that all the premises are true but the conclusion is false. Hint: It should not be possible to accomplish that without changing the grammar of the language or the meanings of the words.

> Statement A: Tuition increases 5 percent per academic year.
> Statement B: I must graduate in no more than two years.
> Statement C: I have legal access to unlimited amounts of cash.

1. Either A, B, or C. Not C. So, A or B.
2. It is not the case that both A and B are true. So, either A is not true or B is not true.
3. Neither B nor C is true. So, B is false.
4. B unless C. Not B. So, C.
5. A only if B. A. Therefore, B.

Write three short declarative statements about any topic which interests you. Fill in the five templates using your statements. Now evaluate each of the arguments created. Is it possible in any of those cases that the argument's conclusion could be false if you assume that all argument's premises are true? The answer should be "no" in all cases. We say that with certainty because validity for these kinds of inferences is based on the structure of our language, not on the topic being talked about.

APPLYING A GENERALIZATION Consider this example of reasoning about individual objects and groups of objects:

- All the books by Michael Connelly feature his fictional hard-boiled LAPD detective, Hieronymus Bosch.[11] *Echo Park* is a book by Michael Connelly. So, *Echo Park* features Detective Bosch.

In this example the first premise states every member of a class of objects (books by Connelly) has a specific attribute (features Detective Bosch). The second premise identifies a specific member of that class (*Echo Park*). And the conclusion that follows necessarily from those two premises is that *Echo Park* features Detective Bosch. Whenever we have a generalization that asserts that a given characteristic applies to each of the members of a class of objects, we can logically assert that a given individual or subgroup of individuals that are members of that class has that characteristic. For example:

- Everyone who installs attic insulation runs the risk of inhaling potentially harmful dust and fiberglass particles. Angela and Jennifer install attic insulation. This means that both of them run that risk.
- Every young woman living in a Muslim country who played in a successful Western style rock band was subjected to numerous hate messages, slurs, and death threats. The young women Aneega, Noma, and Farah lived in a Muslim country and played in the successful Western style rock band known as Pragaash. So Aneega, Noma, and Farah were subjected to numerous hate messages, slurs and death threats.[12] [In this case the premises are true. The **Grand Mufti Bashiruddin Ahmad** declared a fatwa on the band and advised its Muslim members to sing only inside their homes to the other female members of the family, and to wear veils when going out in public.[13]]

If *F* and *G* stand for classes of objects, and if *X* stands for an individual object, then the argument template for Applying a Generalization would work like this:

Premise #1: Every member of group **F** is a member of group **G**.
Premise #2: Individual object **X** is a member of **F**.
Conclusion: So, the object **X** is a member of **G**.

Muslim women in the rock band Pragaash were advised to sing only inside of their own homes.

THINKING CRITICALLY

Classes and Objects

Let **F** be fun-loving people.
Let **G** be college graduates.
Let **H** be high-paid professionals.
Let **X** stand for Xavier.
Let **Y** stand for Yolanda.

Create arguments using each of these templates. Some of the arguments will turn out to be valid, and others will not. Evaluate each using the Test for Logical Strength. Which are not valid? Perhaps none! If you can describe a counterexample, then the argument is valid. Hint: It should be easy to come up with a counterexample showing that #5 is not a valid argument template.

1. If anyone is an **F**, then that person is a **G**. Both **X** and **Y** are **G**. So, **X** is an **F**, and **Y** is also.

2. Some who are **F** are also **G**. Some who are **G** are also **H**. So, some who are **F** are **H**.

3. If **X** is an **F** and a **G**, then **X** is an **H**. As it turns out, **X** is an **F** but not a **G**. So, **X** is not an **H**.

4. Few **H** are **F**. But **Y** is an **H** and a **G**. If anyone is a **G**, then he or she is an **F**. So, **Y** is an **F**.

5. All **F** are **H**. All **G** are **H**. So, all **F** are **G**.

APPLYING AN EXCEPTION If we know that every member of a given class of objects has a certain characteristic, and we also know that one or more specific objects do not have that characteristic, we can logically infer that they are not members of that class. For example:

- Everyone who waits tables has experienced the challenge of trying to be respectful to a rude customer. Alex has never experienced that challenge. That implies that Alex has never worked as a waiter.

- Everyone who works as an attic insulation installer risks inhaling potentially harmful dust and fiberglass particles. Angela and Jennifer have jobs that do not put them at risk for inhaling anything that is potentially harmful. So, Jennifer and Angela do not install attic insulation.

- The numbers 5, 7, 13, and 37 are not divisible by 2 without a remainder. Every even number is divisible by 2 with no remainder. So, 5, 7, 13, and 37 are not even numbers.

The argument template for Applying an Exception works like this:

Premise #1: Every member of group **F** is a member of group **G**.
Premise #2: The object **X** is not a member of **G**.
Conclusion: So, the object **X** is not a member of **F**.

THE POWER OF ONLY *Only* is one of the most interesting words in the language. That word has the power to change the meaning of a sentence depending on where it is placed. Consider this four-part example. Here, first, is a simple sentence:

- Some people objected to being forced to attend.

Now watch how the meanings change depending on where *only* is positioned.

Location of *Only* to Change Meaning	Interpretation of New Statement
Only some people objected to being forced to attend.	Others people did not object.
Some people only objected to being forced to attend.	They did not quit, go on strike, or boycott.
Some people objected only to being forced to attend.	They would have preferred to have been asked or invited to attend voluntarily.
Some people objected to being forced only to attend.	They wanted to do more than attend; they wanted to participate actively.

Here is another example, but this time you fill in the left-hand side of the table by showing where the word *only* would be located to enable the interpretation on the right.

- Some who are students pursue excellence.

Location of Only to Change Meaning	Interpretation of New Statement
Some who are students pursue excellence.	They do nothing but pursue.
Some who are students pursue excellence.	The one thing they pursue is excellence.
Some who are students pursue excellence.	Some students do not pursue excellence.
Some who are students pursue excellence.	They have no other identity besides being students.

Reasoning about Relationships

Natural languages are rich with terms that describe relationships. We use our understanding of the meanings of these terms to make valid inferences about the objects to which the terms apply. For example, the arguments below are valid because of the meanings of the relational terms like *sibling*, *brother*, *sister*, *shorter than*, *older than*, *taller than*, *younger than*, *greater than*, or *equals*. Notice that in ordinary discourse it is not necessary to specify generalizations like "Anyone who is a person's brother is that person's sibling," because those relationships are part of the meanings of the terms. Our understanding of the logical implications of relational terms is part of our comprehension of language. We seldom, if ever, attend to the logical complexity embedded in natural language. Here are some examples of valid arguments built on the meanings of the relational terms these arguments use.

- John is Susan's younger brother. So, they must have the same mother or the same father.
- Fresno is north of Bakersfield. Bakersfield is west of Phoenix. So, Phoenix is southeast of Fresno.
- Six is greater than five. Five is greater than four. Therefore, six is greater than four.
- $(4 + 6) = 10$. $(2 \times 5) = 10$. Therefore, $(4 = 6) = (2 \times 5)$.

TRANSITIVITY, REFLEXIVITY, AND IDENTITY Three relational characteristics we rely upon regularly when using valid reasoning are named Transitivity, Reflexivity, and Identity. Here are two examples of valid arguments based on each, beginning with two examples of transitivity, then a description of the transitivity relationship. After each pair of examples, the relationship is described.

- Tomas is taller than Jose. Jose is taller than Miguel. So, Tomas is taller than Miguel.
- Susan is Joan's ancestor. Joan is Philip's ancestor. So, Susan is Philip's ancestor.

Transitivity Relationship = *If x has a transitive relationship to y, and y has the same transitive relationship to z, then x has the same transitive relationship to z.*

- David is Stanley's neighbor. So, Stanley is David's neighbor.
- Sara is Helena's roommate. So, Helena is Sara's roommate.

Reflexivity Relationship = *If x has a reflexive relationship to y, then y has the same reflexive relationship to x.*

- Leonardo DiCaprio played Jordan Belfort in the 2013 film The *Wolf of Wall Street*. The actor who played Jordan Belfort in that film was nominated for an Oscar. So, Leonardo DiCaprio received an Oscar nomination for his performance in that film.
- The President of the United States was assassinated in 1963. People still remember where they were and what they were doing when they heard that shocking news. John F. Kennedy was the President who was killed that tragic November day in Dallas. So, people still remember where they were and what they were doing the day they heard that Kennedy had been assassinated.

Identity Relationship = *If x is y, then y is x.*

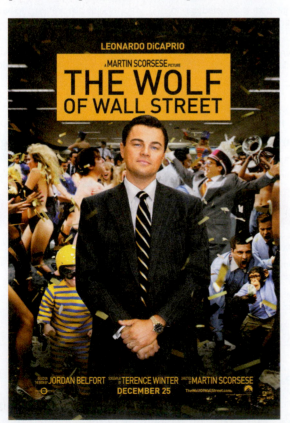

Leonardo DiCaprio, Oscar nominated actor

John F. Kennedy, 35th President of the United States

Sir Arthur Conan Doyle's famous detective calls the arguments he put forth with certainty "deductions." He describes the process of deductive reasoning this way:

> "Eliminate all other factors, and the one which remains must be the truth."
>
> Sherlock Holmes[14]

JOURNAL

It's Elementary!

Is it even possible to follow the advice of Sherlock Holmes on how to figure out the one right answer to a problem? Explain.

8.2 Fallacies Masquerading as Valid Arguments

Just as there are valid argument templates, there are fallacious argument templates. Analysis of the meanings of the terms used and the grammatical rules of the language reveal the source of the error. Precision of thought and expression is the key to avoiding these mistakes when making or evaluating arguments offered as valid inferences. Often, a counterexample that mirrors the fallacious argument template will have the power to reveal the illogical structure, expose the fallacy, and squelch the argument's apparent persuasiveness. As before, in this section please assume that the premises of the example arguments are all true, so that we can focus on their logical flaws rather than their factual inaccuracies.

Fallacies When Reasoning with Declarative Statements

We saw that affirming the antecedent and denying the consequent were two logically correct ways of reasoning with declarative statements. There is a pair of familiar fallacies that mimic those logically correct templates.

AFFIRMING THE CONSEQUENT   Suppose it is true that "If the river continues to rise, then the carpet will get wet." And suppose that we observe that the carpet is wet. It does not follow that the water that wet the carpet came from the river. The wetness may have come from an entirely different source, for example, the dishwasher overflowing, a pitcher of water being spilled, rain coming in an open window, or even old and sadly confused Uncle Joe bringing in the garden hose yet again to water the sofa with flower-patterned upholstery.

The fallacy of Affirming the Consequent follows this invalid pattern:

Premise #1:   If **A**, then **B**.
Premise #2:   **B**.
Conclusion: Therefore, **A**.

But **A** may not be the only condition that brings about **B**. So, it does not make logical sense to believe that **A** must be true simply because **B** is true. Here are more examples of the fallacy of Affirming the Consequent.

- If we put an American on Mars before the end of the twentieth century, then we have a successful space program. We do have a successful space program. So it must be true that we put an American on Mars before the end of the twentieth century.

- If I am a good person, then God favors me with friends, wealth, and fame. God has favored me with friends, wealth, and fame. Therefore, I must be a good person.

DENYING THE ANTECEDENT   Suppose the same hypothetical as before: "If the river continues to rise, then the carpet will get wet." And suppose that we receive the good news that the river has crested and is now receding. It does not follow that the carpet will not get wet. We still must contend with the leaky dishwasher, the open window, and dear old Uncle Joe, the sofa watering man.

The fallacy of Denying the Antecedent follows this invalid pattern:

Premise #1:   If **A**, then **B**.
Premise #2:   Not **A**.
Conclusion: Therefore not **B**.

As before, **A** may not be the only condition that brings about **B**. So, it does not make logical sense to think that just because **A** does not happen, **B** cannot happen. Here are two more examples of the fallacy of Denying the Antecedent.

- If everyone who lived in Mississippi drank red wine daily, then the wine industry would be booming. But some Mississippians never drink red wine. So, the wine industry is not booming.

- If we see a light in the window, we know that there is someone at home. But we do not see a light in the window. So, no one is home.

Fallacies When Reasoning about Classes of Objects

Just as there are logically correct ways of reasoning about classes of objects and their members, there are familiar mistakes we often hear being made. Here are examples of fallacious reasoning about classes of objects. These common errors have earned their own names.

FALSE CLASSIFICATION Suppose "Criminals enjoy mafia movies" and "Cassandra enjoys mafia movies" are both true. It does not follow that Cassandra is a criminal. The same feature or attribute can be true of two groups or two individuals without requiring that one group must

Affirming the Consequent Could Be Called the "*House M.D.* Fallacy"

Between abusing his subordinates, manipulating his friends, and being rude to his boss, Dr. House, played by Hugh Laurie, is called on to diagnose and treat some of the most rare and exotic diseases in the TV series *House M.D.* The popular series ran from 2004 to 2012. The question that drives the drama in each episode is whether or not House will make the right diagnosis before his trial-and-error treatments kill the patient. In the initial scenes of every show Dr. House gives his approval for his team to start medications or do surgeries based on their mistaken ideas about what is really wrong with the patient. Why all the mistakes—apart from there would be no story if he got the diagnosis right the first time? Answer: the fallacy of affirming the consequent. The reasoning pattern the junior physicians on House's team apply goes more or less like this: "If the patient has condition X, then we would see symptoms A, B, C, and D. We do see symptoms, A, B, C, and D. So the patient must have condition X." Watch an episode of *House M.D.* and see if you can pick out the fallacy.

Police dramas often rely on the same fallacy to drive the plot. Early in the stories the detectives reason more or less like this: "If suspect X did the deed, then we would find evidence A, B, C, and D. And, yes, look, here is evidence A, B, C, and D. So suspect X is the felon."

What saves the patient or exonerates the suspect? Strong diagnostic reasoning, which is a thinking strategy that combines pattern recognition with testing aimed at trying to rule out possibilities. For example, something in a medical test—e.g., a given protein showing up in a blood test—implies that the patient could not possibly have condition X. Or the fact that a person was at some other location when the crime was committed definitely rules that person out as a suspect. The testing used in strong diagnostic reasoning is based on the valid argument pattern we described as Denying the Consequent.

Apart from making for enjoyable drama, what problems in real life can result from the fallacy of Affirming the Consequent? Well, if missed medical diagnoses leading to expensive but ineffective medical treatments and the arrests of innocent people were not bad enough already, how about adding comparable mistakes made by other professionals? Have you ever paid an auto mechanic for a repair job only to find out that the mechanic's diagnosis of your car's problem was an honest mistake?

Getting the problem right just might be the most important step in problem solving. We know how to solve all kinds of problems. But applying a solution that does not fit the problem can result in making things worse, not better.

be classified as part of the other group or that the two individuals must be grouped together in all ways. The facts that Emile attended the campus concert and so did 50 students from the local high school does not make Emile a high school student.

Here are three more examples of the False Classification fallacy.

- A good number of residents of Iowa enjoy reading popular fiction. Some who enjoy popular fiction also enjoy windsurfing on their local beaches. So, a good number of residents of Iowa enjoy windsurfing on their local beaches.

- The police profiler said that the rapist was a white male, age 25–35, and aggressive. The suspect is a white male, 28 years old, and aggressive. This establishes that the suspect must be the rapist.

- There are ways of telling whether or not she is a witch. Wood burns and so do witches burn. So how do we tell if she is made of wood? Well, wood floats. And ducks float. So, if she floats, then she weighs the same as a duck and therefore she is made of wood. And therefore . . . , she is a witch! (Condensed from *Monty Python and the Holy Grail* Scene 5: "She's a Witch," 1975.)

In comedy and in real life, there is no surviving fallacious thinking.

Millions have enjoyed the humor that Monty Python created out of this fallacy in the famous "She's a Witch" scene from *Monty Python and the Holy Grail.* If you Google "Witch Monty Python" chances are you will find the scene.

The Monty Python knight's reasoning implies certain death for the poor woman accused of witchcraft, but only if all three premises are true.

Premise #1: If she floats, then she is a witch and we shall burn her.
Premise #2: If she does not float, she'll drown.
Premise #3: Either she will float or she will not float. [Unspoken.]
Conclusion: Ergo, she dies.

FALLACIES OF COMPOSITION AND DIVISION
Reasoning about the relationships of parts and wholes can appear to be valid, but fail because the attribute that applies to the parts may not apply to the whole, or vice versa. Here are some examples:

- It is in each person's financial interest to cheat a little on his or her income tax return. So, it is financially good for the nation if people cheat on their taxes.

- No muscle or joint or organ or cell in your body has the right to give its individual informed consent to a medical procedure. So, why should you, who are composed entirely of those many parts, have such a right?

In the first example, an attribute of individual people who pay taxes is being illogically attributed to the class of objects ("the nation"). The good of each is not necessarily the good of all. The second attempts to withhold from individuals the right to give informed consent because none of our body parts have that right. These examples of the Fallacy of Composition, so called because these fallacious arguments err by reasoning

An Act of Mercy?

Any sparks of humor we might find in the Monty Python silliness are quickly extinguished by the realization that Christians really did burn women to death whom they considered to be witches. Women suspected of witchcraft were first tortured and interrogated to the point of exhaustion. Misfortunes that may have befallen others in their community were interpreted as evidence that the accused had put a witch's evil spell on that unfortunate person. Any blemish on the accused woman's body—a bruise, a birthmark, or a scar from an old wound or burn—could be interpreted as the "mark of Satan," for further confirmation of her guilt.

The tenth and final episode of James Burke's landmark series, *The Day the Universe Changed,* illustrates, given our twenty-first-century worldview, the burning of a woman alive is a horrific killing of an innocent person. But, given their seventeenth-century worldview, the people living in Scotland only four centuries ago interpreted the very same event as an act of mercy. The laws of logic are the same here and now as they were then and there. What has changed? The differences in how the event is seen result from the vastly divergent set of implicit unspoken assumptions that constitute the two worldviews. It is within the context of our "truths" about the world that the laws of logic function. Today in parts of the world where a non-scientific worldview prevails, beliefs in voodoo and magic have a very real influence over the lives and decisions people make. In those communities, it would be "common sense" to fear that some might have the power to cause harm or misfortune simply by thinking evil thoughts and incanting spells. There were witch burnings in Kenya, and New Guinea in 2013 and in Serbia and Russia in 2014. (Google "witch burning" followed by location and year for the news reports.)

Learning to make logical inferences is vital. But logic alone is not enough. Strong critical thinking requires more than skillful inference, analysis, explanation, and interpretation. It requires courageous truth-seeking and the intellectual honesty to reflect from time to time on our own most cherished beliefs and unspoken assumptions. Which of our twenty-first century practices that we see as righteous and sensible will the people in the twenty-fourth century look back on in horror? Google "Witch burning Day Universe Changed" to locate the scene. It is the second scene in the episode titled "Changing Knowledge, Changing Reality." Be advised that the images may be disturbing.

Kepari Leniata being burnt to death in Papua New Guinea for the crime of sorcery. Google "Kepari Leniata Papua New Guinea sorcery" for multiple news reports on this killing, including a report in the *Huffington Post* by Meredith Bennett-Smith on February 7, 2013.

that a group has exactly the same attributes that each of its members have. "I don't know, Bill. Everyone on the Budget Committee is really smart. But, wow, that Committee makes stupid decisions. How can that be?" Simple. What is true of individuals is necessarily true of groups, including how well the group performs. Now consider these three examples:

- The president of the large corporation sent a memo to every vice president, director, manager, and supervisor saying, "In corporations of our size with hundreds of employees we can be certain that 10 percent of our total workforce is performing at a substandard level. Therefore, I am directing everyone in charge of a unit of 10 or more people to immediately terminate one person of every 10 in the unit. Forward the names of your substandard employees to Human Resources by 5:00 pm tomorrow."

- The United States of America has the right to enter into treaties and to declare war. Therefore each of the 50 states has the right individually to declare war or to enter into treaties.

- The average class size at the university is 35 people. Therefore, every class you are taking this term must have 34 other people enrolled in it.

These three examples illustrate the Fallacy of Division, which is the same error, but committed in the opposite direction. Fallacies of Division attribute to each individual member of a group a characteristic that is true of the group as a whole. In the first, an attribute of the class of objects known as the corporation's total workforce is being illogically attributed to each individual small department or unit. In the second, an attribute of our nation as a whole—the authority to enter into treaties—is being ascribed to each of the states that form our nation. In the third, the average class size, which is an attribute of the university, is illogically attributed to each and every class being offered, as if small seminars and large lectures did not exist.

Fallacies of False Reference

Fallacies of false reference occur when reasoning about relationships like identity, reflexivity, or transitivity these most often occur when people think they are talking about the same thing, but in fact are not. The ambiguity of the expressions like "When did we see it?" or "I did it yesterday." can be the source of a mistaken inference if different people interpret "it" to be referring to different things. In another chapter we used an example from *My Cousin Vinny* to illustrate the miscommunication that can arise out of just such an error. In that film the sheriff thought that a young man was confessing to murder when, in fact, he was only saying that he had inadvertently shoplifted a can of tuna fish. A comparable

reasoning mistake occurs when people are not aware that the same object, person, or event may be identified using multiple descriptions.

Suppose that "The dean knows that this year the School of Engineering award for Best Senior Project should go to Team Steelheads." And suppose that "The four members of the team are Karen, Anna, Dwight, and Angela" is true. It does not follow that the dean knows that Karen, Anna, Dwight, and Angela are winners of this year's award. Why? Because the dean may not know that they are the members of Team Steelhead. Knowing, believing, wanting, or intending something when it is described or named in one way does not imply that the person necessarily knows, believes, wants, or intends that very same thing as described or named in another way. That is, unless we add that the person is aware that the two descriptions actually refer to the same thing. Here are two more examples of the fallacy of False Reference.

- Tyler at age 10 has often told his Mom that in college he wants to learn how big buildings and bridges are built. These are subjects addressed in civil engineering. Therefore, Tyler has announced that he plans to major in civil engineering in college. [No. Young Tyler has no idea what "civil engineering" is.]

- Anthony heard that a winner of the 2010 Tour de France used banned performance-enhancing substances. The winner of the 2010 *Tour de France* is Andy Schleck. Therefore Anthony heard that Andy Schleck used banned performance-enhancing substances. [It is not logical to suppose that Anthony knows anything about the cyclist Andy Schleck, including that he is the 2010 winner. As it happens, however, we cannot leave this example without clarifying something. Andy Schleck is the winner of 2010 *Tour de France*. But he was awarded the win after Alberto Contador, the original winner, was disqualified for doping.[15]]

Personal Infallibility?
We Don't Think So

Relying on the grammatical structures of our language, the meanings of key terms, and the laws of mathematics and physics our powers of reasoning enable humans to achieve wondrous technological, computational, and engineering successes. Our species is capable of inferring with certainty the implications of rules, laws, principles, and regulations. This same capability provides endless hours of enjoyment working puzzles and playing games like Sudoku, Spider solitaire, Go, and Chess. The structures defined by the rules of those games determine with certainty the choices we can make as players and the outcomes of each possible choice.

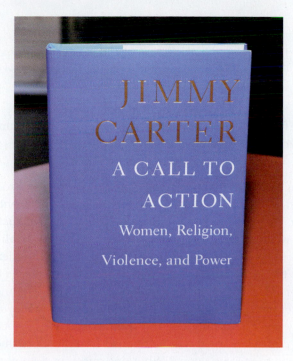

Author, Jimmy Carter, won the 2002 Nobel Peace Prize and served as our 39th president.

But our power to reason with certainty can have more ominous results too. At times, like a freight train thundering recklessly down the tracks, our capacity for certainty drives us headlong toward conclusions that turn out to be patently wrongheaded. We are certain that our assumptions imply those conclusions, so we move ahead perhaps not thinking about whether those conclusions make any sense in their own right. Consider, for example, the ideologically based reasoning used to perpetuate the deprivation and abuse of women and girls.[16]

How can we prevent that ideological freight train from reaching the wrong destination? The answer lies at the starting point. Are all of our beliefs, values, assumptions, and interpretations true? A healthy sense of skepticism, the study of human history, and a great deal of life experience suggests that the probability of personal infallibility approximates zero. Even the most learned, saintly, and wise among us can be mistaken. The chapter on Ideological Reasoning takes up this important theme as it explores the captivating certainty and the often dreadful outcomes our species derives from ideological reasoning.

Summing up this chapter,

when a person offers an argument believing that the truth of the premises completely guarantees the truth of the conclusion how might we evaluate the logical strength of that argument? The answer is clear: If we can find a counterexample, then the argument fails to show that its conclusion must be true given the truth of the premises. But, if there is no possible scenario in which the premises all are true and the conclusion false, then we would say that the premises do imply or entail the conclusion. In that case we describe the argument as valid. Because validity depends on the meanings of structure of the argument, including the words and the grammar of our language, we first examined a number of valid reasoning templates. Then, to arm ourselves against their tempting deceits, we reviewed a roster of fallacies that masquerade as valid arguments.

Key Concept

valid describes an argument or inference such that the truth of the premises entails or implies that conclusion must be true; in other words, it impossible for the conclusion to be false if all the premises are true.

Applications

Reflective Log

Getting the Problem Wrong: The risks associated with what the Fallacy of Affirming the Consequent (which we renamed in honor of the TV character "The *House M.D.* Fallacy") were the extra expense, unnecessary trauma, and risk of death associated with mistaken diagnosis. Review that Thinking Critically box and think about whether you might have ever committed that fallacy or whether you might have been victimized by that fallacy. In either or both cases, describe the situation. What was the fallacious reasoning? What happened as a result? What might you have done differently to have avoided making that mistake? What might the other person have done differently so that you would not have been victimized by their fallacious reasoning?

Individual Exercises

Evaluate arguments: Determine which of these arguments are valid and which are fallacious. In each case assume that all the premises are true, even if it strikes you that one or another of them is actually rather implausible. In each case indicate which valid argument template or which fallacy is exemplified.

1. Everyone who owns a car needs car insurance. Joe just purchased a car. Therefore Joe needs car insurance.

2. Gatorade® is thirst quenching. Tap water is thirst quenching. So Gatorade is tap water.

3. If we drive on the Pacific Coast Highway near San Francisco we can see islands off the Pacific Coast. We can see islands off the Pacific Coast. So we are driving on the Pacific Coast Highway near San Francisco.

4. "I believe the one who brings the hotdogs is supposed to bring the buns too. Somebody messed up," said John. "So, what you're saying is that my mother messed up," said Mary.

5. There are a lot of repossessed condos on the market. The one on Maple Street is less expensive than the place we saw on Palm Ave. And that cute one on Oak Blvd. is priced even lower than that. So the most expensive of the three is the place on Maple.

6. Tweets are short, at most 140 characters. I counted the characters in your last e-mail and there were 1,400. That implies that your last e-mail is nothing but 10 tweets.

7. "Either we'll finish the yard work in time to go to the movie, or we'll enjoy a quiet evening at home," said John. "I don't see us finishing in time for the movie," said Malaya. "It's a quiet evening at home then," said John.

8. If Pepsi tasted better than Coke, then more people would select Pepsi in a blind taste test. And that's just what happened. So, it must taste better.

9. If Pepsi tasted better than Coke, then it would outsell Coke. But Pepsi does not taste better than Coke. So it will not outsell Coke.

10. If the tuition goes up next year, then next fall the freshmen class enrollment will drop. But the freshmen class enrollment will be as high as ever next fall. Therefore next year the tuition will not increase.

Devil and angel: Having died, you find yourself in a room with no windows. You see two identical doors in front of you. There is someone guarding each door. The two guards are wearing identical uniforms. They look exactly alike. A voice, which you recognize as the voice of God suddenly fills the room. God says, "Welcome. An angel guards the door to Heaven. A devil guards the door to Hell. The angel never lies. The devil never speaks the truth. You may ask only one guard only one question. If you ask correctly, the door to Heaven will be opened for you. Good luck, I hope to see you soon." What one question do you ask to identify the door to Heaven with absolute certainty? To see this puzzle worked out watch, after searching, the episode of the *Ricky Gervais Show* that HBO broadcasted on January 28, 2011.

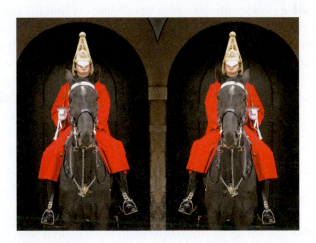

SHARED RESPONSE

Valid Argument or Fallacy?

1. Write one short argument that exemplifies either a valid argument template or one of the fallacies described in this chapter. Post it without identifying what it exemplifies.
2. Select a post by another student and identify the valid argument template or the fallacy which that student used for their example.
3. After your example has received comment, be sure to return and explain what you had intended to exemplify.

Group Exercises

Create your own valid inference examples: Write two valid arguments based on each of the eight valid argument templates described in the chapter:

- Denying the Consequent
- Affirming the Antecedent
- Disjunctive Syllogism
- Applying a Generalization
- Applying an Exception
- Transitivity Relationship
- Reflexivity Relationship
- Identity Relationship

Create your own examples of fallacies: Write two fallacious arguments exemplifying each of these six errors:

- The Fallacy of Affirming the Consequent
- The Fallacy of Denying the Antecedent
- The Fallacy of False Classification
- The Fallacy of Composition
- The Fallacy of Division
- The Fallacy of False Reference

Chapter 9
Warranted Inferences

When you do the numbers, which looks like it is probably the better deal, the public university or the private university? The answer is hidden in the details.

HOW do we evaluate the logical strength of inferences offered as if their conclusions are very probably but not necessarily true?

HOW can we recognize common fallacies related to these inferences?

 ## Learning Outcomes

9.1 Evaluate the logical strength of inferences presented to justify or support the belief that their conclusions are very probably, but not necessarily, true if we take their premises to be true.

9.2 Recognize reasoning fallacies masquerading as warranted inferences.

"Why would you think that Indiana State is less expensive for you than Butler University?" asked Justin.

"Easy," replied his brother Silas. "The in-state tuition and fees at ISU come to something like $8,500, and at Butler, which is private, the tuition and fees are more like $34,500.[1]

Advantage ISU by $26,000 per year! You have to figure that the cost of room and board is a wash. So it comes down to tuition."

"That's not true. You forgot to consider financial aid. My grades are good enough, maybe I will get a scholarship. I've already talked with the financial aid offices at both universities. The people at Butler are saying I'll probably get about $14,500 in scholarship money. For me that brings Butler's tuition down to $20,000. The ISU people were less certain about the status of my scholarship application. They wanted to be conservative, so they talked about maybe $2,500 in scholarships. If that's how it goes, then my ISU tuition would be $6,000. Now the difference is only $14,000 per year."

"So? That's still a lot."

"Yes, but there are student loans too. Both places just about guaranteed that I could make up the rest of what I'd need that way," said Justin.

Silas said, "Which means you can defer starting to pay back the loans until six months after you graduate, right?"

"Right. And let's look at how long it will take me to graduate. I'll transfer in from Ivy Tech with enough credits to be a junior. I could graduate from Butler in two years for sure."

"Well," said Silas, "then it would be two years at ISU too."

"Not necessarily," replied Justin. "I've heard that because the state budget cut backs it is more difficult to get required courses at ISU. It might take an extra year at ISU. But private colleges like Butler work hard to get everyone graduated on time."

"Alright, let's assume that it would take you three years to graduate from ISU, but only two to graduate from Butler. So considering only the tuition minus the scholarships, you're still looking at borrowing $14,000 each year for two years at Butler as compared to $6,000 each year for three years at ISU. It seems clear to me that $28,000 in loans is a bigger problem than $18,000. All in all ISU looks like the better deal financially by about $10,000."

"No, you forgot one other thing," said Justin.

"What?" asked Silas.

"If I graduate from Butler a year earlier, then I can get a full-time job that much sooner. And suppose I find a job that pays maybe $30,000. Or, who knows? Maybe $35,000. In one year of working I will have covered that $10,000 spread. I realize that there are risks and uncertainties. I could be wrong. But financially speaking Butler is probably the better choice given my particular situation."

In this chapter we focus on arguments such that *the premises supply enough support or justification for us to infer with confidence that the conclusion is very probably true, but not necessarily true*.[2] From the context and the evidence at hand we accept these inferences knowing that it is possible that the conclusion might turn out to be false, even if all the premises are true. In the opening example about selecting a college the argument maker, Justin, uses the word "probably" to qualify the force of his claim. Justin is not absolutely certain that Butler University is the best choice financially. And yet, Justin is justified in thinking that Butler probably is the better choice for him financially given the evidence currently at hand.

If the assumption that all the premises are true makes it very probable or highly likely that the conclusion is true, that is if the premises justify or strongly support confidently taking the conclusion to be true, then we will evaluate the argument or inference as **warranted**. Warranted arguments pass the Test of Logical Strength. In this chapter we will expand our tool kit for evaluating the logical strength of arguments and inferences. Our focus here will be on arguments presented to show that their conclusions are very probably, but not necessarily, true. We will also examine a group of common and beguiling fallacies that masquerade as warranted arguments.

9.1 The Evidence Currently at Hand

One way warranted arguments can be distinguished from valid arguments (Chapter 8) is by how new information impacts the reasoning. With warranted arguments new information can lead us to reconsider our conclusions without abandoning any of our original premises. With new information in hand, we may reasonably determine that our original conclusion was mistaken, even though all of our original premises remain true. As you recall from Chapter 8, that cannot happen with valid arguments. With valid arguments, the conclusion is implied or entailed by the premises which means that if the conclusion is false, then one or more of the premises must be false too.

A moment ago we said Justin's conclusion that Butler was probably the best place for him financially was warranted, given the information he had at the time. Let's revisit that example and add some new information. Good news, Justin. Indiana State has decided to award you a full scholarship. Notice that the new information does not contradict anything Justin knew before. It is still true that when he talked to the people at ISU they were uncertain and gave him a conservative response. The news of the full scholarship only expands and updates Justin's knowledge.

Inductive Reasoning

The core idea here is this: A large, important and quite diverse group of inferences justify the confident belief that their conclusion is very probably true given that their premises are all true. The key critical thinking question is how to recognize and evaluate those inferences.

Traditionally the term "induction" named this vast class of inferences. But, as endnote 2 for this chapter indicates, logicians often use more specific names for some of the major sub-groupings. Without inductive reasoning our species would not be able to explain, predict, and in some cases control natural phenomena. We would not have the basic scientific, agricultural, and logistical knowledge that enables us to grow, preserve, and distribute food efficiently. We would not have the scientific and medical knowledge or equipment to enable us to predict, diagnose, manage, and treat diseases. We would not have discovered the multiple contributing factors to climate change and, in turn, the capacity to build models that help us anticipate the impact climate change will have on long term global weather patterns, sea levels, and the habitats of thousands of species of plants and animals, including our own species and those upon which we rely for food.

There are five chapters on various aspects of inductive reasoning in this book: This one, and the chapters on "Comparative Reasoning," "Empirical Reasoning," "Critical Thinking in the Social Sciences," and "Critical Thinking in the Natural Sciences." The organization of the book is driven by its purpose, which is the development of your critical thinking skills and habits of mind. We drew on decades of experience teaching for thinking and no small measure of professional expertise in learning theory when organizing the topics, examples, and exercises. But, yes, if the book were for a different purpose we would of course have organized it differently. For example, had our purpose been to crystallize information into a catalogue of kinds of probabilistic inferences, we probably would have grouped together the five chapters listed above.

How do we understand inductive reasoning? We wrote this after decades of research: "Decision making in contexts of uncertainty relies on inductive reasoning. We use inductive reasoning skills when we draw inferences about what we think is probably true based on analogies, case studies, prior experience, statistical analyses, simulations, hypotheticals, and patterns recognized in familiar objects, events, experiences, and behaviors. As long as there is the possibility, however remote, that a highly probable conclusion might be mistaken even though the evidence at hand is unchanged, the reasoning is inductive. Although it does not yield certainty, inductive reasoning can provide a confident basis for solid belief in our conclusions and a reasonable basis for action."*

*Source: California Critical Thinking Skills Test User Manual, San Jose, CA: Insight Assessment. 2014. Page 22. Used with permission from Insight Assessment-Measuring thinking worldwide. www.insightassessment.com.

None of the premises changed from true to false. Yet Justin's conclusion regarding which institution is the better financial choice for him does change. With a full ride, he can now more confidently conclude that ISU would be better for him financially.

The "Weight of Evidence"

Consider this example, based on a story from the CBS series *CSI*.[3]

- A man is found dead of a gunshot wound to the stomach, his body in a seated position at the base of a tree in a forest. It is deer hunting season. Except for not wearing an orange safety vest, he is dressed like a hunter. His hunting rifle, never having been fired, lies on the ground at his side. The evidence strongly suggests that his death resulted from a hunting accident. The investigator infers that had the man been wearing his orange safety vest, he probably would be alive today.

The investigator's inference is plausible. Although we can imagine alternative scenarios, but in the absence of any further information, we have no basis for evaluating the investigator's inference as other than warranted.

As you could have predicted with a TV cop drama, so it is with the *CSI* story. New facts come to light:

- The time of death was mid-afternoon, a time when deer are not hunted. Deer are hunted at dawn and at dusk. The dead man had not purchased a hunting license. There was gunshot residue on the man's clothing, which indicates that he was shot at very close range. The gun that shot him could not have been more than a foot or two from his body. A $1,000,000 insurance policy had been purchased on his life only two weeks prior to his death. The policy had been paid for with his wife's credit card. The wife is the beneficiary who would receive the money if he should die by illness or by accident.

The initial conclusion, death by accident, looks mistaken in the light of this new information. Now a more plausible conclusion would be that the man had been murdered by his wife or perhaps by someone she hired. Her motive, of course, would be the insurance money.

In the CSI example and in the ISU–Butler example, we can say that the weight of evidence leads us toward one conclusion rather than another. Of course "weight of evidence" is a metaphor. We do not have a method to apply to either example that allows us to measure how much confidence we should have in our conclusion. We know it is not 100 percent, because some other new information might turn up leading us to change our minds again. And we know that our confidence is greater than 50 percent. In the university example, with a full scholarship to ISU, Justin would not say the financial advantage of ISU vs. Butler is nothing but a coin-flip. With the physical gunshot residue evidence and the $1,000.000 insurance policy as motivation,

the detective would not say that the odds that the shooting was murder were only 50-50. How high would you estimate the detective's confidence should be, given the evidence at hand? 75 percent? 90 percent? What do you think?

One tool that would makes it easier to evaluate the logical strength of probabilistic arguments is a systematic method for assigning levels of confidence. We do not have standards in every professional field, but some do. The law, for example, provides a set of increasingly stronger standards that must be met to justify taking various legal actions.[4] The lowest level is "reasonable suspicion." A police officer who observes a vehicle weaving across the lane lines may have a reasonable suspicion that the driver is drunk. If the police officer stops the driver and places the driver under arrest, then the police officer may have "reason to believe" that a search of the vehicle might provide more evidence regarding the DUI, for example, an open container. The standards of evidence continue up from these lower levels to "probable cause for arrest," "credible evidence," and "substantial evidence."

Continuing up the legal standards progression, next comes "preponderance of evidence." As used in legal proceedings "preponderance of evidence" means evidence that provides more than a 50-50 chance that the conclusion is true. That is hardly enough to convict a person of a crime. But it is enough to get an indictment from a grand jury and it is enough to win disputes in civil court over money. A higher standard is "clear and convincing evidence." A jury might base a finding of fact on a witness' testimony because the jury regarded the testimony as substantially more true than false. The highest standard of evidence in legal proceedings is, of course, "proof beyond a reasonable doubt." At this level the evidence is so convincing that there is no plausible or reasonable basis for doubting the truth of the conclusion. Proof beyond a reasonable doubt is strong enough that we would rely upon it and use it as a basis for action.[5]

Notice how much the legal standards at each level call for an unbiased, informed, and fair-minded reasoned *judgment*, rather than a precise mathematical calculation. All the critical thinking skills and all the positive habits of mind are essential for applying the legal standards well.

Proof beyond a reasonable doubt is enough to put a criminal in prison for life. But even this high standard is not 100 percent certitude. A great many people who are found guilty beyond a reasonable doubt really are guilty. Even so, new information may come to light years later to demonstrate that, in some cases, the guilty verdict was mistaken. In 2014 the prizefighter Rubin "Hurricane" Carter died a free man. He was exonerated after spending 19 years in prison, wrongly convicted for a triple murder. During his life Carter became a worldwide symbol of racial injustice.[6] To learn more about Hurricane Carter search the 1999 film starring Denzel Washington. His story inspired others to work, as he did, to achieve justice for people wrongly convicted of murder and other serious crimes. The Innocence Project,

In the eyes of the law, "probable cause for arrest" is a much lower legal standard than "clear and convincing evidence." Check out "How Courts Work" at www.uscourts.gov.

How does the Innocence Project use critical thinking to free dead men walking who are innocent? Yes, "innocent until proven guilty" is the legal standard to be applied to everyone accused of a crime. But how does our system actually function? Locate and watch the HBO award winning documentary *Gideon's Army* for an accurate portrayal of efforts to correct structural injustices in our legal system.

which has exonerated hundreds of innocent people wrongly convicted, is a sobering reminder to us about how difficult and yet how important it is to evaluate the logical strength of arguments carefully. A strong but fair criminal justice system is essential to the rule of law. But a weak or unfair system undermines respect for law enforcement and undercuts trust in the court system. To learn more about the causes of wrongful convictions, such as eye witness misidentifications, improper forensics, false confessions, government misconduct, and self-interested informants, one place to begin your search at the Innocence Project website. Or, Google "social justice film awards" for a rich array of high quality media.

Evaluating Generalizations

A generalization may be based on data gathered systematically or unsystematically. We would be wise to place greater confidence in the claim if it were supported by data gathered more systematically, rather than on simply one or two happenstance personal observations. Consider the following three generalizations. Their conclusions, which are **bolded,** are supported by premises that report personal experiences, conversations focused on these topics, or information derived from historical records or opinion surveys.

1. **People over the age of 60 tend to prefer to listen to oldies.** This claim is based on the data gathered in telephone surveys of persons between the

ages of 60 and 90, which were conducted in Florida, Arizona, Ohio, and Connecticut. In all, 435 interviews were conducted. Participants were asked to identify which type of music they preferred to listen to most. They were given eight choices: Classical, Pop, R&B, Country, Oldies, Broadway, Religious, and Top 40.

2. In May, inspectors from the city sanitation department made unannounced visits to all 20 hotels in the downtown area and to 10 of the other 30 hotels within the city limits. The 10 were

representative of the type and quality ratings of those other 30 hotels. The inspectors by law could demand access to any room in the hotel to look for pests and to evaluate cleanliness. Careful records were kept of each room inspected. In all, 2,000 beds were examined for bedbugs. 1,460 beds tested positive. Based on the data from these inspections, we estimate that **73 percent of the hotel room beds in this city are infested with bedbugs**.

3. I have visited San Francisco maybe seven times over the past 25 years. It is one of my favorite vacation cities. I've gone in the summer and in the winter. And I can

tell you one thing, bring a jacket because **it's probably going to be cloudy and cold in San Francisco if you go in August**.

Notice that in the first example we have a somewhat modest assertion about what people over the age of 60 "tend to" prefer. The second says that it applies to 73 percent of the hotel beds, but not that the infected beds are evenly distributed among the city's 50 hotels. And the third says that it is "probably" going to be cold in San Francisco in August. It is easy to imagine scenarios in which the information in the premises is true but the conclusion may not apply. We can conjure the possibility that someone over 60 does not like oldies. We can imagine that there may be one hotel in the city where most of the beds are not infested. It is no problem to think of the possibility that there should be at least one warm sunny August day in San Francisco. But, developing a possible counterexample does not necessarily diminish the logical strength of a warranted argument.

To evaluate the logical strength of probabilistic generalizations, we need to do more than find one or two counterexamples. We must, instead, examine whether the sampling of cases reported in the premises is adequate to support the probabilistic inferences that are drawn. This means asking four questions and finding satisfactory answers to each of them.

- **Was the correct group sampled?**
- **Were the data obtained in an effective way?**
- **Were enough cases considered?**
- **Was the sample representatively structured?**

WAS THE CORRECT GROUP SAMPLED?   The first example makes a claim about people over the age of 60. The premises tell us that adults between the ages of 60 and 90 were sampled. That is the correct group to sample if one wishes to make generalizations about persons in that age range. It would not do, obviously, to sample people under the age of 60 and then present those data as a basis for a claim about people over that age. One would think that sampling the wrong population would not be a mistake commonly made. But for years, pharmaceutical companies made inferences about children's drug dosages and the effects of various medications on women based largely on studies conducted on adult males. More recently, we have learned that there are genetic factors that affect the rate at which common pain relievers, like the ibuprofen in Motrin, are metabolized. This new finding should influence dosage recommendations for those who are poor metabolizers (e.g., 6 to 10 percent of Caucasians).[7]

WERE THE DATA OBTAINED IN AN EFFECTIVE WAY? In our example about the music listening preferences of adults over 60, we see that the data were obtained via telephone surveys. We might think that a telephone survey may not be as efficient as using a Web-based survey, which would reach many more people and be much more cost-effective. But, upon reflection, it seems reasonable to use the telephone to reach older adults, many of whom may not be comfortable with the use of computers and Web-based survey tools. Finding an effective method to gather data from the sample is often a major challenge for researchers.[8] For example, consider how difficult it is to gather high-quality data about the state of mind of combat veterans in the year after their return from a war zone.

WERE ENOUGH CASES CONSIDERED?   In general, the more cases the better. But there comes a point of diminishing returns. If we are trying to make a reasonable generalization about millions of people who live in major metropolitan areas like Boston, New York, Chicago, or Los Angeles, it is neither necessary nor cost-effective to survey even one percent of a group so large. At some point the distribution of responses simply adds numbers, but the proportions of

responses selecting each possible answer do not change significantly. Social scientists have worked out sophisticated statistical methods to provide a precise answer to the question of sample size. The answer establishes a minimum necessary depending on the kinds of statistical analysis to be conducted and the degree of accuracy needed for the question at hand. For example, to keep us up to date on the likely voting patterns in a forthcoming election, it is sufficient to track what likely voters are going to do within a margin of error of plus or minus 2 percent. Called a "power analysis," the calculations social scientists make begin with a projection of the number of cases expected to fall randomly into each possible category. Scientists can then determine whether the observed distribution varies significantly from the expected random distribution.[9] As a rough rule of thumb, they would want at least 25 cases per possible response category. In our "Oldies" example there are eight categories of music. So, we would need a sample of at least 200 individuals. We have 435, so the sample size is adequate. But we do not have a claim that reports a percentage. In our example the claim reports a *tendency.* Social scientists would not regard a tendency as being a strong enough deviation from random to be called "statistically significant."

WAS THE SAMPLE REPRESENTATIVELY STRUCTURED? We said that 435 was an adequate sample size for our example, but were the 435 representative of the population being talked about in the claim? The claim talks about everyone over the age of 60. Because more than half of the people between 60 and 90 are women, and because women might have different music listening preferences, we would need to be satisfied that the 435 reflected the actual ratio of women and men in that age group. We do not know that

In general, do men and women over 60 like the same genre of music? If we needed to sample at least 400 people when there were eight possible response categories (classical, pop, etc.), now we would need to sample at least 800 people because the number of response categories just doubled. Namely: Men who like classical, women who like classical, men who like pop, women who like pop, and so on.

from the information given. If we hypothesize that music-listening preferences might be related to educational background, race, ethnicity, or socioeconomic status, then we would want to assure ourselves that the sample of 435 was representative of the distribution of those factors among the target population. Because we do not know if 435 is a representative sample, we cannot answer this fourth question in the affirmative. And, as a result, example #1 is not logically strong.

Coincidences, Patterns, Correlations, and Causes

Decades ago scientists first observed that there were a number of cases of heart disease where, coincidentally, the person was a smoker. Further systematic research demonstrated a strong positive correlation between smoking and heart disease. Scientists hypothesized that perhaps smoking was a contributing factor. However, before making a defensible argument that quitting smoking would reduce a person's chances of heart disease, researchers had to explain scientifically how smoking caused heart disease. Researchers demonstrated scientifically that nicotine constricts blood vessels in the heart, which reduces blood flow to the heart muscle, thus causing heart attacks.

The progression from coincidence to correlation to causal explanations marks our progress in being able to explain and to predict events. At first we may observe two events and think that their occurrence might merely be a chance coincidence. Then, as more data are systematically gathered and analyzed, we may discover that the two events are in fact statistically correlated. And, with further experimental

In the heartland people know that lightning can strike twice or more often in the same place.

investigation, we may learn that what had at first seemed like a coincidence actually occurs because of important causal factors. When and if we reach that stage we will have generated a causal explanation.

COINCIDENCES If two events happen to occur together by chance, we call that a coincidence. For example, in 2013 a total of 23 people were killed by lightning in the United States.[10] In 2013 what are the chances that a given individual would have been killed by lightning in the United States, given that the population is roughly 317,300,000? That coincidence has roughly one chance in 13,800,000 of occurring, all else being equal. The qualifier "all else being equal" means that weather patterns do not change substantially and that substantial numbers of people do not behave in ways which increase or decrease their chances of being killed by lightning in the United States, such as becoming residents of another country or standing in an open field holding aluminum rods in the air during lightning storms. But, all things being equal, we can use probabilistic reasoning and statistical facts to calculate the probabilities that a given coincidence might occur.

Although we cannot predict with certainty that the next time you flip a coin it will come up heads, we can predict with a high level of confidence what will happen 50 percent of the time in the long run. We know how to calculate mathematical probabilities for events such as these because we know that each individual outcome occurs randomly with equal frequency. If we roll two regular dice, the result will be two 6s 1 time out of 36 rolls over the long haul. We calculate that by multiplying the chance of rolling a 6 on die #1, which is 1 out of 6, times the chance of rolling a 6 on die #2, which is also 1 out of 6. Then we multiply those odds to get the mathematical probability of both outcomes happening together—the product is 1 out of 36.

PATTERNS Occasionally we see patterns in events that initially appear to be random coincidences. For example, lightning does strike more than once in the same place. That's why people put lightning rods on the tops of buildings. The lightning rod offers an attractive location for lightning to strike. Because the lightning rod is connected to the ground by a sturdy wire, the electrical charge from the lightning is directed safely into the earth, instead of causing damage to the tall building or starting a fire. We do not know where or when the lightning will strike, but we know there will be storms and lightning every year. And we have observed the pattern that lightning is much more likely to strike tall, pointy, isolated objects, like barns in the prairie or skyscrapers in cities.[11] To ignore that pattern would be foolish of us.

The Nurses' Health Study—Decades of Data

One powerful example of research that uses statistical analysis is the Nurses' Health Study (NHS). This project is perhaps the most comprehensive descriptive investigation of health-related behavior ever conducted. Since its inception in 1976, over 238,000 nurses have provided information. The NHS reports findings based on statistical analyses of millions of data points. Some remarkable, unexpected, and important correlations were discovered. Measured expressions like "investigations ... suggested ...", "... is associated with reduced risk ...", and "strong correlations ... support ..." characterize the annual reports. The scientists who conducted this research are presenting probabilistic conclusions. Their conclusions are warranted because the statistical analyses provide sufficient confidence to assert that the relationships on which they report are highly unlikely to have occurred by random chance. Google "Nurses' Health Study" for the website at Harvard.

2009—Early Life Factors and Risk of Breast Cancer

"Epidemiologic investigations conducted by our group and others have suggested that during childhood and early adult life breast tissue is particularly sensitive to factors that influence the likelihood of developing cancer many years later. For example, if the breast is exposed to multiple x-rays or other types of radiation during this early period, the risk of breast cancer rises steadily with higher doses, but after age 40 radiation has little effect. Also, we have seen that being overweight before age 20 is paradoxically associated with a reduced risk of breast cancer for the rest of a woman's life, although subsequent weight gain and becoming overweight after menopause increases risk of breast cancer in these later years. These findings led us to develop sets of questions focusing on diet and physical activity during the high school years....In addition, to assess the validity of the recalled dietary data, we invited a sample of mothers of NHS II participants to also complete a questionnaire about the high school diets of their NHS II daughters; strong correlation between the mother–daughter reports supported the validity of our dietary data.

We have now begun to examine the relation of high school diet and activity patterns to subsequent risk of breast cancer. We have seen that higher intake of red meat during high school years is related to a greater risk of premenopausal breast cancer. Also, higher levels of physical activity during high school were associated with lower risk of breast cancer before menopause. This is particularly important, as many schools do not include regular physical activity in the curriculum, and many girls are now quite inactive during these years." (Nurses' Health Study Newsletter Volume 16, 2009)

2013—Adolescent Alcohol Intake and Benign Breast Disease

Based on the findings reported in 2009 and on the additional data collected about school diets from the daughters of the participants of NSH II, further research was possible. Good science progresses carefully. Five years later this report appeared.

"Alcohol consumption during adulthood is a well-established risk factor for breast cancer. However, less research has been conducted about alcohol consumption during adolescence (when breast cells undergo rapid growth) and later risk of breast cancer. In the NHS II, we found that higher levels of alcohol consumption between ages 18 and 22 was associated with increased risk of proliferative benign breast disease (BBD), a type of breast lesion that is a known risk marker for invasive breast cancer. Compared to non-drinkers, moderate drinkers (less than ½ drink per day) had an 11 percent greater risk of developing proliferative BBD, whereas heavier drinkers (more than ½ drink per day) had a 36 percent greater risk. Each additional drink consumed per day was associated with a 15 percent increase in risk of proliferative BBD. An assessment of alcohol consumption in young women in the Growing Up Today Study, or GUTS (children of the NHS II participants), also showed that drinking between ages 16 and 22 years was associated with increased risk of BBD. These results provide evidence that drinking alcohol during adolescence may increase the risk of BBD. (Nurses' Health Study Newsletter Volume 20 2013.)

Is it only luck that generated the hundreds of millions of dollars needed to build these lavish hotel casinos?

Another pattern that is difficult to miss is the concentration of multi-million dollar luxury casinos in Las Vegas, Atlantic City, and other gambling hubs. Casinos are monuments to the reliability, over the long run, of these calculated coincidences. If 98 percent of the money bet in a casino on any given day goes back to the players as winnings that day, then on an average day the casino can be very confident of retaining 2 percent of every dollar bet. The more money bet, the more dollars that 2 percent represents. Unless more than 100 percent of the money bet is returned to the bettors as winnings, we can be sure that over the long run the bettors go home losers, not winners, and not "breaking even." An individual person winning a specific bet is, considered in itself, a random coincidence. The totality of all those coincidences can be aggregated into a large and highly predictable profit margin for the casino. The best generalization to infer is that, in the end, the casino will very likely separate the chronic gambler from more and more of his or her money.

> "Fables should be taught as fables, myths as myths, and miracles as poetic fantasies. To teach superstitions as truths is a most terrible thing. The child mind accepts and believes them, and only through great pain and perhaps tragedy can he be in after years relieved of them."
>
> Hypatia of Alexandria, (370–415), Mathematician and Philosopher.[12]

CORRELATIONS As in the smoking and heart attack example, when the same coincidence is observed over and

over again, that is, when people see a pattern, they begin to suspect that the events may be related by something more than pure random chance. Even before knowing that one event may be the cause of another, we can determine whether the two are correlated.

Correlations, calculated using statistical analyses, describe the degree to which two different sets of events are aligned. For example, scores on critical thinking skills tests are positively correlated with student success on state licensure exams in a number of health sciences professions.[13] We might wish to speculate about the possible causal relationships of critical thinking skill to academic or professional success. But simply having the correlation in hand can be valuable to those professional programs that have more applicants than can be accepted. The admissions committees can use an applicant's critical thinking skills test score in the way that it uses GPAs or letters of reference, namely as another valuable data point to consider when making its decision to admit or not to admit an applicant.[14]

When a research project reports that a statistically significant correlation has been found between events of kind #1 (scores on a critical thinking skills test) and events of kind #2 (scores on a state's professional licensure examination), that means that the relationship between the two kinds of events is viewed as not likely to be happenstance or chance. Of course, there could be an error in this estimate, but typically the largest threshold for this error is a slim 5 percent. We can be 95 percent confident that the two events are really correlated. Even greater confidence that the events reported did not happen by mere chance can be found in many fields of research in which statistical significance is reported with 99 percent confidence, at 1 percent, or even less (0.001) chance of error. Even so, we remain in the realm of probabilistic reasoning because the warranted inference, which is logically very strong, holds open the possibility that the findings reported may have happened by mere chance. The odds are very definitely against that possibility, however. If the 0.001 confidence level is reached, then the odds that the conclusion is mistaken are 1 in 1,000.

Using statistical correlations as their basis for confidence in their products, manufacturers of over the counter medical test kits do a thriving business. Drug stores like Walgreens sell home tests kits for pregnancy, paternity, colon disease, illegal drugs, blood alcohol levels, and ovulation. These products are used by millions of people. And although these products can be highly reliable, most advertising themselves as 99 percent accurate, that still leaves a 1 percent chance for mistakes. At 1 percent, that comes to 10,000 errors out of 1,000,000 tests. Although the possibilities are remote, a test might be a false positive, meaning that that the

THINKING CRITICALLY

The Devil Is in the Details!

Ever wonder what the return on investment is for graduates from your university with your major? On its public website **PayScale.com** lists the annual return on investment by major for hundreds of institutions. (Navigate to the College ROI Report and select "Best ROI's by Major" from the dropdown menu.) With data from 113 institutions, the top annual ROI for Humanities and English majors is 10.1 percent and the lowest was −3.9 percent. Looking at 840 institutions, for Business majors the top ROI was 12.3 percent down to −3.8 percent per year. Whoa! Does this mean that a humanities major, like Philosophy, is financially comparable to a major in Business?

What's It Worth? The Economic Value of College Majors, a study by the Center on Education in the Workforce at Georgetown University, looked at full-time full-year workers who had completed bachelor's degrees in different fields. That report paints a very different picture. In the Georgetown report, the median salary for Business majors as a group is $60,000. The median annual salary for Humanities and English majors was $47,000. That's 21 percent lower. You can find the Georgetown report on the web by Googling its name.

Why such huge differences? Which one is closer to the truth? Assuming both sources have provided accurate information based on the data available to them, how can we make sense out of the

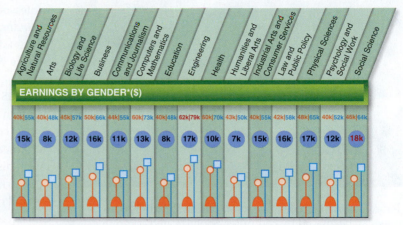

huge differences between what each says about the median salary by major? Hint: "The devil is in the details." Check out the sample sizes and the sources of the information each report uses. This will help you evaluate which is the more credible source.

The Georgetown report showed earnings by major and gender and by race. How do we explain the differences by gender as reflected in this chart from the Georgetown report?

Full-time, full-year workers with a terminal Bachelor's Degree.

- ○ Female Median Earnings
- □ Male Median Earnings
- ● Difference

Source: From What's It Worth? The Economic Value of College Majors, by the Georgetown Center for Education & Workforce. http://cew.georgetown.edu/whatsitworth/. Reprinted by permission.

---

test indicates that someone is a biological parent, is pregnant, is using illegal drugs, is drunk, or has ovulated when those results are not true. Or a test might come back false negative, meaning that the test failed to indicate that the person was in fact a biological parent, pregnant, etc. Rare as false positives and false negatives are, they illustrate the difference between "highly confident but possibly mistaken" warranted inferences and the certainty, which characterizes valid inferences. Depending on one's appetite for risk, with 1 chance in 100 of the test results being wrong, a person might be wise to double check before basing a major life decision on a single test's outcome.

Well-researched correlations can be powerful tools. Consider this possibility. Suppose that writing assignments, which employ grammatically complex constructions, use expected words and expressions, include sentences with greater average word counts, and include fewer spelling mistakes are statistically significantly correlated with higher grades. And suppose that assignments that are missing one or more of those features are

statistically correlated with lower grades. Based on this, we can design computer programs that assign grades by parsing grammar and counting words.[15] The computer does not need to understand the meaning of the essay nor does it have to evaluate the quality of arguments used. The grades assigned by computers can then be checked

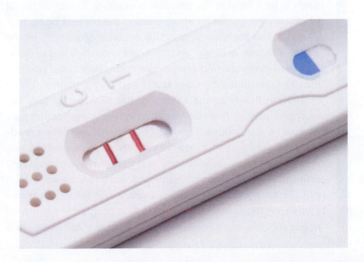

Today writing samples, like those on college admissions tests, can be graded by computer. Sophisticated computer grading programs can generate the same grades as well-qualified humans 99.9 percent of the time, but the computer does its processing without comprehending the meaning of what is written and without applying the four tests of the quality of arguments presented.

against the grades that human evaluators assign to those same essays. Refinements can then be made in the computer program's grading algorithms to achieve ever closer approximation to the results human beings would have produced. When the computer program is refined to the extent that it assigns the same grades as well-qualified human beings to 99.9 percent of the essays, then essay grading can be automated. To assign you the grade your professor would have assigned, the computer never needs to understand what you wrote. This is not science fiction. Automated grading is used by the Educational Testing Service.[16]

CAUSES   Documenting that a causal relationship exists between events requires more than demonstrating a strong correlation. The intellectual challenge of designing research, which is capable of revealing the causal mechanisms at work in nature is important and interesting work. Perhaps this is why many strong critical thinkers find careers in scientific and technical fields attractive. Causal explanations are desirable because they enable us to explain, predict, and control parts of the natural world. In Chapter 14 entitled "Empirical Reasoning" we will explore the powerful investigatory methods used by scientists to achieve causal explanations. In the two concluding chapters we explore the differences between how social scientists and natural scientists seek the best explanations possible.

It is not always possible to move all the way from coincidence to correlation to causal explanation in every field

Grading Written Submissions

If the purpose of grading is to identify which essays fall into which broad groups—for example, "Fail, Pass, High Pass" or "F, D, C, B, A"—and if a computer can manage this faster, with greater consistency, and with an accuracy that matches a well-trained human reader, it seems reasonable to use the computer.

If, on the other hand, the purpose of grading is to advance learning through commenting on the content and presentation of the student's written work, then automated grading does not seem to be a feasible nor desirable alternative. To provide useful feedback, the grader must understand the content being presented, follow the reasoning and the evidence presented, and be able to interpret, evaluate, and comment accurately and usefully.

Well-programmed computers and well-trained graders may assign different grades under certain conditions. These represent threats to the validity of the assigned grade. For example, essays that use information that is not factual may receive higher grades from the computer than human readers who recognized those factual errors. Essays that rely on irony, hyperbole, sarcasm, and humor may receive very different grades from humans and from machines, which presumably would neither recognize nor attend to those stylistic differences. Essays that use plagiarized material might receive a lower grade from the computer because it can check for the replication of text published elsewhere, as compared to a human grader who may not recognize the plagiarized material.

There are threats to the reliability of human graders because humans can become fatigued and less attentive as they grade written submissions for long periods of time. Different human graders may give the same essay different grades because they disagree on the relative importance of various elements in the essay. Humans may be influenced by their personal beliefs, tending to give somewhat higher grades to essays that reflect their point of view. Computers do not suffer from these problems.

If the purpose of grading written submissions is to determine which candidates shall be admitted to highly competitive programs and which shall be excluded, then the threats to validity identified here may lead to unfortunate mistakes. If the purpose of grading written submissions is to determine who shall receive honors, awards, financial support, grant funding, publication, or special privileges, then categorizing essays into broad groups must be refined so that the most meritorious can be validly and reliably identified.

No one would want to be denied admission, funding, or the honor she or he was due because the grader (computer or human) failed to give a written submission its true score.

of inquiry. For example, predicting the behavior of the stock market remains a hazardous and uncertain adventure. Because we do not really know how all the factors that influence the market interact, we are not able to predict with high levels of confidence what the market will do on any given day. Some financial analysts turn out to be right, while others are wrong. Often, it seems as though the analysts announce why the market reacted as it did on a given day only after the day's trading is completed. Then, we hear that the market responded to changes in the jobless rate, the prime interest rate, consumer confidence level, or something else. But those same analysts are not able to use those same factors to predict accurately what the market will do in the future. If their explanations of the past behavior of the market were correct, one would expect that they would be able to make reliable predictions about the market's future behavior. That we are not able to make good predictions about the future leads us to suspect that we do not yet know, beyond the level of coincidences and correlations, what causal factors, individually or in combination with other causal factors, are relevant to explaining the behavior of the stock market. One can only wonder how relevant the factors those prognosticators identify as causes really are.

> "The seeker after truth is not one who studies the writings of the ancients and, following his natural disposition, puts his trust in them, but rather the one who suspects his faith in them and questions what he gathers from them, the one who submits to argument and demonstration."
>
> Ibn al-Haytham, (965–1040), Astronomer and Mathematician.[17]

9.2 Fallacies Masquerading as Warranted Arguments

Just as some fallacies are presented as valid arguments, others are presented as warranted arguments. They draw their power to deceive and persuade from how closely they resemble the genuine article. Detailed analysis often helps us avoid being misled by the following fallacies.

ERRONEOUS GENERALIZATION   Generalizations, even those based on solid evidence and vivid experiences, can be deceptively fallacious, too. At times, we make hasty and erroneous generalizations by relying on far too little information or by exaggerating the importance of one or two particular experiences. The result is a claim that goes beyond what the data can support. Erroneous generalizations tend to spring from and to reinforce preconceptions. Consider these examples:

- The paper showed a picture of the CEO in chains doing the perp walk as he was being led off to jail. Another middle-aged white guy with a $400 haircut! Same as Bernard Madoff, the guy who swindled $170 million out of rich people with his Ponzi scheme. All those corporate thieves are overpaid white guys.

- Many medical professionals recommend a healthy diet and regular exercise. More is always better, right? So the way to be super healthy is to go on a crash diet and exercise as much as possible! Yes?

- Seventy-one percent of the students enrolled in my educational methods course are women. So, women really like my courses.

In each of these cases, even if the premises were true, the conclusion goes unjustifiably beyond what those premises could support. If a person were interested in investigating independently the truth of the claims expressed as conclusions of these generalizations, is there a systematic and effective way to search for the evidence, which might confirm or disconfirm those claims?

PLAYING WITH NUMBERS   Arguments, which use raw numbers when percentages would present a more fair-minded description, or use percentages when the raw numbers would present the more fair-minded description, can be evaluated as fallacies of Playing with Numbers. Arguments that cite statistics or numbers but do not provide sufficient information to make a good judgment about the significance of those numerical data are species of the Playing with Numbers Fallacy as well. For example:

- Six hundred people are affected by the decision you made prohibiting pythons as pets in this apartment complex. I want you to know that 80 percent of the people surveyed said that they wanted you to reconsider your decision. Exactly how many people, you ask? Well, I personally talked to my four roommates and three agreed with me, which makes 4 out of 5, including myself, and that's 80 percent.

- The average salary for postal workers is 5.6 percent higher than the average salary for the employees of the Transportation Safety Administration. This establishes that postal workers are overpaid.

- The National Highway Traffic Safety Administration reports that there were 30,800 motor vehicle fatalities in 2012. Of those 4,957 were motorcyclist fatalities.[18] This means that driving or riding in a car or a truck is six times more dangerous than riding a motorcycle.

Review these examples and add premises or restate the conclusion, or do both to transform each into a warranted argument that gives reasonable justification for believing that the claim—as you may have restated it—is now very probably true. For the third example about traffic fatalities visit the National Highway Traffic Safety Administration website **nhtsa.gov** to get the relevant details. For example note the ratio of motorcycles to other vehicles, or the ratio of total miles per year driven by the different types of vehicles.

FALSE DILEMMA   A real dilemma is a situation in which all our choices are bad, like a person trapped on a window ledge of one of the upper floors of a burning building. But, at times we may think we are facing a terrible dilemma when we are not. Often the world offers more options than we may perceive at first. At times, the consequences of one or another of our options may not be nearly as dreadful as we initially imagine them to be. As the following examples indicate, upon closer analysis at times what appears to be a real dilemma turns out to be a false dilemma.

- The kidnappers have taken eight people hostage and are holding them at a farmhouse just outside town. If the SWAT team assaults the farmhouse, the hostages could be killed. But if we give into the kidnappers' demands for ransom and safe passage out of the country, we'll only be encouraging more kidnappings of innocent people. What can we do?

- If I go to the job interview laid-back and unprepared, I'll blow it. But if I prepare for the interview I could overdo it and be so nervous that I'll blow it anyway. I'm a mess. There's no way to get ready for this interview.

Statistically, who is more at risk, car drivers or motorcyclists?

As these examples show, another good name for this fallacy is "The Either/Or Fallacy" because the situations often appear to be limited to one option or another, but on further examination, additional options emerge. This is true of the first example. Assaulting the farmhouse and giving in are not the only possible options. Negotiating for the release of some or all of the hostages is an option. Waiting until those inside the farmhouse run out of food or water is another option. Blasting the farmhouse with mega decibels of sound and shooting tear gas in through the windows might force the occupants out. In other words, a little creativity can often reveal a way out of a false dilemma.

THE GAMBLER'S FALLACY   Random events, by definition, are not patterned, correlated, or causally connected. But, at times, we make arguments that wrongly assume that what happens by chance is somehow connected with things we can control. We can use "Gambler's Fallacy" as an umbrella term to remind ourselves that random events are, in fact, random and that drawing inferences based on the assumption that they are patterned, correlated, or causally connected is a mistake. Here are some examples of fallacious inferences that attribute more to mere chance coincidences than strong reasoning would warrant.

- If we're going to Vegas, I'll bring my blue socks to wear in the casino. You know, the pair with the word "Winner" embroidered on the side. They're my lucky socks. Although I've lost money plenty of times wearing them, I've never won at slots without those blue socks. So, I won't win a dime from the slots if I don't wear those socks!

- Whenever I leave the apartment, I rub the tummy of the little statue of bronze Buddha we have on the table near the door. It makes me happy to do that because I know that it brings me good karma.

- I just flipped a coin twice and it came up heads both times. So, the next two times I flip it, the coin will come up tails because the chances are 50-50.

- Miguel Cabrera is batting for the Detroit Tigers. Cabrera's batting average this year is .333. This is his third trip to the plate this game. He grounded into a double play his first trip and struck out his second time. So, he's going to get a hit this time.

FALSE CAUSE   This fallacy is one of the most common obstacles to good thinking. The False Cause fallacy is to assume that two events are causally related just because one happens right after the other. This mistake is jumping to the conclusion that the first event must have caused the second event.

THINKING CRITICALLY

Dilemmas Heighten the Drama

The 2010 film *Extraordinary Measures* is based on the true life story of a father's desperate struggle to find a cure for Pompe Disease, a form of Muscular Dystrophy that limits a child's life span to about nine years. Harrison Ford plays the part of Dr. Robert Stonehill, who believes his research may lead to a cure. But Stonehill's research takes a lot of money, more than the father, played by Brandon Frasier, and the researcher are able to get from donations alone. So they formed a research company and then persuaded a venture capitalist to back them with $10 million. But the work was difficult and the expenses were high. There is a dramatic scene about 57 minutes into the story where the father and the researcher face a bitter dilemma. The venture capitalist gives them a choice: Meet an impossibly short deadline to complete their work or sell their company to pay back the venture capitalist. Both options are terrible from the perspective of Harrison Ford's character. He sees this as a dilemma from which there is no escape. But Brandon Frasier's character, the

father of the sick child, sees it as a false dilemma. Locate that scene in the movie and see how Frasier's character and Ford's character grapple with the decision they must make.

- Look, I put the CD into the player and the windshield wipers wouldn't turn on. It has to be that the problem with the wipers is somehow connected to the CD player.

- It's hard to know exactly what made her so angry. She seemed fine when we were talking earlier about what a jerk her former boyfriend was. Then you came in and boom! She exploded. I think it's your fault.

Called *"Post hoc, propter hoc"* ["After this, because of this"], confusing temporal proximity with causality is one of several mistakes grouped together under the heading False Cause Fallacies. Another mistake is to confuse a correlation with a cause.

JOURNAL

Post Hoc, Propter Hoc?

Give an example of when you connected some action you took with a positive result and then found yourself repeating that action in the hope of producing a similar positive outcome. How did that associational inference work out for you? Was it a warranted inference or was it the result of one of the fallacies that we describe in this chapter? Give reasons to support your conclusion.

- Our information shows that in times of economic growth, the hemlines on women's skirts go from below the knee to above the knee. And in times of a bear market when the economy slows down, the hemlines that are considered stylish go down below the knee, at times to mid-calf or even ankle height. I know how we can cure the current recession! All we need to do to pull out of the current recession is to make the fashion designers raise hemlines.

Other mistakes often grouped under the broad heading of False Cause Fallacies result from confusing symptoms, outcomes, or intentions with causes. Here are examples:

- The pressure was intense that day. I had to get from the university to my job, a drive that normally took 25 minutes. But the professor kept us late and then my car wouldn't start. You know there had to be a traffic jam on the freeway that day. And I needed to get to work because I had to make this major presentation. My head was aching and my heart was beating so fast. I felt all sweaty and it was getting harder and harder to breathe. I think that it was all because I couldn't get any air. That's where the pressure was coming from. No air.

- Three years ago we instituted a policy of Zero Tolerance for binge drinking in campus-controlled housing units. Simultaneously, we instituted a non-punitive program of substance abuse counseling. Today we have been honored by the state legislature because the reported incidents of binge drinking have dropped 32 percent compared to numbers from three years ago. The counseling program is why. That program has greatly reduced the number of incidents of binge drinking in campus-controlled housing.

- We wanted it more than they did! And that's why we won.

SLIPPERY SLOPE   Everyone knows that simply beginning something is no assurance that it will be completed. For a variety of reasons, too many good students never finish their degree programs. Not everyone who takes a drink becomes an alcoholic. Not everyone who buys a gun becomes a killer. The Slippery Slope Fallacy makes the false assumption that events are linked together so that the first step in the process necessarily results in some significant, usually bad, result way down the road somewhere. The image conjured by this fallacy is of walking along the edge of a muddy wet ridge. One step over that edge and we slide on our butts all the way to the bottom. Another image associated with this fallacy is the "camel's nose under the tent" image. Once the camel gets its nose under the tent, there is no way to prevent the whole, huge clumsy animal from entering one's well-ordered abode. There is wisdom in avoiding situations that can lead us down the path to major problems. But the fallacy fails to remember that even when we are headed toward trouble we have the power to turn ourselves around.

- If you ever smoke a joint, then you are on the path to perdition. One puff and there is no stopping the inevitable fall. Next it will be snorting coke, then shooting up heroin, leading to addiction with track marks in your arms and hepatitis or worse from contaminated needles.

- I warn you, you had better come to every training session. We start lessons Monday. If you miss the first day, then you'll be behind and you will never catch up.

A person can make a mistake and recover from it. And some of the initial stages that are alleged to be dreadful turn out not to be problems at all. And the middle ground is often the best place to make one's stand. To quote Terence of ancient Rome, "Moderation in all things."

20 Fallacies—Common Yet Misleading Errors of Reasoning (Chapters 7, 8, & 9 Combined)				
Arguments that Fail the Test of Relevance	**Fallacies of Relevance**	Appeals to Ignorance Appeals to the Mob Appeals to Emotion Ad Hominem Attacks	The Straw Man Fallacy Playing with Words Misuse of Authority	
Arguments that Fail the Test of Logical Strength	**Fallacies Masquerading as Valid Arguments**	Affirming the Consequent Denying the Antecedent False Classification	Fallacy of Composition Fallacy of Division False Reference	
	Fallacies Masquerading as Warranted Arguments	Erroneous Generalization Playing with Numbers False Dilemma	Gambler's Fallacy False Cause Slippery Slope	
Fail the Test of Non-Circularity		Circular Reasoning		

Summing up this chapter,

the evaluation of probabilistic reasoning occurs each day of our lives. We evaluate inferences as warranted or unwarranted when talking with friends, working on projects, enduring television commercials, or reasoning through a decision. In this chapter we first worked to strengthen our critical thinking skill of evaluation by considering the impact of new information on extended examples of probabilistic reasoning. It is natural for our minds to think in terms of the progression from coincidence, to perceived pattern, to demonstrated correlation, and then to causal explanation. Although, often it is a mistake to jump to conclusions that events are connected when, in fact they are not. That is why we then worked on the evaluation of arguments that offer to generalize from a limited number of experiences and samplings of data to reach justified claims about the characteristics of larger populations. To protect ourselves from being easily deceived, we reviewed the collection of common fallacies that masquerade as warranted arguments.

Key Concept

warranted describes an inference or argument such that the truth of the premises justifies or strongly supports confidently accepting the conclusion as very probably true, but not necessarily true.

Applications

Reflective Log

To Kill a Mockingbird: Gregory Peck plays the defense attorney, Atticus Finch, in the classic film *To Kill a Mockingbird*. The story is about a young man accused of rape. Toward the end of the trial there is a courtroom scene where Atticus Finch gives his summation to the jury. He must be careful not to alienate the members of the jury, whom he regards as potentially biased against the defendant because of his race. Atticus first argues that the prosecution has not proved that a crime was actually committed. He then argues that the accused, Tom Robinson, could not physically have done the things that the prosecution claims. Atticus, believing that he must do more than make claims and logical arguments establishing reasonable doubt, then addresses a key question. Why would the young woman accuser, a White woman, have lied about being raped by the accused Tom Robinson, a Black man? Atticus says he has pity for the victim and then he argues that by accusing Tom Robinson, she was attempting to rid herself of her own guilt. The defense then attempts to challenge the prejudicial assumption: In the language of those days, "Negros cannot be trusted." Locate the film

and listen carefully to the claims and arguments made by Atticus Finch in his speech to the jury. Transcribe them and then analyze and map the arguments. After the mapping, evaluate them using the skills developed in Chapters 7, 8, and 9. Explain your analysis and your evaluation. Would you have made the summation differently? If so, how?

Individual Exercises

Evaluate the worthiness and explain: Assume that all the premises that are asserted in the arguments below are true. Apply the remaining three tests to evaluate each argument to determine which are worthy of acceptance. Begin with the Test of Logical Strength. Remember, if the argument fails a test you do not have to apply any further tests because, at that point, the argument has been found to be unworthy of acceptance. In each case, give a detailed explanation to support your evaluation. State in your own words why each argument is worthy or unworthy of acceptance. Hint: Be prepared to add implicit but unspoken premises and assumptions. Keep in mind all the things we learned about fallacies and about logical strength from this chapter and the previous two.

1. Anthony was at risk of dying from the severe fall that he took when he was climbing. Many who had the same near-fatal experience become averse to climbing afterward. So, Anthony will surely become averse to climbing after his fall.

2. Susan is John's younger sister. Linda is John's elder sister. So, Linda is Susan's elder sister.

3. I want to buy a boat and you want to buy a car. If we buy a car we can't use it for fishing or to go tubing. But if we buy a boat we can't use it in the city or anywhere else but at the lake. Either way we're stuck.

4. Blood samples taken from the crime scene were type AB. The accused person's blood is type AB. Therefore, the accused was at the scene of the crime.

5. Either we'll study together tonight for tomorrow's exam, or we will both blow it off. I'm too tired to study tonight. So, we're going to blow it off.

6. Whenever I play the lottery, the number I put in is my birthday. If that's not my lucky number, then I don't have one.

7. Randolph knows that John Glenn was a senator. John Glenn was an astronaut. Therefore Randolph knows that John Glenn was an astronaut.

8. Every member of the House of Representatives is under the age of 90. Therefore, the House of Representatives is an organ of government that was created less than 90 years ago.

9. Seventy-three percent of the people surveyed said that they wanted universal health care coverage. Fifty-four percent said that they were worried about the cost of the program or the quality of the care that would be provided. Therefore, the American people are opposed to the President's health care reform legislation.

10. The Mayor has been in office for three months, and our city's economic recession has not gone away. The Mayor needs to take full responsibility for the sorry state of the city's economy.

11. My dear old Uncle Joe has a statue of the Red Faced Warrior on his kitchen table. It faces the side door, and he says that it keeps bad people from coming into his house. He also has a picture of St. Christopher taped to the dashboard of his old Buick and a rosary draped over the rearview mirror. More protection he claims. On the other hand, he never locks his house, and he needs to get his eyes checked!

12. But if we don't study together, then I'm not going to get through the course. And if I don't get through the course, then I'm going to ruin my GPA and lose my financial aid. So if we don't study together tonight, then I'm going to lose my financial aid.

13. We've lost six games in a row; our luck has to change today.

14. We didn't know what to do to improve sales. So, we all started wearing bow ties and navy blue sweaters to work. And look, three weeks later sales are way up. I'm sure it's our new office dress code.

15. It is March tenth and already this year six people have ordered new glasses with plastic frames. Last year only four people had ordered plastic frames by this date. That's an increase of 50 percent. We had better stock up. It's going to be a busy year.

16. Everyone loves ice cream. Children love ice cream. So, everyone's a child.

17. Water is our most precious resource. So, a towel on the rack means "I'll use it again" and a towel on the floor means, "Please replace."

18. The archeological theory that the Clovis people of North America were related to the Solutrean culture of Ice Age France and Spain was based on the similarities in the stone tools used. But new DNA evidence suggests that theory is mistaken. The DNA evidence indicates that the ancestors of the Clovis people came from Siberia in Asia. Since present day Native Americans are descended from the Clovis people, their ancestors were Asian.[19]

19. The suspect has a history of drug abuse. He has no alibi for the time of the murder. The suspect owns a collection of ceremonial knives and the murder weapon was a ceremonial knife. The suspect may have no motive as far as we know right now, but remember that his father was a serial killer. We found fibers at the crime scene, which are consistent with the brand of blue jeans the suspect wears. An eye witness places the suspect at the Fairfield Mall just one hour before the murder. So the suspect must be guilty.

20. Everyone believes that pornography harms people by modeling sexually aggressive behavior in men. But the evidence from recent studies suggests that pornography can have that effect only on men who are already prone to aggressive behavior. Therefore pornography is probably not the problem. Male aggressiveness is the problem.[20]

21. Biologists observed that male crickets on Kauai and Oahu no longer sing. This is due to mutations in their wings, different on the two islands, but both with the same result. Over 20 generations crickets with these wing mutations survived and procreated while the male crickets without the wing mutation all but disappeared. Why? the biologists asked. The answer was that the singing male crickets attracted a species of fly that sprayed baby maggots onto the singing cricket's back. The maggots burrowed into the cricket to feed. Thus killing the cricket. Biologists see this as more evidence that evolution is a natural process that continues to this very day.[21]

What's the truth about colon cleansing? On most issues we can find seemingly credible sources presenting substantially different information. We become confused about what to believe. And if we are unable or unwilling to evaluate the arguments and reasons being presented, we might find ourselves wasting our money or backing the candidate who does not have our interests at heart. But a strong critical thinker sees it as a challenge when two apparently credible sources present highly divergent information: Which is closer to the truth? If selecting an academic major based on faulty information about potential future earnings is not bad enough, making personal health care decisions based on faulty information and weak arguments only adds to one's problems. A service increasingly offered by spas and clinics that seems to be growing in popularity is colon cleansing or colonic hydrotherapy. Lots of colon cleansing products are marketed with celebrity endorsements. The arguments and reasons in support of colon cleansing include enhancing personal well-being, weight loss, and flushing bodily toxins. But there are reasons why colon cleansing is not recommended—for example, that the process itself can cause internal injuries and that its alleged benefits cannot be demonstrated.

You be the judge. Research the reasons given for and against the practice and evaluate them. Figure out which side in this issue is closer to the truth. Search "Colon Cleansing" for spa ads and claims about its advantages. For the other side see, for example, "The Dangers of Colon Cleansing," published in the *Journal of Family Practice*. This is not a 50/50 issue. As compared to those urging caution, those promoting a non-essential service, activity, or product have the greater burden. For they must prove that we ought to do what we need not do.[22]

SHARED RESPONSE

More Than Just a Couple of Cases

To evaluate the logical strength of probabilistic generalizations, we need to do more than find one or two counterexamples. We must, instead, examine whether the sampling of cases reported in the premises is adequate to support the probabilistic inferences that are drawn. This means asking four questions and finding satisfactory answers to each of them.

- **Was the correct group sampled?**
- **Were the data obtained in an effective way?**
- **Were enough cases considered?**
- **Was the sample representatively structured?**

In an earlier shared response exercise, you evaluated the argument that pseudo mature young teens are more likely to experience a variety of problems as young adults. There we asked if one counter example invalidated the probabilistic generalization. Re-evaluate the generalization in light of these four questions. Comment respectfully on other peoples' shared responses.

Group Exercises

Create your own examples of fallacies: Write two fallacious arguments exemplifying each of these six errors

- The Erroneous Generalization Fallacy
- The Playing with Numbers Fallacy
- The False Dilemma Fallacy
- The Gambler's Fallacy
- The False Cause Fallacy
- The Slippery Slope Fallacy

Bedbugs and cold days in August: Evaluate the bedbug example and the San Francisco in August weather example. In each case ask:

- Was the correct group sampled?
- Were the data obtained in an effective way?
- Were enough cases considered?
- Was the sample representatively structured?

When the premises do not provide enough information for a satisfactory answer, explain what information one would have to find, as we did when we noted what would be needed for the sample of 435 to be considered representative of the population of people over the age of 60.

How should the United States conduct the 2020 census? There are two ways to conduct a census. Contact everyone and gather the data being sought, or generalize from well-structured representative samples. This group project invites you to evaluate the methodology used by the U.S. government for conducting the 2010 Census. You are invited to make recommendations for improving that methodology. If you come up with some good suggestions, offer them to your Congressional representatives and the U.S. Census Bureau. Begin your investigation at the U.S. government's census website **census.gov**. Navigate to the methodology page.

To fully evaluate the methodology and make reasonable recommendations, your group will want to consider first and foremost the logical strength of the two alternatives (count absolutely everyone possible vs. make estimates based on samples.) When considering the sampling alternative, keep in mind the importance of sample size and representative structure. For both alternatives, keep in mind the question of the method of gathering data. For example, going door to door will ensure that homeless Americans are systematically excluded.

Other considerations that may weigh on your ultimate recommendations: You should consider the cost (money and time) of the two alternatives, the political consequences of each, and the social value associated with enlisting volunteers in an effort of national scope.

Bonus Exercise

The debate over the "Public Option"

At the end of the July 24, 2009, episode of HBO's *Real Time with Bill Maher*, Maher argues in support of the "public option" to be included in the health care reform legislation, which at that time was being fiercely debated.

The "public option," a provision not included in the final Obamacare (Affordable Care Act) law, would have given tens of millions of uninsured and underinsured Americans the option of purchasing health care insurance at an affordable price. Either the government would provide the program through a not-for-profit agency, or the legislation would permit the establishing of co-ops. Maher's barbed statements included these: "If conservatives get to call universal health care 'socialized medicine,' I get to call private, for-profit healthcare 'soulless, vampire bastards making money off human pain." "I would love to have some journalist ask a Republican who talks about socialized medicine: If it's so awful, how come it's what we have for our veterans?"

Locate and watch Bill Maher's commentary in episode 161 of *Real Time with Bill Maher*. In as fair-minded and nonincendiary a way as possible, present his arguments in support of the "public option." Map his reasons using the techniques presented in the chapter, "Analyze Arguments and Diagram Decisions." Then evaluate his arguments using the four-test process presented in the chapter, "Evaluate Arguments: Four Basic Tests." Remain objective. Resist permitting your personal views on the subject to interfere with the objectivity of your analysis of Maher's views or your evaluation of his arguments.

During the summer of 2009 many conservative political commentators spoke out against the "public option." Research the web for videos and written editorials by political conservatives like Bill O'Reilly, Dennis Miller, and Sean Hannity. With the same concern not to be caught up in the rhetoric, but instead to dig for their reasons and evidence, analyze and map their main arguments in opposition to the "public option." Once you have those arguments analyzed, apply all four of the tests for evaluating arguments. As with the arguments offered by Maher, here too arguments may fail because one or more of their premises are untrue, because the argument is illogical, because the reason is irrelevant, or because the argument is circular. To assist with these tests you might search for commentaries on the arguments, since many media outlets published editorials during those days to refute the arguments of the other side. One example focusing on Sean Hannity that we quickly found five years later was posted by the Media Matters Organization. Google "mediamatters.org/research/200910080006."

Chapter 10
Snap Judgments: Risks and Benefits of Heuristic Thinking

Making snap judgments is like riding a bicycle, once learned we can continue making them with unreflective ease.

HOW does human decision making work, and where does critical thinking fit?

HOW do cognitive heuristics help and harm strong decision making?

 ## Learning Outcomes

10.1 Explain, using examples, the difference between System-1 and System-2 decision making.

10.2 Explain, using examples, each of the cognitive heuristics described in this chapter, including its potential benefits and risks.

Many good judgments we make every day are automatic or reactive, rather than reflective. Consider the ease with which well-trained pilots fly complicated machines safely taking millions of us to our destinations every day. Through training and repetition, veteran pilots have internalized and made automatic a series of complex analyses, inferences, and quick effective judgments that novice pilots often find mentally all-consuming. Automatic reactions are also seen in more "grounded" drivers and in other situations. For example, bike riders often pedal along, paying more attention to the beauty of their surroundings than on shifting gears or maintaining their balance. The process of e-mailing friends is another example. Our fingers tap the keys, but our minds are focused more on composing our messages than on locating the letters on the keyboards. Human beings do not make all their decisions using only their capacity for deliberative reflective thought. Human decision making is more complex.[1] Some judgments, including many good ones, are quick and reactive, not deliberative or reflective. Although some judgments are best made more automatically or reactively, some are best made reflectively.[2] Our real-life critical thinking question is "Which of our reactive judgments ought we to make reflectively?"

For any of us to maximize our personal potential for developing and applying critical thinking to real-life decision making, we first must understand how human problem solving and decision making function in real life. We know that critical thinking, or reflective purposeful judgment, can and ought to be applied to a very large array of vital issues and important decisions. And we know from our experience that we do not always use critical thinking. The fact that we *do* not use critical thinking does not imply that we *ought* not to be using critical thinking.

This chapter and the next one focus on the skill of self-regulation, because monitoring our own decision making and correcting our own decision making turn out to be essential. Taking a moment to "stop and think" is excellent advice for every one of us, authors included. We begin this chapter with a brief synopsis of the cognitive science research on decision making so that we can position critical thinking, and in particular the skill of self-regulation, within that context. We will learn that many reactive judgments are good judgments. But, in some circumstances, reactive judgments can lead to unnecessary risks and mistaken biases. Our work in this chapter is to use self-regulation to become more aware of those circumstances so we can correct ourselves reflectively, using critical thinking, before we make a mistake.

10.1 Our Two Human Decision-Making Systems

Human decision making emerges from the interplay of two cognitive drivers. One is our human propensity toward self-explanation known as argument making. The other driver is the influence on our decision making of mental "shortcuts" known as cognitive heuristics. *Argument making*, as we saw in the previous chapters, is the effort to be logical—that is, to rely on the relevant reasons and facts as we see them when making our decisions. In general, humans value making important decisions as rationally as the circumstances, significance, and content of their judgments permit. This is not to say that we are always successful in this effort. In fact, we often are not. And yet we explain our choices and judgments to ourselves, if not to others, in terms of the relevant reasons and facts—again, as we see them. For example, you ask me why I stayed overnight at a friend's house in another city instead of driving home. I reply that it was late and I was very tired, too tired to drive.

Heuristic thinking is the tendency, which is at times quite useful, of relying on highly efficient and generally reliable cognitive shortcuts when reaching a decision. In the research literature, these mental shortcuts are known as *cognitive heuristics*. These mental maneuvers are as much a part of the human reasoning process as argument making. Cognitive heuristics often enable us to make judgments and decisions more expeditiously and efficiently. Their influences, while often positive, can introduce errors and biases into human decision making.

The "Two-Systems" Approach to Human Decision Making

Research on human decisions made in naturalistic, everyday contexts, describes the interaction of two overlapping decision-making systems.[3] One is reactive, instinctive, quick, and holistic (System-1). The other is reflective, deliberative, analytical, and procedural (System-2). Both valuable systems function simultaneously, often checking and balancing each other.

REACTIVE (SYSTEM-1) THINKING System-1 thinking relies heavily on situational cues, salient memories, and heuristic thinking to arrive quickly and confidently at judgments, particularly when situations are familiar and immediate action is required. Many freeway accidents are avoided because drivers are able to see and react to dangerous situations quickly. Good decisions emerging from System-1 thinking often feel intuitive.[4] Decisions good drivers make in those moments of crisis, just like the decisions practiced athletes make in the flow of a game or the decisions that a gifted

Our self-protective response to any kind of a sudden and unexpected attack is a System-1 decision—automatic and reactive.

teacher makes while interacting with students, are born of expertise, training, and practice. Often we decide first, quickly, and reactively, and then, if asked about our decisions, we explain how we analyzed the situation and we provide the reasons and arguments to explain those snap judgments, which are System-1 decisions. You are suddenly and unexpectedly confronted with an attack dog, you instantly react defensively. It is natural. So what if the owner tries to reassure you with a confident "He won't bite." Your System-1 decision making self-protective reaction kicked in, flooding your body with adrenalin and triggering your natural "fight or flee" reaction. If our ancestors had waited around debating what to do when attacked by ferocious carnivorous predators, our species probably would not be around today. Overt explanations using rationalistic argument making in the case of System-1 decisions are retrospective. We look back at what we did and explain the instantaneous System-1 inferences we made at the heat of the moment.

REFLECTIVE (SYSTEM-2) THINKING System-2 thinking is useful for judgments in unfamiliar situations, for processing abstract concepts, and for deliberating when there is time for planning and more comprehensive consideration. Humans use heuristic maneuvers in System-2 thinking as well, often integrated as components of their logical arguments. Argument making is often part of the inference and deliberation process when making System-2 decisions. And, of course, explanations involve making arguments and giving the reasons we used during our deliberations. When we share our reflective interpretations, analyses, evaluations, and inferences, we are offering explanations. Because of this, critical thinking is self-regulated System-2 thinking. Critical thinking is System-2 thinking focused on resolving the problem at hand and at the same time monitoring

and self-correcting one's own process of thinking about that problem.

As you think about the "two-systems" approach, please avoid all the harsh, rigid, stereotypic, divisive, commercialized oppositional, oversimplified, pop culture dichotomies. We are not characterizing human decision making by expressions and false dichotomies such as "emotion vs. reason," "head vs. heart," "feeling vs. judgment," "intuitive vs. logical," "expansive vs. linear," "creative vs. critical," "right brained vs. left brained," "warm vs. cold," "from Venus vs. from Mars," or "blink vs. wide-eyed." Human decision making is neither this superficial nor this simplistic. We are not saying that normal human thinking is schizophrenic or psychologically disordered in any way. We are not suggesting that some people are only System-1 thinkers while others are only System-2 thinkers.

Normal human beings have and use both systems in problem solving and decision making every day. The two-systems approach to understanding human decision making accounts for the pushes and pulls that normal human beings often describe as part of their decision making. System-1 is the rapid-fire decision making we all experience on some occasions, while System-2 is the more reflective decision making we all experience on other occasions.

Because it is considered more useful for addressing novel and complex problems in a reflective and methodical way, System-2 is the mode of reasoned, informed, and thoughtful problem solving and decision making that a broad undergraduate liberal arts and sciences education cultivates. System-2 is also the mode addressed by

When we make thoughtfully reflective choices, including applying our critical thinking skills, we are using our System-2 decision making.

Model of Two-System Human Decision Making

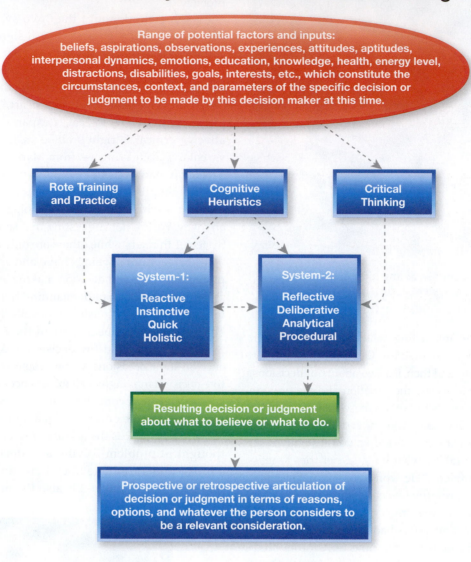

the evidence-based practice and research methods components of one's professional or graduate studies. All levels of education, which aim at improving one's critical thinking—improving one's skills and dispositions to engage successfully in purposeful reflective judgment—is education focused directly on strengthening System-2 problem solving and decision making.

Is the two-systems approach only a helpful way of imagining how our minds work, or is there some basis for it in the neural chemistry of the human brain? In fact, it is the second. Using functional MRI scans scientists can now see the changes in brain activity as a person's thinking moves from one system to the other during learning.[5] System-1 processing appears highly reactive, like a reflex automatically triggered by a stimulus. By contrast, System-2 reasoning is described as much more reflective, analytical, mindful, and meta-cognitive. But System-2 can override System-1, which gives all of us hope that our decisions can be more than knee-jerk reactions.

The Value of Each System

System-1 and System-2 are vital decision-making tools, particularly when stakes are high and uncertainty is an issue. We can often rely on System-1 to get us through our day-to-day activities while engaging System-2 on some other topic of concern. People report they can drive from home to work without remembering any of the hundreds of routine automobile operating decisions necessary to make the trip. Others report being able to drink a cup of coffee and finish a bowl of breakfast cereal almost without noticing because they are so engrossed in the morning news. Have you ever had any of these kinds of experiences in your life—experiences where you did something "without really thinking about it" while your mind was preoccupied with a completely different problem or issue?

We do not store the memories of our System-1 guided actions if we are simultaneously engaged in deliberating about something using System-2. For example, when we are thinking about something else, like a work assignment, a relationship issue, or a financial problem, we are distracted from the simpler System-1 decision making we may be doing, like walking in a familiar place, driving home on a familiar route, or eating lunch. Our mental focus is on the System-2 work, and, during those times, System-1 operates in the background. This is why we may not remember routine System-1 judgments, like why we've walked into a room, whether we've already passed our freeway exit, or if we've already put sugar in our coffee.

System-1 functions in the background or "behind the scenes" more than System-2, but each system is capable of overriding the other. Conflicted decision-making contexts have, through the ages, been described in different ways—"temptation" being only one example. We are drawn one way, but at the same time, pulled the other way. Although we do not accept the implication that the colloquial expressions are scientifically accurate, we can spot oblique references to the behind-the-scenes pushes and pulls of the two systems in the way people ordinarily talk about their decision making. We have all heard people say things like "My gut says to do X, but my brain says to do Y"; "We looked at all the evidence and all the options and yet we don't feel comfortable with where the deliberations are heading"; or "Emotionally I want to do this, but rationally I think I should do that." Some theorists suggest these common ways of talking are evidence that, in certain kinds of ambiguous or complex situations, the two systems might conflict, drawing the decision maker in different directions. In general, this is thought to be an advantage that reduces the chance of making poor, suboptimal, or even dangerous errors in judgment—a natural system of checks and balances, as it were.

Even a good thinker makes both System-1 and System-2 errors from time to time. We misinterpret things, overestimate or underestimate our chances of succeeding, rely on mistaken analogies, reject options out of hand, trust feelings and hunches, judge things credible when they are not, etc. Often mistakes like these are directly related to the influences and misapplications of cognitive heuristics. We all share the propensity to use these heuristics as we make decisions, because at times the heuristics seem to be

Example of System-2 Thinking: Experienced policy makers carefully considering possible responses to budget challenges.

hardwired into our species. Since the critical thinking skill of self-regulation can help us avoid some of these errors if we become more familiar with how they look in practice, let's examine several in closer detail.

> "To paraphrase Socrates, the unexamined thought is not worth thinking."
>
> Pat Croskerry, MD.[6]

10.2 Heuristics: Their Benefits and Risks

Shakespeare called humans the paragon of animals. Aristotle said "rational animals." For Plato, "featherless bipeds" was good enough. Perhaps not the most honorific descriptions, yet humbling and useful reminders that there are times when we base our judgments on unfounded assumptions and fallacious reasoning. The long list of argument fallacies in the table we put at the end of the Chapter 9 titled "Warranted Inferences" does not include all the ways that our decision making can go astray. In the current chapter we consider a whole new set of biases and errors emerging from the *misapplication* of those ordinarily reliable reasoning maneuvers known as "heuristics." Given the natural limitations of human rationality, it turns out that errors in heuristic thinking can result in serious problems when the risks are great and the stakes are high.

The correct application of cognitive heuristics is absolutely essential for day-to-day living. We would exhaust ourselves mentally and accomplish very little if every single judgment was a full-blown reflective decision. We get through the routine parts of our day making quick, automatic reactive heuristic judgments. We rely on these snap judgments because (a) most of the time they are good enough for the purpose at hand; (b) we need to conserve our mental energy for bigger, more important, and less familiar problems that life throws our way; and (c) often,

Example of System-1 Thinking: A well-trained soldier reacting quickly and correctly under fire.

we have no time for reflective thought. This will be clearer as you review the examples and do the exercises in conjunction with each of the following heuristics.

Individual Cognitive Heuristics

Cognitive heuristics are natural human decision-making shortcuts we all rely upon in real life to expedite our judgments about what to believe or what to do. There are potentially beneficial consequences associated with relying on the cognitive shortcuts we'll discuss. In each case we examine the heuristic shortcut or maneuver itself and note potential advantages and disadvantages of relying on the heuristic. A brief, true-to-life vignette and other examples illustrate how that heuristic looks in real life. In most cases a short exercise invites you to apply your critical thinking—and in particular your skill at reflective self-regulation—to occasions in your own life when reliance on that particular heuristic may have resulted in outcomes that were less successful than you had hoped. There are 17 common heuristics described in this chapter. Each is likely quite familiar.

1. SATISFICING AND 2. TEMPORIZING   The first time he was at the beach, young Jerome darted down to the wet sand and watched as a small wave washed up toward him. A wave came in and lapped at his toes and ankles, the chilly wet water sending him scurrying up the sand. He turned and cautiously approached the water a second time. Again he got close enough to just let the water touch the tips of his toes, and scooted up the sand. But not nearly as far as the first time. The third time he approached the surf he anticipated the wave as it approached and, instead of turning to run, he back-pedaled a few steps. Just far enough not to be hit by the salty bubbles. He went just far enough! The kid satisficed, I thought, and, more interestingly, nobody taught him how.

The *Satisficing Heuristic*: Having found an option that is good enough, we take it. We human beings typically do only what must be done to achieve our purposes. In day-to-day living, when faced with choices, instead of expending the resources necessary to identify and then attain the maximally optimal alternative, we decide in favor of an alternative we deem satisfactory.[7] How many times have we read the whole menu in a restaurant compared to reading along only until we spot an entrée that strikes our fancy? We tend to divide the world into "good enough" and "not good enough" and search for a solution until a solution is found that is good enough to attain the desired outcome. Truisms like "If it isn't broken, don't fix it," and "Perfect is the enemy of good" reflect the satisficing cognitive maneuver. Humans satisfice in System-1 and System-2 decision making situations.

- Example (System-1): Being thirsty, how much water would we drink? Only enough to slake our thirst.
- Example (System-2): Seeking a new job, how hard would we look? Only hard enough to find one

The water is so captivating and inviting to the young child. But scary too, like lots of things in life. How far from danger is "far enough"?

that meets whatever are our basic criteria for pay, proximity to home, nature of the work, etc.

- Example (System-2): Having arrested a suspect who had the means, motive, and opportunity to commit the crime, how hard can we expect police detectives to strive to locate other suspects? Satisficing suggests hardly at all because they have a stack of other crime cases needing their attention. The question of the actual guilt or innocence of the subject becomes the concern of the prosecuting attorney and the courts.

The *Temporizing Heuristic*: Deciding that a given option is "good enough *for now*," or temporizing is satisficing's running mate. We often move through life satisficing and temporizing. At times, we look back on our situations and wonder why it is that we have settled for far less than we might have. If we had only studied harder, worked out a little more, or taken better care of our relationships and ourselves, perhaps we would not be living as we are now. But at the time, each of the decisions along the way was "good enough for the time being."

We must not overlook the important potential advantages to satisficing. These include conserving time, money, and energy.[8] If you have to put in 10 percent more effort and time to gain only 1 percent more value, your return on that investment of effort may not be worth the cost. The main disadvantage of satisficing is that we may be mistaken in our estimation of how much is "good enough." Why did the better team lose the game? Because, in underestimating its opponent, the team failed to play up to its own potential. Why did we have trouble on the exam? Because we did not do the homework exercises and study hard enough. Why did my boss not give me a better evaluation compared to my peers? Because I was not productive enough, even though I had thought all along that I was doing just fine. Using our critical thinking in real time,

"It would appear, Hopkins, that your gut feel was only indigestion"

we should take a moment in key situations to be sure our heuristic estimate of "good enough" is really accurate. To achieve greater success we will have to self-correct and recalibrate our sense of how much is enough.

3. AFFECT: "GO WITH YOUR GUT"   "I proposed on our first date. She said no. But somehow we both knew that her response was not going to be her final answer. A few months later we were engaged. More than 40 wedding anniversaries later, we are still in love. Perhaps we have been lucky; our marriage could have been a disaster. Whatever was reflective and rational about that decision—as I recall trying to explain it to her folks and mine—had to have been an effort to build a case for a decision we had already made."

The *Affect Heuristic*: Making a decision based on your initial affective ("gut") response.[9] There is no question that many different kinds of experiences can cause us to respond with joy or sorrow, with desire or revulsion, with enthusiasm or dread. A "gut reaction," that is, an affective response, is a strong System-1 impetus, either positively or negatively, toward the object.[10] It is natural to have the response.[11] That response may be the "first word" on the matter, but System-2 self-regulation demands that we ask ourselves whether that should necessarily be the final word on the matter.

- Example: "Oh, I like those shoes. . . . You know, they would look great with the blue jacket I bought."

- Example: "Did you see his eyes? Pure evil! Made my blood run cold. Believe me, a guy like that, no way should you trust him."

- Example: "Forget it. I don't want to hear about how you think we can balance the budget. You said the 'T' word and I won't have anything to do with that. Read my lips, 'No new taxes!' We all pay too much in taxes as it is."

Our natural, initial affective response to ideas, questions, images, people, events, etc., can have obvious advantages and disadvantages. Research on the relationship between facial and body symmetry, perceived attractiveness, and physical health suggests that first affective impressions we have about another human being as a possible mate are evolutionarily selected for and contributes to the survival of the species. Our System-1 affective reaction can influence us toward embracing a choice that "just feels right" or away from an option that appears frightening or repugnant when our System-2 decision making gets bogged down with too many factors to consider, too many divergent criteria, and too much uncertainty. Were it not for this, some of us might never get unstuck and make a decision when one is needed.

But, what if that initially frightening option is actually the best and most reasonable? For example, what if our fear of the anticipated consequences of radiation or chemotherapy influenced us to reject those options when one or both of them were the best possible cancer treatment options? It may take significant amounts of reflective System-2 reasoning to overcome a powerful System-1 affective response to an idea, but it can be done. And at times it should happen, because there is no guarantee that our affective responses are necessarily always true. Strong critical thinking demands that we check our affective responses. Simply having them is not nearly enough for wise, reflective decision making.

The affect heuristic influences us to make judgments and decisions based on our initial impulsive and subliminal responses. Knowing this, marketing experts coined the expression, "The package is the product," to indicate

THINK CRITICALLY

Examples from Your Life

When "enough" was not good enough: Think of two recent occasions when you were disappointed by how your efforts turned out because of misestimating how much on your part was necessary to achieve your goals. Use your critical thinking skills to make a reasoned judgment regarding how to adjust your sense of "good enough" to increase your likelihood of success in the same endeavors the next time.

When your response was an emotional jolt: Think of two recent occasions when you had a strong initial affective

response to an idea, proposal, opportunity, person, or event. Find one that was positive and one that was negative. Did you reflect on that response, evaluate it, and verify that it was the correct response? If not, this exercise provides the opportunity. Apply your System-2 reflective critical thinking skills to both of those responses. Gather needed information and analyze your response in the light of that new information. Call on your habits of truth-seeking and open-mindedness to support your effort to be as objective as possible in evaluating your initial responses.

Marketing experts know that many of our purchasing decisions are based more on our affective response to the packaging than on our rational reflections on what is inside. Soap is just soap, that is, until it is packaged in either a visually attractive or a plain-wrap uninviting way.

how important the wrapping, the container, and the initial appearance of a product are to making the sale.[12] Certainly a broken residence hall window and an unkempt campus lawn are not necessarily indicative of an academically substandard college. But college recruiters know that these things had better be fixed before prospective students show up for the campus tour. And on reflection, no one would argue that a cabernet in an attractively designed bottle with a classy label is necessarily superior to a cabernet in a generic bottle with a plain looking label.[13] There is no question that first impressions count when choosing a college, choosing a wine, or choosing a mate.

4. SIMULATION   "I was in center field, my favorite position, and the runner at third was itching to tag up and dash for home if the batter hit a fly ball. I imagined what I would do if it were hit to me, how I would run in, position my body, make the catch and fire the ball to the plate on one hop so the catcher could handle the throw easily and tag out the runner. The odds were overwhelming that the batter would hit the ball someplace else. But no! The ball was in the air arcing over the infield and sailing out toward center. I darted to my right, took the fly out of the air with my gloved left hand and made my throw toward the plate. The runner had tagged, leaving early I think. But he didn't have a chance. My throw, just up the third baseline from home, was on target and on time. The catcher put the tag on the runner for the third out. It was like I had made a movie in my mind, watched the movie, and then lived the scene almost exactly."

The *Simulation Heuristic*: Estimating the likelihood of a given outcome based on how easy it is to imagine that outcome.[14] Simulation is a mental process of imagining ourselves doing something successfully or unsuccessfully. Before giving a speech we might "see ourselves" at the podium talking to the audience with confidence, making our point, and delivering our message effectively. Or we may simulate the opposite, seeing ourselves messing up, getting flustered, and forgetting to say things we had wanted to say. If we experience ease in processing a simulation, this influences us to believe that achieving the anticipated outcome is more likely.[15] A person choosing among several options might simulate what it would be like to select an option and then, like making a movie in his or her mind, imagine what life would be like having selected that option. Unless we are being reflective about the actual probabilities that what we picture will actually happen, the simulation heuristic can influence us to select an option that plays out in our minds as the one offering the most desirable result. This might be called "wishful thinking," but whatever it is called, it is not a reflective and well-informed System-2 decision about the actual probability. The same would be true of pessimistically overestimating the likelihood of a bad outcome.

• Example: "You know, I didn't go there to buy a car. But when I was on the lot looking, this salesman came up to me and invited me to sit behind the wheel. Then we went on a test drive, and I could really see myself tooling along I-70 in this baby. So, here it is. My new set of wheels."

THINKING CRITICALLY

See Yourself . . .

Simulate yourself hang gliding off the wind-swept cliffs along the Pacific Ocean. First, see yourself gliding up into the beautiful blue sky, enjoying the grand vistas and the glorious ocean, smelling the salty warmth of the sea air, swooping with silent grace toward the surf, and then lifting effortlessly and joyously on a vector of warm wind with the gulls and pelicans. Take your time. Enjoy the flight. Then when you are ready, ease yourself toward the soft sand and glide slowly to a perfect landing and the admiring approval of your friends. On a scale of 1 to 10, with 10 being "Yes, absolutely," how much did playing that movie in your mind incline you toward wanting to try hang gliding? On a scale of 1 to 10, with 10 being "easy," how easy would hang gliding be?

Now envision a second scenario. See yourself blown along, out of control, harnessed below a tissue-thick nylon wing attached to a flimsy aluminum frame, mentally on the edge of panic, your arms aching, and your back muscles knotted with tension. You are disoriented, high above the jagged rocks and treacherous waves, trying to dodge other hang gliders. Suddenly, you are distracted by the flock of gulls heading your way. You hear the shouts of people below, but are not able to understand what they are saying. You are uncertain about how to land this contraption without breaking both legs. On a scale of 1 to 10, with 10 being "Yes, absolutely," how much did playing that movie in your mind incline you toward wanting to try hang gliding? On a scale of 1 to 10 with 10, being "easy," how easy would hang gliding be?

Notice that neither simulation supplied any concrete information about hang gliding. Neither detailed the actual risks associated with the sport. Neither explained how one learns to hang glide, whether there are safer or more dangerous places to hang glide, or anything else that would have enabled one to make a reasoned and reflective System-2 analysis and evaluation in response to the question about how easy or difficult it would be.

- Example: "I don't know what happened, sir!" said the sales representative to the manager after the failed presentation. "Yesterday I could see myself closing that deal."

- Example: "Day trading. I took it up for a while. Lost a lot of money, too. You know it just seemed like it was going to be so easy. All I had to do was invest in some stocks in the morning and watch them increase in value as the day went along. Then sell them just before the market did its typical end-of-day little dip. Well. Things didn't turn out that way at all. I think the only people who made money on my day trading were the guys who work at the brokerage house."

Psychologist Albert Bandura's research on social learning demonstrates the value and power of simulation to increase attitudes of self-efficacy.[16] Mentors and coaches use the simulation heuristic, (they may call it *visualization*) as a technique to improve performance and to help people anticipate being able to succeed at challenging things. Successful advertising often depends on stimulating simulation. Car ads, for example, often show someone with demographics just like the intended buyers taking great pleasure in driving the model of car the ad is promoting. The idea is that if you match those demographics, you would then be led to see yourself in that car and then want to buy it. The process of simulation is quick, easy, and need not be reflective. In fact, it might be better for the advertiser if you do not reflect too much on the actual costs and benefits of buying that new car. The obvious disadvantage of simulation is the potential to err in estimating the likelihood of the imagined outcomes. This can result in misplaced confidence and unwarranted optimism.

Everyone knows that simulating academic success is not a replacement for actually studying, doing the assignments, and doing well on exams. But along with those things, simulation can be very helpful. Take a moment and see yourself being a successful student by simulating how you will structure your time so that you can read the textbook and do all the exercises and assignments. Simulate how you will be organized, focused, and highly efficient in your use of that study time. See yourself going to class or taking tests justifiably confident in what you have learned, well prepared and ready to demonstrate your knowledge on exams and assignments. Oh, yes, and the critical thinking skill of self-regulation requires that we remind ourselves that we have to carry out the study plans that we have simulated, if we are to have a reasonable shot at achieving the learning and enjoying the success we anticipate.

5. AVAILABILITY "I was doing 75+ heading eastbound on I-96 from Michigan State back home to Detroit, alone, late at night. Darkness had engulfed the rural stretch of interstate. Occasionally, a car heading west passed by on the other side of the wide grassy median. Eastbound was two lanes, and I liked driving in the left lane because it was smoother since the heavy 18-wheelers had not furrowed and gnawed the pavement. But for reasons I'll never know, I decided that night to do the right thing, the thing I'd been taught in driver's education back in high school, and I moved back into the right-hand lane. Then, ahead, just over a slight rise in the interstate, I saw the glare of an approaching vehicle's high beam headlights. It didn't make sense—there

"That could be me! What would I do? Where would I go?"

shouldn't be any traffic heading west directly in front of me. I drove on, never reducing my speed. The lights grew brighter and brighter. I reached the crest of the rise in the freeway just as the other vehicle did. In a shocking blur it roared by, easily doing 75+. Heading west. On the east-bound side of I-96. And, thank God, he was in his right lane too. Moral of the story. Stay to the right, son, or you'll never know what hit you."

The *Availability Heuristic*: Estimating the likelihood of future events based on a vivid memory of a past experience that leaps easily to mind. Let's experiment with a memory. Imagine a conversation you may have had about foods you can't stand. Does a particularly awful experience with that food leap to mind? For example: "I hate mushrooms. Once when I was a kid I got sick on mushrooms at a restaurant." That quick, automatic connection is a manifestation of the availability heuristic. "No mushrooms on my pizza! Please." This heuristic leads us to estimate the likelihood of a future event based on the vividness or ease of recalling a similar past event.[17] Because a past experience leaps vividly to mind or because it was so important, we overestimate the probability that future outcomes will be the same as they were back then. People tell stories of things that happened to them or their friends all the time as a way of explaining their own decisions and warning or advising their friends and family about the future. Often these are helpful because they vicariously increase our own range of experiences. The use of stories makes it much easier for us to remember their lessons or morals. Aesop's fables have more than entertainment value; they remind us not to "cry wolf," not to devalue what we have by coveting something we cannot get (as did the fox with the grapes), and many other solid bits of wisdom. On the other hand, there is always the risk that in the retelling, the actual events may be mistakenly remembered, misunderstood,

or misinterpreted. Whether accurate or not, stories have an unwarranted amount of influence on decisions about what to expect, what to believe, and what to do.

Availability sells. The news media, knowing the power of a compelling narrative, regularly "put a human face" on news reports. They know it is boring to hear newscasters drone on about statistics and abstractions—for example, about how many homes were damaged by a tornado or how many families lost electric power due to the storm. So instead, the news crew will interview an emotionally distraught person. They will take pictures or video of the person, the damaged home and felled trees in the background, looking lost among the scatterings of furniture and the family's ruined and irreplaceable mementoes. This makes abstractions like "terrible tornado," "brutal shooting," "five alarm fire," and "devastating flood," vividly available to us. And because of the availability heuristic, we, unreflectively, jack up our estimate of the chances that we too might become a hapless storm victim—just like that sad person we're seeing in the news report.

The disadvantage of basing judgments on the availability heuristic is that we will wrongly estimate the actual probabilities that a given outcome will occur.[18] Or worse, while we are worrying about the far less likely possibility, we will stop paying attention to threats and problems that are far more likely to happen.

In the aftermath of the horrendous killings of over 30 people at Virginia Tech (VT) in 2007, parents, students, faculty, and staff at the nation's more than 4,200 colleges and universities sharply revised their estimates of the probabilities of a similarly deranged killer's assault on their own campuses. Campus security increased, counseling centers received more funding, legislators held hearings at the state and national levels, and campus authorities updated emergency plans and conducted readiness drills. Although these might have been good things to do, resources are finite. Were these the most urgent things for a campus to do, given all the other risks and threats out there? Probably not. Fire preparedness, weather disaster preparedness, theft detection and prevention, rape and assault protection, food poisoning prevention, and flu epidemic preparedness are just a few projects that address tragically lethal and somewhat more probable eventualities. But all the attention was on the VT situation. It was vividly in mind for administrators, students, parents, and the media. Those other more likely dangers were not on their minds right then. Hence, the disproportionate allocation of time, money, and attention.

JOURNAL
That Reminds Me of the Time When . . .

Provide an example of when someone gave you advice about a really important matter and their only argument was that your situation reminded them of their own or someone else's situation.

---

6. REPRESENTATION   "Uncle John did not smoke cigars at the track, he chewed them. Today he liked the filly—a sleek 3-year-old who looked fast. He would have to find her name in the racing form. But just watching her in the paddock, she reminded him of a horse he'd seen run so well at Bay Meadows a couple of years back. Same markings, same look of a winner in her dark, intense eyes. Hadn't he won a couple of Benjamins at 8 to 1 on that filly? To Uncle John it only made sense to put down a bet on this one to win." Uncle John made the snap judgment that because this horse looked like that other horse, this horse would perform like the other horse.

The *Representation Heuristic*: Making the snap judgment that X is like Y in every way upon noticing that X is like Y in some way. A perceived similarity becomes the basis for assuming that there is an analogical relationship between two things, an analogy that may or may not be warranted.[19] For example, someone might say, "My father and I were alike in so many ways—in our lifestyles and how we thought about things. Dad died a few years ago of lymphoma. He was only 69. You know, as much as I don't like the idea, I probably have about 30 years before lymphoma gets me, too." The speaker in this example is overestimating the probability of contracting a fatal lymphoma or even of dying at age 69. This thinking is disconnected from any System-2 analytical reflection on the scientific evidence regarding the genetic and environmental factors that estimate a person's cancer risks. But absent that self-corrective reflection, we risk allowing the analogical representation heuristic to influence our beliefs and choices unduly.

If the similarity between two things is fundamental and relevant, it's more likely that the analogy will be reliable. For example, suppose your co-worker was fired for missing sales targets. You might draw the reasonable conclusion that you are no different in relevant respects from your co-worker. Thus, if you miss your sales targets, you'll be fired too. Good thinking.

Or the similarity might be superficial or not connected with the outcome, which would make the analogical inference much weaker. For example, we see a TV commercial showing trim, sexy young people enjoying fattening fast foods and infer that because we're young, too, we can indulge our cravings for fast foods without gaining unhealthy excess poundage. This is another example showing that heuristic thought needs to be monitored when it is used to make important decisions. As we develop our critical thinking skill of self-regulation, we become more adept at noticing when our decisions hinge on the analogical representation heuristic. And we can correct ourselves before making a decision that is not well thought out. Self-monitoring and self-correcting one's thinking can help ensure that conclusions are warranted. In a later section entitled "Comparative Reasoning" we will explore the criteria for the evaluation of analogical inferences in detail.

7. ASSOCIATION   "We were having a good time, probably on our third beer, *Sports Center* was on TV someplace nearby, but we're not really paying attention because Bill was talking about how the girl he was seeing really liked dogs, and he did, too. So, he's saying that she has a pit bull. And I have no idea what Harry was thinking but he says, 'How do you think Michael Vick will do this season? He

How about a little "truth in advertising" for a change?

From "pit bull" to "Jet"? System-1, loosened from sound critical thinking, takes full flight with the association heuristic.

was amazing his first year back in the NFL, but his third year in Philadelphia was a bust. So the Eagles dump him and the Jets pick him up?' We all look at Harry because he's on some other planet and say, 'Where did that come from?' And he's like, 'Pit bulls, dogs, dog fights, illegal, prison, Michael Vick.' And then I'm like, 'I wonder if Tiger Woods will pull off a comeback.' And now they're all looking at me. So I'm like, 'Hey, you know! Michael Vick, troubled athlete, big comeback after major issues. Can Tiger do the same? Which reminds me, are we all still on for golf this weekend?'"

The *Association Heuristic*: Connecting ideas on the basis of word association and the memories, meanings, or impressions they trigger. We all have experienced conversations in which one comment seems connected to another by nothing more than word association. Someone might suggest, "Let's take our drinks outside to the picnic table." To which someone else might respond, "Remember the picnic three years ago when Grandpa had his heart attack? I'm never going to that park again." The representativeness, or associational heuristic maneuver, is triggered when a word or idea reminds us of something else. Typically, this is System-1 thinking: reactive, associational, and not critically reflective. For example, one person might associate sunshine with happiness, and another person might associate sunshine with sweaty work picking strawberries. Or, as in the example above, "picnic" with Grandpa's heart attack. The salient negative experience

brought to mind by the mere use of the word *picnic* influenced the speaker to assert the decision never to return to the park where the sad event occurred. This unreflective decision emerged from the System-1 reaction triggered by the word association in this person's mind.

Associational thinking, an unmonitored nearly stream-of-consciousness mind flushing twitter-blab of ideas, is of very little value, logically speaking. But if the associational thinker is also saying out loud everything that comes to mind, it can be creative, frustrating, and entertaining all at the same time. And way too personal! It is rather commonplace in today's culture, and yet we seem unconcerned that judgments made using associational thinking can be very flawed. Instead the media report the results of casual twitter fests and "instant polls" as though these represented our best and most informed thinking on a given topic.

8. STEREOTYPING "I met this Marine, a young corporal, and he was an impressive young man. I could tell just talking to this young soldier that our servicemen and servicewomen are wonderful people." Stereotypes are generalized perceptions that members of one group of people have regarding another group. They shape how we see others and how others see us. The System-1 tendency is to think that everyone in the group has the characteristics, positive or negative, associated with the stereotype. Societal stereotypes tend to evolve slowly.[20]

THINKING CRITICALLY

Last Word to First Word

Listen attentively to a conversation. But do not focus on the topic being discussed, instead focus on the words as they are said. Pay special attention to the last word or expression in a sentence and count how many times the next speaker uses that word or expression as the first thing they say. An associational thinker—and we use the term *thinker* advisedly—often interacts conversationally by connecting what he or she says to the last word in the sentence that the previous speaker

uttered. No, this doesn't make any logical sense. But listen for it nonetheless. Keep a log of which person in the conversation does it the most frequently. And keep track of whether or not the topic of the conversation is actually altered from whatever it was before to whatever topic the associational thinker introduces. Put a clock on the topic. See if any topics at all can last more than three minutes when the associational thinker is in full form.

The *Stereotyping Heuristic*: Making a snap judgment about an entire group based on a single instance. Although an anecdote is not data, we have all heard people draw conclusions about whole groups of people based on their experience with only one or two people who are members of that group. We call this stereotyping or profiling. There are advantages to stereotyping, because it is a highly efficient way of thinking. For example, we tend to stereotype grandparents as loving caretakers. So if I say that I am having Grandma watch my daughter, you are not likely to worry too much about the child. On the other hand, there are risks associated with stereotyping. Profiling groups of people based on unfortunate experiences with one or more of its members can lead to bigotry, prejudice, misunderstanding, and mistrust, to name only a few.

Humans do not have the time to make systematic scientific surveys of everything we may need to know. So, we take the shortcut of basing decisions on relatively few instances. This is what we are doing when we ask a friend if she or he knows a good dentist, doctor, real estate broker, or lawyer. Or if we ask an alumna to tell us how good her college experience was when we are trying to decide where to go to school. The trade-off between effort expended and the reliability of the information derived makes this approach risky. Yes, it's a starting point to get some preliminary information, but it is not an ending point of a thorough investigation. Here again, monitoring one's habits of mind is a good idea.

The tendency to think that our personal experience of a single instance is predictive of what we would find were we to sample more systematically a whole class of individuals can undermine decision making in almost any context. We eat a burger at a fast food restaurant and make a snap judgment about everything on the menu there and at every other restaurant in the same chain. Does this work for paintings by a given artist, songs by a given songwriter, and novels by a given author? What about courses taught by a given professor, patient problems treated by a given health care provider, or building proposals by a real estate developer?

One example of false and negative stereotyping in contemporary America is the idea that all Muslims are terrorists.[21] Like other negative stereotypes based on race, ethnicity, religion, or nationality, this one fuels fear and hatred. In our more reflective moments we realize that Muslim Americans were victims in the 9/11 attacks on the Twin Towers along with Jewish Americans, Christian Americans, and Americans who practiced no religion. We know that Muslim Americans serve with distinction in our armed forces, including side by side with soldiers of other faiths in combat in Afghanistan and Iraq. And we know that millions of American Muslims go to work every day, take care of their families, pay their taxes, and contribute in numerous ways to the quality of our communities. The same is true of millions of African Americans, Jewish Americans, Mexican Americans, Native Americans, Mormon Americans, Catholic Americans, Chinese Americans, etc. But our System-2 reflective considerations about freedom of religion and the rights of others can evaporate if System-1 kicks into overdrive. Negative stereotyping can trigger just that kind of kneejerk defensive hostility. And when that happens, occasionally System-2 is dragged into the skirmish, because all of us are naturally inclined to seek rationalizations in support of our unreflective reactions.

Sensationalist media and unscrupulous politicians relish playing on our weakness for stereotypes. Stereotyping, particularly vicious negative stereotyping, sells papers and garners votes. And, say the unethical journalists and politicians, "Who cares who you have to hurt as long as you make money and win election, right?"

We know that it is difficult to root out the System-1 reactive stereotypic responses. On occasion it takes encountering a remarkable person or story to help us realize that our kneejerk stereotypes about people can get in the way of good judgment. Recently, for example, a 6-year-old little girl was rescued from a kidnapper by a brave man and his wife. Seeing the kidnapper snatch the child, they took immediate action. He chased the kidnapper while she called the police. The man who pulled the child out of

Stereotype breaker, Kent Dolasky

Stereotype breaker, Ayaan Hirsi Ali

the grasp of the kidnapper was honored by the mayor as a hero. The national news picked up the story. Oh, and, as it turns out, he was an illegal immigrant.[22]

Speaking about jarring counterexamples that challenge strong critical thinkers to examine their unreflective stereotypes about people, do you know who Ayaan Hirsi Ali is? Yes, exactly, she is the former member of the Dutch Parliament, native of Somalia, ex-Muslim, feminist who advocates Islamic–Christian dialogue in America.[23] Or do you know Sgt. Maj. Kent Dolasky, retired commandant of the US Joint Special Operations Forces Senior Enlisted Academy with multiple combat tours? Right, he's the army veteran who teaches business at the community college level and founded the Buckets of Hope volunteer organization to assist the homeless in Tampa.[24] And, above all, strong critical thinkers know that none of us are obliged to live out the stereotype that anyone is trying to force upon us.

9. "US VS. THEM"   "I went to Congress to lobby for the reauthorization of the Higher Education Act and to support increased funding for Pell Grants and other forms of non-exploitive student aid. I explained that higher education is a benefit to the person who is fortunate enough to afford to go to college. Research shows consistently higher earnings for college graduates than for those who have not gone to college. But, I added, college education benefits society as a as well. The teachers, nurses, businesspeople, engineers, journalists, social workers, and the like, who attained access to those professions through their college education, provide much needed services for everyone in the community. I was told by one member that he simply did not agree with that. His reason was simple: 'I've heard all that before because it's what the other side says.' I asked

the member to help me understand his thinking better and he replied, 'You see, on the Hill, it's good guys vs. bad guys. They're the bad guys. Whatever they say, whatever they want, whatever argument they make, I don't buy it'."

The *"Us vs. Them" Heuristic*: Reducing decisions to the choice between two starkly opposing options and then rejecting whatever option your opposition favors. This could be named the "good guys vs. bad guys" heuristic as well because applying this heuristic results in an automatic competitive and oppositional relationship. And our tendency, evolving from the earliest survival instincts of our species, is to band together with "our own people" to fight "those other guys." Battle lines are drawn with phrases like "Those who are not with me are against me"; "There can be no middle ground"; "Never compromise"; and "There can be no negotiations."[25] Once our minds apply the Us vs. Them heuristic to a situation, many other decisions about the people or issues involved become very simple. We have no obligations toward "them" or toward anything they want or anything they represent. But, if you are one of "us" we will stand by you through thick and thin.[26] In its most extreme manifestations, the Us vs. Them heuristic can set up the tendency to regard "them" as nonpersons, objects off the ethical radar screen, "others" who can be manipulated or removed without ethical concern. As a nation, we saw this in the torture and prisoner abuses at Abu Ghraib. Called the false polarization effect,[27] this tendency to divide the world into two opposing camps can be a very dangerous approach to problem solving and a potentially explosive and negative strategy for a society or a leader to take.

Let us not be naïve about this. If humans are strongly influenced by Us vs. Them thinking, then it would be

Responsible voters use critical thinking (System-2) to override the partisan reactions triggered in all of us by the Us vs. Them heuristic.

divisions, loyalties, rituals, and rivalries of the Us vs. Them mindset flourish. For example, search and watch the "Pep Talk" scene from *Glory Road*. The coach begins by antagonizing his players with racial stereotyping, and their gut response (affect heuristic) is silent anger and resentment. The coach says that they cannot win the national championship, because they cannot think. He describes them losing the game, they can see it happening (simulation) in their minds, and they become even more agitated because he is the authority figure and he is saying they will lose. They do not want to lose. This is not "just a game." Then the coach changes his tone and evokes the Us vs. Them heuristic to rally the players and unify the team. The short scene ends with one of the players making the point to his teammate that he needs to play good defense (not satisfice), because the usual effort will not be good enough. There are some great "Us vs. Them" moments, simulations, and System-1 affect heuristic appeals to be discovered if you search for the "best movie pep talks of all time."

foolish of us not to take that into consideration when approaching others for the first time. Generosity of spirit and openness are wonderful virtues, but venturing into potentially hostile territory with caution thrown to the wind is seldom likely to be the optimal choice. An advantage of this heuristic is that it orients our thoughts and actions in support of our family, our team, our platoon, our business, our community, "our kind." And, obviously, the disadvantage is that we lose objectivity and impartiality, and we can be prone toward bias and prejudice if we are not reflective. In instances like these, our critical thinking (System-2) must override the pull toward prejudice arising from the misapplication of the Us vs. Them heuristic.

High school might be described as the Kingdom of "Us vs. Them." In the black-and-white thinking that characterizes adolescent cognitive development, the tribal

Journalists, politicians, zealots, coaches, and evangelists of all stripes use our natural tendency to mistrust "those other people"—the ones who are not part of "us," the ones who are different, the ones with whom we disagree. Unscrupulous people make an enemy of the opposition and ascribe to them evil and dangerous intentions. This rallies the troops against the external threat and makes it unnecessary to take seriously what "they" have to say. In the cut-throat competition for high office, campaigners strive to marginalize or even demonize their opposition, engender fear in "us," lest "they" should "get

THINKING CRITICALLY

Is the Infotainment Media Helping or Not?

"If you're not careful, the newspapers will have you hating the people who are being oppressed, and loving the people who are doing the oppressing."

Malcolm X

What role does the infotainment media play in promoting or exposing unfair stereotyping and "Us vs. Them" thinking? Consider stereotypes based age, job status, religion, ethnicity, sexual orientation, educational level, and nationality.

Use evidence, not just personal experience, to come to a fair and accurate evaluation of the role of the media. For example, search "Islamophobia" and read articles on the changes in attitudes toward Muslims over the past 20 years. One perspective is offered by Professor Hatem Bazian in his short piece, "Latent and manifest Islamophobia." Do the same for "poor people" and for "CEOs." If you discover that the media have been fanning the flames of fear, rather than promoting harmony and acceptance, see if you can find another social group that the media has treated in the opposite way.

what they want," "come to power," or "take what is rightfully ours." The risks associated with dualistic thinking are serious, and these risks are compounded when fear and mistrust are set in opposition to loyalty and group identity.

The Us vs. Them Heuristic is a favorite tool of zealots, extremists, hate-mongers, and bigots. Why does it work for them? Too often because, fearing their wrath, the rest of us fail to muster the courage to challenge their caustic and divisive rhetoric with accurate information and sound reasoning. The positive critical thinking habit of truth-seeking requires the courage to ask tough questions and to follow reasons and evidence wherever they lead. History shows us how devastating and explosive religion in the blind service of nationalism can be. That has not changed. So it is not an exaggeration to say that the lives of tens of millions of people may depend on the courage and capacity of educated and truth-seeking men and women to stand up to those whose ambitions or beliefs demand the economic, political, or military annihilation of all of "them."

At this time in our national history the electorate is almost evenly divided between the two major parties. This is why voting is such an important responsibility. In statewide and national elections, political control turns on changing the minds of small percentages of people. A shift of 5 percent one way or the other can empower one party or the other to have control of the one or both houses of Congress, the Presidency, or to win the governorship of a state. Explore how shifting just a few Senate seats can impact control of that house of Congress.

Passing or defeating a statewide referendum or electing a President can depend on shifting just a few percent of the likely voters this way or that. Political parties use wedge issues, like gay marriage, immigration, and marijuana legalization, play on our System-1 heuristic thinking. Can our collective System-2 critical thinking overcome the divisiveness with reasoned judgment?

10. POWER DIFFERENTIAL "I once worked on a senior management team that was headed by a CEO who was the personification of the 'alpha male.' I recall one meeting where the other nine vice presidents and I were sitting along both sides of a conference table, with the CEO at the head of the table. He wanted us to discuss a proposal he had come up with the night before. He presented his idea by handing out five pages single-spaced and talking non-stop for half an hour. Then he said, 'OK, now I'd like to hear from you.' Nobody spoke. Nobody believed he actually wanted to hear our views. Nobody wanted to rock the boat or risk crossing him by pointing out even the smallest flaw or raising even the most tentative counterargument. The CEO waited less than two seconds. When nobody

A Student Body president champions a new resolution. How does the power differential within student organizations affect the work of the group and the sense of group unity?

responded, he said, 'OK, then. That's it. We'll implement this. Now, next topic."

The *Power Differential Heuristic*: Accepting without question a belief as stated by, a problem as presented by, or a solution as proposed by, a superior authority. Social hierarchies abound at home, at work, in government, in religion, and even in recreation. Many are benevolent and respectful. But even in these cases, and certainly in those that are manipulative and abusive, there is a tendency to defer to the individual (or subgroup) in charge. It may be something as benign as agreeing on when to eat dinner or which TV show to watch. The decision to defer—that is, not to dispute or challenge—the decisions of others higher in the social pecking order is natural. It manifests itself in our accepting what "those above us" may decide to have us do. This heuristic leads us to see the world as how our leaders see it and to understand problems and issues the way our leaders describe them to us. Middle managers in a corporate culture are susceptible to similar pressures from senior executives, as are second children from their elder sibling, or junior officers relative to their superiors. But "pressure" is not exactly the correct word, for this heuristic makes compliance with authority the automatic reaction. Thus, when one is out of step with one's "higher-ups," one often feels more discomfort than when one is "going along to get along." In a gang, for example, the power differential between the gang leader and his or her followers, when combined with the Us vs. Them heuristic for viewing the world, can strongly influence gang members to internalize gang rivalries and to agree with violent responses to perceived threats.

There are some advantages to recognizing the realities of power differentials and not bucking the system. Not only can this save cognitive resources, it might save your job and your domestic happiness as well. After all, if the boss wants the client list updated, why not update it? And if your partner wants to go to a movie that might not have been your first choice, why not go anyway? Having people see things your way may not be the highest of all values, even if you are smarter than they are about some things. Societal harmony and domestic tranquility are values, too.

On the other hand, how many times have we seen clearly that the boss was heading the department in the wrong direction, that the team captain was employing an ineffective strategy, that our elder sibling was wrong, or that our leaders were motivated more by self-interest than by the common good? Any full evaluation of the reasoning presented by those in power over us—coaches, teachers, ministers, managers, governmental authorities, or otherwise—should include consideration of whether the benefits derived from the current power structure relationship warrant continuing that relationship or whether it is time to consider seriously other options. In reviewing one's options, do not forget the influence that the satisficing heuristic, discussed earlier, can have on our sense that, however flawed our current situation may be, it is "good enough."

11. ANCHORING WITH ADJUSTMENT "The first book report I wrote as a ninth grader was about the novel *Space Cadets*. My report earned a C−. The teacher, a lover of eighteenth- and nineteenth-century British literature, found scant merit in the silly juvenile novel I had chosen and even

THINKING CRITICALLY

Anchoring on First Impressions

Your personal reputation, positive or negative, can be one of the most difficult anchors to raise. If you have had the misfortune of making a poor first impression at some point in your life, you may know firsthand just how difficult it can be to overcome that unfortunate beginning. But this exercise is about the impressions you have of others. Reflect on the people whom you have met over the past year or two. Think of some whom you initially thought highly of and others whom you did not like at first. Has your general impression of any of these people changed? If yes, describe what the person did or said that was so memorable that you hauled up your anchor from positive waters and dropped it in negative waters, or vice versa. Now reflect on the others, and ask yourself what it would take for you to radically revise your initial opinion of any of them.

What about celebrities? Our opinions of celebrities often anchor on our first impressions and then adjust very slowly, unless the celebrity does something really "out of character." Think about Robert Downey, Jr., drug addict and criminal? Or Robert Downey, Jr., Oscar-nominated movie star? Sherlock Holmes! Or

think about Tiger Woods, all-world golfer or Tiger Woods unfaithful husband. Then there is Justin Bieber, a personality still under construction.

less merit in my futile attempt to state its theme and explore how its author had developed plot and characters. A friend of mine received an A on his report on George Elliot's (Mary Ann Evans') 1861 novel, *Silas Marner*. About halfway through the academic year I was consistently making C–, C, or C+ on my work, and my friend was doing A– or A work. So, we switched. I started writing reports using his name and he wrote reports using my name. My grades (that is, the grades he earned for me) edged up into the C+ and B– range. His grades (that is, the grades my reports earned for him) held steady except for one B+ late in April. Our analysis: In the mind of our teacher from the first paper we submitted in September and throughout that whole year, I was a C student and my friend was an A student."

The *Anchoring with Adjustment Heuristic*: Having made an evaluation, adjust only as much as is absolutely necessary and then only if new evidence is presented.[28] When we are making evaluative judgments, it is natural to locate or anchor our evaluation at some point along whatever scale we are using. If we are being more reflective, we may have established some criteria and we may be working to apply them as fair-mindedly as possible. As other information comes our way, we may adjust our evaluation. The interesting thing about this cognitive maneuver is that we do not normally start over with a fresh evaluation. We have dropped anchor and we may drag it upward or downward a bit, but we do not pull it off the bottom of the sea to relocate our evaluation. First impressions, as the saying goes, cannot easily be undone.

One advantage of this heuristic is that it permits us to move on. We have done the evaluation; there are other things in life that need attention. We could not long endure if we were to constantly reevaluate everything anew. Part of developing expertise is learning to calibrate and nuance one's judgments, refine one's criteria, and adjust the criteria to fit the complexities of the circumstances of judgment. Anchoring with adjustment can reflect a progression toward greater precision, a way to refine not only judgments about particular things, but the criteria applied when making those judgments.

The unfortunate thing about this heuristic, however, is that we sometimes drop anchor in the wrong place; we have a hard time giving people a second chance at making a good first impression. How often have we seen it happen that a co-worker's performance is initially evaluated as sub-par (outstanding) and almost nothing that happens subsequently can move that initial evaluation marker very far from where it started? Subsequent outstanding work (poor work) is regarded as a fluke or an anomaly, not as genuine counterevidence that should result in a thorough reevaluation.

12. ILLUSION OF CONTROL   "They hired me because I was known as a corporate gunslinger. I know how to take a failing organization and turn it around in short order. I kick ass and take names. I hire people who want to bust their butts to get the job done, and I fire the deadwood and anyone who gets in the way of what we're trying to do. Within 90 days I had reorganized the finance division and the technology division. Sales needed major work. That took another three weeks, but I put in the right people and revised our marketing approach. Then it was time to increase productivity and decrease costs in our manufacturing operation. In six months I had stopped the bleeding. In nine, we had bottomed out and were starting to see the signs of a turnaround. We posted our first net profits at the end of my fourth quarter with the corporation. I stayed another two years and then the job got so boring that I had to move on. So, now I'm on the market looking for another company that needs my skill set to save its cookies." The gunslinger's constant references "I did this" and "I did that" give no credit to the team effort it really takes to turn an organization around. Perhaps the gunslinger deserves praise and credit for his or her leadership contributions. But from my own personal experience, I assure you that turning around a large organization that is in real trouble is a group project, not a one-person show. The gunslinger in this example is looking back on the project with an exaggerated and illusory sense of his or her own personal control over how events turned out.

The *Illusion of Control Heuristic*: Estimating the control you have over events by the amount of energy and desire you put into trying to shape those events. When used correctly, this heuristic helps calibrate estimates of our effectiveness and thus helps us gauge how hard we should try. When misapplied, the illusion of control heuristic leads us into snap judgments that are nothing more than wishful thinking. We frequently overestimate our actual ability to control the outcomes of events because we consistently fail to account for contingencies.[29] We overestimate our control of a situation because we underestimate the influences of other people and events. As a result, we imagine wrongly that there is a very strong relationship between whatever we might do and how things are going to ultimately turn out. Wanting a given outcome strongly, we tend to think that decisions we make or actions we take are genuinely instrumental in bringing about or failing to bring about that outcome regardless of the actual contingencies, forces, and factors at work.

13. OPTIMISTIC BIAS AND 14. HINDSIGHT BIAS   Please answer these three questions: Are you any more or less likely than others just like you to contract cancer at your age? Are you more or less likely than others just like you to suffer a debilitating injury in a traffic accident? Are you below average or above average in your ability to get along with others?[30]

THINKING CRITICALLY

In Control of Your ATV

Yamaha makes one of today's most popular ATVs, the Yamaha Rhino. Before going further in this exercise, answer this: Suppose you were given, free of charge, the offer to use as you wish a Yamaha Rhino all day and you had complete access to a beautiful recreational area with hills, streams, ravines, woodlands, and open meadows. Assume that you would not be charged any money, even if you brought the vehicle back damaged. On a scale of 1 to 100, with 100 being "Absolutely, yes!" how likely would you be to accept this offer? After marking down your answer, search and watch the multiple news stories about ATV dangers. (Search "ATV dangers.") Listen to the riders who are interviewed. Do any of them exhibit indications that they may be suffering the influences of the illusion of control heuristic? Explain why. Now, having seen the video interviews you found online, on the same scale of 1 to 100, how likely would you be to accept the offer of the free use of the Rhino? If you changed your answer from the first time, that is OK. Question: If you changed your answer, why did you change? Reflect on your second decision. Did

any of these heuristics play a role: availability, simulation, representation, anchoring with adjustment? Did your sense of risk and possible loss increase or decrease having seen the news story?

The *Optimistic Bias Heuristic*: Tendency to underestimate our own risks and overestimate our own control in dangerous situations.[31] Responding to the third question, most will say they have above average abilities, even though mathematically it cannot be true that most people are above average. On the first two questions above, approximately 75 percent of us will estimate our risks to be lower and about 25 percent will say higher. But, the true answer is that our risks are neither higher nor lower than persons just like us. This natural tendency toward optimistic bias has the evolutionary advantage for our species of providing us with the courage to move ahead in life. The constant dread of serious hazards could be mentally detrimental and debilitating. However, since our risk of hazard is actually no better and no worse than others' just like ourselves, all things being equal, this built-in bias results in poorer and perhaps riskier judgments in some situations. Our sense that we will succeed where others have failed, or that we are not as likely as others to suffer misfortune or the ill effects of bad decisions can lead us to take unnecessary risks.

Please answer these questions: Have you ever felt that you did not receive your fair share of the credit for your contribution to a highly successful project? Were you ever unfairly blamed when things went wrong, even though the unfortunate outcomes were beyond your control?

The *Hindsight Bias Heuristic*: Tendency to remember successful events as being the result of the decisions we made and actions that we took and past failures as having resulted from bad luck or someone else's mistakes.[32] Our human

How does our high level of confidence in our ability to control events and our optimistic sense of youthful invincibility impact our decisions regarding health insurance?

need for accuracy, predictability, and self-justification is believed to motivate this hindsight-biasing behavior.[33] Hindsight bias adds fuel to the fire of our false confidence, for it inclines us to believe that our decisions and actions had a strong positive impact on the outcome of events, or, if things did not turn out as hoped, the fault was not ours. The tendency to take undeserved credit for good outcomes or to shift responsibility to others for undesirable outcomes is something we humans seem to have in common.

We do not mean to suggest that we are mistaken every time we feel unfairly blamed nor that we are mistaken every time we feel in control of a situation. By noting these potentials for wrong judgments, however, we are able to anticipate the possibility of a mistake and correct our thinking before we dig in too deeply to the feelings of pride or resentment that come with being mistakenly praised or blamed. We can use our self-regulation critical thinking skills to monitor ourselves for optimistic bias and hindsight bias so that our estimations about how much we really can control or how much blame or credit we deserve are made more reflectively, and hopefully, more accurately.

15. ELIMINATION BY ASPECT: "ONE STRIKE AND YOU'RE OUT" "I went on four job interviews, which was great because many of my friends were having trouble getting any interviews. The interviewers all wanted me to make a PowerPoint presentation. And, of course, there was a lot of meeting individuals and groups of people. And the mandatory lunch when you have to remember to order lemonade instead of anything alcoholic. All those parts went fine. But at one place there was this guy who kept interrupting my PowerPoint to ask questions. I don't want to work there, not with jerks like him in my work group. This other place was OK, great new computers in fact, but the cubicles were gray and so was the carpet. I just didn't like how blah it looked—too institutional, you know. So, really, it's down to the other two places, and I'm hoping to get an offer from one or both of them real soon."

The *Elimination by Aspect Heuristic*: Eliminating an option from consideration upon the discovery of one undesirable feature. There are simply too many choices! The Excalibur Hotel in Las Vegas boasts a 500-dish smorgasbord. DIRECTV and Comcast offer hundreds of channels. Want to buy a car, rent a downtown condo, enroll in an MBA program, or select a can of soup from the grocery shelf? There are thousands from which to pick. How do we move efficiently through this maze of opportunities? Certainly not by giving our full attention and due consideration to every aspect of every option. Rather, we hack through the choices individually or in whole bunches at a time, pushing the clutter out of our cognitive path as quickly and efficiently as possible. Elimination by aspect is our heuristic strategy. As soon as we identify a "reason why not," we dump that option and options like it. The reason does not have to be monumental. I don't like brown cars or used cars. That's it. For me, the car-buying choices have just been reduced by tens of thousands. Don't like cream sauces? Great, that cuts the smorgasbord problem down by a huge percentage. Don't like to wait behind other folks grazing through the food line? Fine, step around them to an open spot along the buffet and never worry about looking back at the dozens of culinary delights you may have skipped.

In situations where we enjoy a plethora of acceptable choices, the cognitive utility of elimination by aspect cannot be overestimated. However, the price we pay for conserving all that energy and time is clear, too. Applying this heuristic may result in a final selection that does not reflect the best holistic choice we might have made. The used car I refused to consider may have been just as good in every way as a new car of the same make and model, but thousands of dollars less expensive. I will never give that car its due consideration, having eliminated it entirely from view when I rejected it along with all others that were labeled "used." In situations where our choices are limited and where no option is perfect, this heuristic can be a major liability. Because nobody is perfect, balancing the good with the bad is a sign of wisdom. The one strike and you're out approach denies this reality. Political litmus tests, for example, could paralyze a pluralistic democracy. We would all soon become hermits if we tried to select our employees, friends, and leaders on the principle that any one flaw is a fatal flaw.

Do you think retailers know that too many choices can overwhelm System-2, causing us to fall back to our reactive heuristic-driven System-1 responses? If so, isn't that exactly what they want—that we should just buy without thinking through our decisions?

16. LOSS AND RISK AVERSION "Early in my career I was offered an entry-level management position with a new company in a new industry. The company was called Cingular Wireless. I didn't seek the job. And I was a bit surprised when the offer was extended one evening during a dinner party. It would have meant a lot more money than I was earning as a part-time instructor. A job like that would have been the ticket to a lucrative corporate career. But I had a job in the field of higher education, and, with a couple years of experience, I was becoming comfortable in the role of college teacher. I didn't want to lose the identity I had just begun to create for myself. I wasn't sure what it would be like to work in the corporate sector, having all my life been either a student or a teacher, and recently a new mother. My daughter was less than a year old at that time. What if the job with Cingular didn't work out? Somehow the idea of remaking myself into a corporate junior executive seemed too risky and there was too much to lose. So, I thanked the person but declined her offer."

The *Loss and Risk Aversion Heuristic*: Avoiding risk and avoiding loss by maintaining the status quo. Not losing anything, not going backward, at least staying where we are, for most humans, is the preferred default outcome, particularly under conditions of uncertainty. Research demonstrates that most humans are more likely to pass up an opportunity to make a gain rather than risk a loss.[34] Humans psychologically privilege the status quo. Whenever possible, humans take an incremental approach, seeking to avoid uncertainty and the difficult cognitive tasks of weighing and combining information or trading-off conflicting values, rather than opting for more dramatic change. Muddling through personal decisions, attempting to avoid any loss, is the norm rather than the exception. We've all heard the old adage "A bird in the hand is worth two in the bush."

Making decisions on the basis of what we do not want to risk losing can have advantages in many circumstances. People do not want to lose control, they do not want to lose their freedom, and they do not want to lose their lives, their families, their jobs, or their possessions. And so, in real life, we take precautions. Why take unnecessary risks? The odds may not be stacked against us, but the consequences of losing at times are so great that we would prefer to forgo the possibilities of gain to not lose what we have. Can you think of an example of this in your life?

We are more apt to endure the status quo, even as it slowly deteriorates, than we are to engage in change that we perceive as "radical" or "dangerous." Loss and risk aversion have the disadvantages of leading to paralysis or delay precisely when action should be taken. Having missed that opportunity to avert a crisis, we discover later that it requires a far greater upheaval to make the necessary transformations once the crisis is upon us. Worse, on occasion, the situation has deteriorated beyond the point of no return. In those situations we find ourselves wondering why we waited so long before doing something about the problem back when it might have been possible to salvage the situation. History has shown time and time again that businesses that avoid risks often are unable to compete successfully against those willing to move more boldly into new markets or into new product lines.

Uncertainty, risk, and fear of loss are the tools of those who oppose change, just as optimistic bias and simulation are the tools of the proponents of change. There were and continue to be abundant example of both in the protracted and highly politicized debate over Obamacare. And, of course, both sides use satisficing, temporizing, affect, availability, representation, stereotyping. and "Us vs. Them."

17. "ALL OR NOTHING" "I heard that there were going to be budget cuts and layoffs. We all knew that the economy was in the tank. But this is a big university with an annual operating budget over $230,000,000 and more than 1,800 faculty and staff members. So, I figured that the chances that they would cut the course that I was going to take next semester out of the budget had to be about 100,000 to 1. I mean, they probably offer thousands of courses here every

---

THINKING CRITICALLY

Why Privilege the Status Quo?

Reflect on a recent experience in your life that involved making a decision that included some element of risk and potential loss. In a purely objective analysis the *status quo* is only one possibility among many and should not be given any more value than any other state of affairs. But, as you saw in the "Loss and Risk Aversion" section, for human beings, built as we are with an aversion to loss and risk seemingly in our DNA, that is easier said than done. How did you handle the decision you faced? Were you able to give the status quo no more or no less value than any other possible state of affairs? How might a stronger application of the critical thinking skill of self-regulation have affected the decision? In other words, what steps can you take to monitor your own decision making for loss aversion? Write out some questions a person might ask himself or herself that would help the person make a good decision in contexts of risk, uncertainty, and potential loss.

Interrogation–From Confrontation to Confession

Have you ever been interrogated by law enforcement personnel, or have you ever interrogated a suspect? Interrogations involve asking a person several times to repeat what they saw, heard, or did. By repetition details emerge, details which can exonerate an innocent person and which can trip up a guilty person. Repetition can be frustrating and fatiguing, and it tends to reinforce memories, both true and false. Fatigue and frustration are tools that investigators use to break down a suspect's defenses. There is an effective process, known as the Reid technique that interrogators use to move a suspect to confess. At each step in the process both parties are making System-1 and System-2 decisions about what to ask or how to respond.

All things being equal, the advantage goes to the interrogator because the interrogator can follow a proven process and because the interrogator does not have to make claims or give reasons. And, because if the interrogator makes a false statement, there is no downside other than that the person being questioned will realize that perhaps the interrogator is lying. As fatigue sets in the person being questioned, however, falls back on snap judgments and unreflective heuristic thinking. When the interrogator unexpectedly shifts topics or buries a damning assumption deep within a false dilemma, the suspect may agree to something or admit something that implies guilt. Since more crimes are solved by confessions than by forensic evidence, the Reid technique is a powerful and important law enforcement tool. It works so well that its critics say it produces too many false confessions, particularly if applied to children.

The playing field is leveled a bit if the person being questioned knows the nine step process. The person being questioned then knows what the interrogator is trying to do and where the questioning is going to go next. Remember as you read the steps in the process that it is legal for the police to lie to a person suspected of a crime, just as it is mandatory that the police inform the person of their rights, including their right to remain silent and to have legal counsel present.

1. Confront the suspect by claiming to have evidence that the suspect committed the crime. Offer the suspect the opportunity to explain what happened and why. Build in an unspoken assumption that the suspect did commit the crime. For example, "What happened out there? Why did you drive away after the accident with the motorcycle?"

2. Offer the suspect excuses or reasons for the crime. "You didn't know that the motorcyclist was injured, right?" Or, "Were you late for an important meeting?" "I understand, you were just going home so that you could phone in the accident report. Yes?"

3. Do not let the suspect deny guilt. Or, if the suspect denies guilt, do not let the suspect repeat the denial. Denial only reinforces the suspect in the view that he is not to blame. Shift topics if the suspect appears to want to deny guilt.

4. If the suspect offers a reason why he did not commit the crime, attempt to use it to move toward a confession. Ask the suspect to explain in great detail why he could not have committed the crime. If the suspect does not offer a reason, ask for one. Look for inconsistencies. Use any details provided to trip up the suspect.

5. Act as if you are receptive to what the suspect has to say. Appear to be sincere. These are social cues for the suspect to behave in the same way toward you.

6. If the suspect is becoming quiet and listening to the interrogator then move toward offering the suspect different alternative versions of the crime, repeat claims that the evidence is conclusive or that other parties to the offense are implicating the suspect. Interpret crying at this point as implying that the person is guilty.

7. Offer the suspect two options concerning why he committed the crime. Expect the suspect to agree with the more socially acceptable option. But both options imply guilt. The suspect may fail to seize the third option that he is not guilty.

8. Lead the suspect to repeat in front of witnesses his admission of guilt, develop details that corroborate the admission of guilt, and the truthfulness of the confession.

9. Document the confession using video or by getting a written statement.

Source: Based on Zuawski, D., Wicklander, D, et. al., *Practical Aspects of Interview and Interrogation*, Second edition. CRC Press: Boca Raton. 2002.

year. And there are so many other places to save money at a university without cutting academics. So, I planned my work hours and day care around taking that course. And then I go to register and it's not in the schedule. I learned they dropped it for budget reasons. Can you imagine! How am I supposed to complete my program if they cut required courses like that one?"

The *"All or Nothing" Heuristic*: Simplifying decisions by treating remote probabilities as if they were not even possibilities. By and large, when making decisions, we do not calculate Bayesian probabilities. Computers might, but humans do not. But over the millennia as a species, we humans have done reasonably well for ourselves (so far) by operating as if the exact probabilities did not really matter. Instead of thinking that there is precisely a 92 percent chance of this occurring or a 12 percent chance of that occurring, we tend to simplify our estimations and move them toward the extremes. In fact, we behave as if the odds were either 0 (no possibility at all), or 1 (it definitely will happen). Whether the chances are 1 in 100, or 1 in 10,000, do we really think about the mathematical differences in those situations? No. Instead we tend to treat both of them as if the odds were the same, and, in fact, as if they were both zero. The all or nothing heuristic treats these remote possibilities as if they were, for all practical purposes, "impossible." That is, as if the actual odds were 0 in 100 or 0 in 10,000.

When we stop and really think about things, there are all kinds of risky situations. A person walking across the street could be hit by a car. But, really, what are the chances? They are in fact *not* equal to zero. But if even the smallest risk of such a great loss as the loss of one's life were perceived, some of us might never venture out into the world. So, we push that decimal point out further and further in our minds, nullifying the risk, treating it as if it were not present at all. I've ice-skated hundreds of times, so what are the chances that tonight I'll fall and crack my skull? There are thousands of commercial flights each day, so what are the chances of a near miss involving my flight? Sadly, if one of those remote and unfortunate possibilities were to occur, we often think, "I never thought that would happen to me." A main advantage to the all or nothing heuristic is that it balances the paralyzing influences of loss and risk aversion.

Heuristics in Action

In real-world conversations in which we focus on our own issues, cognitive heuristics expedite our thinking by generating ideas, but not necessarily reflectively. Here is an example of a person explaining why he decided to invest in high-tech stocks in late 2007. What could go wrong?

- "I know some businesses fail, particularly those based on technological innovation. But only 3 percent of new ventures failed last year, so I decided that the risk of failure was actually pretty small [All or Nothing], and I decided to go for broke and invest, and . . . you know. . . I'm pretty good at what I do, and I am really watching things closely now so that nothing happens that will threaten my investment. [Illusion of Control] I just don't think I can miss on this one." [Optimistic Bias]

True, it was smart to consider the percentage of businesses that failed, and to do all that one can to run a business well. And the business may not fail, but even the speaker himself would not be likely to invest with confidence were it not for the misuse of heuristic thinking, providing hope, a bit of confidence, and a sense of being in control of the investment. The worldwide economic disaster known now as the Great Recession of 2008 demonstrated that the previous reasoning was a house built on sand.

Often, cognitive heuristics work in tandem with one another. For example, parents often worry about their children getting sick from germs that may be lurking in the environment, like on playground equipment, neighbors' houses, or in public bathrooms. The gut feeling "Germs = Bad!" is an example of the affect heuristic. Fueled by the illusion of control heuristic, many parents set high standards for cleanliness, especially for their daughters. But research suggests that keeping little girls squeaky clean may in fact be the opposite of what they need.[35]

In the following example of a casual family conversation over morning coffee, several heuristics are in play, including association, affect, and stereotyping:

- Husband to wife: "I'm looking forward to retiring. I've worked for 35 years in offices without windows, and, when I'm retired I want to be outside. I can see myself on the fifth tee right now!"

Microbes can be good for you!

- Wife replies: "Same as my Dad; he used to say how much he hated the winter especially going to work when it was dark outside, working in a windowless office all day, and then coming home when it was dark."

- Mother-in-law: "That senior's apartment you showed me was terrible. Only one window! I need more light. I'm never moving to an apartment! You're going to have to drag me out of my house."

In the first paragraph, availability and simulation influence the husband immediately to link the idea of being outside to his vivid and happily remembered hobby [availability]. He sees himself golfing [simulation], projecting how much easier it will be to play golf when retired. As is common with the availability heuristic, he may be overestimating his opportunities to be on the fifth tee. Meanwhile, his wife is still thinking about the original topic, namely retirement. However, she connects her husband's expressed distaste for his windowless office with her father's similar expressions of distaste for the same work environment [representation]. At that point the mother-in-law introduces a new topic, her mind having jumped from "windowless" to an association with darkness [association] and from there to her vividly recalled [availability], negative [affect] experience of recently seeing one dark apartment. Clearly, she is overestimating the

Heuristics and Possible Errors from Their Misapplication		
Heuristic	**Cognitive Shortcut**	**Possible Error from Misapplication**
Satisficing	Having found an option that is good enough, take it. We humans typically do only what must be done to achieve our purposes.	Underestimation of how much is required to satisfy objective.
Temporizing	Decide that a given option is good enough for now.	Underestimation of the growing problems associated with failing to make a long-term adjustment in a timely way.
Affect	Decide based on your initial affective ("gut") response.	First impressions and gut feelings may mislead.
Simulation	Estimate the likelihood of a given outcome based on how easy it is to imagine that outcome.	Overestimation of one's chance of success or likelihood of failure.
Availability	Estimate the likelihood of a future event on the vividness or ease of recalling a similar past event.	Mistaken estimations of the chances of events turning out in the future as they are remembered to have turned out in the past.
Representation	Make the snap judgment that X is like Y in every way upon noticing that X is like Y in some way.	The analogy may not hold.
Association	Connect ideas on the basis of word association and the memories, meanings, or impressions they trigger.	Jumping from one idea to the next absent any genuine logical progression and drawing confused and inaccurate inferences.
Stereotyping	From a single salient instance, make a snap judgment about an entire group.	Profiling and misjudging individuals based on one's beliefs about the group.
"Us vs. Them"	Reduce decisions to the choice between two starkly opposing options and then reject the option your opposition favors.	Unnecessary conflict, disrespect for others, polarization, undermining of the possibility of reasonable compromise.
Power Differential	Accept without question a belief as stated by, a problem as presented by, or a solution as proposed by a superior authority.	Working on the wrong question or problem, applying a mistaken or inadequate solution.
Anchoring with Adjustment	Having made an evaluation, adjust only as much as is absolutely necessary and then only if new evidence is presented.	Failure to reconsider thoroughly, failure to evaluate fair-mindedly.
Illusion of Control	Estimate the control you have over events by amount of energy and desire you put into trying to shape those events.	Overestimation of one's actual power to control or manage events—confusion of desire and effort with effectiveness.
Optimistic Bias	The tendency to underestimate our own risks and overestimate our own control in dangerous situations.	Taking unnecessary risks, putting one's self in unnecessary danger.
Hindsight Bias	The tendency to remember successful events as being the result of the decisions one made and actions one took, and to remember past failures as having resulted from bad luck or someone else's mistakes.	Misjudging the actual extent to which one's actions contributed either positively or negatively to past events and outcomes.
Elimination by Aspect	Eliminate an option from consideration upon the discovery of one undesirable feature.	Failure to give due and full consideration to all the viable options.
Loss and Risk Aversion	Avoid risk and avoid loss by maintaining the status quo.	Paralysis of decision making, stuck in the deteriorating status quo.
"All or Nothing"	Simplify decisions by treating remote probabilities as if they were not even possibilities.	Failure to appreciate the possibilities that events could actually turn out differently than expected—the remote possibility may actually occur.

likelihood that all apartments will be dark. And, given that she has introduced this new topic, rather than join the conversation, this comment has the ring of a bolstering argument for a long-term debate about whether she will agree to move to an apartment. The option of moving to an apartment is off the table as far as she is concerned. And more, not wanting to lose control [loss aversion] over her own life, she expresses her decision to her children—regardless of their obvious age in this context—as a decision she will not permit them to override.

We end this chapter with an example to remind ourselves that heuristic thinking, while generally useful, can lead to some very poor decisions too. Consider this true story. A black high school senior was visiting a college campus with two friends on a recruiting trip. One of the university's white undergraduates accosted the three in the parking lot, questioning their purpose and presence. All the while the student video recorded the younger visitors with her cell phone. The visitors asked why they were being videotaped and the college student replied "just in case". Offended, disillusioned, and a little bit angry about the WWB[36] profiling of the college student, the visitors decided to leave. Moments later the three were coming out of a nearby grocery store only to be met by the campus police who had been alerted by the college student to "suspicious behavior." A series innocent mistakes and misunderstandings? Perhaps. But one based on stereotyping, association, "Us vs. Them," and representation on the part of the college student, the visitors, and perhaps the police too.

Summing up this chapter,

human decision making uses two cognitive systems: System-1 is reactive and automatic; System-2 is deliberative and reflective. System-1 enables us to get through the routine parts of our lives so automatically that we can focus mental energy on difficult problems using the deliberative and reflective powers of System-2. Heuristic thinking is the often quite useful tendency to rely on highly effective cognitive shortcuts when making judgments. This chapter examined 17 common cognitive heuristics, noting the advantages and disadvantages of each. At times, we misapply one or more of those heuristic shortcuts and, so, run the risk that our snap judgments will be mistaken. We can avoid System-1 hasty misapplications of heuristics by using our System-2 self-regulation critical thinking skill to monitor and to correct our judgment-making process.

Key Concepts

System-1 thinking is reactive thinking that relies heavily on situational cues, salient memories, and heuristic thinking to arrive quickly and confidently at judgments.

System-2 thinking is reflective critical thinking that is useful for judgments in unfamiliar situations, for processing abstract concepts, and for deliberating when there is time for planning and more comprehensive consideration.

cognitive heuristics are human decision-making shortcuts people rely on to expedite their judgments about what to believe or what to do.

Applications

Reflective Log

Two Hours: Today or tomorrow keep a written record of all your actions, judgments, and decisions occurring within a two-hour window that begins one hour before your main meal of the day. Make eight very brief log entries, one every 15 minutes. For each entry, list all the actions, judgments, and decisions you made in the prior 15 minutes. Keep track of what you are doing using your System-1 and System-2 thinking. Continue right up through preparing your meal, eating it, and whatever you do afterward until the two-hour period is completed. For example, did you send a text, use the lavatory, think about a relationship, make weekend plans, open a can of soda, or talk with a friend? Did you imagine what it might be like to have more money, listen to music, fret over a problem, or go for a run? Whatever you did and whatever decisions or judgments you made, write them down.

Later, after a couple more hours have passed, go back and review your list of all your actions, judgments, and decisions you made. Count the number that you would classify as System-1 and the number you would classify as System-2. Are there any that you classified as System-1 that, in retrospect, you wish that you had reflected about more before acting or deciding as you did? In view of this little personal experiment, are their ways to build more critical thinking self-monitoring and self-correcting into your daily life?

Individual Exercises

Estimate your chances: Watch the local or national news on TV this evening and look for the story in which the victim of a crime, a disease, an economic misfortune, or an accident is interviewed. Don't worry. You'll find that story because, as they say in the business, "If it bleeds it leads." The more empathetic the victim, the better. The more the victim is like you in terms of age, gender, socioeconomic status, the better. On a scale of 1 to 1,000, with 1,000 being "extremely likely," estimate the chances of the same or a similar event happening to you. After making your estimate, check on the Internet to find the actual statistical likelihood that such an event will happen to you. We believe you will find that your chances are less than 1 in 1,000.

Have you ever been profiled? Were you ever the object of someone else's use of the stereotyping heuristic? To answer this, think of a time when you might have been treated a certain way, either positively or negatively, by someone else simply because of something about your age, gender, style of clothing, race, or accent.

Closer to home: Clubs, community groups, and professional organizations are not immune to the dangers of the misapplication of the Us vs. Them heuristic. On the other hand, the benefits of this heuristic include that it gives people energy and a sense of urgency to be working to defend their own, to compete for resources, and to feel justified in their beliefs and actions. Recall the last decision-making meeting of a club or organization to which you belong. In what ways did the Us vs. Them heuristic influence your group's thinking about people, about threats or opportunities, about problems or issues? Reflect on those influences. How might your group's decisions have been different had it not been for the sense of "Us" vs. "Them" that this heuristic engendered?

Leadership's challenge—Do thinking and motivating get in each other's way? The capacity to cultivate a group culture that fosters reflective, respectful, and fair-minded decision making and problem solving can be a great asset to a leader. If trusted not to revile, belittle, or ridicule subordinates for their ideas and suggestions, the leader can benefit immensely. Decisions can be openly discussed and refined before being implemented. Problems can be analyzed and options considered, with each person feeling encouraged to bring his or her best thinking forward. At the same time, intentionally triggering heuristic thinking by using association, "Us vs. Them," and loss aversion scenarios, for example, can be a powerful tool to motivate people to take action. Based on your own experience, what are some specific things leaders can do to foster a climate that is highly receptive to critical thinking and self-regulation? What are some things that undermine that good climate? Give examples.

Two decimal places too many? Reflect on how often you approach key decisions with your own personal litmus test, sorting choices by looking for a single flaw or reason to eliminate as many as possible as quickly as possible. For example, reducing the list of job applicants this way, "Let's eliminate every applicant whose GPA is less than 2.70." In this example, the first important System-2 question is why should we look at GPA at all, and the next reflective question is why does 2.70 make the cut, but 2.69 not? What is the evidence that GPA is such a precise measure as that? Going back to your own litmus test decisions, apply your critical thinking skills, and ask yourself whether there is good evidence to support using that single criterion as a make-or-break decision point?

Explain it to Grandma or Grandpa: Critical thinking is nothing new. Human beings have been relying on our reflective System-2 thinking from—well—from our beginning. Today we call this purposeful reflective judgment about what to believe and what to do "critical thinking." And we talk about its core skills and the positive habits of mind that incline us to use those skills. We caution ourselves against relying too heavily on snap judgments and we discipline ourselves to be reflective and thoughtful. The question is, do our grandparents use critical thinking or not?

If you are fortunate enough to be able to talk with one of your grandparents, please ask him or her if he or she uses critical thinking to solve problems and make decisions. Since the chances are overwhelming that he or she will not understand your question if you use the expression *critical thinking*, you will have to find some other way to ask the question. If you are not able to talk with any of your grandparents about critical thinking, then your challenge is to find someone else with whom you can have the conversation. The catch is that the person has to be at least 40 years older than you.

The challenges of this exercise, in addition to simply having the conversation, are to explain what you are learning about critical thinking and to see how much of what you describe is something that the older person may have also learned. Is there something the older person knows about strong critical thinking that you may not yet have learned?

SHARED RESPONSE

Not All Bad, Not All Good

How do cognitive heuristics help and harm strong decision making? Be sure to provide your reason(s), not just your opinion. And, comment respectfully on the reasons others offer.

Group Exercises

Discussion question—Would you or would you not? Make a snap judgment: Yes or No. Suppose you are thinking about having a child and you can be tested for hundreds of genetic diseases that you might pass on to that child. Assume the genetics test is free. Would you be tested? Now, reflect on the judgment you just made. Which heuristics in your case may have influenced you? Was there an element of fear and risk, afraid of knowing perhaps, even a quick association popping to mind about a genetic disease? Did a stereotype come to mind toward which you perhaps felt some aversion? OK, now put that initial snap judgment aside, and consider reflectively what a responsible person who is thinking about becoming a parent would do if given the opportunity. Before you decide this time, first learn more about the potential for genetic tests, and about the options for informed decision making once one has a fuller knowledge of one's own genetic heritage. Check out the pros and cons of using a commercial genetics ancestry locator company, like 23 and Me, for example, and research the concerns expressed by the Food and Drug Administration and the National Human Genome Research Institute.

Discussion question—How did you decide today? Reflect on the choices you made today—for example, your choices of what you ate at one of your meals. Replay in your minds how you made that decision. Assuming that you are like the rest of us, you probably did not really give equal and due consideration to all of your potential options. That's OK. Heuristic snap judgments can be good things; for one, they are highly efficient and they conserve time and energy. Think now about the foods that you could have eaten, but decided not to choose. Share with the others in your conversation group the basis upon which you eliminated the ones you did not select. Was it by weighing all the pros and cons of each choice? Or was it via a snap judgment to reject a given option? For example, did association (memory of prior bad experience), affect ("looked gross"), or elimination by aspect ("too large a portion") play a role in your System-1 decision making? Talk about the choices you did make. Which cognitive heuristics played a role in those? For example, representativeness ("reminded me of something my Mom makes that tastes really good, so I thought this would taste good, too."), or satisficing ("I was in a hurry and I just grabbed the first thing that looked halfway edible").

Chapter 11
Reflective Decision Making

All things considered, neighborhood oil rigs on the pathway to beach—a good decision or not?

WHY do we feel so confident in our choices that we seldom change our minds?

WHAT specific critical thinking strategies can we use to improve our decision making?

 ## Learning Outcomes

11.1 Explain dominance structuring and how it impacts our ability to consider our options in a full and fair-minded way.

11.2 Describe and apply the strategies used by strong critical thinkers thoughtfully to manage, monitor, and self-correct their decision making.

"Locals refuse to budge in battle with an oil company." Hermosa Beach has a decision to make. It has been a long time coming, but the referendum is finally on the ballot. Will we permit E&B Natural Resources to drill for oil, or will we say no? Everyone has heard the arguments pro and con for years. E&B has the legal right to drill. So if the citizens say no, then the city must pay the oil company $17.5 million over the next 20 years. But, if the citizens say yes, then E&B will pay the city as much as $451 million spread over the next 35 years from the billions E&B will be making from the oil. E&B plans to sink 36 wells from a small site, about the size of three lots, located in a quiet residential neighborhood at 6th Street and Valley. The shafts will spider out below the homes and arc under the beach and the ocean floor to reach a vast oil deposit in the shale rock 3,000 feet down.[1]

Opponents warn that property values will plummet. Who will want to buy a house where there could be toxic spills? Think of the fire hazard, the health risks, the eyesore, the constant noise, and the nasty oil odors fouling air we breathe. Think of globs of thick tarry oil washing on to the sandy beach with every wave. The oil company says the risks are being greatly exaggerated. New technologies and current laws make drilling safe and clean. Sound and sight abatement is already part of the plan. Other communities are benefiting from drilling, why not Hermosa Beach too? Oh, and remember, the money. $3.8 million will go to the schools each year. The rest will go to parks, public services, and to put all the city's ugly overhead utility wires underground. These improvements will increase property values!

The interesting thing is that both sides are locked in. Neither side is listening to the other. Not anymore. Every "fact" is contested, every "study" is flawed, every claim is challenged, and every expert opinion is maligned. All motives are questioned. Yes, we will vote. But, no, we will not be doing any more System-2 deliberating.

For reasons that will be explained in this chapter, it is very hard for human beings to reverse a decision once made. The best opportunity to exercise our critical thinking is while we are still considering options. We can improve decision making by using our critical thinking skills and habits of mind to thoughtfully manage, monitor, and self-correct our own decision-making process. In this chapter we are focusing on the quality of the decision-making process. In the second part of this chapter we will explore specific strategies aimed at fostering reflective decision making. When the stakes are high and when we have the time to think things through carefully, our best chances for a good decision-making outcome is to call on the full power of our reflective System-2 thinking, that is on the full power of our critical thinking skills and habits of mind.

But, before getting into the decision-making strategies, we first will explore the psychological phenomenon that is the natural human tendency to lock into a decision. Once we commit to a given decision option, we gain confidence that our choice was the best one and that the other options would have been mistakes. Called **dominance structuring**,

THINKING CRITICALLY

What Can We Learn from Popular Fiction?

Are you capable of enduring trust in the face of almost overwhelming contradictory evidence? Some will risk their lives and fortunes believing that the person they love is worthy of unconditional loyalty, trust, financial support, and emotional investment. Belief against all odds is the dramatic engine in the amazingly creative and engaging *Girl with a Dragon Tattoo/Millennium* trilogy by Stieg Larsson. In the second book of the trilogy, the protagonist Mikael Blomkvist is convinced that his estranged friend, Lisbeth Salander, has been wrongly accused of a triple murder. Despite compelling circumstantial evidence and shocking revelations about Lisbeth's psychological background, Blomkvist believes she is innocent of those crimes. Using his powerfully honed skills as an investigative reporter, he launches his own investigation into the murders. Fortunately for Blomkvist, the lead police investigator, Officer Bublanski, possesses strong critical thinking skills himself. So, while all the other police investigators appear to have locked in on the idea that Salander is guilty and while they have set about building the case for her

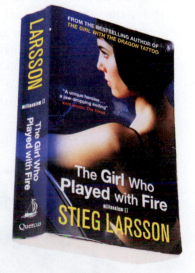

arrest and prosecution, Bublanski at least tries to maintain an open mind. He urges his colleagues to investigate other possible perpetrators—a fool's errand perhaps, given so much evidence of Salander's guilt. All three books in this trilogy are great reads, suspenseful, beautifully plotted, and artfully written. All three remind us about a danger we all risk, namely jumping to mistaken conclusions about other people and what motivates them. Did you ever discover that your judgments about a person were mistaken? How might one avoid making that kind of mistake?

this is an extremely valuable human characteristic. With confidence in the choice we have made, we are able to take action and to persevere during difficulties. We would hardly be able to accomplish anything were we to constantly reconsider every decision and change our minds. Our natural tendency toward dominance structuring helps us to be resolute and to sustain our commitments. But with the benefits come risks. Because dominance structuring tends to lock us into a decision, this tendency can occasionally lock us into an unwise decision. The critical thinking skill of self-regulation and the habit of truth-seeking are our best hopes for identifying those occasions and guarding against hanging onto poor decisions. In this chapter we first unpack dominance structuring so we can see how it works. Then we consider critical thinking strategies for managing the potentially negative consequences of premature dominance structuring.

11.1 Dominance Structuring: A Fortress of Conviction

Once human beings have made a decision, we almost never change our minds. Looking back on our choice as compared to other options, we often feel that ours was so obvious and others were so poor that it is a wonder that we considered them possibilities at all. Maybe we do not need to work on the skill of self-regulation after all because we are seldom, if ever, wrong. We say to ourselves, "Others may disagree, but that's their issue." Things may not turn out as we had expected, but that's just bad luck or someone else's screwup. Right? Be honest; there are plenty of times when we all have thought exactly that. Why? Part of the answer may be that we really do a good job of making sound decisions. And part of the answer, whether our decisions are objectively wise or foolish, is our tendency toward dominance structuring. To appreciate the thought-shaping influences of dominance structuring, consider the arguments presented in this next example.

"Yeah, Sure I can be open-minded."

"I Would Definitely Go to the Doctor"

A woman who has made a decision was invited to describe her decision-making process in detail to a trained interviewer. The narrative below is a brief excerpt from the transcription of that much longer interview.[2] The interviewer and the woman are talking about the possibility that she might discover a worrisome lump during a breast self-examination. The excerpt begins with the interviewer asking the woman whether she would go to see her health care provider if she were to discover a change in her body that caused her to worry about the possibility of breast cancer.

INTERVIEWER: "You're very religious. Could you see yourself waiting a while before going to the doctor and praying instead?"

RESPONDENT: "Oh, no. For one thing, God is a wonderful God; he made doctors. You know, my mother-in-law—I'm divorced, I was married then—she had had a heart attack. And, she definitely would pray instead of go to the doctor. She loved the Lord, and she remained in God's will [and was fortunate not to die]. But at times people have to understand that God doesn't make things as complicated as people kind of want to make it. And it's not about religion; it's about God, your personal relationship with Him. And God, He made some [people] become doctors to want to help. You know that's how I feel. You know, I'll say this until the day I die and go back to the Lord. I'm a practicing Christian; I love the Lord. I just know God works within common sense. That's why He gave us a brain, you know. And I would definitely go to the doctor. "

Review the decision map showing the respondent's arguments. For this individual the option not selected ("I would pray for a while instead of going to the doctor") has virtually no support. She considers whether going to the doctor means that she is not being sufficiently trusting in God, but abandons that line of reasoning. She is pulled by the availability heuristic as she recalls what her mother-in-law would do, but she resists that pull, saying that God does not make things that complicated. Although in the end she offers only two arguments directly supporting her decision, it is clear from the interview and the map that all her thinking has moved inexorably and confidently in that direction. Not going to the doctor is, for her, not really an option. The problem in her mind was how to explain that to her deeply religious friends.

Were we to evaluate the arguments the woman makes using the standards and strategies presented in Chapter 7 entitled "Evaluate Arguments: Four Basic Tests," we would find them wanting. For example, comparing herself to her mother-in-law could well have led the respondent

Decision Map—"I Would Definitely Go to the Doctor."

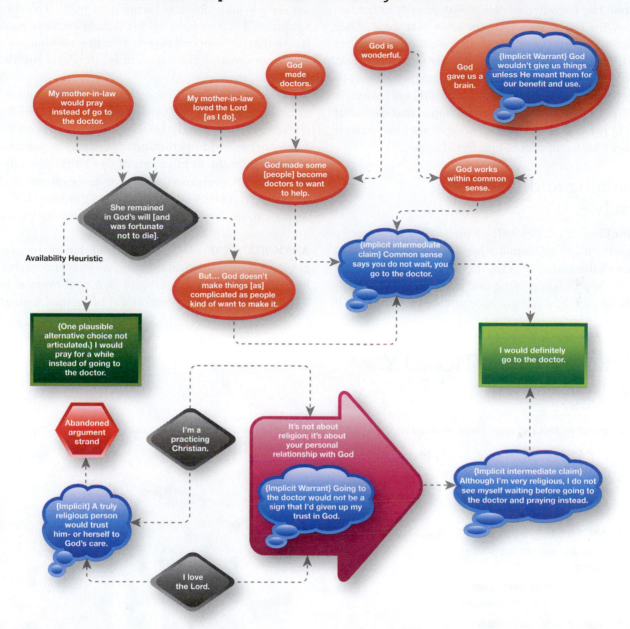

to infer that she did *not* need to see the doctor right away. The mother-in-law, a close family member, and, like herself, a woman of faith with a potentially severe illness, would delay seeking medical help. Ergo, following out the analogy, the woman being interviewed should also delay. The respondent's other arguments rely on belief statements about what God intends or how complicated God wishes things. But humans cannot know the mind of God. Therefore, we cannot establish the truth of premises about what God may want, intend, or think. This makes the soundness of those two arguments highly questionable. And yet, whatever their individual logical weaknesses might be, taken together her arguments are, for her,

persuasive explanations that she would indeed go to the doctor. She is firm in that decision. From the longer narrative, which is not reproduced here, we can infer that she is not an uneducated or illogical person; therefore to understand what is happening we have to dig deeper into her purposes for telling the story as she does.

As it turns out, this woman is using her reasoning skills to explain a decision, not to make a decision. Going to the doctor was always to her the more sensible of the two choices. For her this was a System-1 decision—Sick? Go to the doctor! What she needed to do was explain that choice in the light of her deeply religious views and in the context of having relatives (and perhaps friends) who use religion to delay seeing a doctor for a possibly dangerous symptom. Her cognitive challenge was actually rather formidable. She had to deal with the issue that some of her friends and the people at her church would interpret her going to the doctor as showing that her faith was weak. Notice that she does not bother to explain why going to the doctor would be valuable to her health, only why it's OK not to leave it to God. And also notice that she is not doubting her faith. But she does achieve her goal of creating a rationale to support her preferred option.

Explaining and Defending Ourselves

Our thinking capacities helped us survive as a species through the many millennia when we were anything but the most formidable species on the planet. Today our capacity for problem solving and decision making helps us achieve our personal goals, whatever they may be. If learning the truth helps achieve our goals, then we apply our skills to the problem of learning the truth. If needing to feel justified that we have made the right decision, particularly if that decision cost people their lives, is vital, we will apply our thinking skills toward creating and sustaining that justification.

Objectivity in decision making is something we prize. Yet objectivity can be very difficult for us when we already have a strongly held opinion on a given issue. Truth-seeking and open-mindedness incline us toward objectivity in the application of our skills of analysis, interpretation, evaluation, inference, and explanation. But unless we also invoke the sixth critical thinking skill, self-regulation, we may fail to achieve the objectivity we seek.

A POORLY CRAFTED ASSIGNMENT For many years I gave my students critical thinking assignments expressed like this example: "Gun control is a controversial issue in our nation. Take a position for or against legislation

THINKING CRITICALLY

Pro or Con

Let's try a little thought experiment. Indicate whether you are pro or con on each of the following policy proposals:

	PRO	CON
1. Legislation permitting death with dignity (assisted suicide)	_____	_____
2. Banning abortion	_____	_____
3. Licensing well-armed private militias	_____	_____
4. Scholarships for immigrant non-citizen college students	_____	_____
5. Legalization of payment for sex between consenting adults	_____	_____
6. Capital punishment	_____	_____
7. Applying campus nondiscrimination policies to religious student clubs	_____	_____
8. Requiring two years of public service of all citizens after high school	_____	_____
9. Increasing the retirement age for Social Security to 70	_____	_____
10. Statehood for Puerto Rico	_____	_____

Pick one of the 10 proposals and write down all the good reasons *for your position*, pro or con. All of them, please. After you have finished, write down all the good reasons for the other position, the one that *is not your view* of the matter. Thank you, and we'll come back to this in a moment.

banning all sales of handguns. Research the issue and defend your position with the best arguments possible. In doing so, please consider the arguments for the other side and explain why they are mistaken."

As it turned out, that was a terrible way to give a critical thinking assignment. Why? Because my students would do exactly what I had asked, in *exactly that order*. If they did not already have a point of view on the matter, they would first take one side or the other. Often their System-1 heuristic thinking played a big role in determining which side they took. Some were "pro-gun" and some had poignant personal stories of gun violence that made them "anti-gun." Some would knock one side or the other out of contention in their minds using the one-rule decision-making tactics of elimination by aspect: "If she'd had a gun to protect herself, she'd be alive today" or "You don't need an automatic pistol to hunt deer." Then, after they had taken a side in their minds, they would search for reasons and information that supported their point of view, but not reasons or information that opposed the view they had adopted. This was energetic investigation, but it was neither truth-seeking nor fair-minded. Their minds were pretty much already made up on the subject. Next they would write a paper laying out all the good reasons for their points of view. But, no matter which side they took, they struggled to say anything good about the opposing point of view. Their papers, by the way, were often well organized and logically presented. Like the woman talking about her decision to see the doctor, my students could explain their decisions and defend them. But they had not reflected on whether or not they were the best decisions. *Critical thinking is not the holding of a belief; it is the process of reflective judgment by which we come to the belief.*

The problem was my own, not my students'. I wanted my students to give due consideration to both sides of a controversial issue and to think about it in a fair-minded, objective, informed, and well-reasoned way. But that was not what the instructions said. What I had done instead was invite students to build a dominance structure around one option and to bolster their perspective by fending off all counterarguments. I should have said, "The right to bear arms has become a major issue in our country. Come to class on Monday next week prepared to discuss this issue. I may ask you to take either the pro side or the con side with regard to a possible piece of legislation relating to gun control. Open your mind to either possibility. Be ready to present either side effectively. And be ready for the third possibility, which is that I will assign you to listen and then to adjudicate the class discussion by evaluating objectively the reasoning presented by your peers. Study the issue, inform yourself about the arguments in favor of and opposed to gun control. Be ready to speak intelligently and fair-mindedly on the topic of the right to bear arms

and gun control legislation, no matter which of the three jobs I give you on Monday in class." If critical thinking is a process, then I should have found a way for my students to demonstrate that they are able to interpret, analyze, infer, explain, evaluate, and self-regulate. Only after the full, informed, and fair-minded discussion would it have made sense to invite students to then take a reasoned position on the matter.

> "A fanatic is one who can't change his mind and won't change the subject."
>
> Winston Churchill[3]

The challenge for critical thinking is not unlike the problem of building a new house on a lot where an older house already stands. Without doing damage to the land or the neighborhood, we need to remove the old house, salvaging anything that may be of value, before we can build the new house. It takes similar skill and sensitivity to perform the same operation on opinions. Truth-seeking and open-mindedness need to be cultivated as much as possible so that we can be prepared to revisit our opinions with objectivity and judiciousness. In my life there have been more than a few times when my dearly held but ultimately mistaken opinions on controversial matters had to be abandoned so that sounder, more informed, and better-reasoned opinions could take their rightful place. But it is never easy to change one's mind about an opinion that has been firmly held—and this makes the job of self-regulation that much more difficult. To understand why most of us have a very hard time changing our minds, let's explore the psychological process of deciding on "the best available option."

Moving from Decision to Action

Whenever we are presented with a problem, our cognitive heuristics and our capacity for logical reasoning play critical roles in the natural human quest to find some resolution that we can assert with plausible confidence to be our best available option. We shall call this option the *dominant or superior option* in any given context. In decision making we move, more or less quickly, through a process that includes sorting through options. We discard the implausible ones, identify one or more promising options, evaluate it or them on the basis of our decision-critical criteria,[4] and select the option we come to judge to be superior.[5] Psychological research by Henry Montgomery and others, as we shall see, is consistent with the idea that both argument making and cognitive heuristics are central factors in our search for a dominant option—to move us from cognition to action. In times of uncertainty, when action is needed, dominance structuring is a necessary strategy for

THINKING CRITICALLY

Pro or Con Revisited

Let's go back to the exercise in which we requested that you write down all the good reasons for your and for the other side of one policy proposal. Please count up the number of good reasons you put down for your opinion and then count all the good reasons for the other side. If you are like most of the rest of us, it was easier to list more reasons in favor of your point of view than against it. Was that true? Did you list more in favor of your view than the opposing view? Do you think you listed the strongest reasons against your point of view? Most of us do not take the time necessary to discover exactly what those are. Most of us act as if those who disagree with us have flimsy arguments when compared to our own. But we would unwise to assume that those who disagree with us are idiots.

Now, looking only at your side, what information or what new considerations would lead you to change your mind?

Please attempt to be as forthright and honest as possible. If there is absolutely no possibility, no new information, no event, no change in circumstances, that you could change your mind, then write that down. What about the people with whom you disagree? Assuming they are as reasonable as you are, is there anything that ought to lead them to reconsider and to change their minds? If your point of view is reasonable, fair-minded, and well-founded, then surely if they knew what you know, then they should change their minds. If you agree, then flip it around. If you knew what they know, and if you saw the world the way they do, then perhaps it is you who should agree with them. Both sides cannot be the right side. The whole exercise is predicated on the assumption that there is a pro and a con that diverge. Or, perhaps you have worked out a viable compromise policy position.

---

deciding between alternatives and swinging into action. Montgomery describes the human search for a single dominant option among our many possible choices in any given context as having four phases:

- pre-editing
- identifying one promising option
- testing that promising option for dominance
- structuring the dominance of the option selected[6]

PHASE 1: PRE-EDITING In the pre-editing phase, we start by selecting a group of possible options and a number of attributes that we think are going to be important as we decide which option to finally pick. Take, for example, the problem of hiring one new employee from a large applicant pool. We want to interview only a small group of highly qualified candidates. We want them to have relevant work

experience, education, employment test scores, and the like. We may have a concrete set of characteristics in mind for the final choice: someone with strong communication skills, enthusiasm for the position, and a schedule that permits that person to work the hours we might require. Our selection of these criteria shows good reasoning, for they are in fact crucial to finding the best person for the job. And we expect further evidence of reasoning in the systematic approach taken to identify potential candidates by advertising the position and screening the applicants to cull the list down to a group of interviewees. But when the applications come in, we don't exhaustively rate every candidate on every decision-critical attribute. Rather, at this early pre-editing stage we look for reasonable ways to make the decision easier and more efficient. We eliminate as many alternatives as possible with as minimal an expenditure of effort as must be committed to the task.

Typically, we use the elimination by aspect heuristic and the satisficing heuristic to make our work go more quickly. We toss every applicant who is missing any single qualifying condition (insufficient education, low employment test scores, or no relevant work experience), and we retain only those we judge to be good enough for a second look. We may cluster the applications into broad categories such as "well-qualified," "qualified," and "marginal." If we do cluster them like that, we will quickly eliminate all but the "well-qualified." Pre-editing can be brutally expeditious, and yet there is good reason for this. In real life we do not have the time or the resources to deliberate in detail about the cases we already know are not going to make the cut. What's the point?

Our natural eagerness to shortcut through large numbers of options was captured in a lyric from "The Boxer" by Paul Simon and Art Garfunkel, where the poets said that we tend to hear what we want or expect to hear and then to ignore or disregard all the rest.

PHASE 2: IDENTIFYING ONE PROMISING OPTION The second phase of the search for dominance is the identification of a promising option. We do this by *finding one* alternative that is more attractive than the others on at least one critically important attribute. There are many reasons why one choice may emerge as very attractive and be judged optimal. Perhaps this choice is most in tune with our values or current desires. Or perhaps the choice is the least threatening or the most economical. Whatever the source of the attraction, once this choice is identified, it becomes our "favored" or "promising" option. Using our hiring example, suppose there are four finalists who have passed through our initial screening process, and we plan that a committee will interview them all. And suppose that candidate number one has the most job experience, number

two is most energetic, number three is most analytical, and number four is the most congenial. It is possible the committee will immediately discover its consensus candidate. But it is more likely that different members of the committee will find different candidates to be optimal for different reasons. Each member of the committee has a different favorite. Thus, the stage is set for a difference of opinion as to which candidate should be the one hired.

PHASE 3: TESTING THE PROMISING OPTION   Having identified a promising option, we begin almost immediately to test it against the other options. We do this by comparing our promising alternative to the other options in terms of the set of **decision-critical attributes**. Typically, we focus on seeing whether our promising option has any salient disadvantages or major drawbacks. Returning to our hiring example, suppose that five years of relevant work experience is a decision-critical criterion. If our favored candidate has seven years of relevant work experience, we will interpret that to mean that our candidate is not at a disadvantage on that criterion. That our candidate may not have as many years of experience as some other candidate is not a problem. We are not going to argue the potential positive advantage of more years beyond the minimum five. Our focus will only be to assure ourselves that our favored option does not fall short of the mark on any decision-critical factor. But what if our candidate does fall short? In that case some of us may argue that the disadvantage is not fatal to our favorite's candidacy. In fact, if we are attracted to candidate number four because of his or her congeniality, we are likely to argue that even if candidate four has only two years of experience, this is really more than enough. At this point, we are not looking to prove that our candidate is the best; rather we want to be sure that our candidate has no fatal flaws.

Job Candidate Options

Most Experienced

Most Energetic

Most Analytical

Most Congenial

If our promising alternative is "comparable to the others," "about as good as the others," "neither better nor worse than the others," or "good enough" on the other decision-critical attributes, the promising alternative becomes the "to be chosen" alternative. Our initial preference for that candidate, *who was the first one we found whom we liked*, wins out. We become more and more firm in our choice. We will not abandon our "to-be-chosen" option easily. Once we begin to appraise and anchor on a given promising option, we seek to establish a rationale for selecting this promising or "to-be-chosen" option over the others, and this means we transition nearly seamlessly into phase 4.[7]

> The detective "began to worry that he was 'locking in,' a problem he saw with other cops all the time, the sure sense that something was just so, when it wasn't."
>
> John Sandford, *Mortal Prey*

PHASE 4: FORTIFYING THE TO-BE-CHOSEN OPTION In the final phase, we restructure our appraisals of the options so as to achieve the *dominance of one option over the others*.[8] This restructuring can be more or less rational, more or less in touch with reality, and, hence, more or less likely to lead to the intended and desirable results.[9] One way we restructure the decision so that our "to-be-chosen" candidate comes out on top is by de-emphasizing those decision-critical attributes on which our promising candidate may be weaker. Another way is to bolster our candidate by increasing the significance of an attribute on which our candidate is stronger. A third way is to collapse attributes into larger groupings; for example, we could combine education and job experience into the single attribute, "background experience." Now we can hire someone with more education but very little job experience, overriding our concern for job experience per se. Or, because we do not favor candidate number one who has the most job experience, we may need to diminish this apparent strength. We might argue that work experience is an advantage of candidate number one, but some detail about that work experience (for instance, that the person had never served in a supervisory role) is a disadvantage, so the one can be said to cancel the other. And, because of this, we might argue, candidate number one is not the person to hire.

The process of *de-emphasizing, bolstering, trading off, and collapsing* attributes continues until we find that one alternative stands above the others as the dominant choice. Acute reasoning skills are vital to this complex and dynamic process of making comparisons across attributes. Obviously, one might be able to quantify within a given attribute—for example, by comparing two candidates on the basis of their years of relevant background experience. But it is not clear

how one would compare—for the purposes of possible trade-offs—communication skills against, say, energy or loyalty. And yet, we will make arguments in support of the to-be-chosen alternative as the decision maker's search continues for a dominance structure to support this choice above all others.[10] When the decision is being made by committee, and the stakes are high, this process can become interpersonally difficult, stressful, political, and, in the worst situations, ruthless.

When is dominance structuring complete? There are three indicators. First, unless they are intentionally dissembling, people who have made their choice will tend to describe themselves as having decided, rather than as still thinking or as undecided. Second, people who are locked into a given choice tend to dismiss as unimportant, refute, or abandon all arguments that appear to be leading to a decision other than the one they embrace. Third, when asked to explain their choice, people who have built a dominance structure to fortify their selection often present with some enthusiasm a plurality of arguments supporting their chosen decision and they tend to recite rather unconvincingly a minimum number of arguments supporting any of the other possible options.

JOURNAL

Locked In?

Give an example of when you locked in on a choice prematurely, and then regretted it later. What could you have done differently?

Benefits and Risks of Dominance Structuring

The result of dominance structuring is confidence, whether reasonable or unreasonable, in the option we have decided upon. Dominance structuring supplies us with enough confidence to motivate us to act on our decisions and to sustain our efforts. Obviously, the more unreasonable, biased, irrational, and unrealistic we have been in our dominance structuring, the greater the risks of a poor decision. On the other hand, if we have made the effort to be reasonable, truth-seeking, informed, open-minded, and neither too hasty nor too leisurely in coming to our decision, then there is a greater chance that the decision will be a wise one. And we would be foolish not to be confident in it and not to act on the basis of such a decision. It is hard to know what more we could want when we need to make an important decision that involves elements of risk and uncertainty.

It would be a mistake to think of this human process as intentionally self-deceiving or consciously unethical or unfair. Rather, what cognitive scientists like Montgomery offer is a description of how human beings bolster confidence in their judgments under conditions of uncertainty. Humans seek to establish a strong and enduring rationale for the belief that one alternative dominates over others. This strong rationale impels us to act and sustains our continuing to act on the basis of that belief. We surround our choice with a rationale for its enduring superiority to the other choices. This strategy allows us then to move forward, with confidence in the quality of our decision.

Understanding the power of dominance structuring explains why it is so difficult for us to reconsider a choice once it has been made or why the criticisms of our choices seem unpersuasive. Once we have dominance structured around a choice, the virtues of other options are less compelling to us and their vices appear larger than they may in fact be. When the dominance structure has been created, it is not uncommon to hear people describe the results of their deliberations with phrases like "When we looked at it, we really didn't have any other choice," or "Hey, at the end of the day it was a no-brainer!" These mantras are evidence that the decision maker has elevated one option to the top position and discredited or discounted all other options. Having done that, it often is unclear to the decision maker why any of the other options were ever considered viable in the first place.

Searching for dominance in conjunction with elimination by aspect, satisficing, and anchoring with adjustment involves cognitive risks. First, we risk making poor decisions due to a lack of due consideration of all reasonable alternatives. Second, we risk being blind to the chance that our choice might be seriously flawed or need revision. At some level, we recognize these potential problems in human decision making. Our judicial system, for example,

---

THINKING CRITICALLY

Organic Foods

Proponents of organic foods maintain that they are natural, taste better, healthier, more environmentally sustainable, and purchasing them supports local small farmers. We should put aside the first reason, "they are natural." The Black Plague was natural and so are salmonella and botulism. Tornadoes, polio, and selfishness are natural. Pain and death are natural. The argument "It is natural, therefore it is good" is fallacious. But the four other reasons . . . well, those seem plausible. Of course, there's the issue of cost. Organic foods tend to be more expensive. So, for the sake of this exercise, let's eliminate that factor from the other side of the equation. Assume that you have  plenty of money to spend on food. Would you buy organic? Yes or no? If no, why not? If yes, what would it take for you to change your mind? What if all four reasons were knocked down, would you still buy organic? What if all four reasons disappeared and the assumption that you had plenty of money was removed?

To see dominance structuring in action, after you write your answers to the questions above, search and watch "Organic" from *Penn and Teller: Bullshit*! (Showtime, Season 7, Episode 6). Remember, our focus in this chapter is not on the pro or con arguments about buying organic. Our concern is how we humans can hold onto a decision (in this case, to buy organic foods) even though we come to realize that all of our reasons for doing so are misguided. Unscripted, the people in the video display how our shared, human psychological tendency to dominance structure around a decision continues to have the power to influence our behavior even after we no longer accept our original reasons for that decision. A 2011 NPR-Thomson Reuters Health Poll survey of 3,000 people about their attitudes regarding organic foods found that their reasons included "(36%) an eagerness to support local farms," "(34%) desire to avoid toxins," belief that organic foods were "(17%) better for the environment," and that organic foods "(13%) taste better." Why do we believe these things? Is there serious science backing up these claims, or is it just novelty, social conformity, and clever marketing? What would it take for us to change our minds?

Critical Thinking Skills Map to Leadership Decision Making

Successful professionals with leadership responsibilities, like those in business or the military, apply all their critical thinking skills to solve problems and to make sound decisions. At the risk of oversimplifying all the ways that our critical thinking intersects with problem solving and leadership decision making, here are some of the more obvious connecting points:

- **Identify Critical Elements**
  - *Analyze* the strategic environment, identify its elements and their relationships
  - *Interpret* events and other elements in the strategic environment for signs of risk, opportunity, weakness, advantage

- **Project Logical Consequences**
  - *Infer,* given what is known with precision and accuracy within the strategic environment, the logical and most predictable consequences of various courses of action

- **Navigate Risk and Uncertainty**
  - *Infer,* given the range of uncertainty and risk in the strategic environment, the full range of the possible and probable consequences of each possible course of action

- **Assess Decision Options**
  - *Evaluate* anticipated results for positive and negative impacts
  - *Evaluate* risks, opportunities, options, consequences
  - *Explain* the rationale (evidence, methodology, criteria, theoretical assumptions, and context) for deciding on the integrated strategic objectives and for the planning and action parameters that compose the strategy

- **Double Check Everything**
  - *Self-regulate* at every step review one's own thinking and make necessary corrections.

© 2013 Measured Reasons LLC, Hermosa Beach, CA Used with Permission. From Jan 2013 briefing "Critical and Creative Thinking" for Joint Special Operations Forces Senior Enlisted Academy, MacDill AFB.

generally provides for appeals to be made to some person or judicial panel other than the one that rendered the initial decision. We know that once people have fixed their minds on given results, it is very difficult for them to change their judgment. In everyday life, who is there to review our decisions for us if we do not do have the habit of truth-seeking and the skill of self-regulation so that we can review them ourselves?

Dominance structuring is a powerful influence on individual and group decision making. Our discussion may seem a harsh critique of human decision making. However, no rebuke is implied or intended. Nor is any praise. The description of dominance structuring is meant to be exactly that: a description of how human decision making works based on empirical investigations. At times we do well, at other times not.

OK, given that we humans naturally engage in dominance structuring, and given that the process has many benefits but some risks, does that mean that we cannot improve our decision making? No. Developing strength in critical thinking is all about improving our decision making process. We are human beings, not machines, so we are not going to replace dominance structuring with some other process. But we can adapt. The question for strong critical thinkers with a positive habit of truth-seeking becomes "What steps can we take to improve our decision making process and realize better outcomes given that we tend toward dominance structuring?"

11.2 Self-Regulation Critical Thinking Skill Strategies

Because dominance structuring is an automatic System-1 tendency, we do not ask ourselves whether we wish to engage in dominance structuring or not. We just do it. And, again, for the most part that is a good thing, particularly in contexts of uncertainty when a decision is needed and action is required. But, sometimes, premature dominance structuring is a mistake. It can lock us into a less than optimal decision. Fortunately, System-2 decision making is capable of overriding and intervening. There are many strategies to mitigate the risks of dominance structuring around a less than optimal choice. These strategies rely on the critical thinking skill of self-regulation. Using self-regulation we can monitor our individual and group decision making, and we can make corrections in our decision-making processes to protect ourselves against premature dominance structuring around a lesser option. Some of these strategies will be familiar and obvious, but others may be new to you. What's important is that we use our self-regulation skills to monitor decision making and make midcourse corrections should we begin to lock in prematurely. And that can happen, because our preferred option, after all, appears to be rather strong as compared to the others.

"Ongoing cognitive debiasing [e.g. monitoring one's own thinking for errors and self-correcting] is arguably the most important feature of the [strong] critical thinker and the well-calibrated mind."

Pat Croskerry, Geeta Singhai, and Silvia Mamede[11]

So, we will be tempted to take shortcuts and to achieve closure prematurely on our preferred option, fortifying it psychologically even against the onslaught of our original precautionary intentions.

Precautions When Pre-Editing

BE SURE ABOUT "THE PROBLEM" What we take to be the problem can limit our imaginations about possible solutions. For example, if the problem is "Our team is not going to meet the deadline," our solutions include working harder, putting in more time, or reducing the quality of the work to complete it on time. But if the problem is "Roy is not doing his share of the work," then our solutions include talking with Roy about the importance to the team of his fulfilling his responsibilities, giving some of Roy's work to other team members, replacing Roy on the team, or excluding Roy from the work effort and the resulting credit for the team's accomplishments. As we saw in Chapter 2 entitled "Critical Thinking Mindset and Skills" the crew of *Apollo 13* was able to identify the right problem; it was the oxygen. But if they had interpreted the problem to be instrumentation, it is difficult to see how they would have survived. Through training and experience, we learn all sorts of ways of solving all kinds of problems. But if we interpret the problem incorrectly, we are very apt to decide upon a solution that will be ineffective or inappropriate.

SPECIFY THE DECISION-CRITICAL ATTRIBUTES Before beginning to work on a solution, be clear about the standards to be applied when evaluating options and minimum thresholds that an acceptable option must meet. If two years of work experience is an expectation for hiring, then say so and stick to it. If a non-stop

flight is, in your judgment, a requirement for your next vacation trip, then don't compromise on that standard. On the other hand, if a non-stop flight is desirable but not essential, then don't elevate a secondary criterion to the level of "mandatory." If the decision must be made after you hear from your friend next week on Monday, but before the opportunity lapses next week Thursday, then hold to that time frame. People with strong critical thinking skills and habits of mind protect themselves from making suboptimal decisions by establishing primary and secondary criteria and negotiating the secondary ones but holding firm to the primary ones.

BE CLEAR ABOUT WHY AN OPTION IS IN OR OUT Even at the pre-editing phase, make a reflective and deliberative judgment as to why each option should remain in contention or be eliminated. It will be impossible in most cases to give full consideration to every conceivable option. We need to eliminate large numbers of options early in the process so we can conserve time and energy to focus on those that remain. Real estate salespeople know this, and so they will ask prospective buyers and renters about their price range and how many bedrooms they need. These two parameters alone will enable agents to avoid wasting their own time and their clients' time on properties that are too expensive or not the right size.

Suppose you are looking to rent a two-bedroom apartment for less than $900 per month near school. A computer search or a friend who is a real estate agent can provide a list of a dozen apartments within minutes. Because you were clear about why an option was in (near the campus, two bedrooms) and why an option was out (cost more than $900), each and every one of the apartments will be a viable possibility. Your chances of making a poor decision or falling in love with a place you cannot afford or that does not meet your needs are reduced considerably. Suppose that a safe neighborhood and proximity to the metro system are also major considerations for you. Now, with clarity about five criteria, the choices become fewer and the next step, identifying the promising option, is more manageable.

✔ **CHECK LiST**

"Apartment Must Haves"

☐
☑ Under $900/mo
☑ Two bedrooms
☑ Near campus
☑ Near metro stop
☑ Safe neighborhood
☐

Precautions When Identifying the Promising Option

SCRUTINIZE OPTIONS WITH DISCIPLINED IMPARTIALITY When you first start considering a problem, it is too soon to become the champion of one alternative over another, and you'll need to discipline yourself to assess strengths and weaknesses without becoming enamored of any specific option. If there are four apartments to look at, prepare your mind to look objectively at each. In practice, this can be more difficult than it seems, especially because many professional real estate agents often use the following tactics. First, an agent shows an acceptable property, a weaker one second, the best one third, and a lesser-quality property fourth. Psychologically, this puts the client at ease because, after two less-than-fully-desirable options, the third option looks really good, adjusting upward from where the client had first anchored. Seeing a less-acceptable fourth option helps lock the client in on the third option. Although the salesperson may never have heard of Professor Montgomery and dominance structuring, he or she knows how to wield these decision behaviors. The agent might ask the client to note the positives of one apartment over the other, guiding the dominance structuring process along. The agent will have a fifth to show, if the client insists, but the agent is hoping that the client will lock in on one that is "good enough." The way *not* to be shepherded into a decision we might later regret is to decide beforehand that we will not let ourselves make any decision about the options, not even a tentative decision, until we have examined each with equal scrutiny.

LISTEN TO BOTH SIDES FIRST A variation on the previous strategy is the mental discipline not to decide until we have heard the other side of the story. Judges instruct juries not to decide until after the prosecution and the defense have both completed presenting their cases and made their closing arguments. Parents discover that it is not good enough to hear only one child's story about who started the fight and why. They know that they must hear the other child's side of the story. We all have a natural tendency to believe the first credible report we hear and then use that belief to critique subsequent reports. Has this ever happened to you? Can you think of a time when you were involved in a situation or a disagreement with another person that resulted in that other person telling a third party what happened, only to find that when you tried to explain your side of the story to that third party they seemed to have already made up their minds about you? We as authors can think of a few examples with co-workers, friends, and even some family members where this has happened to us in the past. It takes a set of practiced critical thinking self-regulation skills and a strong habit of open-mindedness to resist coming to a premature decision regarding which side to believe.

Precautions When Testing the Promising Option

USE ALL THE ESSENTIAL CRITERIA As obvious as this seems, we often do not use all the decision-critical criteria after identifying our promising option. We like the apartment in the complex that has the well-equipped workout room, and so we elevate that new factor to the status of a major consideration. But our initial set of essential factors did not include that consideration. It may have been on our desirable list, but it was not on the essentials list. Instead, we err by neglecting one or more of our initially essential criteria, for example, the proximity to the university or the cost. Strong critical thinking habits of mind incline us toward sticking to our initial criteria and applying all of them to this candidate and to all the other candidates. If a new and important criterion emerges during the decision-making process, then we would want to revise the list of decision-critical criteria and initiate a new search. There may be others that have great recreational spaces. As we first envisioned our set of criteria, great recreational space was

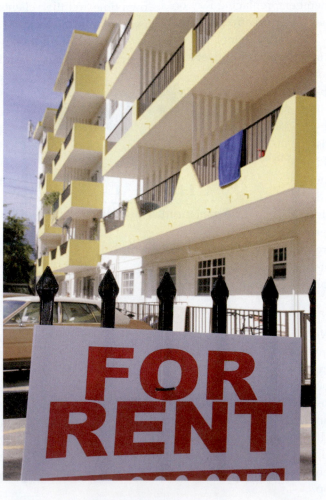

not among them. Until we saw this apartment, that consideration was not an essential factor. No matter whether we stick with our initial set of criteria or initiate a new search with a new set of criteria, the important thing is that we apply all of them if they are all considered essential.

TREAT EQUALS AS EQUALS The tendency toward dominance structuring privileges the promising option over all the other candidates by orienting our thinking around whether that one option has any obvious disadvantages. If the favored option has no obvious disadvantages, then it will become the to-be-chosen option. I like the apartment in the complex with the great fitness room. So, I ask myself whether it has any major disadvantages as compared to the other choices. It's pricey, but I can stretch. It isn't as close to the university, but it's not too far either. I wish the second bedroom were bigger, but I can live with that. Nope. No major disadvantages. Notice that in this process I did not give all four options a fair-minded evaluation, seriously comparing them on each criterion. Instead of truth-seeking, I threw objectivity to the wind and settled for an apartment that was more expensive, further from the university, and too small. And I did not even look at the other two criteria, safety and proximity to the Metro.

DILIGENTLY ENGAGE IN TRUTH-SEEKING AND REMAIN IMPARTIAL Truth-seeking helps us follow reasons and evidence wherever they lead, even if they go against our preferred or favored option. This is an active process. We must discipline ourselves to go out and find the needed evidence and consider all the reasons, pro and con. Being *diligent* in truth-seeking means that we give fair-minded consideration to options and ideas even if they go against our preconceptions or cherished, but perhaps unreflectively held, beliefs. Impartiality helps us maintain our objectivity. But we all know that it is hard to be impartial in some situations. If the stakes are high for us or if people we care about are involved, it is very difficult. Strong critical thinking demands that we recognize contexts in which impartiality is difficult to maintain. In those cases, if others are involved, the judicious thing to decide is that someone else should decide. In legal matters, when a potential juror is deemed to be at risk of not being impartial, that person is excused from being a juror. A judge who is at risk of not being impartial in a given case asks that the case be moved to a different judge. But in our daily lives, we cannot remove ourselves from judging or excuse ourselves from the responsibility of making decisions. We must, instead, make a conscious and deliberative effort to decide objectively. The habit of truth-seeking and the skill of self-regulation are irreplaceable assets in doing this.

Precautions When Fortifying the To-Be-Chosen Option

BE HONEST WITH YOURSELF The complex processes at work in the final stage of dominance structuring can be difficult to manage unless one is deeply committed to making honest evaluations. But, if there are good reasons, we can de-emphasize a given decision-critical criterion relative to another. In the apartment example, price may be more important than proximity to the campus. At other times, a criterion cannot be de-emphasized. Safety, for example, might have been a major consideration in the pre-editing phase. If that were the case, then it would be intellectually dishonest to argue at this point that it is no longer a factor to consider seriously. When bolstering we may be tempted to exaggerate the virtues of our to-be-chosen option and exaggerate the vices and shortcomings of the other options. But exaggeration would be less than fully honest. Yes, our favored candidate does have advantages, and yes, the other options have flaws, but we should use self-regulation to monitor our evaluation so that we do not blow these advantages or these flaws out of proportion.

Trading off one criterion for another can be straightforward if the two have the same metric. For example, proximity to the university and proximity to the metro can both be measured in time and distance. So, we can more easily decide whether being a little closer to the metro and a little further from the university is acceptable or not. But when two criteria are measured on different metrics, the trade-offs can be more difficult. How much safety should one trade to get a lower rent? How much smaller

can that second bedroom be to live closer to the university? Again, we need self-regulation skill to monitor and correct, if needed, our tendency to trade away too many important things to get that one feature that attracts us so much. Collapsing criteria is not going to work when the criteria are as different as those in the apartment example. It is hard to imagine price and safety as one criterion. But in the hiring example earlier in the chapter, it could be reasonable to collapse work experience, volunteer experience, and maybe service-learning experience. If we can expect that the person learned job-relevant skills even though he or she may not have had a paying job, then collapsing makes sense.

Critical Thinking Strategies for Better Decision Making

TASK INDEPENDENT TEAMS WITH THE SAME PROBLEM Military commanders, realizing the risks of poor decisions, occasionally set two independent teams to work on the same problem. The theory behind this strategy is that if the two teams make the same recommendations, then that recommendation is probably the best option. If the teams make divergent or conflicting recommendations, then that provides the commanding officer the opportunity to listen impartially and objectively as each team explains why its recommendation is superior.

THINKING CRITICALLY

Should He Live or Should He Die?

In December 2005, Arnold Schwarzenegger, then governor of California, faced a difficult decision. Should he grant clemency to a high-profile inmate on death row, Mr. Stanley "Tookie" Williams? The death penalty, as a social policy, had come under considerable criticism. Many well-known Californians called for Governor Schwarzenegger to commute Mr. Williams' sentence to life without possibility of parole. Many Californians believed that Mr. Williams had demonstrated for several years that he was a "changed man." As a convicted murderer he deserved life in prison, but he was not the same person he had been decades earlier, and he did not, in their view, deserve at this time to be punished with death. Some saw him as a symbol of why the death penalty should be abolished. After deliberating on the matter, Governor Schwarzenegger decided against clemency, so Mr. Williams was executed. The governor posted a document on the Internet describing his decision-making process. Search by "Schwarzenegger Williams clemency decision" for the decision and for comments on it.

The governor's statement explains his decision. First, map that decision. Your map will show that the governor provides two primary lines of reasoning supporting his decision. One ends in the claim that Mr. Williams is, in fact, guilty (as determined by the jury at his trial), and that there is no other basis for clemency given that he is guilty. The map should also show additional bolstering arguments supporting the conclusion that Mr. Williams should not be granted clemency: The gangs he formed continue to do violence; his attempted escape risked the lives of law enforcement officers; and the murders he committed were brutal in nature. The governor entertained five considerations, which indicated that a decision would be needed [mapped using diamond shapes]: (1) claimed innocence, (2) claimed redemption, (3) a lack of apology, (4) fairness of the trial, and (5) good works while in prison. Several of these were endorsed as important considerations in the public debate prior to the governor's decision.

Second, examine the map that reflects your interpretation of this document to see if there is a discernible dominance structure surrounding and supporting the chosen option. Were the strongest arguments for the option not chosen identified and given due consideration? Does the map reflect that the governor applied appropriate standards in an appropriate way? Discuss your response to these two questions with due consideration to maintaining your own objectivity, truth-seeking, and fair-mindedness. These are not easy questions because the chances are that you, like most of the rest of us, have an opinion about the death penalty. And, if so, then you, like the rest of us, have probably built a dominance structure to support your opinion on that policy question. Thus, objectivity and impartiality must be self-monitored during this discussion.

Third, evaluate the governor's arguments individually and his decision holistically. Apply the four tests for evaluating arguments presented in Chapter 7, the Holistic Critical Thinking Scoring Rubric presented in Chapter 1, and what you have learned about heuristic thinking and dominance structuring in Chapter 10 and this one. We worked this exercise ourselves, and we put our map of the governor's explanation in the Appendix.

DECIDE WHEN IT'S TIME TO DECIDE Particularly in group decision-making situations, there is a tendency to decide prematurely. Time for discussion is short, and some people always seem ready to decide faster than others do. People can become impatient, and the urgency of other matters can lead us into the trap of "Ready, Fire, Aim." We can mitigate the tendency toward premature decision making by first setting out a plan for making the decision that identifies all the steps that will be taken first. In group decision making, this can be very helpful, for it establishes a set of expectations and assures time for the diligent inquiry and deliberation that is due an important decision. Obviously, it would be equally unwise to fail to make the decision when opportunities are being missed and the costs of delaying are mounting up. That said, sticking to an initial plan for when and how a decision needs to be made, including the time frame, fact finding, option development, and consultation, can be very helpful.

ANALYZE INDICATORS AND MAKE MIDCOURSE CORRECTIONS Health care and business professionals employ this strategy. They frequently measure progress and make necessary adjustments if the relevant outcome indicators do not show the expected improvements. This strategy is the critical thinking skill of self-regulation made operational. When a patient is in the hospital, the clinicians monitor all the patient's bodily systems to be sure that the treatment plan is having the desired effect. If any of the many tests that are performed show that the patient's condition is not improving, then the medical team makes changes in the patient's treatment. In business settings, people monitor sales revenues, expenses, cash flow, accounts payable, and accounts receivable on a regular basis. They review data to monitor progress toward revenue targets or to be sure they are staying within budget allocations. If any of the numbers look problematic, they make midcourse corrections. The same idea applies to decisions we make to improve or change our life situations. If we monitor the effects of those decisions and we do not see the results we planned, we need to make midcourse corrections.

CREATE A CULTURE OF RESPECT FOR CRITICAL THINKING All of us, and leaders in particular, can increase the likelihood of better decision making by creating a culture of respect for critical thinking. We do this by modeling and encouraging positive critical thinking habits of mind. We do this by inviting, acknowledging, and rewarding the constructive use of critical thinking skills. We do this by showing respect for people even if they advance ideas and opinions that differ markedly from our own. We can model respecting people's effort to think well even if we do not accept their ideas. As leaders we would be wise to invite people to supply their reasons for their recommendations, rather than only their votes or their recommendations, as if the reasons were unimportant. As leaders we must give truth-seekers enough latitude to raise difficult questions without fear of reprisals. We must be willing to listen, to reconsider, and to be persuaded by good arguments. At the same time, we must use these same tools when presenting our final decisions—sharing not just the choice made, but providing the reasons for that choice.

Summing up this chapter,

dominance structuring is the natural tendency we have to fortify our decisions in our own minds so that we can move forward with confidence to act on those decisions, particularly in contexts of risk and uncertainty. The many advantages of dominance structuring include persistence when the going gets tough, confidence that we have made the right choice, and the courage to act even though some uncertainty may remain. With these advantages there are also risks. The choice may not have been a good decision in the first place. Or conditions may have changed, making the choice no longer optimal. But unless we are monitoring our decision making and self-correcting along the way, dominance structuring can lock us into a bad decision or prevent us from making needed changes. There are many critical thinking strategies that we can use to guard against the pitfall of poor decision making. These strategies share two common themes: cultivate and practice the critical thinking habits of mind, especially truth-seeking, and apply strong critical thinking skills, especially self-regulation. Use these strategies to monitor decision making every step of the way and correct the process as often as needed.

Key Concepts

dominance structuring is the psychological process through which humans achieve confidence in their decisions. The four phases of dominance structuring are pre-editing, identifying one promising option, testing that promising option for dominance, and structuring the dominance of the option selected.

decision-critical attributes are those criteria the decision maker deems to be important and relevant for the purpose of evaluating options.

Applications

Reflective Log

Decisions that change your life: Picking an apartment is a relatively benign matter compared to decisions that have the potential to radically alter the course of your life. Imagine these four possibilities:

1. Considering whether you should get married.

2. Deciding whether you need help with a drinking, gambling, or drug problem.

3. Deciding whether to make an embarrassing apology to someone.

4. Dealing with another request from a member of your family for a loan.

Step 1: Select one of the four possibilities. Think about the problem as it might play out in your life and how you would go about deciding what you should do. Simulate the entire decision. Then, draw it out in a decision map or write out an explanation of your decision process.

Step 2: Examine your completed map or written explanation for dominance structuring. Evaluate your decision process to see whether you applied the critical thinking strategies to ensure that you make as good a decision as possible.

Individual Exercises

Recall a past decision: Consider a time when you needed to deliberate over a decision under conditions of uncertainty about an important issue. Perhaps, for example, you pondered the question of which college to attend, which apartment to rent, or whether to accept a job offer. How well does the four-stage process described above in MOVING FROM DECISION TO ACTION fit with your decision-making experience in that case? Were a number of conceivable options quickly eliminated in pre-editing? Did one option begin to appear rather attractive to you for some particular reason? Did you weigh that option against a few other possibilities to be sure that yours did not have any major disadvantages? Did you do any mental trading off, bolstering, grouping of criteria, or de-emphasizing of criteria that might initially have seemed important? In the end, after you had made your decision, do you recall thinking that the choice you made was rather obviously the best option among those realistically available at the time? If you answered "yes" to all the questions, which would be fine, then it would appear that you were dominance structured around that option. If you answered "no" to one or more of these questions, then reflect on what happened to derail the natural tendency toward dominance structuring in your particular case. If you do not feel that you were dominance structured around your preferred option, what new information or new considerations would have led you at the time to have made a different decision?

Preparing for a future decision: Consider a decision coming up in your life. Reflect on the issues and concerns that are leading you to make this decision. What exactly is "the problem" you must resolve with this decision? What are your decision-critical criteria? Which are essential and

which are important but only desirable? Are there any minimum thresholds that must be met for an option to be considered viable? How do you plan to scrutinize your options? How will you be sure that you have heard all sides? Is there a way for you to assure yourself that none of the essential options will be dropped out of the equation before you make your decision? How do you plan to ensure that you have diligently engaged in truth-seeking, maintained your objectivity, and impartially evaluated all the options prior to selecting a favorite? How will you determine when the time has come to make the decision? What factors will you monitor after you have made your decision, so that you can know whether a midcourse correction is needed? This exercise does not invite you to make that important decision. It invites you to lay the groundwork for making that decision by applying the critical thinking strategies of self-regulation.

Can we question what we were raised to believe? For many of us, the religion we say we belong to is the one into which we were born and raised. From childhood we were instructed to believe certain things and pray in certain ways. As children we accepted what we were told by people in authority over us. Many of us eventually grew comfortable with those beliefs, rituals, and practices of a particular religion. Yes, there may have been questions and doubts, but somehow or other we fought through those. Moving away from the religion of our youth can feel like stepping into an abyss. We may have no sense of how we could replace it. What should we believe instead? What basis would we have for our sense of right and wrong, were it not connected to religion? What would we make of our place in the universe, if we were not somehow part of a Grand Plan, and watched over by a loving Creator? How would our family members respond? Who would we be, if we were not a _____?

There are answers to these questions. But make no mistake about it, the answers for any of us are not easily won. The first challenge of this exercise is to recognize how much we dominance structure around the religion of our youth. Meditate on that for some time. Ask yourself when, if ever, you actually sat down and compared point for point the religion of your youth in an objective, open-minded way with two or three of the other major world religions. For most of us, the answer is never. Oh, maybe we learned to defend our religion from the attacks and criticisms people may hurl at it. But, few of us have laid out the options side by side and reviewed their pluses and minuses point by point. Many of us fortify the dominance structure holding up our religious convictions by discounting objections and ignoring inconsistencies.

Part two is this challenge: Ask yourself what it would take for you to thoughtfully and intentionally examine the religion of your youth. Not reactively, not angrily ping-ponging off of some dreadful tragedy or upsetting news report. But with all due deliberation, considering the evidence as we know it, the reasons as we see them, the nature of the human condition as we understand it. One way for us to examine the religion we were born into would be to ask, what we would need to find, to learn, to know that would result in our reflective decision to say to ourselves in the privacy of our own heart and mind that, well, not to put too fine a point on it, sorry but as good as it might have been for our youth, the religion we were born into is simply untrue?

SHARED RESPONSE

Full and Fair Consideration?

How does dominance structuring impact our ability to consider our options in a full and fair-minded way? Give a real-life example. Be sure to provide your reason(s), not just your opinion. And, comment respectfully on the reasons others offer.

Group Exercises

What would it take? You are on the governor's select committee of senior advisors, and the governor has asked you to make a recommendation and supply your reasons. Here's the situation: A serial killer who brutally rapes and tortures for days before murdering his victims was cornered by FBI agents and, while trying to escape, was shot and suffered a non-lethal head wound. Now lying in a private room in a state hospital, the killer, who is in a coma, is being kept alive by a feeding tube. Doctors say that he will never recover from the coma because of the severity of the head wound he suffered. Although there is no doubt about his guilt, he has never been arrested, indicted, or put on trial. The governor has been receiving political pressure from many sources saying that the killer should not be kept alive. They want the governor to order that the feeding tube be removed, which will cause the killer to starve to death. Others, hearing of this, have sent a flurry of messages to the governor that say that all human life must be respected, reminding the governor that this person has not been convicted of any crimes by a jury.[12] The governor has asked you to advise on the question: "Withdraw the feeding tube or not?" After discussing this with your group, write down your recommendation and your reasons. Also write down your reasons for *not* recommending the opposite.

After you have written down your recommendation, write down what it would take for you to change your mind and recommend the opposite. If that is not a possibility, explain why not.

Wishy-washy flip-floppers: If judiciousness is a positive critical thinking habit of mind and if strong self-regulation skills and honest truth-seeking can guide us to revisit our decisions and change our minds, why is it that, in the United States, a leader who changes his or her mind is criticized for being wishy-washy? And why is it that a politician who learns new information and comes to a new position on an issue is criticized for flip-flopping?

Bonus Exercise

Death in the West

In 1979, the BBC aired a Themes Television Documentary on smoking. It featured gut-wrenching interviews with American cowboys from Montana and other Western states that were dying of lung cancer, emphysema, and heart disease. Their doctors were interviewed and hypothesized that smoking was the cause of these men's illnesses. The documentary also shows interviews with executives from Philip Morris, the manufacturer of Marlboro cigarettes, which used the "Marlboro Man," a handsome, rugged, healthy, independent-minded cowboy, on all their advertising. The executives offered reasons why we should not believe that cigarettes were causally connected to these diseases. Nevertheless, the documentary's message was that smoking was a serious health risk. Because of the potential loss of millions of dollars in revenue from the sale of Marlboro cigarettes, Morris sued the BBC. The documentary was suppressed as part of the court settlement. It may be that only underground copies are available. If you happen to find a copy to watch, you will see dominance structuring in action. The physicians who cared for

Come to where the flavor is. Come to Marlboro Country.

the dying cowboys believe that smoking caused their diseases. The Philip Morris executives appear sincere in their claims that cigarette smoking is safe. Even the independent clinical psychologist who is interviewed suggests that the Philip Morris executives needed to think of themselves as people doing worthy labor, not as ruthless purveyors of disease and death. And this insight came several years before the initial research on dominance structuring was published. Search for and watch the documentary. (Search "Thames Television 1979 documentary Death in the West.") Map the arguments made by the Philip Morris executives in favor of smoking and opposed to those who would argue that smoking is dangerous.

Bonus Exercise

"Brown or Wilson?"

The names of Michael Brown and Darren Wilson will forever be linked in the minds of the people of Ferguson, Missouri. The tragic killing in the summer of 2014 of young Mr. Brown by Officer Wilson drew the attention of the entire nation. As the facts slowly emerged and as the crowds of protestors marched, people began taking sides. Many demanded justice for what they regarded as the murder of an unarmed Black man by the police officer. Many stood by the police officer for what they regarded as a regrettable but justifiable act of self-defense in the line of duty. And then more facts emerged. But apparently those who had already locked in on one side or the other could no longer hear or process any facts that went counter to the position they had already taken.[13] The challenge of this exercise is to examine the dominance structuring of people on both sides. Why do some

so strongly support Officer Wilson, and why do others so strongly condemn him? Do not take one side or the other in this yourself, or, if you already have, put your own beliefs in the matter aside for a moment. Get all the facts you can from the news about Mr. Brown's killing. Then try to figure out what it would take to persuade a reasonable person who supports the police officer and a reasonable person who condemns the police officer to open their minds to the possibility that they are mistaken. Yes, this is a very difficult challenge given all the psychology involved in dominance structuring and all the emotion associated with issues of race, duty, violence, self-defense, guns, and death. But, and this is the important part, but, if we are to make progress as a community then we must learn how to think about and to talk about these difficult topics with respect and with an open mind.

Chapter 12
Comparative Reasoning

Marine Colonel George Connell, left, controls his contempt for the CBS journalist, Mike Wallace, center, who is arguing with Air Force General Brent Scowcroft, right.

HOW can we recognize comparative reasoning?

HOW can we evaluate comparative reasoning?

WHAT are the uses, benefits, and risks of comparative reasoning?

 ## Learning Outcomes

12.1 Explain comparative reasoning and how it impacts our understanding of novel situations.

12.2 Apply correctly the five criteria for the evaluation of comparative reasoning.

12.3 Describe the uses, benefits, and risks of comparative reasoning.

"The reporter is supposed to shout, 'Americans, these guys are about to attack you,' and then you die. Is that the problem here?" demands veteran CBS News anchor Mike Wallace of Air Force General Brent Scowcroft. "Yes, you should warn our troops!" is the answer the general wants to hear. But that is not the answer Wallace gives. The hypothetical—you are an American TV news journalist who is embedded with enemy troops who are about to ambush a platoon of American soldiers. Your options—videotape the ambush for the evening news or warn the American platoon.

The program *Ethics in America* brought together military officers, journalists, and government officials to debate this hypothetical as a way of exploring the relationship between one's responsibilities as a professional journalist and one's responsibilities as a fellow American. Mike Wallace and Peter Jennings—at the time two of the best-known, most respected, and widely watched TV journalists in the nation—struggled mightily with the high-stakes hypothetical. As Mike Wallace is speaking, another panelist, USMC Colonel George M. Connell, is seething with contempt for the journalist. The Marine colonel is wondering if he should order American Marines to rescue a reporter pinned down by enemy fire, if that same reporter didn't have the courage to risk his own life to save a platoon of Americans. To see how Wallace answers the general and whether the colonel would, in fact, send Marines to rescue a journalist for whom he has "utter contempt," watch this powerful video free at Annenberg Learner. (Search "Annenberg Under Orders Under Fire part 2." The clip we will focus on here is about 12 minutes long.)

The key discussion starts at 31:18 when Harvard Law School professor Charles Ogletree presents the hypothetical to ABC News anchor Peter Jennings. After clarifying the question Jennings visibly struggles with the ethical dilemma. At one point, 34:47, Jennings pauses nearly 12 seconds to ponder what he would do. No experienced television personality would knowingly create that much "dead air time." But, for Jennings, the problem is very high stakes. He infers that should he decide to warn the Americans about the ambush, the enemy will immediately kill him. Ogletree turns to CBS News veteran reporter Mike Wallace and presents the same problem. He too struggles. First Wallace tries to apply the expectations of his professional role as a journalist to the situation. But that approach fails, and at 38:48 Wallace admits he does not know what his ethical duty is. Is he an American first or a journalist first?

Then, trying a different approach, Mike Wallace proposes an analogy. He says a reporter's ethical obligations in a combat zone are comparable to the reporter's duties in any U.S. city. If a reporter knew that a murder was about to be committed on the streets of an American city,

then the reporter would be ethically bound to call the police or to try to warn the victim. "Now," says Wallace, nervously moving his hands along the top of the table, "now . . . you take that and apply it to a war zone. And, I think . . ."

This video, like the others in the *Ethics in America* series, show the challenges associated with reasoning through a novel high-stakes problem. After you have watched Colonel Connell tell whether he would or would not "send Marines to save a couple of journalists," (42:36) ask yourself if the comparison that Mike Wallace tried to make—between warning the soldiers and warning the potential murder victim—is a good analogy or not. But keep your evaluation of Wallace's analogy tentative for now. Moving forward, we will explore the specific criteria for evaluating analogies, like Wallace's. It will be interesting to compare your reasons for your preliminary evaluation of his analogy with your thoughts about the analogy after you have reviewed those criteria.

12.1 Recognizing Comparative Reasoning
Our Minds Crave Patterns

Shaped by hundreds of thousands of years of natural selection, animal intelligence and particularly human intelligence has developed its powers of pattern recognition. Those of our ancient ancestors who learned how to recognize what they could eat and distinguish that from what would eat them had a greater likelihood of survival and with that a higher chance to reproduce. By providing adaptive advantage, the genes for pattern recognition were passed down through the long history of the evolution of our species. Reading the patterns in the movements of the stars and the moon, our ancestors eventually learned to anticipate the changes of the seasons, the migrations of the animals they used for food, and the times for planting and harvesting. Aberrations in the expected patterns, like the emergence of a comet or lunar eclipse, were interpreted as having meaning too. Perhaps the comet foretold a plague, or perhaps a blood moon meant the death of the king.[1]

When our species turned its gift of pattern recognition toward social interactions it saw recurring behaviors that led some people to be trusted as friends and others to be vanquished as enemies. In ancient times, different primitive civilizations, trying to understand the patterns that shaped good fortune and misfortune, endowed their pagan gods with the familiar patterns of behavior they saw in human interactions. This god was capricious, that god was vengeful, other

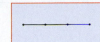 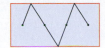 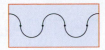

How many patterns can our minds make out of four dots inside a rectangle? Easily more than four.

gods acted out of courage, or jealousy. Fecund gods made the crops grow, drunken gods encouraged debauchery. Humans squabbled, and so must the gods. But the squabbles of the gods had an impact on human events. Down through the millennia for most members of our species life was harsh, unpredictable and short. Natural dangers, diseases, and predators abounded. If the gods had anything to do with what was happening, then perhaps appeasing them or pandering to them might influence those gods to be a little more generous, or at least a little less hurtful. Working the pagan gods certainly must have seemed worth a try.

To learn more about how our gift for pattern recognition sparked a deeper and sounder method for understanding of the origins of our planet watch the March 23, 2014 episode of *Cosmos: A Space Time Odyssey*, narrated by Neil deGrasse Tyson. You can search by that description or by its apt title: "When Knowledge Conquered Fear."

Today the members of our species continue to use our amazing capacity for pattern recognition. A jogger listening to music hears the first three musical notes and recognizes the song immediately as one of her favorites. An experienced poker player studies all the other players at the table looking for each person's tells. A partner arriving home smells the delicious dinner that has been prepared and knows immediately what seasonings were used and what culinary delights await. A gossip says, "Well, if you ask me, I'd say he's a narcissist. Did you see how he looked at himself in the mirror?" A political commentator editorializes with, "Yet another in a long line of foreign policy failures for the current administration." An expert diagnostician examines a patient complaining of a sore back and pain radiating down his right leg and says, "I think you have a herniated disk. Let's do an MRI."

We crave patterns so much that we impose them on natural phenomena. Thousands of years ago humans looked to the starry skies and saw hunters, dippers, dancers, spears, lions, bears, birds, and body parts. Today a child looks up at the white cotton candy clouds and says "Mommy, I see a face in the clouds! Look. And there's another one!" We are so good at recognizing patterns that we can tell when a familiar pattern is not being followed. A college student returns to his room and sees immediately that the books and papers on his desk are not exactly the way he left them. The student thinks, "Something isn't right here. Has someone gone through my things?" But just because we can "see" a pattern does not mean that the pattern is really there. Just for the fun of it, how many patterns can you make out of four dots inside a rectangle? There is no single right answer to this, because our minds are able to impose any number of different patterns. It reminds us of the line in the film *American Hustle* that says people see what they are looking for.

Pattern recognition is fundamental to human learning.[2] We all try to understand novel experiences by integrating them with what we already know. We notice something that looks familiar about the new experience, something, which we believe we can understand because of its familiarity, and we then try to expand our understanding of the larger new experience from that initial point. And in this stretch, projecting the familiar on to the unfamiliar as a way of seeking understanding, we have comparative reasoning.

Comparative reasoning can be helpful. A transfer student notices how many of the procedures at their new institution are similar to those at their prior institution. Even the names of some of the offices and departments are the same. Yes, there are differences to be learned, for sure. But the differences are easier to deal with once the student sees how similarly the two institutions operate. An employer asks a job applicant about prior work experience hoping to learn that the applicant has at least a year or two. The employer believes that the prior experience will make it much easier for the new hire to learn the new job; there will be similarities in the basic routines of the workplace. The candidate with prior experience can link what is new about this job to what was learned at previous workplaces. The similarities will make the transition to the new job easier than if the applicant had no prior work experience.

This approach, projecting our more familiar expectations on less familiar contexts, is, of course, full of potential risks and problems. Not knowing the dining customs in Italy, a visiting American reinforces the stereotype of the "ugly American" because at the trattoria he became irate when no waiter appeared to offer him a drink as soon as he sat down. As the history of our species shows, we can be so very wrong to think that we understand the new experience based only on that initial impression that it has something in common with our more familiar experiences. Betting that they could influence the pagan gods to show mercy to their village, our ancestors raised the ante all the way to sacrificing their own children to those false deities. Seems both foolish and tragic, we know—killing your own smart, beautiful, healthy, obedient child whom you love so dearly because somehow you got it in your head that a petulant and fickle god demanded the child's blood sacrifice. What a sad waste of a life.

THINKING CRITICALLY

What Is God to Do?

We wonder, and so we will ask, to what lengths would we go today to try to influence the outcomes of events? Would we pray to God to lift a famine or avert a flood? What would we sacrifice? How about something less important? Do we really think that God, the Almighty Creator of the Universe, will be influenced by our silent prayerful wishes to quietly tip the outcome of a sporting event in our favor, rather than allowing our opponent to prevail? And what if the opponent prayed as we did and was as worthy as we were? What then, if we think of God in the way that we think of a loving parent, is God to do when two good children earnestly pray for conflicting outcomes? What human pattern should God follow then?

Comparative, Ideological, and Empirical Inferences

Human beings draw inferences and offer explanations in most situations using one of three fundamental reasoning strategies. We use *comparative reasoning* (this-is-like-that), *ideological reasoning* (top-down from core beliefs), or *empirical reasoning* (bottom-up from observations to generalizations). Each of the three offers advantages and disadvantages. In this chapter on comparative reasoning and in Chapters 13 and 14 we will explore each of the three fundamental modes of human reasoning. In this way you will be able to make the most effective use of your critical thinking across the widest possible array of contexts.

Comparative reasoning (or this-is-like-that thinking) enables us to make interpretations, draw inferences, or offer explanations by relying on something that is more familiar to understand something that is less familiar. For example, one wintery bright February in Minneapolis—St. Paul two roommates were talking about climate change as they stepped through the residence hall doors and out into the brittle morning cold. "Climate change! Are you kidding me? Look around. We need snowshoes to get to class today!" The other, ever the serious student, replied, "Your problem is that you're too close to see the big picture. It's like you have your nose pressed up against the

TV screen and can see only a couple of pixels. Step back and the pattern is as clear as Hi-Def."

We use comparative reasoning, as in the climate change example, to explain abstract ideas. We use it when giving advice, too. For example, a grandparent might tell you a story that relates your current problem to something similar that happened to that grandparent and then use that to suggest how you might handle your current problem. The legal system's reliance on precedents is a form of comparative reasoning. In appealing to precedent a lawyer is arguing that the judge should treat the current case a certain way because it is so much like a previous case; it thus deserves to be handled the same way that case was handled. Imaginative engineers and scientific investigators use comparative reasoning when they develop and apply theoretical models in the creative search for novel solutions to problems. We will explore the creativity, complexities, and uncertainties of comparative reasoning in this chapter.

How This Chapter Connects to Others

So that you know the plan, and so that you can get a preliminary sense of the contrasts between the three modes of reasoning, here is how this chapter on comparative reasoning relates to other chapters in this book. Chapter 13, entitled "Ideological Reasoning," focuses on the strengths and weaknesses of drawing inferences from axioms, principles, or core beliefs and values to determine their specific applications. In high school plane geometry, for example, we begin with a set of first principles—axiomatic assumptions—about lines and points, and from these we infer the theorems they imply. A person with strongly held political or religious principles will use this same mode of reasoning to draw inferences about specific legislative proposals. For example, if I begin with the principle that all human life is sacred, I am likely to oppose specific legislative proposals that would permit euthanasia because of the belief that euthanasia, the taking of a life, ought not to be permitted. As we shall see in Chapter 13, ideological reasoning begins with our core beliefs and values, and then seeks to draw valid inferences

Breaking Down Comparative Reasoning		
Elements	**Mike Wallace's Example**	**Climate Change Example**
Feature or features of interest	A journalist's ethical responsibilities.	Proximity (lack of distance in space or time) to specific events.
Less familiar object, event, concept, or experience	An American journalist warning an American platoon in a combat zone that it is about to be ambushed by the enemy.	Achieving the perspective needed to perceive long-term global weather patterns.
Assertion of useful likeness or similarity	is analogous to	is like
More familiar object, event, concept, or experience	An American journalist warning an innocent person in a U.S. city when the person is about to become the victim of a crime.	Stepping back from a TV to see the whole picture rather than being so close to the screen that only a couple of pixels are in view.

about what those core values and beliefs entail. As we saw in Chapter 8, valid inferences leave no room for doubt, if the starting point beliefs and values are all true. This absolutist thinking turns out to be both a strength and a weakness of ideological reasoning. Chapter 16 on "Ethical Decision Making" examines how we use both ideological reasoning and comparative reasoning when deliberating moral, ethical, or policy issues.

In Chapter 14 we explore empirical reasoning, which moves from particular observations toward hypotheses, generalizations, and theories intended to explain those observations. Because of the possibility that our theories, generalizations, and explanations might be false, this mode of reasoning is probabilistic. In its most refined and sophisticated form, empirical reasoning is scientific investigatory reasoning that progresses, as we saw in Chapter 9 entitled "Warranted Inferences," from coincidence to correlation toward causal explanations so accurate that we can predict and control events. Chapter 14 extends that discussion by exploring the rigor, power, and limitations of scientific investigatory reasoning. Critical thinking in the social sciences and critical thinking in the natural sciences take empirical reasoning into these two captivatingly intersting domains of human learning.

When using comparative reasoning, we apply our critical thinking skills. We make interpretations, offer explanations, and draw inferences about that which is less familiar by comparing it to that which is more familiar. As we saw in Chapter 10, on snap judgments and heuristic thinking, at times comparative reasoning can be automatic, reactive System-1 thinking. The representativeness heuristic, the simulation heuristic, and occasionally the affect heuristic are examples of making quick, reactive comparisons. The fruit of System-2 comparative reasoning, with its more deliberative effort to explicitly consider points of comparison and contrast, is often an analogical argument. Mike Wallace's effort in the opening video clip is an attempt to find a useful comparison when trying to solve a difficult and unfamiliar problem. Mike Wallace tried to understand his ethical responsibilities in a combat situation by considering his ethical responsibilities in a comparable, but not identical, situation that he had experienced

before—namely warning an innocent person that he or she is about to become the victim of a crime. Fortunately Wallace had positive critical thinking habits of mind, which lead him to admit that his analogy did not provide an obvious answer, as he had hoped it would.

> "Reserve your right to think, for even to think wrongly is better than not to think at all."
>
> Hypatia of Alexandria, (370–415), mathematician and philosopher.[3]

Comparative reasoning, whether System-1 or System-2, is basically the reliance on a more familiar image, idea, or experience to shape or guide how we think about something that is less familiar. We are employing the word *reasoning* broadly to include comparisons used to illustrate, clarify, or explain our ideas as well as comparisons used to draw conclusions.

Gardens of Comparatives

Just as there are myriad flowering plants in a well-tended garden, people cultivate an exceptional variety of ways to express comparative reasoning. To communicate our insights about why "this is like that" our species employs stories, metaphors, and similes. Most comparative reasoning does not appear as a fully developed argument with reasons and claims. But no matter how they are presented, comparisons can shape our judgments about what to believe or what to do. Judicious critical thinkers must be alert to the rich variety of ways we use comparisons to express our thinking. Here are several examples. Each is a bit different from the others, but they all have one important feature in common: In each example, the speaker is attempting to interpret or to explain something, or to draw an inference about something, by comparing that thing to another thing the speaker believes to be more familiar to the listener.

- We awaken in this world like an abandoned baby left on a doorstep. No note telling who we are, where we came from, or how our universe came to be.[4]

Pattern or Not?

Is GM guilty of corporate manslaughter? The answer to that may depend on whether or not a jury sees a pattern of cover-up and intentional negligence in how the automaker dealt with complaints about faulty ignition switches leading to fatal accidents.[5] Pattern or not?

Are hospitals in Mexico so overcrowded that pregnant women cannot be admitted when they are about to give birth? That is what the Mexican health officials say. But women's rights advocates disagree. They see a pattern emerging of poor women in labor being turned away, forcing them to give birth in parking lots or on the lawn outside.[6] Pattern or not?

Does economic stability contribute to economic instability? Hyman Minsky thought so as he studied the Great Depression. The "Great Recession" of 2008 gave economists the opportunity to revisit Minsky's theories. Perhaps Minsky was right in thinking that the banking system is not as benign as most economists once believed.[7] Pattern or not?

Do mega tech companies, like Facebook and Google, long to act with impunity, as if they are above the law? Some suggest parallels to the once dreaded East German secret police, the Stasi, in the comments attributed to the leaders of these tech giants, comments like that those with nothing to hide have nothing to fear, and we could develop even more ideas if only they were not illegal.[8] Pattern or not?

Does each group's pursuit of its own interest result in less for all? The once booming Greek shipyard at Perama is in economic desolation. Many say the workers brought it on themselves because their powerful labor unions, high wages, and lavish benefits programs chased the shipping away.[9] Seeing automakers opening factories in other cities and states, some of us from Detroit, the "Motor City," would tell a similar story. Pattern or not?

Do I unknowingly contribute to my own interpersonal strife? In *Games People Play*, Eric Berne M.D. describes common but avoidable patterns in dysfunctional interpersonal transactions. He calls them "games." But they are not fun games. You may know about the cycle of abuse, and about enabling alcoholism. But have you ever been drawn into a game of "Ain't It Awful," "See What You Made Me Do," "I'm Only Trying to Help," or "Bring Me a Rock, No Not that Rock"? Patterns worth knowing about and avoiding? Yes! We recommend this 1964 book, which just might be the first great self-help book.

- Think of the world as a clock. Just as a clock could not have come into existence unless there was a clockmaker, so there also must be a God who made this wonderfully complex world.

- You can make John the club's treasurer, if you want. But with the way he manages money doing that would be like skydiving without a parachute.

- *Minecraft* is a metaphor for life: survive, befriend, imagine, experience, collaborate, and create.

- Time is a great river. We float on that river, like leaves borne along by the rush of seasons, spun by the turbulence of events beyond our control, knowing only that we are being carried into the infinite sea of eternity.

- In the movie *Traffic*, Michael Douglas' character reminds us that in the war on drugs the so-called enemies may include our own children. How, he wonders, it is even possible to make war against your own children?[10]

- You pull the trowel over the wet cement with the same kind of motion you would use to apply frosting to a freshly baked cake.

- The National Center for Science Education Web site proposes this analogy: "Evolution is only a theory in the same way that Universal Gravity is only a theory."

- How do I know that my furry fireside friend, Blue, understands when I tell him it's time to go out for a walk? Well, I think that your average dog is about as smart as your average two-year-old.

- Author Tom Franklin explains how an unexpected event can expose all the hidden secrets of a person's past life in his novel *Crooked Letter, Crooked Letter*: "Time packs new years over old ones but those old years are still in there, like the earliest, tightest rings centering a tree. . . . But then a saw screams in and the tree topples and the circles are stricken by the sun . . . and the stump is laid open for all the world to see."[11]

- The people at the Family Bank care about each other. And we care about you. When you bank with Family Bank, you're not just customers, you're family.

- God forgives the sinner who repents in the same way that a loving father forgives a prodigal son who returns to the family.

- Animal rights activist: "We did not steal any animals from the lab. We rescued those monkeys because they were the helpless victims of torture."

- Last year, the CEO said we were all on the same team. Then the economy goes south and he wants our suggestions for downsizing. Sort of reminds you of asking for volunteers to play Russian roulette.

- One productive way of thinking about how our minds work is by using the computer model of list processing, as suggested by Allen Newell. Just like computers, our minds store problems and tasks as lists, and our mind always works on the first thing in a list, the others coming to the fore only after the first is dealt with.[12]

As the examples illustrate, comparative reasoning can rely on images, comparisons, parables, allegories, fables, models, metaphors, and similes. We can use comparative reasoning to illustrate ideas, to offer interpretations, to make arguments, to give reasons, to explain our thinking, and to simplify concepts. As Mike Wallace did in the video clip, we can use these skills to help ourselves understand new ideas, unfamiliar objects, and abstract concepts.

Comparisons have the power to persuade people, to shape expectations, to alter attitudes, and to evoke emotions.

Powerful Comparisons Connect Intellect and Emotion

In his September 20, 2001, speech to the U.S. Congress former president George W. Bush said, "Al Qaeda is to terrorism what the Mafia is to crime."[13] By comparing al Qaeda to the Mafia, he communicated that al Qaeda was responsible for terrorism on a very large and organized scale, in the same way that the Mafia is responsible for crime on a large and organized scale. In addition, the former president's comparison evoked the same loathing toward al Qaeda that the public feels toward the ruthless, criminal Mafiosi. As a tool for communicating his ideas, Mr. Bush's comparison was powerfully effective, for it touched the American public at both an intellectual and an emotional level. Because they often communicate at the emotional level as well as the intellectual level, comparisons are among the most persuasively powerful devices in our culture.

Knowing that vivid comparisons can move hearts as well as minds, speechwriters, songwriters, and poets strive to associate their ideas with memorable comparisons as these examples illustrate.

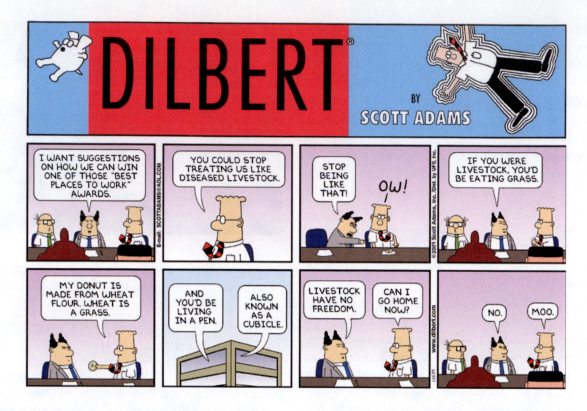

- A gift to the town's economy, the proposed metro line will ribbon through our downtown business district and gracefully glide north to the airport, the bow on our gift wrapped present.

- Like a knife thrust into the town's heart, the proposed metro line will sever existing transportation arteries and slice residential neighborhoods apart deeply wounding our community.

Although neither has supplied much by way of facts and figures, clearly the author of the first supports a proposal to build a metro line from the airport to the central city, whereas the author of the second opposes the proposal. Who would not want a gift wrapped in a beautiful ribbon? On the other hand, nobody would permit their streets and neighborhoods to be stabbed to death. Well-crafted comparatives, skillfully used, can dispose us for or against people, proposals, and points of view even before we have fully engaged our System-2 reflective judgment. As critical thinkers we must keep our guard up.

JOURNAL

Being a College Student Is Like …

Provide a powerful example of comparative reasoning that connects intellect and emotion, and which completes the sentence "Being a college student is like …"

12.2 Evaluating Comparative Inferences

Comparisons are like a fine set of carpentry tools—you have to know a tool's purpose, or else it will be useless to you. Several factors contribute to the merit of a comparison (like the one in the previous sentence). Before specifying the evaluative criteria more formally, let's first look informally at how we might evaluate a couple of examples.

- "Competition in today's business climate is like war. Companies that have good strategic plans will outcompete their opposition; they will gain market share the way an army gains ground in a battle. Lean, mean, and nimble, they will be ready to attack new opportunities and defend against threats and assaults from all sides. Their loyal troops will do whatever it takes to make the business successful, including doing battle with marketing campaigns and orchestrating superior manufacturing productivity. And in the end, they will prevail. So if you want your company to win out over the competition, hire our consulting firm. We have the know-how to make you a winner."

"Let your plans be dark and impenetrable as night, and when you move, fall like a thunderbolt."

Sun Tzu, *The Art of War*[14]

- "A seagull is like a sailboat. The gull's tail is like the boat's rudder. The gull's body is shaped like the boat's hull. A lot of gulls are white, and so are a lot of sailboats. Gulls often fly in flocks, and sailboats are often seen in bunches, too, called regattas. The gull's feathery wings remind me of the billowing sails. Gulls probably float on the surface of the air the way a sailboat floats on the surface of the water."

The first comparison, "business is like warfare," is the stronger of the two. It is based on several points of comparison that seem both apt and central, specifically the struggle to gain market share, the importance of being able to adapt quickly to changing conditions, and the assets of good communications, efficient manufacturing, and loyalty. The analogy is productive in another way as well, for the maker of the analogy could have extended the comparison by adding comments about corporate espionage and sabotage but did not.

The second comparison is weaker. Yes, the gull's tail functions like a rudder. But the gull's body does not function like a hull; it only looks like a hull—and then, not very much like one, given the legs hanging down or dragging behind. Gulls do not float on the air by displacing their weight in that gaseous medium the way a boat displaces its weight in water. The similarities of color and visual appearance are superficial, not structural or functional. The hull of a sailboat holds up the mast, which lifts and holds the sail. When birds are in flight, the lifting is done by the wings, not the body. The physics of how a wing functions is the opposite of a sail. A sail catches wind and is pushed along. In contrast, the speed of the air passing over the top of a wing, as compared to the speed of the air passing under the wing, creates lift and pulls the wing upward. The physics of flight is not the same as the physics of floating. All in all, it is a rather poor analogy indeed.

Do the Four Tests of Acceptability Apply?

The analyses and evaluations offered may appear to stray a bit from the four tests for the worthiness of arguments. Let's apply those four tests to our two examples to see how useful they are for evaluating comparative reasoning.

First Test: Are the premises all true? The key premise in both cases is the one that asserts the similarities: "business is like war" and "a seagull is like a sailboat." Based on the analyses, our first thought when applying this test would be to evaluate "business is like war" as true and "a seagull is like a sailboat" as false. Unfortunately, the words *true* and *false* are not optimal for evaluating a sentence that asserts a comparison. Those two terms offer us only two options when, in fact, our evaluations are more nuanced. Going back to our examples, we would want to say that "business is like war" is *more true* than "a seagull is like a sailboat." But expressions like *more true* or *more false* have no place in the world of logic. In addition, the two (waging war and sailing) are not connected in any way that would permit us to say that one is "more true" than the other. Words like *apt, insightful, vivid, silly,* and *superficial* are better words for evaluating sentences that assert comparisons. As we shall see, we use these insights to come up with more precise criteria for evaluating comparisons than "true" or "false."

Second Test: Are there counterexamples and how difficult is it to imagine them? This question helps gauge the logical strength of the analogy. We do not have refined statistical tests to apply to comparative inferences. But we can categorize comparisons as *more or less plausible*. And, yes, there are counterexamples to consider. Let's look at the stronger of the two analogies. Some businesses form partnerships with other businesses, and some acquire and merge with their competitors by purchasing their stock. Behaviors like these suggest that business is not always like war. Do these observations mean that the analogy is illogical? No, that would be too negative. What this *does* show is that comparative reasoning reveals points of dissimilarity as well as points of similarity. We will need to make a more refined judgment about the utility of the points of comparison. We will build this insight into the more refined set of criteria provided in the next part of this chapter.

Third Test: Are the premises relevant to the truth of the conclusion? The conclusion is the assertion about the characteristics of the unfamiliar object (business in the first case and gulls in the second). At first, we may not see how warfare is relevant to understanding business or how boats are relevant to understanding gulls. The burden is on the maker of the analogy to show that the comparison is relevant. In both of our examples, the argument maker offers observations to establish the relevance of the comparison.

Fourth Test: Does the truth of any premise depend on the truth of the conclusion? This can be tricky, because for many of us, business is more familiar than warfare, and gulls or birds in general may be more familiar than boats. But comparative inferences should flow from what we know about war to what we can project to be true about business, and from what we know about boats to what we can project to be true about gulls. Both of our examples have problems with this test. Many businesspeople have never been in combat. Likewise, many people within the general public have no firsthand combat knowledge. Therefore, for many people, the comparison depends more on imagination of what war might be like than on actual warfare experience. The same goes for boating. More of us have watched birds fly than have built or skippered a sailboat.

Based on the application of the four tests we developed, neither comparison establishes that its conclusion is true or justified. *But the purpose of comparative reasoning is to illustrate, illuminate, suggest, or hypothesize.* It would be expecting too much if we were to demand that comparative reasoning should prove that a conclusion is true. Our four tests of acceptability may be a little heavy-handed. Comparative inferences will almost always come up short on those four tests.

Yet some comparisons do appear to be stronger and more useful than others. Why is that? Because in some cases, the points of comparison are based on shared functional, structural, central, and essential features. However, in other cases, the points of comparison are based on shared features, but they are unimportant, trivial, superficial, decorative, or happenstance. We'll analyze this generalization in a moment and come up with five specific criteria to use when evaluating comparative inferences.

Five Criteria for Evaluating Comparative Reasoning

Why is comparative reasoning so potentially valuable? Its value comes from the possibility that comparative reasoning could lead to new insights, hypotheses, and dimensions as we try to understand something unfamiliar. If the comparison is reasonable, then some salient feature of the more familiar object is also a salient feature of the less familiar object. Evaluation depends on the congruence between the two objects. "Are they alike enough in important ways or not?" *The more pervasive the essential similarities are, the more relevant the comparison is, and therefore the more credibility a conclusion based on those similarities will have.*

Comparative inferences, including analogical arguments, draw their power from the perceived relevance and pervasiveness of the fundamental parallelism between the situations or objects being compared. Superior comparative inferences are *familiar, simple, comprehensive, productive,* and *testable.*[15] Let's break down each of these features in turn.

FAMILIARITY Suppose that a speaker offers this analogical argument: "Don't put John in charge of buying groceries! That would be like asking Queen Cleopatra to do the laundry." But suppose that the listener has no idea who Queen Cleopatra was. This lack of familiarity with the object of the comparison would quash the analogy like an elephant stepping on a snail. Familiarity is the first criteria for a successful comparative reasoning process. Successful comparisons direct the listener's attention to that which is more familiar. Now, consider this example:

The simulation heuristic heightens our sense of familiarity by enabling us to imagine experiences we may never have had.

- A coach trying to teach an 11-year-old how to swing a baseball bat: "The right way to swing a baseball bat is with the same motion you use when you swing a long-handled ax into the trunk of a pine tree."

These days, the number of children who learn to swing a baseball bat is higher than the number of children who learn to swing a long-handled ax. The coach's comparison fails because the child is probably entirely unfamiliar with ax swinging as the object of comparison. Maybe if the child was at summer camp and the camp counselor was trying to teach about chopping trees, the camp counselor could say, "Swing the ax like you would a baseball bat." This might work, because there is a better chance that the child is familiar with how to swing a baseball bat.

Earlier we looked at the following example about hiring John as the club treasurer.

- You can make John the club's treasurer, if you want. But with the way he manages money doing that would be like skydiving without a parachute.

This comparison works, but not because most of us have ever personally experienced skydiving. It works because most of us have seen people skydiving on television or in a movie, so we can simulate the process. And we can easily realize that it would be suicidal to skydive without a parachute. The simulation heuristic makes skydiving familiar enough that we can understand the comparison. For most people, it would be far less effective for the argument maker to have offered this analogy:

- You can make John the club's treasurer if you want to, but if you ask me it would be like ingesting massive quantities of sodium chloride.

The point is the same, but this comparison is less effective because most people are not as familiar with consuming toxic amounts of salt as a means of self-destruction. **Familiarity** is the quality of a comparison that expresses the degree of knowledge the listener has about the object to which the unknown is being compared.

SIMPLICITY **Simplicity**, a virtue for comparisons, is a measure of the relative complexity of the comparison. The less complicated—that is, the simpler—the comparison is, the better the comparison. Simpler comparisons are often more readily understood and remembered.

- In 1971 President Nixon announced our nation's war on drugs.

Using the brutal image of war to characterize a law enforcement policy is simple, familiar, and easy for the general public to remember. And, as politicians from both parties knew at the time, the analogy, however misguided it might be, had far more emotional impact and voter appeal than any detailed description of the actual policy. Not sure about that? Here's an alternative:

- In 1971 President Nixon announced a get-tough law enforcement policy that has evolved into a concerted, long-term, resource-intensive, multi-agency, multinational effort aimed at the interdiction or destruction of illegal substances, associated seizing of assets, the arrest and criminal prosecution of persons found to be importing, manufacturing, distributing, selling, shipping, or possessing those substances.

The powerful but simple and memorable image of "WAR!" captures the listener's imagination, even if it does not communicate anything to the listener about what exactly the policy will entail, other than it will be brutal.

Consider another example. A young American couple wants to take a romantic vacation in Italy. Seeking advice about places to go and hotels to book, the couple is told, "If it's your first trip, you'll want to see Venice, Florence, Rome, and the Amalfi Coast. Not to worry, these days making hotel reservations in another country is as easy as buying books through Amazon.com." Suppose that the young couple is familiar with buying books online at Amazon.com, and because of that familiarity the couple knows that there are several required steps. They had to establish an account and, in so doing, they had to enter a lot of personal data, such as their address and credit card information. Then they had to search for the book they wanted and wade through the pop-ups that appear on the screen as they did so. Then they had to navigate through

Swing a long-handled ax like you would a baseball bat.

the checkout process. Familiar, yes. And, for this couple it is simple enough too. They have been through the Amazon.com registration and purchasing process successfully. They know roughly what to expect as they go online to book a hotel in Venice.

COMPREHENSIVENESS The process of booking hotel reservations in another country may seem daunting for people who have never done it before. Comparing that process to the process of using Amazon.com offers another benefit. It provides the young couple with a single comparison that includes all the major steps in the process. The virtue of simplicity must be balanced with the importance of **comprehensiveness**. One comparison is more comprehensive than another to the extent that it captures a greater number of central or essential features. The question is, "Does the comparison capture enough of the critical elements?" Let's revisit the example about the camp counselor teaching someone how to swing a long-handled ax into a tree.

- Counselor to the camper: "Hold the handle like you would a tennis racket. Set your feet apart like you would if you were getting ready to push something heavy. And swing like you would if you were going to hit a nail with a heavy hammer."

Three comparisons were needed because none was comprehensive enough to apply to the whole effort. On the other hand, the counselor might have said:

- "Swing an ax like you swing a baseball bat."

That single comparison covers everything relevant, including how to hold the ax, how to stand, and how to swing.

Suppose that the counselor and the camper are in a gymnasium, not at the campground. And suppose that the camp counselor does not have an ax, but has a broom handle. And suppose instead of a tree, in the gym there is a volleyball net held up by two steel poles. The camp counselor could simulate the skill using the broom handle and pretending that one of the poles is a tree. The counselor might say, "Swing the ax like this." This demonstration would rely on the camper's capacity for comparative thinking, just as do the verbal explanations. This demonstration works as a comparative explanation because the camper can see the grip, the positioning of the feet, and all the relevant movements of the legs, hips, torso, arms, and wrists, even without an ax in hand or a tree in sight. And although swinging a broom handle into a steel pole only simulates swinging an ax into the soft wood of a living pine, the demonstration is a more comprehensive comparison than the words alone are.

PRODUCTIVITY **Productivity** is the capacity of a comparison to bring to mind unexpected new ideas that go beyond the points of comparison initially mentioned. Productive comparisons are so rich that exploring the comparison more deeply reveals or suggests additional possible implications. For example, comparing the government's policies on illegal drugs to a war allows us to anticipate that there will likely be "innocent victims" of the war on drugs. Harm to innocent victims, collateral damage, is a foreseeable consequence of waging war. Innocent victims of war deserve our compassion. Using the comparison to war also suggests that some people are going to be regarded as "the hated enemies." In war, we use all of our military might to destroy the enemy. Wartime propaganda engenders hatred for a nation's enemy. So if we are waging war on drugs, we can expect to commit considerable effort to destroying the hated enemy—whomever that may turn out to be.

This, in turn, raises an interesting problem: At times, a productive comparison can suggest something that is both unexpected and troubling. In non-metaphorical wars, the innocent victims are not the hated enemies. But what if one's brother or sister becomes a drug user and then, to support

his or her habit, becomes a pusher? In situations like that, the "war on drugs" comparison does not help us understand what has happened or how we should behave toward our brother or sister. Should we have compassion for the person, hate the person, help the person, report the person to the authorities, or what?

Consider the productivity of comparing avatars to real people. In virtual worlds, like the galaxy we can explore through *Second Life*,[16] I am my avatar. Avatars, however they may look and whatever they may do, tell us something about their creators. Researchers, noting the many points of comparison between avatars and their creators are studying avatar faces and avatar behavior to see whether it is possible to identify the people controlling them. In fact, because identity theft can happen to avatars too, virtual people should get ID checks.[17] The solution applied in the familiar case to genuine people is being extended, by analogy, to the virtual world. And, why not go further? How about bank accounts and drivers' licenses too? With the integration of GPS technology, accident avoidance radar, infrared linkages, holographic projection systems, and on-board navigation systems, within a few short years we will be seeing avatars driving not only along the virtual highways of Internet space, but along the potholed cement thoroughfares of the real world.

How productive is it to think of avatars as if they were real people? How can you extend the comparative reasoning? What else might your avatar need or be able to do? Perhaps climb a mountain or play a sport that you've always wanted to enjoy but did not have the physical strength to accomplish? Perhaps stand watch for you during an anxious time of fretful waiting? How about taking your final exam for you, or committing a crime for you? If your avatar commits a crime, do you go to jail or does your avatar?

TESTABILITY The "war on drugs" comparison productively suggests consequences, including the unexpected and confusing one we just talked about—that a member of our own family might be both an "innocent victim" and a "hated enemy." Should we treat our addicted siblings or children who become small-time pushers as the hated enemy? We may not approve of what they are doing, and we may seek treatment for them, but most of us are not likely to think of them as "the enemy" or to treat them as such. That the comparison would lead us to do so diminishes its value. It is a weaker comparison because it implies this unacceptable consequence.

We call this criterion testability. **Testability** is the capacity of a comparison to project consequences that have the potential to be shown to be false, inapplicable, or unacceptable. If there is a war on drugs, then our siblings and children might be our hated enemy. For most of us, "hated enemy" does not apply to family members.

One tactic for testing a comparison is to ask if there are crucial incongruities between the objects being compared. Going back to an earlier example, suppose that in response

to the idea that stealing experimental animals is really a kind of rescuing of innocent victims, a person objected by saying, "No, under the law, animals are property, not persons. Therefore, they cannot be considered victims in any sense that would excuse you from the legal consequences of your having taken property without authorization." This objection points out that one of the consequences of that comparison does not apply—under the law, animals are property, not persons. This might change someday, but that day is not yet upon us. One of our other examples compared the CEO's request for downsizing options to Russian roulette. That comparison can be evaluated as misleading in this way: "Not really, because in Russian roulette, you have to hold the pistol up to your own head, but what I plan to do is to recommend eliminating someone else's department, not my own."

The criterion of testability enables us to evaluate the acceptability of a proposed comparison. In general, we should prefer comparisons that have the potential to be testable as false, inapplicable, or unacceptable. Some comparisons simply cannot be falsified in principle. Consider this example: Like having a loving aunt or uncle, each of us has a guardian angel who watches over us, protects us from danger, and helps us know right from wrong. This comparison is familiar, simple, and productive. The many ways that a loving aunt or uncle might help us in our lives suggest a reasonable level of comprehensiveness as well. Unfortunately, there is no way, in principle, to test whether or not the comparison is true, applicable, or appropriate, at least none that these two textbook authors have been able to imagine so far.

> "Analogies, it is true, decide nothing, but they can make one feel more at home."
>
> Sigmund Freud[18]

12.3 Models and Metaphors Shape Expectations

Creative Suggestions vs. Solid Proofs

Comparative inferences are best used to explore assumptions and to tentatively shape expectations about new situations. "Don't worry," a mother tells her three-year-old child as they approach a house the child has never before seen. "Visiting Great Uncle Bill is like visiting Grandpa." The comparison is meant to reassure the child and establish positive expectations in the child's mind.

Consider this suggestion: "What if we were to think about a classroom as a social network? How would that modify the educational process? Would we need a professor, or grades? Could we educate ourselves without an authority figure controlling what is learned, when and how? How about assignments and due dates?" The idea is familiar, simple, and productive. Is the suggestion comprehensive and is it testable?

Analogies suggest alternatives, possible explanations, and hypotheses. But analogies are not proofs. So, before we fire all the faculty, we should analyze and test the "Social Network Model" of education. If it is the best way to learn chemistry, history, a foreign language, business, psychology, or nursing, then great, we can talk about how to scale it up and make education available to tens of thousands of people using that model. But only if it works when tested, not simply because it seemed like a good idea at first.

Comparisons, termed "models," are relied upon in engineering to imagine possible solutions to structural puzzles. Models, not in a physical but in a conceptual sense, are used in science to suggest promising hypotheses for further testing. While creative comparisons can be richly suggestive of new ideas, comparative inferences are notoriously inadequate to the task of serving as final proofs of those ideas.

Unfortunately many people define science as a body of knowledge, as if scientists seek and then find "the truth." Those same people become confused when scientists disagree. And that is because many people try to understand science (less familiar) by analogy to religion (more familiar). Religions do not change their "truths," and, if there are disagreements, then one group or the other is simply wrong. The analogy fails, however. The mistake is fundamental. Science is not a body of known truths, it is a process of refining our models of how the universe and everything in it function.[19] The scientific process tests models, which are intended to explain natural phenomena. If the model is found wanting, then it is improved or replaced with other models. These new or improved models are then tested. Experiments that show a model is in some way incomplete or inaccurate are important positive steps forward. These disconfirmations of our previous understandings enable scientists to help us to understand the universe better. Disconfirmations enable us to achieve deeper and more comprehensive explanations, and hence provide a reliable basis to predict, and possibly to manage, natural phenomena. Religion is not a process of coming to know how the universe functions. A religion is a set of interconnected beliefs about the universe accompanied most often by an associated group of customs and rituals. The comforting models and reassuring metaphors offered to us by religion, example, "God is like a loving father" are not testable, they are to be taken on faith. That is why it is such a problem for any religion if one of its articles of faith is questioned. At the same time questioning articles of faith is exactly what science is all about.

The Center of the Universe for Two Thousand Years

Imagine an ox cart on a country road. There are two ways to get the cart moving and keep it moving. One is to push it; the other is to pull it. Being very familiar with carts and the effort required for a man to push a cart along muddy country roads, Aristotle, and those influenced by his philosophical writings prior to Copernicus, drew comparative inferences about the movements of the Sun, the Moon, the planets, and the stars. The common sense, late fifteenth-century European view of the universe, which everyone in those days took to be God's design for things, placed Earth firmly in the center. Everyone could see these heavenly bodies moving in great circles overhead. Like the cart, they needed to either be pushed or pulled along their paths. A good job for angels, perhaps. How could we see them, if they were being pushed along a hard surface? The answer was that the surface was transparent, a "crystal sphere," totally encompassing Earth. Not familiar with crystal spheres? Think of a giant glass fishbowl. The heavenly object—for example, the Moon—was resting on a crystal sphere. An angel pushed it along, like a man pushing

a cart. When we looked up, we saw the moon through the transparent crystal. And we could note the path it had traveled and predict where it was going because the path was a perfect circle. Heavenly motion was perfectly circular. On Earth, however, if you propel a cart along a flat and level path or drop a rock from a tower, you can see that the cart or the rock will move in a straight line. For 2,000 years, Aristotle's views dominated our understanding of how the natural universe worked. Every object had its own particular nature, and it always behaved in certain predictable ways because its nature made it act that way.

Circular motion in heaven, straight-line motion on Earth, some Greek who's been dead for 2,500 years or so—who cares? Well, as it turned out, just about everyone of European heritage was affected in one way or another when the Aristotelian comparisons for understanding how the universe worked came undone. And who would have thought that it would be about the motion of Mars and the arc of cannonballs? Search and watch Episode 5, "Infinitely Reasonable," of the terrific BBC history of science series *The Day the Universe Changed* to see how the Aristotelian model of the universe was unraveled. That episode begins with the astronomer-priest Copernicus and continues through Galileo and a letter he wrote to a female friend saying that Aristotle, and everything that depended on his view of the universe, was quite simply false. What do you imagine would be the immediate aftermath once Church authorities realized that the bulwark, upon which rested all European civil and religious power in those days, was wrong?

The comparative inference used by Aristotle—understanding the cause of motion in the way that you understand how a man pushes or pulls a cart—was a powerfully valuable comparison. It endured for two millennia as a scientific principle. The insight that an object is predictable because of how it is made remains a powerfully valuable idea, although today we do not appeal to an object's "nature." Instead, depending upon what the object is, we talk about its organic composition and function, its chemical structure, its genetic heritage, or its physical properties.

Aristotle thought that like a cart, the Sun, Moon and stars could move only if they were pushed or pulled along.

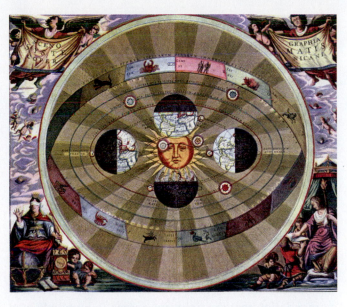

Copernicus placed the Sun at the center, with the Earth and planets in elliptical orbits—radical, crystal sphere shattering, stuff!

The Many Uses of Comparative Inferences

Comparative reasoning is widely used in legal argumentation. Attorneys will appeal to precedents when arguing about the interpretation or the applicability of points of law. The basic character of the appeal to precedent is the assertion that the case now in question is so much like the prior case that the ruling that applied there should apply here. That argument depends on how much the new case is analogous to the prior case.

The short version of the appeal to precedent is used whenever we make an argument structured like this: "We had a situation sort of like this before and that time we did such-and-such." As in this example:

- Someone said we should turn off the air conditioner when we are stuck in a traffic jam on a blisteringly hot summer day. We didn't believe it until last summer when our car overheated on a day just like this. We were stuck in traffic and we kept the AC running. Not too smart of us. So I say this time we close that puppy down and just deal with the heat!

Comparative reasoning is used in discussions of ethics, such as to compare cases and infer obligations.

- Making a promise to help your sister rake the leaves is the same as when Dad made the promise to take you to the movie. Even though he was tired, Dad had to keep his promise to you. He took you to the movie. Remember? So you have to keep your promise to your sister. You go outside now and help her rake the leaves.

THINKING CRITICALLY

Simplicity and Hypothetical Entities

In the "Infinitely Reasonable" episode, the writer and presenter, James Burke, notes the application of the simplicity criteria by Copernicus. Can you spot how Copernicus used this criterion? First the Catholic Church was unconcerned about the "mere lines and circles" drawn by the astronomer-priest. Why? How are the hypothetical orbits of Earth and the Sun, which Copernicus introduced, similar to other scientific ideas, like "atoms," "germs," and "genes"? Hint: Think of objects that exist theoretically and are used to explain observations but cannot themselves be observed—angels, for example. Is it possible to devise a scientific test to establish the existence and the properties of orbits, atoms, germs, genes, and angels? In each case,

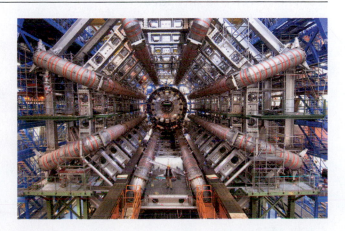

why or why not? What about the so-called "god particle"? If there is no conceivable test that would reveal its existence, does that mean it does not really exist?

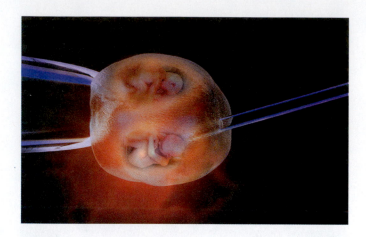

In the next example, the genetic similarity of human beings and human stem cells is used as a basis for the policy recommendation that the rights we accord to human beings should be accorded to stem cells.

- Because human stem cells can be cultivated and grown into human organs and potentially cloned into whole persons, we should think of stem cells as potential human beings. We are never justified in taking the life of an innocent human being. So geneticists should not be allowed to experiment with human stem cells.

In business and professional life, arguments like the following are commonplace.

- The CEO's misuse of corporate funds was bad enough, but the way upper management lied to keep the board from learning the truth was far worse. That deceit was a cancer that spread throughout upper management. And, like a cancer, it had to be mercilessly eradicated. Everyone had to go, even if it meant firing some people who never had any idea about what was going on. When you cut out a tumor, you have to remove some good tissue too, because you can't risk leaving a single bad cell or the cancer will return.

Comparative reasoning is powerfully persuasive. This can be a major benefit of the use of comparative reasoning, and, at the same time it can be a serious liability. In the previous example, if we accept the characterization of the board's deceit as "a cancer," then it follows that we should treat that deceit with the

same aggressive therapies. If we were to be persuaded that upper management did not lie to the board but that its failure to notify the board could be explained in some other reasonable way, then using the reference to the Big C would only inflame passions and impel us toward responses that were disproportional, if not inappropriate.

A comparison's persuasive power depends heavily on the suggested parallelism. For example, consider this argument for the claim, "Women should not insist on raising their children alone."

- Comedian Chris Rock first acknowledged that women were fully capable of raising their children by themselves. Then he stated something almost everyone agrees with, namely that children need fathers. Then he reminded the audience at the Apollo Theater that just because a person could do something does not mean that the person should do it. To make his point he said that just because people *could* drive a car with their feet, it does not imply that people *should* drive a car with their feet.[20]

The response Chris Rock received from the audience was loud and enthusiastic. The vivid comparison brought home his point. It was an easy and humorous image for the audience to visualize. And, if raising children alone is like driving your car with your feet, you can see how awkward, clumsy, risky, and foolish that would be. To balance and complement the work done by the comparison on the negative side of the claim, the comedian bolstered the affirmative aspect of the claim with the observation about children needing fathers. From the other remarks he had made in the same context, it was clear to that audience that Chris Rock was really speaking to both of a child's parents, calling for them to stay in a parental relationship with their child.

Map 1

People are capable of driving a car with their feet only, but that does not imply that they should drive that way.

Women have the capability to raise their children alone.

Children need fathers as well as mothers.

Just because you can do something a certain way does not imply that you should do it that way.

Women should not insist on raising their children alone.

The persuasive power of comparisons, analogies, and models derives in part from our natural propensity to use heuristics like simulation, representation, and association, which were explained in Chapter 10 on heuristic thinking. Comparisons are built into the language we use. We say that standard household electric current *flows* through the wiring in our homes and businesses. We know that if the wires are not connected to the sources, the electricity would not flow through them to our computers, lights, and appliances. The comparison is to water flowing through pipes. But if that were true, then electric current should be gushing out of every open socket in the wall. Obviously, there is more to it than what the simple and familiar image of flowing water conveys.

However persuasive they may be, logically speaking, comparative inferences are seldom, if ever, acceptable proofs of the *truth of their conclusions.* Comparing electricity to flowing water, as useful as that image might be for some purposes, does not prove that electricity can be expected to behave just like flowing water in all contexts. Comparisons are helpful for suggesting initially promising approaches to understanding unfamiliar things. Comparisons can be memorable and compelling. They have the power to shape individual and group decisions. Comparisons can be humorous, emotionally evocative, and powerfully motivating. Their simplicity and familiarity often lead to a false sense of their relevance and applicability. The strong critical thinker with a healthy sense of skepticism and a good nose for weak logic will be cautious when comparisons and metaphors, rather than sound arguments, are used as substitutes for solid explanations or as calls to action.

Summing up this chapter,

comparative reasoning projects aspects of things that are more familiar onto things that are less familiar. The most useful comparisons are those that are based upon structural, functional, central, and essential features to *suggest* how we might understand that which is less familiar based on what we know about that which is more familiar. Although powerfully persuasive, comparisons are risky.

Their soundness, logical strength, and relevance can easily be questioned. Comparative reasoning can captivate our imaginations and move us emotionally. But, comparative inferences are notoriously weak and unreliable, from a logical point of view. We can evaluate comparative inferences using five criteria: familiarity, simplicity, comprehensiveness, productivity, and testability.

Key Concepts

comparative reasoning (or this-is-like-that thinking) is the process of using what is more familiar to make interpretations, explanations, or inferences about what is less familiar.

familiarity, in the evaluation of comparisons, is the degree of knowledge the listener has about the object to which the unknown is being compared.

simplicity, in the evaluation of comparisons, is a measure of the relative absence of complexity.

comprehensiveness, in the evaluation of comparisons, is the extent to which a comparison captures a greater number of central or essential features.

productivity is the capacity of a comparison to suggest consequences that go beyond those mentioned in the initial comparison.

testability is the capacity of comparisons to project consequences that have the potential to be shown to be false, inapplicable, or unacceptable.

Applications

Reflective Log

Time travel—Evaluate the evaluations: Time travel— the stuff of great science fiction! Is time travel really possible? If the time-space continuum loops back upon itself, like tangled yarn, then perhaps there are places so close together that passages from one point in the string to another point in the string would not be impossibly distant. Consider the following two comparisons. The first is by an advocate of the dynamic view of time, and the second is by an advocate of the static view of time.

Advocate of the dynamic view of time: Like wind rushing by our faces, time whisks from the past to the future, pausing but for the smallest instant in this moment we call the present. The past is unreal and the events it contains are no more. The future is unreal, and the events that will become are not yet. Only the fleeting present—that place where past and future join—is real. And even that reality is lost into the past as quickly as it is conceived. Think, you who flit on life's stage for your one tiny moment of existence—how should you use what precious little time you have?

Advocate of the static view of time: Time doesn't pass; we do. We move through time as if we were driving along an interstate highway. The highway stretches ahead of us and behind us to places we may never visit. We get on the highway at birth and exit at death. We move along, like those in the cars beside us, at a constant rate of speed. So, looking from car to car it seems we are not moving, but looking at the mileposts flashing by, like the weeks and months of our lives; we are steadily going along. Along this highway, there are places that came *before* or *after* or that occurred *simultaneously* with others. The past and the future are real places.

Before reading further, stop for a moment and write your own evaluation of the two comparisons, "time is like the wind" and "time is like an interstate highway."

After entering your own evaluations into your log, read the following two critiques. The first applies to the dynamic view and the second to the static view.

Critic of the dynamic view of time: Your analogies are charming, but your thinking is confused. If only the present is real, how can we measure the *passage of time*? Any measurement must be against some external standard. But do you want to argue that there is some kind of time outside of time? Also, consider the present. According to you, it is the point at which the unreal past touches the unreal future. In that case, it is so infinitesimally tiny as to have no duration in itself. Thus, the present is unreal too. But if time is the accumulation of present moments, you might as well say that time is entirely unreal. There is no past, future, or present.

Critic of the static view of time: You make it sound like all I have to do is make a U-turn and I can go back in time. That's absurd. Also, by your analogy, if I step on the accelerator, I can shoot ahead of the other cars and, in effect, speed myself into the future. That is also absurd. Your problem is that you are thinking of time as analogous to your concept of space. However, our movement in space from one place to another does not imply we can move in time from one present to another.

Evaluate the critics' evaluations. In what respects are the two critiques strong or weak? How might an advocate of each of the two views of time respond reasonably to the criticisms offered? If you disagree with both of the critics or if you agree with both of the critics, then explain what your view of time is. Just for fun: Is time travel possible?

Individual Exercises

Evaluate Mike Wallace's analogy: Reconsider the analogy Mike Wallace attempted to draw between warning American soldiers about the ambush and warning a person that he or she was a murderer's intended target. This time, apply the five criteria by asking:

1. How familiar, as compared to the combat zone situation, is the prospect of warning someone about a crime that is about to be perpetrated?

2. Is the comparison simple and straightforward enough for us to understand the basic idea and simulate what it would be like to warn the victim of the crime?

3. What are the critical elements in the two situations and how well are they captured by the comparison?

4. Is the comparison productive enough to provide useful guidance or indications of how we might behave in the unfamiliar combat zone situation?

5. Are there any crucial incongruities that undercut the comparison of the behavior of a civilian journalist in a combat zone to the behavior of journalists at home?

Evaluate Father Tom's story about the man who lived by the river: Episode #14, "Take This Sabbath Day," from season 1 of *The West Wing*, first aired on February 9, 2000. In that episode, President Josiah "Jed" Bartlet, played by Martin Sheen, must decide whether or not to commute a murderer's death sentence. He has less than 48 hours to make his decision. The episode features an array of powerfully presented arguments—economic, ethical, political, religious, and legal. Pushed and pulled by those considerations, President Bartlet, a Catholic, eventually calls his wise old friend, a priest, played by Karl Malden, for guidance. The priest tells the president that he reminds him of a man who lived by a river. The man hears a radio report warning that the river was going to flood, possibly trapping the man in his own home. The story is, of course, meant as an analogy to Bartlet's situation. Evaluate that comparison using the standards of familiarity, simplicity, comprehensiveness, productivity, and testability. Search "The West Wing February 9 2000" to locate this episode.

Jon Stewart admits Charlton Heston was right: After the tragic massacre at Columbine High School in 1999, people advocating stricter gun control legislation protested against the National Rifle Association's (NRA) planned convention in Colorado. They argued that it was disrespectful and insensitive of the NRA to meet so close to the site of such a tragedy. Jon Stewart, host of *The Daily Show*, admitted he was wrong to have supported those protesters since his views would have abridged the Second Amendment rights of law-abiding citizens who were members of the NRA. In 2010 others protested the location of a Mosque near Ground Zero using very similar arguments. To see Stewart admit his mistake and to see the comparison of the 1999 arguments with the 2010 arguments watch the opening nine minutes of the August 19, 2010, *Daily Show*. The sequence is entitled "Extremist Makeover Homeland Edition."[21] There are two places in that sequence that Stewart uses comparative reasoning. The first, about five minutes in, has to do with hand-lettered highlighted index cards. The second, and more important, begins about 7 minutes and 20 seconds into the sequence, where Stewart invokes the arguments made by Charlton Heston in defense of the NRA's exercise of its First Amendment rights. Stewart says that the 2010 case of a Muslim Community Center is analogous and that Heston's arguments apply now as much as they did more than a decade ago. Evaluate both of the examples of comparative reasoning in the August 19, 2010, *Daily Show* opening sequence.

"Ticking Time Bombs" A loving father buys what he believes are new tires and has the family car serviced so his 19-year-old son and some friends can take it on vacation. He gets the phone call all parents dread. There was an accident. His son was killed. The car's "new" tires had sat unsold in the retailer's stockroom for so many years that they were dangerously old. On the highway one exploded causing the driver to lose control. An emotionally gripping comparison leaps to the minds of parents and young people. "That could be my child." "That could be me!" Search and visit this *20/20* news feature.[22] Evaluate the commentator's use of comparisons like "ticking time bombs," "museum of death," and "cryptic code." What exactly are the statistics on auto crashes resulting from exploding tires? Why do the automobile manufacturers and the tire manufactures not agree on the recommendation that no tires should be sold as new if they are more than six years old? If selling a product that you know is dangerous and is ethically wrong, which is what one of the attorneys in the video asserts, then what ethical responsibilities do retailers have regarding the sale of "aged tires?" Can you think of any comparisons that would support your position with regard to the ethics of that situation?

SHARED RESPONSE

Comparative Reasoning

What are the uses, benefits, and risks of comparative reasoning? Give a real life example of a misleading comparison. Be sure to provide your reason(s), not just your opinion. And, comment respectfully on the reasons others offer.

Group Exercises

The "Free Enterprise System" model: One of the basic economic beliefs associated with doing business in the free enterprise system is the "law of supply and demand." When the supply of goods or services is greater than the demand, prices go down. When the demand is greater than the supply, prices go up. For example, in times of weather emergencies, merchants selling ordinarily plentiful commodities like food, electric generators, fuel, flashlights, tarps, and fresh water are beset by unquenchable demand because people are trying to stock up. So prices rise. Showing the reverse process, the prices of homes and automobiles dropped during the 2008–2009 recession because consumer demand fell sharply.

Two areas of our economy seem to defy the law of supply and demand. One is public higher education, where tuition and fees do not increase to the level that market demands would sustain. If this fit the free enterprise model, then the consumers—that is, the students—would be charged much more. The second area that does not appear to fit the model is health care. In the case of health care, the consumers, sick or injured people in need of care, do not "shop around" looking for the best deal. Also, the charge for a medical procedure is the same whether a lot of people or only a few people need that service.

First, evaluate the comparison of public higher education to the classic model of the free enterprise system. How can comparing public higher education to a business operating in the free enterprise system help us understand higher education better, and in what ways does the idea not fit? Second, evaluate health care services against the classic model of the free enterprise system. How does comparing the services provided by health care professionals, hospitals, emergency rooms, insurance providers, and pharmaceutical companies to businesses functioning in a free enterprise system help us better understand health care services? How might the comparison cause us problems because it does not fit?

A third enterprise that may or may not fit the model of the free enterprise system is organized religion. Organized religion provides services for the benefit of the faithful, including prayers and religious ceremonies. Many people give money to those organizations and receive those services. In some cases, the money is given voluntarily as contributions; in other cases, the money is in payment of a fee. In still other cases, the money is given voluntarily, but the amount is established by the religious organization on the basis of some metric, like 10 percent of a person's income. Religious organizations need the money they receive to pay their employees, rent or buy buildings used for worship, and acquire the equipment and supplies needed to provide services. Evaluate the comparison of organized religion to the free enterprise model and the applicability of the law of supply and demand.

Rock-paper-scissors: Is there a pattern when humans play? The game should be winnable one chance in three, if both players randomly select rock, paper, or scissors each round. But one experiment with large numbers of students saw a pattern in what was supposed to be random behavior.[23] Humans apparently make their decisions non-randomly. If a person wins a round, the person tends more often than not to select the same object in the next round. Win with rock, do rock again. If a person loses a round the person tends to change objects, but not randomly. The person tends to go to the next object in the game's name. Lose with rock, tend to select paper next time. Lose with paper, go with scissors. If these human decision patterns are genuine, and you know it, then you should be able to win more than one out of three times in the long run, provided that you are playing against a person who is unaware of these natural human tendencies. Your group may wish to experiment. For example, suppose you hosted a Rock-Paper-Scissors tournament. Most wins out of 100 rounds is the winner of the tournament. Invite lots of other people to participate. Let 75 percent of them play as they wish. Recruit the other 25 percent to assist you. You do not have to tell them what you are checking, just ask that they play according to your instructions. If they agree, instruct that if they win a round they play the same object the next round. But if they lose a round, they should select the object that would have won. If they lost to a rock, play paper. If they lost to paper, play scissors. If they lost to scissors, play rock. Instruct the 25 percent not to tell anyone that they are assisting you. If the clued-in 25 percent on average do better than the other 75 percent, this would tend to disconfirm the hypothesis there is no relationship between whether a person wins or loses a round and what they select to play in the next round.[24] Keep track of wins and losses as the data to use for purposes of testing the hypothesis. Because the 25 percent are your confederates in this little experiment, ethically you probably ought not to reward them if they are more successful than the other competitors in the tournament.

Chapter 13
Ideological Reasoning

Tracey and Maggie Cooper-Harris are legally married. Tracey served 12 years in the U.S. Army. The Department of Veterans Affairs denied Tracey's application for the same level of additional compensation as other married veterans are entitled to receive. Internal appeals were denied. Is it right to permit that kind of discrimination?

HOW can we recognize ideological reasoning?

HOW can we evaluate ideological reasoning?

WHAT are the uses, benefits, and risks of ideological reasoning?

 Learning Outcomes

13.1 Explain ideological reasoning and its implications for beliefs and actions.

13.2 Apply correctly the criteria for the evaluation of ideological reasoning.

13.3 Describe the uses, benefits, and risks of ideological reasoning.

"Fifty-nine percent support same-sex marriage."[1] This 2014 statistic stands in sharp contrast with the 2009 Gallup opinion polls. Then 59 percent opposed same-sex marriage. In 1997, the year when many of today's college students were born, 68 percent opposed same-sex marriage.[2] As of November 30, 2014, same-sex marriage was legal in 35 states and the District of Columbia, and banned in 15 states.[3] In October 2014, the U.S. Supreme Court declined to take up the issue during 2014–2015.

Given the statistics and the trends, should we infer that same-sex marriage is no longer an issue in the United States? Absolutely not. No more so than that the 1973 Supreme Court decision in *Roe vs. Wade* resolved the ideological conflict at the root of the abortion vs. choice issue. And no more so that the Court's 1954 *Brown vs. Board of Education* decision irradiated racial prejudice. There are many who strongly oppose same-sex marriage on religious grounds, in spite of the dramatic changes in public opinion. There are many who are profoundly opposed to abortion, even though the Court has affirmed a woman's right to elect to terminate her pregnancy. A person's deeply held beliefs and core values do not change simply because of shifting public opinion, legislation, or court decisions. It is our great good fortune as a nation that nearly all of us believe in obeying the law, even if we may disagree with one or another specific statute.

"Marriage" is not easy to define well. Consider its history and the different purposes that marriage was expected to serve down through the millennia. In some times and places the purpose of marriage was strictly economic. In those cultures a wife was her husband's property. In some times and places the purpose of marriage was procreation. In those cultures a man could divorce his wife if she was barren. Some today say marriage is about love, which implies that if love ends, so does the marriage. Christianity says marriage is sacred, a sign of God's love for the Church. But marriage does not signify that same thing to people of other religions, nor to people who are not religious. Some cultures permit honor killings if a married woman is raped by someone other than her husband. Some cultures permit children to be taken in marriage or to be given in marriage by their parents. Marriage has been used to form political and economic or strategic alliances between families, tribal groups, and empires.[4]

But social mores and attitudes change over time. Because so many intricate situations arise, because the consequences of each difficult decision can be long term and psychologically and economically expensive, and because so many vulnerable people are involved, a pluralistic society like ours must rely on legislation to sort out what "marriage" should mean. But, we must not ask ourselves "What was marriage in our grandparents' time?" or "What is marriage today?" No, instead we need to consider "What marriage should be during the first half of the twenty-first century?"

To begin to address the massive question of the future meaning of marriage, let's first consider a few of the intricate situations and complex questions that need to be resolved. Here is a list to get you started. Think for a moment about each question before expressing your initial tentative opinion. In every case explain exactly what your reasons are for that opinion. Remember not to lock-in prematurely. Be prepared to revise your opinions about some of the earlier questions based on the thoughts prompted by later questions in the list.

1. Should a State that has banned same-sex marriage be required by law to recognize same-sex marriages performed legally in another State?

2. If a religious community is opposed to divorce or same-sex marriage, should the law permit that community to expel a devout member who becomes divorced or who enters into same-sex marriage?

3. Should a private employer be permitted to consider a person's marital status when evaluating job applicants or when deciding on a person's salary?

4. If its owners object to divorce or same-sex marriage on religious grounds, should a private business be legally permitted to fire an employee who gets divorced or who enters into a same-sex marriage?

5. If its owners object to same-sex marriage on religious grounds, should a private business located in a State that has banned same-sex marriage be legally permitted to refuse service to same-sex couples who have been legally married in another State?

6. Should couples who cannot have children or who refuse to have children be allowed to get married?

7. Should a same-sex married couple be allowed by law to be foster parents, should the couple be allowed to adopt children, should the couple be allowed to have a biological child through in vitro fertilization?

8. If a legally married lesbian couple gets a divorce, and if one of the women is the birth mother of a child they had been raising as a couple, should both parties be granted visitation or shared child custody rights if the birth mother strongly objects?

9. Should the living spouse of a legally married same-sex couple be entitled to the same benefits from the U.S. Department of Veteran Affairs as are provided to the spouses of other veterans?[5]

10. When a military veteran's widow dies, should the widow be allowed to be buried in a military cemetery if the deceased husband is buried there and if their marriage was a legal same-sex marriage even though the State where the cemetery is located has banned same-sex marriage?

11. If their religion demands it, should the male relatives of a married woman be permitted by law to perform an "honor killing" if they establish beyond a doubt that she has had an extramarital affair?

12. Should a parent be permitted to pay a financial debt by offering a child in marriage?

13. What should the minimum age and the maximum age be for a person to consent to be married?

14. Should two adults who live together for seven years and who acknowledge each other as spouses be recognized by the government as having entered into a common law marriage for all legal purposes including medical and tax benefits, inheritance, child support, and possible alimony payments?

15. Should a person who is legally incompetent owing to mental illness be permitted to marry?

16. Should biological siblings be legally permitted to marry, should people who are siblings by adoption be permitted to marry, should a parent be legally permitted to marry his or her biological or adopted child? What if agreeing not to have children were part of the marriage contract?

17. Should the law permit a man or a woman to be married to more than one person at the same time?

18. Instead of limiting marriage to two people only, should three or more people be legally permitted to marry each other?

19. It is sci-fi now, but when the day comes that we can manufacture robots who look human and who can express human emotions and display human intelligence, should a human being be legally permitted to marry such a robot?

20. If, as the Supreme Court says, corporations are persons too, should a human being be legally permitted to marry a corporation?[6]

Having thought about these questions and clarified your reasons in your own mind, write your own personal definition of "marriage." The ideal personal definition must reflect your heartfelt beliefs and core values about marriage. Set aside your personal definition for a moment. Now write a legal definition of "marriage." The ideal legal definition must take into account that ours is a

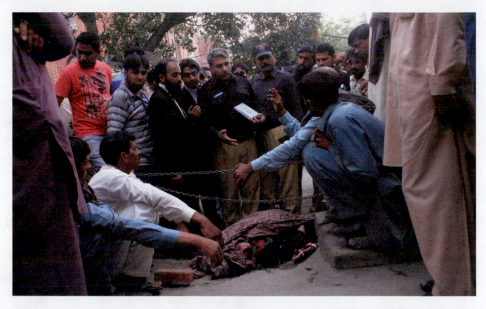

Just because some were raised to believe that a husband's honor is more valuable than a wife's life does not make that ideology true. In fact, "We were raised to believe X," never makes "X" true.

nation of 360,000,000 people endeavoring to live together in a diverse, pluralistic, multi-cultural, economically complicated, global twenty-first century democratic society. The legal definition fails if it simply forces any one group's traditions, political agenda, or religious ideology on every other group. The legal definition succeeds if it ensures maximal individual freedom while at the same time protecting the innocent and vulnerable among us from harm. Any restrictions your legal definition imposes must be no more than the minimum necessary to resolve all 20 questions in way that is internally consistent, comprehensive, enforceable, predictable, just and fair to everyone.

Consider both your personal definition and your legal definition. Can you reconcile your personal definition and your legal definition? Or, are your personal beliefs and values in conflict with the legal definition you wrote?

"Our freedoms are often acquired slowly, but our country has evolved as a beacon of liberty in what is sometimes a dark world...It has been over forty years since Mildred Loving[7] was given the right to marry the person of her choice. The hatred and fears have long since vanished and she and her husband lived full lives together; so it will be for the same-sex couples. It is time to let that beacon of freedom shine brighter on all our brothers and sisters. We will be stronger for it."

Christopher Piazza, Circuit Judge,
Pulaski County, Arkansas[8]

13.1 Recognizing Ideological Reasoning

As long as same-sex marriage was a political wedge issue, it attracted enough voters to the polls to determine the outcome of elections. Conservatives who came out to vote against same-sex marriage predictably voted for conservative candidates. Same for liberals. If they showed up to vote for same-sex marriage, since they were already in the voting booth, they typically voted for liberal candidates.

But, politics and public opinion aside, are their good arguments for or against same-sex marriage?

We might see the issue as a matter of conflicting rights. There is the *right of the people of a State* to pass laws or to amend their State's constitution. On the other hand, there is the *right of individuals* to marry the person whom they choose. If the courts determine that the U.S. Constitution protects an individual's right to marry the person of his or her choice, then the voters in a given State will not legally be permitted to ban same-sex marriage. Constitutional rights cannot be stripped away, even by majority vote. But if the courts determine that same-sex marriage is not a constitutionally protected right then the voters of each State are free to exercise their right to establish State laws permitting or banning same-sex marriage.

These two points of view are based on the concept of rights. The rights of individuals and the rights of the voters. These are high level abstractions, "important ideas," "first principles," "beliefs we cannot compromise." We often make important decisions by applying high level first principles to specific situations. In the case of same-sex marriage, we are mindful that ascribing a right to a person or a group of people implies that others would be in the wrong if they tried to prevent that person or that group from exercising that right. The freedom to exercise one's rights is a core value in our society. Whenever the rights of different people come into conflict, it is necessary to consider which rights take priority. To help resolve the matter we reference a higher level principle, if there is one. And, in this case there appears to be a principle that takes priority,

Map 1–Conflicting Rights

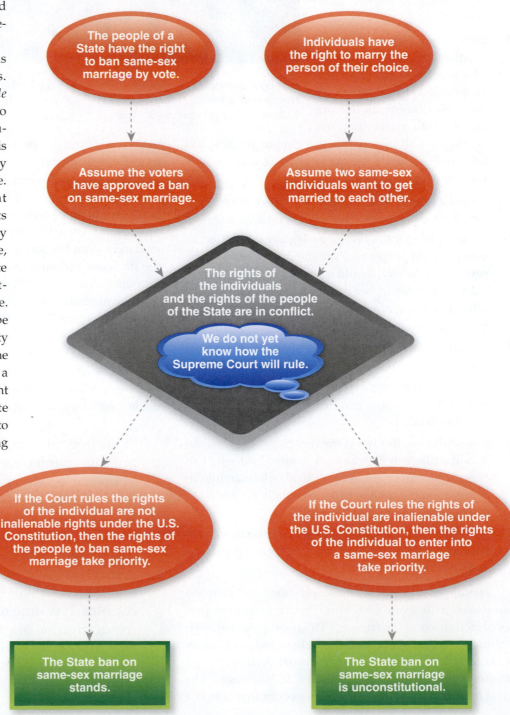

The people of a State have the right to ban same-sex marriage by vote.

Individuals have the right to marry the person of their choice.

Assume the voters have approved a ban on same-sex marriage.

Assume two same-sex individuals want to get married to each other.

The rights of the individuals and the rights of the people of the State are in conflict.

We do not yet know how the Supreme Court will rule.

If the Court rules the rights of the individual are not inalienable rights under the U.S. Constitution, then the rights of the people to ban same-sex marriage take priority.

If the Court rules the rights of the individual are inalienable under the U.S. Constitution, then the rights of the individual to enter into a same-sex marriage take priority.

The State ban on same-sex marriage stands.

The State ban on same-sex marriage is unconstitutional.

namely that inalienable constitutional rights cannot be removed from a person by any agency of government, including by majority vote. This is one of the most fundamental principles of the American democratic system; it is affirmed in our Declaration of Independence. From these two broad and powerful absolutes ideals ("honor all rights" and "give priority to inalienable constitutional rights"), we can reason down to the specific case at hand. If X is an inalienable constitutional right, then X cannot be removed by majority vote. The decision map for a rights-based interpretation of the same-sex marriage issue would look like Map 1.

At the time we are writing this edition, we do not know what the U.S. Supreme Court will rule with regard to the right of individuals to marry the person of their choice. If it is determined to be an inalienable constitutional right, then State level bans on safe-sex marriage will be struck down.

A second conflicting pair of arguments in the same-sex marriage debate is based on religious convictions and ethical first principles. The argument to ban same-sex marriage could be expressed this way. Our religious convictions tell us that God intends marriage to be the sacred union of one man and one woman. Same-sex marriage is an unnatural violation of the way God has defined marriage. The laws of God take priority over the laws of the nation. Same-sex marriage is always wrong. The laws of the nation should be based on the laws of God. Same-sex marriage should be legally banned. The ethical argument against banning same-sex marriage could be expressed like this: Ethically we ought always to treat one another as we would want to be treated. None of us would want to be forced to follow the dictates of a religion that was not our own religion. Therefore it is unethical for one religious group to impose its morality on anyone who is not a member of that group. Specifically, no religious group should be permitted to prevent people who are not members of their religion from entering into a legal marriage. This applies to same-sex marriage. Therefore same-sex marriage should not be banned. Map both of these arguments.

Both of the pairs of arguments described above are examples of **ideological reasoning** or **top-down thinking**. Ideological reasoning begin with abstract generalizations that embody first principles, core values or broad generalizations that are taken to be rock solid truths. Reasoning then proceeds down from the high mountain to apply these initial principles to specific situations.

THINK CRITICALLY

Is Media Objectivity Possible?

The media love to spotlight the inflammatory rhetoric and offensive behavior of extremists. The more outrageous the claim or the deed, the more social media attention it receives, and the more the mass media networks make of it. Hey, as the saying goes, "It sells papers." At the same time, a favorite ploy of ideologues and politicians is to condemn the media as biased. This way, if the person likes how he or she was treated in a certain news story, then ho-hum, that's how it should be. But if the person does not like the story, then the person can whine "See, I told you so. Look how I was misrepresented by the biased media."

Whatever the advantage or disadvantage to the media corporations or the individuals who may be seeking attention, the net result is that the public's quotient of general cynicism increases. We tune out, disengage, decide it's all noise, and that none of it makes any difference. The tragedy is that public cynicism is just like public outrage. Both ends of that spectrum undercut reasoned discourse and erode our democracy.

We often hear that news coverage of ideologically controversial events is biased and slanted, rather than objective and fair-minded. People accuse news organizations of pandering, sensationalizing, failure to fact check, and confusing hype and entertainment for solid reporting. Anything to increase

followers or viewers and, thus, to sell more advertising. And occasionally those accusations are true. But after all, news corporations are in business to make money. Right?

If you could improve media coverage to make it more objective without suppressing free speech, what policies would you put in place?

Ideological reasoning is an important and widely used way of thinking. It offers many benefits, such as in the practice of law. This mode of reasoning comes into play whenever religion, ethics, politics, rules, laws, regulations, or policy matters are the focus of concern. As we saw both sides in the same-sex marriage debate can and do use ideological reasoning when making their respective cases to the voters and to the courts. Advocates for one side argue that the high ideals associated with ethics, personal liberty and civil rights imply that same-sex marriage should be permitted. Advocates for the other side argue that our shared religious convictions and our democratic principle mean that the majority rule takes priority.

It would be a mistake to oversimplify the situation. There are people who believe that the right of the individual to marry the person of their choice is not protected by the U.S. Constitution. They may agree that a person has that right if the person lives in a State that has legalized same-sex marriage. But, if the people of the State decide by majority vote to ban same-sex marriage, then it should be banned. And, on the other side, there are deeply religious people who do not believe that God has necessarily decreed that same-sex marriage is deeply sinful. They find the Biblical evidence unconvincing. And, even some verses of the Bible were totally unambiguous on that point, these religious people prefer to "err on the side of mercy, grace, justice, love of neighbor. . . . and on the side of gospel, which makes all things new."[9] To make matters even more complicated, there are extremely conservative Christians who maintain that our nation should base all our laws on the Christian religion. They know this amounts to imposing their version of Christian standards of behavior on the hundreds of millions of their fellow Americans, including a great many Christians who believe that the laws of the nation should not reflect any single religious perspective. True, these extremely conservative Christians would never accept having Sharia law imposed or strict Orthodox Judaic law imposed.

The Government of the United States is in no sense founded on the Christian religion.

The Treaty of Tripoli Article 11

John Adams

Ideologically based reasoning, exemplified by both sides in this heated controversy over same-sex marriages, is pervasive and important in human affairs. We use it to make inferences and to explain our point of view on specific issues of the day. As strong critical thinkers, we must understand how it works, what its uses are, and what its potential benefits and risks are. Above all, we must learn to appreciate ideological reasoning for what it can achieve and, at the same time, be able to apply it and evaluate it objectively and fair-mindedly. Before we look at its evaluation and applications, both reasonable and unreasonable, we must learn to recognize ideological reasoning so we can distinguish it from comparative reasoning and from empirical reasoning. To help us be able to recognize ideological reasoning, we will first look briefly at three more sets of examples and then, based on the examples we've developed, we will quickly be able to identify three distinguishing characteristics of ideological reasoning.

Examples of Ideological Reasoning

Consider the following pairs of ideological arguments. Beginning with broad axiom-like first principles and generalizations, each speaker reasons to specific applications. As is often the case with opposing ideological positions, there is precious little room for compromise.

IMMIGRATION POLICY

1(a). By definition, if a person enters this country illegally, that person is breaking the law. All lawbreakers are criminals. Criminals should be prosecuted. I support legislation that is tough on crime. That is why I support a constitutional amendment that requires the incarceration and deportation of all illegal immigrants.

1(b). Government policies and laws that destroy the family unit are bad. The family is sacred, and it is fundamental to our American way of life. That is why I oppose the constitutional amendment, which would rip a family apart by deporting a parent, or even a child, if the person is not in this country legally.

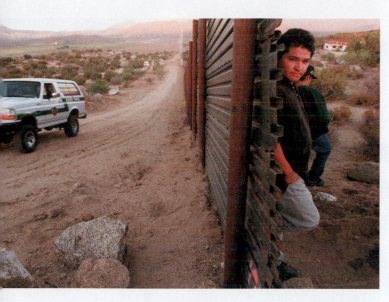

Is this a dad or a criminal? Blocking illegals vs. supporting families—exactly how should we frame the immigration policy question?

GOD'S EXISTENCE

2(a). The space-time continuum extends outward, forward, and backward infinitely from the present-here-and-now moment. It follows that there can be no reality whatsoever other than the universe, for there can be no time nor space outside the infinite vastness that is the space-time universe. Ergo, there is no God sitting outside our naturally infinite time-space continuum. Nor is there any such place as Heaven or Hell, nor any time when we shall receive eternal happiness or eternal pain. There is no place outside space nor any time after the end of time.

2(b). Every natural thing that exists today—the matter and energy that is this universe, this galaxy, this solar system, this planet, all the animals and plants, each one of us—every natural thing comes from prior natural

How would the universe be different in some noticeable way if it were or if it were not divinely created?

causes. We would not exist were it not for our parents, for example. If we could go back in time, we would never find anything that came into existence on its own without a prior cause. Given that the natural world exists, it follows that something had to get this whole huge chain of causes going. Something had to set it all in motion. And that something had to be outside of the natural universe, for without a force outside nature, the whole long causal process would never have begun. Thus that first creative mover had to be supernatural. We call that First Cause by the name "God." Ergo, God exists.

HUMAN NATURE

3(a). People are fundamentally good. Most people will keep their word and to try to do what is right for their fellow human beings most of the time. It is wrong to take away our freedom. This is why I support those who would maximize individual liberties and reduce the number of bureaucratic rules and regulations that legislators and administrators are constantly trying to impose on our personal and commercial interactions.

3(b). People are fundamentally bad. If they can get away with something they will; they can be counted on to exploit every advantage in an effort to advance their own interests. This is why we need tougher laws and detailed regulation of commerce. More individual liberty will lead only to greater societal disintegration and the inevitable exploitation of the poor by those who have the means to do so.

In the first pair of arguments about immigration policy, one speaker appeals to the value of enforcing our laws while the other appeals to the value of the family. Each comes up with a different conclusion. The first would deport people who entered the country illegally, without reference to the fact that a given person might be the parent or the child of someone else who is in the country legally. The second would attend to that family relationship and not deport the person. Starting the policy discussion from those two opposing positions will make a legislative compromise a challenge to negotiate. On the other hand, perhaps both speakers share both values. A first step might be agreeing that enforcing the laws and protecting families are both core commitments.

The second pair of arguments takes on a challenge that many regard as intellectually impossible: proving beyond a doubt either that God does exist or that God does not exist. Theological conceptualizations of God are not static; they have changed throughout human history and from culture to culture. So have our scientific conceptualizations and theories about the nature of the universe. Thus, in different historical eras and in different cultures, we may or may not find people making arguments for or against the existence of

These images of Adam and Eve and the Vietnam War depict very different sides of human behavior. Are we all potentially devoted lovers or brutal warriors—or both? Explain why.

God or gods, as conceived of in those times and places. The Judeo-Christian monotheistic view of the universe dominated European culture for centuries. From that cultural perspective, many philosophers proposed arguments for God's existence. One question this pair of arguments raises for the critical thinker is "To what extent does or should our understanding of the universe influence our theological ideas?"

The arguments in the third pair both begin with a core belief about human nature. One says human nature is fundamentally good, another that it is fundamentally bad. The debate about our fundamental moral character goes back millennia. Are we the innocent creatures originally designed for life in a Garden of Eden, or are we self-indulgent brutes never more than the collapse of a government away from barbarism? The truth is probably some place between the two extremes. The issue is not likely to be resolved any time soon. And although there are anecdotes and historical examples, which might be cited to support both sides of that dispute, it is difficult to know when, how, or whether it can ever be fully resolved. But notice that, at the purely ideological level, one's stance on this question tends to propel one toward specific applications. If we're basically good, then trust us and give us more freedom. If we're basically bad, then protect us from each other with more governmental or religious controls on our behavior. Ideological reasoning, even about ideas that cannot be resolved, has important consequences for policies and practices that profoundly affect our lives.

Three Features of Ideological Reasoning

There are three distinguishing features of ideological reasoning: (1) It is deductive in character; (2) the ideological

premises are axiomatic; and (3) the argument maker takes the ideology to be true more or less on faith.

Before unpacking each of the three, we need to take note of the word "ideological." The root of *ideological* is "idea." The concept behind our use here of ideological as applied to reasoning is that the reasoning begins with ideas that express concepts, opinions, beliefs, or principles. The contrast would be reasoning that begins with descriptions of events, observations, or experiences. Our use of the term *ideological* is meant to be value-neutral. In other words, thinking is neither good nor bad simply because it is ideological as we are using the term here. Some people hear "ideological" or "ideology" and associate negative connotations with those words. And there is no question that some specific ideologies are quite dangerous. But *ideological thinking*, as we use the term, is not about a specific good or bad ideology. Rather, it refers to the way in which arguments are made beginning with general ideas, such as concepts, opinions, beliefs or principles, and moving down from these abstractions to their specific applications.

IDEOLOGICAL REASONING IS DEDUCTIVE IN CHARACTER For the most part, the conclusions of ideological arguments are presented as certainties. Qualifiers like *probably*, *maybe*, or *perhaps* are seldom, if ever, found in ideological arguments. There might be a citation of a book, author, or other "authoritative" source. There will seldom be references to correlations, data, experimentation, or systematic investigation unless those references support the author's preconceived ideas. Unlike courageous truth-seekers, ideologues look for facts that support their points of view, not facts that disagree. If research is cited, an example used, or a comparison made, the purpose is anecdotal or illustrative, not evidentiary. For example, "Same-sex couples do not make good parents. Let me tell you about the sad case of little so-and-so who had two daddies until they wanted to get a divorce."

Ideological Reasoning or "Top-Down Thinking"

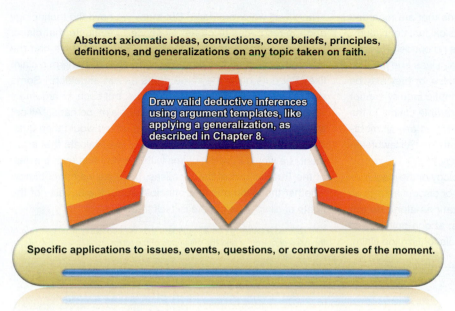

Abstract axiomatic ideas, convictions, core beliefs, principles, definitions, and generalizations on any topic taken on faith.

Draw valid deductive inferences using argument templates, like applying a generalization, as described in Chapter 8.

Specific applications to issues, events, questions, or controversies of the moment.

- Everyone should have the right to marry the person whom he or she chooses.
- God intended that marriage should be between a man and a woman.
- All lawbreakers are criminals.
- The family is sacred.
- The space-time continuum extends outward, forward, and backward infinitely.
- Every natural thing that exists today comes from prior natural causes.
- People are fundamentally good.
- People are fundamentally bad.

Not all deductive reasoning is ideological. To categorize ideological reasoning as deductive is like categorizing trees as plants. Doing so does not imply that all plants are trees. Describing ideological reasoning as deductive focuses on the certainty with which ideological thinkers endow their conclusions. Ideological thinkers present their conclusions as if the conclusions were entailed or implied by the premises of their arguments. They intend and often believe that their conclusions cannot possibly be false, given their ideological starting points. Ideological arguments move from general ideas to specific applications. If the general ideas are true, then their specific application must be true, too. In the chapter "Valid Inferences," we described this valid argument template, it is named "Applying a Generalization." The observations about ideological reasoning, particularly about its benefits and risks, do not apply to all valid inferences. There are many kinds of valid inferences that are not ideological at all.

IDEOLOGICAL PREMISES ARE AXIOMATIC As in high school plane geometry, axioms are simply a set of *first principles, starting points, or assumptions.* For example, "All right angles are equal." From the axioms we proved that other statements (theorems) were true. In ideological reasoning the key assumptions, whether spoken or unspoken, are those that embody a community's or individual's deeply held beliefs and core values. These, for that person and that community, are axiomatic. The ideas, concepts, principles, or beliefs that ideological thinkers use to initiate their arguments represent the axioms from which other ideas or specific applications follow, much like theorems in geometry. We saw absolute convictions, including those listed here, in the previous examples:

THE ARGUMENT MAKER TAKES THE IDEOLOGICAL ABSOLUTES ON FAITH To the person or the community making an ideological argument, the first principles are so profoundly obvious that they require no demonstration. Ideological thinkers do not require or expect independent scientific confirmation of their first principles. The opposite, in fact. They try to bend science to fit their preconceptions. Ideological reasoning begins with the conviction that the axiomatic first principles express good ideals, worthy purposes, and true beliefs. Similarly, ideological thinkers consistently regard their absolutes as immune from disconfirmation. Evidence scientifically gathered cannot, in principle, demonstrate to the argument maker that these absolutes are mistaken.

We talked about the strategies of confirmation or disconfirmation as two independent ways to evaluate a claim. We might, for example, ask a person who believes that people are fundamentally good, "What would it take to convince you that you are wrong about that?" If the opinion is held by that person as a matter of faith, then the person would probably reply quite honestly, "Nothing. You could never convince me otherwise." We would expect the same reply from a person who holds as a matter of faith that people are fundamentally bad. The same holds for people who believe any of the other six statements in our list as matters of personal faith.

Because the argument maker sees the truth of his or her own ideology as self-evident, that person might at times become impatient, frustrated, or even angry with a listener who disagrees. A listener who cannot see the truth of those axiomatic first principles may appear to the argument maker to be uneducated, unintelligent, or perhaps even malevolent. This would be an unfair assumption on the part of the argument maker, of course.

Metaphysical Claims

The term metaphysical refers to assertions that are regarded as being true or false, independent of physical facts or circumstances. A claim is metaphysical if there is no conceivable evidence that could establish whether the claim was true or false. The claims might be true, they might be false, or they may be nonsensical. But whatever they are, scientific inquiry cannot confirm or disconfirm them. The eight example claims in the "Ideological Premises Are Axiomatic" section are all metaphysical in this sense of the word. One of them, "All lawbreakers are criminals," appears to be a tautology.*

It may be impossible given the technology or the resources at hand in a given time or place to confirm or disconfirm a given claim, but those kinds of practical limitations alone do not make a claim metaphysical. For example, at one point it was technologically impossible to confirm or disconfirm the claim,

"There was water on Mars." But today we have the technology and the resources to gather evidence to evaluate that claim. By contrast, there is no conceivable way, even if we had the technology and the funding, to confirm or to disconfirm a claim like "Pet cats have the same rights as pet angelfish." Some may wish to argue that the claim is true, but such an argument would depend on another metaphysical claim, perhaps, "All pet animals have the same rights." That argument would then qualify as ideological reasoning. And when we evaluate that argument, we would have problems with the very first test, the Test of the Truthfulness of the Premises, because we cannot know whether the axiomatic first principle about the equality of the rights of all species of pets is itself true.

*We defined a *tautology* as a statement that is necessarily true by virtue of the rules of grammar and the meanings of the terms used.

Consider what we learned on reflective thinking about how dominance structuring gives us confidence to act on our choices and convictions. Once we realize that axiomatic convictions are held to be truly independent of potential confirmation or disconfirmation, it is easier to understand how powerfully motivating they can be. In the grip of unquestioned axiomatic beliefs any community might readily become convinced that its particular view of the world is right and every other view is wrong. So powerful can a community's worldview be that some within that community are moved to become martyrs or warriors. They are willing to make the ultimate sacrifice to protect and defend their community's worldview.

Our level of faith and conviction is no measure of the truth of the beliefs we hold so dear. Our devotion to a cause is no measure of the worthiness of the values for which we may be prepared to die. We might be tragically mistaken, believing something that is not true, prizing something that is not worthy. Aristotle and the people of ancient Greece believed that slavery was an ethically acceptable practice. The economics of ancient Rome depended on slave labor as a given. Sending her mighty legions to conquer and enslave others was righteous and self-evidently reasonable. Slavery was accepted as part of the cultural fabric of several of the original 13 colonies that formed the United States. There were men and women of those times and places who were as convinced of the rightness of slavery as we, today, are convinced that it is wrong. By no means are we advocating relativism in this matter. Recall the "Levels of Thinking and Knowing" chart in the section on cognitive development. There we said that "Truth-Seekers" and "Sages" were at higher and more sophisticated stages of intellectual development than "Relativists." To move beyond relativism, we need to expand the domain of critical thinking by courageously and objectively examining those beliefs that we hold as articles of faith. Perhaps some of the things that we hold to be true and righteous are

What part of "Do unto others as you would have others do unto you" did the defenders of slavery not understand? Perhaps we can begin to appreciate the horrendous crime against humanity that is slavery, by watching the Academy Award–winning film *Twelve Years a Slave*.

as wrongheaded as slavery. That we believe them does not make them true.

As authors of a textbook on critical thinking, we realize the importance of applying the critical thinking skill of self-regulation, guided by the habit of truth-seeking and a healthy sense of skepticism to ourselves as well. Yes, we are concerned to help you realize that there are pitfalls associated with unwittingly accepting any ideology as if it were immune from well-reasoned examination and thoughtful evaluation. But that same advice cuts both ways. As the authors we must ask ourselves, are we so blind to our own wrongheadedness on some issue—be it political, religious, social, cultural, or whatever—that we are being critical of the tiny speck in our brother's eye but missing the branch in our own eyes?

13.2 Evaluating Ideological Reasoning

To evaluate ideological reasoning, we will apply the four tests for the worthiness of an argument. These are the four questions those tests ask: (1) Are all the premises true? (2) Is the argument logically strong? (3) Are the reasons relevant to the claim being made? and (4) Is the argument non-circular? Let us consider each question in sequence.

Are the Ideological Premises True?

The test for the truthfulness of the premises is perhaps the most important test for ideological reasoning. If the premises are taken as true, then the listener could be well down the path to believing the conclusion. To apply this test, we must consider each premise one after another. Some will be spoken and others will be implicit. They all require individual attention.

Given that strongly held beliefs and core values often function as the implicit but unspoken guiding ideology, it may be challenging to bring all the unspoken assumptions to the surface for examination. And yet, for ideological inferences, the key issues revolve around the truthfulness of those axiomatic ideological premises themselves. These are the very premises that the argument maker takes on faith and expects the listener to take on faith as well. For critical thinking, the question is, "How can we tell whether the premises expressing the speaker's ideology

Applying the Test of Truthfulness of the Premises

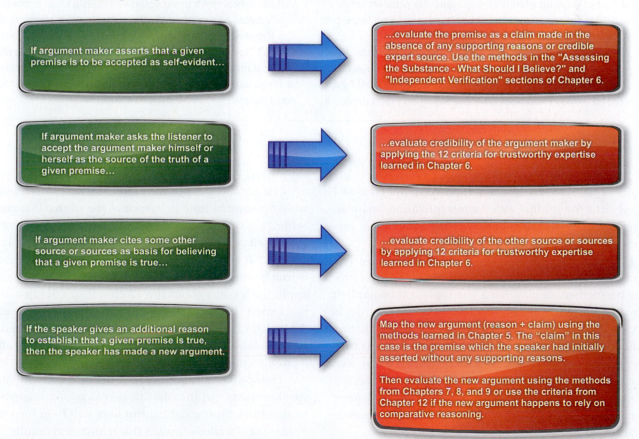

If argument maker asserts that a given premise is to be accepted as self-evident… → …evaluate the premise as a claim made in the absence of any supporting reasons or credible expert source. Use the methods in the "Assessing the Substance - What Should I Believe?" and "Independent Verification" sections of Chapter 6.

If argument maker asks the listener to accept the argument maker himself or herself as the source of the truth of a given premise… → …evaluate credibility of the argument maker by applying the 12 criteria for trustworthy expertise learned in Chapter 6.

If argument maker cites some other source or sources as basis for believing that a given premise is true… → …evaluate credibility of the other source or sources by applying 12 criteria for trustworthy expertise learned in Chapter 6.

If the speaker gives an additional reason to establish that a given premise is true, then the speaker has made a new argument. → Map the new argument (reason + claim) using the methods learned in Chapter 5. The "claim" in this case is the premise which the speaker had initially asserted without any supporting reasons.

Then evaluate the new argument using the methods from Chapters 7, 8, and 9 or use the criteria from Chapter 12 if the new argument happens to rely on comparative reasoning.

THINKING CRITICALLY

Faith Enduring Adversity: The Book of Job

Critical thinking is not something invented by scientists or philosophers of the modern or postmodern eras. There is evidence of vigorous critical thinking, including lively debates and arguments, in many historically significant documents, the Bible among them, and in many religious traditions as well. The reasoning, as we would expect, particularly in prescientific times, tends to be ideological in character, but the skills of analysis, interpretation, inference, self-regulation, evaluation, and explanation are all evident.

Consider, for example, the question "Why does God, who is all good and all powerful, permit innocent people to suffer evil?" The question has been around for thousands of years, and there are no easy answers. To say that evil is unreal is playing with words. To say that all evil is natural, like the tragic consequences of bad weather or unfortunate accidents, is to ignore the evil that men and women do to each other intentionally on occasion. To say that God gives us free choice so the evil we do is something God is permitting, but does not approve of, seems to contradict God's goodness. No loving parent would permit his or her children to rape and murder one another. This issue, known as "the problem of evil," is a classic concern of people raised in the Judeo-Christian tradition. To offer the metaphysical claim that a particular evil is all part of a grand plan only sidesteps the problem momentarily. We naturally want to know why that evil had to be part of the plan.

The problem of evil is addressed in powerfully straightforward way early in the Judeo-Christian Bible. The book called *Job* is worth reading. That book tells the story of a wealthy and blessed man named Job. One day Satan and God decide to test his faith. They have a bit of a wager over the question of what it might take for Job to abandon his conviction and trust in God. Their approach is to test him by visiting upon him and his household all manner of evil and misfortune.

What is most interesting is how Job behaves in response to the adversity sent his way. Apply your critical thinking skills to the arguments used by the three main characters in the story: God, Job, and Satan. Map and evaluate their arguments. In the final analysis, is Job's faith an example of ideological reasoning or not—that is, does it have the three characteristics of being deductive in character, axiomatic, and immune from both confirmation and disconfirmation?

Suppose God and Satan had tried a different ploy. Instead of taking away all the good things in Job's life, suppose that they only sent him more blessings. Would that have been a tougher challenge to his faith? Some might argue that it is more difficult for the coddled and comfortable to sustain their faith, than for the poor, oppressed and desperate. Is there any experience or set of circumstances that can logically lead one to infer that if God does exist, then God is not currently taking an active interest in the lives and fortunes of all the individual human beings?

For a contemporary rendering of the story of Job, watch the 2009 Coen brothers' film, A *Serious Man*. How to interpret that allegorical film's unexpected ending is a topic of considerable interest on the Internet. Question: In what respects does this film deviate from the classic Biblical version of the story of Job? Does that deviation alter or reinforce the core philosophical message about how difficult it is to understand why at times bad things happen even to those who try hard to be good people?

---

are true or false?" Here is where we need to integrate and to apply in a thoughtful way the interpretation, analysis, inference, and evaluation skills that we examined in earlier chapters.

The first possibility to consider in applying the Test of the Truthfulness of the Premises is that the speaker provides no further backing for a given explicit or implicit premise. The speaker simply asserts it or takes it as true. In this case we can use the methods described for evaluating claims to see whether or not we should agree that it is true. If speaker has asserted something that is factually false, that will come out when we fact-check. Statistics don't lie, but people do. A healthy sense of skepticism is the best defense strong critical thinkers have when an ideologue starts making fact-checkable claims.

The second possibility is that the argument maker would present himself or herself as the source that stands behind a given premise. The person might say, "Trust me when I tell you . . ." or "Based on all my experience I know that . . ." If the speaker wants us to believe the premise is true because of his or her own credibility, then we can apply the lessons about the 12 characteristics of a credible expert. We can use those lessons to assess whether the maker of an ideological argument is, in fact, a credible source whose word we should trust regarding the truth of a given premise.

The speaker's third option is to cite a source that the speaker trusts and that the speaker is asking the listener to also trust. Strong critical thinkers will then turn their evaluative attentions toward that source and inquire as to its worthiness. Suppose, for example, that the argument maker states, "It is in this reference book that XYZ," "I saw it on the Internet that XYZ," "My buddy at work says that . . . ," or "Someone on *Oprah* said XYZ." We would then demand reasons why any of these sources should be trusted as experts on the topic XYZ. We developed a full set of expectations for evaluating the credibility of sources, and we can apply those to see whether we should or should not trust the source that the speaker now offers.

The fourth possibility is that the argument maker could offer a reason why the ideological premise is true. In effect, this creates a new argument. The premise we had been questioning is now the conclusion of this new argument. Its reason is the reason newly given. This tactic of providing an additional reason simply pushes the problem one step back. For example, "I believe that chimpanzees and humans have the same rights because all animals that are self-conscious and can feel pain have the same rights." Providing a reason for an ideological claim invites strong critical thinkers to evaluate that new argument. The first question might be "Why do you believe that all self-conscious animals that can feel pain have the same rights?" The next question might test the implications of that conviction by asking, "Do you really believe that worms, sparrows, kittens, small children, and carpenter ants have the same rights?"

Value Judgments

We all make judgments that express priorities. We authors, like many of you, prefer clean water to impure water, moderate exercise to a couch potato's sedentary existence, and intelligent discourse to loudmouthed stubbornness. And, as you know, we give priority to all of the positive critical thinking habits of mind over their negative polar opposites. But we have not asked you to agree with us about the positive critical thinking habits of mind as a matter of faith. Instead, we considered several reasons why critical thinking was valuable for you individually and for us as a society. We connected the skills and the habits of mind to that core idea of critical thinking. Therefore, the value of the habits of mind, like the value of the skills, comes from the value of critical thinking as purposeful reflective judgment. If there are superior ways to judge what to believe and what to do, we do not know what they are.

Taking it a step further, we have recommended that you should strengthen your skills and fortify your habits of mind. These recommendations are based on the value that we see for you and for all of us in using critical thinking. More than that, this book contains a number of other value judgments about critical thinking. We have urged that we try to be more reflective and use self-regulation to protect ourselves against premature dominance structuring and from risky reliance on System-1 judgments when more reflection should be used. To support our advice and explain our value judgments, we have used arguments, examples, and research. Some people might think that value judgments are automatically unreliable, false, or nonsense. We do not agree with that assumption. And we do not know how a rational person could argue for that assumption. Arguing that value judgments should neither be made nor accepted is arguing for a specific value judgment! So, let's agree that people make value judgments. The critical thinking question this raises is the question of judiciousness. Are our value judgments reasonable, well founded, carefully considered, and thoughtfully applied with sensitivity to the complexities of real-world situations? Recall the "Sage" level of cognitive development. That is the quality of value judgment we should be striving to attain.

To explore some interesting personal value judgments and moral dilemmas and to see whether you would make the bargains with the devil (or is he an angel?) that are offered, watch an episode or two of *The Booth at the End*. This remarkable series is somewhat reminiscent of the more thought provoking episodes of the classic *Twilight Zone*. We found it on **hulu.com.**

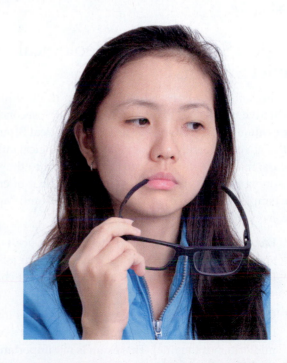

If the speaker offers a reason or reasons why one of the original premises is true, we simply apply our tools for evaluating arguments to that new argument. We could map the argument, then use the four tests. If the speaker happens to use comparative reasoning to make a new argument that his or her original premise was true, we would apply the criteria for evaluating comparative thinking.

> "The world is a dangerous place to live; not because of the people who are evil, but because of the people who don't do anything about it."
>
> Albert Einstein, genius[10]

Depending on the context and the importance of the issue, we may decide not to push things this far. Good judgment is always a virtue. If the issue is trivial, we may not want to keep asking "Why should I believe you about that?" so aggressively that we end up risking an important friendship or relationship. But if the ideological argument is going to be costly and risky, then good judgment requires that we push the Test of the Truthfulness of the Premises with vigor. It is too easy to let ideological first principles slip by unchallenged. Strong critical thinkers do not want to do that. But because these first principles often express beliefs and values that we happen to share, we can drop our guard at times. And it is exactly in those times that we are vulnerable to making mistakes. We do not want to sing the critical thinker's lament, "Oh, but I should have asked more questions before I believed so-and-so or agreed to such-and-such. Ah, but it all sounded so sensible at the time."

Logical Strength and Ideological Belief Systems

Ideological arguments, which are often the product of deductive reasoning, generally will pass the second test for evaluating arguments—the Test of Logical Strength. Although occasionally a fallacy slips in or a logical mistake occurs, many ideological arguments adhere to the valid reasoning patterns described in Chapter 8. They often use the templates for "applying a generalization" and "applying an exception." For example:

- Lazy people don't deserve handouts. Cecelia and street people like her who don't have regular jobs are lazy. So, you shouldn't give her any pocket change when you see her begging for a handout.

- Cheating is unethical only when the exam is important. But this course is not in my major and it's only a midterm, not the final. This exam is not important. So, it's OK to cheat on this exam.

- Jesus has made it clear that the most important commandment is to love our neighbors as we love ourselves. No nation that structures its health care policy so that tens of millions of its citizens are systematically denied access to adequate health care is practicing love of neighbor.[11] Jesus would be very disappointed in all of us, voters and leaders alike, for our part in permitting so many millions of our neighbors to be treated so badly. This implies that Christians should be among the strongest advocates of universal health care.

When considering these examples, keep in mind that one or more of the premises may be false. But for the sake of illustrating the logical strength often found in ideological reasoning, let us, only for the moment, assume that they are all true.

Ideological belief structures often contain internal contradictions. Buddhism, Islam, Taoism, Newtonian physics, Aristotelian cosmology, Scientology, communism, fascism, democracy, Marxism, and feminism can all be reasonably described as ideological belief systems of one kind or another. Each contains inconsistencies, small or large, as is evident from the internal disagreements that theorists and proponents of those systems experience. Some, like Buddhism and Marxism, embrace inconsistency. Some, like Newtonian physics and Aristotelian cosmology, gave way to superior conceptualizations, such as the theory of relativity. Some, like democracy and feminism, struggle with inconsistencies.

As a rule of thumb, all ideological belief systems that are "isms" are prone to internal inconsistencies. It is always possible that internal inconsistencies can be explained or resolved. As we shall see in Chapter 14 on empirical reasoning, the internal inconsistencies, called *anomalies*, in scientific belief systems often provide the impetus for further research and the generation of new knowledge. In ideologies that do not employ empirical investigation as a source of new knowledge, inconsistencies can be resolved by debate and the examination of founding documents. One belief will survive and be embraced as dogma, and the other will be branded a heresy.

What should we do if our beliefs lead to contradictions? In that case, strong critical thinking would require us to revise or abandon one or more of our beliefs. That is the only logical way to resolve the contradiction that inconsistent beliefs create. Unfortunately, in our opinion, proponents of ideological systems too often give themselves permission *not* to think critically about their own beliefs. Instead, they use escape clauses when challenged about the internal contradictions in their beliefs, using phrases such as "Well, we call that a mystery" or "If your faith were stronger, you would understand." The other unfortunate tactic ideological thinkers at times employ is resorting

Ideologies Spawn Wars

The terrible twenty-first century violence between the Muslim and Christian political parties in the Central African Republic, and the deadly terrorist attacks by Boko Haram and ISIL extremists in Nigeria and the Middle East today are ideologically driven. But not by ideology alone. They are also fueled by governmental incompetence, economic strife, Us vs. Them thinking, fear, outrage, and plain old mean-spirited vengefulness. Terrorism and war seldom have only one cause. But too often ideology is one of their many causes.

During the nineteenth century, remarkably different ideologies took heart from the expression "survival of the fittest" and the scientific weight that Darwin's evolutionary theory had already garnered. In the 1800s three writers whose ideas greatly influenced world leaders and world events a century later—Ernst Haeckel, William Sumner, and Karl Marx—pressed Darwinian ideas, misinterpreted and wrongly applied, into the service of their ideologies. To appreciate how each invoked evolution,

search for and watch the episode entitled "Fit to Rule" from the series *The Day the Universe Changed*.

The twentieth century saw tens of millions of human beings killed as these global ideologies clashed. Nazism, with its theory of Aryan supremacy and programs of "racial hygiene," manifested Haeckel's misuse of Darwin's ideas. Capitalism, which free of government regulation produces an ever widening gap between the very rich and everyone else, manifested Sumner's misapplications of Darwin. And Communism, with its belief in the inevitability of the rise of the proletariat working class, revealed Marx's misconceptions about Darwin. As history has demonstrated, the power of ideologies like these not only to shape policies but to destroy tens of millions of human lives cannot be overestimated. Science made subservient to ideology will always pose a grave danger for us all.

Haeckel's nineteenth-century misinterpretations of Darwin spawned the brutal genocides perpetrated by twentieth-century Nazism.

Sumner's nineteenth-century misinterpretations of Darwin spawned the greedy dog-eat-dog excesses and recurring market collapses of unrestricted twentieth-century capitalism.

Marx's nineteenth-century misinterpretations of Darwin spawned failed economics and the crushing misery of twentieth-century communism.

to donkey cart terms: "You see, true freedom means . . ." or "True racial supremacy means that we have . . ."

If the truth of their absolute convictions is challenged, weak critical thinkers are likely to try to fend off those challenges with fallacious or unverifiable rationales such as: "It's just common sense; everyone knows that . . ."; "Our tradition has always taught that . . ."; "It is a fundamental principle of our founders that . . ."; "Inspiration and revelation are the sources of . . ."; "I was brought up this way";

"It's what my parents always told me"; "It's what I learned in kindergarten"; or "We'll all find out the truth some day after we're dead."

But, having registered our concerns about how weak critical thinkers respond when problems are evident in their ideological reasoning, it is important to note that people with stronger critical thinking skills respond differently. When inconsistencies are found, those with stronger reasoning skills who are advocates of the

When should an ideology be set in stone?

positive results. Why? Proponents of large-scale ideological systems, like religions, metaphysical worldviews, and political and economic world-views declare their ideologies to be relevant to everything. In the United States, commentators advocating liberalism and conservatism provide strongly held opinions on virtually all topics. The initial problems that some Christian theologians had with Darwin, for example, grew out of a belief system that presumed that, in the act of creation, God must have made every animal at the same time. Later theologians refined their theory of creation so that it would be consistent with the scientific evidence. The inconsistency was resolved, and the Church and its belief system could continue to be presented as relevant to all God had created, which of course, is everything.

Our fourth test, non-circularity, produces consternation as well. The arguments used by ideological thinkers typically pass this test. They are not circular for the most part. Yes, it would be circular to argue that God exists

ideology try to address and to remove those inconsistencies. Understanding the power of dominance structuring to bolster their preferred opinion, we would expect those advocates not to abandon ship if they can plug the leak. Their efforts generally take the form of reframing the definitions of key terms, modifying or qualifying core beliefs, or refining the language used to express the ideology to remove the "apparent" contradiction.

We are talking here about advocates who are devoted to an ideology and who have strong thinking skills. We did not say that they also had strong critical thinking habits of mind. Nor are we saying that they have a healthy skepticism.[12] If they did, then their responses would also have to include the possibility of abandoning the ideology in whole or in part. And some people do exactly that. For example, a recent study focused on the religious beliefs of ordained clergy in the Protestant Church of the Netherlands. Traditional Christian beliefs, for example belief in life after death, a personal God, or the Divinity of Jesus, were not universally affirmed. In fact, one in six of the clergy in that denomination were agonistics or atheists.[13]

> "Fix reason firmly in her seat, and call to her tribunal every fact, every opinion. Question with boldness. . . ."
>
> Thomas Jefferson[14]

Relevancy, Non-Circularity, and Ideological Reasoning

For the big "isms," our third test for evaluating arguments, the Test of Relevancy, tends to yield unambiguously

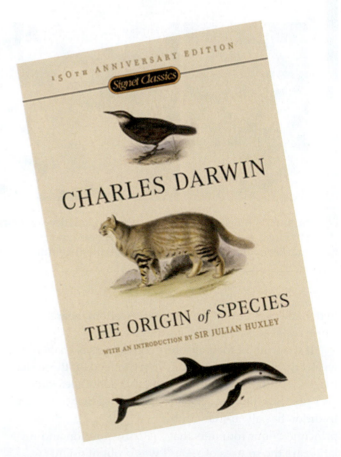

How could a study of beetles and birds cause so much trouble?

THINK CRITICALLY

Which Comparison Is Better?

We could use your assistance with something. We authors are unsure which comparison works better. One of us likes to compare ideological thinkers to people riding a merry-go-round, the other author likes to compare ideological thinkers to people on board an express train. Here is what we mean:

Conversing with ideological thinkers is like talking with people on a train. There is no doubt which direction the train is moving because that is pre-determined. The passengers are on board voluntarily and they enjoy speed and the sense of community that mass transit offers. Viewed externally, the express train is rushing by but stuck on a particular track and full of riders who cannot get off even if they wanted to until the train reaches its destination.

Conversing with advocates of ideological systems often feels like a ride on a merry-go-round—a lot of movement but not much progress! To those watching from the side, the riders appear to be going no place fast, but they are generally enjoying the experience. To those riding, the spectators seem to be rushing by, while the merry-go-round represents the steady and predictable force of their well-ordered universe with every other horse and rider exactly in the place where they belong.

Using the criteria developed in the Section on Comparative Reasoning, decide which is the better comparison. Or, come up with a third possibility. Email your advice to: **pfacione@measuredreasons.com**.

---

because the Bible says so, and then to argue that the Bible is true because it is the word of God. But that is not generally how strong critical thinkers who are religious people would frame their arguments. And, yes, it would be circular for a Marxist to argue that the proletariat will prevail over other economic classes because that is the inevitable result of world historical economic forces, and then to argue that belief in those forces is based on the expectation that the proletariat will prevail. But, again, that is not how strong critical thinkers who are Marxists would frame their arguments.

13.3 Uses, Benefits, and Risks of Ideological Reasoning

Ideological reasoning offers many benefits. First and foremost, our shared ideologies define and shape our communities and give individuals a strong sense of identity. We know who we are by reference to our ideological belief systems. For example, "I am a liberal, a member of the Democratic Party, and a Christian."

Second, ideological convictions enable us to escape the suffocating malaise of relativism. The core values of an ideological belief system guide our thinking about right and wrong, good and bad, and obligatory and optional.

Third, ideological reasoning offers an efficient way of addressing novel questions. Our "isms" often provide ready answers to new questions we may not have the time or the

expertise to answer for ourselves. Suppose, for example, that we genetically modify food grains so that rice, corn, and wheat provide nourishment that is the equivalent of the protein from eating meat. People with deep convictions that anything God did not create naturally is clearly bad might advocate bans on the genetic manipulation of foods. People deeply convinced that God intended human beings to use their powers of reason to solve problems, like world hunger, might advocate expanding the use of genetically altered foods.

JOURNAL

Must I Be Who I Was Raised to Be?

By a process known as "Excommunication" many of the world's largest religions reserve the right to expel members who publicly advocate positions which that religion officially opposes. In 2014, for example, Kate Kelly, a lifelong Mormon, faced excommunication for repeatedly and publicly advocating gender equality within the practice of Mormonism, including permitting women to be lay clergy. A spokeswoman for the Church of Jesus Christ of the Latter Day Saints said that the Church wants everyone to feel welcome and free to raise questions. But, said the spokeswoman, no person can "dictate to God what is right for his Church." Kate Kelly said that her Mormon faith was part of her identity, that it was not something that excommunication could "wash off." *

Can a person change his or her core religious, national or political identity? Can they become someone other than who they were born and raised to be?

*Price, M. L. & McCombs, B., "Mormon woman awaits decision on excommunication," Associated Press News, June 23, 2014.

"I do not feel obligated to believe that the same God who has endowed us with sense, reason, and intellect has intended us to forgo their use."

Galileo Galilei[15]

The benefits are also the risks. Ideological reasoning is pervasive in our culture, and it can be powerfully persuasive. We noted that our ideologies shape the character of our communities and our personal identities as members of those communities. Ideological belief structures are socially normative—those who disagree are seen as outsiders, ignorant, mistaken, abnormal, or dangerous. Socrates (470–399 BCE.) was convicted of the capital offense of corrupting the youth of ancient Athens because he taught them to reason for themselves and to question the unsubstantiated beliefs of the leaders of that city-state.[16] Take heed, you who write books about critical thinking!

Because ideological convictions often seem to be immunized against scientific confirmation or disconfirmation, it can be difficult for us to see them as mistaken. For example, we know of no scientific test to determine whether the individual is more important than the social collective. We have not found a scientific way to verify or falsify the belief that knowledge is superior to ignorance, but most of us believe it is. There is no scientific way to investigate the claim that it is the will of God that America be destroyed. Ideological convictions that are neither testable nor falsifiable can be called "metaphysical," as explained earlier in this chapter.

Ideological reasoning constrains and empowers. Our axiomatic core convictions have life-shaping consequences. Differing political orientations generate dramatically divergent visions of human society. Not

The Soul of the Matter

We might wonder why people raised in other cultures or other religious traditions than ours believe such strange things. But few of us question our own fundamental axiomatic beliefs and cultural values. Our ideologies are just as powerful in determining how we see the world as theirs are. Like colored lenses on a camera, ideologies skew and shape how humans behave and what they think. If anyone questions our cherished beliefs and core values, our natural tendency is to react defensively and to regard the questioner as an enemy. Tolerance and respect for others come when we realize that nobody has the right to impose their beliefs or ways of living forcefully on everyone else. But, it is fair to question.

A great many of us were born into a very large tribe that believes human beings have immortal souls which survive after our bodies die. As children we may have wondered where our souls go after we die. Many of us were socialized to believe that the souls of good people are rewarded while the souls of evil people are punished. We may have been taught that there were places called Heaven and Hell, although nobody knew where those places were in the map of the universe. And, as children, many of us trusted and believed.

Most of our tribe conceived of our soul as our conscious mind and individual personality. Post-mortem reward or punishment makes no sense unless it can be experienced, which implies a conscious mind. And since the rewards and punishments are allotted to each individual based on how they lived their bodily lives, the implication is that our souls are not absorbed into one massive amalgam or group mind, but rather endure as individual persons.

As we matured more questions may have come to mind. We may have wondered how our consciousness could endure after the brain died. Since bodies suffer illness, injury and the deterioration of aging, many of us wondered how long souls might endure once freed. Our tribe's answer is that souls are immortal. They endure forever. That may be absolutely wonderful for a person who is mentally healthy. But it seems unfair to think of the soul of an Alzheimer's victim enduring for eternity. Who would that person be? The damaged and demented personality they were at the end of their lives? Or would the soul be the person who they had been before ravaged by disease? We cannot jump to the conclusion that the soul will revert to its healthy younger self. But if we do, then we open the door to asking whether all of us can elect, after we die, to be the person we were at some earlier time in our life. If not, why not? If so, can we really go backward and think as we once thought, as if the rest of our lives had never happened? And what about the soul of a child who dies, does it ever mature to the fullness of what it would be as a mature adult?

As we matured other questions may have arisen. For example, we might wonder whether the souls of dead people can communicate with one another. Communication as we know it requires body parts. But souls not only have no voice and no hands with which to generate language, they have no eyes, no ears, nothing with which to perceive language. And souls have no brains with which to make meaning or achieve understanding. It would be torture to suffer an eternity unable to communicate. Eternal solitary confinement? A ticket to insanity.

Okay, we'll stop. You get the point. A lot of what we were taught as children was important guidance for how to live an ethical and productive life. But some of our unexamined metaphysical ideas planted in our brains during childhood may not be as sensible as they seemed to us as children. Tempted as we are to quote Socrates' comments about the unexamined life, we have decided to quote another member of our ancient tribe.

"When I was a child, I spoke and thought and reasoned as a child. But when I grew up, I put away childish things." First Letter of Paul to the Corinthians 13:11

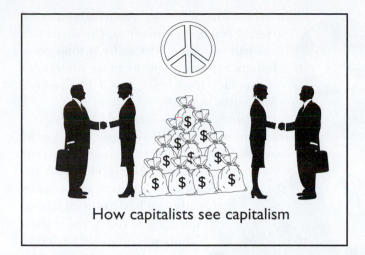

How capitalists see capitalism

How libertarians and socialists see capitalism

How socialists see socialism

How capitalists and libertarians see socialism

How libertarians see libertarianism

How socialists and capitalists see libertarianism

Why do we hold our own ideology in high esteem, but have only negative opinions about the competition?

surprisingly, people who are deeply convinced that their way is "the only right way" often seek to change or to destroy those institutions and people who threaten "the only right way." History offers many examples: the Christian Crusaders, the Taliban, the Nazis, the Stalinists, the Klan, racists, zealots, fanatical terrorists, true-believers, suicide bombers, and bigots of all stripes, shapes, and stenches who use ideological reasoning to motivate their followers and try to destroy those who disagree.

The benefits and risks of ideological thinking revolve around the power of ideologies to structure our individual and collective way of seeing the world. In the middle of the twentieth century many Americans saw the world as a place of conflict between two global powers, the United States and the Soviet Union, each dominated by opposing ideologies: constitutional democracy and communism. The film *Good Night and Good Luck* shows what can happen when unscrupulous ideological bullies, like Senator Joseph McCarthy, gain political power. True, McCarthy regarded himself as doing battle against the communists, who were regarded as ideologues and enemies of the United States. Although his goal may have been consistent with the defense of the rule of law and individual freedom, McCarthy's methods turned out to violate those very ideals.

It takes courage to challenge powerful people who are using their ideological stance to cause harm. That decision is never an easy one, because there is always the risk that you and yours will be targeted. One of the scenes in the film *Good Night and Good Luck* reenacts a conversation as it might have occurred at CBS when the journalists Edward R. Murrow and Fred Friendly decided to take on Senator Joseph McCarthy. The film includes actual footage of the

David Strathairn received an Oscar nomination for his portrayal of the courageous, truth-seeking journalist Edward R. Morrow in *Good Night and Good Luck*.

Senator bullying witnesses who have been called to testify before his committee. The whole film is worth watching. McCarthy is long gone. But not his tactics. How can we protect our democracy from being twisted by today's ideological bullies?

Hundreds of years ago, the English statesman and philosopher John Locke described the habit of talking and listening only to those who agreed with the beliefs and opinions one already holds as a basic type of flawed thinking.[17] Today the critical thinking community refers to the habit first described by Locke as a failure of courageous truth-seeking. James Howard Griffin's extraordinary book, *Black Like Me*,[18] describes the power of ideologies to shape our perceptions of reality. In that book, he tells about his life-shaping experiences as a white man living as a black man in America's deep South in the late 1950s. There are many other powerful examples in literature and film that help us simulate what the world is like from another's perspective. Trying to see the world through the eyes of another is a valuable way of expanding our sensitivities and monitoring our tendency to accept beliefs uncritically.

Summing up this chapter,

ideological reasoning begins with our deeply held convictions and core values. From these generalizations we reason, top down, to specific implications about how we should live and what to think. Ideological reasoning is deductive in character, meaning that the conclusions of ideological arguments are intended to be taken as valid. Ideological premises are taken as axiomatic, meaning they are our starting points—the givens. The argument maker takes the ideology to be true more or less on faith. Ideological reasoning is important and useful because it shapes our community, our culture, and our individual identities. It guides our thinking on policy questions and reflects our value judgments.

It helps us know what we should think when we do not have the time or the expertise to address new questions on our own. The risks associated with ideological reasoning are as great as the benefits. On close examination, ideological arguments often fail the Test of the Truthfulness of the Premises. Because strong convictions may be mistaken, we can easily find ourselves advocating and defending views that are ill-conceived and harmful. History shows the dangers of ideological reasoning though the wars, genocides, and human misery caused by ideologues and their followers. Ideologically driven extremists will not only fight for their beliefs, they will kill for them.

Key Concept

ideological reasoning (or **top-down thinking**) is the process of thinking that begins with abstractions or generalizations that express one's core beliefs, concepts, values, or principles and proceeds to reason top down to specific applications. Ideological reasoning is deductive and axiomatic. The argument maker takes the ideological premises on faith.

Applications

Reflective Log

A military draft: A nation can legislate mandatory service in the armed forces. Known as "the draft," the United States used forced conscription to build the armies it needed to fight World War II, the Korean War, and the Vietnam War. If drafted, a person must leave his or her school, job, and family to serve for a specified period of time, typically two years, in the armed forces. Draftees become soldiers. And some soldiers give their lives in combat. Those who try to escape their duties, known as "draft dodgers" are prosecuted and imprisoned. Assume that the nation's military leaders evaluate the readiness of the armed forces and determine that the national defense requires that a military draft should be established now. Assume that men and women between the ages of 18 and 35 will be subject to the draft as recommended to the President and the Congress. Assume that the proposal to institute a draft is going to be taken up by Congress next week and that you have the opportunity to offer your advice to your state's representatives and senators. Although the nation may or may not be at war at the moment when the legislation is being considered, it is reasonable to assume that the nation could be at war at some point in the future. Considering what you know about the nation, its ideological convictions, and its history, what would you recommend and why? Assume that you are the right age to be drafted into the military and that you are otherwise fully qualified and eligible to serve. That is, assume that whatever law is passed, if there is a draft, you may be one of the people conscripted to serve.

Individual Exercises

Evaluating our own convictions: All of us have beliefs that we hold with such conviction that they might be considered "immune" from being proven wrong, at least in our own minds. But a strong conviction might still be mistaken. Strong critical thinkers strive to protect themselves from the error of being strongly committed to mistaken beliefs. Critical thinkers ask themselves what evidence or arguments might be developed that should lead reasonable, fair-minded people to realize that some of their strongly held opinions are mistaken. Or, they ask what possible life experience might come along to dislodge the dominance structuring that they have built in their minds to prop up a mistaken belief. This five-step exercise invites you to ask yourself these same questions relative to your beliefs about each of the statements listed below. Some of the statements address serious topics; others address matters that may not be of great concern to you. But, whether the issue is profound or trivial, we can find ourselves holding beliefs with unwarranted conviction. And that is something that strong critical thinkers seek to avoid. This exercise unfolds in five steps.

Step 1: Mark "True," "False," or "Uncertain" by each statement below to reflect your current opinion about each.

1. Same-sex couples make excellent parents.

2. America is the greatest nation on earth.

3. There would be fewer homicides if more people owned guns.

4. Treating others as we would wish to be treated is the most important ethical principle.

5. Like Australia, our country should decriminalize and regulate prostitution.

6. The good of the many is more important than the good of the one.

7. Teaching children to think for themselves undermines parental authority.

8. Given that the life on earth has survived five mass extinction events, we should repeal the Endangered Species Act.

9. Western education is evil.

10. Lazy people don't deserve handouts.

11. Pets have rights, just like people do.

12. You can accomplish more if you are feared than if you are loved.

13. Climate change is real, but it is not all bad.

14. There was a time when dinosaurs and human beings inhabited the earth together.

15. The K-12 Common Core is dangerous because it may teach children to think for themselves.

16. Women must cover their heads and bodies in public places.

17. Paranormal psychic phenomena are real.

18. Ghosts, the spirits of the dead can return to (haunt) certain places and times.

19. Democracy is the best form of government ever invented.

20. God is love.

21. Humans, like other animals, are simply elements in the natural world.[19]

22. Generosity of spirit engenders generosity in return.

23. The term *person* or *persons* includes every human being from the moment of fertilization, cloning or the functional equivalent thereof.[20]

24. If the United States was founded by Christian people, then it must be a Christian nation.

25. Conscientious stupidity is more debilitating to a democracy than public cynicism.

Step 2: Having asserted your opinion about each statement, reflect on the risks associated with dominance structuring and create some mental space for yourself so that you can complete this exercise with your habits of truth-seeking, open-mindedness, and objectivity fully engaged.

Step 3: Looking only at the ones you marked "True," write down what evidence or arguments you would accept as proof that each statement is *false*. If no possible evidence or argument could persuade you that the statement is false, is there any experience you could imagine that would lead you to abandon your commitment to the truth of that statement?

Step 4: Looking only at those that you marked "False," write down what evidence or arguments you would accept as proof that each statement is *true*. If no possible evidence or argument could persuade you that the statement is true, is there any experience you could imagine that would lead you to abandon your commitment to the falsehood of that statement?

Step 5: Looking now only at the statements that you marked "Uncertain," write down the process you could use to gather information and make an informed, fair-minded, and reasoned judgment about what to believe with regard to the truth or falsity of that statement. That is, how would you use your critical thinking skills and habits of mind to make that purposeful reflective judgment?

When ideologies clash—Money: In the film *Capitalism: A Love Story*, writer Michael Moore strongly suggests that contemporary American Capitalism is at odds with Christianity, Socialism, and Democracy. Whatever your personal beliefs, these four ideologies are, in fact, influencing your life, your leaders, and the laws by which we live. We recommend you view the film as part of your effort to learn about these major ideologies. But, keeping an open mind, do not limit your learning to one filmmaker's interpretation of these four ideologies. Develop a *well-reasoned and factually informed* analysis of each. In light of your learning and in light of the actual facts as can be demonstrated by trustworthy scientific studies, evaluate the claim that contemporary American Capitalism is at odds with Democracy, Christianity, and Socialism. If it is your view that it is at odds with any one of them (and it cannot be compatible with all of them because of the differences between the three), then how should we reconcile these ideological conflicts in real life—that is, what government policies and personal practices would be the wisest to pursue?

When ideologies clash—God: Bill Maher's film, *Religulous*, features interviews with several believers representing several different major world religions. The film, a comedic documentary about a serious subject, challenges viewers to examine the assumptions behind their own beliefs. The film culminates in the claim that today's conflicting religious ideologies clash so violently that they could trigger global nuclear war. Map the reasons developed throughout the film, which support that dire warning. Remember that the reasons may be demonstrated more than spoken, for example, that in spite of their claims to be peace loving, some religious leaders treat non-believers as if they deserved to be purged from the planet. Evaluate the film's major argument using the criteria developed in Chapter 7. Given that human nature has not changed much in 100 years, today are we as much at risk of global ideological war as were the people of the twentieth century?

SHARED RESPONSE

Social Media–Asset or Liability?

Is today's glorious abundance of social and mainstream media—including television, print, Web, and social networking—a net benefit for reasoned public discourse and a flourishing democracy, or a net liability? This surprisingly complex question drives Season 3 of the celebrated HBO series *The Newsroom*. When you give your response, be sure to provide your reason(s), not just your opinion. And, comment respectfully on the reasons others offer.

Group Exercises

Discussion—What ideals would you go to war to defend? Throughout history people have gone to war. On many occasions, religious ideologies, political ideologies, or economic ideologies have been at the root of those conflicts. The Crusades, World War II, and the American Civil War might be seen as examples of such conflicts, at least in the minds of some leaders and some combatants; ideological reasoning played a major role in explaining why each war was unavoidably necessary. Discuss with your peers the ideological beliefs and core values that, in your considered judgment, would make war unavoidably necessary. Beyond self-defense and the defense of the lives of your family and other members of your community, are there principles, fundamental beliefs, and core values worthwhile to defend with your life and to protect the lives of those you love by waging war? Is freedom worthwhile? Is democracy? Would you go to war to end slavery, to prevent genocide, to free children from forced labor, to rescue fellow citizens from illegal detention in a foreign country, to protect commercial shipping on the high seas, or to save whales from being slaughtered for human food? Would you fight to regain your homeland, or to gain access to clean water? Would you go to war to free your ethnic group from an oppressor nation? If none of these is a worthwhile endeavor to you, is there anything that you personally would go to war to defend or to protect? Remember that whatever your group's answer might be, you should expect that your answer works in reverse as well. That means that you should expect others to do no more and no less, should they perceive your behavior as demanding from them an identical bellicose response. Be prepared to give the very best reasons possible for either the view that war would be the appropriate response of last resort in a given situation or that war is never an appropriate response no matter what the situation. When considering the "no matter what" alternative, be sure to include in your reflections "self-defense and the defense of the lives of your family and other members of your community."

Discussion—Why do we believe what we believe? Discuss each statement or set of statements below in turn and, as a group, examine as objectively as possible the reasons why the statement or set of statements may be true or may be false.

1. Everyone believes in the same God, just by different names.

2. Given what we now know, chimpanzees should be accorded the same rights as humans.

3. Life is fundamentally unfair.

4. There is no reasonable possibility of solving the problem of world hunger in the next 50 years.

5. Over 2 million aliens, originally from some other planet, are being secretly held in a concentration camp 200 kilometers outside Johannesburg, South Africa.[21]

6. Before today's 20 year olds reach retirement age, humans will have made it impossible for our species to live on earth.

7. When humans and machines elegantly merge, a singularity will pour forth, and it will bring to an end the ravages of old age, illness, and perhaps even death.[22]

8. If the sugar lobby has its way, 90 percent of all Americans will be obese by the year 2050.

9. A large middle class provides social stability not found in countries where there are only the very rich and the very poor.

10. And now these three remain: faith, hope, and love. But the greatest of these is love.[23]

Project—Conflicting principles and conflicting positions: Select one of the following conflicts and prepare a well-researched report on the core beliefs, values, and assumptions that fuel each side in the dispute:

1. The conflict between Israel and Palestine in the Middle East.

2. The conflict over fracking as a method of extracting petroleum.

3. The conflict between Libertarianism and Socialism.

4. The conflict over immigration reform in the United States.

5. The conflict between religion and atheism.

Chapter 14
Empirical Reasoning

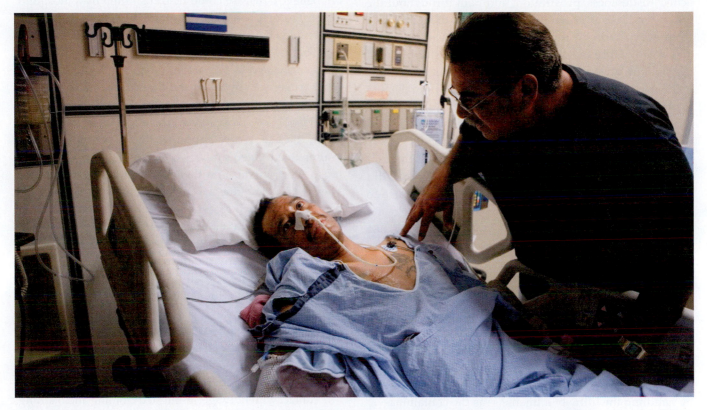

Sadly, Yellow Fever claimed the life of Javier Garcia in California in 2007. But there was no epidemic, no panic in the streets, no sense of being out of control. Contrast that with what happened when Yellow Fever ravaged North and Central America in the nineteenth century killing tens of thousands each year. Using empirical reasoning, we discovered how to control the spread of this disease and how to care for those who become infected. The same for tuberculosis, the flu, HIV/AIDS, and Ebola. Empirical reasoning is the only effective tool our species has for explaining, predicting, and controlling natural phenomena.

HOW can we recognize empirical reasoning?

WHAT are the steps in conducting an investigation scientifically?

WHAT are the benefits and risks of empirical reasoning?

 ## Learning Outcomes

14.1 Explain empirical reasoning and how it works as a self-corrective process.

14.2 Apply empirical reasoning correctly.

14.3 Describe the uses, benefits, and risks of empirical reasoning.

"Yellow fever!" The cry struck dread and panic into the hearts of the residents of port cities from New Orleans to Philadelphia during the eighteenth and nineteenth centuries. Epidemics of yellow fever ravaged the population. Its symptoms include nausea and vomiting, chills, headaches, restlessness, prostration, and pain throughout the body. Victims suffer irregular fever, jaundice, bleeding from every bodily orifice, delirium, convulsions, coma, and death.[1] Once the disease took hold of a city it spread throughout, mysteriously killing some but not others. The epidemics raged, and tens of thousands died until the first frosts of late autumn.

Called "Yellow Jack," no one knew where the disease came from, how to treat it, or how to stop its spread. Quarantines did not work. Closing doors and windows did not work. Burning tar to "disturb the miasma" did not work. The disease seemed to jump from house to house through the city, afflicting men and women, old and young, black and white, prosperous and poor.[2] People fled cities by the thousands in fear. Commerce collapsed; cities declared bankruptcy. Thinking it was a Divine plague, religious leaders advocated moral reform and closing dance halls. Physicians, not knowing any better, treated the sick with purging and bleeding. Nurses and family members tried to ease the pain, to comfort, and to console. Many, but not all, of those physicians, ministers, nurses, and family members contracted the illness themselves. Why? Was it by touching the sick person, by breathing the same air, by handling the filthy bed linens? Was the contamination in the blood, the feces, the food, the furniture, the clothing, or the dying person's breath? Nobody knew. But unless someone could figure out exactly how the disease was transmitted, there would be no hope of containing or controlling it.

In the late 1870s a Cuban physician, Carlos Juan Finley, presented a theory about the cause of the disease. He hypothesized that the dreaded fever, which annually plagued his homeland, was carried from person to person by, of all things, a mosquito.

He had gathered empirical data and mapped the locations where the mosquito was prevalent and where the fever occurred. Looking at the two maps, he realized that the locations overlapped. He saw the correlation. But a correlation is not a cause, and the physicians of his day did not believe a disease could be transmitted by a mosquito. When Finley presented his work in 1881 at a scientific meeting in Havana, he was completely ignored.

That is, until 1900. That year the U.S. Army marched into Panama and faced the same enemy that had destroyed other armies sent by Spain and France. The generals knew that the U.S. troops being sent to Panama risked annihilation by Yellow Jack. To lead the effort to combat yellow fever, the U.S. Army appointed a young major named Walter Reed. Reed and his colleagues thought Finley's mosquito transmission theory might have some value. They worked to refine the theory, but in October 1900 there had been only two cases to examine. Without more data, Reed's group could not rule out other possible causes. The most widely accepted explanation at the time was that germs transmitted by the filthy clothing and bedding of yellow fever victims caused the epidemic. The *Washington Post* labeled Reed's ideas about mosquitoes "silly and nonsensical."

To test his hypothesis that mosquitoes were the cause, Reed needed to create an experiment that would show two things: First, that the disease was transmitted by contaminated mosquitoes and, second, that it was not transmitted by contact with filthy, germ-infested clothing and bedding.

To obtain the volunteer human subjects his experiment would require, he offered each willing person $100 in gold. At a remote location known as Camp Lazear, Reed set up two identical huts and divided the volunteers randomly, sending some to live for several days in Hut #1 and others to live for several days in Hut #2. Both huts were screened to prevent the entry of any mosquitoes. Hut #1 was loaded with filthy clothing and bedding in which yellow fever victims had slept, bled, vomited, and died. No one in Hut #1 became sick with yellow fever.

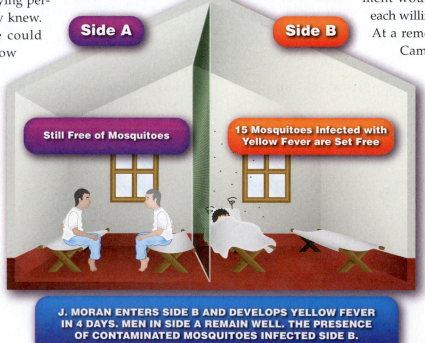

Side A — Still Free of Mosquitoes

Side B — 15 Mosquitoes Infected with Yellow Fever are Set Free

J. MORAN ENTERS SIDE B AND DEVELOPS YELLOW FEVER IN 4 DAYS. MEN IN SIDE A REMAIN WELL. THE PRESENCE OF CONTAMINATED MOSQUITOES INFECTED SIDE B.

Interior of Walter Reed's experimental Hut #2. Why is there a screen dividing the hut into two chambers, A and B?

Hut #2 was divided into two chambers by a screen that permitted the air to circulate between the two chambers. Infected mosquitoes were released into one side but not the other. As predicted, only the volunteers in the chamber where the infected mosquitoes had been released became ill. None of the other volunteers in Hut #2's other chamber contracted yellow fever, even though they were breathing the same air as the sick volunteers.

Walter Reed was able to design a test that demonstrated that a widely held idea was probably false and that another idea (mosquitoes can bring sickness and death to humans) must be regarded as a vital new insight. It was an insight of great importance to public health. www.pbs.org offers extensive details about the objective, preparation, protocol, data, and conclusions from Walter Reed's classic use of empirical reasoning in his Camp Lazear experiment.[3]

> "I think science and biology is tremendously exciting, as you can find so many fascinating things—and it gets more and more fascinating."
>
> Elizabeth Blackburn, 2009
> Nobel Laureate[4]

14.1 Recognizing Empirical Reasoning

Our capacity to anticipate what comes next and then to devise ways to affect the outcomes of events and processes is absolutely fundamental to our survival as a species and to our current planetary dominance. We look for cause-and-effect relationships to explain, and hence to predict and control. The opening sequence of classic film *2001: A Space Odyssey*[5] dramatizes the basic idea: You hit your rival over the head hard enough and he dies! But your arm is not long enough and your fist is not hard enough, so you make a tool, a club, to get the job done. The film suggests

This scene from *2001 A Space Odyssey* depicts the dawn of tool-making as the primate realizes a leg bone can become a weapon.

that progress from the bone used as a club to interplanetary space travel is simply a matter of filling in the blanks.[6]

Tens of thousands of years later we are still working on filling in those blanks. Today our species is using the map of the human genome and research on gene expression to mount a genetic counterattack on diseases like cancer. Advances gained through empirical reasoning permit us to ask ourselves questions that eclipse the understanding of scientists working in Reed's or Finley's day. What makes a cancerous cell's DNA express itself in different ways at different points in the tumor's growth? What are the mechanisms that turn the protein receptors off and on and, hence, make one kind of therapy effective and another ineffective at different points along the way?

The correct answers to these questions and to others like them come only as the fruit of empirical arguments. Investigators, using the same kind of reasoning that Reed and Finley used, begin with a theory about how or why something happens in the natural world. They form a testable hypothesis, gather data by observation and experimentation, and use those data to evaluate their hypothesis. Empirical investigations are often designed to see whether a hypothesis can be disconfirmed. By showing how our understandings are mistaken, we reveal the limits of our current understanding and are best positioned to refine our explanations and make more precise predictions. If we assume that two things are at best randomly related, like the habitat of a given species of mosquito and the incidences of yellow fever, but then learn that the data show we are mistaken about that, we can then refine our ideas. We can note that there is a correlation. And, noting that, we can begin to investigate empirically just exactly what that correlation might mean for purposes of explaining, predicting, or controlling the occurrences of the dreaded disease. In this chapter, we will explore this kind of "bottom up" thinking, known as empirical reasoning. Our purpose in this chapter is to achieve a solid and detailed understanding of scientific empirical reasoning. Science is a broad topic and covers a wide range of disciplines. Critical thinking in the social sciences and critical thinking in the natural sciences delve into the questions and research approaches that characterize each.

Characteristics of Empirical Reasoning

Empirical reasoning is *inductive in character, open to self-corrective revision*, and *the argument makers take their empirical premises to be true on the basis of interpersonally verifiable experience*. Thus empirical reasoning contrasts with ideological reasoning on all three key characteristics. Recall that in Chapter 13 we described ideological reasoning as deductive in character, axiomatic, and taken on faith.

EMPIRICAL REASONING IS INDUCTIVE Describing scientific investigations as inductive in character means that the conclusions reached are probabilistic. Scientists would be the first to insist on this. They strive to remain open to the possibility that the conclusions they reach based on empirical reasoning might need to change! Recall our discussion of coincidences, correlations, and causes in "Warranted Inferences," Chapter 9. We noted there that the analytical and inferential tools used in empirical reasoning, like statistical tests, afford confidence levels that approach 1 in 100 or 1 in 1,000. But even with such high levels of confidence, the conclusions drawn remain probabilistic. Scientists use observations and statistical analyses to draw warranted inferences with varying levels of confidence. The inferences drawn remain probabilistic even when our statistical analyses permit us to have very high levels of confidence such as only 1 chance of error in 10,000.[7] Although it turned out that Finley was right about the mosquito being the vector that transmitted the yellow fever virus from one person to another, he *might* have been wrong. His correlations that mapped the mosquito's habitat and the areas where the disease was found may have been correct, but there just might have been some third factor he had overlooked.

> "The kernel of scientific outlook is a thing so simple, so obvious, so seemingly trivial, that the mention of it may almost excite derision. The kernel of scientific outlook is the refusal to regard our own desires, tastes, and interests as affording a key to the understanding of the world."
>
> Bertrand Russell[8]

EMPIRICAL REASONING IS SELF-CORRECTIVE   The second important feature of empirical reasoning, namely that it is self-corrective, is vital to the progress made using investigative methods. Crime dramas like *CSI* and *Law & Order* unfold like mystery novels. They reveal clues and bits of information along the way so that the viewer can form hypotheses about "who done it." Clever writers arrange the story so that the criminal's identity is concealed as long as possible. But the writers organize the flow of information to the viewer so that various characters can be ruled out as the possible criminal. The viewer then revises his or her theory of the crime so that it explains all the data, old and new. The process of scientific inquiry is similar, except that there is nobody orchestrating the moment at which the data will be made known to the investigating researcher. The researcher is responsible for devising the means to acquire the kind of data that will be relevant and revise his or her hypothesis, if necessary, as new information is gained.[9] To answer empirical research questions, investigators examine data gathered using instruments specifically designed to find the kinds of data that they expect might exist. We would not have invented the microscope had we not thought that perhaps there were important things to learn by looking at objects in more detail than the unaided human eye can reveal.

> "One is always a long way from solving a problem until one actually has the answer."
>
> Stephen Hawking, Physicist[10]

EMPIRICAL REASONING IS OPEN TO INDEPENDENT VERIFICATION   A third feature of empirical reasoning is that premises that report data or the results of statistical tests are open to scrutiny and independent verification by the entire scientific community. Investigatory inquiry is a community activity. Other scientists are not only welcome, but they are encouraged to gather additional data, to re-create experiments, and to recalculate statistical findings. The observations, databases, and findings scientists use and report are subjected to the scrutiny of other investigators. Replication studies (do overs) are used to verify that the observations and findings reported by the original scientist can be duplicated by other scientists working independently. If we were to replicate today the experiment Reed conducted in 1900, we should expect to find, as he did, that the only people who become infected are those who are exposed to yellow fever by the infected mosquitoes. Our belief in the truth of the premises, observations, and findings, does not depend on whether we have faith and trust in Reed. *Science is not a matter of faith in the word of others*. Science is based on the fact that if others conducted the same experiments, they would get

Forensic scientists use empirical reasoning to gather evidence that can exonerate or convict.

Empirical Reasoning or Bottom-Up Thinking

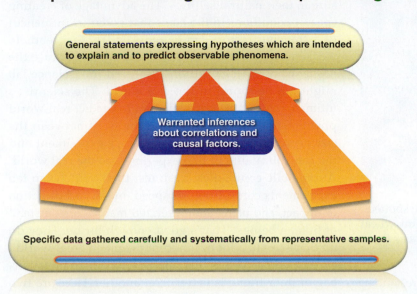

General statements expressing hypotheses which are intended to explain and to predict observable phenomena.

Warranted inferences about correlations and causal factors.

Specific data gathered carefully and systematically from representative samples.

is very probably false, demands that a curious investigator inquire next whether the sugar might be a contributing factor to the diabetes. An empirically testable hypothesis that two phenomena are entirely unrelated except perhaps by random chance is known as a **null hypothesis**. Null hypotheses not only invite further inquiry if they are shown to most probably be false, they help the investigators maintain a level of objectivity during their work. Science is not about trying to confirm pet theories. Instead of going all macho about how using torture on prisoners of war is an effective way of gaining useful information about the enemy, it is wiser to first test that empirically. The null hypothesis might be stated this way, "Torturing prisoners does not produce reliable intelligence."[12]

the same results. The commitment of the scientific community to make the arguments, databases, analyses, and other aspects of the empirical reasoning process open to others for independent verification can lead to collaborations that advance our scientific understanding of phenomena. For example, unprecedented advances in Alzheimer's research have been achieved because of a 2003 agreement between The National Institutes of Health, the Food and Drug Administration, as well as industry, university, and nonprofit researchers to combine their independent efforts into a shared database that the Alzheimer's research community could access.[11]

Hypotheses, Conditions, and Measurable Manifestations

An empirical investigation begins with a hypothesis. The hypothesis often can be expressed as a supposition, such as "If things of a certain kind are placed under certain conditions, then we will be able to observe certain phenomena." Or a hypothesis can be expressed as a general statement: "Certain kinds of objects behave in certain ways under certain conditions."

Hypotheses are often expressed as negatives, asserting that two phenomena are not connected. If scientists can show with a high degree of confidence that a negative hypothesis is false, the critical thinking habit of inquisitiveness impels us to figure out how they are connected. For example, "There is no connection between the percent of refined sugar in children's diets and the occurrences of childhood Type 2 diabetes." Discovering that the data establish that the hypothesis

"We thought there might be some relationship between telomerase, telomere length and the survival of stem cells, but it was really exciting to see it."

Carol Greider, 2009 Nobel Laureate[13]

Here are some example hypotheses. Some are null hypotheses; others assert there is a relationship.

- If the *Salmonella* bacterium is exposed to temperatures greater than 140 degrees Centigrade for more than 30 seconds, nothing will happen. (Evidence shows that the Salmonella bacterium will die.)

- Married couples who experience unanticipated severe financial problems will experience no changes in their relationship. (Evidence shows they will likely experience more anger and fight more than they did prior to their financial problems.)

- The reflexes of a person who drives a motor vehicle for five or more hours without a rest period will have deteriorated by 30 percent or more as compared to his or her reflexes after only one to four hours of driving.[14]

- In our new program, we train sixth graders to tutor third graders in reading and math. Our hypothesis is that the test scores of the sixth graders and the third graders will be significantly higher than the scores of their peers who were not involved in this tutoring program.

- The majority of Silicon Valley start-up tech companies spend all their investment capital before their technology product is ready to bring to market.

"Gluten Free" is selling so well now that we have spotted it on soft drink cans. Did anyone ever actually think wheat was an ingredient in diet cola? Apparently so. Check the results of searching "gluten free diet cola."

- Gluten-free is really big right now. So, if our restaurant advertises that our menu offers several gluten free selections, we will see an increase in our lunchtime business.

Arguments expressing empirical reasoning include statements describing the particular states of affairs that the researchers strive to create experimentally or to measure in their natural settings. The advantage of creating specific conditions in the lab is that potential influences of extraneous factors can be reduced. Yet that tends to weaken the *generalizability* of the findings because the highly controlled conditions achieved in a science lab might not be found in the real world. The scientist's ultimate purpose is to explain and to predict real-world phenomena. There is always a trade-off between the strict controls possible in a laboratory experiment and the generalizability of that experiment to the real world. Automobile companies crash test their vehicles in lab experiments controlling for speed, mass, and direction of impact, and using computerized mannequins instead of human beings. That's good enough for us. They do not have to kill a lot of innocent people in "real-world" experiments to prove that one way of designing an airbag or door frame is better than another. Here are two examples in which the investigators note the difference between the controlled experimental environment and the real world. Under the circumstances, trade-offs must be made.

THINKING CRITICALLY

Measurable Manifestations

The six example hypotheses above illustrate measurable manifestations of hypotheses in six different subject areas: biology, psychology, human performance, education, economics, and marketing. Here are five more examples that are only partially completed. Please complete each one by expressing one or more measurable manifestations of the hypothesis proposed. Add additional statements that clarify or expand upon the descriptions of the exact conditions under which the behavioral manifestations you predict will occur. Explain, in your own words, why the clarifications or expanded descriptions are helpful.

- If we apply a solution made up of water and laundry bleach to mold growing on the surface of a glass dish, then the mold, which is a fungus, will _____.

- In our experimental teacher training program, we have each college student spend a semester as a math and science tutor for seventh or eighth grade students. Our regular teacher training program does not include the semester tutoring. Our hypothesis is that the college students in our experimental program will _____ as compared to the students in our regular program.

- One of the sources of energy consumption is household electricity usage. Electricity is used to heat water, cook or refrigerate food, and to operate lights and consumer appliances. LED bulbs last many times longer than comparable incandescent or florescent bulbs, and require far less energy. So, we can predict that if the average consumer were to replace household light bulbs with LED bulbs, he or she would save _____.

- Fashion magazine models, many of whom are teenagers, risk malnourishment and severe eating disorders. If the fashion industry were to adopt mandatory body mass requirements to protect the health of these people,

_____.

- Domestic dogs, like their pack animal ancestors, behave in accord with a social hierarchy. The lesser animals in a pack will follow the lead of the dominant animal. Obedience and subservience are expected, and violation of the rule of the pack is punished. We can expect that if dog owners displayed more _____, then their pet dogs would _____.

- Rather than risk accidents on the open road where our subjects and other people as well might be injured or killed, we can check the reflexes of men and women of different ages by having them drive on a closed track in dry weather. Of course, driving on a closed track in dry weather is dull as compared to driving on the open road under differing weather and traffic conditions.

- If we divide the sixth graders and third graders into two groups each, we can train one group of sixth graders to tutor one group of third graders. If we ensure that all other known relevant factors are held constant (e.g., that otherwise they receive instruction in the same subjects by equally competent teachers in identical learning environments), then we should see statistically significantly higher test scores for the experimental group students [third graders who were tutored and their sixth grade tutors] as compared to the control group students [third graders who were not tutored and sixth graders not in the tutoring program]. But how can we ensure that the other known relevant factors are held constant?

> "Measure what is measurable, and make measurable what is not so."
>
> Galileo Galilei[15]

14.2 Conducting an Investigation Scientifically

There are many steps involved in investigating an empirical question logically, systematically, and in a way that allows others in the scientific and professional community to verify the results through replication. Any place along the way an investigator can introduce error through technical, conceptual, methodological, or reasoning mistakes. And yet, because the process can be monitored and corrected by the investigator or others on the research team, science is exceptionally robust from the perspective of the reasoning to be used. All our critical thinking skills and habits of mind are engaged when we set out to determine, using empirical reasoning, what we should believe. And as in Reed's situation, it turns out that a measure of cleverness and bit of creativity are needed just to figure out how to test one's hypothesis.

Perhaps the First Recorded Empirical Investigation

A driving sense of scientific curiosity impelled the Head Librarian of Alexandria in North Africa to wonder how to explain this extraordinary observation: on one day each

At high noon on June 21, the sun casts no shadows down the walls of this well. But it casts shadows at other places at that same date and time. Eratosthenes asked, "Why?" 2,200 years ago.

year, June 21, at noon in a city 800 kilometers to the south, the sun cast no shadows. "Would I see this same lack of shadow everywhere?" To approach an answer to this question, the librarian first had to ask the question with more specific detail. "Do sticks, towers, columns, and obelisks cast shadows in Alexandria at noon on the summer solstice?" wondered that librarian. He experimented and observed that they do. "But how is that possible?" And then he thought of an explanation: "Perhaps the Earth is not flat, but curved." His next question was how to test that hypothesis.

That librarian, whose name was Eratosthenes, was a person of extraordinary accomplishment and learning. Although 2,200 years ago science as we know it did not yet exist, inference, analysis, and truth-seeking were alive and well in Egypt and its greatest center of learning, Alexandria. Eratosthenes drew the inference that the only way that there could be a shadow in the one city and not in the other is if the Earth were curved, instead of flat. He needed more data to either disconfirm his idea that the Earth was curved or to find evidence that supported his insight. It was easy to measure the length of the shadows in Alexandria at the appointed date and time. But, without any other way to measure the distance, Eratosthenes had to hire a man to pace out the exact distance between Alexandria and the city to the south where the sun cast no shadows on June 21 at noon. Eratosthenes needed that data point to calculate the curvature of the Earth. Then by using geometry (thank you, Euclid), he could estimate the Earth's circumference. Search and watch episode 1 of the classic 1980 Carl Sagan original *Cosmos* series. (Search "Shores of a Cosmic Ocean" "Eratosthenes" and "Carl Sagan.") About 31 minutes into the episode Carl Sagan explains clearly the empirical reasoning Eratosthenes used. Eratosthenes was able to infer that the Earth was approximately 40,000 kilometers in circumference, an amazingly accurate calculation. (Oh, and for some reason, we forgot and then needed to rediscover more than a millennium and a half later that the world was round. Oops! Our bad!)

Just Because the Null Is False Does Not Make the Opposite True

Normally, science proceeds by ruling things out. The scientific process incrementally refines our understanding of the universe. By disconfirming the null hypothesis ("A is not related to B.") and by assuming that *every other theory, measurement, contextual variable, and precondition is true and accurate*, we infer that there is some relationship between A and B. The next step, normally, is to refine our understandings of A and/or B so that we can make another null hypothesis involving the refined concept(s) and see if we can then experimentally disconfirm that one.

But look at all the things scientists must assume are just fine: data generation and data gathering conditions, theories about what might possibly be relevant to observe, various measurement strategies, the quality of the measurement instrumentation, and the statistical procedures for handling and for analyzing data once they are collected. Scientists do trust those things. But they also know that each one of them was itself the object of empirical investigation at one time or another. Because they understand all these factors must be assumed to be true in order to test a given hypothesis, careful scientists avoid saying "X is *certainly* true." They might say, "X is true to a scientific certainty," but that means that we should hold an extremely high level of confidence in X. There should be no reasonable doubt about X. But, as scientists using empirical reasoning we are not justified in saying "Ah look, we disconfirmed the null hypothesis. So its opposite must be true."

True example: "We have 40 years of data across multiple studies that confirm the positive correlation between taking a course in critical thinking and improvements in the students' pretest to posttest critical thinking skills scores. It would be a mistake, therefore, all things being equal, to say that growth in critical thinking and taking a course in critical thinking are unrelated." The null hypothesis is false. Does that mean, therefore, that taking a critical thinking course causes students to become more skilled at critical thinking and more motivated to use those skills? No, that jump from "A is not unrelated to B" to "A causes B" assumes too many things. And, even if the course were a contributing factor, it is almost always an indication of a reasoning error when we hear that any given event is attributed to one and only one cause.

But, maybe it is not the course at all, but the teaching methods that result in the perceived growth. Or maybe the students grew in skills or mindset simply because they were in school and it was the net effect of several educational experiences. Or perhaps they just tried harder on the posttest. Maybe it was something about the way the students studied, in teams rather than individually perhaps, that produced the effect. Or maybe the apparent growth will not manifest itself when the students have to solve problems or make decisions beyond the classroom. That said, if you asked us whether we think that taking a good critical thinking course can contribute meaningfully and measurably to improvements in students' critical thinking, our answer would be that we are very highly confident, based on all the data we've seen, that, yes, it can.

In pretest to post-test educational experiments, the *California Critical Thinking Skills Test* and the *California Critical Thinking Disposition Inventory* measure college level critical thinking skills and mindset.

Steps in the Process: An Extended Example

At some point during their college years, or soon after, many students find themselves working in an office. They may work in an office on campus, or during a summer job, or perhaps after graduation to pay the bills before they land a job closer to their intended career field. Many people work in group office environments for many years. The job can have its good points and its bad points. Lately, the collective productivity of office workers, which in the past may have been taken for granted, has become a serious concern for cost-conscious employers. With millions of men and women working in group offices, even a small increase or decrease in productivity can have an unexpectedly large impact on the nation's economy as well as the company's bottom line. How much does the workplace environment affect the motivation and the productivity of group office workers?

Some might leap to the conclusion that improvements in the workplace environment would mean predictable increases in motivation and productivity. Others might be

" Instead of *cubicles*, we call them *interconnected productivity centers.* "

In the earlier paragraphs we already addressed Step 1—the importance of the question of the productivity of workers in group office settings. Investigating a factor that might improve motivation and productivity for millions of people is a worthy inquiry. Undertaking an investigation that involves the application of our knowledge of psychology to answer this question could be useful to millions of people and businesses.

It is both challenging and interesting to design and to execute a strong plan to test a complicated idea. Each step along the way we benefit from refinements in the investigatory process that are included because previous investigators may have learned the hard way that this or that step was essential to making a tightly reasoned empirical inquiry. We can ask important questions and we can test important ideas using empirical methods. It takes training in research methods—often a requirement of undergraduate and graduate programs—to learn how to apply the broad sketch of empirical science provided here to the specific context of one's professional field and academic discipline. But, in general, the specific investigatory steps are more or less the same for empirical disciplines.[17] Strong critical thinking skills and a positive critical thinking mindset apply across the board.

skeptical about that. Whatever one's initial thoughts, the question cannot be satisfactorily resolved without investigating the facts. Spending money to improve the workplace environment for group office workers may or may not make cost-effective positive changes in their motivation and productivity. Merely speculating about the issue is not an adequate response, not if you are the owner of the company and greater productivity would mean more profits for you.

The "Steps in a Scientific Investigation" table describes in detail how a team of researchers would scientifically investigate this question.[16] One column describes each step in an empirical investigation. The next column applies that step to the office productivity example. In the first step, the investigators articulate the question they are expecting to investigate. Unless the investigator expects to fund the research work himself or herself, simply raising a question is not adequate to secure the funding for conducting that research. Today researchers must explain why a question is significant enough to warrant attention and a commitment of resources. This real-world financial reality is reflected in the table. Critical thinking is the tool investigators use to take into consideration all the problems that need to be overcome to engage in a productive empirical inquiry.

What are the factors which affect office worker productivity?

Steps in a Scientific Investigation		
The Steps in the Investigation	**Running Example Using a Social Science Observational Study of Workplace Productivity**	**The Scientific Investigator's Thinking and Argument Making Responsibilities**
Identify a problem of significance.	(1) How does the office environment affect the productivity and job motivation of employees working in a group office setting?	Explain to the funding agency why this problem is important, and why resources should be used to study this question.
Form a hypothesis that describes what we can expect to happen under certain conditions.	(2) Suppose we currently believe: **The more noise and distractions, the more confined and the less personal the workspace, the lower the productivity and motivation of workers will be.** This is a hypothesis that can be studied. Notice that this is a correlational hypothesis at this point, not a causal hypothesis.	Explain what all the terms in the hypothesis mean ("noise," "workspace," "productivity," "distractions," "motivation," etc.) Explain what the hypothesis asserts.
Review the scientific literature to see what can be learned from the work of others about this hypothesis or similar hypotheses.	(3) The lit review is for the purpose of informing our investigation. It can help with many practical problems in future steps (e.g., we may learn how those investigators measured "noise," "distractions," "productivity," and "motivation"). The lit review is not for the purpose of proving we are right.	Before accepting the published conclusions, evaluate the scientific merit of each study. Were the premises true? Are the arguments logically strong? Were all the relevant factors considered?
Identify all the factors related to the hypothesis and the phenomenon of interest that it will be important to measure, control, or monitor.	(4) We will measure noise, distractions, personalization of the workstation, window view, productivity, traffic, and motivation. And we will measure things about the workers that might also affect motivation and productivity (e.g., years of experience, knowledge of the job, the importance the worker attaches to his or her assignments).	Explain why each of the factors is potentially relevant to the hypothesis (e.g., People with more experience may be more productive. People who are new to the job may be more motivated. People who think their assignments are "unimportant" may be less motivated.).
Make each factor measurable.	(5) Noise - number of decibels Personalization of the workstation - number of family pictures and personal knickknacks displayed, Traffic - the number of persons who pass within 3 feet of the person's chair. Window views - presence or absence of an unobstructed view out through an exterior building window located within 7 feet of the person's chair. Productivity - phone and e-mail messages sent and received in a randomly selected one-hour period. Motivation - statements affirming desire to work as recorded during a personal interview. Experience - years in the job. Job Knowledge and Importance - scales in an employee survey.	In the proposal to acquire the resources to conduct this study be sure to: Justify the chosen measure of each factor. For example, why use an interview, instead of a survey questionnaire, to gather data about motivation? Explain and justify the costs of this project. you will need to consider all costs for carrying out data collection.
Ensure that the experimental conditions can be met.	(6) We will determine that there will be a sufficient number of office workers for the study, that their supervisors have authorized the research, that the research has been reviewed and approved by relevant human subjects review boards, that the provision has been made to secure the informed consent of the persons who will be the experimental subjects. We will decide how we will gather the measurable data, including the information on work experience, who will conduct the interviews, who will count the personal items in each workstation, who will count the phone calls and e-mails, etc.	In your proposal, answer 'why' and 'how' questions for every decision made about setting up these experimental conditions.
Design a procedure to ensure that the data gathered will reveal the full range of possible observations.	(7) We will study a enough workers in their usual workplace to assure that we have a range of conditions for each important variable: enough people in both quiet and noisy conditions, enough in solitary and well visited areas, enough in range of a window view and not. We need to determine how we will observe working conditions for these employees without our behavior influencing productivity as a result of our study. We decide to use data from our security cameras to measure Traffic.	Explain that study design to be used will be observational, rather than experimental. Demonstrate that there are enough employees in enough varying conditions to make the needed observations. Explain that the people being studied will be protected from unacceptable risks, in this case how their work productivity will not be diminished.
If possible, run a pilot of at least some portion of the study to test the feasibility of your design plan.	(8) From the pilot, we learned that we need to assure that there are enough employees in our study sample who have more years on the job. We will widen our participant group to include more office workers. We learned that the work associated with email is variable. We will count E-mails with an automated count of messages opened and messages sent from each person's desktop PC, smartphone, or tablet through the network servers. Messages greater than 100 words will be counted as 1.5 messages. Interviews will follow a protocol of questions to be asked. Etc.	Demonstrate that the study is feasible and that whatever amounts of error the measurement tools themselves might introduce is an acceptably small amount. Anticipate practical problems and justify the decisions about those problems. Finalize the budget for the study, and consider what you will do when you receive fewer resources that you have requested.

Steps in a Scientific Investigation		
The Steps in the Investigation	**Running Example Using a Social Science Observational Study of Workplace Productivity**	**The Scientific Investigator's Thinking and Argument Making Responsibilities**
Conduct the study/experiment and gather the data.	(9) Divide the workers into three groups. Make all the measurements and conduct the interviews. Record all the data for analysis.	Provide focused effort to assure that the research is completed.
Conduct appropriate analyses of the data.	(10) Statistical analysis shows that productivity is statistically significantly higher in quieter working environments. Traffic by the desk and noise together accounted for 31 percent of the variance in productivity. Differences in motivation were not statistically significant. Etc.	Demonstrate that the study's planned observational conditions were satisfied, that the data were recorded correctly, that the correct analyses were used, and that the math is right.
Interpret the findings and discuss their significance.	(11) If workplace distractions are limited, noise is reduced, and traffic is minimized, then one can expect modest increases in productivity. These findings may be of interest to interior design architects and supervisors who configure group workplace settings.	Demonstrate that the interpretations being made are reasonable and justifiable, given the data. The claims must not exaggerate the findings.
Critique the findings.	(12) When we carefully critique the design of this study we discover some flaws In our plan. Moving some of the workers to new environments and leaving others In familiar workstations had a possible effect on our findings. Moving employees is disruptive so It would be best to conduct future studies by initiating changes in the work environment itself (add sound proofing or add noise). Select participants in consideration of existing window views.	Identify and describe any limitations of the completed study. Describe how these might be handled in a future study. Explain why the additional research would be valuable in its own right or because of its potential to refine applications of the current findings.
Publish the research.	(13) To contribute to a better understanding of the workplace, we will submit a paper reporting this investigation for possible publication in the XYZ Journal of Office Productivity. Our paper will describe each step of our question, or methods, our measurement tools, our results, and our interpretation of those results.	The investigator must reason through questions such as "Who may need to see the results of this investigation?" to decide on an appropriate scientific or professional journal in which to seek publication.
Design a follow up study that will deepen and extend our knowledge.	(14) Some believe that open space work areas, where groups are in relatively constant communication, are most productive of innovative ideas. (Hypothesis) What are the questions we will need to ask and answer to show whether this belief Is anything more than a myth?	This step further explains to the funder, the scientific community, and the public if necessary, why studying this claim Is important.

Scientific Inquiry Is the Critical Thinking Process in Practice

Scientific inquiry, when executed by fair-minded, truth-seeking people with strong critical thinking skills and a positive critical thinking mindset, is exhaustively systematic and unwaveringly honest.

Evaluating Empirical Reasoning

A rigorous and thorough investigatory process, like the one described in the "Steps in a Scientific Investigation" table, relies on all four of the tests for the worthiness of an argument presented in Chapter 7. *The truthfulness of the premises* is in part ensured by the accuracy of the measurements made and the descriptions of the conditions under which the investigation was conducted. There are additional theoretical assumptions being made, of course. In the example, which showed how to apply the psychological theories about human motivation and productivity to a workplace setting, the theoretical assumptions were presented as true.

We might wonder if those assumptions are true, of course. In the example we could choose to measure noise, distractions, and views of exterior windows, but not the color of the flooring or the height of the ceiling. When we do this we are making certain assumptions about whether those factors we choose not to measure could plausibly be relevant. Perhaps we should also measure the air temperature, on the theory that it is difficult to work when you are too cold or too hot. In an empirical investigation, even one that is tightly controlled and designed, there will always be assumptions that may be questioned. That said, any issues about the truthfulness of any of the premises should have been addressed by the investigator when the study was being designed and by the reviewers who evaluated the merit of the project's possible contribution to knowledge development. If all of those checks fail, empirical investigations are still open to independent verification through replication.

The *test for logical strength* is also addressed in the research design of a study. That is why the investigators consider which statistical tests are the appropriate ones to use, given the kinds of data they are gathering. That is also why they consider any and all possible factors that might have a relationship to the outcome of the investigation. The investigation, if it is thoughtfully designed and carefully conducted, should supply ample grounds for well warranted inferences with regard to the probable truth or falsity of the hypothesis.

But if there are errors in logical strength, these should emerge when independent investigators endeavor to replicate and extend the study. Suppose, for example, that an independent inquiry determines empirically that the air temperature (something not measured in our study) had an impact on productivity and more of an impact than any of the other environmental factors we measured. In that study, workers in a group office were less productive when the office was too hot or too cold. In this case we would refine our collective understanding about the relationship of workplace environment and worker productivity.

Observations: In most offices there are fewer managers than workers. Managers tend to wear suit jackets, but workers tend not to wear jackets or sweaters. Managers are more likely to walk around in the office work environment, while most workers tend to stay seated at their workstations. Hypothesis: Managers will prefer a lower air temperature, while workers will prefer that the office be warmer.

Instead of saying that environment does not count, we would say that it continues to make a difference, but that the element in the environment that is most important to control appears to be the air temperature. We would suggest that management makes sure it is warm enough, but not too warm, in the winter, and cool enough, but not too cold, in the summer.

The same observations can be made about the *test of relevancy* and the *test of non-circularity*. All the factors relevant to testing the hypothesis or to observing the phenomenon in question should have been identified by the investigators as they designed their empirical research. If the investigators missed any or were not able to account for one or more factors, they should note this in their discussion of their research findings. Similarly, a well-designed and well-executed project can be expected not to be circular. But expectations can be mistaken. Ideally, if the empirical reasoning behind the research plan fails the test of relevancy or the test of non-circularity, that should be picked up by the investigative team or project reviewers very early in the process. The research study should not move forward until those issues are addressed.

An evaluation of a researcher's empirical reasoning also occurs as a part of Step 13, when the researcher submits her or his written findings for publication in a scholarly journal. A research manuscript typically undergoes a process known as *peer review*. Through the peer review process the researcher's ideas, methods, and inferences about the findings are scrutinized by others who are experts in the same field of study. These expert reviewers analyze the research in terms of the evaluation steps we have described in this chapter. The peer review process is designed to screen out research that violates one or more of the four tests of the worthiness of an argument. If the work is good, but not quite good enough to be published, the peer review process works to indicate to the researcher how the work might be revised so that it meets the scholarly journal's standards for rigorous research. The peer review process is generally accepted by the scholarly community as the best available means for ensuring the quality of a scientific investigation, but it has its critics too who point out that the peer review process can be slow, ineffective, or inconsistently applied.[18]

Even with the peer review process, errors happen. From time to time poor research ends up being published. So, it is always a good idea not to take for granted that any of these four tests are somehow automatically passed simply because the reasoning is empirical, or simply because consistently making precise and accurate predictions depends on knowing how to explain the causes that bring about the phenomenon of interest.

- If we eliminate the mosquitoes that carry yellow fever, we can prevent the disease from spreading.
- If we travel to a place 1,600 kilometers south of Alexandria, we will see shadows cast by the sun in the opposite direction of those we see in Alexandria on June 21.
- If we eliminate distractions and keep the air temperature moderate for the workers, we will increase employee productivity among workers in group office settings.

We human beings want to ensure our health, safety, survival, and, to the extent possible, our happiness by controlling our lives and the world around us. If we can explain and predict a given phenomenon, then we may be able to prevent it from happening or make it happen when we want it to happen.

- If we can prevent the spread of the disease, we will save a lot of lives.

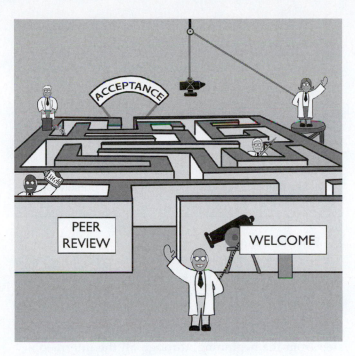

The chances of publishing in a high-quality, peer-reviewed scientific journal are comparable to the chances of a professional baseball player hitting 100 mile per hour fast ball.

a study appears in print. That would be a mistake. Just because something is published in a professional or scientific journal does not mean it passes the four tests. Of course, with all the checks and balances, especially the process of independent peer review, the chances are high that the material published in professional and scientific journals can be trusted. Even so, note that the table, in Step 3, calls for the investigators to make their own independent evaluation of the merits of the arguments in other published papers that may be found in the literature.

14.3 Benefits and Risks Associated with Empirical Reasoning

Empirical reasoning is used when we want to explain, predict, or control what happens. These are three powerful and interconnected purposes. Explanation helps us understand why.

- Why do some people catch yellow fever and not others?
- Why does the sun cast a shadow at one place and not at another?
- Why does environment affect workplace productivity?

Predictions, accurately made, enable us to anticipate what is likely to happen under certain conditions. But

The highest quality journals publish only a fraction of the articles submitted for consideration. Search "Acceptance Rates Scientific Journals" to get a sense of how competitive it is to publish in the most prestigious peer-reviewed journals.

- Because the Earth is a sphere, we can save fuel by taking a polar route when flying from Chicago to Moscow.
- If we can increase employee productivity, we will make more money.

Empirical reasoning offers the promise of explanation, prediction, and control, but empirical reasoning can be complicated. And errors can occur. It would be a mistake to think that a hypothesis was not true simply because an empirical inquiry failed to provide us evidence that supports that hypothesis. Empirical reasoning is probabilistic. So, it would be a mistake to think that findings that have been established with a high level of confidence can never be rejected, revised, or refined. Confirmatory findings *support* a hypothesis. The scope of questions that guide empirical investigations is very broad, but not universal. For instance, some questions, like those involving policy matters, require good judgment in addition to good information.

> "Science is a way to keep from fooling ourselves — and each other."
>
> Anne Druyan, Executive Producer, & Steven Soter, Astrophysicist[19]

JOURNAL

What Did They Mean?

What are Anne Druyan and Steven Soter referring to when they say that science keeps us from fooling ourselves and others? Give an example.

Scientific inquiry, when executed by fair-minded, truth-seeking people with strong critical thinking skills and a positive critical thinking mindset, is exhaustively systematic and unwaveringly honest. It anticipates the consequences of choices and intermediary judgments and decisions. It demands well-reasoned justifications at every step from the beginning, through all the intermediary

---

Dear Friends,

As you probably have already detected from what was said earlier about comparative, ideological and empirical reasoning, I have major reservations about two of the three forms of reasoning. But even in my own life, I cannot do without using all three, at least on occasion.

I enjoy using comparative reasoning because it generates fresh insights and novel and creative ways of looking at things. I know people are too easily persuaded by vivid and emotionally impactful analogies. I worry that comparative reasoning can mislead people, unless we remember that just because an idea is new or clever does not mean it is good! Comparisons are not proofs. They are suggestions about how to look at things in a new light-"war stories" that may not fit today's problems, models that need to be tested.

I admire well-designed empirical reasoning that is truth-seeking, systematic, comprehensive, and self-corrective. When done well, it is objective, modest, cumulative, and empowering. With empirical reasoning we can cure diseases, extend life and improve the quality of life, build safer structures, grow enough food for everyone, travel quickly and comfortably to faraway places, communicate at the speed of light, reverse global warming, and even restructure DNA. But we can also build devastating weapons, unleash biological or chemical plagues, or accelerate climate change. Empirical reasoning is definitely a high-risk, high-reward invention. Even so, I agree with Dallas County Judge Clay Jenkins who said that science is "what separates us from other mammals"[20] In context he meant it is always better to base decisions, even policy decisions, on scientific facts, rather than on fear, superstition, wishful thinking, and ignorance.

Some arguments, including those that capture my political and ethical stance on many issues, although informed by facts empirically discovered are best expressed using ideological reasoning. And yet, ideological reasoning, which does address those value-laden concerns, has many drawbacks. Ideologies can force compliance and can quash independent inquiry, but they are terrible at achieving reasoned accord among people, except perhaps among their own set of true-believers. Perhaps this is because the starting points for ideological arguments must ultimately be taken on faith, and because, unlike empirical reasoning, ideological reasoning provides no workable mechanisms for collaborative self-correction. Ideologies demand too much mindless conformity, spawn too much violent repression, and engender too much foolish and prideful "my way or the highway" for me. No thanks. I'll stick with science.

Yours,

Peter A. "Dr. Pete" Facione
Lead Co-Author-Think Critically

stages in the investigation, all the way to the presentation of the results. It demands the application of all of our critical thinking skills: analysis, interpretation, inference, explanation, evaluation, and reflective self-correction. The scientific mindset includes following reasons and evidence wherever they lead, courageously pursuing the inquiry, being systematic, being confident in the power and process of reasoned inquiry. That mindset reflects the attributes of the ideal critical thinker.

Empirical investigation and the application of our critical thinking skills and habits of mind to scientific inquiry are fundamentally *group endeavors*. It is the community that determines what is most important to study. Science progresses when the entire scientific community can evaluate the merits of a scientific investigation through replications and refinements of the original investigation. Replication and refinement yield either disconfirmation of the original investigation's findings or generation of support and possible improvements of the original findings.

The scientific community uses a process of reasoning that has a built-in capacity for objective self-monitoring and self-correcting through independent inquiry. It is this capacity that gives empirical reasoning an advantage over comparative reasoning and ideological reasoning. Empirical reasoning calls for the application of the four tests of the logical quality of arguments at every stage of scientific investigation. The results are evident in our increasing knowledge of how the natural world works, and in the technological, biomedical, and engineering benefits humans have achieved over centuries by using scientific inquiry.

> "There are in fact two things, science and opinion; the former begets knowledge, the latter ignorance."
>
> Hippocrates, Greek Physician (460–377 BCE)[21]

Perhaps nothing illustrates the ageless insight in the quote from Hippocrates better than the current debate among Evangelical Christians over climate change. Older, more traditional evangelicals tend to dismiss science out of hand when the empirical evidence conflicts with their ideologically derived opinions. Their rejection of evolution is one example. But younger evangelicals accept that the empirical reasoning produces vital information, the reality of climate change being one important example. While traditional evangelicals reject the idea of climate change on ideological grounds, younger evangelicals are leading faith-based environmentalist projects. To appreciate how hard a tradition bound ideological thinker must work to resist the evidence of climate change, and how hard his daughter must work to try to persuade him to accept the empirical science, search and watch episode 1 "Dry Season" of season 1 of the Showtime series *Years of Living Dangerously*.

> "Being able to adapt our behavior to challenges is the best definition of 'intelligence' I know."
>
> Neil deGrasse Tyson, Astrophysicist[22]

Summing up this chapter,

empirical reasoning moves bottom up, from specific observations and measurable data to generalizations that explain why things happen. Empirical reasoning is inductive, that is, probabilistic in character. Conclusions reached by empirical reasoning are warranted inferences that remain open to revision in light of new information. Empirical observations can be verified by other independent investigators. Experiments can be replicated. Calculations can be checked by other scientists. These features make empirical reasoning fundamentally self-corrective. The purpose of empirical investigation is to generate new knowledge through which we can explain, predict, and possibly control what happens. Empirical reasoning is the best process our species has as yet invented for determining what to believe about the universe, the galaxy, the planet, and all natural phenomena, including ourselves.

Key Concepts

empirical reasoning (or **bottom up thinking**) is that process of thinking that proceeds from premises describing interpersonally verifiable experiences in order to support or to disconfirm hypotheses, which, in turn, are intended to explain and predict phenomena. Empirical reasoning is fundamentally inductive, self-corrective, and open to scrutiny and independent verification by the entire scientific community.

null hypothesis is an empirically testable hypothesis that two phenomena are entirely unrelated except perhaps by random chance

Applications

Reflective Log

Comparative, ideological, and empirical reasoning: Chapters 12, 13, and 14 describe comparative, ideological, and empirical reasoning. Each of these major strategies of thinking is best suited for some applications, but not for others. Each has its strengths and weaknesses. All things considered, what are the relative strengths and weaknesses of comparative, ideological, and empirical reasoning? As a truth-seeker who must make reasoned and purposeful judgments about what to believe or what to do in real life, which of these forms of reasoning is the most valuable? Explain why, give examples, and present your perspective as clearly as possible in your own words.

Individual Exercise

Evaluate reports of empirical research: Scientific studies are constantly being reported in newspapers, magazines, television, and the Internet. Because television synopses tend to provide the findings but not describe the methods or the data, we will focus this exercise on the fuller descriptions provided in newspaper, magazine, and Internet reports. Locate an article published within the last 30 days that reports on the findings of a scientific study. Read and analyze that article carefully. Using the table "Steps in a Scientific Investigation," determine how many of the steps are covered in the magazine or newspaper article. Based on what you learn about the scientific study from the article, evaluate the quality of that scientific research.

To inform your evaluation you will want to judge how well the study, as reported by that magazine or newspaper, fulfills the demands of each step in the table. Remember that you are reading another person's synopsis of someone else's research.

Want more of a challenge? Find the scientific publication where the research was originally reported. Evaluate the scientist's presentation of his or her research findings in light of the "Steps in a Scientific Investigation" table. Each step should be addressed someplace or other in that scientific publication, unless the scientific journal placed word limits on reports it would accept for publication.

SHARED RESPONSE

Empirical Reasoning

What are the benefits and risks of empirical reasoning? Give a real life example of a misleading interpretation of empirical reasoning. Be sure to provide your reason(s), not just your opinion. And, comment respectfully on the reasons others offer.

Group Exercises

Design the initial steps in a scientific investigation: The National Climate Assessment reports on the findings of a team of more than 300 experts. They studied the hypothesis that the harmful effects of climate change are now manifesting themselves in all 50 U.S. states.[23] Their report is available at an interactive website so you can check region by region what was found as well as the supporting evidence. Search by National Climate Assessment U.S. Global Change.

1. Is this a significant problem? Why do you make that judgment?

2. What testable hypotheses are implied by the claim, if it were true?

3. Let's assume that you have performed a thorough review of the scientific literature and that it has been helpful in suggesting factors to measure and ways of measuring them. And let's assume that, through this literature review, you have learned what other investigators have discovered about the potential implications of the sea level rising.

4. What factors related to these hypotheses should we measure either to disconfirm a given hypothesis or to acquire evidence that tends to support the hypothesis? Remember to think about all the ways that various factors might confound the evidence you might wish to gather.

5. How could those factors be measured?

Science and policy: The fear of Ebola, and a lack of scientific understanding about how and when a person with Ebola was contagious, caused powerful waves of fear to wash over the population in the late summer of 2014. Ignoring the science, but responding instead to the opinion polls, Governors quarantined people who might have been exposed to Ebola even though those people were symptom free. Instead of being shown compassion and respect, those people who permitted themselves to be quarantined were stigmatized by frightened and ignorant friends and coworkers. Question: How should policy makers respond when the science tells us one thing but the general public believes and fears another thing?

Symmetry, sexual attractiveness, and smell: Hypothesis: Heterosexual women find men whose faces are more physically symmetrical to be more sexually attractive and to smell better than men whose faces are less physically symmetrical. How might we test this hypothesis? Suppose you had access to a sufficient number of willing volunteers including men whose facial and physical symmetry you could measure and women who were

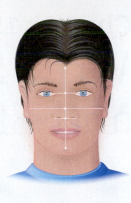

willing to provide you with their opinions about which of these men looked more sexually attractive and smelled better. Design an experiment to test the hypothesis expressed above. The challenge is to describe the steps your experiment would follow, if it were conducted. You do not have to actually conduct this experiment, just design it. Remember to find some way not to let extraneous factors confound your data. For example, control for the possible influences of cologne or certain foods, like garlic. Be sure too that the women are not influenced by a man's facial expressions, weight, height, or personal charm. Find a strategy for gathering data, which will prevent the women from being influenced by something that a lab assistant might say or do.

After you have recorded the design for your experiment, search the Internet for recent articles on symmetry and sexual attractiveness. Among them you will find peer-reviewed studies conducted by a Stanford undergraduate.

Chapter 15
Write Sound and Effective Arguments

Critical thinking and effective writing are skill sets that support one another.

WHAT critical thinking questions do effective writers ask?

HOW do effective writers synthesize, organize, and develop their presentations?

HOW do writers evaluate the soundness and effectiveness of their written work?

 ## Learning Outcomes

15.1 Explain how strong critical thinkers analyze the rhetorical situation in terms of author, audience, purpose, and presentation.

15.2 Demonstrate the use of strong critical thinking by organizing and developing an effective presentation.

15.3 Evaluate the effectiveness of written presentations using the Rubric for Evaluating Written Argumentation.

Sooner or later we all need to make our case. With their cover letter job applicants must make the case that they are worth serious consideration. Editorialists and bloggers must persuade as well as inform. If you prepare a project proposal, PowerPoint presentation, budget request, marketing plan, letter of recommendation, fundraising e-mail, or policy decision, you must lay out your arguments in a sound and effective manner. Even a "30-second elevator speech" is meant to inform and to impress in a memorable way, all in less than a minute. *Everyone with a college education is expected to be able to write sound and effective arguments.*

Knowing that effective writing is essential for our success, wouldn't it be great if we could approach writing the way that professionals do? What do the pros think about when they must prepare a sound and effective argument? How do they decide what to say and in what order, and what not to talk about at all? And how do they approach a reluctant listener with an unpopular idea? Surely they think about a lot more than grammar, spelling, and punctuation. But what?

Most professional writers followed educational paths very much like yours or ours. From the earliest grades, we were all taught how to spell and formulate grammatically correct sentences. In middle school we were given repetitive practice in writing concise multi-paragraph essays. (We can hear our junior high teachers' voices now: "it must be no longer than 1,000 words!" "one paragraph for each idea" "where's the topic sentence?") In high school we were expected to use sources to support our opinions, to present reasons pro and con, and to develop "thesis statements."

In our college-level basic writing courses we learn about the "rhetorical situation" as we discover how important it is to be mindful of the purpose of the writing we are asked to produce. Whether you are considering a major or a career in the social sciences, the natural sciences, mathematics or computer sciences, the arts, humanities, business, education, law enforcement, or engineering—or whatever—in college you are asked to write. This chapter is not meant to cover the content of a college writing course. This chapter does not substitute for a course on writing across the curriculum or within your major. Instead, this chapter demonstrates *how to use your critical thinking skills in creating sound and effective written arguments in your college work and in your chosen profession.*

To achieve its purpose, this chapter focuses on what it means to *think like an effective writer.*

15.1 What Critical Thinking Questions Do Effective Writers Ask?

Analyzing effective writing (and speaking) reveals certain basic elements. In all or almost all situations *a specific author* intends to *communicate* with a *specific audience* for a *specific purpose.* For the purpose of persuasive writing, the author's strategy is to communicate *reasons* that will lead the audience to believe that a *claim or conclusion* is true and to decide to act on the truth of that conclusion. The claim being proven may be an assertion the author wants the audience to accept, or a recommendation that the author wants the audience to follow. Ideally the author's arguments will be *worthy* as defined in Chapter 7 on evaluating arguments. That is the author will use true and relevant premises, and logically strong, non-circular reasoning to establish the claim.

An **author's case** can be thought of as all of the pros and cons along with the supporting evidence, arguments, and counterarguments that the author presents to the audience to establish the truth of a given statement or the wisdom of a given recommendation. Using our decision mapping analytical tools from Chapter 5, we can map out the author's case. With this analysis in hand, we can then evaluate the *soundness* of the author's case using the evaluative methods presented throughout this book. But there's more. Using the rubric for evaluating written argumentation, presented at the end of this chapter, we will also be able to evaluate the *effectiveness* of the author's case.

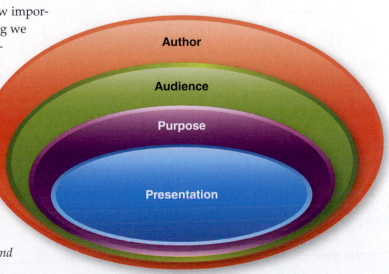

Rhetorical Situation –
The Interactive Combination of Four Elements

The Rhetorical Situation

Effective writing is like custom-made clothing—tailored to fit. Before they set fingers to typing, effective writers already are thinking about the key situational elements: As the specific author they have an intention to communicate with a specific audience for a specific purpose and in a specific way. Effective writers know who they are as authors and they strive to understand exactly who their intended audience is. Effective writers have a clear sense of the context within which they are communicating, and they are clear about the purpose of the communication. Effective writers are systematic and thorough: They do the research and then they present well-reasoned arguments grounded in solid evidence. Effective writers are good critical thinkers who know what questions to ask and what methods to use. And they can evaluate their written product and apply their writing skills to real-world situations. To think like an effective writer we must apply our own critical thinking skills to discover our own answers for these same issues.

To become an effective writer the first thing we must do is apply our critical thinking skill of analysis to the rhetorical situation. **Rhetorical situation** refers to the interactive combination of four elements: a *specific author* using a specific mode of communication or *presentation* to engage a *specific audience* for the *specific purpose*. The purpose of persuasive writing is to make the author's case. The successful author who understands his or her audience and who has researched the topic well will organize and present a sound and effective case. The case will persuade a reasonable audience by means of presenting sound reasons and credible evidence. To achieve this, an effective writer asks himself or herself four key questions. The questions emerge directly from the rhetorical situation. Before doing anything else, the effective writer will ask:

1. Who am I, as author?
2. Who is the intended audience? What do they believe and value?
3. What is the purpose and what are the circumstances of my communication?
4. How should my case be developed and be presented?

Let's think about each one of these four broad and highly interconnected questions the way that a writer would.

Think Author

Sound and effective writing comes from someone. It is not anonymous. A person gives the writing a voice. Voice is power. Voice communicates meaning, passion, and intensity. We can ignore words on a page. We can ignore "believe X." But it is very hard to ignore a voice that we respect. Voice says that there is a real person saying "I believe X." So now we have to take X more seriously because someone whom we respect believes X and wants us to believe X too. The first thing an effective writer must do is to discover his or her voice. The 2010 Academy Award–winning Best

Don't Be Bart—Honesty Works

Occasionally a writer fudges the truth. Writers of non-fiction have been discovered intentionally using false premises, claiming that their conclusions are logical when they knew that they were not, relying on fallacies to deceive a gullible audience, or using circular reasoning. We do not condone this. We think it is a mistake at many levels. We believe that sound and effective argument making should never knowingly employ falsehoods, be illogical, rely on fallacies, or build circular arguments. Not only is it manipulative, insincere, and disrespectful of the audience; it is also a sure way to alienate the strong critical thinkers in that audience. If an audience discovers that a writer is being deceitful, the audience will reject the message as well as the messenger. These admonitions hold true in social media as well! Like Bart Simpson on a bad day, authors of e-mails, blogs, tweets, Facebook posts, or other online comments may be prone to exaggerate the truth or outright fabricate the claims they are making about themselves or other individuals.

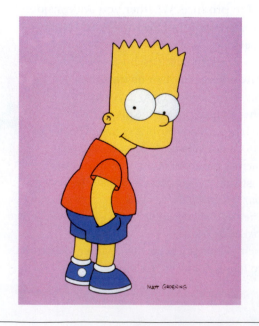

Film, *The King's Speech*, makes that point most eloquently. When you watch it, pay particular attention to the scene in which the king, played by Colin Firth, is finally able to break through his lifelong anger and frustration with the stunning realization that he indeed has a voice.[1] The story is much more than a tale about a man overcoming the stammering and stuttering he had experienced since childhood. It shows how a king grows to understand that he has something he must say to his nation. It tells us all that we too can have an effective voice, if we learn how to control it.

We thought about who we were as authors to prepare to write this book text for you. We shared our biographies with you because we wanted you to know that we were real people with a genuine desire to assist you to become stronger critical thinkers. Yes, we wanted you to know too that we had the academic and real-world professional creds to write a book like this. And we often shared personal anecdotes and stories to illustrate various ideas. It would be hard to miss that one of our concerns is to combat intolerance and hate, which explains many of the examples we elected to use. Another concern is to promote healthy living, which explains another bunch of examples. But more than either of those things, we really wanted to share our passion for learning, our belief that learning needs to connect to real-world experiences, and our commitment to the value of critical thinking in all dimensions of life. We hope that our voice has been clear and strong from Chapter 1 all the way through the book.

FIND YOUR VOICE Suppose you are asked to write an editorial or blog for the college newspaper about "life as a college student." Your very first question needs to be: "Who am I, as author?" Take a moment and think about how you would respond. Here are some responses students have shared with us over the years.

- I am a female college student who just graduated from high school last year. I am majoring in International Relations and I want to work at the United Nations. My  parents are alumni of this university. I attend full-time, and I am living on campus in the residence halls. I like to have fun, like anyone else, but I worry that there are some people in my residence hall that overdo it. There is too much drinking, at least that's what I'm seeing. Maybe I'm wrong and I shouldn't judge. But it bothers me.

- I am a 22-year-old male in ROTC and getting my college education. I come from a military family and look forward to serving my country after I graduate just like my father and  my older brother and sister did. I don't know where I'll be deployed, but wherever it is, I'll be a second lieutenant and my unit's communications officer. It really bothers me that so few Americans understand all the good our armed services do, or why we need to confront terrorism. But, either you take the battle to the bad guys or they will bring it to you.

- I am an Indian woman who is studying part-time to be an early childhood educator while raising my two children with my husband of 22 years. We moved to the United States a few years ago for my husband's work. I was a preschool teacher in Mumbai for many years, but I must now  become recertified in this country. This does not make sense to me. I know more than many of my teachers. But I will humbly comply, because I must get certified or I cannot do what I love, which is to take care of the little ones.

- I am the oldest of three children and the first person in my family to go to college. I live at home with my mom and dad, my little sister and brother, and my grandparents. I drive to campus for my classes then I leave to go to my job. Between that and my homework, I don't have a lot of time for my friends. Some of 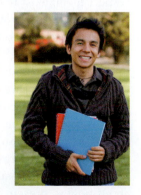 the people in my courses are full-time and will graduate years before me. Frankly I envy them at times. But other times I think that they have no clue about what it is like to make it in today's world. I'm the assistant night manager at a *Chipotle* restaurant now, but my major is chemical engineering and someday I'm going to own that restaurant and five more like it.

Effective writers think about themselves as authors as they prepare to draft a written case. They ask questions such as "How can I draw on my past experiences when talking about this topic?" "What makes me a

Six Minutes to Persuade Millions

It was February 18, 2014, and NBC Network had captured a large late night audience by broadcasting the Sochi Winter Olympics. Throughout the Olympic coverage the network promoted Jimmy Fallon as the new host of their marquee *Tonight Show*. Hype and anticipation overflowed as the new host took the stage for the first time to replace the legendary Jay Leno. For millions of viewers this would be their first look at the new host. Jimmy Fallon absolutely needed to connect with them. He needed to be himself, not Jay. He needed to be respectful of the past but also to assert that he was now the new face of the *Tonight Show*, and would be for perhaps decades to come. Tens of millions of dollars, not to mention his career, rode on how he handled that opening six minutes. A heck of a rhetorical situation—one that required a lot of critical thinking before setting fingers to keyboard.

To see how he handled himself, his audience, the context, and the mode of presentation so effectively, search and watch the opening monologue of episode 1 of *The Tonight Show Starring Jimmy Fallon*.

credible person to argue for this claim?" "Do my attitudes about this topic make me unfairly biased, or can I be open-minded about this topic?" "What are my attitudes toward my intended audience—do I like them, respect them, trust them, fear them—and how do I want those attitudes to show through in my writing?" "What do I need to learn about the topic and about the audience before I start writing?" "What is my motivation for writing this—what do I want to get out of this communication?" "Why do I care about this topic?"

Ultimately, effective writers will consider how their backgrounds influence the assumptions that they make about the audience and the purpose for the communication. Effective authors consider the perspectives they will take on particular issues and make conscious decisions about how to present themselves and their positions on the topic.

THINK ABOUT WHO YOU READ   Along with thinking about what you like to read, think about *who* you like to read. Favorite authors are like favorite musicians, actors, professors, and artists. Many of us enjoy reading our favorite authors so much that we pre-order their next novel. Why? In part because we enjoy hearing that author's voice.

Identifying the author's voice is a key piece of enjoying and understanding what we read. We can apply our critical thinking skills to the author of a written piece to analyze and interpret a piece of writing. Thinking

about the author's background, attitudes, and purpose can help us explain the decisions that the author made in constructing the piece. Why did the author take that position? Why did the author interpret this situation in the ways that he or she did? How did the author's assumptions about the world influence the analysis and evaluation of situational events and social relationships?

These questions are particularly fascinating to ask when we are reading written argumentation intended to elicit a particular attitudinal or emotional response from the reading audience. Take, for example, the autobiographical narrative of Elizabeth Najeeb Halaby, the American-born woman who is the last wife and widow of the late King Hussein of Jordan. In *Leap of Faith: Memoirs of an Unexpected Life*, Queen Noor encourages the reader to see the Middle East through her eyes, providing a more sympathetic perspective on the history of that region, a region that may not be familiar to most of her reading audience.

Think Audience

Effective writers do not write for themselves; they write for their audience. An effective writer seeks to establish a relationship *grounded in trust*. Before putting pen to paper, the author must think critically about the intended audience. Who will be reading or hearing this? How do I get the audience's attention and keep it? How shall I express my arguments to this audience in the most effective way

American-born author Elizabeth Najeeb Halaby, last wife and widow of the late King Hussein of Jordan, uses written argumentation to elicit a more sympathetic understanding of the Middle East.

possible? Is the audience friendly or hostile to the position I am going to take? Will this be my only chance to communicate to this audience?

WHAT DOES THE AUDIENCE CARE ABOUT?
Effective writers connect with the receptivity of their audience by appealing to the audience's core values, perspectives, and shared interests. To do this effective writers research their audiences. They learn about the background, experiences, interests, and goals of audience members. To craft a sound and effective case, an author draws on what is known or safely assumed about the audience to make critical thinking decisions about how to organize ideas and orchestrate the presentation of those ideas.

When constructing an effective argument, an author needs to know what will be convincing to an intended audience, what will move them to respond in the way the writer is seeking. Take, for example, the long-running reality television show *Hell's Kitchen*.[2] Each season, 20 chefs compete against one another to avoid elimination and win the ultimate prize: a coveted position as

executive chef in a named fine-dining establishment. Each episode serves as the evidence for or against each competitor's claim that they are the most deserved of the prize. For any TV show to remain successful season after season, its producers, directors, writers, and actors must demonstrate over and over again to its audience that the show is worth watching. The production team considers their audience very carefully as they craft show after show. Will the viewing audience be interested in knowing how to prepare the dishes that are served in the *Hell's Kitchen* restaurant? Are viewers considering careers in the culinary arts? Do viewers enjoy watching Gordon Ramsey yell at the bumbling chefs who seem to have forgotten all of their training and are ready to turn on one another at the drop of a poofy white hat? The importance of retaining and expanding the viewing audience (numbers of people, not waist sizes) certainly influences production decisions of many kinds, such as who will have the opportunity to be contestants? How should audience analysis influence editing which footage to include in each broadcast?

The fruit of strong and weak critical thinking is constantly on display in the flood of TV shows, films, recordings, concerts, and live theater offered for our

Does it take strong critical thinking skills to solve the problems like those faced on *Hell's Kitchen* by expert chef star Gordon Ramsey?

Every production decision requires well-trained critical thinking skills, focus and mental discipline, and knowledge of every element in the rhetorical situation.

entertainment. The professionals who write, direct, edit, produce, or perform in the most successful of these are keenly aware of their target audience. But perhaps none more so than the people working on long-running TV series. How can we writers, directors, actors, and producers create (author) TV show after TV show (presentation) on the same topic in a way that is fresh and entertaining for the viewers (audience) and persuades them to tune in again next time (purpose)?

Effective writers never take the audience for granted. They ask themselves, "Who cares and why?" "For whom am I writing?" "Why might they be interested in what I have to say about this topic?"

WRITING FOR YOU   Yes, we asked ourselves these very same questions as we prepared to write this book. We (author-element) wanted to communicate the value of critical thinking (purpose-element) by writing a terrific book that teaches how to build critical thinking and apply critical thinking to real-world problems and decisions (presentation-element). But those three elements alone did not complete our rhetorical situation. We needed also to think a lot about *you.*

You, the college student, are our most important audience. We knew that we wanted to write this book *for you.* We knew that today's college student represents multiple and complex backgrounds in terms of age, race/ethnicity, religious affiliation, gender, sexual orientation, health, family obligations, work responsibilities, interests, economic status, experiences, subject matter knowledge, skills, and belief systems. Because of the many faces in today's college classroom, we knew it was crucial for us to

present many different real-world examples in the text scenarios and in the exercises. We also knew it was necessary to represent multiple perspectives on controversial issues; to show respect for the incredible diversity of the thousands of readers; to show sensitivity in our narratives, opening vignettes, and images you see on each page. We wanted you to see yourselves in the book and to know that it really was *written for you.*

Written presentations often have multiple audiences, some not even intended by the authors. (We see that with tweets that go viral and "reply all—oops!" e-mails that circulate too widely and end up embarrassing their authors.) There was a *known* secondary audience for this book, namely your instructors. And so we authors thought a lot about how the book would be received and used by the faculty teaching critical thinking. For example, we wondered whether all the possible instructors would be familiar with the kinds of teaching tools and tactics that we planned to use in the book. Thinking that some instructors might be new to teaching for critical thinking, we wrote a variety of instructor resources to accompany this book. Because our main purpose was for you to build your critical thinking skills and develop strong critical thinking habits of mind, we decided to supply your instructors with all the support we possibly could provide so they, in turn, could help you get the most out of this book.

WHO IS YOUR AUDIENCE?   "Write a paper on . . . !" One rhetorical situation you are highly likely to encounter as a college student is this: You (author) are asked by your instructor (audience) to write a paper (presentation) in which you research a topic and then take a position and defend your view (purpose). Many students, as they begin thinking about the topic they will write about, think about their opinion on that topic. We have two things to suggest. First, we suggest not taking one side or the other on an issue until after thoroughly researching it. This suggestion helps avoid the problem of locking-in prematurely, as described in Chapter 11 on reflective decision making. Our second suggestion: Think audience!

Who is the audience for the paper you are assigned to write? Many professors answer this question for you by identifying a target audience when they make the writing assignment. The professor might say, "Assume that you are writing a letter to the editor," or "Imagine that you are posting a blog for the whole world to see online," or "Write a paper that could be submitted for publication in a

THINKING CRITICALLY

A Dozen Office E-Mail No No's

The tactics of successful written communication extend to the workplace and to its most prominent mode of sharing information and ideas, namely e-mail. Assume you are working in a typical office and suppose your boss has asked you a question by e-mail and expects an e-mail response. What are some of the dos and don'ts of that rhetorical situation? Having worked many years as administrators in large, complex organizations, we have learned, the hard way, some communication tactics:

1. Brevity is next to godliness—say it all on one screen.

2. Focus—no more than one topic per e-mail.

3. Never delegate problems or work upward to your boss—do the work, solve the problems, communicate solutions.

4. State the benefits of your proposal, not the shortcomings of someone else's.

5. Never propose something that is against company policies.

6. Don't display ignorance of management directives.

7. Be upbeat and positive, but not unreasonably optimistic.

8. Make your case using good reasons and accurate information.

9. Get it right the first time—follow-up corrections only make you look bad.

10. Irony does not play well in e-mails, nor do snarky comments.

11. Don't assume everyone has read the relevant background material.

12. Expect that if the higher-ups like your idea you will be asked to write it up in greater detail.

If there are tactics for successful e-mail communications at work, are there also tactics for effective workplace text messages between employees and bosses? If so, what are they?

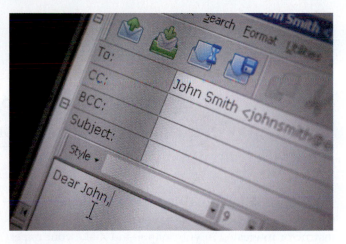

professional journal in your major." Or "Write a memo to your employer." Whenever the professor does specify the audience you can apply your analytical skills to determine how best to organize and express your ideas for that specific audience.

But what if the professor gives a writing assignment that does not include a specification of the intended audience? It is difficult to write for some imaginary, disembodied, unspecified audience about whom we know nothing. Professional writers would not attempt that. So, why should college students? We have two suggestions to offer. First, ask the professor to specify a target audience for the assignment. If that does not work, then as a last resort, imagine that the audience is the professor who made the assignment. Many college faculty are not entirely comfortable with being seen by their students as the rhetorical audience. So it is very likely that the first suggestion will work better.

However, if you are left with no option other than thinking of the professor as your audience, then proceed

on the basis of that assumption. What do you know about that instructor and how can that knowledge help you to be more successful as a writer on this assignment? Begin with questions like this, "What can I assume that my instructor is looking for in this assignment?" Part of the answer to this will be in the grading criteria the instructor has described in the course syllabus and, more importantly, in any scoring rubrics and examples of the work of prior students that the instructor has shared. Another part of the answer to this comes from realizing what subject field standards the instructor is likely to apply. If the instructor is teaching writing or one of the humanities or arts disciplines, then the instructor is more likely to expect you to focus on analysis, interpretation, careful inference, and thoughtful evaluation. Your writing craft, important for all subject fields, may play a larger role in this instructor's assessment of your work. If the instructor is in the social or behavioral sciences or one of the professional fields then you can be sure that he or she will apply the standards appropriate to that discipline to your work.

"I call it, 'Research Paper Lite.' It contains a third fewer facts, but you'd never know it."

As you think about the instructor as your audience you will also want to ask yourself: what will get the instructor interested in your paper and make your paper stand out as compared to the other papers the instructor will also be reading? Writing is like golf: The best golfers compete against themselves, but golf is a sport, not just a pastime and competition with other players cannot be avoided. When a professor assigns a grade to a paper the professor typically uses an abstract grading standard like a scoring rubric, and the professor draws on his or her experience and expertise, measuring your work against the work of other students past and present. So it makes sense to ask yourself what will help your paper stand out as compared to the papers other students submit. What will keep the instructor focused and interested in what you have to say all the way through to the end of your paper? Instructors, being human, appreciate an engaging example, a clever turn of phrase, an apt metaphor, a concise and well-documented presentation, relevant quotations, well-crafted prose, accurate and informative graphics, insightful analyses, reasonable interpretations, and fair-minded presentations that offer a balanced, respectful, and objective approach to the topic at hand. Wit and irony are appreciated too, but only if all the other elements are present. You will want to ask yourself what to avoid so the instructor will not respond negatively. For example, you will

want to avoid grammatical errors, punctuation mistakes, and misspellings. Your instructor may react negatively to slang, profanity, and flippant comments. The instructor may have warned against overgeneralizations, claims that are not supported by evidence or quotations that are inserted without appropriate citations. You can bet that the instructor will expect your work to be well organized and easy to follow, and be alienated by a paper that is nothing more than a swamp of mushy and marshy disjointed paragraphs.

SAME AUTHOR AND AUDIENCE, DIFFERENT PURPOSE Let's keep the same author (you) and the same audience (your professor) in this next example, but we'll change the purpose and the presentation. Suppose you want to communicate with one of your college professors that you are thinking of majoring in that professor's discipline and you wonder what careers people with that major are likely to pursue. Three elements in the rhetorical situation are clear. You (author) want to talk about possibly majoring in the discipline (presentation) so you can find out what career potentials it offers (purpose). The remaining element, the professor (audience), is more of an unknown now.

Yes, you have been taking classes from this professor, but now you are going outside of that relatively

Effective Writers Apply All Six Critical Thinking Skills By Asking

Think Author (Myself)

Interpretation—What about me makes me a credible author on this topic?

Analysis—What biases might I have in relation to the topic or issue?

Inference—Why am I motivated to undertake this communication?

Evaluation—Do I have the necessary knowledge and experience to write about this?

Explanation—How is my background influencing my perspective on this issue?

Self-Regulation—How can I remain open to considering alternative points of view or counter-evidence?

Think Audience

Interpretation—Who is the audience for this communication?

Analysis—Is the audience receptive to the argument?

Inference—What will build credibility and trust between me and the audience?

Evaluation—Was the desired response achieved?

Explanation—Why does the audience need to hear this argument?

Self-Regulation—How do shifts in the audience's mode or knowledge change the argument?

Think Purpose

Interpretation—What is the cognitive or behavioral purpose of this communication?

Analysis—What situational factors enhance or limit the effectiveness of this communication?

Inference—If the purpose is achieved, what will the audience do?

Evaluation—Are the reasons presented appropriate to the audience and to the purpose?

Explanation—How does the historical (economic, cultural, interpersonal, etc.) context influence the evaluation of evidence?

Self-Regulation—What could be done to refine the purpose and adjust better to the circumstances influencing this communication?

Think Presentation

Interpretation—Should the argument be an oral, written, or visual communication?

Analysis—How should the argument be structured so that it is optimally persuasive?

Inferences—If I use this rhetorical device, how will the audience react?

Evaluation—Are style requirements being met?

Explanation—How did word choice influence the impact of the communication?

Self-Regulation—Will further revision and rewriting improve the strength of the communication?

---

well-defined context. Now you are seeking to communicate person-to-person about an academic discipline that might become your chosen major and shape your college studies and possibly your professional life after college. What do you know about this professor as a professional scholar and educator in that field? Maybe you sensed the professor's passion for the subject matter, or you were intrigued by the kinds of questions the professor's discipline explores. But talking with your professor is not like talking with a friend over coffee or with a family member around the kitchen table. So, strategize. How will you communicate with this professor? E-mail, text message, phone call, Facebook connection, drop by during office hours, or catch the professor after class? And what will you say (Probably not, "Yo, Doc. Dude, your major is sick, man! Hook me up."). How will you communicate your interest

in the subject area and your concern that the subject you decide to major in should also further your professional aspirations after graduation?

Smart and strategic writers consider all of their audiences, including the non-human ones. This example may also apply to you. Suppose that your essay is going to be read and graded by a computer. Although abhorrent to faculty in a great many disciplines, this is happening more and more with group assessment instruments like the CLA.[3] It is also happening with college and graduate school entrance exams like the SAT and GMAT that individuals take.[4] What do computers look for when they evaluate an essay? Will the computer be able to tell that you are using irony, hyperbole, or sarcasm effectively? Will the computer be able to detect the differences in the quality of the critical thinking expressed in your analyses,

What if the machine grading your exam can't tell the difference between sense and nonsense?

interpretations, inferences, explanations, or evaluations? Or will the computer's scoring algorithm focus on syntax, spelling, average sentence length, average word length, sentence structure, and word choice?[5] For more on the plusses and minuses of computer-graded written work visit " Grading Written Submissions" in Chapter 9.

Think Purpose and Circumstances

"What exactly am I trying to accomplish?" And "How will I achieve it?" These are two of the most important questions an effective writer asks. Sound and effective writing is a matter of purpose and strategy, not just topic, word count, and sentence structure. A clear purpose is essential. Our advice: don't write it if you don't know why you're writing it.

But when you do know why, don't stop there. Make sure your audience knows too. When an author fails to communicate her or his thesis or goal, the audience is left to wonder "What's the point?" The audience is likely to tune out even if they care about the topic. They simply will not want to hear about it from that author.

Before producing words on the computer screen, effective writers clearly define the goal or purpose of their written communication and they think carefully about their strategy for achieving that goal. Imagine yourself creating a battle plan. "My goal is to persuade this audience of the truth of this claim. To achieve this goal I must do this, this, and this. And in accord with rules of engagement I will use sound and well-documented arguments." The overall strategy for leading the audience to believe that a claim is true and to act on the truth of that claim is communicating worthy arguments.

THINK TACTICS   Strategy is the big picture approach. But successful campaigns are also tactical. Strong critical

thinkers drill down into the details. As effective writers they ask tactical questions like these:

- "My case rests on three strong arguments, but which one should I put first and which one will I close with?"

- "I have a lot of abstract concepts and solid statistical information to build upon, but is there a vivid comparison or a gripping narrative that I can use to illustrate my point?"

- "This audience is apt to react negatively to me as an outsider unless I somehow let them know that I really do understand their issues and concerns, so how can I build that into my presentation?"

- "This audience is impatient, so how can I make my key point powerfully clear as early in my presentation as possible?"

For example, suppose you are taking a marketing course and the professor has made this assignment: *Prepare a 5–7-page paper with references addressing this topic: "How to improve brand X's recognition in television advertisements."* Right away you recognize that your professor is giving you some freedom in defining how you will approach your written response. What are some questions you could ask to think about your purpose when writing this paper? We can interpret this paper topic to mean that our paper has to include a marketing strategy for a brand of our choosing. To be effective you will need to write more than your personal opinions. At a minimum you will need some quotes from successful ad agencies' Web sites and from books describing the social science theories that apply to successful marketing. Ask yourself, what other source material might be useful? Perhaps a couple of extended examples showing what works when advertising the brand you decided to talk about.

Our Purpose and Strategy

This book aims **to strengthen critical thinking skills and nurture the courageous desire to seek truth by following reasons and evidence wherever they lead**. . . . Our approach is simple, practical, and focused. To build . . . skills we have to **use them**. To build . . . positive habits we have to **engage**. . . . [We use] questions, exercises, video clips, controversial examples, contemporary issues, practical life problems, classic quotes, science, technology, religion, politics-all these and more . . . **whatever it takes**.

From the Preface to *Think Critically*

Effective writing, like accomplishing one's mission, requires tactical problem solving and decision making.

CLUES FROM CONTEXTUAL CUES   Take advantage of situational and contextual cues. For example, you know you are writing a paper *for a college class*. Therefore a goal should be to present your written case using the format, language, and style appropriate for an academic paper.[6] And since your professor declined to tell you anything about an intended audience, you infer that the audience is your professor. You also know that the professor is going to be reading lots of papers and so you will want yours to emerge as one of the best. Tactically it might make sense to select products from a brand that the professor might see himself or herself using and then to suggest a marketing approach that might appeal to the professor's demographic. This could help capture the professor's interest, as compared to talking about products and brands that the professor is not likely to care anything about. Again, this is a tactical suggestion. Every situation is different when we get to the level of tactics. You need to apply your critical thinking skills to plan your own approach, given what you know about *your* audience.

Another context cue: This paper is for this course, not some other course. So it makes sense to be sure to incorporate the ideas, theories, and concepts that this professor and the text for this course have been addressing in this part of the syllabus. Professors do not typically assign papers that are unrelated to the material they have been covering in that part of the course. Having shown your knowledge of this course, it is always useful to then think about how you will show that you can connect and integrate what you are learning in this course to other relevant knowledge gained in other courses.

Sound and effective written work typically revolves around one main controlling idea or purpose. Know your main claim. Write it out. Work it word for word until it expresses exactly what you intend to communicate. Of course, you cannot know what your main claim is with regard to a controversial topic until you research the topic open-mindedly, learn about it, and consider the various points of view objectively. But after you have engaged your powers of reasoned reflective judgment, set forth your considered opinion on the topic. Having done so, you can marshal your reasons and evidence, showing how you make the case for your claim and also how you consider and address the major counterarguments. Map everything out: claims, rejected options, reasons, assumptions, counterarguments, and responses to them. Creating the outline for your paper is relatively straightforward from that point, *because you have done the thinking and organized your own ideas*. You have already worked carefully through your side and the other side in doing your background research.

Your paper becomes the document that presents the fruit of those mental labors in an orderly progression so that your audience can follow the path of your logic. A typical progression might be this:

- Here's the question or problem this paper is addressing.
- Here are the main possible options as discussed in the relevant literature.
- Here are the pros and cons of each of the main options.
- Because of the research I've done, this is where I come down on this topic, and here are my reasons.
- Yes, I am aware of potential problems and objections to my point.
- Here are the important ones and here is how I would propose to address them.
- Here is how we will know that the approach I am proposing is working.
- This is the bibliography of sources upon which this paper relies.

STAGES OF WRITING: DON'T TRY THIS ON CAMPUS

DENIAL   BARGAINING   PANICKING   REGRET

Nick M. Sambaluk — University Daily Kansan

15.2 Organize and Develop Your Presentation

Whatever the medium, book, term paper, report, exam essay, Prezi show, e-mail, tweet, screenplay, etc., a presentation cannot be effective unless it reaches out and grabs the audience's attention. To do this the author has to do more than lay out the facts like fish fillets on crushed ice in the supermarket. The author has to share something of himself or herself—passion for the topic, concern for the audience, significance of the purpose, something real, something human, or something that communicates the value of the work. Even formal scientific publications include a paragraph addressing the reason why the research is important.

Reach Out and Grab Someone

"How will I get my audience's attention?" is a key question effective writers ask themselves. But it is slightly different from the question that hangs up many less experienced writers. They tend to ask, "How will I start my paper?" That question is almost on target because it focuses on the vitally important opening paragraph. But it is slightly off target too, because it focuses on the author instead of the audience. In general it is a good idea to eliminate "I" whenever possible. The audience should be the focus, not the author. You can see the contrasting results by comparing these two "draft opening paragraphs" to a paper about the economy.

Ho Hum Nap Time Draft	Okay, I'd Like to Read Some More Draft
In this paper I want to talk about the economy. There are a lot of things happening. I will first describe the current economic situation. The question for this paper is should a person invest in the stock market now or should I wait until the economy improves. I will say wait. Then I will explain why it is a bad time to buy stock and then I will talk about safer possibilities, like investing in government bonds.	Like a wind whipped wildfire devouring homes in a California canyon, economic storms are ravaging world markets. What do smart people do when they see a fire leaping toward them? They think safety and survival above all. The economic equivalent is investing in government bonds. Now is no time to venture naively into the out of control economic wildfire by buying stocks. This paper explains why.

There are many ways to grab your reader's attention. Vivid images, like a California wildfire, work. Apt comparisons are effective. In the example draft venturing into the stock market is compared to venturing out into a wildfire. Mixing in short punchy sentences, along with longer more detailed sentences, works too. By contrast, limp, tepid prose, navel-gazing introspection, and pedantic elitism are likely to alienate even a willing audience.

Successful writers and presenters show the audience that they care about them and that they are passionate about their topics. The audience can tell if the caring is real and the passion is genuine. If so, the audience will most often connect. We know an extraordinary math professor who teaches statistics. The course is required and students are often leery of taking a statistics course. But across the board they all praise the effectiveness of this particular professor as being the reason for their academic success in a class they were dreading. We asked some students why they thought this professor was so effective. Their response was that she was both knowledgeable and passionate about statistics, and she had an uncanny ability to express her excitement about statistics while teaching the concepts the students needed to learn. Students said they looked forward to her classes because she was so enthusiastic about stats and energized to work with them on real-world examples. She made a hard subject understandable and doable. For her the key to a successful presentation was her love for her subject and her passion to help her students learn it and be able to apply it.

Crafting a Presentation

As far as the technical aspects of a written presentation go, there are many fine sources offering useful guidance about the craft of writing. We derived this list, for example, from the College Board.[6]

- Once you have selected your topic, keep your focus narrow and manageable.

- Establish a clear thesis statement early—be specific and compelling.

- Use headings and subheadings to guide the reader.

- Assemble evidence to support claims—include interpretations of evidence.

- Be fair-minded and balanced in presentation—be sure to give pros and cons.

- Cite sources using appropriate style (MLA, APA, Chicago, etc.). There are publication manuals and resources on the Internet to assist with the stylistic requirements.

- Never plagiarize. Use quotes or paraphrasing, depending on the style of the discipline, and always provide citations.

- Use appropriate terminology and vocabulary and consider word choice appropriate to your audience. Most professors prefer if students' papers avoid overgeneralizations, colloquialisms, idioms, slang, profanity, pretentious rhetoric, problematic vagueness, and problematic ambiguity.

- Avoid parenthetical expressions.
- Follow format requirements: margins size, sentence spacing, page numbering, font size, meaningful title, endnote styles, footnote styles, list of works cited at the end.
- Write, rewrite, and polish your writing.
- Proofread your work, read it aloud, ask someone else to check it too.

"I think the following rules will cover most cases:
(i) Never use a metaphor, simile, or other figure of speech which you are used to seeing in print.
(ii) Never use a long word where a short one will do.
(iii) If it is possible to cut a word out, always cut it out.
(iv) Never use the passive where you can use the active.
(v) Never use a foreign phrase, a scientific word, or a jargon word if you can think of an everyday English equivalent.
(vi) Break any of these rules sooner than say anything outright barbarous."

George Orwell[7]

Crafting an effective presentation matters for textbook writers, too. Given our purpose and our audience, we then thought about the presentation itself. Here are four examples. You be the judge. Did they work?

- We knew we needed to include many varied examples of real-world situations and current events focusing on issues and situations that college students of all kinds could find interesting. Otherwise you might be less motivated to engage the examples and less likely to benefit as much from the book text. So all the examples in Chapter 3, which is about problem solving, focus on college students and how they can achieve success by being better problem solvers.
- Not wanting to cause any readers to feel excluded because a given term or example related only to people who were in some major, we selected examples and exercises with great care and we explained all the key terms and technical vocabulary needed. Someplace or other in this textbook there is an example that fits your major, no matter what your major is, including undeclared.
- To keep the pages fresh and interesting to read we avoided bland droning discourse *about* critical

thinking as an academic concept, and instead focused on writing *for* critical thinking. Hence the focus on application and integration of critical thinking into life and learning.

- Realizing that most people learn best "from examples to theories" instead of "from theories to examples," we opened each major chapter with an illustrative example, and we often organized subsections and paragraphs so that the examples came above the explanatory text.

"Genius is 1 percent inspiration and 99 percent perspiration."

Thomas Alva Edison, Inventor[8]

Good News: Writing Is Work

We cannot speak about genius, but we can say from experience that sound and effective writing is at most 10 percent inspiration and at least 90 percent perspiration. We think this is good news, because it means that people who put in the required effort can become more effective. If writing were largely about inspiration, then we all would be in trouble because inspiration is difficult, if not impossible, to learn.

So, if writing is basically digging in and working hard, then what are the things that need to be done? Effective writers seeking to build a reasonable and credible case are diligently methodical. They take the time and spend the energy to do things like

- Develop a clear, arguable, and relevant thesis statement
- Inform themselves about the topic by doing solid research
- Draft a solid, well-organized outline
- Double check the credibility of their sources
- Prewrite, write, and rewrite their presentation.

AN ARGUABLE THESIS STATEMENT AND SOLID RESEARCH   Organizers use social media to notify people about the time, place, and purpose of protests and demonstrations. Recently organizers planned to hold a demonstration on one of the subway platforms used by San Francisco's Bay Area Rapid Transit (BART). Concerned about possible injuries or deaths if protestors or passengers should fall off the platform into the path of a train or on to the electric rail, BART officials made the decision to shut down cell phone coverage. Effectively this prevented planners from organizing their demonstration, which was to be held in protest to an

What would you do if you were in charge of BART and you learned that people were using social media to organize a big protest demonstration against the BART system?

earlier shooting of an individual by armed BART security guards.[9]

Suppose the professor teaching your English course gives this assignment: "Write an arguable thesis statement about BART's decision to close down cellular communications. Was it a violation of the First Amendment or a prudent business decision?" Analyze the following draft thesis statements and distinguish the arguable statements from those, which are off-topic or for which no plausible case can be developed.

1. Free speech protections extend to cellular communications.

2. A business has an obligation to protect its customers from foreseeable harm.

3. Freedom of speech is the cornerstone of an open society.

4. BART administrators have the right to restrict access to the BART-owned property, including its communications systems.

5. Concern for possible injury was not a sufficient cause for BART to have prevented peaceful protests.

6. What is wrong with BART?

We can imagine developing arguments in support of the first five, but not #6. That one is a question, not a claim. It assumes that there is something wrong with BART. But the grammatical structure is wrong because it suggests that the paper is going to be an investigation, rather than the defense of your position on this issue. A careful interpretation of the professor's prompt is always in order. "What is the professor asking me to do?" An arguable thesis is going to be a *claim* as we have used the term throughout this book. A claim is a statement that the maker of an argument is endeavoring to show to be true or probably true. #6, a question, does not fit that criterion.

The other candidates are contenders. But some are better than others. We suggest that #1, #2, and #3 do not meet the objective of the professor's assignment as well as #4 and #5 do. Those first three, while relevant, are expressions of principles and values that could be useful as premises in topdown ideological arguments, but they are not focused on BART. The assignment calls for claims that assert that the decision made by the BART officials was either the right one or the wrong one. #6 is not only vague, but it is not about BART's decision at all. A clear and arguable thesis statement for a class assignment always draws upon a careful interpretation and analysis of the professor's question prompt. The professor said to talk about "BART's decision." Only #4 and #5 fit the demand. The next step, after researching the issue thoroughly and with an open mind to both sides of the issue, would be to analyze and then evaluate the reasons for and against the BART decision.

MAP OUT THE ARGUMENTS PRO AND CON—THEN OUTLINE YOUR CASE Our recommended tool for analysis is the argument and decision mapping process detailed in Chapter 5. Lay out the competing positions. What kinds of considerations would you expect to find in your review of the arguments in the BART example? In addition to doing the research, think about how you would make the strongest possible case for both sides. You might bring in principles like protecting innocent people from harm, affirming the rights of free speech, affirming the rights of business owners to control the use of their own property, and affirming the importance of laws that give priority to free speech over other lesser considerations.

As you do the research it is important to get all the reasons on the table. *Work backward from conclusion to reasons and then to reasons for the reasons.* Dig out the implicit and explicit assumptions. Diagram and color-code the counterarguments and statements that reveal invitations to further deliberation. Discover where lines of reasoning have been abandoned. Once you have mapped the terrain in detail you can add your own additional reasons,

"BART'S Decision—Draft"

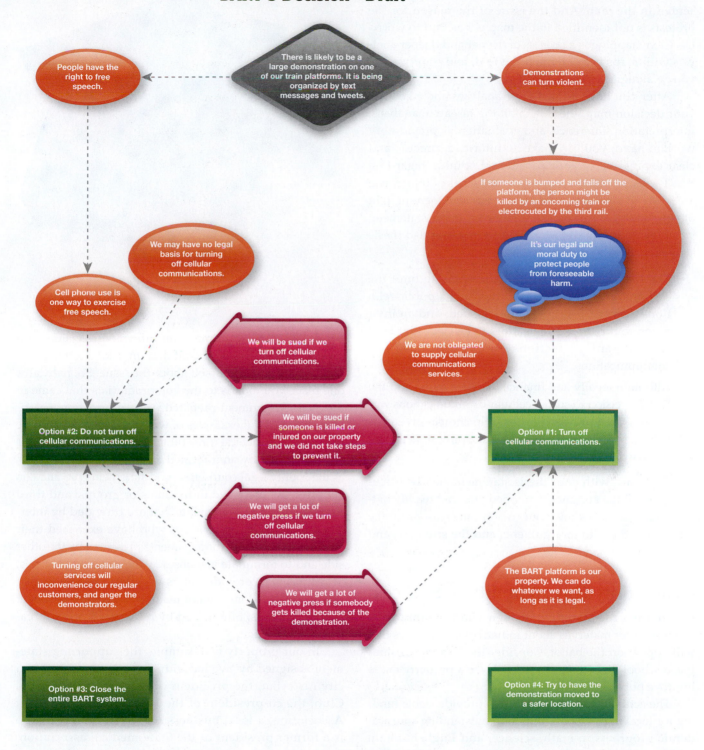

extend, or defend arguments that have come under criticism, and amplify the map until you have fully expressed the relevant reasoning. And then, using the basic tests for the quality of arguments developed and for evaluating the credibility of claims, apply your critical thinking skills of evaluation to the elements in your decision map. Are the arguments worthy? Are the initial premises they rely upon credible?

To give you more of an idea of how a decision map related to the BART example might be developed, we've provided some preliminary ideas in the draft map. That map is underdeveloped. You'll see that four options are identified. Maybe there are more options. Arguments and counterarguments are anticipated only for two of the options in the map. A more refined map would explore arguments for and against the other options as well.

There are unspoken assumptions that are not yet presented in the map. And the issue of the reason for the protests is not identified in the map either. Not to worry. Decision mapping is a process of deeper and deeper analysis with maps being refined, revised, and improved as you go along.

After you have refined your analyses and filled out your decision map, then, with all the research, analysis, interpretation, inference, and evaluation as preparatory work in hand, you can make an informed, precise, and clear expression of your considered opinion regarding BART's decision. Now, having done the heavy lifting, you are ready to write your arguable thesis statement in light of your analysis. As you formulate your thesis statement, you may now want to offer an even more refined thesis statement. How about one of these?

- The BART decision, while it appeared to limit the corporation's financial liabilities, was a public relations disaster, a sure way to get sued, and an invitation to jurists and legislators to be clear that First Amendment protections do extend to cellular communications.

- Although legally and financially risky, in the end the BART decision to curtail cellular communications was the only mature and responsible choice, given the risks to innocent bystanders that the protestors appear to have disregarded.

And now, with your thesis statement clearly articulated and all the arguments mapped, you can readily outline your case. You know your reasons, the reasons for the other side, the counterarguments and the strengths and weaknesses of each.

Evaluating the Credibility of Sources

If you are a registered voter then you probably have received voter materials about initiatives or measures that will appear on the ballot. Consider the following example, a school district's proposal to levee a property tax to improve public education:

The actual initiative proposed to provide stable funding for local high schools, maintain outstanding core academic programs in math, science, and English, retain highly qualified teachers, provide programs that prepare students for college and careers, and provide classroom materials like books and science equipment. Shall the Mountain Ridge Joint Union High School District be authorized to levy $35 per parcel annually for six years, with citizen oversight, an exemption for seniors, no funds for administrators' salaries, and every dollar staying in local high schools? (Yes/No.)

Like most voters, you probably have had limited exposure to the actual language of this property tax

proposal. Wanting to make an informed decision, you prepare to apply your critical thinking skills to the question by informing yourself about the issue. So, naturally, one place you look is to the voter materials that came in the mail. Government-prepared voter information materials provide useful examples of written arguments because they typically include three things: First an analysis of the ballot measure by an informed and impartial party, such as the county legal counsel; second statements pro and con supplied by interested individuals or groups; and third rebuttals to those statements that are provided by interested individuals and groups who have exercised their legal rights to review the arguments presented by the other side and to formulate responses.[10] The point of all of this, of course, is to provide voters with information so that important decisions are not made by knee-jerk System-1 snap judgments, but instead by reflective System-2 reasoned deliberation.

In our property tax example, the supporting statement is signed by five individuals: a local resident and city historian, the president of the Home and School Club, the co-president of the Parent Teacher Student Association, a local business owner, and an MD who is a former president of the State medical association. A rebuttal to the pro argument is presented by someone who describes himself simply as a concerned voter. This same individual submitted a position statement against the ballot measure. The rebuttal to the opposition is signed by the district school board president and its budget advisory committee members, two different chairmen of local charitable foundations that support education, as well as an alumnus of the district who is identified as a Rhodes Scholar. Without having access to the position statements of either side in this issue,

How credible are ballot initiative signature drive workers?

but simply based on your life experience and what you learned in Chapter 6 about evaluating sources, which side of the issue appears to have more initial perceived credibility? Why?

Mindful of the risks as well as the benefits of System-1 heuristic thinking, we want to avoid jumping to the conclusion that the "concerned voter" is automatically less credible than the various individuals and groups that have come out in support of the ballot measure. By the same token, we don't want to jump to the conclusion that because it is a tax increase it is automatically a bad idea or that because the money is for schools that it is automatically a good idea. All of these "fast and furious" one-rule decisions can lead us to problems. In California, where we live, cleverly deceitful authors of ballot initiatives know that too many of us are likely to rely too heavily on our System-1 reactions instead of digging deeper into the ballot measures. So they disguise their intentions by using misleading titles for their initiatives. For all we know in California, some outfit with a title-nobody-could-be-against, like "Taxpayers Who Love Democracy," might sponsor an initiative perhaps named "The Freedom of Communication for All Act," which, if passed, would actually regulate or restrict various modes of communication. We never know. In our state it's important to apply System-2 and read the fine print.

How might we activate our System-2 thinking to evaluate the credibility of sources? Recalling the guidance in Chapter 6, we can start by asking whether the individual or group has the relevant expertise. Ideally our source, the person or people who are authoring the message, will enjoy all 12 of the positive characteristics of a trustworthy source. The list is straightforward. We've reproduced it here for you.

Suggestions for Identifying Credible Source Material

1. Select appropriate databases. As powerful as it is, we suggest not limiting your searches to Google and Google Scholar. In addition, use the subject matter–oriented databases in your campus library.

2. Search for source material before finalizing your thesis. One mark of a strong critical thinker is the realization that everyone has their point of view, including the investigator. To avoid biased searches that only produce evidence to support their preconceptions, strong critical thinkers intentionally discipline themselves to hold off taking sides or formulating their thesis until after the research is completed.

3. Be your own best critic. Once you have taken a tentative position on an issue, discipline yourself to search for relevant counter-evidence to that position. It will either strengthen your case to be able to account for the counter-evidence, or lead you to reconsider, which is what maturity of judgment and strong critical thinking would require.

4. It is better to list several good sources than to list every possible document that might remotely apply. Refine your search to produce a manageable number of sources. Narrow your keywords, define your audience, limit the time frame to only the past few years, seek sources that give even-handed overviews, or that are fundamental or seminal works.

5. Evaluate the credibility of the sources. Find out who the author is, what the basis is for the claims being made, who manages the Web site where those claims are posted. Check the credentials of all proponents and opponents, evaluate the methods used in the source materials, establish that the material is authentic, reliable, and based on facts rather than a clever hoax. Remember Chapter 6; don't end up on a blind date with Godzilla and contributing money to save the tree octopi of the Pacific Northwest.

TWELVE CHARACTERISTICS OF A TRUSTWORTHY SOURCE

- Learned in topic X
- Experienced in topic X
- Speaking about X
- Up-to-date about X
- Capable of explaining the basis for their claim or their advice about X
- Unbiased
- Truthful
- Free of conflicts of interest
- Acting in accord with our interests
- Unconstrained
- Informed about the specifics of the case at hand
- Mentally stable

Prewriting, Writing, and Rewriting

When the time comes to set fingers to keyboard, the actual process of writing an effective essay is commonly described as having three phases: *prewriting, writing,* and *rewriting.*[11] Within each of these phases there are specific steps that can yield a higher-quality final written product. Here is what we and others suggest.[12]

PREWRITING: Organizing my thoughts—strategic decisions about presenting my case. Grab the audience's attention, explain your purpose, and describe the order in which your case will unfold the various arguments and counterarguments pro and con and the supporting documentation. Be sure to do the following:

1. Identify a topic, problem, or question as clearly as possible.
2. Develop a clear, focused, plausible, and arguable thesis statement.
3. Gather relevant evidence and credible source material.
4. Prepare a decision map that organizes all the arguments pro and con, from which you can then outline the entire presentation of your case, section by section.

WRITING: From the title to endnotes, put together one complete draft. Be sure to:

5. Draft a strong, clear, succinct introduction telling the reader what to expect.
6. Draft the body of your essay, focusing on main ideas and sub-ideas. Stick to your outline, or if a change is needed, change the outline too. Don't soar off into a free flight of opinions or irrelevant digressions after

doing all the work of organizing your ideas and researching your topic.

7. Draft the conclusion, which summarizes your views and reminds the audience of the issue, its importance, and the main thesis you have defended.

REWRITING: Check it. Fix it. Make it sing your song.

8. Rewrite the draft for clarity, flow, style, and interest. Delete repetitious material. Smooth out transitions. Be sure that the structural organization is clear to the reader so that the reader does not get lost in the details.
9. Check the craft before launching by reviewing the entire draft for mechanical or organizational errors, grammatical issues, misspellings, missing citations, sentence fragments, etc. Make edits as warranted and reread.
10. If available, incorporate feedback from peers, external reviewers, or the instructor.

> "Thinking like an effective writer means carefully, thoughtfully, skeptically evaluating potential information resources for credibility, authority, and bias, being unwilling to settle for the borderline-relevant, easy-to-find, pops-to-the-top-of-a-Google-search source, and taking the time to rigorously critique all the information that goes into your work."
>
> *Gail Gradowski, University Librarian*

Two Practical Tips

Extremely successful and influential writers, like George Orwell and Stephen King,[13] offer interesting and candid guidance on how to practice the craft more effectively. We know we are not in their league. So, sticking with the theme that writing is 90-plus percent perspiration, we do have some practical tips to suggest.

JOURNAL

Telling Your Compelling Story

What compelling story do you want to tell? How could you use the practical suggestions offered in the section "Organize and Develop Your Presentation," and the critical thinking questions that effective writers ask, to organize your ideas and to sequence how you tell your story to your audience?

A writing session arcs like a workout session: warm up, hit your stride, cool down.

We find it helpful to copy and paste the outline for our written work right into the document file that will become the first draft. This gives us the architectural structure, the red steel as it were, that we can then build upon. The outline provides us with the heading, sub-heading, and all the reminders of what we planned to say and where we planned to say it in the flow of the essay. The more detailed the outline, the better. Add notes that represent the evidence you plan on using in your case, a clever example or analogy that you want to use, quotes that fit well at various points. And don't forget to identify your sources. They can go into the outline too! There is nothing that wastes more time than placing an important quote or piece of evidence in your outline only to realize later that you have forgotten where you found it. Many of the examples in this textbook started out as reminders typed in a different font color or as track-changes comment balloons so we would remember where to best use them. The endnotes and the Internet search suggestions were included so that the finished text could be enriched with real-world examples when we came back through to rewrite and to polish the rougher drafts.

Secondly, there is an arc to the quality of writing that can be produced in a single sitting. Much like it takes a runner time to warm up and settle into a comfortable pace, the effective writer is likely to notice that when she or he first sits down to write, the quality of the work may not be as strong as it will become once the writer has become more connected and engages with the writing activity. And again, like the runner who will experience fatigue over time that will inevitably compromise his or her pace, the writing will exhibit a peak in writing quality and ultimately begin to show signs of fatigue.

In our experience there are at least two lessons to be learned from becoming aware of this writing quality arc. First, it is highly improbable that a high-quality written communication can be produced in a single session. Second, to improve the weaker beginning and ending sections of a writing session it often works to start by reviewing, and editing the writing completed during the *previous* session. Like applying overlapping roof shingles to keep the rain out, each session overlaps the previous a bit and is, in turn, overlapped by the session that follows. Using reviewing and editing the previous session as a warm-up, it is easier to move forward into the new material, having settled in to a writing groove. Overlapping the arcs in writing quality is more likely to produce writing that is consistent in its quality from start to finish rather than work that is choppy, disconnected, and uneven.

15.3 Evaluating Effectiveness

We know how to evaluate the worthiness of arguments to be sure that they are sound, logical, non-fallacious, and non-circular. So if the arguments we produce in our written work meet those standards, then we have the "sound" part of "sound and effective" covered. But how do writers determine that their presentations are effective? To assess the potential for their written arguments to be effective, writers first assure themselves that they have correctly analyzed, interpreted, and addressed each element in the rhetorical situation. And second, as with all writing, the writers attend to the craft and mechanics of writing.

Features of Sound and Effective Written Argumentation

What are the features of effective written argumentation? We shared many of them in the discussions about the rhetorical situation and the methods of developing the presentation. Here again are a few of the most important points to remember when your goal is to persuade reasonable people that your position on a given topic is the correct one or that your recommendations are worth accepting:

- An effective written presentation addresses a clear and manageable thesis in a way that is appropriate for the intended audience and the mode, purpose, and context of the communication.

- The reasons and claims are focused on supporting a focused and plausible thesis statement.

- The author has delivered a fair-minded and balanced discussion of the pros and cons, analyzed the relevant evidence, addressed key assumptions, and presented a credible case in a thorough and objective manner.

Effective Writing is Passionate, Persistent, and Personal

Dear Peter,

When a publishing contract presented the wonderful opportunity to write our book, *They Poured Fire On Us From the Sky*, big challenges came with it. What did we want the book to do? How do we do it?

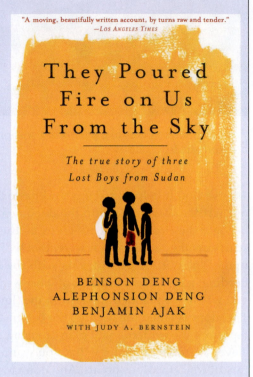

I'd met my co-authors three years earlier and never before had I seen so much hope in anyone's eyes, or known anyone with so much pain in their past. As little boys, war destroyed their homes, villages, and families in Southern Sudan. They fled a thousand miles barefoot across deserts and mountains, through bullets and lions, and then languished for years in a refugee camp in Kenya. The conflict still raged in Sudan, their loved ones suffered silently, they wanted their story to speak for those who couldn't speak for themselves.

Their story had altered my perspective forever so I knew it would impact other Americans. Between us, we'd determined what we wanted the book to do. Next we had to analyze how to do it.

How should we tell it? Should it be my interpretation as a non-fiction or fictionalized true story? The old adage of writing, "Show. Don't tell." swayed me otherwise. A memoir that maintained the integrity of their voices would be the most effective.

Compelling storytelling has an arc. We had a large collection of handwritten journals, emails, and text files filled with gems of compelling anecdotes, fresh metaphors, and lush descriptions, none of it in order, or with dates or place names that could be found on a map. Like assembling a 3D jigsaw puzzle without a picture to follow. The content was extraordinary, but also one huge ongoing crisis with the structure of a plate of spaghetti. How do we explain so many potential story arcs? We chose the human story: the five year separation and eventual reunion of the brothers. For a year my office was wallpapered with notes and outlines pasted on one big arc that ran clear around the room. To deliver the most powerful message, that structure was vital.

Judy A. Bernstein

- The writing style is concise and coherent, and the author uses headings and an organized sequence of ideas and transitions to connect the paragraphs into a flowing essay.
- The author communicates a detectable voice, perspective, or personality and demonstrates respect for the audience and the audience's capacity to reach reasonable conclusions if presented with the relevant information.
- The written presentation is mechanically error free in terms of grammar, punctuation, spelling, and citations.

Top Ten Ways to Earn an "F" on a Writing Assignment

1. Plagiarize. Represent someone else's work as if it were your own.

2. Quote sources that are not credible or not even real.

3. String together direct quotes without adding context or interpretation.

4. Speed-write the essay and skip the proofreading.

5. Include gross factual errors or blatant misrepresentations of ideas.

6. Display close-minded hostility to opposing viewpoints.

7. Ramble aimlessly just to reach the required paper length.

8. Make errors in spelling, punctuation, grammar, and capitalization.

9. Use clichés, profanity, emoticons, jargon, and vacuous buzz words.

10. Misunderstand the assignment, disrespect the subject matter, insult your audience, and write on the wrong topic.

"I didn't think of it as someone else writing my term paper, I thought of it more as a guest blogger situation."

A Tool for Evaluating Critical Thinking and Writing

What standards do strong critical thinkers use when evaluating the soundness and effectiveness of their writing? Written presentations are generally evaluated in terms of the accuracy and efficacy of four domains: (1) *content*, which includes all assertions and supporting evidence; (2) *organization*, which includes the clarity of paragraph arrangement and effectiveness of transitions between paragraphs; (3) *mechanics*, which includes grammar, spelling, punctuation, and vocabulary; and (4) *style*, which includes formatting and, when appropriate, citation style. These domains can be further represented by two overarching categories: *the author's demonstration of critical thinking through the writing, and the author's command and competency at the craft of writing.* Strong critical thinking and masterful writing competency will be observed in a sound and effectively written argumentation. But, like any two independent but compatible sets of skills, strength in one does not ensure strength in the other. Both must be evaluated independently.

Let's assume you have organized, developed, and written a presentation that presents your well-researched best judgment about what to believe or what to do. And now you want to evaluate it yourself, before you hand it in to your professor or share it with whomever your intended audience may happen to be. We have an evaluation tool to share with you: The *Rubric for Evaluating Written Argumentation.*[14]

The *Rubric for Evaluating Written Argumentation* (REWA) is designed to provide detailed feedback on how written material that is intended to argue persuasively on behalf of a given claim, opinion, or recommendation might be improved. As you can see by reviewing the REWA, it addresses eight different aspects of sound and effective writing:

> **Purpose and Focus**
>
> **Depth of Thought**
>
> **Thesis**
>
> **Reasoning**
>
> **Organization**
>
> **Voice**
>
> **Grammar and Vocabulary**
>
> **Mechanics of Presentation**

How to Apply the *Rubric for Evaluating Written Argumentation*

Because each of the eight rows on the *Rubric for Evaluating Written Argumentation* addresses a different aspect of sound and effective writing, each aspect should be evaluated separately. When using the REWA give yourself a score on each row separately. The REWA offers exactly four evaluative options. From highest to lowest the four are: *Highly Developed, Developed, Underdeveloped,* and *Substandard.*

Rubric for Evaluating Written Argumentation © 2011 Gittens, C.A., & Measured Reasons LLC. Reprinted with Permission. www.measuredreasons.com			
	Highly Developed	**Developed**	**Underdeveloped**	**Substandard**

	Highly Developed	Developed	Underdeveloped	Substandard
Purpose and Focus	The writer has made insightful and mature decisions about focus, organization, and content to communicate clearly and effectively. The purpose and focus of the writing are clear to the reader and the organization and content are well chosen, sophisticated, and/or persuasive.	The writer has made good decisions about focus, organization, and content to communicate clearly and effectively. The purpose and focus of the writing are clear to the reader and the organization and content achieve the purpose as well.	The writer's decisions about focus, organization, or content sometimes interfere with clear, effective communication. The purpose of the writing is not fully achieved.	The writer's decisions about focus, organization, or content interfere with communication. The purpose of the writing is not achieved.
Depth of Thought	The information presented reveals the writer's assimilation and understanding of the material. The writer is convincingly aware of implications beyond the immediate subject.	The information presented reveals the writer appreciates and understands the material. The writer seems aware of implications beyond the immediate subject.	The information presented reveals that the writer has only partially assimilated or understood the material. The writer shows some awareness of implications beyond the immediate subject.	The information presented reveals the writer's lack of assimilation and understanding of the material. The writer's assertions lack awareness of implications beyond the immediate subject.
Thesis	Has a highly developed, defendable assertion that provides focus and direction to the essay. Uses sources to support, extend, and inform, but not substitute for the writer's own development of ideas.	Has a clear recognizable assertion that provides focus and direction to the essay. Uses sources to support and inform writer's own development of ideas.	Uses relevant sources but lacks variety of sources and/ or the skillful combination of sources necessary to support a central assertion.	Lacks a clear, recognizable assertion and/or lacks adequate sources.
Reasoning	Substantial and well-reasoned development of ideas. All key assumptions are made explicit. Credible evidence is germane, and accurately analyzed and fair-mindedly interpreted. Displays strong critical thinking skills and habits of mind. (See *Holistic Critical Thinking Scoring Rubric*.)	Offers solid reasoning. Most key assumptions are recognized or made explicit. Most inferences are accurate, most examples are on point.	Offers some supporting evidence. The case includes some examples that are too general, not interpreted, or not clearly relevant to thesis.	Offers simplistic, underdeveloped, fallacious, circular, or irrelevant arguments. Includes exaggerations, faulty reasoning, factual errors, biased statements, etc. (See *Holistic Critical Thinking Scoring Rubric*.)
Organization	Sequencing of ideas within paragraphs and transitions between paragraphs flow smoothly and coherently throughout the paper. The writer shows clear effort to assist the reader in following the logic of the ideas expressed.	Sequencing of ideas within paragraphs and transitions between paragraphs make the writer's points coherent and easy to follow.	Sentence structure and/ or word choice sometimes interfere with clarity and coherence. Needs to improve sequencing of ideas within paragraphs and transitions between paragraphs to make the writing easy to follow.	Ineffective sentence structure, word choice, transitions, and/ or sequencing of ideas make reading and understanding difficult.
Voice	The writer's tone or control of language consistently reflects a confident or authoritative central "voice" or "personality." The writer shows clear discernment of and effective engagement of intended audience.	The writer's tone or control of language generally reflects a confident or authoritative central "voice" or "personality." The writer shows appropriate and consistent awareness of intended audience.	A central "voice" or "personality" is evident, though inconsistent in minor ways. The writer shows little or inconsistent awareness of a particular audience.	The writer's tone or general control of language is so lacking in consistency that little central "voice" or "personality" is evident. The writer lacks awareness of a particular audience.
Grammar and Vocabulary	Sentence structure is complex and powerful. The writer has used vivid, purposefully crafted, and varied sentence styles and lengths. The writer displays a broad range of vocabulary, with effective, accurate, and contextually appropriate word usage.	Sentences are effective and varied in style and length. Grammar or usage errors are minimal and do not distract the reader from understanding the intended meaning. The writer displays a satisfactory range of vocabulary and accurate and appropriate word usage.	Sentences show errors in structure. The writer uses limited variety in sentence style and length. The writer displays a limited range of vocabulary. Errors of diction and usage are evident but do not interfere significantly with readability.	Sentence structure is simple, with practically no variety in sentence style and length. Frequent errors in sentence structure interfere with readability. The writer displays an extremely limited vocabulary. Diction and syntax errors make communication confusing or unintelligible.
Mechanics and Presentation	Written response is virtually free of punctuation, spelling, or capitalization errors. The writer utilizes an appropriate and attractive format, presentation, and style (citations) for the assignment.	Written response contains only occasional punctuation, spelling, or capitalization errors. The writer utilizes an appropriate format, presentation, and style (citations) for the assignment.	Written response contains many punctuation, spelling, or capitalization errors. Errors interfere with meaning in some places. The writer makes some errors in format, presentation, or style (citations) for the assignment.	Written response contains many severe punctuation, spelling, or capitalization errors that hinder communication. The writer utilizes inappropriate format, presentation, or style (citations) for the assignment or the formatting is absent.

For example, you might read an essay you have prepared for your Introductory English Composition course and realize that you should evaluate your Purpose and Focus, Depth of Thought, and Thesis (the first three rows) as "Developed," your Reasoning, Organization, and Voice (the middle three rows) as "Underdeveloped" but your Grammar and Vocabulary, and Mechanics of Presentation as simply "Substandard." You know right away that you need to spend more time on these last categories for sure. And you know that you could improve the middle ones as well. By engaging in this self-evaluation and addressing these categories you should be able to improve your essay and, in turn, improve your effectiveness as a writer—and your grade too!

As you can see, in the REWA each row can have a different evaluation decision. This is great! It tells you, the author, where your case needs more work to maximize its effectiveness. Contrast the REWA with the *Holistic Critical Thinking Scoring Rubric* (HCTSR) presented in Chapter 1. When applying the HCTSR to evaluate the quality of the critical thinking manifested in a presentation, we have to arrive at a holistic overall qualitative evaluation of *critical thinking* as either "strong," "acceptable," "unacceptable," or "weak." Unlike the HCTSR, the *Rubric for Evaluating Written Argumentation* does not provide an overall or composite score. Instead it yields eight separate scores, one on each aspect of the written argumentation.

Whenever you are evaluating a written presentation, whether your own work or the work of another person, we strongly recommend that the REWA and the HCTSR be used in tandem. This way a person can accurately focus their evaluative attention on each of the specific criteria as expressed in the two rubrics. Otherwise the tendency is to confuse, omit, or collapse the different individually important criteria. Employing both rubrics allows for both the holistic evaluation of the soundness of the critical thinking exhibited in a piece of writing (HCTSR) and a detailed analysis of the effectiveness of the writing (REWA). Remember that the HCTSR assigns a single rubric score or evaluation decision that represents the best overall characterization of the critical thinking being displayed. By contrast, the REWA analyzes eight separate aspects of the writing and so it provides for eight scores.

Summing up this chapter,

sound and effective written argumentation requires the consideration of four key elements of the rhetorical situation: Author, Audience, Purpose, and Presentation. Effective writers carefully and fair-mindedly articulate the reasons in support of the claim that is their central purpose in writing. The reasons and claims are focused on supporting a focused and plausible thesis statement in a way that is designed to reach and to persuade the intended audience. The author communicates a detectable voice, perspective, or personality, and demonstrates respect for the audience and the audience's capacity to reach reasonable conclusions if presented with the relevant information. Sound and effective writing is achievable because it is only about 10 percent inspiration, but about 90 percent largely practiced effort. The *Rubric for Evaluating Written Argumentation* is a useful tool for assessing your own writing on eight essential dimensions: Purpose and Focus, Depth of Thought, Thesis, Reasoning, Organization, Voice, Grammar and Vocabulary, and Mechanics and Presentation.

Key Concepts

author's case includes all of the pros and cons along with the supporting evidence that the author presents to the audience to establish the truth of a given statement or the wisdom of a given recommendation.

rhetorical situation is the interactive combination of four elements: a specific author is using a specific mode of communication or presentation to engage a specific audience for the specific purpose.

Applications

Reflective Log

Analyze your own prior writing: Select one research paper or persuasive essay that you have written for a course this term or in a previous term. Write a reflection about the process you went through when preparing and writing that paper/essay. As you write this reflective piece provide as many details as you can recall. How long did you spend working on the paper? What process of gathering evidence did you engage in? What sources did you use? Did you select the sources or were they provided to you? What planning steps did you use when preparing to write? How much editing and rewriting did you engage in? Using the HCTSR and REWA, evaluate the critical thinking and the writing that you displayed. Now, re-read your reflection and add a final paragraph: What is the relationship between my writing process and my critical thinking evaluation? How might I change my approach to preparing written cases in the future to reflect stronger critical thinking?

Individual Exercises

Why? Why do you suppose that every chapter of this book invites you to contribute to a Reflective Log, a Writing Space, a Journal, and a Shared Response?

Apply the REWA. Select an editorial published in your city or campus newspaper. Evaluate it with the REWA. Working individually or with a writing partner, research and write an opinion piece on the same topic. Submit it to campus or city newspaper as a letter to the editor.

Penn Jillette on connecting with the audience: On August 16, 2011, magician Penn Jillette, of the duo Penn & Teller, was interviewed on the NPR radio program *Talk of the Nation*.[15] Jillette was on the show to discuss his book, *God, No! Signs That You May Already Be an Atheist*. When listeners phone in during the interview, the host, Neal Conan, often puts them on the air. One caller identifies himself as a fellow magician and conveys the struggle he has forming an emotional or deep connection with his audience during his performances. The caller wonders if Jillette ever experienced a similar struggle. Review the discussion of audience and the importance of establishing a connection with the audience to make an effective case. Write up an analysis of this rhetorical context in terms of author (the magician), audience, purpose, and presentation. Explain how these four elements strain the soundness and effectiveness of the magician's case. Search "Penn Jillette Talk of the Nation" to locate the program at the NPR web site and hear Penn Jillette's explanation.

Research for campus president: Consider the following situation: You are the leader of a group of students known as the *President's Student Advisory Council*. An issue has come up on campus regarding food sold in the student cafeteria. The president of your institution is seeking your advice about the sale of genetically engineered foods on campus. The president wants you to prepare a written recommendation, which responds to the following question: Should the campus sell or serve foods that have been genetically modified? The president has asked that you consider the arguments on both sides of this issue, and recommend whether to continue to offer genetically modified foods on campus. For this letter you must gather at least four credible sources of evidence. Your evidence must represent strong arguments for both the pro and con sides. Describe each source as well as how and where you obtained it. Provide an analysis of the source's credibility. After reviewing the source evidence, what recommendation would you make to the president and why?

The Internet is a liar's paradise: Strong critical thinkers treat Internet sources with a healthy skepticism until they thoroughly check the credibility of those sources. Nobody wants to be tricked into including factual errors and outrageous inaccuracies in their written assignments. A case in point: Suppose you have been given the assignment of writing a paper for your American History course on the effectiveness of Dr. Martin Luther King's non-violent, civil disobedience in undermining the culture of racial segregation in the United States. A search on the Internet produces the following possible sources:

—http://www.thekingcenter.org/
—http://www.martinlutherking.org/
—http://en.wikipedia.org/wiki/Martin_Luther_King, Jr
—http://www.kinginstitute.info/

Visit each of these Web sites and evaluate their credibility using the tools presented here in Chapter 15 and earlier in Chapter 6. Get past the home pages. Be sure to analyze each site completely. (HINT: One of these is a hate site intended to mislead gullible searchers.) What observations can you make about the author(s) and their credentials, organizational affiliations, accuracy of their "information," and hidden or not so hidden biases?

Does the Web address alone influence your perception of the credibility of the source? How accurate was that perception in light of what you observed by reviewing each Web site? How can we use our critical thinking skills of analysis and evaluation to determine whether these are sources that we should trust enough to cite in our written assignment?

SHARED RESPONSE

Marketing Matters

Go to your college's public admission Web page and consider the arguments implicitly and explicitly made there for why people should apply. Evaluate those arguments using the REWA. Be sure to provide your reason(s), not just your opinion. And, comment respectfully on the evaluations others offer. [Your class may wish to consider synthesizing these evaluations into positive recommendations that could be shared with the Director of Admissions.]

Group Exercises

Artificial sweeteners: In June 2011 a number of newspaper and Internet news sources reported the findings from a study linking the consumption of diet soda to increased waistlines over time and increased sugar levels in the blood stream. Researchers hypothesize that it may be the artificial sweeteners in the diet soda that are boosting people's appetites as well as blood-sugar levels.[16] Assume that you are an intern in the legal department of Standard Sodas Inc. Your supervisor asks you to join her team in crafting a response letter to the public. The letter will be posted on the company's Web site. The team must develop a sound (logical and truthful) and effective (persuasive) written case for why consumers should continue to consume Standard Diet Soda.

Employer exploitation of fashion models: This project is intended for a group of three to five students working collaboratively. It can serve as a cumulative final paper in a course on writing and critical thinking.

    Hypothetical question: *Should student leaders at your college initiate or join a national effort by college students to secure legislation regarding working age, body mass, nutrition, etc. to prevent the fashion industry employers from endangering the physical or mental health of runway models?*

    Context: Ethical business practices suggest that employers should not put workers at unnecessary risk. The impact of culturally relative notions of physical beauty in our media-intensive society can have significant negative effects on the behavior and health of impressionable people of all ages, but particularly the youth. To what extent should an employer's freedom be limited, if at all, in the interests of the workers or of society? Employers who knowingly exploit workers, and industries that unnecessarily endanger impressionable young people, have traditionally come under scrutiny by college students seeking to build a more just and humane society. Often through boycotts and by seeking legislative changes or by insisting that the institution alter its investment practices, students at many of the nation's colleges have awakened their school's social consciousness to unacceptable business practices, whether in the United States or abroad. Some of the world's largest corporations and most entrenched business have been moved to alter their policies by the efforts initiated by college students. The fashion industry, in these respects, is no more formidable or exceptional than other industries. And, more than the harm done to their workers, the images of men and women, which the fashion industry presents as "desirable" and "beautiful" have potentially profound effects on people, particularly high school and college aged people. Hence efforts to secure legislative changes in the United States and in

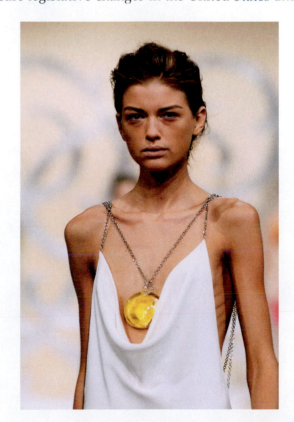

Europe initiated by that segment of the population would carry special economic and political significance for that industry.

Assignment: Fully research this topic in all of its historical, social, political, ethical, and scientific dimensions. Make a well-reasoned, fair-minded, scientifically complete and accurate, articulate, informed, well-organized, scholarly, ethically wise, humanly sensitive, and technically feasible recommendation that answers the *hypothetical question* stated above.

Audience: Write so that your recommendation may be transmitted to and read and understood by your colleague students, by intelligent college-educated members of the general public, the officials at your college, newspaper editors, and legislators. Your written presentation may include charts, images, video clips, or tables as your project team deems appropriate. There is no word limit or page limit on this assignment other than the limits you impose on yourselves when being mindful of your audience.

Due date: To be established by your instructor.

Chapter 16
Ethical Decision Making

Value judgment: "Regardless of the possible benefits and potential risks, cheating is fundamentally dishonest, disrespectful, and dishonorable." Ethical Imperative: "Don't cheat."

WHAT kinds of values or principles might be called "ethical imperatives"?

HOW is ethical decision making different than decision making in general?

HOW does critical thinking help when faced with divergent ethical imperatives?

 Learning Outcomes:

16.1 Explain ethical imperatives using examples.

16.2 Distinguish ethical decision making from decision making more broadly understood.

16.3 Explain how strong critical thinking skills and positive habits of mind assist in deciding what to do when ethical imperatives diverge.

"Yes, I do feel bad about it," said the college student on the telephone. "I'm a good student, I work hard, and I need to get into medical school. If I cheat, I get an A. If not, maybe an A- or B+. Not good enough."

"But what about the other students?" replied the journalist, "You're not being fair to them. If you cheat you'll alter the grading curve. You'd be hurting everyone else in the class!"

"No. You have it wrong. Most of them are cheating too. So the curve is already altered. If I don't cheat I'm only putting myself at a disadvantage."

While the student responded, the journalist was taking notes and recording the phone call, looking for material on a story about academic dishonesty at the college. "What if you're caught? You could be expelled," said the journalist.

"Not going to happen. I've learned a lot of tricks since junior high. But even if the professor sees me cheating, what is he going to do? First he has to prove it. And even then I might only get a warning and maybe have to retake the exam or the course. What are the stats on students who are actually expelled for cheating? Miniscule, I'm sure."

"You said that you feel bad about cheating, but maybe you're also enjoying the excitement too," observed the journalist.

"There's a little bit of a rush, I suppose. Like, if I use a paper from **SchoolSucks.com,** will the professor discover it on **Turnitin.com?** Or if a buddy texts me the answers to a multiple-choice exam, will the professor see me using my phone? But, yeah, in the end I'm not happy needing to cheat. I don't like to think of myself that way. It's not like I'm a jock who has to have the athletics department tutor do my homework for me so I can stay eligible."[1]

"I can see that you're intelligent," replied the journalist. "And yes, the 2014 report of a massive scandal at University of North Carolina involving 1,500 athletes over 20 years was a huge embarrassment.[2] But let's not stereotype athletes. Not all athletes cheat and not all cheaters are athletes. In 2013 Harvard expelled 70 students for cheating.[3] In 2010, hundreds of undergraduate business students had to retake a mid-term exam because of cheating.[4] A GMAT scandal seriously affected thousands of aspiring graduate students in 2008.[5] In 1994, 24 seniors were expelled for cheating from the U.S. Naval Academy only a month before graduation.[6] In 2005, 21 students, including some graduate students, were expelled or withdrew from the University of Virginia for honor code violations involving cheating.[7] And more recently cheating scandals have rocked other nations.[8] In January 2012 the CBS show *60 Minutes* ran a story, 'The Perfect Score,' about felony fraud indictments for an organized network of college-aged brokers and test-takers who charged high school students thousands of dollars to take the SAT for them.[9] Why all the cheating? What do you think is happening?" asked the journalist.

"Can't tell you." replied the student. "Bad things happen. But none of that is about me."

After pausing for a moment to think, the journalist said, "Okay. Let's talk about you. Can you say more about not wanting to think of yourself as a cheater?"

"Look. My parents brought me up to be an honest person. No way am I going to become the Bernie Madoff or the John Edwards of the medical profession. When I finish medical school and start my professional practice, people are going to come to me expecting that I know how to help them. I won't be cheating then because I don't want to hurt anybody."

"So, you're saying it's okay to cheat until you get what you want?" asked the journalist. "I understand. Hey, look at Cam Newton. He was accused of academic dishonesty in college, and then he goes on to win the Heisman Trophy and become the #1 overall in the NFL draft. Now he's making millions as the quarterback for the Carolina Panthers.[10] You know what they say: If you're not cheating you're not trying."

"I don't know about Cam Newton. But you are one cynical journalist!" said the student. "Or are you just baiting me—trying to get a good quote or something? Hey, I get it now. You're recording this phone call. Right? I didn't give you permission to do that!"

"So, can I quote you in the story about cheating in college?" responded the journalist.

"No way!" said the student. "Let me be clear. If you use my name in a story about cheating, I'll sue you. My reputation is at stake. And I'm not going to rat out my friends."

Undaunted, the journalist pushed harder. "But you admitted you cheated in college and that you have been cheating since junior high school. You say you've thought it through, and you've decided that the benefits to you outweigh the risks. And you claim to believe that your cheating does no harm to any other students—or at least it does not harm any of the other students who are also cheating. In other words, you claim that your cheating is justified. Yet now you threaten to sue me for simply reporting what's true? If you're ashamed, stop cheating. If not, what's your problem? If cheating is justified, why are you hiding what you're doing? Or is it that you know deep down that it is unethical to cheat?"

The line was quiet for a second then the student said, "This conversation is over!"

The ethical question is not "Do people cheat?" but "Is cheating unethical?" Although cheating is commonplace, the majority of students who admit to cheating still feel some level of guilt about it.[11] Intentional misrepresentation is dishonest. It would be dishonest to submit, as if the work were my own, a term paper that I did not write. It would be dishonest to hand in a paper into which

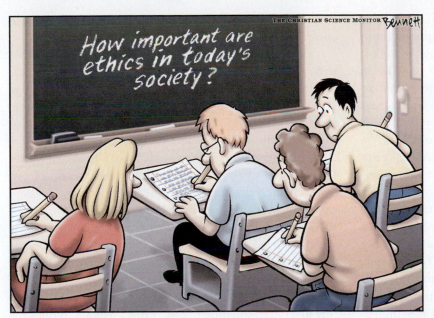

I had copied a block of text without using quotation marks and giving proper credit to the author of that text block. I am intentionally misrepresenting my actual knowledge when I copy someone else's answers during an exam, or use prohibited aids, like notes inked on my wrist. I am intentionally misrepresenting the truth if I make up false citations, or present myself as having completed a program or earned an academic degree when in fact I have not. If this reminds you of some of the things we talked about in Chapter 6 on evaluating the credibility of sources, you would be right. There we were concerned to maintain a healthy skepticism and to use critical thinking to protect ourselves from being deceived by claims others may make. In the case of academic dishonesty the situation is reversed. Here we are concerned not to intentionally mislead or deceive others about the extent of our knowledge and academic accomplishments. Because we believe that the ethical ideal is not to be dishonest, we feel guilty if we do cheat. Cheating is not consistent with our sense of ethics.

The term **ethics** refers to a set of behavioral ideals or moral principles that guide us in determining right and wrong. We can think of these ideals and principles as a set of core values and beliefs.[12] The source of these core ethical values and beliefs for most human beings is a combination of family upbringing, pressure to conform to the standards of one's peer group, social mores, organizational culture, and religious heritage.

In response to the question "How important are ethics in today's society?" we might consider the negative impacts of unethical business practices on innocent people. Was it ethical for General Motors (GM) to conceal dangerous ignition design defects for a decade or more? When the corporate deceit came to light we learned that GM knew that the defect had contributed to at least 42

deaths and 58 injuries.[13] Or what about the 15 percent of recreational triathletes trying to get an edge on their competition by brain doping?[14] Is that just about their own health risks? Or is the cheating affecting the sport as well as taking unfair advantage of their more honest competitor? And what will we learn from the class action lawsuit against 23 and Me, the genetic testing company, alleging misleading advertising, making medical claims that have never been federally approved, and providing their customers with meaningless test results?[15] Or consider the ethical lapses by Veterans Administration hospital bureaucrats who directed that appointment requests not be logged so that they could appear to be providing timely care to veterans when, in fact, they were not.[16]

Except perhaps when we are in college or when we suffer a major misfortune, we seldom scrutinize the cluster of ethical values and beliefs by which we have been living. For the most part, we are unreflectively comfortable with them. Oh, perhaps we wonder why our views about right and wrong, which seem so obviously true to us, are not more widely shared by people of other age groups, professions, countries, religious traditions, or historical eras. For most of us that is either just a point of curiosity, or at most a source of concern only because those others, with their strange and unorthodox views, might somehow cause us problems. Of course, they look at us the same way. Which begs the question "Could they be correct about right and wrong and we be mistaken?"

Ethics Content vs. Ethical Decision Making

For concise overviews of ethics content knowledge such as major ethical theories, thinkers who wrote about ethics, and branches of ethics—for example, Virtue Ethics, Feminist Ethics, Computer Ethics, Business Ethics, Environmental Ethics, Pacifism, Pragmatism, Plato's Ethics—we suggest the *Stanford Encyclopedia of Philosophy*. Here our focus is on the *process* by which we make reflective decisions about ethical questions. We are not attempting to summarize the ethical theories that have rich and deep philosophical roots. Instead, this chapter is a practical guide for how we can and should apply strong critical thinking to the important ethical issues and concerns that arise in all areas of our lives.

A strong critical thinker and truth-seeker engages questions that challenge fundamental assumptions about what is right and what is wrong. It is not enough to deflect them by saying "This is how I was raised," or "This is what we've always believed." For a strong critical thinker there is no good excuse for not examining core values, moral opinions, and ethical ideologies. They shape our decisions about what to do in such powerful ways. We saw in Chapter 13, "Ideological Reasoning," how risky not reflecting on the truth of our core beliefs and assumptions can turn out to be. We should never assume that our core beliefs and values are right simply because they feel comfortable. Although they may have been inherited and although they are widely shared, they may still be terribly mistaken. There was a time, not so long ago, for example, when anti-Semitism was prevalent and comfortable in many social, professional, and business circles in the United States. That certainly did not make anti-Semitism ethical. (To see the socially acceptable anti-Semitism of WWII England amply dramatized, search and watch episode 2 of season 1 of *Foley's War*.)

This section on ethical decision making challenges us to be reflective about our core values and ethical opinions by applying our critical thinking to our ethical opinions. This can be risky. Why? Simple: they may not stand up to scrutiny. We may discover that we have no good reasons for those beliefs. Then what? Will our personal system of ethical beliefs and values fall apart like a house of cards? Will we try in vain to steer the relentless torrent of our own critical thinking away from the crumbling conceptual sandcastles that we once thought of as our unassailable ethical edifices? Or, put another way, will we have the integrity to ask tough questions about our ethical beliefs and the courage to follow reason and evidence wherever they may lead?

"Some questions," say those averse to truth-seeking, "are just too frightening to ask." "Ask anyway," replies the truth-seeker, "for although we may not easily or quickly

How "Ethical Decision Making" Connects

This chapter connects conceptually with the other parts of *THINK CRITICALLY* at many points. Ethical issues provide the opportunity to see the value of critical thinking in the section on "critical thinking in a free society" in Chapter 1. In Chapter 2 the ethical obligations of a jury to follow the law and the evidence in coming to a verdict are central to the example from 12 *Angry Men*. That same chapter raised the question "Is a critical thinker automatically a good person?" The question of the ethical obligations we have toward our friends emerges in the examples in Chapter 3. Successful problem solving, as explained in that chapter, includes working through ethical problems that might arise as we pursue success in college.

Chapter 5 on argument mapping uses an ethical issue, the question of the sale of guns to children, as a central example. Chapter 6 on evaluating claims begins with the tragic story of how moral failure can lead to hate and homicide. The "Levels of Thinking and Knowing" discussion about cognitive development in that chapter will be revisited in this chapter as one way of understanding moral development.

Chapter 7 on evaluating arguments features a Reflective Log ethics exercise, "The Ethics of Fallacious Argumentation." Chapter 8, "Valid Inferences," opens with a current ethical dilemma, the sale of human organs harvested from healthy but economically desperate people. Chapter 9, "Warranted Inferences," uses the ethical pursuit of equal justice for all people under the law twice. It is used, first in conjunction with The Innocence Project, and its second use

is illustrated in the film *To Kill a Mockingbird*. The discussion about System-1 and System-2 thinking from Chapter 10, and the discussion about how to protect ourselves from locking in prematurely on a given choice, from Chapter 11, will both figure prominently in this chapter's approach to ethical decision making.

The chapters titled "Comparative Reasoning" and "Ideological Reasoning" are important because these are the two modes of reasoning most used when endeavoring to make a reflective ethical decision. The example that leads off the Chapter 12 on comparative reasoning is an ethical question: Should the reporter imbedded with the enemy warn the platoon of his countrymen that it is about to be ambushed by the enemy and, for doing so, be killed on the spot? The issue of same-sex marriage, which opens Chapter 13 on ideological reasoning, raises ethical questions for a great many people in the United States and in other nations around the world. The feature "Nineteenth-Century Ideologies and Twentieth-Century Wars" illustrates the uncountable devastation and human suffering that can result from taking one's ideological beliefs and core values as imperatives that demand the annihilation of all who do not believe and live by that same ideology. A sobering thought. For in this we are no different from people of a century ago. Ideological conflicts can ignite violence today just as they could then. The ethical virtue of tolerance and the ethical maturity to see the humanity in other people may be all that stands between any of us and the violence that can erupt from ideologically fueled self-righteousness, anger, and hate.

come to a satisfactory answer, knowing the question but not seeking its answer is not satisfactory either."

In our quest to understand how decision making applies to matters of ethics, we will first summarize briefly three of the major approaches ethics theorists offer as guidance in addressing questions of ethics. Then we will turn to ethical decision making, noticing that ethical concerns can arise when making decisions about all kinds of different topics. We complete this section with the challenging question of how to think critically about ethical matters when the relevant ethical imperatives pull us in different directions. Let's begin with the phrase in the previous sentence, *ethical imperatives*. What might they be?

> "Corporate executives and business owners need to realize that there can be no compromise when it comes to ethics."
>
> Vivek Wadhwa, Stanford Center for Corporate Ethics[17]

16.1 Ethical Imperatives

- Keep promises.
- Tell the truth.
- Live in harmony.
- Obey the law.
- Act responsibly.
- Treat other people the way you want to be treated.
- Bring about more good than harm.
- Be moderate in all things.

The previous eight sentences are examples of ethical imperatives. Imperatives in general are expressions intended to shape behavior.[18] Commands, like "Close the window" are imperatives; so are warnings like "Don't text while skateboarding." **Ethical imperatives** are intended to shape or guide behavior by expressing core values and beliefs about what is morally right or morally wrong. Ethical imperatives express behavioral ideals and moral principles by pointing out what we ought to do or ought to refrain from doing.[19]

One way ethics theorists group ethical imperatives is by how we should think about the ethical questions that each particular imperative recommends.[20] Broadly speaking, the imperatives gravitate to one or another of three basic approaches. One set advises us to consider the *consequences* of our actions and policies for ourselves and for others. Another set says we should make ethical decisions by reference to our *duties* regardless of what the consequences might be. And a third group of imperatives guides us to think more about how we might consistently *cultivate virtues and root out vices*.

Think Consequences

In city councils and school boards across the nation we expect that proposed new policies will be evaluated by first asking whether or not they are likely to bring about more benefits than harm to the people affected. It is always a challenge to achieve consensus about governmental regulations and social policies in pluralistic democratic society. As a way to think through the pros and cons of alternative social policies, many ethical theorists advise that we focus on the foreseeable consequences of each alternative. The policy option we should select, according to this approach, is the option that will produce the greatest net benefit for the greatest number of people. If one option benefits many people and another benefits only a few, and if the costs associated with each option are the same, then it seems wise to go with the option that benefits the most people.

Giving due consideration to the consequences of our choices is a sensible approach. But that does not make it easy to execute. There are lots of dimensions to the due consideration of consequences. Consider, for example, a proposal that all income be taxed at a flat rate of 15 percent. For a working parent making the minimum hourly wage that 15 percent could take a large bite out of the money available for rent, food, clothing, health care, and bus fare. For a

Making ethical decisions about public policy in a pluralistic democracy demands that we consider many factors, among them the foreseeable positive and negative impacts of each option.

wealthy individual without family obligations who makes a six-figure salary working at a job that provides medical benefits and a transportation and housing allowance, the 15 percent may mean not being able to enjoy quite as lavish a vacation or new summer wardrobe this year. We can foresee that the proposed policy of taxing all income at 15 percent would result in a smaller absolute dollar tax bill for the hourly wage working parent, but a more intensely negative impact on that person and the children in that household. So it seems reasonable that we should take the intensity of the negative and positive impacts into consideration along with the number of people affected.

We probably should think too about how long the negative or positive results might last. For example, although college tuition is expensive and studying is not often enjoyable, the economic and social benefits of a college education endure for decades. On the other hand, those economic and social benefits are someplace in the future and there is a measure of uncertainty about whether I shall ever personally realize those benefits. Contrast that with spending the tuition money with my friends on a blowout *Hangover II*–quality Vegas holiday right now! That could be intensely enjoyable. Should we not also consider how near to hand and tangible the gains might be as compared with nebulous possibilities off in the future? But then too, while we can foresee the possibility of having a lot of fun, we should also give due consideration to the many potentially negative consequences of that choice. Realistically they range from a brutal hangover and not having any money left to live on afterward, all the way to being mugged, getting killed or injured in a drunken auto accident, catching some terrible disease, etc. And those are only the possible negative consequences for us. Should we not also consider the possible negative consequences to others?

That last question raises an interesting ethical issue. A strong critical thinker will explore the question "Consequences for whom?" If we wish to be ethical is it sufficient to consider only ourselves and our own family and friends, or should we not also consider the beneficial and harmful foreseeable consequences to others?

How broad is the circle of those whom we should consider? Does it include, for example, one or more of these?

- our communities (e.g., using city revenues for schools and parks)
- our shareholders (e.g., manage the business to ensure large stock dividends)
- our nation (e.g., immigration reform that benefits workers and the economy)
- all people everywhere (e.g., world peace, or the eradication of malaria or world hunger)
- all future generations (e.g., establishing a trust fund for the grandchildren)
- all potential individuals (e.g., human clones)
- pets (e.g., rescuing dogs and cats trapped after a terrible flood)
- food sources (e.g., the animals we slaughter for our food)
- unnamed other species (e.g., reducing deforestation to preserve endangered species)
- robots (e.g., sophisticated machines that mirror human intelligence artificially)

As business leaders know, investments require capital. When evaluating anticipating investment opportunities, the goal is to identify the one that will provide the greatest net return.[21]

But shrewd investors take another factor into consideration as well, namely the *opportunity cost*. If the available capital is invested now and a better opportunity emerges in the near future, then they will not be able to take advantage of that opportunity. If we take a yearlong lease today and next month rental rates fall, then we will not be able to take advantage of those lower rates. From the perspective of ethical theories that focus on consequences, opportunity costs figure into the evaluation of options. If we are moved by the value of a particular goal—for example, providing senior citizens with comfortable pensions—and as a result we pledge our resources to that goal, then we

Consequences for whom? Pets trapped by a natural disaster, intelligent robots, vacationers who may want to enjoy the beach?

How Broad Should My Circle of Ethical Concern Be?

First separate the ethical question and the factual question. As a question of fact we might ask a person who they most often take into consideration when making ethical decisions. Most of us would say we take into account how their decisions will affect those who are the closest to us— our family, our friends, our co-workers. But "everyone who lives in my town," "everyone who goes to school here," and "everyone in the nation" are seldom answers one hears.

Perhaps we *ought* to hear about those larger circles of affected people more than we do. That is the ethical question. Whom ought we to take into consideration, given that our choices can have a significant impact on the lives of a great many people we may not know or may seldom, if ever, think about?

In desperate times, when danger is all around and things are out of our control, it makes psychological and practical sense to constrict the circle of ethical concern. Smaller is safer. And from the ethical perspective, we cannot hold people responsible for things they cannot control. The battlefield is often a test not only of courage but of ethics. If you have not served as a soldier in combat, it is difficult to appreciate what that experience is like or how profoundly it can affect a person. The film *Restrepo*, winner of the 2010 Grand Jury Prize for best

Are military rules of engagement the equivalent of battlefield ethics?

documentary at the Sundance Film Festival, follows a platoon of U.S. soldiers deployed in Afghanistan's Korengal Valley for one year. Free of moral judgment, this National Geographic production is a gripping study of human behavior under the constant stress of combat. It is a film to experience first, and then to reflect upon in its entirety. Search for and watch this documentary. At the end several of the soldiers are interviewed after they completed their tour of duty. How would you evaluate their comments?

may find ourselves unable to respond to other worthy purposes, such as education, transportation infrastructure, or national security.

If you have the impression that in the real world it is difficult to determine with precision the exact quantity of good consequences over bad consequences, you would be correct. We can try creating a moral calculus by assigning dollar values to various outcomes, but that would only push the problem back one level. Suppose, like an insurance company, we decided to say that the loss of a hand or a foot in an industrial accident was worth X dollars, but the loss of a life was worth Y dollars. Yes, that might make it easier to do the math when we are trying to figure out how much money to pay out for an accident claim or how much money to charge a policy holder. But the obvious questions strong critical thinkers would ask are "Why X?" and "Why Y?" Where did those numbers come from and how can we justify them? Does every human life have the same dollar value?

Ethical decision making that considers only the consequences of our choices often leaves us uncertain about how to proceed even when we have to choose between two apparently equal outcomes. Suppose a corporate CEO convicted of felony embezzlement and a decorated war veteran both needed to be transported to the trauma center in a hurry. Suppose that our transport vehicle could only take one of the two. And suppose that the one who is left behind would have a significantly lower chance of

survival. Which one ought we to transport first? Most of us would say the decorated war veteran has the stronger claim from the ethical point of view. But if both would benefit equally as a consequence, and if consequences were the only things we could take into consideration, then we should flip a coin to decide which gets transported. Purely in terms of consequences to that individual there is no way to put greater value on the one than on the other. The imprecision and uncertainty often found when consequences only are being considered places us squarely in the realm of the probable rather than the certain.

If we applied comparative reasoning to this problem, the choice of which person to save might be resolved like this: Transporting the war veteran first would be like securing a national treasure as compared to transporting the convicted embezzler, which would be more like squandering precious resources to salvage a poisonous reptile. While both deserve some consideration, the felonious embezzler is less deserving than the war veteran. But given the case as presented, looking strictly at consequences that argument cannot be made. Or we might find ourselves guesstimating the relative amount of good vs. bad consequences a given course of action might produce. That is why ethical decision making in real-life contexts goes beyond consequences to include core values and principles. Do we not have a duty to try to rescue the innocent and perhaps heroic person before trying to rescue the criminal?

Suppose a CEO convicted of embezzlement and a decorated war veteran both needed to be transported to the trauma center. Suppose each has an equal chance to live, if transported. But we can transport only one. How should we decide? Why?

Think Duties

Down through the ages communities of like-minded people have relied on the sayings of religious figures, traditions, written codes, commandments, or other expressions of duties to guide their ethical decision making. For example:

- Protect children.
- Respect other people's property.
- Tell the truth.
- Remain faithful to your spouse.
- Don't drink and drive.
- Fulfill your agreements.
- Obey the law.
- Give 10 percent of your income to charity.
- Treat others as you want to be treated.
- Honor your parents.

These mandates are ethical imperatives that express our duty to behave or not to behave in the specified ways. We can phrase them as commands or as statements. As statements they express moral principles. For example: "One should strive to ensure that innocent people suffer no harm," and "One ought always to speak the truth." The grammar is less important than the ethical idea. Either way of expressing these ideas works because as commands or as statements of principle we understand that they assert that we have certain ethical responsibilities and duties.

Ethical decision making by reference to duties leaves consequences out of the equation. Principles like "Always tell the truth" are not meant as pragmatic suggestions; telling the truth may or may not generally lead to a greater preponderance of beneficial as opposed to harmful consequences. When it comes to duty, outcomes are beside the point. A duty imposes an ethical obligation. In other words, it is our duty to tell the truth,

Is It Ethically Acceptable to Con a Con?

There is a lot of cheating in college, and occasionally it is the college student who is cheated. College students are often the targets of swindles, cons, and scams. While some scams victimize innocent people, many actually depend on the victim being a bit unethical too. Here are three classic cons that target college students.

Pyramid Scheme: Pyramid schemes are illegal. Ever wonder about those miracle medicines, consumer cosmetics, or kitchen utensil companies that are always looking for new distributors? The con artist brings a crowd of people to a hotel conference room on the promise of easy money. With the help of a couple of shills, they generate a frenzy of enthusiasm for the company's wonder product, whatever it might be. "If you don't sign up today, you're going to miss this golden opportunity." "This product is

great! It sells itself." Recruiters sign up the gullible new distributors as fast as possible, demanding payment up front for non-returnable inventory. If the operation is illegal, it quickly becomes apparent that more effort is put into recruiting new distributors than into actually selling the products. Your payment goes half to the recruiter and half to "the company." You get stuck with the inventory because when you try to sell it, you quickly discover that nobody really wants it.

Advance Payment Loan: You need money and someone offers to loan you what you need even though you have no obvious way to repay the loan and your credit rating is poor. You only have to pay a loan fee in advance and fill out some paperwork. You pay the fee. The paperwork hits snags and delays pile on delays. Then for some obscure reason the loan is denied. Oh, and one other thing, you forfeit the loan fee.

Pigeon Drop: You're in a mall or a large shopping center and someone approaches you claiming to have found a wallet with a large amount of cash. The con artist asks you what to do with the wallet and, while you are talking it over, the con artist says he wants to do the right thing and call someone else to get some advice. Typically the con artist calls his "boss" to ask what to do. The word comes back eventually that the money is illegal, perhaps stolen. The con artist says that the boss suggests that the two of you might simply divide the found treasure. But, because the money is illegal, the con artist proposes to see if the boss has any suggestions about how to cover the trail so the authorities do not come after you to seize the money. The boss offers, through the con artist, to help with that. But it will take some time. You get drawn into the problem solving. Eventually the boss suggests that each party needs to show "good faith." The con artist goes to his ATM and withdraws a few hundred dollars to be given to the boss as his good faith money. If you want your share you have to put in an equal amount. The con artist, or an accomplice, takes all of the money to the boss who is going to give you back your "good faith" money and your share of the found money once it is laundered. You are told exactly when and where the boss' office is located so you can go there and collect your money. You go at the appointed time and, of course, there is no office, no boss, and no money.

Our thanks to the National Association of Bunco Investigators (NABI) Web site for these cons. Visit the NABI Website

In *The Sting*, Newman and Redford team up to run the big con on another con man.

for more about swindles and cons that target college students and others. Thieves are clever, the list is long. Perhaps the principle "Two Wrongs Don't Make a Right" applies here. But maybe not. Is it ever ethical to con a con? Apropos that question, you might enjoy the 1973 Best Picture Oscar award–winning film, *The Sting*, with Paul Newman and Robert Redford. The entertaining 2007 comedy *Ocean's Thirteen*, directed by Steven Soderbergh, is another in that genre.

regardless of the consequences. Ethically we want police officers to tell the truth when they are called as witnesses in a criminal trial. We do not want them fabricating evidence or distorting the facts so that the prosecution can

gain a conviction. And we do not want defense witnesses to lie under oath even if their lies would help an innocent person from being convicted. Our judicial system works because core ethical principles, like telling the truth, are observed by all parties, independent of how that might affect the ultimate outcome of the case. The goal is justice under the law. As much as we might rejoice at our friend's acquittal or be saddened at his conviction, our ethical duty if called as witnesses is to tell the truth.

Motive and intention have an important place when thinking about ethics in terms of duties rather than consequences. If our intention is pure, then we are considered to be acting ethically even if the results of our behavior are largely unfortunate. We can imagine one brother innocently saying to another, "I only meant to help by telling our Dad about your money problems." And having the other brother reply, "Look, that's my business, not his. Don't ever do that again." On the other hand, if we try to borrow money from a friend with no intention of paying back the loan, then we are acting unethically. That one day we enjoyed an unexpected windfall and used it to repay the loan makes no difference.

Respect for other people is an important ethical duty. We value human life and we regard it as unethical, in all or

"Do you swear to tell the truth, the whole truth, and nothing but the truth?"

In striking down a California law prohibiting violent video games, the U.S. Supreme Court was upholding the constitutional right of free speech.

almost all circumstances, to take another's life. We commit significant resources to rescuing, rehabilitating, and healing people who are in trouble, in need, or sick to save lives. Another way we respect others is to accord them personal autonomy and freedom of choice. On the basis of these principles we respect the rights of competent adults to make their own choices, to enter into contracts, and to live their own lives as they wish provided that they do no harm to others in the process. Protecting innocent people from undue harm is another way we show respect for others. Ethically we ought to do what we can to help children get a good education; to provide them food, shelter, and health care; and, because they are unable to protect themselves, to ensure that they are not victimized by predators of any kind.

When a community is homogenous, the boundaries between ethics, tradition, religion, and law can be blurry. In those communities the laws often reflect the traditions and religious values of the community. Our duty to obey the law becomes one with our religious duties and our community traditions. This is often the case in any nation that does not carefully maintain the separation of Church and State. At one time throughout the United States one could find towns and cities that had ordinances prohibiting pornography, violent video games, sodomy, interracial marriage, public dancing, gambling, and selling alcoholic beverages on Sundays. The majority of people in those communities may have regarded these statutes as sensible, given their personal ethical values and religious convictions. But these kinds of statutes are regularly struck down by the U.S. Supreme Court, and not because the Court is opposed to religion or to ethics. Rather,

as with the 2011 ruling regarding violent video games,[22] it is not that the Court condones violence, but that the Court is upholding a higher principle. The U.S. Constitution is grounded in a set of ethical principles like freedom of speech, personal autonomy, and equal rights under the law. Although there may be adverse consequences, the Supreme Court often rules that the power of government to encroach into our private lives should be limited. As in the Supreme Court, ethical decision making on the basis of core beliefs and ethical values must always weigh the relative prominence or importance of those principles. Duties can conflict. Not every principle is of equal significance. Just because a given principle fits one's own lifestyle, is traditional, or is consistent with one's upbringing does not mean that it can be imposed by law or by majority vote on everyone else in the community.

Because ethical principles express a person's core values and beliefs, they are seldom easily forsaken or compromised. Making ethical decisions based on our duties as we see them is "top down" thinking as described in Chapter 13 on ideological reasoning. One begins with a general ethical principle (e.g., be honest) and then applies the principle to a specific situation (e.g., cheating on exams is dishonest) to draw a moral conclusion (e.g., one ought not to cheat on exams). Ideological reasoning is deductive in character, the ethical imperative is treated as axiomatic, and the maker of the argument often takes the ethical first principle to be self-evidently true or true as a matter of faith.

It is not merely a literary accident that the phrase "we hold these truths to be self-evident" is in the *Declaration of Independence*. That document exemplifies top down ideological reasoning. Beginning with its bold assertion of divinely instilled inalienable rights, the document uses ethical principles as initial axiomatic premises. In a century that was dominated by topdown monarchies and religious institutions,

"It doesn't *matter* that you never got caught!"

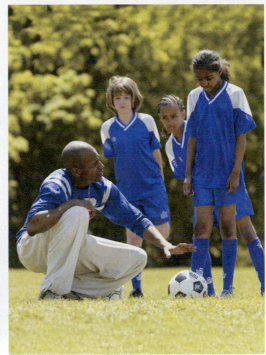

Decisions are not ethically neutral simply because they are about business, educational, personal, or public policy issues.

the authors of the *Declaration of Independence* intended it to establish a top down ethical justification for their break with the British Empire and the war for independence that would ensue. And, ironically enough, a top down justification for the bottom up democracy they hoped to established was the result.

One cautionary note: Rigid adherence to first principles can produce painful results, as we saw in the chapter titled "Ideological Reasoning." If we make ethical decisions heedless of consequences we are not exhibiting strong critical thinking. In Chapter 2 we noted that the positive critical thinking habits of mind include endeavoring to anticipate consequences and recognizing that many judgments are not "black and white" but instead involve shades of gray. A century ago in America it was a self-evident ethical axiom in European immigrant neighborhoods that interfaith marriage was morally wrong. It was a son's or daughter's duty to marry inside the family's religious faith and, if at all possible, to marry someone with the same European ethnic heritage. Irish Catholics ought not to marry German Lutherans, and certainly not Polish Jews. Grounded in strong family traditions and deep religious convictions this principle was self-evident in those communities. Today most Americans regard the marriage between two

people of different faiths or different ethnic backgrounds as unproblematic from the ethical perspective.

We are not advocating ethical relativism. Far from it, instead we are pointing out that the first premise of an ideological argument may turn out not to be true for any number of reasons. In this case perhaps it was prejudice and fear that made late nineteenth-century and early twentieth-century European immigrants so sure of the rectitude of their moral position on interfaith marriage. Or perhaps it was a protectionist attitude aimed at preserving their European languages and social customs in this strange "New World." Whatever the basis, they held that ethical opinion and articulated that principle with conviction. Those European immigrants can be admired for their courage in leaving their villages and families to immigrate to this distant country. But strong critical thinking also enables us to think through core ethical principles, values, and beliefs for ourselves. Yes, we want to consider our duties as we make our ethical decisions. But no, the great grandchildren of those European immigrants are not obligated to burden their hearts unreflectively or bind their minds uncritically to the ethical opinions of their great-grandparents.

Think Virtues

At the beginning of this book we described the positive critical thinking habits of mind as personal attributes. These habits dispose us to seek the truth, to proceed systematically, to inquire, and strive to learn. At one point we suggested that the positive critical thinking habits of mind were virtues, as contrasted with vices like intellectual dishonesty, intolerance, disorganization, indifference, and imprudence.

Critical thinking habits are not the only valuable personal attributes. Ethical virtues are too. For millennia good people have displayed virtues such as generosity, truthfulness, trustworthiness, compassion, humility, loyalty, helpfulness, and friendliness. They strive always to live harmoniously with others. They take responsibility for themselves and their own actions. They don't have to be begged, embarrassed, or incentivized to do their fair share; instead they pitch right in, willingly taking up their portion of the work at hand. Behaving in these ways is engrained in their character.

> "This is my simple religion. There is no need for temples; no need for complicated philosophy. Our own brain, our own heart is our temple; the philosophy is kindness."
>
> 14th Dalai Lama[23]

A virtuous person does not make ethical decisions by tabulating consequences. If they see a stranger in need they offer a helping hand. Virtuous people do not make ethical decisions by pondering the precise nature of their duties. They speak truthfully, they share what they have with their friends, and when it is their turn they take out the garbage. Yes, on occasion virtuous people may slip. They may not always be as generous, helpful, honest, or friendly as they could be. But knowing people like this, we realize that those occasions are isolated exceptions. When they are at their best they practice these virtues with ease and grace.

Yes, it is possible to go overboard. How much compassion is too much? At what point does my generosity put other people at risk? If we were to give all of our wealth to feed the poor, how would our own families survive? A virtuous person needs a measure of wisdom and balance. Moderation is not a shortcoming. Suppose a friend calls and asks us to lend a hand with a home improvement project. We could quit our jobs so that we could give all our time and energy to our friend. But we are no less virtuous if we give only Saturday and part of Sunday to the friend's project. *Virtue is not measured in the quantity of the good produced. Virtue is measured by a person's tendency to respond or not to respond whenever the need or the opportunity arises.*

Vices work the same way. If we are habitually surly, gluttonous, selfish, boastful, deceitful, disloyal, unhelpful, hostile, indifferent to the needs of others, and generally unpleasant, cantankerous, and obnoxious troublemakers, then the occasional nice thing we might do will only be regarded as out of character for us.

While it may be difficult to get a clear fix on exactly what our duties as a virtuous person might be, or exactly how to predict the consequences of our well-meaning efforts to live a virtuous life, those concerns are less important. From time to time a virtuous person may be uncertain about how to act in a given situation or disappointed by the unanticipated negative consequences of something done with the best of intentions. Yet for the most part a virtuous person lives life confident that he or she is being true to them self, acting in accord with his or her best tendencies, and trying to bring a small measure of happiness and harmony to those whom he or she encounters.

The real difficulties come when that virtuous person is suddenly faced with specific ethical dilemmas. Questions like abortion, capital punishment, the torture of enemy combatants to learn vital information, immigration reform, and the many ethical issues on the frontiers of science are not easily resolved by simply acting virtuously. Acting virtuously, because it is something that we are habituated to doing, requires little reflection. Acting out of a spirit of kindness, friendliness, loyalty, or generosity is a natural, spontaneous automatic response for the virtuous person. But virtuous behavior does not resolve complex dilemmas, it simply avoids them. They still exist, like hungry dogs that sooner or later must be fed.

In Chapter 10 on snap judgments and heuristic thinking we describe the "Two-Systems" approach to human decision making. In a person for whom virtuous behavior is a habitual automatic, spontaneous, reactive response, System-1 thinking drives the decision making. But when novel or complex ethical issues arise, a vague System-1 response, like "I'll just do the right thing," is inadequate for strong critical thinkers. They realize that the issue needs to be analyzed, relevant information carefully assembled, and each option thoughtfully examined. Our more reflective decision-making system, System 2, must be engaged. The success of System 2 depends on our critical thinking skills. We need to guard against prematurely locking in on a given response to dilemmas like those listed above. In other words, we must apply our critical thinking skills to come to a well-reasoned reflective judgment about those matters. The ethical virtues are highly desirable, and they ought to be cultivated and practiced. But simply being a virtuous person is not sufficient in itself as a way to thoughtfully resolve complex, high-stakes, multi-dimensional, ethical dilemmas.

16.2 Decision Making and Ethical Decision Making

If we mentioned leadership decision making, journalistic decision making, or culinary decision making, people would know that we were talking about how to solve problems and make decisions as leaders or journalists or chefs. And, no matter what the topic, money, time, and effort almost always factor into decision making about that topic. For dedicated business professionals, military leaders, college students, lawyers, engineers, designers, coaches, and chiropractors alike, the decisions that they face often include considerations like how much does each option cost, how much time will it take, and how much effort do we have to invest to accomplish our purpose. Assessing those factors accurately is part of what one learns by experience and professional training.

So how does a person prepare to become successful as a decision maker in a given domain? We have always said that critical thinking alone was not sufficient to ensure success. Knowledge, dedication, training, and ethical courage are also essential. Legality is another factor we often find influencing decision making across a range of professional domains.

Decisions made by players and coaches in sports must take into account the rules of the game. Business decision makers know that a myriad of rules and regulations apply to their decisions about employees, product safety, finances, etc. When teachers and school officials make educational decisions, they factor in the policies, rules, and regulations of their school district, their school site, and their board of education. Health care providers and patients often consider the rules and regulations health insurance providers have as they decide on a course of treatment.

Ethics, like money, time, effort, and applicable regulations, is another consideration that arises in a great many decision-making contexts. Decisions are not ethically neutral simply because they are about business, military, medical, educational, technological, personal, social, economic, religious, or public policy issues. In fact, it is the opposite. The more people who might be affected by a decision, the more important it is to weigh the ethical merits of the options under consideration. Yes, people can choose to ignore the ethical dimensions of a given problem, just like they can choose to ignore any other dimension of a problem. "Politics aside, this is what we should do." Or "Hey let's spitball this as if money was not an issue." Or, "I don't care how much time it takes, I want this project completed!" But, of course, ignoring a factor does

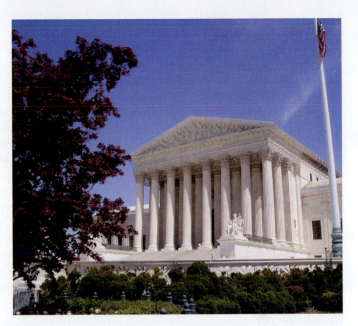

"Justice Under Law" is inscribed across the cornice of the U.S. Supreme Court Building. Does this imply a potential ethical conflict? Is it possible to have justice without law, or law without justice?

not mean that the factor is irrelevant. It only means that the decision maker intends not to let that factor be part of the equation when solving the problem at hand.

Reactive and Reflective Ethical Decision Making

Because ethical decision making is fundamentally decision making applied to ethical concerns, the general theory of decision making detailed in the chapters on "Snap Judgments" and "Reflective Decision Making" apply. Because our cultural heritage, upbringing, and socialization contribute so much to our sense of what is ethical and what is not, many times our first response to an ethical question is a System-1 reaction. We saw this with ethical decision making based on habitual virtues. But it is not limited to only that way of thinking about our ethical responsibilities. We generally do not call on our System-2 resources until we realize that the question at hand is more complicated than we might first have realized. Our System-2, more reflective ethical decision might be rather different from our first System-1 impulsive reaction.

While they are ordinarily reliable, if misapplied thinking heuristics described in the chapter on "Snap Judgments" can result in biases and errors. Misapplications of heuristics, like Us vs. Them, Illusion of Control, Affect: "Go with your Gut," and Power Differential, can infect ethical decision making in the same way they can infect decision making in other domains.

THINKING CRITICALLY

Duty vs. Consequences

Conflicts between duty-based ethical decision making and consequences-based ethical decision making generate powerful drama. Many wonderful films reveal the powerfully divergent forces of these two contrasting approaches to ethical decision making. Nominated for seven Academy Awards, the 1962 classic *Mutiny on the Bounty* is one of the best. As you watch the film, remember that, in those days, for a seaman or an officer to refuse the direct order issued by the captain of a vessel at sea warranted the most severe punishment. First officer Fletcher Christian, the character played by Marlon Brando, must consider the consequences for himself as well as for the crew if he decides to lead a mutiny. We wonder what we would do if we were to find ourselves faced with a comparable ethical challenge.

The clash between a naval captain and his executive officer in times of great crisis is the theme of the 1995 film *Crimson Tide*. The captain of a U.S. nuclear submarine, played by Gene Hackman, and the vessel's second in command, played by Denzel Washington, disagree about how to interpret an order that appears to sanction launching nuclear missiles. Is there a war going on, and should they launch the missiles as ordered, or have they misunderstood the situation and the command from fleet headquarters? Should the second in command carry out the order of the captain to launch, or refuse that order and risk court-martial for treason and mutiny? Depending on whether or not the missiles are launched, the consequences for himself, the crew, the nation, and the world are huge.

All of these films use a military context. Identify a film that portrays the conflict between duty-based ethical decision making and consequences-based ethical decision making in a non-military context, and describe that ethical dilemma.

A scene from *Mutiny on the Bounty*.

JOURNAL

What if You Disagreed?

Give an example of when you disagreed with an authority figure about ethical duties or ethical obligations. Describe the situation and the reason(s) you disagreed. How did you resolve the conflict that time? What ought you do next time?

The Us vs. Them heuristic can mislead us into treating others as if they were not due to the same level of respect or did not have the same rights we have. The Illusion of Control heuristic can result in putting others or ourselves in danger because we imagine ourselves able to manage events even if we are drunk or high. The Affect heuristic can lead us to make impulsive, uninformed, and unreflective decisions about the ethics of a given situation. The Power Differential heuristic may result in our not thinking an ethical issue through for ourselves, but instead relying on the opinions of powerful and influential people, even though those opinions are flawed. These are only examples. Other heuristics may also be misapplied in ethical decision making just as in decision making involving other matters. We suggest you might want to quickly review how the heuristic thinking shortcuts might be misapplied when ethical questions arise.

The problem of locking in too soon to a particular option—that is, premature dominance structuring as described in Chapter 11, "Reflective Decision Making"—can infect ethical decision making. It is always difficult for any of us to give due consideration to alternative views once we have locked in on a particular choice. In matters of ethics the same human psychology applies. The precautions in the same chapter's section on "Self-Regulation Critical Thinking Skill Strategies" are so valuable in reminding us that making good decisions about ethical issues, or any other issues, requires due deliberation. Here

THINKING CRITICALLY

By Nature Saints or Savages?

If all the structures of society and law were stripped away, would human beings be fundamentally good or fundamentally evil? The question is fun to consider, although it may turn out to be unanswerable because it is difficult to imagine how it would be approached experimentally. Or is it? Shortly after the horrors of World War II William Golding produced *Lord of the Flies*, the riveting story of a group of boys suddenly separated from all other human contact and social institutions. Golding won the Nobel Prize for Literature. Film adaptations appeared in 1963 and 1990. There are no adults in Golding's fictional story. So perhaps savagery would not be the outcome in a more realistic scenario.

With its mild climate, plentiful fresh water, game, and edible plants, Easter Island once supported a population approaching 20,000. Then came the ecological disaster of deforestation and ever-dwindling food supplies. The island could not sustain so large a human population, and the humans could not leave the island, for the large trees from which they had made their boats were no more. Anything and everything that could be used for food was tried and yet communities fell apart, people starved, thousands died. Survivors abandoned their huts and walled themselves into underground caves. Cannibalism had come to Easter Island. Locate and watch the National Geographic documentary titled *The End of Easter Island*. To what extent are ethical imperatives conditioned by the wealth and resources our community has at its disposal? And the follow-up question: If social policies inexorably drove a group of people to lives of hopeless desperation, would they not be justified in acting in their own self-defense? Assuming violent rebellion is off the table, what sorts of self-defense initiatives would be justified? How bad would things have to become for that group before the assumption about violent rebellion was nullified, if it ever could be nullified? Explain your answer with reasons and historical examples.

The people of Easter Island destroyed their environment, and then, desperate and starving, they savaged one another. Any lessons here?

are some of the questions described there that are of particular relevance to ethical decision making:

- Have we analyzed the issues at hand well enough to clarify the ethical dimensions of the problem? For example, in the academic cheating scenario we opened with, the core ethical concern is the student's academic integrity, even though initially the student may have ignored that concern, preferring to regard the problem simply as a tactical question about how to get a good grade on a particular exam.

- Have we identified the factors that are critical to deciding the ethics of the matter? For example, have we foreseen beneficial and harmful consequences of various options, or the rights and duties of the people involved, or the justice or injustice of various options?

- Have we scrutinized all the viable options with disciplined impartiality, respectfully taking into consideration the interests and concerns of people on all sides of the matter? For example, did the student in the opening scenario consider the harmful impact of his decision on the grades of those students in the course who did not cheat on exams?

- Are we treating equals as equals by being fair to all involved and diligently avoiding favoritism? For example, it would be unjust for the professor in the course to punish all the students simply because some had cheated.

Informed ethical decision making requires a knowledge base. To be useful our System-2 reflections must be based on solid information. We need to know with a reasonable level of confidence what the foreseeable and likely consequences of our actions will be. We need to know what our duties are in a given situation. We need to have information that enables us to analyze options accurately, to draw reasonable inferences about what we ought to do or ought not to do. Ethical decision making is much more than System-1 reactions, impulses, or feelings. It includes applying all the critical thinking skills and positive critical thinking habits of mind that we have talked about throughout this book to make informed and reflective decisions.

16.3 Thinking Through Diverging Ethical Imperatives

A close friend asks to borrow your car for the day so she can hurry home to see her family. But you need the car to get to work today. Your friend says you can call in sick. She tells you she needs the car because there is some kind of family emergency. You remember that you had promised your boss that you would come in to work today. What to do? Friendship, generosity, and compassion impel you toward loaning your friend the car. But you don't want to break the promise you made to your boss and you have a responsibility: to fulfill your commitment to your job by showing up when you are scheduled to work. You don't want to lie. Not only is lying wrong, it's not who you are as a person. You don't casually lie just because it may happen to suit your desires at the moment. But what if you say no to your friend? Will that harm the friendship? And what about her family that needs her? Will her family suffer unnecessarily because she can't come to their aid and all because you refuse to loan your car?

The situation described above is typical of day-to-day ethical problems that come our way. A decision is needed. We appear to have a couple of clear choices. And the relevant ethical imperatives pull us in different directions. How do strong critical thinkers make ethical decisions in circumstances like these?

Prioritize, Create, and Negotiate

Faced with divergent ethical imperatives, strong critical thinkers summon their thinking skills to explore reasoned solutions using one or more of three strategies: clarify priorities, creatively seek other alternatives, and negotiate a resolution by finding common ground. How might these three be applied to the problem of whether or not to loan the car to the friend?

ESTABLISH PRIORITIES In this case analyzing the situation and setting priorities provides a path to a reasonable solution. Yes, friendship and generosity are important. But so is personal integrity. Lying and shirking your work responsibilities are not part of your character. Yes, the friend has needs, but one person is not ethically obligated to take on the burden of a friend's needs at the expense of one's own integrity. In fact, if this friend were more respectful of your personal integrity, the friend would not have suggested so glibly that you lie to your boss and blow off your job. In terms of your priorities, it would be reasonable to tell the friend that she will simply have to find some other way to solve her transportation problem. If she respects you, this should not cause grave harm to your friendship. Or, put another way, if your decision does lead her to discount your friendship, then that should be a signal that perhaps the relationship was not as sound as you might have thought.

CREATE ADDITIONAL OPTIONS But suppose you do not want to put the friendship at risk. Instead you take the second approach and think creatively about other options to suggest to your friend. You might propose that she call a taxi, that she rent a car for a day, that she ask one of her family members to come and pick her up, that she take a bus or the subway, or ride her bike, or borrow a car from someone else. Or, instead of going to the family to offer her help, that she phone her family and offer to help in some other way, or that she simply apologize for not being able to get there today and, instead, plan to go another day. In other words, in this case as with many apparent ethical

The Virtues of Friendship and Ethical Courage

In the critically acclaimed 1987 film *Cry Freedom*, a white journalist, played by Kevin Kline, must confront the divergent imperatives of his profession, the law, and his own humanity. Set in South Africa during the apartheid era, the film focuses on the friendship between the journalist and Steve Biko, a black man imprisoned for speaking out against South Africa's oppressive, racist apartheid policies. Denzel Washington earned an Academy Award nomination for his portrayal of Biko in this film. The movie is a study in the consequences of political corruption, racial discrimination, violence, and oppression. This is another of those films that lead us to hope that we might have the moral courage displayed by these two friends.

In the film Cry Freedom, *Kevin Kline plays a journalist who must decide if he can find the courage to rescue his friend.*

Government enforced orthodoxy as documented by the Spanish painter Francisco Goya (1746–1828).

dilemmas, there are options. It may take a few minutes to identify alternative choices, and so a strong critical thinker will allow time for some creative thought and reflection. Instead of accepting the situation as a stark, either A or B, we can often find choice C, D, E, or F, if we take our time and think things through.

NEGOTIATE BASED ON EACH PARTY'S INTERESTS

Let's suppose your friend rejects all those options, comes up with nothing creative on her own, and instead keeps returning to her request, "Look, just please loan me your car." Even at this point it might be possible to negotiate a resolution. The car is not the issue. It is only a means by which you and your friend hope to achieve your own interests. You have an interest in getting to work. Your friend's interest is to get to her family. Strong critical thinkers will strive to analyze the situation, often working together, to identify each party's interests and then to suggest, refine, and evaluate possible resolutions aimed at allowing each party to achieve some or all of their interests.

You may be able to negotiate a resolution that fulfills the most important interests of both parties. For example, you could propose to loan your car to your friend after you get home from work. Or you could offer to drop your friend at her family's house on your way to work. Or you could offer to take your friend with you to your job and then loan her the car, knowing that one of your co-workers would give you a ride home after work.

If the interests of both parties cannot be completely fulfilled, you may be able to negotiate a resolution that enables each party's interests to be partially fulfilled. For example, you could use the car to get to work and then ask to be permitted to leave early so that you can make the car available to your friend. Your friend will have to tell her family that she will be coming, but that her arrival will be delayed until the car is available.[24]

PERSONAL CONSISTENCY AND RESPECT FOR OTHERS

We have a friend who enjoys joking that he is "a man of principle" because he can come up with a principle to suit his every whim. He may be joking, but there are people who cannot seem to keep their ethical imperatives straight.

Without clarifying our points of view in greater detail, it would be inconsistent of us to deplore the use of force by the police against protesters at one moment, but then to pound the table demanding that the police do more to ensure public safety, law, and order. Unless we refine our point of view, we cannot gush about wholesome family values but get all self-righteous and indignant about refusing to grant the rights of citizenship to "anchor babies."[25] It would be inconsistent of us to ardently advocate for free speech but resent it when people march against causes we favor. We cannot logically argue that above all other values human life is sacred and also support capital punishment. We cannot logically stand firmly on the side of choice but oppose assisted suicide. We cannot make limited government our top priority but then refuse to consider repealing the statues and regulations prohibiting pot or prostitution. Without helping constructively to find ways to achieve these divergent goals, we cannot demand lower taxes and at the same time insist on good roads, sturdy bridges, clean parks, safe neighborhoods, clean drinking water, effective schools, modern hospitals, wholesome food, protection

Is There a Fitting Punishment for False Beliefs?

In a free society founded on the separation of Church and State, there ought to be no punishment for so-called "false" beliefs. Behavior is another thing, however. If religious differences lead us to cause harm to others, then that behavior needs to be examined. For if we have violated the law by what we have done, then we deserve a punishment that fits our crime. But what about communities where Church and State are not so clearly demarcated? For example, in December 2014 Al Shabah proudly took credit for killing non-Muslims in Kenya. ISIS claims a religious basis for its war to establish a Muslim state in Iraq and Syria.

Buddhist monks have historic political and military involvements in Japan and Korea. And as recently Spain, barely 200 years ago, affords us another example of the brutal consequences that can result from governmentally sanctioned enforcement of religious beliefs in a Christian country. To appreciate how the awesome power of orthodoxy through coercion can terrorize a society, search for and watch the 2006 film *Goya's Ghosts*. Are there any examples today in the U.S. where extremist religious orthodoxy joins with the coercive power of the state to force non-believers either to conform or to be severely punished?

from terrorists, security in our later years, affordable health care, high-quality college educations with low tuition, consumer protections, reliable commercial transactions, a robust and effective judicial system, a strong military, the economic benefits that come from scientific and technological research, and reductions in the national debt.

Consistency may be the hobgoblin of small minds, but it has its value when it comes to ethical decision making. When we realize that we are being inconsistent in applying our ethical principles, it is time to step back and reconsider our positions. It is time to sharpen our analyses, to demand greater precision of thought and expression, and to pay more careful attention to the actual facts of the situation. If we wish to be taken seriously as critical thinkers and ethical decision makers, then our opinions cannot be crispy autumn leaves floating on a mountain lake, blown this way and that by whatever small breeze might come along. Ethical decision making is not about picking and choosing among ethical imperatives as if they were designer fashion accessories.

Strong critical thinking about complex and difficult social policies demands that we respect those with whom we disagree. And this means that we are not likely to see high-quality decision making occurring if the people involved are merely showing off for the cameras or staging shouting matches to amp network ratings. That may be good entertainment, but it seldom if ever results in the resolution of our most vexing policy issues. Strong critical thinkers follow reasons and evidence wherever they lead, even if they go against cherished beliefs or preconceptions. Strong critical thinkers take seriously the points of view of those with whom they may disagree. Instead of regarding that person as a fool or as an evil person, if the disagreement is genuine and the conversation is sincerely intended to explore ways to resolve the issue at hand, then a strong critical thinker will seek to discover the basis of the ethical disagreement. Does the other person have a different set of ethical priorities? Perhaps the anticipated consequences are balanced differently. Perhaps there are duties involved that may not be immediately apparent to me. Has the other person found an alternative approach that I might have overlooked? Is there a way for us to negotiate a resolution that fulfills the interests of both of us, either completely or partially?

APPLY THE "GOLDEN RULE"—DO UNTO OTHERS AS YOU WOULD HAVE OTHERS DO UNTO YOU There is a strategy for bringing a measure of resolution even to the most difficult ethical problems, and that simply is to consider what would happen if the situation were reversed. Ask yourself, "If someone else were in my situation and I was going to be affected by that person's decision, how would I want that person to behave?" Would you want them to lie to you, to take advantage of you, to break their promise to you, to cheat you, or to cause harm to you or to your loved ones by what they decided to do? No, certainly not. So, whatever you would want the other person to do or not to do is what you ought to do or ought not to do.[26]

Another way to explore this same idea is to ask "If everyone were to do what I propose to do, how would things come out?" If everyone were to lie on the witness stand, how well would the judicial system work? If everyone were to shirk their work responsibilities, how well would the community or the family or the business survive? If everyone were to think only about how to satisfy their own desires and ambitions, how enduring would friendships be? How loving would families be? Individual choices make a difference because they define mutual expectations and set standards of acceptable behavior, high or low. A person who hopes to be treated respectfully would be wise to treat others respectfully.

If every factory were to dump its waste materials into the river, what would happen to the quality of the city's drinking water? If everyone in the residence hall or the apartment regularly was rude and uncivil toward one another, invaded each other's privacy, and appropriated each other's property at will, how awful would it be to live in such a place? These last two examples lead to one final thought. Ethical decision making is not only about what individuals decide but also about what businesses, groups of people, government agencies, and whole communities decide with regard to how they ought to act when they are at their best.

"What if everyone were to ...?" The Chicago River prior to regulations concerning waste disposal.

Summing up this chapter,

strong critical thinkers, when engaging an ethical question reflectively, will consider their options in light of the consequences of each and in light of their ethical duties. Bringing about the greatest preponderance of beneficial over harmful consequences for the greatest number of people is an important ethical value. But estimating which course of action will actually result in the greatest net balance of positive over negative outcomes is often difficult and fraught with uncertainty. In addition to considering our ethical responsibilities and the foreseeable consequences of our actions, our personal vices and virtues influence the choices we make. Ethical virtues are habits, which impel us to react and to respond ethically as if it were the natural thing for us to do. Typically these are System-1 judgments. Like the positive critical thinking habits of mind, ethical virtues can be taught, cultivated, nurtured, and practiced.

Ethical decision making can be difficult because ethical imperatives can diverge or conflict. Strong critical thinkers apply three strategies when working through ethical questions and dilemmas involving divergent imperatives: (1) set priorities, (2) attempt to find additional options and alternatives, and (3) negotiate options aimed at fully or partially achieving the most important interests of all the parties involved.

Personal, social, professional, and political problems involving diverging ethical imperatives can be emotionally and intellectually difficult to resolve. Strong critical thinkers approach those challenges mindful that reasonable people can disagree. They strive for consistency in the application of ethically significant beliefs and values. And strong critical thinkers with a well-developed moral compass strive to treat those with whom they disagree not as evil people or as fools, but with respect.

Key Concepts

ethics refers to a set of behavioral ideals or moral principles that guide us in determining right and wrong. We can think of these ideals and principles as a set of core values and beliefs.

ethical imperatives are intended to shape or guide behavior by expressing core values and beliefs about what

is morally right or morally wrong. Ethical imperatives express behavioral ideals and moral principles by pointing out what we ought to do or ought to refrain from doing.

Applications

Reflective Log

Extraordinary rendition: Does the end ever justify the means? The War on Terror has resulted in some ethically challenging practices and policies in many countries. Faced with the duty to protect innocent people from harm, nations have tightened security, increased surveillance, and gone to great lengths to discover and thwart terrorist plots. As in every war, knowledge of what the enemy is planning is a huge advantage. To acquire that knowledge some nations have sanctioned enhanced interrogation methods and arranged with other nations to have suspected terrorists handed over for questioning. Ordinarily two countries might have a treaty permitting either country to transfer a suspect it has arrested into the custody of the other country. But what if one

country sends a team of operatives into another country to capture and extract a suspected criminal without the knowledge or cooperation of that other country. And what if the suspected criminal is then transferred to a third country where the laws permit interrogation methods that we might regard as torture, or where prisoners do not have the legal right to an attorney or to a speedy trial? Called extraordinary rendition, is this practice ethical? As you reflect on this, consider other examples where people have proposed that the end might indeed justify the means. What consequences do you foresee for your country if it embraced the notion that if the goal is important enough any means that leads us to that goal is ethically defensible?

Individual Exercises

Conflicting duties to church and state: The 1964 film *Becket*, nominated for 11 Academy Awards, dramatizes the conflict between duty to one's sovereign and duty to one's God. Richard Burton's moving portrayal of the Archbishop of Canterbury shows the depth of that character's internal struggle. King Henry II, played by Peter O'Toole, cannot abide that his former friend and drinking buddy now places religion above obedience to his king. The 1966 film *A Man for All Seasons*, winner of six Academy Awards, tells a similar tale of the internal moral conflicts that must be addressed by a person of conscience. Sir Thomas More, played by Paul Scofield, could simply sign the oath of loyalty to his king, Henry VIII. But, refusing, he risks trial and the death penalty for high treason.

Archbishop Becket and Sir Thomas More, as portrayed in these classic films, were "persons of conscience" who would rather die than compromise their religious convictions. Fortunately their religious convictions did not impel them to kill other people. Only their own lives were in jeopardy because of their interpretation of their religious duties.

What about today? If they should diverge, which ethical duties deserve priority—those of Church or those of State? Explain why. And if we should fail in either, what punishments should we expect? Explain why. And today, if a religion should be interpreted as imposing the ethical duty to perform "honor killings" or to kill non-believers, should the laws of the nation say that such a killing is justified or excused? Explain your answer by reference to good reasons and solid evidence.

Research and report on both sides of this centuries old ethical conflict: What ethical principles support each side of this debate? What would it be like to live in a nation if its laws permitted any and every kind of behavior that any citizen might regard as his or her duty because of a religion-based set of moral beliefs? If such a life seems intolerable, then in what sense, if any, should a nation's laws be "grounded in religious values" or "express the religious values" of the community?

Anything goes these days—not! Three stories are described briefly below. With each is a question or two. Select one event. Investigate the details of that event and its aftermath, beginning with the reference provided. Identify the ethical issues and then comment intelligently on those issues by analyzing the alternatives, describing foreseeable consequences, identifying duties and ethical principles that are relevant, and form reflective ethical decisions about the question or questions asked. Be careful not to jump to conclusions. Do not base your answers only on the one news event presented. In each case you should be able to find other stories that impel you toward the opposite conclusion if you are using only System-1 thinking. Use your critical thinking skills and be sure to consider all the possibilities.

Story 1. After Ameneh Bahrami was blinded and disfigured by acid, the Iranian court ordered her attacker be imprisoned and blinded. Blinding is part of the punishment for his brutal crime under Sharia law. Although jailed, the attacker has not yet been blinded. Years passed and Ameneh demanded the full measure of justice. However, organizations like Amnesty International oppose the blinding. First Question: If the victim of a crime is not satisfied with the punishment the courts apply, does the victim have the right to demand a greater punishment until the victim is satisfied that punishment is great enough? Second Question: In a case like Ameneh's, when the justice system fails, does the victim have the ethical right to exact justice? What if you lived in a

Orson Wells, playing Cardinal Wolsey, accuses Thomas More, played by Paul Scofield, of treason for not signing the oath of loyalty to King Henry VIII.

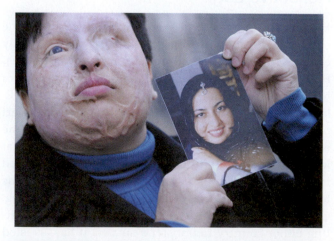

In the tradition of "an eye for an eye," the Iranian court ordered that the man who intentionally attacked Ameneh Bahrami with acid should himself be blinded.

country where rapists routinely went unpunished because the justice system was incompetent, corrupt, or indifferent, and what if someone you loved were raped? Would those facts change the ethics of the situation?[27]

Story 2. In November 2014, 90-year-old World War II veteran Arnold Abbott was arrested in Fort Lauderdale, Florida for giving meals to homeless people. And in 2011 the Orlando, Florida police arrested more than 20 activists who were handing out food to the homeless in a city park. Giving food to the homeless is illegal in both of those Florida cities.[28] In response to the 2011 arrests, the hacker collective known as Anonymous declared war on the city. Their assault came in the form of so many demands on the city's tourist information Website that its servers could not keep pace. Called a DDoS (Distributed Denial of Service) attack, this tactic effectively closed down a Web site. Similar DDoS attacks have occurred more frequently in recent years. Some are directed at businesses, but most are directed at government websites. Question: Is cyber vigilantism ethically acceptable? Question: Who, if anyone, was harmed, and who, if anyone, is ethically responsible for compensating individuals who might have become the innocent victims of all of this?

Story 3. In 1985 a former KGB agent gave an interview describing how a government might go about brainwashing its own population. The four phases are demoralization, destabilization, crises, and normalization. In the first phase the educational system is weakened and the population is fed useless information until it no longer is able to assess the facts. Destabilization involves undermining the economy, foreign relations, and the national defense system. The crises phase is brought about by a sudden, unexpected, imminent threat. In response to the crises the government puts in place emergency measures after which follows the normalization process, which affirms and institutionalizes the new status quo. Question: Is it the government's responsibility to provide for the education of the people, if by education we mean to include developing strong critical thinking? Question: Is it the government's ethical responsibility to ensure that the population has easy access to full and accurate news and information? Since an affirmative answer to either of these questions would cost billions, who is ethically responsible for picking up the bill?[29]

Video take three: Select one story other than the one you used in the previous exercise. Present the story and the questions to three people who are not in this course. With their permission, capture their responses on video. Use the argument and decision mapping techniques presented in Chapter 5 to analyze those responses, to identify how they came to their ethical decisions. Look for examples of thinking about consequences, considering duties and ethical principles, spontaneously responding in an ethically virtuous way, System-1 thinking, System-2 thinking, comparative reasoning, or ideological reasoning. Look for efforts to set priorities, to find alternatives, or to negotiate resolutions. Look for consistency, respect for those who might reasonably disagree, and the strategy of using the Golden Rule. Comparing these elements in each of the three video responses, determine which of the three responses manifests the best application of critical thinking to ethical decision making.

SHARED RESPONSE

Ethical Decision Making

How is ethical decision making different than decision making in general? Give examples. Be sure to provide your reason(s), not just your opinion. And comment respectfully on the response others have shared.

Group Exercises

How much? Realistically speaking, exactly how far ought a society go to save the lives of children in need of health care? Obviously, the answer to this question is a moving target, for it depends on the resources available, the state of scientific knowledge and medical technology in that society, and the responsibilities that the society has to meeting other ethical demands being made on its resources. But the question does not go away just because the answer in the early part of the twenty-first century may be different in one country than in another, or may be different in the same country than the answer would have been 70 years ago. So, to be specific, how much money, ethically speaking, should your country appropriate next year for diagnosing, treating, and preventing childhood diabetes? Begin your inquiry by first investigating the prevalence and the causes of childhood diabetes in this country. Then compare that disease to other childhood diseases to understand the scope of the problem. Consider the consequences of addressing the problem aggressively now or of postponing action for a period of years. And consider the many other reasonable demands being made on the limited resources available to your country. Come up with a specific recommendation and explain the basis for your recommendation by referencing the information you have developed about this illness, other child-hood illnesses, and the budgetary constraints you have discovered.

Is world peace possible? Do all humans, for all their cultural and social differences the world over, basically progress through the same stages of moral development? According to Lawrence Kohlberg, we do. According to Kohlberg, human moral development proceeds sequentially through six stages. The first two stages are self-focused. Initially decisions about what one ought to do or ought not to do are based directly on avoiding punishment. "If I am a bad boy, daddy will punish me!" At the second stage satisfaction of our own needs is our paramount concern. "What's in it for me?" "If I do my chores will you pay me?" Conventional morality is evident in stages three and four. A stage three ethical decision maker seeks the approval of others, the peer group, people whom they respect, people whose approval matters to them. A person at the fourth stage of moral development in Kohlberg's theory focuses mainly on rules, codes, and laws. This person is likely to equate ethics with legality. A person at stage five makes ethical decisions based on the community values behind the laws, codes, and rules. Ethical decision making that reaches the final stage, stage six, moves past the limits of one's own society and into the realm of universal ethical principles and a profound respect for persons. At level six (a level Kohlberg says few people reach), a person can appeal to ethical principles and standards beyond those of one's own society. In the way that Gandhi or Martin Luther King, Jr. or Jesus pointed out the need for moral change, a person at level six can seek to infuse his or her own society with a higher sense of moral right and wrong.[30] Assume Kohlberg's theory of moral development is true. Discuss its implications for achieving world peace based on finding common ground with people who may have been raised in communities with different traditions, cultures, political systems, and religious traditions far different from our own. What would we have to do within our own society to prepare the general population for the prospect of making peace with people whose tradition, culture, political system, and religious heritage are so unlike our own?

Chapter 17
The Logic of Declarative Statements

When every dollar helps, a systematic and logical approach to routine budget management makes a tangible difference

HOW can we express the logical relationships among declarative statements?

HOW can we translate between symbolic logic and a natural language declarative statement?

HOW can we detect the logical characteristics of declarative statements?

HOW can we test two declarative statements for implication and equivalence?

HOW can we test an argument composed of declarative statements for validity?

Learning Outcomes

17.1 Identify negations, conjunctions, disjunctions, and conditional declarative statements.

17.2 Translate simple and compound natural language declarative statements to and from symbolic notation.

17.3 Identify tautologies, inconsistent statements, and contingent declarative statements using truth tables.

17.4 Test declarative statements for implication and equivalence using truth tables.

17.5 Test arguments composed of declarative statements for validity using truth tables.

Joan rubbed her tired eyes and picked up the pencil once more. Taxes! What a bother. But every dollar helps! If I could get some money back for Seth's child care, that would be great.

Thankfully Joan's 6-year-old son, Seth, went to sleep each night at 8:00, which meant Joan could plan on a couple of precious quiet hours. A single parent, there was always so much to do. During the day Joan worked at Hendrix Manufacturing in the Shipping and Billing Department. After work she took courses through Valley County Community College. She attended class once a week at the college, on Saturdays. She participated in the other sessions online from her apartment. Most nights if she was not logged in to a class session, she studied. But not tonight. Tonight was income tax night!

Joan picked up an envelope marked "Seth expenses," and pulled out a fist full of cancelled checks. Most were made out to Mrs. Marta Ramirez, the neighbor who took care of Seth after school. I don't know what I would do without Marta's help, thought Joan. Every morning Joan dropped Seth at school. Marta picked him up when school was out. And Marta took care of Seth until Joan could get home from work. Wow, she thought, there's $2,400 in cancelled checks to Mrs. Ramirez. Joan realized she had paid Mrs. Ramirez almost 10 percent of the $28,500 she had earned working at Hendrix that year. Joan knew that some employers offered benefits programs that covered a portion of their employees' dependent care expenses. But Hendrix Manufacturing did not. Joan found a slip of paper from Mrs. Ramirez acknowledging the payments and showing a business address and a government ID number. Joan recognized the address as Mrs. Ramirez's home, and thought that the ID number was probably her Social Security number.

After Joan's divorce, five years ago, there had been no money. Her ex-husband, a deadbeat of the first magnitude, missed more child support payments than he made. So Joan withdrew from college and took the first decent job she could find. For the first few months Joan and little Seth lived with her parents. But as soon as she had enough money, Joan got her own apartment. Well, all of that is ancient history, thought Joan. What doesn't crush you makes you stronger! Now, five years later, Joan had the skills and the confidence to reason through lots of things for herself. Like tax returns!

She pulled IRS Publication 17 down from the government Web site, and scrolled through the PDF to the section on "Child and Dependent Care Credit." Okay, first, do I even qualify to claim a tax credit for Seth's day care? She saw a page full of conditions. Some were easy. Yes, the money she had paid Mrs. Ramirez was for the care of her dependent child, Seth. Seth was under the age of 13. Joan paid for Seth's care so that she could work at Hendrix. The list went on and on. Joan was about to chart out all those conditions when she turned the page and saw a diagram. Lots of boxes, arrows, Yeses and Nos. Joan studied the diagram, working her way through. Hum, things are looking promising, she thought. The IRS document said she needed to use Form 2441 to claim the tax credit. So she downloaded it from the IRS web site. I could get six or seven hundred dollars back! Not bad for an hour or so spent analyzing the logic of a bunch of income tax rules.

Hum . . . I wonder what else I can find. How about educational expenses? It's not just books. I bought a new computer this year so I could take courses online. And each month I have to pay for the Internet connection too.

In this chapter we explore the power of the *Logic of Declarative Statements*. Joan used that power to make the valid and financially valuable inference that she qualifies for the child care tax credit. Tax regulations are complicated. But Joan was able to work systematically through the long series of conditions. It was worth the effort. Her analysis led her to infer that she should complete the income tax form to claim a tax credit for the child care expenses. We can express the relevant facts of Joan's case as a series of declarative statements:

- Joan incurs expenses for the care of Seth.
- Seth is Joan's dependent child.
- Seth is under the age of 13.
- Joan earned $28,500 for the year as an employee of Hendrix Manufacturing.
- The child care expenses allowed Joan to work.
- Joan pays Mrs. Ramirez to provide the child care for Seth.
- It is not the case that Mrs. Ramirez is Joan's dependent.
- Mrs. Ramirez is not Joan's parent.
- Mrs. Ramirez is not Joan's child.
- Joan is single.
- Joan knows Mrs. Ramirez's name, address, and government ID number.
- Joan had expenses for only one child, Seth.
- Because she receives no dependent care benefits at all, Joan will not be excluding $3,000 dependent care benefits.

Joan reasoned through the complex income tax regulations, answering "Yes" or "No" to the questions in the Figure "Can You Claim the Credit?" She inferred that she qualified for the tax credit. In fact, she reasoned to the conclusion that there is no way that she does not qualify, given the applicable tax regulations and the facts of her situation. If she is correct, her inference would be logically valid as described in Chapter 8. And, she saves herself some money.

Drawing valid inferences and evaluating inferences for logical validity is important for success in today's complex, legalistic world. The primary goal of "The Logic of Declarative Statements" is to develop a *reliable* way to test for logical validity for the first level of logic declarative statements. We first introduced this level of logic, in Chapter 8.

A second, also very practical goal is to refine our skills in the analysis and interpretation of logical relationship between statements—both as these relationships are expressed in a natural language, such as English, and in the notation of symbolic logic. When we were in college we both found the precision with natural language gained by the study of logic to be an unexpectedly huge and widely applicable lifelong benefit.

How will we reach our goals? To generate a reliable method of testing arguments for validity at the level of the logic of declarative statements, this chapter follows a simple four-part program: First we will focus on how to express simple declarative statements, negations, conjunctions, disjunctions, and conditional statements in symbolic notation. With these tools in hand, we develop interpretive and analytical skills so we can translate between English and symbolic logic notation. The symbolic notation will probably remind you of basic algebra. At least that's what it reminds us of, except without numbers. We learn to rely on a small set of simple symbols and alphabet letters to express the relevant logical relationships between declarative statements, much as algebra uses a few familiar mathematical symbols to express addition, subtraction, and other relationships between positive and negative numbers.

Next we develop our skills at using a tool called a "Truth Table" to determine the logical characteristics of individual statements and pairs of statements. Truth tables are reliable tools to test declarative statements to see if one implies another or if two are equivalent to one another.

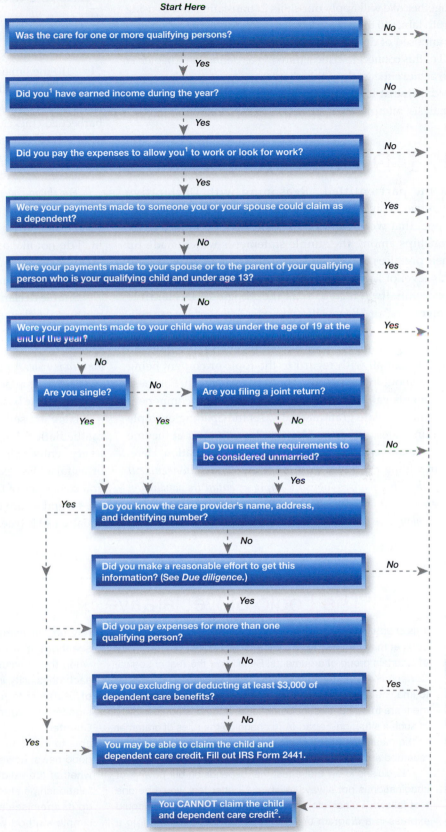

Logic Decision Tree: Can You Claim a Tax Credit for Dependent or Child Care Expenses?

Start Here

- Was the care for one or more qualifying persons? → **No**
- ↓ *Yes*
- Did you[1] have earned income during the year? → **No**
- ↓ *Yes*
- Did you pay the expenses to allow you[1] to work or look for work? → **No**
- ↓ *Yes*
- Were your payments made to someone you or your spouse could claim as a dependent? → **Yes**
- ↓ *No*
- Were your payments made to your spouse or to the parent of your qualifying person who is your qualifying child and under age 13? → **Yes**
- ↓ *No*
- Were your payments made to your child who was under the age of 19 at the end of the year? → **Yes**
- ↓ *No*
- Are you single? → *No* → Are you filing a joint return?
- Are you single? ↓ *Yes* ; Are you filing a joint return? ↓ *Yes* ... *No* →
- Do you meet the requirements to be considered unmarried? → **No**
- ↓ *Yes*
- Do you know the care provider's name, address, and identifying number? (*Yes* →)
- ↓ *No*
- Did you make a reasonable effort to get this information? (See *Due diligence.*) → **No**
- ↓ *Yes*
- Did you pay expenses for more than one qualifying person?
- ↓ *No*
- Are you excluding or deducting at least $3,000 of dependent care benefits? → **Yes**
- ↓ *No*
- You may be able to claim the child and dependent care credit. Fill out IRS Form 2441.

You CANNOT claim the child and dependent care credit[2].

[1] This also applies to your spouse, unless your spouse was disabled or a full-time student.
[2] If you had expenses that met the requirements for last year, except that you did not pay them until this year, you may be able to claim those expenses on this year's return. See *Expenses not paid until the following year* under *How to Figure the Credit*.

"Evaluating Arguments for Validity," puts all the pieces together. We will apply our skills in translating and in using truth tables to the practical business of evaluating arguments composed of declarative statements for validity. How does all of this connect to critical thinking as defined in Chapter 1? To achieve the goals of this chapter we must exercise, apply, and refine at least four of the core critical thinking skills: analysis, interpretation, inference, and evaluation.

17.1 Declarative Statements

In the part entitled "Reasoning with Declarative Statements" in Chapter 8, we identified a group of arguments that were valid because of the grammatical relationships among the simple statements which made up their premises and conclusion. The driving insight behind this level of logic, often called the "Logic of Statements" (occasionally referred to as the "Logic of Declarative Statements" or "Propositional Logic"), is that we can reliably evaluate these arguments for validity by looking only at those grammatical relationships even if we have no expertise at all with regard to the topic or content being talked about in the premises and the conclusion. For these arguments validity comes down to how their component statements relate grammatically. As the opening example demonstrates, we do not have to be an expert at income tax regulations to follow the logic of Joan's situation. Here, as in Chapter 8, **valid argument** is defined *an argument such that its premises logically imply or entail its conclusion which makes it impossible for all of its premises to be true and its conclusion to be false.*

Simple Statements

The smallest unit of measure for the Logic of Statements is the simple declarative statement that asserts that something is true. Four quick examples: "I enjoy barbecued chicken." "In 2010 the Japanese economy was remarkably healthy." "Cotton farming has transformed Brazil's vast savannah." "Seth is Joan's child." As it happens, it is true that I enjoy barbecued chicken. The statement about the Japanese economy is false. The statement about cotton farming in Brazil is true. And the statement about Seth is true within the fictional context of the opening story for this section.

For the purposes of the Logic of Statements, we will assign the value "true" or the value "false" to every statement. As we will see below, we can assert that a statement is not true, as in "I do not like barbecued ribs." And we can assert combinations of statements too. For example, "Either I enjoy barbecued chicken or I like barbecued ribs."

Simple declarative statements are the sentences people use to make claims, to give reasons, to assert beliefs, and to express their opinions. A **simple statement** *is a grammatically correct construction in a given language used to assert that an idea is true.* A prime example of a simple statement is a sentence that attaches one predicate to one subject: "Janet is going to the beach."

Here are seven natural language examples and two mathematical language examples of simple statements. Every sentence in this list can be evaluated either as true or as false. For example, #1 is true by virtue of the general consensus of the critics and readers of popular fiction. #2, #4, and #7 are historical facts. Equation #8 is false, but equation #9 is true. We may not know the truth value (true

---

How "The Logic of Declarative Statements" Connects

This chapter connects conceptually with the other parts of this book at many points by providing a reliable test of the validity of a certain group of arguments. Recall how the Test of Logical Correctness first presented in Chapter 7 relied on our capacity to imagine a situation in which all of the premises of an argument are true and its conclusion false. If there is no possibility of such a situation—apart from changing the rules of grammar or the meanings of the words—then the argument should be regarded as valid.

Logicians know that a test that depends on our powers of imagination is not always reliable. A better test would be one that follows a clear, step-by-step process—one that we could express in a diagram or a table, or perhaps program into a computer.

In the current chapter we will develop such a procedure. Within the domain of the Logic of Statements, we need not rely on our imaginations only to come up with possible scenarios that might make an argument's premises true when the conclusion is false. We will be able to consider each possibility in a simple and systematic way. The Logic of Statements provides us with the tools to evaluate a significant group of arguments for validity. And yet, as Chapter 8 illustrates, at this level of logic, we will not be able to evaluate every possible argument for validity. The good news, however, is that we will have a solid test to see whether the validity of an argument depends on the logical relationships among the declarative statements that make up its premises and its conclusion. And, the powerful yet simple method we will have developed works, no matter what the topic or content of that argument might be—including income tax rules and regulations!

or false) of a given statement—for example #3, #5, and #6—but we will proceed on the working assumption that each has exactly one truth value, either true or false.

1. John Sanford's highly successful *Prey* series novels are captivating thrillers.

2. Kim Clijsters won the U.S. Tennis Open Championship in 2009 and 2010.

3. Sally and Broderick met online.

4. In 1265 the Mongols sacked the Gareja Monastery.

5. Michele believes that drinking water before meals results in weight loss for adults.

6. Luella read in *The Economist* that capitalism is thriving in South Korea.

7. Vancouver hosted the 2010 Winter Olympic Games.

8. $(2 + 2) = 6$

9. $(3 \times (4 + 5)) = (12 + 15)$

As this initial point in our exploration of logic we must limit our evaluation of declarative statements to two values only: "true"/"false." There is no third option. If a statement is not true we will regard it as false. If a statement is not false we will regard it as true. The Logic of Statements, being a very elementary level of logic, provides for no other possibilities. Expressions like "probably true" or "might be true someday" do not fall within the scope of the Logic of Statements.[1]

Let's use the lowercase alphabet letters *p*, *q*, *r*, and *s* to stand for simple statements. We can assign any simple statement to any one of the letters. In the Logic of Statements these letters work just like the familiar *x*, *y*, and *z* do in algebra. They are variables. In algebra the variables, that is the letters, stand for numbers and are used in equations: $(2x + 2y) = 2(x + y)$. In logic the variables stand for statements. Here are four quick examples:

Let p stand for "I do like frozen yogurt."

Let q stand for "The abacus is obsolete."

Let r stand for "We met online."

Let s stand for "The Valley of the Kings is on the Nile."

Negations

Besides asserting that something is true, people often assert that something is not true. These sentences, for example, make the claim that something is false.

- I do not like frozen yogurt.
- It is not true that the abacus is obsolete.
- It is false to say that the Valley of Kings is on the Nile.
- No way did you drive from Toronto to Windsor in less than three hours, man!
- The sum of $7 + 3$ does not equal 9.

A **negation** *is a grammatically correct construction used to assert that a statement is false.* As the examples illustrate, there are many ways in a natural language, like English, to express a negation.

Remembering that a letter stands for a statement, it is easy to express the negation of that statement. All we need to do is put the symbol ~ (called a *tilde*) to the left of the letter, as in ~p.[2] If p stands for "I do like frozen yogurt," what do you suppose that ~p means? Right. It means "It is not the case that I do like frozen yogurt," or, more idiomatically expressed, "I do not like frozen yogurt."

Suppose that we associate the value "true" with p. The negation of p would then be a false statement. Yes? If it is true that the Valley of the Kings is on the Nile, which it is, then it is a mistake to say that the Valley of the Kings is not on the Nile. OK. Flip it around. Suppose that we assign the value "false" to p. What then is the value of ~p? If "the abacus is obsolete" is a false statement, then "it is not the case that the abacus is obsolete" becomes a true statement. It is easier to see the effect of negation using a table. In fact, let's say that the table below defines the operation called "negation" for the purposes of the Logic of Statements.

Negation Truth Table	
p	**~p**
T	F
F	T

The "Negation Truth Table" completely describes the function of negation as far as symbolic logic is concerned. In this definitional table, p can stand for any statement whatsoever, no matter how complex. The row below the

Kim Clijsters, two time U.S. Tennis Open Champion

horizontal line of the negation truth table tells us that if any given statement, p, no matter how complex is true, then the negation of that statement is false. The second row tells us that if p is false, then the expression ~p is true. Remember at this level of logic there were no other possibilities but "true" and "false." The table covers all the possibilities. There are no other cases to consider. Logicians call a table like this one a "truth table." A simple shortcut way to remember how negation functions in symbolic logic is this: *Let A stand for any symbolic logic statement whatsoever, the value of ~A is the opposite of the value of A.*

Let's apply negation, as defined by the truth table above, to ~q. If we negated ~q, we would get ~~q. What, then are the possible values of ~~q? Starting out there are two possibilities only: that q is true or that q is false. The two possible values of q are shown in the left-hand column of the truth table below. First we need to find the value of ~q so we can then find the value of its negation, ~~q. The middle column represents that first step, showing us the value of ~q in both cases. The right-hand column then displays the value of the negation of ~q, which is ~~q.

q	~q	~~q
T	F	T
F	T	F

Statement Compounds: *And, Or, If… Then,* etc.

In conversation we express important relationships among statements with words like *and, or,* and grammatical constructions like *if* ____, *then* ___. Here are six examples.

10. Worldwide the percentage of workers over the age of 55 is growing, **and** many older adults are reentering the workforce each year.

11. France will increase the retirement age to 62, **or** the French government will have to raise taxes to cover the projected costs of its national pension program.

12. **If** cable TV cooking shows continue to be popular, **then** we can start a business selling high-end kitchenware.

13. **If** we cannot start a business selling high-end kitchenware, **then** we can open a cooking school.

14. **Either** we can start a business selling kitchenware **or** we can open a cooking school.

15. We can start the kitchenware business **but also** we can open a cooking school.

Notice how the words in **bold orange** not only connect the simpler statements, but also express logically significant relationships between the statements that they connect. Let's examine these relationships more closely.

CONJUNCTIONS   One of the most familiar logical structures is the assertion that two things are both true, for example, sentences #10 and #15. Here are three more quick examples of conjunctions. "I just changed my major to Accounting, and yet I still hope to graduate next year." "My favorite subject is Finance, but I really enjoy Graphic Arts too." "Joan pays Mrs. Ramirez to take care of Seth after school, although Mrs. Ramirez would be willing to provide the care for free."

We commonly use words like *and, but, however, although, furthermore,* and their synonyms to express conjunctions. A **conjunction** *is a grammatically correct construction used to assert that two statements are both true.* Let's use the ampersand (&) to express conjunction in the language of symbolic logic. We can use parentheses for punctuation, to mark the beginning and the end of a conjunction. For example, (p & q) is the grammatically correct conjunction formed by combining the two statements p and q. Suppose that (r & s) is another conjunction. We could write a statement that is the conjunction of both of those examples: ((p & q) & (r & s)). As long as both component statements are grammatically correct constructions themselves, we can form the conjunction of those two statements using the ampersand and a pair of parentheses. For example:

$$(\sim p \ \& \ \sim q)$$
$$((\sim p \ \& \ q) \ \& \ \sim p)$$
$$(\sim(p \ \& \ q) \ \& \ (r \ \& \ q))$$

The conjunction (p & q) asserts that p is true and that q is true. And if both are true, then the conjunction itself would be a true statement. Otherwise, it would not be true. The truth table below defines the meaning of conjunction in the language of the Logic of Statements.

Conjunction Truth Table		
p	q	(p & q)
T	T	T
T	F	F
F	T	F
F	F	F

There are four rows needed because there are four possible combinations to consider. Both component statements might be true, both might be false, or one of them might be true when the other is false. The only condition that results in a conjunction being true is if both of its component statements are true. The simple shortcut way to remember the conjunction function in symbolic logic is this: *Given any two statements, p and q, the expression (p & q) is true only in the situation where p is true and q is true, otherwise (p & q) is false.*

Logicians always build 4-row truth tables with the rows in the order shown here, starting with the case where both component statements are true, and ending with the case where they are both false. The colors are optional, of course. Logicians use basic black on white. But because the colors can help us see the key relationships better, we've used them occasionally in this book for their educational value.

DISJUNCTIONS   Example sentences #11 and #14 assert that one or both of two component statements are true. Here are three more quick examples. "On Monday we often enjoy watching *2 Broke Girls* or sometimes we watch the NFL football game." "Either I'll buy orange juice or I'll buy grapefruit juice." "Either Joan studies at night after Seth goes to sleep, or she relaxes by reading a novel."

The *either ___ or ___* construction obviously offers us the opportunity to say that each alternative may be the true alternative. A **disjunction** *is a grammatically correct construction used to assert that one or both of two statements are true.*[3]

THINKING CRITICALLY

Where Might We Be Without Logic?

Logic is the study of the inferential structures manifested in language and thought. There are many wonderfully interesting levels of logic, beyond the Logic of Statements. Chapter 8 offers a brief glimpse at the Logic of Classes and the Logic of Relationships, for example. Each level builds on earlier levels and reveals even more about the complex and intricate inferential structures of reasoning. To me, each level of logic is progressively more captivating and more powerful.

As abstract as it may seem at first, logic is immensely practical. The programming in the computer chips that run our communication and power grids, our cars, our phones, and our electronic games is based on the kinds of logical relationships that we begin exploring in the Logic of Statements. Personally, I found that the study of logic improved my ability to analyze and interpret language, to evaluate arguments, and to make well-reasoned inferences.

As I write this I'm working on my laptop while flying in a Boeing 757 between LA and San Francisco. The engineering physics that permits us to build this flying machine, the radar that keeps us on our flight path, and the automation that makes for a smooth takeoff and landing are all based on the solid bedrock of logic. Although it is purely speculation, flying at 37,000 feet, I wonder what life might be like had logic not been invented. My guess is that my trip from LA to San Fran would mean I'd be walking the wagon-rutted road, called the El Camino Real, which has connected those towns since the days of Brother Junipero Serra. It would take weeks to hike the 350 miles, and I probably would need to bunk down each night at a mission inn along the way.

Life without the invention of logic? A goofy hypothesis? Perhaps. Logic in one manifestation or another, like mathematics, has been around for several thousand years. Logic has been part of the college core curriculum since the invention of universities, centuries ago. That kind of longevity would be highly unlikely if logic offered no practical benefits. Think about it. What would our lives be like without all the medical, transportation, communication, manufacturing, entertainment, and military technology made possible because our species invented logic? Using the tools of logic we continue to be able to study, display, systematize, validate, improve, and extend our powers of reasoning. Try this to see what I mean: Empty your pockets, backpack, and apartment of everything that has a computer chip (don't forget to get rid of your car, microwave, phone, TV, and the thermostat that controls your heating unit). Whatever's left is roughly where we'd be without logic.

Built in 1777, Mission Santa Clara de Asís, where Santa Clara University is now located, was one link in the chain of missions along the El Camino Real established by Junipero Serra and his Franciscan brothers between 1769 and 1823. From San Francisco de Solano to San Diego de Alcalá, 21 in all, each mission in the chain was located about a day's journey by foot from the next.

71559   SANTA CLARA DE ASIS MISSION, CALIFORNIA   FOUNDED JANUARY 12, 1777 BY PADRE TOMAS

In example #11, both component statements might be true. That is, France may increase the retirement age and raise taxes too. The same for example #14. We can do both, open the kitchenware business and open a cooking school. Hey, why not put our school inside the kitchenware store? Our cooking students might become our best kitchenware customers.

Let's use a v-shaped wedge to express a disjunction in the language of the logic. Again, parentheses punctuate the beginning and the end of the disjunction. For example, (p v q) is the disjunction of the statement p and the statement q. The statement (p v q) asserts that either p is true, or q is true, or they both are true. We can form more complex disjunctions out of other grammatically correct constructions. For example:

$$(r \text{ v } (p \text{ v } q))$$
$$((q \text{ v } r) \text{ v } (p \text{ \& } q))$$
$$(\sim p \text{ v } \sim q)$$

This truth table defines the meaning of disjunction in the language of the Logic of Statements. The shortcut way to remember this truth table and the function of disjunction in logic is this: *Given any two statements, p and q, the expression (p v q) is true in every situation except the one where p is false and q is false.*

Disjunction Truth Table		
p	q	(p v q)
T	T	T
T	F	T
F	T	T
F	F	F

If you are thinking that English is not nearly so cut and dried, you would be right. The English construction *Either _____ or _____* can at times be problematically ambiguous; we are using it to include the possibility of both being true. Logicians call this the *inclusive* sense of the disjunction. But on occasion that construction in English is used to assert one or the other of two alternatives is true, but to exclude both of them being true. For example: "Either I will study or I will go work out," spoken in a context where I clearly do not have the time to do both. Let p stand for "I will study" and let q stand for "I will go work out."

Do we need to amend our definitional truth table for disjunction? No. We can handle the exclusive sense of *Either _____ or _____* using the tools we already have at hand. In the language of symbolic logic we can express the idea that I will do *one or the other, but not both,* (that is the *exclusive* sense of the disjunction) this way:

$$((p \text{ v } q) \text{ \& } \sim (p \text{ \& } q))$$

There is nothing ambiguous about this symbolic logic statement. It says, "Either p is true or q is true, but it is not the case that both p and q are true."

Whenever we are translating from English to symbolic logic our goal is to represent faithfully the logical relationships intended by the speaker. Chapter 4 about clarifying ideas shows how to resolve problematic ambiguity and vagueness through careful attention to purpose and the context. Instead of creating exceptions to the rules of logic, whenever we confront problematic ambiguity or vagueness in a natural language statement, we will clarify using logic's basic building blocks.

In the story that opened this chapter, Joan had to satisfy a number of conditions to qualify for the income

Operations that appear to be complex at first can often be broken down into negations, conjunctions, and disjunctions. For example: "Do not continue the train on the current track. Switch the train first to this track and then on to that track. Taken in the order given, these switches will enable the train to reach its destination safely."

tax credit. We can express each condition as a disjunction using the grammatical, but somewhat awkward, construction "Either it is false that _____ or it is true that _____." For example:

- Either Joan does not qualify for the tax credit or Seth is Joan's dependent.
- Either Joan does not qualify for the tax credit or Seth is under the age of 13.
- Either Joan does not qualify for the tax credit or Mrs. Ramirez is not Joan's parent.

Let p stand for "Joan qualifies for the tax credit" and let q stand for "Seth is Joan's dependent." We can express the first of the three examples in symbolic logic notation as (~p v q). The truth table for (~p v q) below shows that this expression is false only in the case that p is true and q is false. The four combinations of starting values for p and q are given in the two left-hand columns. Before we can calculate the value of (~p v q) we must first determine the value of ~p. So the table gives ~p a column of its own. The formula (~p v q) will be true in all cases when the formula on one side or the other of the v is true. Looking at the values under the ~p column and under the q column we can see that there is only one row when both are false. That is in the second row shaded light blue.

p	q	~p	(~p v q)
T	T	F	T
T	F	F	F
F	T	T	T
F	F	T	T

Speaking about the inclusive sense of *or*, I saw this odd sign in the window of Scotty's Restaurant in Hermosa Beach. Surely the restaurateur is not trying to warn the public that pizza is not food—as if the response to a customer trying to place a phone order would be, "Sorry, buddy, but you can order pizza or you can order food, but not both!" The only way this curious sign makes sense is for the *or* in the sign to be inclusive. "Hey, in addition to that pizza, do you want some other food? Maybe a salad?"

CONDITIONALS   Instead of using the expression *Either not ___, or ____.* another way to express the same conditions that apply in Joan's case would use the construction *If _____, then _____.* Our three examples can be restated this way:

- If Joan qualifies for the tax credit, then Seth is Joan's dependent.
- If Joan qualifies for the tax credit, then Seth is under the age of 13.
- If Joan qualifies for the tax credit, then Mrs. Ramirez is not Joan's parent.

THINKING CRITICALLY

Quick Check Exercise—Identify the Negations, Conjunctions, and Disjunctions

1. To earn a baccalaureate degree, a student must complete 120 semester units, fulfill the requirements of a major program of study, and complete the university's general education requirements.
2. Courses taken at another institution cannot be used to satisfy university general education requirements.
3. Every student must complete two courses in the humanities or two courses in the fine arts.
4. Every student must complete three courses in science, or the student must complete two courses in science and one in mathematics.
5. Units in remedial course work do not count toward the completion of 120 semester units.
6. Every student must complete one course in critical thinking, two courses in writing, and four courses in a foreign language.
7. International students do not have to complete the foreign language requirement.
8. University courses may be completed either on-campus or online.
9. All freshmen must enroll in the Freshman Seminar Program.
10. All seniors are automatically members of the University Alumni Association.

The *If* _____, *then* _____. construction expresses a conditional assertion. When we use it, we are saying that if the first statement is true, then the second statement is true. Exactly as in Chapter 8, the first statement in the conditional is called the *antecedent*. The second is called the *consequent*. A **conditional** *is a grammatically correct construction used to assert that if an antecedent statement is true, then a consequent statement is true.* Here are two quick examples of conditional statements. "If I enroll in the Tuesday evening section of American Literature, then I can take Canadian Studies on Mondays." "If I major in Chemistry, then I do not have to take any general education sciences courses." And, again, here are the two examples of conditional statements from earlier, #12 and #13:

- **If** cable TV cooking shows continue to be popular, **then** we can start a business selling high-end kitchenware.
- **If** we cannot start a business selling high-end kitchenware, **then** we can open a cooking school.

We will use an arrow (→) along with opening and closing parentheses as our symbols to express conditional statements. For example (p → q) means "if p, then q." A conditional statement is going to be false just in the situation when the antecedent statement is true but the consequent statement is not true. "If Joan qualifies for the tax credit, then Seth is Joan's dependent" is false if it turns out that Joan does qualify, but Seth is not Joan's dependent. The table below defines the meaning of a conditional in the Logic of Statements. The simple shortcut for remembering this definitional truth table goes like this: *Given any two statements, p and q, the expression (p → q) is false only in the situation where p is true and q is false, otherwise (p → q) is true.*

Conditional Truth Table		
p	**q**	**(p → q)**
T	T	T
T	F	F
F	T	T
F	F	T

In the section on disjunctions in this text we used (~p v q) to express the idea that Joan does not qualify for the tax credit unless Seth is Joan's dependent. In this section we use (p → q) to express the same idea. Just as there are two correct ways to express the relationship

THINKING CRITICALLY

Logic Circuits

Different people learn in different ways. Some like explanations in words, some like charts and tables. Some want to see examples first, others like to see definitions first. And some like to use analogies. One interesting analogy that some of us find helpful compares logic functions to electrical circuits. If this analogy does not help you, don't worry. It doesn't help everyone. But, because it helps some people, we have included it here.

An electric circuit connects a power source to an electrical device—for example a ceiling light, in a circular pattern. If the circuit is complete, electric power flows from the source to the device and back to the source.

Everyone knows that if the switch is put in its "on" position, as in the diagram on the left, then the circuit is completed and the ceiling light turns on. When the switch in the "off" position, as in the diagram on the right, then the circuit is incomplete and the ceiling light will be off. Substituting "T" for "on" and "F" for "off" we can express these same ideas.

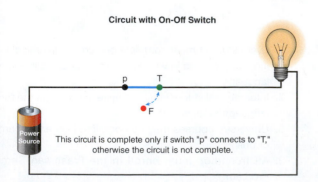

Circuit with On-Off Switch

This circuit is complete only if switch "p" connects to "T," otherwise the circuit is not complete.

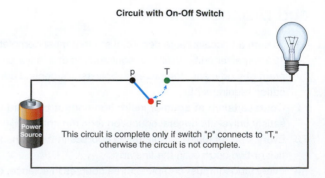

Circuit with On-Off Switch

This circuit is complete only if switch "p" connects to "T," otherwise the circuit is not complete.

The switch, labeled "p," can rotate back and forth between only two points: the "T" and the "F". The diagram on the right shows the switch at "F" and, so, the circuit is incomplete.

Now think about how negation works. Negation turns the value of 'p' to its opposite. So if 'p' is True, then ~p is False. In terms of light switches, this would mean that the electrician who wired the circuit connected the wires so that to turn the light on the switch must rotate to F instead of T. We can picture that way of wiring a circuit using the "Negation Circuit" diagram.

Negation Circuit

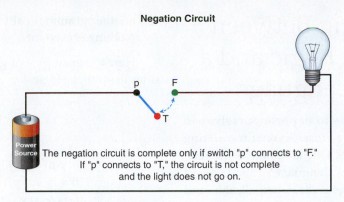

The negation circuit is complete only if switch "p" connects to "F."
If "p" connects to "T," the circuit is not complete
and the light does not go on.

We can describe the circuits for conjunction and disjunction too. Compare the statement in each diagram to the simple shortcut explanation given in italics by the definitional tables for conjunction and disjunction. You should see that the conditions that turn on the light are analogous to the conditions that make the conjunction or the disjunction true.

Conjunction Circuit

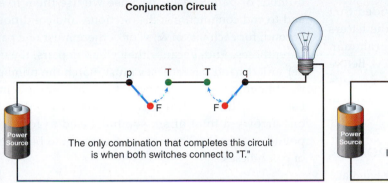

The only combination that completes this circuit
is when both switches connect to "T."

Disjunction Circuit

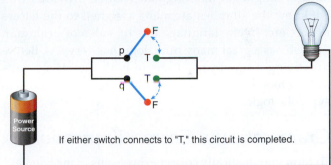

If either switch connects to "T," this circuit is completed.

How can we describe the conditional function using the electrical circuit analogy? We know that the only condition under which the conditional (p → q) is false is when the p is "T" and the q is "F." So we will have to draw a circuit that is incomplete in that situation only; otherwise no matter the position of the two switches, the circuit will have to be complete so that the light can turn on. Does this work?

Conditional Circuit

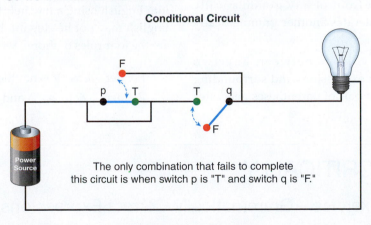

The only combination that fails to complete
this circuit is when switch p is "T" and switch q is "F."

between "Joan qualifies for the tax credit" and "Seth is Joan's dependent" in English, there are two correct ways to express that relationship in symbol logic. If the two English expressions communicate the same thing, then the two symbolic expressions must communicate the same thing. In the Logic of Statements this means that the two formulas should have the same values when we look at their truth tables. And they do. The truth table for (~p v q) is false only in the second row. And the same is the case with the truth table for (p → q). It shows false in one row

only, namely the second row. The truth table below illustrates this point.

p	q	~p	(~p v q)	(~p → q)
T	T	F	T	T
T	F	F	F	F
F	T	T	T	T
F	F	T	T	T

17.2 Translating Between Symbolic Logic and a Natural Language

Now that we have the tools to express ourselves in two languages, we can take a closer look at translating between those two languages. One language is the relatively economical, if not stark, language of the Logic of Statements. The other language is the rich, malleable, and nuanced natural language we use every day. In our case, English.

As you will see, grammatically correct expressions in symbolic logic notation are easy to translate into a natural language, like English. That is, provided that we know the simple statements assigned to the letters *p, q, r,* etc. Every language has its rules of grammar. English has a great many rules, logic has very few. Before practicing a few translations in both directions, let's focus a moment on grammatically correct expressions in symbolic logic.

Grammatically Correct Expressions

To form grammatically correct expressions in the language of symbolic logic we need only three basic rules.

- First, a statement letter, like p, q, r, etc., by itself is a grammatically correct expression.

- Second, placing ~ in front of any grammatically correct expression generates another grammatically correct expression.

- Third, placing &, v, or → between any two grammatically correct expressions and surrounding the whole thing with a pair of parentheses generates

another grammatically correct expression. That's it. Nothing else counts.

Here are examples of grammatically correct expressions in symbolic logic:

> r
>
> s
>
> ~q
>
> ((s v p) → ~q)
>
> ((r v (p & ~p)) → ~~~r)
>
> ((~(s & q) v ~(r & ~p)) → (p & (r v q)))

Question: How can we know that we have the right number of parentheses? Well, first, there must be an even number of parentheses, because we use them to start and to end conjunctions, disjunctions, and conditionals. Second, for each use of &, v, or → there must one pair of parentheses. And, because they come in pairs, the number of left-hand parentheses must match the number of right-hand parentheses. Look at the last example in the list above. There are three ampersands, two wedges, and one arrow—a total of six symbols used to form compound statements. That means there should be six pairs of parentheses.

Translation to English

If we know what each statement letter stands for, we can render grammatically correct symbolic logic expressions into English using a few helpful guidelines. The resulting English may not be elegant, but it will be accurate. Here are the four rules of thumb we'll need:

> Render ~A as "It is not the case that A"
>
> Render (A & B) as "A and B"

THINKING CRITICALLY

Quick Check Exercise—Grammatically Correct Expressions

Identify those expressions in this list that are not grammatically correct symbolic logic expressions. Explain what mistake or mistakes each grammatically incorrect expression contains. Hint: only the last two are grammatically correct expressions.

1. q~

2. (p ~ q)

3. p & q

4. (p)

5. ((p →) v q)

6. (r & s v p)

7. (r v (~p & q)

8. (A & B)

9. ~(~p)

10. (((r & s) = s) v s)

11. p → (p & p)

12. (r → p) → (p r)

13. ((q & (r v p)

14. ~~~~q

15. ~(~(~(p v r) & (s & q)) & ~(p → ~r))

Render (A v B) as "Either A or B"

Render (A → B) as "If A, then B."

To illustrate our translation rules, let's assign some simple English statements to p, q, and r.

Let p stand for "It is raining."

Let q stand for "The lawn is wet."

Let r stand for "The sidewalk is wet"

Given these interpretations of p, q, and r, the table below shows accurate translations of the symbolic expressions. In some cases an accurate translation may be somewhat clunky. The column on the right suggests a way of expressing the English that may be a bit more elegant:

Statement in Symbolic Logic	Accurate Translation	More Elegant Rendering
~ r	It is not the case that the sidewalk is wet.	The sidewalk is not wet.
(p & q)	It is raining and the lawn is wet.	
(p & (p & p))	It is raining, and it is raining and it is raining.	It's raining and raining and raining!
(p → (q & r))	If it is raining, then the lawn is wet and the sidewalk is wet.	If it is raining, then the lawn and the sidewalk are wet.
((r v q) → p)	If either the sidewalk is wet or the lawn is wet, then it is raining.	If the sidewalk or the lawn is wet, then it is raining.
(~~q & ~p)	It is not the case that it is not the case that the lawn is wet, and it is not the case that it is raining.	The lawn is wet and it is not raining. [Note: In English a double negation cancels itself.]
((r → q) & (q → r))	If the sidewalk is wet, then the lawn is wet; and, if the lawn is wet, then the sidewalk is wet.	The lawn is wet if, and only if, the sidewalk is wet.
(p & (p & p))	It is raining, and it is raining and it is raining.	Wow, is it raining! [In English repetition signifies emphasis.]

Translating to Symbolic Logic

Translation to symbolic logic begins with the realization that natural languages like English offer a variety of grammatically correct ways to express negations, conjunctions, disjunctions, and conditionals. The table below lists some of the more common ways. In this table **A** and **B** stand for any statement no matter how complex. In other words, we are using **A** and **B** as placeholders. For the most part, in ordinary everyday discourse, the expressions in the left-hand column can be rendered into symbolic logic notation using the construction in the right-hand column. But there are going to be exceptions, so we need to practice strong critical thinking by applying our interpretive and analytical skills when clarifying the speaker's intended meaning. As Chapter 4 on clarifying ideas reminds us, context and purpose, not grammar alone, are the determining factors when trying to understand what something means.

English Construction	Symbolic Logic Construction
It is not the case that A. It is false that A. A is untrue. Not A. A is not the case. Don't believe A. A? No way!	~ A
A and B. Both A and B. A, but B too. A, however B. Although A, B. A but also B. A moreover B. A, what is more B. A even though B.	(A & B)
Either A or B. A or B. A, unless B. If not A, B. A, otherwise B. A or else B.	(A v B)
If A, then B. If A, B. B, if A. B, provided that A. A only if B. Not A unless B. B, on the condition that A.	(A → B)

EXAMPLE: TRANSLATING A TELEPHONE TREE Call any big company, like Verizon, DIRECTV, or United Airlines and you will get a telephone tree built almost entirely on the Logic of Statements. We all know the drill, "If you are calling for technical support, press 1. If you want to know your account balance, press 2. If you want to place an order, press 3. Otherwise stay on the line and your call will be answered by the next available agent." Basically that telephone tree instruction is an exercise in the Logic of Statements. In fact, we can render it symbolically like this:

$$((((p \rightarrow q) \vee (r \rightarrow s)) \vee (p^1 \rightarrow q^1)) \vee (r^1 \& s^1))$$

In this translation we are interpreting the statement letters as follows:

- p = You are calling for technical support.
- q = [You should] press 1.
- r = You want to know your account balance.
- s = [You should] press 2.
- p^1 = You want to place an order.
- q^1 = [You should] press 3.
- r^1 = [You should] stay on the line.
- s^1 = Your call will be answered by the next available agent.

Notice, that to make this translation we needed more than four statement letters. We can create as many more letters as we may need by adding superscripts to our basic four, for example, p^1, p^2, q^1, q^2, etc.

The actual translation of the example telephone tree begins with the realization that it is fundamentally a disjunction. One or another of the first three situations will apply to your case, or you should stay on the line and speak to an agent. And, looking closely at each of those three possible situations, we recognize them as conditionals. Then,

looking at what happens if none of the three conditionals apply, we see that two statements will be true. That is a conjunction. So, the instruction comes to "conditional #1, or conditional #2, or conditional #3; or conjunction."

WHAT THE TELEPHONE TREE EXAMPLE TEACHES ABOUT TRANSLATION The process of translating from English into symbolic logic requires the application of our critical thinking skills of analysis and interpretation. First we have to determine whether the sentence we are seeking to translate is a declarative statement. The claims and conclusions that are used to make arguments are declarative statements, for example. Only sentences used to make assertions can be translated into this level of symbolic logic.

The declarative statements that this level of logic can handle are negations, conjunctions, disjunctions, conditionals, and simple assertions. This realization suggests the second thing our analysis should seek to determine: the overall structure of the statement we are trying to translate. In the case of the telephone tree example it was a disjunction. When translating, always preserve the statement's overall logical structure.

Then, once we know what the overall structure is, we begin analyzing the component parts, if any. In our telephone tree example we saw that on the left-hand side of the overall disjunction there were three conditional statements, while on the right-hand side there was a conjunction. Again, we will want our translations to preserve these internal structures.

Once we have determined the structure of the statement, including any internal statements that it might include, we are in an excellent position to identify the simple statements that the statement letters will represent. As we identify each simple statement we can assign a statement letter to it. We're looking for a one-to-one match here.

THINKING CRITICALLY

Quick Check Exercise—From Symbols to English

Accurately translate each of the following. Add a more elegant rendering in those cases when the accurate translation seems somewhat awkward or clunky. Use the interpretation of the statement letters given here:

p = "My son has chickenpox."
q = "I have to stay home from work."
r = "I need to take care of my son."
s = "My son is contagious."
t = "I need to call my boss."

1. p
2. $(p \rightarrow s)$
3. $(\sim p \rightarrow \sim s)$
4. $(\sim s \rightarrow (r \& q))$
5. $((r \vee q) \rightarrow t)$
6. $(p \rightarrow t)$
7. $(p \vee \sim p)$
8. $((p \rightarrow s) \& (s \rightarrow t))$
9. $(((q \& r) \& t) \vee \sim p)$
10. $(\sim s \rightarrow (\sim p \& (\sim r \& \sim t)))$

Procedure for Translating from Natural Language into the Logic of Statements

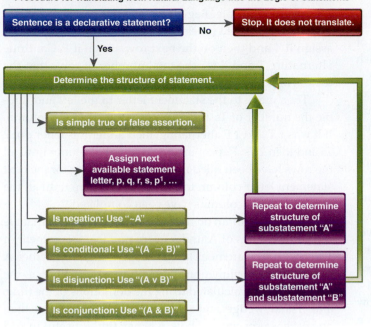

The translation process can be described in the diagram shown here. The process continues until each simple assertion has been assigned its own unique statement letter. Along the way, as the overall structure of the statement is determined, and as the structure of the sub-statement(s), if any, are determined, we insert the parentheses or the special characters that stand for the different functions (negation, conjunction, disjunction, conditional).

17.3 Detecting the Logical Characteristics of Statements

Different symbolic logic expressions have different interesting characteristics. Some are true no matter what values we assign to their statement's letters. Others are false no matter how we assign the values true or false to their statement letters. And some turn out to be true in some circumstances and false in others. The Logic of Statements provides an accurate and reliable way to determine exactly which are which. Given any grammatically correct expression in the language of the Logic of Statements, we can use truth tables to determine the truth value of that expression.

Remember not to assign two statement letters to the same simple statement, and not to assign two simple statements to the same letter. We do not want to turn something like "It is raining or it is not raining," which should be rendered (p v ~p), into the mistaken translations (p v ~q) or (p v q). Careful interpretation and precise analysis are our defenses against mistakes.

THINKING CRITICALLY

Quick Check Exercise—From English to Symbols

Accurately translate each of the following.

1. I take courses at United Community College (UCC).
2. UCC offers online courses.
3. If I work part time, then I graduate next March.
4. Either I work part time or I work full time.
5. If I work full time, I fall behind in my courses.
6. If I fall behind in my courses, I do not graduate next March.
7. Although I work part time, I take courses at United Community College.
8. UCC offers online courses or I do not take courses at UCC.
9. I do not take courses at UCC unless UCC offers online courses.
10. I do not graduate next March unless I work part time.
11. I graduate next March only if I work part time.
12. I work part time otherwise I do not graduate next March.
13. I neither work full time nor take online courses at UCC.
14. Hey, I work part time if, and only if, I do not work full time.
15. I do not both work full time and graduate next March.

Building Truth Tables

A truth table for a grammatically correct expression in symbolic notation, call it **A**, is intended to display the value of **A** under every possible assignment of truth values to each of the statement letters in **A**. Each row of a truth table is intended to represent one of the possible assignments of true or false to each of the statement letters in **A**. The full table will then show us the value of the formula, **A**, under all of the possible assignments of true or false to each of its different statement letters. Search "Truth Table Facione Video" for our YouTube video on how to build truth tables.

The first step in building the truth table for **A** is to count how many *different* statement letters are used in **A**. That will determine how many rows the truth table must have. One statement letter gives us a 2-row truth table. Two statement letters give us a 4-row truth table. Three statement letters give us an 8-row table. Four statement letters give us a 16-row table. Five statement letters and we have a 32-row table. And, in general, if the number of statement letters is n then the number of rows of the truth table will be 2^n.

The columns on the left-hand side of a truth table for **A** display the possible assignments of truth values to each of the statement letters in **A**. These statement letter columns are organized alphabetically, even if the statement letters appear in some other order in **A**. The rows of a truth table are always organized in a predictable order. The top row is always the row that assigns "true" to all the statement letters in **A**. And the bottom row always assigns "false" to all the statement letters. The middle rows, if any, also follow a standard pattern—one that is

easier to describe with the following chart. These patterns are easy to duplicate. Begin with the right-most statement letter, the one that comes the latest in the alphabet. First assign it T and then on the next row assign it F. Continue alternating T and F for the total number of rows that the table will need – 2, 4, 8, 16, 32, 64. . . .

Then move to the statement letter to the left and double the number of Ts and Fs used in the previous column. If it was 1 T and 1 F alternating, then under this letter put 2 Ts and then 2 Fs. Repeat moving down the column until all the rows have been filled in. Do the same thing for the next statement letter column to the left. And so on, until all the statement letter columns have been completed.

The final column on the right-hand side of a truth table shows the values of **A** under every possible assignment of T and F to its statement letters. Depending on whether **A** is a negation, conjunction, disjunction, or conditional, the values of **A** are calculated using the definitions of the tilde, ampersand, wedge, and arrow. But if **A** includes more than one of those special symbols, we may find it useful to add intermediate columns to our truth table. It is easier to keep track of each of the different logical operations inside of **A** if we create an intermediate column for each one.

Suppose, for example, that **A** is this expression: ((p & q) → ~q). This expression is a conditional statement with two distinct statement letters. The antecedent is a conjunction. The consequent is a negation. Given that there two statement letters, the truth table for this expression will have exactly four rows. We can begin building the truth table by putting the columns for the statement letters on the left-hand side and the column for the whole conditional expression itself on the right-hand side.

Patterns for the Assignment of Values to Statement Letters

Row	One Letter	Two Letters		Three Letters			Four Letters			
1	T	T	T	T	T	T	T	T	T	T
2	F	T	F	T	T	F	T	T	T	F
3		F	T	T	F	T	T	T	F	T
4		F	F	T	F	F	T	T	F	F
5				F	T	T	T	F	T	T
6				F	T	F	T	F	T	F
7				F	F	T	T	F	F	T
8				F	F	F	T	F	F	F
9							F	T	T	T
10							F	T	T	F
11							F	T	F	T
12							F	T	F	F
13							F	F	T	T
14							F	F	T	F
15							F	F	F	T
16							F	F	F	F

p	q		((p & q) → ~q)

We then fill in the values under the statement letters. We start with the q and assign T to the top row, F to the second, and alternate T and the F until we have completed that column. There are going to be exactly 2^n rows, where n is the number of different statement letters. In this example case that would be 2. So 2^2 or 4 rows. We then fill in the values of T and F under p, first with two Ts and then with two Fs. Our table at this point will look like this:

p	q		((p & q) → ~q)
T	T		
T	F		
F	T		
F	F		

To calculate the value of the conditional, we need to know the values of its antecedent and its consequent. Let's add two columns to the table, one for the antecedent (p & q), and the other for the consequent ~q.

p	q	(p & q)	~q	((p & q) → ~q)
T	T			
T	F			
F	T			
F	F			

Now we can easily calculate the values of the conjunction and the negation that are the two intermediate columns. Use the truth table that defined conjunction for the ampersand, and use the truth table that defined negation for the tilde. When we do that, we get these results:

p	q	(p & q)	~q	((p & q) → ~q)
T	T	T	F	
T	F	F	T	
F	T	F	F	
F	F	F	T	

We can now determine the values for the conditional statement. Remember our simple shortcut for the condition function: A conditional statement is false only in the case when its antecedent is true and its consequent is false. That combination occurs in the top row only. So the final truth table will look like this, with F only in the top row. It helps to align the values of an expression directly beneath the letter or symbol being evaluated. In this case it would be the →.

p	q	(p & q)	~q	((p & q) → ~q)
T	T	T	F	F
T	F	F	T	T
F	T	F	F	T
F	F	F	T	T

One more example, this time with three statement letters. This truth table answers the question: "What are the values for every possible assignment of "true" and "false" to the component statement letters of the expression "((~(r → p) v (~p → r)) v q)?" There are three distinct statement letters in the expression. So we are going to create an 8-row table. First we organize the three columns with the statement letters in alphabetical order, and put the expression to be evaluated in the far right column. We have to remember to leave some space in between for the intermediate columns.

p	q	r					((~(r → p) v (~p → r)) v q)
T	T	T					
T	T	F					
T	F	T					
T	F	F					
F	T	T					
F	T	F					
F	F	T					
F	F	F					

Next we analyze the expression itself to see what form it takes. It turns out to be a disjunction, with one side being a statement letter and the other being another complex disjunction. We already have a column for the statement letter, q, but we could use an intermediate column for that complex internal disjunction, as shown below:

p	q	r				(~(r → p) v (~p → r))	((~(r → p) v (~p → r)) v q)
T	T	T					
T	T	F					
T	F	T					
T	F	F					
F	T	T					
F	T	F					
F	F	T					
F	F	F					

Let's break that larger expression into its component expressions. The first is a negation of a conditional, and the second is a conditional with its antecedent being a negation. Let's put those two expressions into intermediate columns too.

p	q	r			~(r → p)	(~p → r)	(~(r → p) v (~p → r))	((~(r → p) v (~p → r)) → q)
T	T	T						
T	T	F						
T	F	T						
T	F	F						
F	T	T						
F	T	F						
F	F	T						
F	F	F						

We should create a column for (r → p) and another for ~p, just so we do not confuse ourselves later. Here is how our table looks with those two columns added and with their values filled in. (In longer tables, numbering the rows makes talking about specific calculations easier.)

	p	q	r	~p	(r → p)	~(r → p)	(~p → r)	(~(r → p) v (~p → r))	((~(r → p) v (~p → r)) v q)
1	T	T	T	F	T				
2	T	F	F	F	T				
3	T	F	T	F	T				
4	T	F	F	F	T				
5	F	T	T	T	F				
6	F	F	F	T	T				
7	F	T	T	T	F				
8	F	F	F	T	T				

Notice that (r → p) is false only in row 5 and row 7, where its antecedent, r, is true and the consequent, p, is false. Otherwise it is true. Now let's fill in the next two intermediate columns that are the negation of (r → p) and the other conditional that has ~p as its antecedent. That conditional will be false only on the rows were ~p is true and r is false. This occurs on rows 6 and 8 only. So we get this result.

	p	q	r	~p	(r → p)	~(r → p)	(~p → r)	(~(r → p) v (~p → r))	((~(r → p) v (~p → r)) v q)
1	T	T	T	F	T	F	T		
2	T	T	F	F	T	F	T		
3	T	F	T	F	T	F	T		
4	T	F	F	F	T	F	T		
5	F	T	T	T	F	T	T		
6	F	T	F	T	T	F	F		
7	F	F	T	T	F	T	T		
8	F	F	F	T	T	F	F		

We have only one more intermediate column to complete, and it is a disjunction. It will be false only when the formulas on both sides of the v are false.

	p	q	r	~p	(r → p)	~(r → p)	(~p → r)	(~(r → p) v (~p → r))	((~r → p) v (~p → r)) v q)
1	T	T	T	F	T	F	T	T	
2	T	T	F	F	T	F	T	T	
3	T	F	T	F	T	F	T	T	
4	T	F	F	F	T	F	T	T	
5	F	T	T	T	F	T	T	T	
6	F	T	F	T	T	F	F	F	
7	F	F	T	T	F	T	T	T	
8	F	F	F	T	T	F	F	F	

The expression we initially targeted for evaluation is a disjunction with q as one alternative. Looking at the values under the column we just added and under q, we see only one row where both are false. That is row 8. And that tells us that out of the eight possible assignments of values to the three statement letters, there is only one assignment that results in the expression ((~(r → p) v (~p → r)) v q) being false. The completed truth table looks like this:

	p	q	r	~p	(r → p)	~(r → p)	(~p → r)	(~(r → p) v (~p → r))	((~(r → p) v (~p → r)) v q)
1	T	T	T	F	T	F	T	T	T
2	T	T	F	F	T	F	T	T	T
3	T	F	T	F	T	F	T	T	T
4	T	F	F	F	T	F	T	T	T
5	F	T	T	T	F	T	T	T	T
6	F	T	F	T	T	F	F	F	T
7	F	F	T	T	F	T	T	T	T
8	F	F	F	T	T	F	F	F	F

Tautologies, Inconsistent Statements, and Contingent Statements

In the Logic of Statements we use truth tables to learn the value of a complex statement under each possible assignment of "true" and "false" to its component statement letters. In the example above the statement we were investigating came out true under seven possible assignments, but false under one assignment. A statement that comes out true under at least one assignment and false under at least one assignment can be called "contingent" because its value is contingent upon the particular assignment of true or false to each of its statement letters. For the purposes of the Logic of Statements, a **contingent statement** *is a grammatically correct expression that turns out to be true under at least one possible assignment of truth values to its component simple statements and false under another possible assignment of truth values to its component simple statements.* The

statements (p & q), (p v q), and (p → q) are all contingent statements. Each one comes out true on at least one row of its truth table and false on at least one other row of its truth table.

But what about statements that always come out true or always come out false? In Chapter 6 on evaluating claims we had terminology for statements like those. The first we called tautologies; the second group we called inconsistent or self-contradictory statements. We can apply that same terminology to the grammatically correct expressions of symbolic logic. For the purposes of the Logic of Statements, an **inconsistent statement** *is a grammatically correct expression that turns out to be false under every possible assignment of truth values to its component simple statements.* The expression (p & ~p) is an inconsistent statement by this definition. Its 2-row truth table will have F as its value on both rows. The inconsistency in this statement springs from its apparent effort to assert both p and not-p at the

Who Ate the Pizza?

Five roommates, Abe, Bob, Carl, Dave, and Ziggy, share an off-campus apartment. On Monday night they had leftover pizza and so they put it in the refrigerator. On Tuesday when Ziggy went to get some of that pizza he found that it had all been eaten. Later Ziggy confronted his four roommates to find out who ate the pizza. Each roommate made one statement. The person who ate the pizza lied; his statement is false. The other three statements are true.

Which one ate the pizza? Here are their four statements:

Abe: I was in class all day.
Bob: Carl ate the pizza.
Carl: Bob's statement is false.
David: Carl's statement is true.

same time. Because of this internal conflict the statement can also be described as "self-contradictory." The term "self-contradiction" is an alternative way of characterizing a statement that is inconsistent at this level of logic.

The concept of a tautology can also be expressed in the Logic of Statements. A **tautology** *is a grammatically correct expression that turns out to be true under every possible assignment of truth values to its component simple statements.* Obviously the Logic of Statements does not contain all possible tautologies as described in Chapter 6, nor does this level of logic contain all possible inconsistent (self-contradictory) statements. This is because there are additional ways to create statements that are internally inconsistent or tautological in English, ways that become evident only at levels beyond the Logic of Statements.

We can use truth tables to accurately and reliably determine whether a grammatically correct expression at the level of the Logic of Statements is a tautology, an inconsistent (self-contradictory) statement, or a contingent statement. Every statement we evaluate will fall into exactly one of those three categories. Looking at its values on each row of its truth table, we can tell which it is. If we see a column of all Ts, then the statement is tautology. If we see a column of all Fs then the statement is inconsistent. If we see a mix with at least one T and at least one F, then the statement is contingent.

17.4 Testing for Implication and Equivalence

If you were told that both p and q are true, then you would be correct in saying that q by itself is true. And if someone were to say that you were wrong about that, your logical reply would be, "No, that's not possible. It cannot happen that q is false if we are certain that both p and q are true. If (p & q) is true, that implies that each component is true on its own." Implication is an important logical relationship between statements. We can

THINKING CRITICALLY

Quick Check Exercise—Tautology, Inconsistent Statement, or Contingent Statement

Using truth tables, classify each of the following as one and only one of the following:

Tautology (True under every interpretation of its statement letters)

Inconsistent statement (False under every interpretation)

Contingent statement (True at least once and false at least once)

1. (p & ~p)
2. ~(p & ~p)
3. (p → (q → p))
4. ((p → q) → (p & ~q)
5. (((r → s) & ~s) → ~r)
6. ((r → s) → (~s → ~r))
7. ((~r & ~p) & p)
8. ((p ∨ s) ∨ (~r & p))
9. ((s & (s → q)) → q)
10. (((s ∨ q) & ~ q) → s)

define it this way: *In the Logic of Statements* **A implies B** *if there is no interpretation of the statement letters of A and B such that A is true and B is false.*[4]

We can check for implication at this level of logic using truth tables. All we need to do is form the expression $(A \rightarrow B)$ and then build its truth table. If $(A \rightarrow B)$ is a tautology, then A implies B. Otherwise not. Why? Because if $(A \rightarrow B)$ is a tautology, then there is no possible interpretation of its statement letters such that A is true and B is false. But, if that case should arise, then we would spot an F in the truth table's right-hand column. For example, here's a table that shows that (p & q) implies q.

	p	q	(p & q)	((p & q) → q)
1	T	T	T	T
2	T	F	F	T
3	F	T	F	T
4	F	F	F	T

The only row on which the antecedent of the conditional is true is row 1. But in row 1 the consequent, q, is also true. So the conditional is a tautology; that is, it is true under every possible interpretation of its statement letters. The antecedent statement, (p & q) implies the consequent statement, q. We could also define implication at this level of logic like this: *In the Logic of Statements* **A implies B** *if the grammatical expression generated by the structure* $(A \rightarrow B)$ *is a tautology.*

Question: How many of the rows of that truth table did we really have to calculate fully to answer our question about whether the conditional was a tautology? Think about it for a moment. Did we really have to fill in all the intermediate values on rows 1 and 3? No. Because on those rows q was true, which means that the conditional would come out true no matter what the value of its antecedent turned out to be.

If we are given (p & q), can we write (q & p) instead and still mean the same thing? Well, if (p & q) implies (q & p) and if (q & p) implies (p & q), then Yes. Let's check. Here's a truth table that evaluates both $((p \& q) \rightarrow (q \& p))$ and $((q \& p) \rightarrow (p \& q))$.

p	q	(p & q)	(q & p)	((p & q) → (q & p))	((q & p) → (p & q))
T	T	T	T	T	T
T	F	F	F	T	T
F	T	F	F	T	T
F	F	F	F	T	T

Both of the conditional expressions are tautologies. The implications hold, in both directions. In English we could

express this relationship this way, "(p & q)" is true if, and only if "(q & p)" is true.

The English expression "if, and only if" has come up a couple of times in this chapter. Let's analyze it. We can translate "p only if q" part using the conditional $(p \rightarrow q)$. And we translate "p, if q" part using the conditional $(q \rightarrow p)$. The *and* in "if, and only if" indicates that we are dealing with the conjunction of those two parts. So we would get the expression $((q \rightarrow p) \& (p \rightarrow q))$. Here is its truth table.

	p	q	(q → p)	(p → q)	((q → p) & (p → q))
1	T	T	T	T	T
2	T	F	T	F	F
3	F	T	F	T	F
4	F	F	T	T	T

Only on row 2 and row 3 is the expression false; otherwise it is true. Because it is such a common expression, we might want to define a more economical way of expressing "if, and only if" in symbolic logic notation, one that does not require three pairs of parentheses, two arrows, and an ampersand. Many logicians refer to the expression "if, and only if" as a *biconditional*. They use a triple bar $\equiv$ and represent this logical relationship as $(A \equiv B)$. An expression using the triple bar will be false whenever there is a different value on the two sides; but when both sides are true or both sides are false, the biconditional statement will be true. The truth table below defines the biconditional in the Logic of Statements.

Biconditional Truth Table		
p	**q**	**(p ≡ q)**
T	T	T
T	F	F
F	T	F
F	F	T

Let's see what happens if we build the truth table for $((p \& q) \equiv (q \& p))$. We should expect it to be a tautology because we have already established that the first side implies the second side and the second side implies the first side.

And, in fact, it turns out to be a tautology. At this level of logic, if two statements have identical truth values under every interpretation of their statement letters, then the two statements are equivalent. We can define the equivalence of two statements this way: *In the Logic of Statements* two statements, **A and B, are equivalent** *if, and only if, the biconditional* $(A = B)$ *is a tautology.*

p	q	(p & q)	(q & p)	((p & q) ≡ (q & p))
T	T	T	T	T
T	F	F	F	T
F	T	F	F	T
F	F	F	F	T

17.5 Evaluating Arguments for Validity

It is time to put all the pieces of this section together so that we can accurately and reliably test an argument for validity at this level of logic. An argument is valid, as we said at the beginning of this section, if it is impossible for all of its premises to be true and its conclusion false. Consider an argument with two premises, which we will name *A* and *B*, and with a conclusion, named *C*. If we form the following conditional, we would be expressing the assertion that the premises A and B together imply C.

$$((A \ \& \ B) \to C)$$

Suppose that there was no assignment of truth values to the simple statements that make up A, B, and C, such that the conditional came out false. On every row of its truth table, in other words, ((A & B) → C) comes out true. It is a tautology, therefore. And, moreover, the truth table demonstrates that "it is impossible for all of its premises to be true and its conclusion false." That means that the argument is valid! We have an accurate and reliable way of testing for the validity of arguments at the level of the Logic of Statements!

Testing an argument for validity at this level of logic can be accomplished in three easy steps:

1. Form the conditional that uses as its antecedent the conjunction of the argument's premises and as its consequent the conclusion of the argument.

2. Build the truth table for that conditional statement.

3. Examine the truth table to determine whether the conditional is a tautology. If that conditional is a tautology, the argument is valid at the level of the Logic of Statements.

Two quick clarifications: If there are more than two premises in the argument, we expand the antecedent of the conditional so that it is a longer conjunction that includes all of the argument's premises. And, the expression "at this level of logic" is important because some arguments that fail the test for validity in the Logic of Statements turn out to be valid at more sophisticated levels of logic. Chapter 8 presents many examples of this.

Testing Symbolic Arguments for Validity

The following example illustrates how to test arguments in symbolic logic notation for validity. The argument to be evaluated is this:

> Premise #1:   (q v r)
>
> Premise #2:   ~r
>
> Conclusion: q

First we form the conditional that uses the conclusion as its consequent:

$$((\underline{\hspace{2cm}}) \to q)$$

And then we add the conjunction of the two premises as its antecedent. And we get this formula.

$$(((q \ v \ r) \ \& \ ~r) \to q)$$

After we form that conditional, we build the truth table for that conditional.

We then inspect the table to determine whether or not the conditional is a tautology. And it is a tautology. So the argument is valid at this level of logic.

THINKING CRITICALLY

Logic Circuits Again

Earlier we developed an analogy between the functions at this level of symbolic logic and electrical circuitry. Think about the biconditional function. We know that it is false whenever the values on both sides are different, and otherwise it is true. Examine the diagram. Does this diagram capture the idea behind the biconditional function? If so, the circuit should be complete only if both switches are in the T position or both are in the F position.

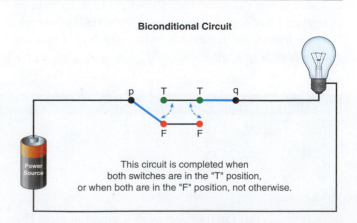

Biconditional Circuit

This circuit is completed when both switches are in the "T" position, or when both are in the "F" position, not otherwise.

THINKING CRITICALLY

Quick Check Exercise—Implication and Equivalence

Using truth tables, for each pair of statements below, determine whether the statement in column A implies the statement in column B. If (A → B) is a tautology, then A does imply B, otherwise not.

Using truth tables, determine whether each pair of statements in columns C and D below are equivalent. If (C ≡ D) is a tautology, the two statements are equivalent, otherwise not.

	A	B
1	(p & q)	((p & p) v p)
2	r	(q v r)
3	(q & ~q)	s
4	s	(q → q)
5	((q v r) & ~r)	q

	C	D
6	(r v r)	~~r
7	(~p v q)	(~q → ~p)
8	(q & ~q)	(r & ~r)
9	(p → p)	(q v ~ q)
10	((q v r) & ~ r)	q

q	r	(q v r)	~r	((q v r) & ~r)	(((q v r) & ~r) → q)
T	T	T	F	F	T
T	F	T	T	T	T
F	T	F	F	F	T
F	F	T	T	F	T

Now consider this example:

Premise #1: (p & q)

Premise #2: (p → r)

Premise #3: (q → r)

Conclusion: r

First we form the conditional that we will later test using a truth table. The conditional will have the letter r, which is the argument's conclusion, as its consequent. The antecedent of the conditional needs to be the conjunction of the premises. But there are three of them. So we will need to use parentheses to be sure that we capture them all. Because we are building a conjunction, the grouping can go either this way ((A & B) & C) or this way (A & (B & C)). Let's use the second option and generate the conditional's antecedent as:

$$((p \& q) \& ((p \to r) \& (q \to r)))$$

Putting that antecedent with the consequent to form the whole conditional we get:

$$(((p \& q) \& ((p \to r) \& (q \to r))) \to r)$$

The next step is to build the truth table for this conditional. When you complete yours it should look like the one below.

The right-most column of the truth table shows all Ts. The conditional is a tautology. And, so, the argument we are evaluating is valid at this level of logic.

p	q	r	(p → r)	(q → r)	(p & q)	((p → r) & (q →r))	((p & q) & ((p → r) & (q → r)))	(((p & q) & ((p → r) & (q → r))) → r)
T	T	T	T	T	T	T	T	T
T	T	F	F	F	T	F	F	T
T	F	T	T	T	F	T	F	T
T	F	F	F	T	F	F	F	T
F	T	T	T	T	F	T	F	T
F	T	F	T	F	F	F	F	T
F	F	T	T	T	F	T	F	T
F	F	F	T	T	F	T	F	T

Paradoxes of the Logic of Statements

There is something a bit strange about the way the concepts of implication and equivalence operate at this level of logic. You might have sensed something curious when working through "Quick Check Exercise—Implication and Equivalence." Look back for a moment at #3 in the first five pairs. When you formed the construction (A → B) for that pair, the A part was the inconsistent statement (q & ~q). No matter what we put as the B part, the implication will hold. At this level of logic, a self-contradictory statement implies any statement whatsoever. But we would not find it credible to argue in real life for the claim, "32 teams qualify for the FIFA World Cup" based on the reason "I own a dog, but I do not own a dog." From the critical thinking perspective it would be unwise to accept an inconsistent reason as the basis for believing a person's claim. As Chapter 7 on evaluating arguments explains, the first test of an argument's acceptability is the Test of the Truthfulness of the Premises. An argument with a self-contradictory premise cannot pass that test. The same for an argument that has two premises such that their conjunction forms an inconsistent statement. Here's the paradox. Given that A is inconsistent, why would we say that A implies B in the Logic of Statements when, as strong critical thinkers, we clearly would not accept A as a reason for B?

Equally puzzling is what #4 in that set of implication exercises demonstrates. Notice that when we construct (A → B) for #4, the B statement is a tautology. There is no way in such a case to have (A → B) come out false. So, no matter what the A statement is, according to the Logic of Statements, that statement implies our tautology, B. But from a critical thinking perspective, we do not need a reason for B. If B is a tautology, then it is true. End of story. No need to make an argument for B.

Consider #8 and #9 in the part of the exercise that asks us to test for equivalence, we find two more curiosities. Notice that the two statements in #8 are equivalent according to the Logic of Statements, same for the pair of statements in #9. But the two statements in #8 do not talk about the same content. Whatever simple declarative statement q is assigned to represent, it is not the same simple statement that r is assigned. Suppose q is "My pet cat loves to sit facing away from the TV." And suppose r is "The price of gold keeps rising." In our everyday discourse we would not expect to find statements about my pet cat and statements about the price of gold to be equivalent. They are not even on the same topic. But, as #8 illustrates, in the Logic of Statements, every inconsistent statement is equivalent to every other inconsistent statement. And, the example in #9 illustrates that at this level of logic every tautology is equivalent to every other tautology.

With regard to implication and equivalence, how should we resolve these differences between the treatment of these concepts in the Logic of Statements and how these same concepts apply in everyday real-world discourse? Recall that in this chapter where implication and equivalence were first introduced, the connections with how those terms are used in everyday discourse seemed rather solid. And they were. So what happened?

The way out of this puzzle is to notice that meaning at this level of logic is not in any way connected to the topic or content of a given statement. But in everyday discourse, interpreting what a statement means not only includes the topic and content of each statement; meaning includes the context and purpose for which the statement is used as well. Some use the expression "semantic meaning" to talk about the actual content of the statements in natural language and "pragmatic meaning" to talk about the context and purpose for which the statements are being used. But the Logic of Statements operates below the levels of semantic meaning and pragmatic meaning. It operates at a purely grammatical level, a level some would refer to as the level of "syntactic meaning." Syntactic correctness is a precondition for semantic correctness.

Think of it like this. I am visiting a country, say Thailand, and I want to communicate in Thai. But my Thai language skills are really weak. I make the effort and say a few words to you in Thai. Suppose you have been speaking Thai since birth. So there is every reason for me to hope that you will understand me. But if I mess up my Thai grammar, my effort to communicate with you will, in all likelihood, fail. But if I express myself in a grammatically (syntactically) correct way in Thai, then we might communicate successfully. I would still have to know enough Thai vocabulary (semantic level), and there are probably going to be many awkward moments because of contextual and social miscues on my part as I learn how to communicate in Thai (pragmatic level).

Long story short, the way that the terms *implication* and *equivalence* are defined and tested at the level of the Logic of Statements is sufficient for evaluating grammatical relationships between declarative statements for those two characteristics. But this level of logic is not designed to do more than to look at syntax. And there is much more to implication and equivalence as we look at the semantics and pragmatics of natural language communication. The challenge, and the fun, for logicians comes in trying to design ever more advanced levels of logic that are capable of capturing or replicating the much more sophisticated and intricate ways that humans reason and communicate logically with one another. Natural language processing, voice recognition software, expert systems, and artificial intelligence are some of the fascinating and still developing products of the efforts by logicians, engineers, and computer scientists to respond to this challenge.

THINKING CRITICALLY
Quick Check Exercise—Are These Symbolic Logic Arguments Valid?

	Argument 1	Argument 2	Argument 3
Premise	(p → q)	(p ≡ q)	r
Premise	~q	(q → s)	p
Conclusion	~p	s	(q v r)

	Argument 4	Argument 5	Argument 6
Premise	(q → s)	~(p → q)	(r v s)
Premise	r	~(q → r)	(r → ~q)
Premise	~q	q	(s → ~q)
Conclusion	~s	~r	~q

Testing Natural Language Arguments for Validity

To evaluate natural language arguments for validity within the context of the Logic of Statements we need only translate them into symbolic notation prior to applying the three-step process described above. In Chapter 5 on using maps to analyze arguments there is a full discussion of how to identify an argument's implicit and explicit premises and its conclusion. Having found those statements, we can translate the argument into symbolic logic and then apply the same process as we used for the example arguments that were already in symbolic notation. Here are the steps:

1. **Translate natural language premises and conclusion into symbolic logic notation.**

2. **Form the conditional ((conjunction of the premises) → conclusion).**

3. **Build the conditional's truth table.**

4. **If the conditional is a tautology, then the argument is valid.**

In Chapter 8 there were a group of arguments that committed the fallacy described there as "Denying the Antecedent." Let's check one of them using symbolic logic. Here is an example that commits that fallacy: "If the front wheels keep making that annoying scratching-noise, then the brakes need attention. The noise stopped. So the brakes do not need attention." To evaluate the argument

for validity, we first translate it into symbolic notation. For convenience sake, as we assign statement letters we can paraphrase the English as long as we preserve the meaning of each simple statement.

> Let p stand for "The wheels make an annoying scratching noise."

> Let q stand for "The brakes need attention."

We do not need a third statement letter because we can treat "The noise stopped," as ~p. Contextually, this is the apparent intent of the speaker. Our translation of each of the premises and the conclusion becomes:

$$\text{Premise \#1:} \quad (p \rightarrow q)$$
$$\text{Premise \#2:} \quad {\sim}p$$
$$\text{Conclusion:} \quad {\sim}q$$

Forming the conditional that takes the conclusion as its consequent and the conjunction of the premises as its antecedent we get:

$$(((p \rightarrow q) \,\&\, {\sim}p) \rightarrow {\sim}q)$$

If the argument commits the fallacy of denying the antecedent, then we can expect that the truth table will show that the conditional we just formed is false in at least one row. Before building the truth table, can you think of an interpretation for p and q that will make it come out false? Hint: If we assign true to q, then ~q will come out false. What would p have to be so that the antecedent of the conditional comes out true? That's right, p would have to be false.

	p	q	(p→ q)	~p	((p → q) & ~p)	~q	((p → q) & ~p) →~q
1	T	T	T	F	F	F	T
2	T	F	F	F	F	T	T
3	F	T	T	T	T	F	F
4	F	F	T	T	T	T	T

On row 3 of the table above the conditional is false. This means that the argument is invalid at the level of the Logic of Statements.

Let's test this argument for validity. "Joan is not going to benefit by several hundred dollars of Federal income tax credit. Why? Because Joan qualifies for the dependent

care income tax credit only if all 13 bullet statements at the beginning of this chapter are true. But one of those statements is false. If she does not qualify, she does not benefit.

To evaluate this argument we must be sure we have correctly identified the conclusion and the premises. In this case the claim being argued for (the conclusion) happens to be expressed in the first sentence. The other sentences express premises that explain the reason the speaker offers in support of that claim.

> Let p = Joan benefits by receiving several hundred dollars of tax credit.
>
> Let q = Joan qualifies for the dependent care income tax credit.
>
> Let r = All 13 statements are true.

In making these assignments of letters to the simple declarative statements used in the argument, we edited the English to make our analysis of the argument's structure more transparent. But in editing we preserved the basic meaning of each of those statements. Keeping with our convention, we assign the first statement letter alphabetically to the first simple declarative statement in the argument we are analyzing. The structure of the argument, as symbolized in the Logic of Statements, is this:

> Conclusion: ~p
>
> Premise #1:   (q → r)
>
> Premise #2:   ~r
>
> Premise #3:   (~q → ~p)

As we form the symbolic logic conditional for which we will construct a truth table, we must be sure to use the argument's conclusion as the consequent in that conditional. The conclusion is listed first, because that was the order of the sentences in the original English. But it still goes as the consequent in the conditional expression.

$$((((q → r) \,\&\, {\sim}r) \,\&\, ({\sim}q → {\sim}p)) → {\sim}p)$$

p	q	r	~p	~q	~r	(q → r)	((q → r) & ~r)	(~q → ~p)	(((q→r) & ~r) & (~q → ~p))	((q→r) & ~r) & (~q → ~p)) → ~p
T	T	T	F	F	F	T	F	T	F	T
T	T	F	F	F	T	F	F	T	F	T
T	F	T	F	T	F	T	F	F	F	T
T	F	F	F	T	T	T	T	F	F	T
F	T	T	T	F	F	T	F	T	F	T
F	T	F	T	F	T	F	F	T	F	T
F	F	T	T	T	F	T	F	T	F	T
F	F	F	T	T	T	T	T	T	T	T

Summing up this chapter,

logic provides tools for evaluating the validity of certain kinds of arguments. At the initial level of analysis, logic focuses on the grammatical relationships among declarative statements. The Logic of Declarative Statements, using symbolic notations, permits us to express simple assertions, negations, conjunctions, disjunctions, conditionals. We can translate these expressions from symbolic notion into a natural language, like English, or from a natural language into symbolic notation. Using truth tables we can detect certain logically relevant characteristics of declarative statements—for example, we can determine which are tautological, inconsistent, or contingent. And we can determine whether one declarative statement implies another or is equivalent to another declarative statement.

We can use the tools and skills of the logic to evaluate arguments composed of declarative statements for validity. The procedure includes these four basic steps:

1. Translate an argument's premises and conclusion into symbolic logic notation.

2. Form the conditional that is: ((conjunction of the premises) → conclusion).

3. Build that conditional's truth table.

4. If that conditional is a tautology, then the argument is valid

Natural language is much richer than the notational language of the Logic of Declarative Statements. We can express only a limited range of the logical power of natural language using the tilde, ampersand, wedge, arrow, and triple bar. The validity of a great many arguments can be revealed only at levels of logical analysis that go beyond the tools presented in this chapter. Chapter 8 describes some of those further levels of logic. It is fun to explore how to express those relationships using more advanced levels of symbolic logic. But those joys are for another time.

Key Concepts

valid argument is an argument such that its premises logically imply or entail its conclusion, which makes it impossible for all of its premises to be true and its conclusion to be false.

simple statement is a grammatically correct construction in a given language used to assert that an idea is true.

negation is a grammatically correct construction used to assert that a statement is false.

conjunction is a grammatically correct construction used to assert that two statements are both true.

disjunction is a grammatically correct construction used to assert that one or both of two statements are true.

conditional is a grammatically correct construction used to assert that if an antecedent statement is true, then a consequent statement is true.

inconsistent (or "self-contradictory") statement in the Logic of Statements means a grammatically correct expression that turns out to be false under every possible assignment of truth values to its component simple statements.

contingent statement in the Logic of Statements means a grammatically correct expression that turns out to be true under at least one possible assignment of truth values to its component simple statements and false under another possible assignment of truth values to its component simple statements.

tautology in the Logic of Statements means a grammatically correct expression that turns out to be true under every possible assignment of truth values to its component simple statements.

Statement A implies statement B in the Logic of Statements if there is no interpretation of the statement letters of A and B such that A is true and B is false.

Statement A implies statement B in the Logic of Statements if the grammatical expression generated by the structure $(A \rightarrow B)$ is a tautology.

Statement A and statement B are equivalent in the Logic of Statements if A and B have the same truth value under every interpretation of their statement letters.

Statements A and B are equivalent in the Logic of Statements if, and only if, the biconditional $(A = B)$ is a tautology.

Applications

Reflective Log

Find a reliable shortcut: After we've been using truth tables for a while, the truth table method can become a bit tedious. The stated advantage of the truth table method is that truth tables consider every possible case. On the other hand, if our purpose is to evaluate an argument for validity, considering every possible case may not be necessary. As soon as we find one case, which invalidates the argument, the other cases no longer matter. Think about it. We are looking at a conditional statement. The particular conditional is the one that uses the argument's conclusion as its consequent and the conjunction of the argument's premises as its antecedent. If the consequent is true, then no matter how the antecedent comes out, the whole conditional will be true. Therefore, we only need to consider those cases where the consequent comes out false. If in any one of those situations the conjunction of the premises comes out true, then we need look no further. That argument is not valid at this level of logic. While truth tables are good, there must be shortcuts. Design a reliable shortcut procedure of evaluating arguments for validity. Hint #1: Begin your procedure with the step that says, "Assign values to the statement letters which make the consequent come out false." Hint #2: Given that the first assignment of values probably did not cover all the statement letters, what if you could then extend the assignment of values to those other statement letters such that the antecedent came out true? If you could, how much further would you have to look to be sure that the argument was not valid at this level of logic?

JOURNAL

The Advantages of "If p, then q"

This chapter required us to translate between natural language declarative statements and symbolic logic. What are the advantages that the careful analysis of language provides when trying to interpret exactly what is being said? Answer by giving an example from your own experience and explain your example.

Individual Exercises

Check for equivalence: In Chapter 8, the table "Grammatically Equivalent Structures" asserts that several pairs of expressions are logically equivalent. Double-check these pairs using truth tables.

Translate and evaluate: Use truth tables to evaluate each of these arguments for validity.

1. Unless Seth is Joan's dependent, she cannot claim a tax credit for Seth's care. Unless Joan pays for Seth's care to be able to work, she cannot claim a tax credit for Seth's care. Seth is Joan's dependent; and Joan pays for Seth's care. So Joan can claim a tax credit for Seth's care.

2. Joan cannot claim a tax credit for Seth's care. Unless Seth is Joan's dependent, she cannot claim a tax credit for Seth's care. Therefore Seth is not Joan's dependent.

3. Joan can claim a tax credit for Seth's care. Unless Joan pays for Seth's care to be able to work, she cannot claim a tax credit for Seth's care. So, Joan pays for Seth's care to be able to work.

4. Joan has child care responsibilities but she does not have difficulty finding time for study. Either Joan has child care responsibilities or Joan is a college student, or both. Therefore Joan is a college student and she does not have a difficulty finding time for study.

5. Mrs. Ramirez is not Joan's parent. Joan pays Mrs. Ramirez to care for Seth. If Joan pays Mrs. Ramirez to care for Seth, Joan may qualify for a tax credit, provided that Mrs. Ramirez is not Joan's parent. Therefore Joan may qualify for a tax credit.

Federal Family Medical Leave Act (FMLA): The U.S. Department of Labor requires certain employers to provide up to 12 weeks of unpaid leave, with no loss of other medical or other benefits to employees for any of the following reasons: incapacity due to pregnancy, birth or adoption of a child, to provide care for a spouse or child or parent with a serious health condition, etc. To be eligible for an unpaid leave under FMLA, an employee must have worked for the employer for at least 12 months, put in at least 1,250 hours of service during those 12 months, and if at least 50 people are employed by that employer within 75 miles. Using your critical thinking skills and the tools developed in this chapter, determine in each of these cases whether or not the employee's request for an unpaid leave from work fits the FMLA specifications. Explain your answers.

1. William has worked for the city's largest chain of supermarkets for two years. The supermarket chain employs 840 people in locations within 60 miles from the store where William works. He puts in 30 hours each week. He requests FMLA leave to care for his mother who will be undergoing hip heart valve surgery next week.

2. Evelyn, pregnant with her first child, requests FMLA to give birth. Evelyn has worked five years full time at the front desk greeting people and making appointments for a group of three dentists.

3. Six months ago Tyler purchased a car dealership and works there too as full-time sales manager. He employs 65 other people and, as the owner, he has routinely turned down requests for unpaid leave. Tyler and his wife are adopting a child and he wants to give himself 12 weeks of unpaid leave so that he can maintain his health benefits. Does Tyler qualify for FMLA?

SHARED RESPONSE

Sick as a Dog

Consider these facts: The family dog has a tumor. The preliminary lab tests say it is either a bug bite or a cancer. If it is a bug bite, then the treatment is a cortisone injection. If it's a cancerous tumor, the treatment is an operation. We cannot afford to pay for an operation. If we give the cortisone injection, then if the tumor is a bug bit it will disappear in four days. We can afford the injection.

A family is facing the facts presented above. The dog is the family pet. Logically, what should the family do, and how should the family make this decision? Be sure to provide your reason(s) and any additional premises that you need in order to make your arguments logically strong. Comment respectfully on the responses other share.

Group Exercise

"The Teeter-Totter Coach Challenge": In American-style football each team can play exactly 11 people at a time. Twelve players are eager to get into the game. Except for the numbers on their uniforms, the coach simply cannot tell one person from the other because they are all the same height and in their helmets and pads they all look so much alike. The coach knows, however, that 11 of the 12 are exactly the same weight. The twelfth person is a different weight. But the coach does not know if the twelfth person is heavier or lighter than the others. Oddly enough there is a teeter-totter (balancing scale) available. It is big enough to hold as many players on each side as the coach might wish. We could put six players on one side, and six on the other, for example. In that case, the teeter-tooter would shift from its natural level state so that one end went up and the other side went down. And the coach could infer from that shift that one of the six players on the side that went up was lighter than the other five on that side of the teeter-totter, or one of the six players on the side that went down was heavier than the other five on that side of the teeter-totter. The coach, a logic star, realizes that by using the teeter-tooter exactly three times, he can figure out precisely which of the 12 players is a different weight than the other 11, and he will have figured out also whether that player happens to be heavier or lighter. How will the coach use the teeter-totter to achieve this?

Appendix
Extend Argument-Decision Mapping Strategies

The mapping strategies first introduced in Chapter 5 make the reasoning used in decision making clearer and much easier to follow. Argument and decision maps can be applied in many practical ways. In this section you'll see examples of maps used not only to analyze the relationships of claims and reasons, but to express the kinds of arguments being made, to express the evaluation of arguments, and to expose the reasoning strengths and weaknesses of important and complex multioption decisions. This section builds the critical thinking skills and habits of mind that we've been strengthening all through this book. The key is that the mapping strategies work at a practical level because

they reveal the thinking being used, and thus enable all of us to apply our interpretive and evaluative skills to that thinking—once we've secured a correct analysis, of course.

Mapping the Sequence of Arguments

Map 1 This map displays an interviewee's explanation of why she cannot quit smoking *at this time*. As you can see, the map displays two possible conclusions and three watershed realizations that a decision was called for. One

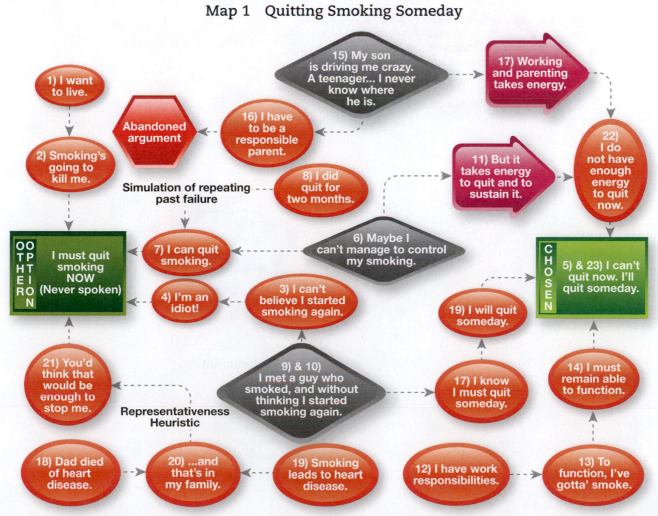

Map 1   Quitting Smoking Someday

argument strand leading from one of the watershed ideas is abandoned. The interviewee who is providing this account of her ongoing decision offered five more arguments supporting quitting smoking now and four arguments for quitting later. This shows that she is seriously entertaining the idea of quitting and in fact is using the Temporizing Heuristic (described in Chapter 10) to sustain the ongoing, but shaky, decision to continue with smoking for the time being. We might infer from this that the dominance structuring (discussed in Chapter 11) around the "continuing to smoke" option may not be impervious.

The sequencing of a person's thoughts can often be a clue that a person is on the verge of a new decision or realization. *To capture the data about the order in which this interviewee presented her arguments we can add numbers inside the shapes.* The numbers represent the order of the interviewee's claims and reasons. This technique preserves the chronology of the interview, revealing how the interviewee first argues for quitting smoking (phrase 2: "Smoking is going to kill me"). Although the person never

declares that she must stop smoking, it is an implicit statement in the first things she says (1: "I want to live, 3: "I can't believe I started smoking again," and 4: "I'm an idiot" [for doing so.]). But then the person's defenses begin to build. The temporizing starts rather early in the interview, as the person explains why this was not the time to try quitting (phrase 5). The interviewee's arguments also reveal unwarranted beliefs that there are beneficial effects of the nicotine addiction (phrase 13 "To function, I've gotta smoke"). If our purpose were to evaluate the reasoning, and not simply to analyze it, we could further augment the argument map by inserting "(True)" and "(False)" by each statement that we were sure was true or false.

Mapping Forms of Inference

Look closely at Map 1 and you'll spot another enhancement. On two of the arrow lines we've indicated the name

Map 2   We Need Groceries

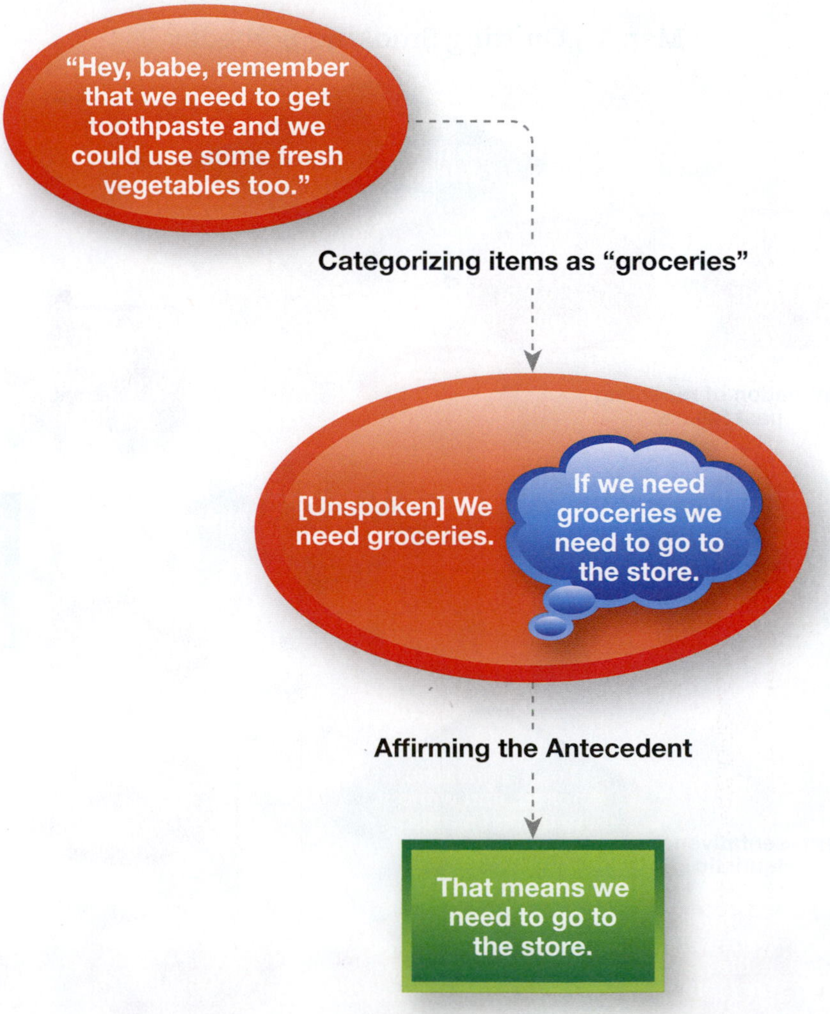

"Hey, babe, remember that we need to get toothpaste and we could use some fresh vegetables too."

Categorizing items as "groceries"

[Unspoken] We need groceries.

If we need groceries we need to go to the store.

Affirming the Antecedent

That means we need to go to the store.

of the reasoning used to move from one oval to the next. "Simulation of repeating past failure" indicates that the Simulation Heuristic described in Chapter 10 operated as the person's thinking moved from phrase 8 to phrase 7. She spoke phrase 7 first, then explained how she came to that idea with phrase 8, but without much self-confidence, having already revealed her relapse in phrase 3. *Introducing information on the arrow lines is a way of displaying how the analyst is interpreting what the interviewee is saying.* You'll see another interpretive insertion on the arrow line between phrase 20 and phrase 21. There the analyst suggests that the interviewee is using the Representativeness Heuristic, as the memory is fresh in her mind and close to her life.

Heuristics are not the only forms of inference that we can add by name to the arrow lines of an argument or decision map. We can insert the names of any fallacies, valid argument templates, or statistical tests that the argument maker uses to draw his or her inferences.

Map 2   This map indicates the critical thinking skills used. In Map 2 one of the valid rules for drawing inferences we discussed in Chapter 8, Affirming the Antecedent (also called "Modus Ponens"), is noted on the arrow line leading directly to the conclusion. The argument maker logically infers the conclusion without needing to speak aloud the two implicit statements in the intermediate claim. The argument maker reaches the first of those, "We need groceries," by applying a basic critical thinking sub-skill listed in Chapter 2, categorization. *Reference the logic used by the argument maker to infer the conclusion by inserting its name on arrow line.* Whether the argument maker used a logical argument pattern or a fallacious reasoning, if it has a name we can display it on the arrow line.

Mapping Supporting Explanatory Information

Map 3   This map uses overlapping ovals, creating something that looks like an upside-down "Mickey

Map 3   Which Students Value Truth-Seeking?

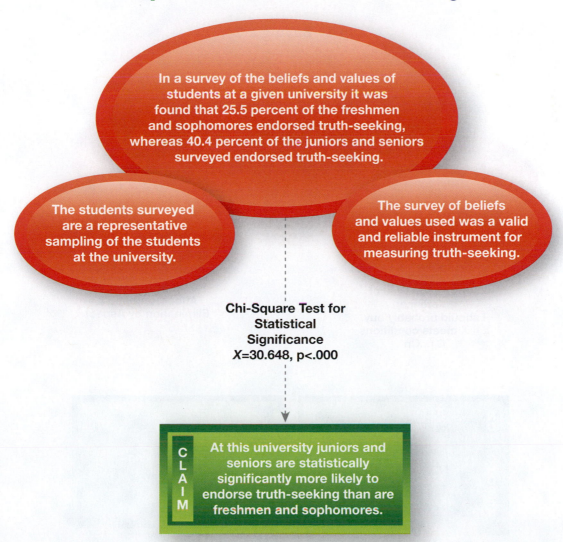

In a survey of the beliefs and values of students at a given university it was found that 25.5 percent of the freshmen and sophomores endorsed truth-seeking, whereas 40.4 percent of the juniors and seniors surveyed endorsed truth-seeking.

The students surveyed are a representative sampling of the students at the university.

The survey of beliefs and values used was a valid and reliable instrument for measuring truth-seeking.

Chi-Square Test for Statistical Significance
$X=30.648$, $p<.000$

CLAIM

At this university juniors and seniors are statistically significantly more likely to endorse truth-seeking than are freshmen and sophomores.

Mouse" hat. The overlapping oval on the left shows that the data in the large central oval are supported by good methodology—specifically that the sample was representative. The right side's overlapping oval indicates that the claim in the center is based upon the application of a measurement instrument which the argument maker believes to have been valid and reliable. Argument makers often rely on well-established research methodologies or decision-critical factors in making a key claim. We can best interpret these elements as parts of a complex claim itself, rather than as separate reasons for the claim. *To display a complex claim that includes explicit justifications and explanations of that claim itself use overlapping ovals.*

Map 3 also notes on the arrow line leading to the conclusion that the argument maker applied a commonly used analysis for statistical significance called a Chi-Square Test. As indicated with Map 2, we can show this on the arrow line. The label on the arrow line in Map 3 is shorthand for saying "The argument maker applied a Chi-Square statistical test to determine the likelihood that the observed results happened to come about merely by

random chance is less than one chance in 1,000." Another option would have been to put this same information into a third oval that overlapped the larger oval above. Either way works to communicate the basis for the statistical analysis that, itself, then justifies our confidence in the conclusion. Breaking out each element and displaying it offers a map that better displays the complexity of the thinking yet keeps that reasoning easy to understand and interpret correctly. This is particularly helpful when the reasoning involves several complex steps, like scientific reasoning as described in the chapter on empirical reasoning, Chapter 14.

Mapping the Decision System

Map 4 This augmented decision map draws from what we learned in Chapter 10 about systems of reasoning. Here, the notations of System-2 and System-1 reasoning are both present. The application of the rule called *substitution* is the

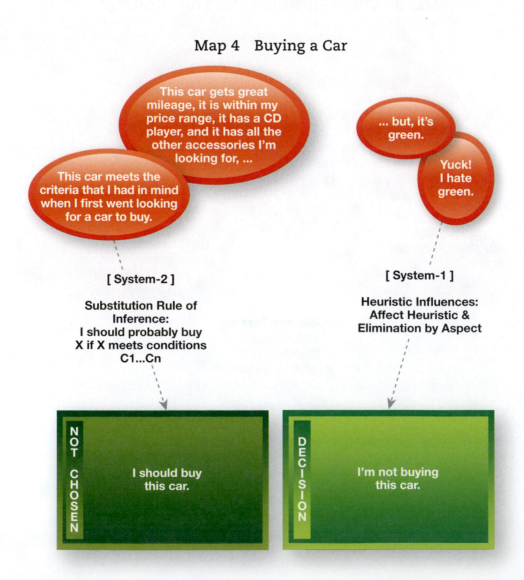

Map 4   Buying a Car

more reflective System-2 inference that *would* have led the person to buy the car, but the System-1 negative affective response to its color gave the buyer pause. Ergo, this car was not purchased by this decision maker!

Less Is More

Map 5 We can increase the information on a map or, if it helps in a given context, we can strip out information. In Map 5 I have stripped out the arguments so that the map reveals the overall pattern of the decision making divorced from the specific content of the argument. The numbered "P" ovals are the reasons the speaker gave in favor of ("pro") attending a given college, and the "C" ovals are ("con") arguments the speaker made concerning attending that college. And we've added evaluations of the arguments (discussed in Chapter 7) as "sound" or "unsound" based on the truthfulness of the premises and the logical strength of the speaker's original arguments. Now the map clearly shows which option was the one that was best supported, in our judgment, by the decision maker. The dominance structuring we talked about in Chapter 11 emerges strongly in this next map too. In the end, this person decided to attend Michigan State University (MSU). What was particularly

interesting was that a few of the arguments the person considered both for and against attending MSU were not sound. This is an instance of the fourth stage of dominance structuring, as we learned in Chapter 11, by a person who does not seem to be the world's best critical thinker.

Schwarzenegger's Denial of Clemency

Map 6 Here is a map of Governor Schwarzenegger's reasoning in his denial of clemency for Stanley "Tookie" Williams, explored in Chapter 11's exercise. We invited you there to map his reasoning as expressed in the statement he published. The map you produced would likely have been rather complex, since the reasoning you were mapping was itself rather complex. And you would probably have had to make more than a couple drafts before you were satisfied that your analysis was reasonable. Take a moment and study Map 6.

Assuming this map is a reasonably accurate analysis, how would you evaluate that reasoning? In particular, what should we make of the two abandoned lines of reasoning? What would have been the result had they

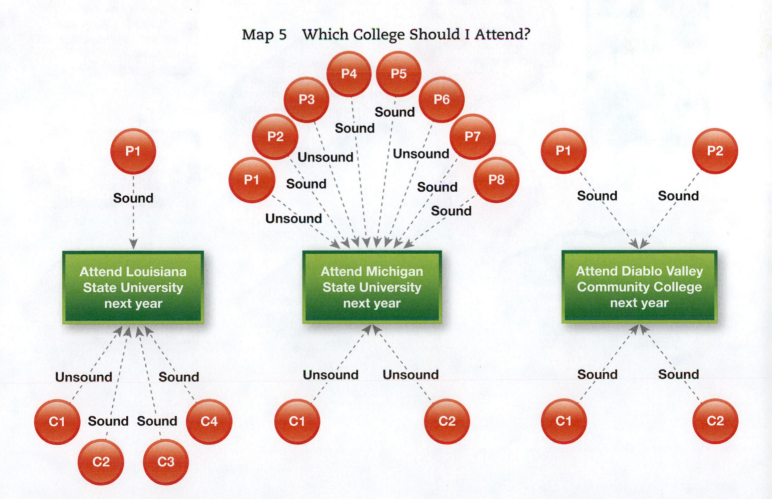

Map 5   Which College Should I Attend?

Map 6   Governor Arnold Schwarzenegger's Argument for Denying the Death Row Appeal for Clemency of Stanley "Tookie" Williams

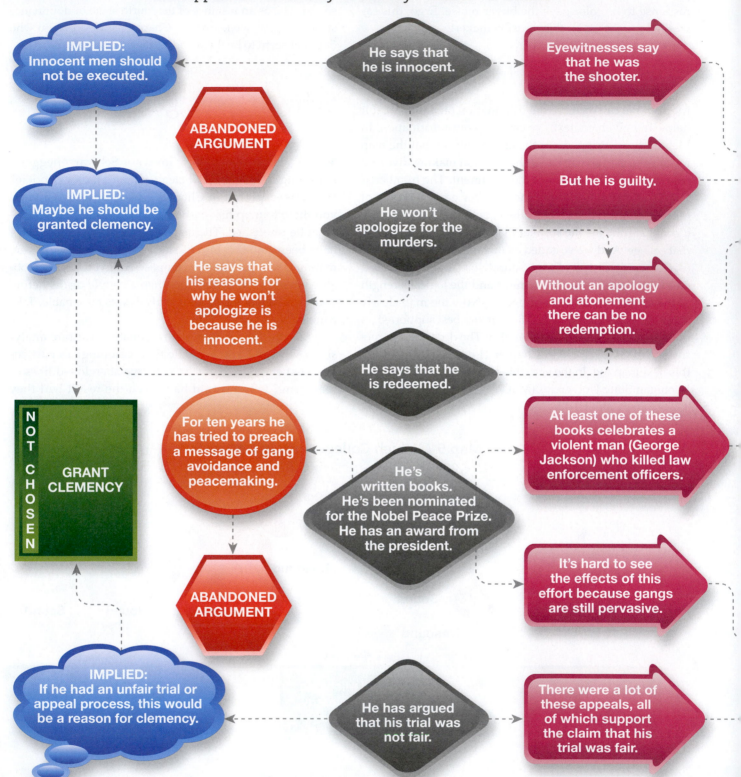

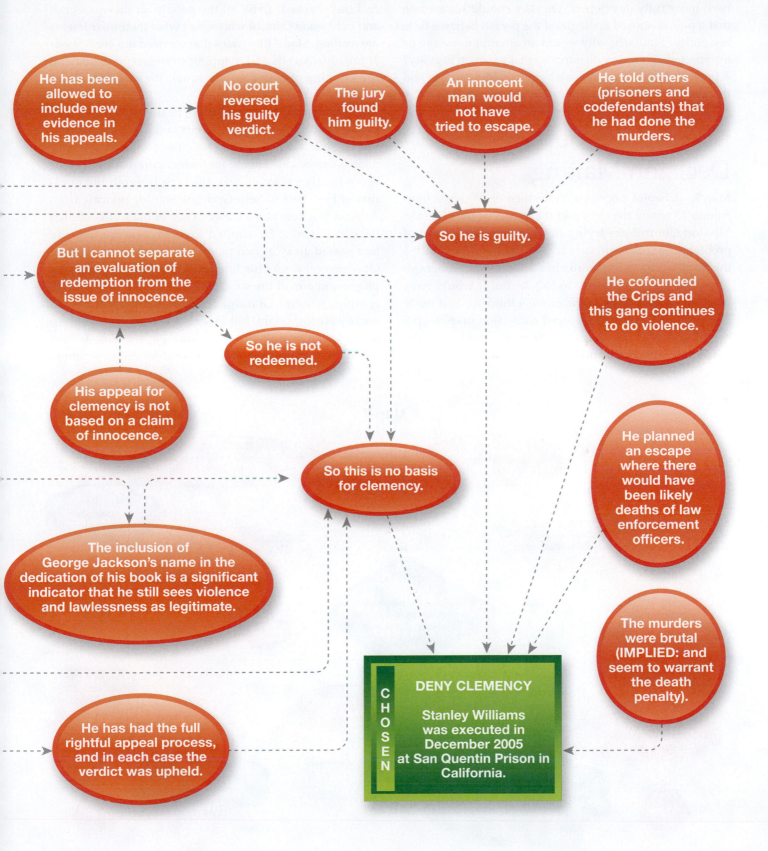

He has been allowed to include new evidence in his appeals.

No court reversed his guilty verdict.

The jury found him guilty.

An innocent man would not have tried to escape.

He told others (prisoners and codefendants) that he had done the murders.

So he is guilty.

But I cannot separate an evaluation of redemption from the issue of innocence.

He cofounded the Crips and this gang continues to do violence.

So he is not redeemed.

His appeal for clemency is not based on a claim of innocence.

He planned an escape where there would have been likely deaths of law enforcement officers.

So this is no basis for clemency.

The inclusion of George Jackson's name in the dedication of his book is a significant indicator that he still sees violence and lawlessness as legitimate.

The murders were brutal (IMPLIED: and seem to warrant the death penalty).

CHOSEN

DENY CLEMENCY

Stanley Williams was executed in December 2005 at San Quentin Prison in California.

He has had the full rightful appeal process, and in each case the verdict was upheld.

been more fully developed? Or, why should we assume that a person should apologize if the person believes he is not guilty? Similarly, why would an attempt to escape be interpreted as a reason to suppose that a person is guilty? A good argument map reveals both the strong points and the weak points of a decision maker's thinking.

Mapping Group Decision Making

Map 7. Chapter 2 opens with the memorable scene from Apollo 13 where the crew and the people at the Houston Mission Control are trying to figure out what kind of problem the spacecraft was having. There we described the thinking by using words in sentence and paragraph form. Perhaps it was easy to follow. But it would have been even easier to trace the group's thinking as it made that vital decision had we used a decision map. Map 7 begins with the realization that there is a problem on the spacecraft. This realization is communicated to Houston

and then backed up by all the people on the spacecraft and in Mission Control who report what their instruments are reading. Map 7 illustrates that we need not confine our argument analysis and mapping strategies to displaying the thinking of a single individual. We can map group decisions too.

Mapping a group decision can be useful, but challenging too. As many college students and instructors know, figuring out how to best care for older parents and grandparents can be challenging for their children. About a year ago a family we know was working through the question of how best to help Grandpa Stanley relocate from Arizona to a new home closer to one of his adult children back in Chicago. He wanted to move because his wife had passed away as had many of his retirement friends. Over several weeks his four adult children discussed by phone and e-mail the various options. The decision was complex because Grandpa Stanley's needs and preferences were important, but so were the needs and abilities of the various adult children and their families. To sort out all the options and relevant considerations, a couple

Map 7

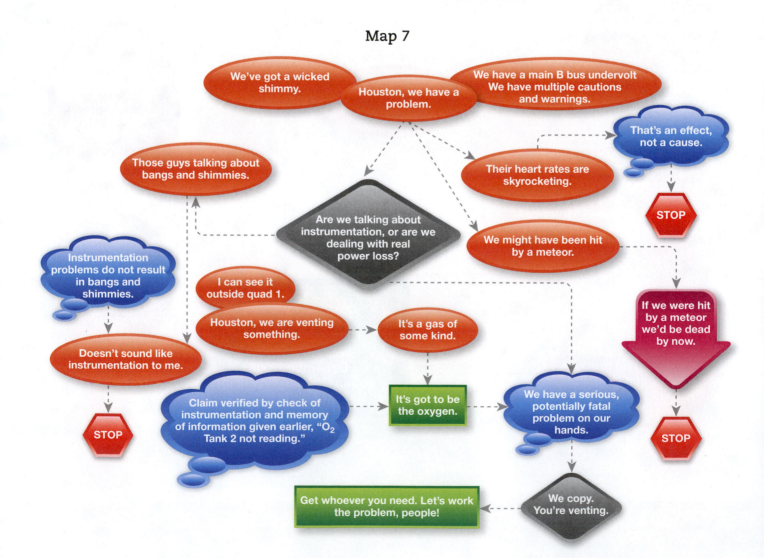

of huge decisions maps were drawn up and circulated. In the spirit of "let the chips fall where they may" the maps were accurate to a fault. All the options and reasons, weak and strong, were displayed, along with all the abandoned lines of reasoning. Which child was too busy with work, which had medical problems of his own to deal with, etc. all made it into the map. Given how families can be, all this truthfulness risked reopening old conflicts because the map exposed an unverifiable assumption and an occasional fallacy in the reasoning of one or another adult sibling. Eventually it was all happily resolved. Grandpa Stanley is resettled near two of his sons on the north side of Chicago. He occasionally rides the Red Line to Cubs games. With millions of other Cubs fans, Stanley yearns to cheer his team as World Series victors—someday. The adult siblings are all still close friends. The decision maps have been put away, perhaps someday to be shared with the great-grandchildren, but maybe not. There are things that are important, and then there are other things that are more important. Strong critical thinkers make judgments.

Research Applications

There are still other ways we can effectively use our mapping techniques for practical and for scholarly purposes. Advanced students interested in pursing the idea of using decision maps to compare how different people make comparable decisions, for example, would find the book *Thinking and Reasoning in Human Decision Making: The Method of Argument and Heuristic Analysis*, useful (Facione and Facione, The California Academic Press, 2007). The mapping techniques presented in this appendix and in Chapter 5 are drawn from that book; from our many years of collaborative research; and from our shared goal of making the analysis, interpretation, and evaluation of complex human decision making more scientifically objective and open to replication by other investigators. In this work, critical thinking and scientific inquiry, as discussed in Chapter 14, go hand in hand. When we use empirical reasoning, if our maps do not agree, we can compare our analyses to see what the best interpretation might be.

Glossary

Actions are processes or conditions whereby something is done or accomplished.

Analysis identifies the intended and actual inferential relationships among statements, questions, concepts, descriptions, or other forms of representation intended to express belief, judgment, experiences, reasons, information, or opinions.

Analytical means that a person is habitually alert to potential problems and vigilant in anticipating consequences and trying to foresee short-term and long-term outcomes of events, decisions, and actions. "Foresightful" is another word for what "analytical" means here.

Anomalies are solid scientific findings that are not consistent with prevailing theories.

Argument refers to the combination of a person's claim and the reason or reasons a person presents in support of that claim.

Author's case includes all of the pros and cons along with the supporting evidence that the author presents to the audience in order to establish the truth of a given statement or the wisdom of a given recommendation.

Claim refers to the statement that the maker of the argument is seeking to show to be true or probably true.

Cognitive heuristics are human decision-making shortcuts people rely on to expedite their judgments about what to believe or what to do.

Comparative reasoning (or **this-is-like-that thinking**) is the process of using what is more familiar to make interpretations, explanations, or inferences about what is less familiar.

Comprehensiveness in the evaluation of comparisons, is the extent to which a comparison captures a greater number of central or essential features.

Conclusion is another way of referring to an argument's claim.

Conditional is a grammatically correct construction used to assert that if an antecedent statement is true, then a consequent statement is true.

Confident in reasoning means that a person is trustful of his or her own reasoning skills to yield good judgments. A person's or a group's confidence in their own critical thinking may or may not be warranted, which is another matter.

Conjunction is a grammatically correct construction used to assert that two statements are both true.

Considerations or **rationale** are other terms used to refer to reasons.

Contingent statement in the Logic of Statements means a grammatically correct expression that turns out to be true under at least one possible assignment of truth values to its component simple statements and false under another possible assignment of truth values to its component simple statements.

Critical thinking is the process of purposeful, reflective judgment. Critical thinking manifests itself in giving reasoned and fair-minded consideration to evidence, conceptualizations, methods, contexts, and standards in order to decide what to believe or what to do.

Decision-critical attributes are those criteria the decision maker deems to be important and relevant for the purpose of evaluating options.

Disjunction is a grammatically correct construction used to assert that one or both of two statements are true.

Dominance structuring is the psychological process through which humans achieve confidence in their decisions. The four phases of dominance structuring are pre-editing, identifying one promising option, testing that promising option for dominance, and structuring the dominance of the option selected.

Empirical reasoning (or **bottom up thinking**) is that process of thinking that proceeds from premises describing interpersonally verifiable experiences in order to support or to disconfirm hypotheses, which, in turn, are intended to explain and predict phenomena. Empirical reasoning is fundamentally inductive, self-corrective, and open to scrutiny and independent verification by the entire scientific community.

Evaluation assesses the credibility of statements or other representations that are accounts or descriptions of a person's perception, experience, situation, judgment, belief, or opinion; also assesses the logical strength of the actual or intended inferential relationships among statements, descriptions, questions, or other forms of representation.

Ethics refers to a set of behavioral ideals or moral principles that guide us in determining right and wrong. We can think of these ideals and principles as a set of core values and beliefs.

Ethical imperatives are intended to shape or guide behavior by expressing core values and beliefs about what is morally right or morally wrong. Ethical imperatives express behavioral ideals and moral principles by pointing out what we ought to do or ought to refrain from doing.

Expert refers to someone who is both experienced and learned in a given subject matter area or professional practice field.

Explanation states and justifies reasoning in terms of the evidential, conceptual, methodological, criteriological, and contextual considerations upon which one's results were based; also presents one's reasoning in the form of cogent arguments.

Fallacies are deceptive arguments that appear logical, but upon closer analysis, fail to demonstrate their conclusions.

Familiarity in the evaluation of comparisons, is the degree of knowledge the listener has about the object to which the unknown is being compared.

Good argument/worthy argument is an argument that merits being accepted as a proof that its conclusion is true or very probably true.

Ideological reasoning (or **top-down thinking**) is the process of thinking that begins with abstractions or generalizations that express one's core beliefs, concepts, values, or principles and proceeds to reason top down to specific applications. Ideological reasoning is deductive and axiomatic. The argument maker takes the ideological premises on faith.

Inconsistent (or "self-contradictory") statement in the Logic of Statements means a grammatically correct expression that turns out to be false under every possible assignment of truth values to its component simple statements.

Inference   identifies and secures elements needed to draw reasonable conclusions; it forms conjectures and hypotheses, it considers relevant information, and it reduces or draws out the consequences flowing from data, statements, principles, evidence, judgments, beliefs, opinions, concepts, descriptions, questions, or other forms of representation.

Inquisitive   means that a person habitually strives to be well-informed, wants to know how things work, and seeks to learn new things about a wide range of topics, even if the immediate utility of knowing those things is not directly evident. An inquisitive person has a strong sense of intellectual curiosity.

Interpretation   is an expression of the meaning or significance of a wide variety of experiences, situations, data, events, judgments, conventions, beliefs, rules, procedures, or criteria.

Judicious   means that a person approaches problems with a sense that some are ill-structured and some can have more than one plausible solution. A judicious person has the cognitive maturity to realize that many questions and issues are not black and white and that, at times, judgments must be made in contexts of uncertainty.

Language community   is a community in which people share an understanding of the meanings of words and icons. Dictionaries were invented to record a language community's conventions for what its words shall mean.

Make an argument   refers to the process of giving one or more reasons in support of a claim.

Motivation   is a term used to represent the internal and external forces that stimulate, maintain, and regulate human behavior and influence our decision for action or reaction in social situations.

Natural science   refers to the systematic empirical inquiry into the causal explanations for the observed patterns, structures, and functions of natural phenomena from the subatomic to the galactic in scope.

Negation   is a grammatically correct construction used to assert that a statement is false.

Null hypothesis   is an empirically testable hypothesis that two phenomena are entirely unrelated except perhaps by random chance.

Open-minded   means that a person is tolerant of divergent views and sensitive to the possibility of his or her own possible biases. An open-minded person respects the right of others to have different opinions.

Participant   means an individual who performs, shares, or engages in something. In social science research, participants are sometimes referred to as subjects, informants, or actors.

Problem solving   is moving from the point at which we initially realize that we have a difficulty which requires our attention to that point where we regard the difficulty as being sufficiently resolved for the current time and circumstances.

Problematic ambiguity   is the characteristic of a word or expression which can have multiple meanings such that uncertainty about exactly which meaning applies in a given context for a given purpose results in troublesome misunderstandings.

Problematic vagueness   is the characteristic of a word or expression having an imprecise meaning or unclear boundaries such that uncertainty about precisely what is included in that meaning or excluded from that meaning results in troublesome miscommunications in a given context or for a given purpose.

Productivity   is the capacity of a comparison to suggest consequences that go beyond those mentioned in the initial comparison.

Reason   those sentences in the argument that are used to show that the conclusion is true or that it is probably true.

Rhetorical situation   is the interactive combination of four elements: a specific author is using a specific mode of communication or presentation to engage a specific audience for the specific purpose.

Self-contradictory statement   is a sentence that is false entirely because of the grammatical construction and the meanings of the words used to form the sentence.

Self-regulation   is a process in which one monitors one's cognitive activities, the elements used in those activities, and the results educed, particularly by applying skills in analysis, and evaluation to one's own inferential judgments with a view toward questioning, confirming, validating, or correcting either one's reasoning or one's results.

Simple statement   is a grammatically correct construction in a given language used to assert that an idea is true.

Simplicity   in the evaluation of comparisons, is a measure of the relative absence of complexity.

Situation   means the physical, social, and cultural circumstances or surroundings that define the phenomenon of interest.

Social science   is the systematic empirical study of the patterns, structures, and functions of human behavior, individually or in groups, within society.

Sound argument   is an argument with true premises that also passes the Test of Logical Strength.

Statement A implies statement B in the Logic of Statements   if there is no interpretation of the statement letters of A and B such that A is true and B is false.

Statement A implies statement B in the Logic of Statements   if the grammatical expression generated by the structure $(A \rightarrow B)$ is a tautology.

Statement A and statement B are equivalent in the Logic of Statements   if A and B have the same truth value under every interpretation of their statement letters.

Statements A and statement B are equivalent in the Logic of Statements   if, and only if, the biconditional $(A \mathrel{K} B)$ is a tautology.

Statistical significance   is a term used in statistical analysis to represent the probability that an obtained result has not occurred by chance.

System-1 thinking   is reactive thinking that relies heavily on situational cues, salient memories, and heuristic thinking to arrive quickly and confidently at judgments.

System-2 thinking   is reflective critical thinking that is useful for judgments in unfamiliar situations, for processing abstract concepts, and for deliberating when there is time for planning and more comprehensive consideration.

Systematic   means that a person consistently endeavors to take an organized and thorough approach to identifying and resolving problems. A systematic person is orderly, focused, persistent, and diligent in his or her approach to problem solving, learning, and inquiry.

Tautology   is a statement that is necessarily true because of the meanings of the words.

Tautology in the Logic of Statements   means a grammatically correct expression that turns out to be true under every possible assignment of truth values to its component simple statements.

Testability   is the capacity of comparisons to project consequences that have the potential to be shown to be false, inapplicable, or unacceptable.

Testable hypothesis   is one that can be shown to be false by reference to empirical evidence.

Trusted source   on topic X is a person (or the words of a person) who is learned in X, experienced in X, speaking about X, up-to-date about X, capable of explaining the basis for their claim or their advice about X, unbiased, truthful, free of conflicts of interest, acting in accord with our interests, unconstrained, informed about the specifics of the case at hand, and mentally stable.

Truth-seeking   means that a person has intellectual integrity and a courageous desire to actively strive for the best possible knowledge in any given situation. A truth-seeker asks probing questions and follows reasons and evidence wherever they lead, even if the results go against his or her cherished beliefs.

Valid   describes an argument or inference such that the truth of the premises entails or implies that conclusion must be true; in other words, it is impossible for the conclusion to be false if all the premises are true.

Valid argument   is an argument such that its premises logically imply or entail its conclusion which makes it impossible for all of its premises to be true and its conclusion to be false.

Warranted   describes an inference or argument such that the truth of the premises justifies or strongly supports confidently accepting the conclusion as very probably true, but not necessarily true.

Endnotes

Chapter 1

1. Ray Marshall and Marc Tucker, *Thinking for a Living: Education and the Wealth of Nations* (New York: Basic Books, 1992).

2. "It Takes More than a Major: Employer Priorities for College Learning and Student Success." Hart Research Associates, Washington DC. April 2013, page 1

3. Karl Popper, *The Open Society and its Enemies*, Vols. 1 & 2 (New York: Routledge, 1945, 2002).

4. Thurgood Marshall, Former U.S. Supreme Court Justice. STANLEY v. GEORGIA, Supreme Court of the United States, 394 U.S. 557, April 7, 1969.

5. Salaheddin, S and Salama, V., "Islamic State Group Issues New Curriculum in Iraq," Associated Press, September 15, 2014.

6. Brooks, R., "China's Biggest Problem? Too Many Men," CNN Opinion, March 4, 2013.

7. "Megadroughts," Bob Varmette. Fort Stockton Pioneer. August 4, 2011.

8. Anne Rice, *The Vampire Lestat* (New York: Ballantine Books, 1985).

9. The Delphi method begins by inviting all the experts to respond to an initial set of questions about the topic of interest. The project's coordinating research director, who cannot be one of the experts, has responsibility for compiling results, sharing those results with the roster of participating experts, and asking whether they agree, disagree, or want to propose clarifications or revisions. The research director also moves the project forward by asking questions that arise from the material being generated by the experts. This process is repeated over and over again as the group slowly comes to consensus on major points. The research director keeps track of those points of consensus. The research director invites more comment on areas that are still unclear or on which there is disagreement. The experts may end up not agreeing on everything. But after several rounds, there usually is enough accord on key points that the process can be drawn to a close. To do this, the research director writes up the points of apparent agreement and verifies that the experts are in accord. In this particular Delphi research project focusing on critical thinking, it took six rounds of questioning and 16 separate group communications back and forth before consensus was achieved. One very important thing about the Delphi process in general, which was true of this particular project as well: Because the group is made up of experts whose names and reputations are well known to the other experts, the Delphi process calls for omitting their names when the research director circulates their remarks and opinions to the other members of the group. That way the group sees each expert's arguments and explanations, but not knowing who the author is, the others in the group will not be overly influenced by any positive or negative opinions they may have about that other expert. The ideas speak for themselves. This account of the Delphi research process comes from the person who was the project director for the effort to achieve an expert consensus regarding the meaning of critical thinking, namely, the author of this textbook. As such, he was not a contributing expert on that 46-person panel.

10. American Philosophical Association, *Critical Thinking: A Statement of Expert Consensus for Purposes of Educational Assessment and Instruction*, also known as *"The Delphi Report"* (ERIC Doc. No. ED 315 423) 1990. Executive summary available through Insight Assessment, San Jose, CA, **www.insightassessment.com**.

11. Some use the word "meta-cognitive" when referring to the skills of self-monitoring and self-correcting. We will unpack these ideas in much greater detail in Chapter 2.

12. "Air France crash 'due to pilot and technical failings," BBC News, July 5, 2012. **http://www.bbc.co.uk/news/world-europe-18720915**

13. "San Francisco plane crash caused by pilot's inexperience with onboard computers," The Verge, December 12, 2013. **http://www.theverge.com/2013/12/12/5202954/asiana-214-crash-pilot-misunderstood-auto-throttle-system**

14. "Yosemite-National-Park-Vernal-waterfall-accident-3-hikers presumed dead," Nbcnews.com, July 20, 2011 **http://www.nbcnews.com/id/43815801/ns/us_news-life/t/hikers-who-went-over-yosemite-falls-presumed-dead/#.UvJlGpWPKpo**

15. Pretest and posttest studies by the authors and by many other scholars using objective measures of critical thinking have documented gains. For example see **http://files.eric.ed.gov/fulltext/ED327566.pdf**. See also **http://www.insightassessment.com/CT-Resources / Independent-Critical-Thinking-Research**.

16. © 2009, Peter A. Facione, Noreen C. Facione, and Measured Reasons LLC, Hermosa Beach, CA. USA. Original publication 1994. Permission is hereby granted by the copyright holders to students, faculty, staff, or administrators at public or nonprofit educational institutions for unlimited duplication of the *Holistic Critical Thinking Scoring Rubric* when used for local teaching, assessment, research, or other educational and noncommercial purposes, provided that no part of the

scoring rubric is altered and that "Facione and Facione" are cited as authors. Download PDF from Insight Assessment. **www.insightassessment.com**.

17. Katz, A. "Four Years Later, Haiti's Troubled Recover Haunts Its Future," Time.com. January 12, 2014.

Chapter 2

1. Allen Newell, *Toward Unified Theories of Cognition* (Cambridge, MA: Harvard University Press, 1990); Paul Slovic, Baruch Fischhoff, and Sarah Lichtenstein, "Behavioral Decision Theory," *Annual Review of Psychology* 28 (January 1977); Henry Montgomery, "From Cognition to Action: The Search for Dominance in Decision Making," *Process and Structure in Human Decision Making*, Ed. Henry Montgomery and Ola Svenson (Chichester, UK: John Wiley & Sons, 1989) 23–49; Allen Newell and Herbert Alexander Simon, *Human Problem Solving* (Englewood Cliffs, NJ: Prentice Hall, 1972).

2. The descriptions of events in this paragraph and the paragraphs that follow are based on the 1994 book *Apollo 13*, by Jeffery Kluger and Jim Lovell (Boston: Houghton Mifflin) and on subsequent dramatizations of the events described in that book including the 1995 film *Apollo 13*, directed by Ron Howard with technical consultation provided by the book's authors, Lovell and Kluger.

3. Quotes about critical thinking – Mill to Zinn. February 12, 2014. **http://www.procon.org/view.resource. php?resourceID=005439**

4. Sir Arthur Conan Doyle (1892), *Adventures of Sherlock Holmes*, Harper & Brothers.

5. Peter A. Facione, Noreen C. Facione, and Carol A. Giancarlo, "The Disposition toward Critical Thinking: Its Character, Measurement, and Relationship to Critical Thinking Skill," *Informal Logic* 20(1)(2000): 61–84; Peter A. Facione, Noreen C. Facione, and Carol A. Giancarlo, "The Motivation to Think in Working and Learning," *Preparing Competent College Graduates: Setting New and Higher Expectations for Student Learning*, Ed. Elizabeth A. Jones (San Francisco: Jossey-Bass Publishers, 1997) 67–79; Peter A. Facione, Carol A. Giancarlo, and Noreen C. Facione, "Are College Students Disposed to Think?" (ERIC Doc. No. ED 368 311) April 1994; Peter A. Facione, Noreen C. Facione, "Profiling Critical Thinking Dispositions," *Assessment Update* (5)2 (1993): 1–4; Carol A. Giancarlo and Peter A. Facione, "A Look across Four Years at the Disposition toward Critical Thinking among Undergraduate Students," *The Journal of General Education* 50(1) (2001): 29–55.

6. H. C. Triandis, "Values, Attitudes and Interpersonal Behavior," *Beliefs, Attitudes, and Values. Nebraska Symposium on Motivation*, Ed. Herbert E. Howe (Lincoln, NE: University of Nebraska Press, 1980); Icek Ajzen and Martin Fishbein, "A Theory of Reasoned Action: Some Applications and Implications," *Beliefs, Attitudes, and Values. Nebraska Symposium*

on Motivation, Ed. Herbert E. Howe (Lincoln, NE: University of Nebraska Press, 1980).

7. Peter A. Facione, Carol A. Giancarlo, Noreen C. Facione, and Joanne Gainen, "The Disposition toward Critical Thinking," *Journal of General Education* 44(1) (1995): 1–25; Peter A. Facione, Noreen C. Facione, and Carol A. Giancarlo, *User Manual: The California Critical Thinking Disposition Inventory* (San Jose, CA: California Academic Press, 1992, 1994, 2001, 2007, 2014); Noreen C. Facione and Peter A. Facione, "Externalizing the Critical Thinking in Knowledge Development and Clinical Judgment," *Nursing Outlook* 44 (1996): 129–136; Peter A. Facione, "Empirical Methods of Theory and Tool Development for the Assessment of College Level Critical Thinking and Problem-Solving,"*Report, Conference on Collegiate Skills Assessment*, Washington, DC: NCES, U.S. Department of Education, 1992; Elizabeth A. Jones, Steven Hoffman, L. Moore, G. Ratcliff, S. Tibbetts, and B. Click, *Essential Skills in Writing, Speech and Listening, and Critical Thinking for College Graduates: Perspectives of Faculty, Employers, and Policy Makers, Project summary*, U.S. Department of Education, OERI Contract No. R117G10037, University Park, PA: National Center for Postsecondary Teaching, Learning, and Assessment, Pennsylvania State University, 1994; Elizabeth Jones, Steven Hoffman, L. Moore, G. Ratcliff, S. Tibbetts, and B. Click, *National Assessment of College Student Learning: Identifying the College Graduates' Essential Skills in Writing, Speech and Listening, and Critical Thinking*, Washington, DC: National Center for Educational Statistics, U.S. Department of Education, Office of Educational Research and Improvement, OERI publication NCES 93-001, 2005.

8. John Dewey, *How We Think* (Boston: D.C. Heath & Co., 1910).

9. Transcript of March 9, 1995 CBS *60 Minutes* Crawford Stahl interview. February 9, 2014 **http://archive.tobacco. org/Documents/950319crawford.html**

10. George Carlin, Life Is Worth Losing, recorded and broadcast live by HBO, November 5, 2005 at the Beacon Theater, New York.

11. Stephen D. Brookfield, *Developing Critical Thinkers: Challenging Adults to Explore Alternative Ways of Thinking and Acting* (San Francisco: Jossey-Bass Publishers, 1987); Lauren Resnick, Education and Learning to Think (Washington, DC: National Academy Press, 1987); Chet Meyers, Teaching Students to Think Critically (San Francisco: Jossey-Bass Publishers, 1986).

12. The findings of expert consensus are published in *Critical Thinking: A Statement of Expert Consensus for Purposes of Educational Assessment and Instruction* (ERIC Doc. No. ED 315 423) 1990. The research was undertaken originally as a project of a committee of the American Philosophical Association (APA), published by The California Academic Press, Millbrae, CA. In 1993 and 1994, the Center for the Study of Higher Education at Pennsylvania State University undertook a study of 200 policy makers, employers, and faculty members

from two-year and four-year colleges to determine what this group took to be the core critical thinking skills and habits of mind. That Pennsylvania State University study, under the direction of Dr. Elizabeth Jones, was funded by the U.S. Department of Education Office of Educational Research and Instruction. The Pennsylvania State University study findings, published in 1994, confirmed the expert consensus expressed in the APA report.

13. From Peter A. Facione, American Philosophical Association, *Critical Thinking: A Statement of Expert Consensus for Purpose of Educational Assessment & Instruction*, (also known as *The Delphi Report*). Copyright © 1990, The California Academic Press, 217 La Cruz Ave., Millbrae, CA 94030. All Rights Reserved. Reprinted by permission.

14. The descriptions of what characters do and think in this paragraph and those that follow are based on the book *12 Angry Men: A Play in Three Acts*, by Reginald Rose (London: Penguin Books, 1955), and Reginald Rose's later adaptation of that book for the 1957 United Artists film *12 Angry Men*.

15. The United Artists 1957 film version of *12 Angry Men* was nominated for three Academy Awards. Fifty years later the film *12 Angry Men* was selected for preservation in the United States National Film Registry by the Library of Congress as being "culturally, historically, or aesthetically significant." Do not miss DVD scene #10 where the two main protagonists argue about how a streetwise killer would hold a switchblade knife.

16. Cosmos—A Space Time Odyssey, FOX Television, Episode 13 "Unafraid of the Dark," June 8, 2014

17. Why "we" some times and "I" other times? There two co-authors. But because the book often illustrates key points with personal stories and because the two of us have had different life experiences we occasionally use the work "I" for the sake of accuracy. When we use the word "I" we intend that one of us, but not both of us, have had a particular experience that we both agreed to describe for you to help illustrate a point. Thanks for understanding the difference between what "we" authors are saying together and what one or the other of us is describing as a personal experience.

18. Used with permission from Insight Assessment-Measuring thinking worldwide. **www. insightassessment.com**.

19. Mathematicians and computer scientists would describe this as a "recursive function," meaning that the function can be applied to itself. We can analyze our analyses. We can evaluate our evaluations.

20. Quotes about critical thinking—Mill to Zinn. February 12, 2014. **http://www.procon.org/view.resource. php?resourceID=005439**

21. Table © 2009, 2011, 2014 *Test Manual for the California Critical Thinking Skills Test*, published by Insight Assessment, San Jose, CA. Used with permission of the publisher.

22. M. Neil Browne and Stuart M. Keeley, *Asking the Right Questions*, 9th ed. (Pearson, 2009).

23. Based on Table 3, "Consensus list of critical thinking cognitive skills and subskills," and Table 4, "Consensus descriptions of the core critical thinking skills and subskills" from American Philosophical Association, *Critical Thinking: A Statement of Expert Consensus for Purposes of Educational Assessment and Instruction*. Also known as "*The Delphi Report*" (ERIC Doc. No. ED 315 423) 1990.

24. Visit the "research" tab of the Insight Assessment website for numerous citations to our work and the work of other scholars and researchers.

25. "Mark Twain.

26. By permission. From Merriam-Webster's Online, by Merriam-Webster, Inc. (**www.Merriam-Webster.com**).

Chapter 3

1. "Cochelle, "Dedication of the Heart" found in Lucile Davis, Cesar Chavez 'Cesar Chavez: A Photo-illustrated Biography', Capstone (1998).

2. *Women in America*, U.S. Government, the White House, March 2011). **http://www.whitehouse.gov/sites/default/ files/rss_viewer/Women_in_America.pdf**.

3. Sylvia Earle, quoted in Cindy Griffin (2014), *Invitation to Public Speaking - National Geographic Edition*. Cengage Learning.

4. We use "IDEAS" as a mnemonic device to assist in remembering the five steps. Note that each step, as described above, has two parts. The two parts of each step supplement each other. We could have merged the two parts grammatically, but at the risk of losing one or the other of them. However, if it is easier to remember the steps, one might describe them this way:
   - Identify the problem and the priorities.
   - Determine, gather, and digest relevant information.
   - Enumerate options and consequences.
   - Assess the options and make a preliminary decision on which one appears to best fit the situation.
   - Scrutinize the process carefully and self-correct as necessary before making a final decision.

5. Arthur W. Chickering and Linda Reisser, *Education and Identity*, 2nd ed. (San Francisco: Jossey-Bass, 1993). Arthur Chickering's model and other approaches are discussed in *Student Development in College: Theory, Research, and Practice* by Nancy J. Evans, Deanna S. Forney, and Florence M. Guido. (San Francisco: Jossey-Bass, John Wiley & Son, 2009).

6. Berra, Yogi, *The Yogi Book: I Really Didn't Say Everything I Said!* (Workman Publishing Company, 2010).

7. Lyubomirsky, Sonja, *The How of Happiness: A New Approach to Getting the Life You Want* (The Penguin Press, 2007).

8. Albert Schweitzer.

9. Lions for Lambs, screenplay by Matthew Michael Carnahan, MGM/United Artists, 2007.

10. Kahneman, D, "The Focusing Illusion," in Brochman, J. (Ed), *This Book Will Make You Smarter*. New York: Harper Perennial, p. 49.
11. Oprah Winfrey.
12. "Rainn Wilson explores 'life's big questions'" **Salon.com**, December 15, 2012.
13. Erik H. Erikson, *Identity: Youth and Crisis* (Austen Riggs Monograph) (New York: Norton, 1968). **http://www . quotationspage.com/quote/603.html**.
14. Richard Dawkins, *The God Delusion*, (Boston: Houghton Mifflin Company, 2006).
15. Paul Tillich.

Chapter 4

1. Jerome Lawrence and Robert Lee, *Inherit the Wind* (New York: Random House, Ballantine Books, 1955).
2. Paul E. Koptak, "What's New in Interpreting Genesis," *The Covenant Quarterly* LIII (1) (February 1995): 3–16. February 21, 2014 at **http://www.religion-online.org/ showarticle.asp?title=19**.
3. Bible defenders and Bible detractors will both find the article "The Bible is Dead; Long Live the Bible," by Timothy Beal most interesting. He speaks directly to the question how the Bible is read and interpreted. For example, does it have a single right meaning? Does it answer questions, or does it raise questions? What was its historical context and purpose? Professor Beal's article appeared online in the *Chronicle of Higher Education,* April 17, 2011. It is drawn from his new book, *The Rise and Fall of the Bible: The Unexpected History of an Accidental Book*, published by Houghton Mifflin Harcourt.
4. Grossman, Joanna L, "The Supreme Court on the Social Security Rights of Posthumously Conceived Children," *Verdict.* May 29, 2012. **http://verdict.justia. com/2012/05/29/the-supreme-court-on-the-social- security-rights-of-posthumously-conceived-children**.
5. Grossman, Cathy Lynn, "Who's Mom? Legally biologically, it's no easy answer." *USA Today*, December 9, 2012.
6. Used with permission from Insight Assessment-Measuring thinking worldwide. **www. insightassessment.com**.
7. Jared Diamond, *Guns, Germs, and Steel* (New York: Norton, 1997).
8. Schroer, William J., "Generations X, Y, Z and the Others." *The Social Librarian*. February 22, 2014. **http://www. socialmarketing.org/newsletter/features/generation3.htm**
9. *My Cousin Vinny*, Palo Vista Productions, dir. Jonathan Lynn, writ. Dale Launer, perf. Joe Pesci, Ralph Macchio, and Marisa Tomei. 1992.
10. Andreas Teuber "Original Intent or How Does the Constitution Mean? *The London Review of Books*, 10(7), (March 1988) **http://people.brandeis.edu/~teuber/ origintent.html**.
11. For example, often the jury in a criminal case is asked to deliberate about the perpetrator's intent as one of the elements when determining guilt or innocence, as in the case of murder in the first degree.
12. Page 1062, "The Constitution of the United States of America Analysis and Interpretation." U.S. Government Printing Office, Washington DC, 2013. (Includes analysis of cases decided by the Supreme Court of the United States to June 26, 2013) Prepared by the Congressional Research Service, Library of Congress. Kenneth R. Thomas, Editor-in-Chief.
13. Roger Fisher, William L. Ury, and Bruce Patton, *Getting to Yes: Negotiating Agreement Without Giving In* (New York: Penguin Books, 1983).
14. Dawkins, Richard. *The God Delusion*. Houghton Mifflin Harcourt. (**www.hmhco.com**) iBooks.
15. Margaret Wheatley, It's An Interconnected World, Shambhala Sun, April 2002.
16. "Stinking Fish and Coffee: The language of corruption," *BBC News Magazine*, July 10, 2013.
17. Tariq Ramadan, The power of counterpower. Gulf News September 4, 2012.
18. © 2013, "Today I Will Be," Jerome Jesse Facione. February 25, 2014. **http://hellopoetry.com/jerome-facione/**
19. *The Wall Street Journal*, "Why Violence Is Vanishing," September 24, 2011.
20. "Living Ohio Man Donald Miller Ruled 'Legally Dead,'" *BBC News* US & Canada, October 10, 2013.

Chapter 5

1. "Measles Vaccination," Vaccines and Immunizations, Department of Health and Human Services: Centers for Disease Control, October 20, 2009, October 27, 2009 **http://www.cdc.gov/vaccines/vpd-vac/measles/default. htm**.
2. "Argument," *Merriam Webster's Online Dictionary*, June 22, 2009 **http://www.merriam-ebster.com/dictionary/ argument**.
3. "Parents' Guide to Childhood Immunization," Centers for Disease Control and Prevention, June 22, 2009 **http:// www.cdc.gov/vaccines/pubs/parents-guide/default.htm**.
4. Pinto, R. C., University of Windsor, The relation of argument to inference. Paper available on the web (March 4, 2014) at **http://www.dwc.knaw.nl/DL/ publications/PU00010684.pdf**.
5. There is a contextual element relating to scientific research that a fuller analysis of the reason might include; if the question "But if even 1 case occurs, then why not call it a side effect?" were raised, then the premise added might be, "When two events occur together so rarely that their coincidence cannot be distinguished from pure chance, then we do not have sufficient reason to regard either as the cause of the other."
6. Which is not to say we always know our own minds well enough to articulate all of our own assumptions. At times our own assumptions become clear to us only during the give and take of discussing our ideas with other people.

7. Successful communication depends on the intentions of the speaker concerning what he or she is trying to convey and on the beliefs of the speaker with regard to the knowledge of the listener. If the speaker believes that the listener is not aware of information that is essential for correctly interpreting what is being said, then it would not be sensible for the speaker to expect that the listener should understand the message. For more on this the reader may wish to search and explore the rich literature regarding the intricate relationships between communicating, meaning, believing and intending, for example, P. Facione, "Meaning and Intending," *American Philosophical Quarterly* 10(4) (1973): 277–287.

8. A 2010 Pew Research Center survey shows that nearly 75 percent of Americans favor legalizing medical marijuana and that just over 40 percent are of the opinion that all marijuana should be legal. According to a 2008 Gallup poll that percentage was 35 percent, which itself is about triple the 12 percent who held that view when Gallup surveyed Americans in 1969. In January 2014 NBC News reported that 55 percent of Americans now favor decriminalizing pot for personal use. **http://nbcpolitics.nbcnews.com/_news/2014/01/27/22470647-poll-majority -of-americans-support-efforts-to-legalize-marijuana**

9. BBC Monday, May 9, 2011, "Blurred lines in California's Cannabis Capital" as reported by Vishva Samani.

10. Rose, Reginald, *Twelve Angry Men—A Play in Three Acts* (London: Penguin Books, 1955). The 1957 film version was nominated for three Academy Awards and in 2007 the film was selected for preservation in the United States National Film Registry by the Library of Congress as being "culturally, historically, or aesthetically significant." The El Train scene begins roughly forty minutes into that United Artists film. The fair-minded juror who leads the reasoning is played by Henry Fonda.

11. That people make arguments in their efforts to reason through their decisions is clear. The number of arguments can vary widely, particularly if the decision is one of those important ones that needs to be reaffirmed on a frequent basis, like deciding not to seek a diagnosis for a worrisome symptom, or deciding not to take disciplinary action against a problem employee. Noreen C. Facione and Peter A. Facione, "Analyzing Explanations for Seemingly Irrational Choices: Linking Argument Analysis and Cognitive Science," *International Journal of Applied Philosophy* 15(2) (2002): 267–286.

12. The mapping conventions presented here are drawn from Peter A. Facione and Noreen C. Facione, *Thinking and Reasoning in Human Decision Making: The Method of Argument and Heuristic Analysis* (Millbrae, CA: The California Academic Press, 2007). Used with permission from Insight Assessment-Measuring thinking worldwide. **www.insightassessment.com**.

13. Source: The mapping conventions presented here are drawn from Peter A. Facione and Noreen C. Facione, *Thinking and Reasoning in Human Decision Making: The Method of Argument and Heuristic Analysis* (Millbrae, CA: The California Academic Press, 2007). Used with permission from Insight Assessment-Measuring thinking worldwide. **www.insightassessment.com**.

14. See related stories in the news. For example, Smietans, B., "Anti-Bias Policies Drive Some Religious Groups off Campuses," *USA Today*—Most Popular, April 2, 2012.

15. Amos, J. "Missouri Gun Murders 'Rose after Law Repeal'," BBC News—Science and Environment—Feb 17, 2014.

16. Peter A. Facione and Noreen C. Facione, *Thinking and Reasoning in Human Decision Making* (Millbrae, CA: The California Academic Press, 2007) 58.

Chapter 6

1. Williams, R., "Women Aviators Finally Fill Cockpits of Military Aircraft," *American Forces Press Service*. March 19, 2003.

2. National Museum of the US Air Force, "WASPS: BREAKING GROUND FOR TODAY's FEMALE USAF PILOTS" printable fact sheet *Posted 2/8/2011*.

3. Gomez, Mark (July 21, 2009). "S.J. woman was a trailblazing pilot during World War II." *San Jose Mercury News*. Retrieved July 22, 2009.

4. Marcus, G., "Cognitive Humility," in *This Will Make you Smarter*, Brockman, J. Ed., New York: Harper Perennial. p. 40.

5. Fernyhough, C., *Pieces of Light*, New York: Harper Collins, 2013.

6. "Yelp admits that a quarter of reviews submitted could be fake," *BBC News–Technology*, September 27, 2013. This story was prompted by a sting operation by the Brooklyn city attorney's office, which set up a fake yogurt shop. Search optimization firms were found to be paying freelance writers to make up fake reviews. These firms sell their services to small businesses to help them be found in Internet searches and thus attract more business. Except this yogurt shop did not exist. See "Fake yogurt shop snares 'astroturf' online reviewers," *BBC—Business*. September 24, 2013. Nineteen firms were fined a total of $350,000.

7. "Anonymous online critics must be identified, says court," *BBC News–Technology*. January 13, 2014.

8. Patricia M. King and Karen Strohm Kitchener, *Developing Reflective Judgment* (San Francisco: Jossey-Bass Publishers, 1994). My formulation presented here is a reformulation of work by King and Kitchener. Scholars who were instrumental in expanding our understanding of cognitive development include B. Bloom, W. Perry, L. Kohlberg, J. H. Flavel, M. Fischer, and J. Piaget, to name only a few of the many.

9. "Expert," Wikipedia, the Free Encyclopedia, July 27, 2009. **http://en.wikipedia.org/wiki/Expertise**

10. Janet Yellen. The Magazine of the HAAS School of Business at the University of California. Berkeley HAAS Fall 2012 from "A Force at the Fed" by Russ Mitchell.

11. Kahneman, D., 2012, *Thinking Fast and Slow*, New York: Farrar, Straus and Giroux.

12. In Chapter 10, we will revisit statements like this in the context of "heuristic thinking" and "System-1 decision making." Highly trained individuals have so internalized their problem-solving and pattern-recognition skills in the domain of their expertise that they make automatic, reactive decisions. Often, these are quite reliable and appropriate. The difficulty for critical thinking is that we cannot know that in a reflective and carefully explained way. But let's save this conversation for later.

13. Plato, "*The Republic Book* III, 389 b-c," *The Collected Dialogues of Plato*, Ed. Edith Hamilton (New York: The Bollingen Foundation, 1961), p. 634.

14. Pope Francis, Inconsistency of Pastors and Faithful Undermines Church's Credibility, News.va 15 April 2013.

15. **http://www.factcheck.org/2014/03/misleading-abortion-attack-in-Michigan**. Posted and updated March 14, 2014.

16. Mark Silva, "Obama, McCain: U.S. Citizens," The Swamp: Tribune's Washington Bureau, October 25, 2008 and July 27, 2009. **http://www.swamppolitics.com/news/politics/ blog/2008/10/obama_mccain_us_citizens.html**

17. Weiner, R., "Stefan Frederick Cook: Soldier Won't Deploy Over Obama Birth Certificate." *Huffington Post*, Politics Section. Posted August 14, 2009.

18. Google "GOP reject birthers" for 2011, 2012, and 2013 news stories on rejection of birther movement by GOP.

19. Alex Koppelman, "Why the Stories about Obama's Birth Certificate Will Never Die," Salon.com, December 5, 2008 and July 27, 2009. **http://www.salon.com/news/feature/2008/12/05/birth_certificate/**

20. Bomford, A., "How environmentally friendly are electric cars?" *BBC News Magazine*. April 11, 2013

21. Secretary of State John Kerry, January 2012. Reported in the *Executive Summary of the International Religious Freedom Report for 2012*. US Department of State, Bureau of Democracy, Human Rights and Labor.

22. Aaron Sorkin, "The Newsroom" (pilot), HBO Entertainment, 2012.

23. See "Call for 'fat-year' measurement," *BBC News–Health*, August 34, 2011.

24. Benjamin Edelman, "Red Light States: Who Buys Online Adult Entertainment?" *Journal of Economic Perspectives*, 23(1) (Winter 2009): 209–220.

25. White, E., "Nurses, family bond online as Iranian dies in US," *AP News*. February 11, 2014.

26. Enda Brady, "Image of Virgin Mary Found in Tree Stump," *Sky News*, July 10, 2009 and August 21, 2009. **http://news.sky.com/skynews/Home/World-News/Virgin-Mary-Tree-Stump-Depiction-Found-InRathkeale-Ireland/Article/200907215334913**

27. Steven Miller Design Studio, July 27, 2009. **http://www.stevenmillerdesignstudio.com/**

28. Rogers, J., "Study: Playing Music Helps Sharpen Kids' Brains," *Associated Press*. September 2, 2014.

29. Stephen Barrett, M. D., "Q-Ray Bracelet Marketed with Preposterous Claims," *Quackwatch*, January 6, 2008 and July 27, 2009. **http://www.quackwatch.com/search/webglimpse.cgi?ID=1&query=Q-Ray**

30. Michael Higgins, "Placebo Effect a Key Issue in Trial over Pain Bracelet," *Chicago Tribune*. August 23, 2006.

31. The power bracelet bankruptcy and Kobe's lost $400K were reported by several news outlets. For example: **http://content.usatoday.com/communities/gameon/post/2011/11/kobe-bryant-400k-endorsementcompany-bankrupt/1; http://www.huffingtonpost.com/mobileweb/2011/11/21/powerbraceletslawsuit_n_1105559.html**; and **http://www.ocregister.com/articles/company-328232-balancepower.html**

32. This exercise is based on Greg Brown, "Evaluating a Nutritional Supplement with SOAP Notes to Develop CT Skills," *Critical Thinking and Clinical Reasoning in the Health Sciences*, Eds. Noreen C. Facione and Peter A. Facione (San Jose, CA: California Academic Press, 2008), pp. 198–201.

Chapter 7

1. In Chapter 5 we said that the premises are those statements, explicitly asserted or contextually assumed and implicit, which comprise a reason offered on behalf of a claim. A person may offer more than one reason for a given claim. Each reason is a set of premises. The "Truthfulness" presumption about argument making says that we expect each and every premise that constitutes a given reason to be, in fact, true.

2. Brainyquote.com, March 26, 2014. **http://www.brainyquote.com/quotes/quotes/b/bertrandru103632.html**

3. Peter Facione and Donald Scherer, *Logic and Logical Thinking* (New York: McGraw-Hill Publishing, 1978).

4. People studying logic learn that there are a couple of peculiarly paradoxical cases in which the premises cannot possibly all be true and the conclusion false. One is a case in which the premises are inconsistent with each other. In that case it is impossible for them all to be true, because if one of the inconsistent pair of premises is true, then the other in the pair will necessarily be false. In that odd situation, the argument will pass the test of logical strength. Not to worry—it will fail the test of the truthfulness of the premises. The other odd case is the situation in which the conclusion of the argument is a tautology, and again the argument will pass the test of logical strength, because it will not be possible ever for the conclusion to be false. Again, not to worry, because the test of relevance eliminates these kinds of arguments from being considered acceptable. The test of relevance requires that the basis for believing in the truth of the claim should be the reason given and not some independent consideration. A tautology is true no matter what reason is given; in fact, the reason is entirely irrelevant to the truth of the claim. Therefore, an

argument with a tautological conclusion fails the test of relevance.

5. Irving M. Copi and Carl Cohen, *Introduction to Logic* (New York: Macmillan Publishing, 1990), pp. 52–53.

6. "National Safety Council Calls for Nationwide Ban on Cell Phone Use While Driving," National Safety Council, July 27, 2009.

7. John Searle, *Speech Acts: An Essay in the Philosophy of Language* (Cambridge, UK: Cambridge University Press, 1969).

8. Many frequently repeated mistakes in reasoning have earned themselves names as fallacies. To list them all would not be possible. That is one reason for approaching the evaluation of arguments in terms of the four tests. There are many fallacies we will describe in Chapters 8 and 9 that fail the test of logical strength. Obviously, those seven fallacies described in this chapter are arguments that also fail the test of relevance. We could have named "circular reasoning" as a common fallacy as well, but we already have the test of non-circularity. Being able to recognize common fallacies is a way to become more proficient in applying the tests of logical strength, relevance, and non-circularity. And it is fun, too, to see how we all are, at times, misled by the clever fallacies that commonly infest everyday conversation.

9. Aristotle, *On Sophistical Refutations*, trans. W. A. Pickard-Cambridge, 350 b.c.e., July 27, 2009; J. Machie, "Fallacies," *The Encyclopedia of Philosophy*, Vol. 3, Ed. Paul Edwards (New York: Macmillan Publishing, 1967), pp. 169–179; Hamblin, C. L., *Fallacies* (London: Methuen, 1970); John Chaffee, *Thinking Critically* (New York: Houghton Mifflin, 2003).

10. The prejudicial belief expressed in the first sentence was widely accepted for decades. Doug Williams went on to lead the Pittsburgh Steelers to victory in Super Bowl XXII. He received the 1988 Super Bowl MVP award for his performance that day as quarterback.

11. The local Chamber of Commerce has no special expertise or legal authority either in educational curricular or educational policy matters.

12. Prior, A., C. Lejewski, J. F. Staal, A. C. Gram, et al., "The history of logic," *The Encyclopedia of Philosophy*, Vol. 4, Ed. Paul Edwards (New York: Macmillan, 1967), pp. 513–571.

13. Paraphrased from the novel, *Rough Country*, John Sandford (New York: Putnam's, 2009).

14. William C. Rhoden, *Third and a Mile: The Trials and Triumphs of the Black Quarterback* (Bristol, CT: ESPN Books, 2007). This excerpt from Chapter 5 examines the fitful start to the 12-year NFL career of James Harris: William C. Rhoden, "The James Harris story: a long, painful road," February 12, 2007 and July 27, 2009. **http://sports.espn.go.com/espn/blackhistory2007/news/story?id=2762569**

15. Shukman, D., "Scientists hail synthetic chromosome advance," *BBC-Science & Environment*. March 27, 2014.

Chapter 8

1. Mosbergen, D., "Overdose Risk Is Staggering; Acetaminophen Safeguards Remain Insufficient," Huffington Post Healthy Living, September 24, 2013.

2. Dinsmore, J., HBO Series: Documentaries. November 5, 2013. "Tales from the Organ Trade."

3. "Deductive and Inductive Arguments," Internet Encyclopedia of Philosophy: A Peer Reviewed Academic Resource. March 26, 2014. Hamby, B. personal email correspondence October 27, 2013 and subsequent exchanges; Massey, G., *Understanding Symbolic Logic* (New York: Harper & Row Publishers, 1970); Kneale, W. and M. Knealw. *The Development of Logic* (Oxford: Clarendon Press, 1964).

4. Sagan, C., Cosmos: A Personal Voyage. Episode 1, "The Shores of the Cosmic Ocean." September 28, 1980.

5. Many logicians categorize arguments offered believing that the conclusion must be true if all the premises are true as "deductive." These theoreticians would describe the reasoning involved as deductive inference. There is much to recommend this terminology. However, we have elected not to embrace the adjective "deductive" because that word is defined differently by various disciplines and groups of theoreticians. But, more importantly, many instructors including ourselves have found that it offers fewer benefits than liabilities, when the purpose is teaching for critical thinking, to employ that adjective.

6. Aristotle, *Metaphysics*,1802, Cambridge, Mass.: Harvard University Press.

7. Massey, G., op. cit. uses the term "deductive principles" to refer to valid deductive argument templates.

8. The word *consequent* in "Denying the Consequent" refers to the second part of an "If___, then___" statement. That is the part after "then ___". The part that comes before is the "if ___" part, or the *antecedent*. So, the hypothetical is constructed "If *antecedent*, then *consequent*."

9. Logicians call this pattern *modus tollens*.

10. Logicians call this pattern *modus ponens*.

11. Another false premise. Connelly writes very enjoyable books featuring other characters too. But, again, assume that the premises in these examples are true. Go with the flow on this, so that the focus can be on the logic.

12. Way, M., "How Did Pragaash, Kashmir's First All-Girl Rock Band, Ignite the Kashmiri Muslim Establishment?" February 7, 2013. *Noisey Music by Vice* posting found online March 31, 2014 at **http://noisey.vice.com/en_uk/blog/how-did-pragaash-kashmirs-first-all-girl-rock-band-ignite-the-kashmiri-muslim-establishment**; Sharma, B., "Online Abuse of Teen Girls in Kashmir Leads to Arrests" India Ink, February 8, 2013, India Blogs NYTimes.com.

13. Sharma, B., "Online Abuse of Teen Girls in Kashmir Leads to Arrests" India Ink, February 8, 2013, India Blogs NYTimes.com. posting found online March 31, 2014 at **http://india.blogs.nytimes.com/2013/02/08/online-abuse-of-teen-girls-in-kashmir-leads-to-arrests/?_php=true&_type=blogs&_r=0**

14. Sherlock Holmes -The *Sign of Four*, Chapter 1: "The Science of Deduction." **http://www. sherlockholmesquotes.com/Sherlock-Holmes-on-Deduction-and-Deductive-Reasoning.html**

15. Cycling News. Post found March 31, 2014 at **http://www. cyclingnews.com/tour-de-france/race-history**

16. Carter, J., 2014. *A Call to Action: Women, Religion, Violence and Power*.

Chapter 9

1. Indiana State University is located in Terre Haute, Butler University is located in Indianapolis, Indiana. The statistics cited in this opening story are approximations of the 2013–14 data published on the *US News and World Report*'s Education Web site: Visit the web pages for their respective undergraduate admissions offices for more precise and up to date information on tuition and fees.

2. Researchers in the field of Informal Logic would categorize some, but not all, of the examples in this chapter as "Inductive." Other examples they recommend categorizing as "Abductive" or "Conductive." A helpful summary of the Informal Logic categorization is provided by Leo Groarke, "Informal Logic," *The Stanford Encyclopedia of Philosophy* (Spring 2013 Edition), Edward N. Zalta (ed.). There is no question but that elaborating definitional schema expedites communication within a given disciplinary language community. Although, too often, that very goal is frustrated when speaking across the fence with the members of a neighboring disciplinary language community where those same words are used with different meanings. As valuable as technical definitions are for other purposes, they can be impediments when *teaching for thinking*. Like so many of our colleagues who teach critical thinking in open-admissions general education courses, we have found that the less we rely on the technical vocabulary of any one discipline or professional field the more successful our students are in applying their critical thinking skills and in developing the positive habits of mind. We take to heart the "to name it is to tame it" error described in the box "About Technical Vocabulary" in Chapter 5.

3. The story as told here is derived from *CSI* episode 212, "*You've Got Male*" (episode #12, season 2), which first aired on December 20, 2001. The story as it is told in the *CSI* episode includes yet another twist that is not revealed as it is recounted in our chapter. Hint: "murder or accident" is a false dilemma if there are other possibilities. In the original script we learn that the wife did not purchase the life insurance policy, even though her credit card was used.

4. U.S. courts information provided online by the U.S. government. For criminal cases see **http://www.uscourts. gov/FederalCourts/UnderstandingtheFederalCourts/ HowCourtsWork/CriminalCases.aspx**. For civil cases see **http://www.uscourts.gov/FederalCourts/ UnderstandingtheFederalCourts/HowCourtsWork/ CivilCases.aspx**.

5. Legal Information Institute, Cornell University Law School. April 27, 2014 "Burden of Proof," Legal Dictionary at The Free Dictionary by Farlex, April 7, 2014. **http://legal-ictionary.thefreedictionary.com/ Standard+of+proof**

6. Beacham, G., "Prizefighter Rubin 'Hurricane' Carter Dies at 76." AP-Sports. April 20, 2014

7. Margaret K. Ma, Michael H. Woo, and Howard L. McLeod, "Genetic Basis of Drug Metabolism: Genetic Polymorphisms in the CYP Isoenzymes," *American Journal of Health-System Pharmacy* 59(21) (2002): 2061–2069. Also found at Medscape Today, August 10, 2009.

8. Raymond M. Lee, *Doing Research on Sensitive Topics* (London: Sage Publications, 1993); Delbert Charles Miller, *Handbook of Research Design and Social Measurement* (London: Sage Publications, 1991).

9. Scott Maxwell and Harold Delany, *Designing Experiments and Analyzing Data* (Belmont, CA: Wadsworth Publishing, 1990).

10. NOAA National Weather Service Lightning Safety 2013 Fatalities by State. April 9, 2014. **http://www. lightningsafety.noaa.gov/fatalities.htm**

11. NOAA National Weather Service Lightning Safety Myths and Facts. April 9, 2014. **http://www.lightningsafety. noaa.gov/facts_truth.htm**

12. *Little Journeys to the Homes of Great Teachers* by Elbert Hubbard (New York: Roycrafters), 1908.

13. Karen B. Williams, Colleen Schmidt, Terri S. I. Tilliss, Kris Wilkins, and Douglas R. Glasnapp, "Predictive Validity of Critical Thinking Skills and Disposition for the National Board dental hygiene examination: A Preliminary Investigation," *Journal of Dental Education* 70(5) (2006): 536–544; Kenneth L. McCall, Eric J. MacLaughlin, David S. Fike, and Beatrice Ruiz, "Preadmission Predictors of PharmD Graduates' Performance on the NAPLEX," *American Journal of Pharmacy Education* 15; 71(1) (2007): 5; The CCTST total score is a prepharmacy predictor of successful licensure as a pharmacist (NAPLEX test). Age, advanced science education courses, and previous BS or MS degree were not significantly correlated with NAPLEX; J. Giddens and G. W. Gloeckner, "The Relationship of Critical Thinking to Performance on the NCLEX-RN," *Journal of Nursing Education* 44(2)(2005): 85–89. CCTST total scores were higher in participants who passed the NCLEX-RN.

14. The power of a correlation to predict results depends on how strong the correlation is. Typically a correlation is reported as a decimal value between 0 and 1. For example, "the correlation of X and Y is 0.31." Researchers use this number to calculate how much the change in X can predict changes in Y, and vice versa. That calculation is simple. Called the "variance," it is correlation squared. If college success (measured as GPA) is correlated at 0.40 with critical thinking skill, then we could infer that 16 percent of the variation seen

in college GPA is predictable based on differences in critical thinking skills.

15. Randy M. Kaplan, "Using a Trainable Pattern-Directed Computer Program to Score Natural Language Item Responses," Educational Testing Service, Research Report #RR-91-31, 1992, August 10, 2009.

16. Donald E. Powers, Jill C. Burstein, Martin Chodorow, Mary E. Fowles, and Karen Kukich, "Comparing the Validity of Automated and Human Essay Scoring," Educational Testing Service, Research Report #RR-0010, 2000, August 10, 2009; Bloom, M., "Computers Can Score Essays As Well as Humans, Study Finds," *Ohio State Impact*. April 12, 2012 and April 10, 2014. **http://stateimpact.npr.org/ohio/2012/04/12/computers-can-score-student-essays-as-well-as-humans-study-finds/**

17. Sabra, Abdelhamid I. "Ibn al-Haytham" *Harvard Magazine* September-October 2003. **http://harvardmagazine.com/2003/09/ibn-al-haytham-html**.

18. U.S. Government, National Highway Traffic Safety Administration. April 10, 2014. **http://www-nrd.nhtsa.dot.gov/Pubs/812006.pdf**

19. "Ancient American's Genome Mapped," BBC News–Science & Environment. February 13, 2014.

20. Fidgen, Jo., "Do We Know Whether Pornography Harms People?" *BBC News Magazine*, June 25, 2013.

21. Webb, J., "Crickets in Two Places Fall Silent to Survive," BBC News – Science & Environment, May 29, 2014.

22. Mishori, R., A. Otubu, and A. Jones, "The dangers of colon cleansing," *Journal of Family Practice* 60(8) (2011): 454–457. Published Online May 5, 2011. Science Express Index.

Chapter 10

1. Herbert Alexander Simon, *Models of Man: Social and Rational* (New York: Wiley, 1957).

2. Facione, P. and N. Facione,. *Thinking and Reasoning in Human Decision Making* (San Jose, CA: The California Academic Press, 2007).

3. Thomas Glovitch, Dale Griffin, and Daniel Kahneman, Eds. *Heuristics and Biases: The Psychology of Intuitive Judgment* (Cambridge, UK: Cambridge University Press, 2002); Daniel Paul Slovic Kahneman, and Amos Tversky, Eds, *Judgment under Uncertainty: Heuristics and Biases* (Cambridge, UK: Cambridge University Press, 1982); Steven A. Sloman, "Two Systems of Reasoning," *Heuristics and Biases: The psychology of intuitive judgment*, Eds. Thomas Glovitch, Dale Griffin, and Daniel Kahneman (Cambridge, UK: Cambridge University Press, 2002); pp. 379–396; Daniel Kahneman and Dale T. Miller, "Norm theory: comparing reality to its alternatives," *Heuristics and Biases: The psychology of intuitive judgment*, Eds. Thomas Glovitch, Dale Griffin, and Daniel Kahneman (Cambridge, UK: Cambridge University Press, 2002); pp. 348–366.

4. My research colleagues and I recommend avoiding use of the word *intuition*. We are puzzled by claims of justified true beliefs—knowledge—that go beyond observations or direct personal experience and yet are not preceded or preconditioned by some degree of interpretation, analysis, or inference, whether reflective or unreflective. Perhaps there is such a thing as intuitive knowledge, ineffable, immediate, mystical, and true. Even so, by definition such knowledge, if it is indeed knowledge, is beyond the scope of inter-subjective verification and science. That which is said to be "known" by intuition is, by definition, placed outside possible connections with other evidence-based, replicable, or falsifiable knowledge. Hence, other humans cannot, in principle, confirm or disconfirm that what is asserted to be known by means of intuition. "Special knowledge," available only to one, is always and ever to be suspect. Healthy skepticism demands that it be rejected. We respectfully decline to drink that Kool-Aid. Another reason we have deep ethical concerns about appeals to "intuition" as a basis for justifying beliefs as true or decisions as reasonable is that we seek accountability for knowledge and for action. In matters of importance, including the decisions made in professional practice contexts—such as medicine, law, government, business, and the military—some appeal to "gut feelings" or "intuition" because they are either unable or unwilling to explain their judgments. In effect, they seek the cover of "intuition" because they do not wish to explain their judgments, they cannot explain their judgments, or they do not want to permit others to evaluate those judgments or those explanations. How do we know this? Our research team includes people with many decades of professional practice experience involving health care, management, legal, and leadership responsibilities. We realize the fundamental inadequacies of appeals to intuition and gut feeling. These experiences, in part, motivated us to look more deeply into decision making.

5. Croskerry, P., "Audio Interview," New England Journal of Medicine, 2013. 368: 2445–2448. June 27, 2013.

6. Croskerry, P., "Audio Interview," New England Journal of Medicine, 2013. 368: 2445–2448. June 27, 2013.

7. Shelly E. Taylor, "The availability bias in social perception and interaction" *Judgment under Uncertainty: Heuristics and Biases*, Eds. Daniel Kahneman, Paul Slovic, and Amos Tversky (Cambridge, UK: Cambridge University Press, 1982), pp. 190–200; Baruch Fischhoff, "Attribution theory and judgment under uncertainty," *New directions in attribution Research*, Eds. John. H. Harvey, William John Ickes, and Robert F. Kidd (Hillsdale, NJ: Erlbaum, 1976); Herbert Alexander Simon, *Models of Man: Social and Rational* (New York: Wiley, 1957).

8. Gerd Gigerenzer, Jean Czerlinski, and Laura Martignon, "How good are fast and frugal heuristics?" *Heuristics and Biases: The Psychology of Intuitive Judgment*, Eds. Thomas Gilovich, Dale W. Griffin, and Daniel Kahneman (Cambridge, UK: Cambridge University Press, 2002), pp. 559–581.

9. Paul Slovic, Melissa Finucane, Ellen Peters, and Donald G. MacGregor, "The affect heuristic," *Heuristics and*

Biases: The Psychology of Intuitive Judgment, Eds. Thomas Gilovich, Dale W. Griffin, and Daniel Kahneman (Cambridge, UK: Cambridge University Press, 2002), pp. 397–420; Norbert Schwarz, "Feelings as information: Moods influence judgments and processing Strategies," *Heuristics and Biases: The Psychology of Intuitive Judgment*, Eds. Thomas Gilovich, Dale W. Griffin, and Daniel Kahneman (Cambridge, UK: Cambridge University Press, 2002), pp. 534–547.

10. Oswald Huber, "Information-processing operators in decision making," *Process and Structure on Human Decision Making*, Eds. Henry Montgomery and Ola Svenson (Chichester, UK: John Wiley & Sons, 1989) pp. 3–21; Allen Newell and Herbert Alexander Simon, *Human Problem Solving* (Englewood Cliffs, NJ: Prentice Hall, 1972).

11. Paul Slovic, Melissa Finucane, Ellen Peters, and Donald G. MacGregor, "The affect heuristic," *Heuristics and Biases: The Psychology of Intuitive Judgment*, Eds. Thomas Gilovich, Dale W. Griffin, and Daniel Kahneman (Cambridge, UK: Cambridge University Press, 2002), pp. 397–420.

12. Phillip Waite, "Campus Landscaping in Recruitment and Retention: The Package Is the Product," presented at the 2007 annual Noel Levitz conference on enrolment management, Orlando, FL, 2007.

13. Business students may be interested in how the Turning Leaf brand applied a "Blue Ocean" Business strategy to this and made tremendous gains in a very competitive market. Chan Kim, W., and Renee Mauborgne, *Blue Ocean Strategy* (Boston, MA: Harvard Business School Corporation, 2005).

14. Koehler, D. J., "Explanation, Imagination and Confidence in Judgment," *Psychological Bulletin* 110 (1991): 499–519; Koch, S. J., "Availability and inference in predictive judgment," *Journal of Experimental Psychology, Learning, Memory and Cognition* 10 (1984): 649–662.

15. Daniel Kahneman, Paul Slovic, and Amos Tversky, Eds. *Judgment under Uncertainty: Heuristics and Biases* (Cambridge, UK: Cambridge University Press, 1982); Amos Tversky and Daniel Kahneman, "Availability: A Heuristic for Judging Frequency and Probability," *Cognitive Psychology* 5 (1973): 207–232.

16. Albert Bandura, "Self-Efficacy: Toward a Unifying Theory of Behavioral Change," *Psychological Review* 84(2) (1977): 191–215; Albert Bandura, "Self-Efficacy Mechanism in Physiological Activation and Health-Promoting Behavior," *Adaptation, learning and effect*, Eds. J. Madden, IV, S. Matthysse, and J. Barchas (New York: Raven Press, 1989).

17. Norbert Schwarz and Leigh Ann Vaughn, "The availability heuristic revisited: Ease of recall and content of recall as distinct sources of information," *Heuristics and Biases: The Psychology of Intuitive Judgment*, Eds. Thomas Gilovich, Dale W. Griffin, and Daniel Kahneman (Cambridge, UK: Cambridge University Press, 2002) 103–119; Daniel Kahneman, Paul Slovic, and Amos Tversky, Eds. *Judgment under Uncertainty: Heuristics and Biases* (Cambridge, UK: Cambridge University Press, 1982), p. 11.

18. Daniel Kahneman, Paul Slovic, and Amos Tversky, Eds. *Judgment under Uncertainty: Heuristics and Biases* (Cambridge, UK: Cambridge University Press, 1982); Irving Lester Janis and Leon Mann, *Decision-Making: A Psychological Analysis of Conflict, Choice, and Commitment* (New York: The Free Press, 1977).

19. Paul Rozin and Carol Nemeroff, "Sympathetic Magical Thinking: The Contagion and Similarity 'Heuristics.'" *Heuristics and Biases: The Psychology of Intuitive Judgment*, Eds. Thomas Gilovich, Dale W. Griffin, and Daniel Kahneman (Cambridge, UK: Cambridge University Press, 2002), pp. 201–216; Daniel Kahneman and Shane Frederick, "Representativeness Revisited: Attribute Substitution in Intuitive Judgment," *Heuristics and Biases: The Psychology of Intuitive Judgment*, Eds. Thomas Gilovich, Dale W. Griffin, and Daniel Kahneman (Cambridge, UK: Cambridge University Press, 2002), pp. 49–81. In the early heuristics literature, "representativeness" covered a wide range of things. Here we use "representation" as the name for some and "association" as the name for others. At times, these heuristics are found in the literature under the title "similarity."

20. Ball, J., "Stereotypes 'evolve like language,' Say researchers." BBC News–Science & Environment. Sept. 8, 2012.

21. "Bigotry against Jews and Muslims on the Rise, Says US" BBC News–US & Canada. May 20, 2103.

22. Katrandjian, O., "Illegal Alien Who Saved Child Is Center of Debate on New Policy for Illegal Immigrants," *ABC News*, August 20, 2011.

23. Deborah Solomon, "Questions for Ayaan Hirsi Ali, The Feminist," *New York Times Magazine*, May 21, 2010, p. 14.

24. Wyant, A. M., "Offering Hope by the Bucket," Tip of the Spear, MacDill AFB: US Joint Special Operations Command. April 2012.

25. Dualistic thinking divides the world into black and white with no shades of gray. For dualistic thinkers, all problems have right answers or wrong answers only. But psychological dualism is a broader construct. It is better understood in the context of cognitive development. The "Us vs. Them" dynamic, as cognitive heuristic, can influence decisions made by people whose cognitive development has progressed beyond dualistic thinking in many domains.

26. David Berreby, *Us and Them: Understanding Your Tribal Mind* (New York: Little, Brown and Company, 2005).

27. Robert J. Robinson, Dacher Keltner, Andrew Ward, and Lee Ross, "Actual vs. assumed differences in construal: 'Naïve Realism' in intergroup perception and conflict," *Journal of Personality and Social Psychology* 68 (1995): 404–417.

28. Amos Tversky and Daniel Kahneman, "Judgment under uncertainty: heuristics and biases," *Science* 185 (1974): 1124–1131; Gretchen B. Chapman and Eric J. Johnson,

"Incorporating the irrelevant: Anchors in judgments of belief and value," *Heuristics and Biases: The Psychology of Intuitive Judgment*, Eds. Thomas Gilovich, Dale W. Griffin, and Daniel Kahneman (Cambridge, UK: Cambridge University Press, 2002), pp. 122–138.

29. Thompson, S. C., W. Armstrong, and C. Thomas, "Illusions of Control, Underestimations, and Accuracy: A Control Heuristic Explanation," *Psychological Bulletin* 123(2) (1998): 143–161.

30. Myers, D., "Self-Serving Bias," in Brochman, J. (Ed). *This Book Will Make You Smarter*. New York: Harper Perennial, p. 37.

31. Schultz, T. R., and D. Wells, "Judging the Intentionality of Action-outcomes," *Developmental Psychology* 21 (1985): 83–89.

32. Baruch Fischhoff and Ruth Beyth, "'I Knew It Would Happen'—Remembered Probabilities of Once Future Things," *Organizational Behavior and Human Performance* 13 (1975): 1–16.

33. Irving Lester Janis and Leon Mann, *Decision Making: A Psychological Analysis of Conflict, Choice, and Commitment* (New York: The Free Press, 1977).

34. James G. March and Chip Heath, *A Primer on Decision Making: How Decisions Happen* (New York: The Free Press, 1994); Daniel Kahneman, Paul Slovic, and Amos Tversky, Eds. *Judgment under Uncertainty: Heuristics and Biases* (Cambridge, UK: Cambridge University Press, 1982); Irving Lester Janis and Leon Mann, *Decision Making: A Psychological Analysis of Conflict, Choice, and Commitment* (New York: The Free Press, 1977); Daniel Kahneman and Amos Tversky, *Choices, Values, and Frames* (Cambridge, UK: Cambridge University Press, 2000); Paul Slovic, "Limitations of the Mind of Man: Implications for Decision making in the Nuclear Age," *Oregon Research Institute Bulletin* 11 (1971): 41–49.

35. **http://www.npr.org/blogs/health/2011/02/04/133371076/how-keeping-little-girls-squeaky-clean-could-make-them-sick**

36. Walking While Black

Chapter 11

1. Montero, D. "Oil and Water," *Easy Reader–An Edition of the Register*, Hermosa Beach, CA. April 17, 2014.

2. The interview excerpt and the associated decision map are published in Noreen C. Facione and Peter A. Facione, *Thinking and Reasoning in Human Decision Making* (Millbrae, CA: The California Academic Press, 2007) 108–111. Used with permission from Insight Assessment-Measuring thinking worldwide. **www.insightassessment.com**.

3. Halle, Kay. *A Treasury of Winston Churchill's Wit*. Cleveland, OH: World Publishing Company, 1966. p. 308.

4. "Decision-critical criteria" is a short phrase that refers to those criteria the decision maker deems to be important and relevant for the purpose of evaluating options. Two people working together to make a decision often agree to use the same decision-critical criteria because they both think that the same things are important and

relevant when evaluating options. That said, they may not agree on the relative priority or importance of their various criteria. "Tastes great!" NO, "Less filling!"

5. Henry Montgomery, "From cognition to action: the search for dominance in decision making," *Process and Structure in Human Decision Making*, Eds. Henry Montgomery and Ola Svenson (Chichester, UK: John Wiley & Sons, 1989), 23–49.

6. Henry Montgomery, "From cognition to action: The search for dominance in decision making," *Process and Structure in Human Decision Making*, Eds. Henry Montgomery and Ola Svenson (Chichester, UK: John Wiley & Sons, 1989), 24.

7. Henry Montgomery, "From cognition to action: the search for dominance in decision making," *Process and Structure in Human Decision Making*, Eds. Henry Montgomery and Ola Svenson (Chichester, UK: John Wiley & Sons, 1989).

8. Henry Montgomery "Decision Rules and the Search for a dominance structure: Towards a process model of decision making," *Analyzing and Aiding Decision Processes*, Eds. Patrick Humphreys, Ola Svenson, and Anna Vari (Amsterdam/Budapest: North Holland and Hungarian Academic Press, 1983), 343–369.

9. Henry Montgomery, "From cognition to action: the search for dominance in decision making," *Process and Structure in Human Decision Making*, Eds. Henry Montgomery and Ola Svenson (Chichester, UK: John Wiley & Sons, 1989), 26.

10. Henry Montgomery "Decision Rules and the search for a dominance structure: Towards a process model of decision making," *Analyzing and Aiding Decision Processes*, Eds. Patrick Humphreys, Ola Svenson, and Anna Vari (Amsterdam/Budapest: North Holland and Hungarian Academic Press, 1983), 343–369.

11. Croskerry, P., Singhai, G., and Mamede, S., "Cognitive debiasing 2: impediments to and strategies for change," BMJ Quality & Safety. First published online August 30, 2013. October 2013, Vol. 22. Supplement 2.

12. This scenario about a serial killer was inspired by Michael Connelly's novel *The Scarecrow* (New York: Little, Brown and Company, 2009).

13. Washington, J. "No Gray Area: Beliefs Shape Views of Brown Killing," AP News. September 1, 2014.

Chapter 12

1. This paragraph and the next are paraphrases from the narrative of "When Knowledge Conquered Fear," Season 1, Episode 2 March 23, 2014, *Cosmos: A Space Time Odyssey*, narrated by Neil deGrasse Tyson. FOX Television.

2. Anderson, J. R., Cognitive Psychology and Its Implications, 7th Ed. (New York: Worth Publishers, 2009); Shaffer,. D. R. and Kipp, K., Developmental Psychology: Childhood and Adolescence, 9th Ed. (Belmont, CA: Cengage, 2013).

3. Osen, L.M., *Women in Mathematics*. Cambridge, MA: MIT Press, 1974, pp. 21–32.

4. Paraphrased from *Cosmos: A Space Time Odyssey*. FOX Television. Season 1, Episode 2. "When Knowledge Conquered Fear," March 23, 2014.

5. Hartmann, T. "Shouldn't GM Get the Death Penalty for 57 Cent Premeditated Murder?" Blog: Thom Hartmann Program. April 3, 2014.

6. Licon, A. G. "Activists: Mexican women giving birth in street," AP News. March 28, 2014.

7. "Did Hyman Minsky find the secret behind financial crashes?" BBC News Magazine. March 24, 2014.

8. "Google under fire from European media tycoon," BBC News Technology. April 18, 2014.

9. Paphitis, N. "Greek seaside town highlights unemployment drama," AP News. Feb. 13, 2014.

10. *Traffic*, Hollywood, CA: Universal Studios, dir. Steven Soderbergh, perf. Michael Douglas, Don Cheadle, Benicio Del Toro, Dennis Quaid, and Catherine Zeta-Jones, 2000.

11. From Tom Franklin, *Crooked Letter, Crooked Letter*, William Morrow (2010). Copyright © 2010 Tom Franklin. All rights reserved.

12. Allen Newell, *Toward Unified Theories of Cognition* (Cambridge, MA: Harvard University Press, 1990).

13. Carolyn Lochhead and Carla Marinucci, "Freedom and Fear Are at War," The *San Francisco Chronicle*. September 21, 2001, September 1, 2009. **http://www.sfgate.com/politics/article/FREEDOM-AND-FEAR-ARE-AT-WAR-MESSAGE-TO-2877442.php**

14. *Art of War*, Sun Tzu.; Samuel B Griffith. Art of War. Clare, 1963.

15. Michael Scriven, *Reasoning* (New York: McGraw-Hill, 1976).

16. **http://SecondLife.com**

17. **http://www.bbc.co.uk/news/technology-14277728**

18. Freud, Sigmund. *New Introductory Lectures on Psychoanalysis*, translated and edited by James Strachey (New York: W.W. Norton, 1965). p. 72.

19. Gershenfeld, Neil, "Truth is a Model," *This Will Make You Smarter*, Ed. Brockman, J. (New York: Harper Perrennial, 2012), 72.

20. Chris Rock, *Chris Rock: Bigger and Blacker*, HBO Productions, writ. Chris Rock, perf. Chris Rock, 1999.

21. **http://www.thedailyshow.com/watch/thu-august-19-2010/extremist-makeover—homeland-edition**

22. **http://abcnews.go.com/Video/playerIndex?id=4826897**

23. Morgan, J. "How to win at rock-paper-scissors," BBC News–Science & Environment. May 2, 2014.

24. You may recognize this as the "Null Hypothesis." The null hypothesis proposes that there is no relationship between the events being observed.

Chapter 13

1. Craighill, P.M, and Clement, S. "Support for same-sex marriage hits new high; half say Constitution guarantees right." *The Washington Post–Politics*. March 4, 2014.

2. Jones, J.M., "Majority of Americans continue to oppose Gay marriage," Gallup Politics. March 27, 2009.

3. On November 6, 2014 the U.S. Court of Appeals for the Sixth Circuit upheld bans on same sex marriage in four states. Only weeks before, on October 5, the U.S. Supreme Court announced it would not hear appeals by states where bans on same sex marriage had been overturned by their regional U.S. Circuit Courts. See also, "Gay Marriage," at **http://gaymarriage.procon.org/view.resource.php?resourceID=004857**

4. Everitt, L., "Ten key moments in the history of marriage." *BBC News Magazine March* 13, 2012.

5. See the landmark in favor of the plaintiffs in the *Cooper-Harris* case, August 29, 2013. The Southern Poverty Law Center (SPLC)brought the case to court when the Cooper-Harris family could not find any for-profit legal firms that would take the case. The plaintiffs challenged the constitutionality of parts of the Federal Defense of Marriage Act (DOMA). You can easily find the ruling at **www.splcenter.org** (the SPLC website). Just put "Cooper-Harris" into the website's search field, top right.

6. If you own corporate stock, and if a corporation is a person, do you own part of a person? And if a person owns a percentage of or all of another person, then is that owner a slaveholder. Perhaps a corporation should not be considered a person, even if the U.S. Supreme Court prefers to use the analogy.

7. Mildred Loving, a black woman, married Richard Loving, a white man. The State of Virginia prosecuted Richard and sentenced him to prison for marrying across racial lines. In 1967 Mildred Loving appealed to the Supreme Court and won. Mildred died in 2008. Martin, D., "Mildred Loving, who Battled Ban on mixed-race marriage, dies at 68." *New York Times*. May 6, 2008.

8. Public document–ruling on the case of M. Kendall Wright, et al. v. State of Arkansas, et al. Circuit Court of Pulaski County, Arkansas. Second Division. Case No. 60CV-13-2662.

9. "Lutherans accept Clergy in 'Lifelong' same-sex relationships," **CNN.com**. August 21, 2009, September 2, 2009.

10. BrainyQuote, Albert Einstein quote. May 9, 2014. **http://www.brainyquote.com/quotes/quotes/a/alberteins143096.html**

11. If a health care professional is making this argument, then to analyze it properly we should inform ourselves about the meaning of "access" in that language community. "Access to adequate health care" is more than "has some level of health insurance" or "can go to an emergency room." Adequate health care, as defined by health care professionals, includes three things: screening, diagnosis, and treatment. These three are necessary not only to manage a person's care but also to prevent illness and to mitigate the morbidity and mortality associated with disease discovered at an already acute or advanced stage.

12. Chapter 2 clarifies the differences between critical thinking skills and critical thinking habits of mind.

13. R. Pigott, "Dutch rethink Christianity for a doubtful world," BBC News Europe. August 5, 2011.

14. "Thomas Jefferson Quotes," Brainy Quote. September 2, 2009.

15. "Galileo Galilei," Wisdom Quotes. September 2, 2009.

16. Plato, *Euthyphro*, trans. Benjamin Jowett, 380 b.c.e., September 2, 2009; Ian Kidd, "Socrates," *The Encyclopedia of Philosophy*, Vol. 7, Ed. Paul Edwards (New York: Macmillan Publishing, 1967), 480–486.

17. John Locke, "Of wrong assent or error" in *Essay Concerning Human Understanding*, 1690, Book IV, Chapter XX.

18. John Howard Griffin, *Black Like Me* (New York: Signet, 1961).

19. S. Hirst, 2006, *I Am the Grand Canyon: The Story of the Havasupai People*, (Grand Canyon, AZ: The Grand Canyon Association), xiv.

20. This is the language of Mississippi ballot initiative "Proposition 26." It was designed by its supporters to put a stop to abortions. It implied that abortion is the taking of a human person's life, which would be a homicide. In November 2011 Mississippi voters rejected this ballot initiative.

21. The premise of the popular 2009 sci-fi film District 9.

22. The "Singularity Movement" is a utopian vision of golden future when the human mind and technology interact at such a deep level that the two will have become one and a new and superior intelligence will have emerged from that union. See, Vance, A. "Merely Human? So Yesterday," *The New York Times*, Sunday Business section page. June 13, 2010.

23. *Paul's First Letter to the Corinthians*, The Holy Bible, Chapter 13, verse 13.

Chapter 14

1. Richard L. DeGowin, *Diagnostic Examination*, 6th ed. (New York: McGraw-Hill, 1994,), 945.

2. Bob Arnebeck, "A Short History of Yellow Fever in the U.S.," 30 January 30, 2008, September 3, 2009. **http://www.geocities.com/bobarnebeck/history.html**

3. Lest we think that plagues of unknown origin no longer ravage and kill, consider the thousands of young men dying of kidney disease in Central America. Nobody knows why. Pesticides, food poisoning, chronicxdehydration, chronic fatigue, what? And why only the men, and not the women? For more on this medical mystery see the *BBC Science* report "Mystery Kidney Disease in Central America Dec. 11, 2011. Along with the mystery illnesses, some of our old enemies are not dead yet too. As we noted earlier in the book, polio is making a most unwelcome comeback in 2014. And as we write a second case of the deadly MERS Coronavirus has been discovered in the United States. Visit the Center for Disease Control for details.

4. Signy, H. "Exclusive interview with Professor Elizabeth Blackburn," Reader's Digest Asia. July 30, 2010.

5. 2001: *A Space Odyssey*, Warner Brothers Studios, director Stanley Kubrick, performers Gary Lockwood and Keir Dullea, 1968.

6. At three key places in this film an obelisk is visible on-screen. One interpretation is that the obelisk's presence indicates moments of extraterrestrial intervention into human affairs; another is that these are moments of supreme insight, or perhaps divine inspiration. The first appearance of the obelisk is just before the man-ape creature realizes that he can use a leg bone as a tool to club another creature to death. This fictional depiction of the first realization of leg-bone-as-killing-tool includes moments intended by the filmmaker to show deliberation and stimulation. Whether the idea came to the man-ape by insight, extraterrestrial intervention, or divine inspiration is immaterial. What is important is that the man-ape considered the notion and decided to act on the hypothesis that a leg bone could be used to kill. Whatever its source, subsequent events supported that hypothesis.

7. Comparative reasoning, discussed in Chapter 12, is probabilistic too. But because the points of comparison might be conceptual, rather than experimental, comparative reasoning is not empirical.

8. "Classic Quotes," The Quotations Page, September 3, 2009. **http://www.quotationspage.com/quote/24972.html**

9. See, for example, "Ex-sceptic says climate change is down to humans," *BBC News–Science & Environment*. July 20, 2012.

10. Goodreads. > Stephen Hawking > Quotes > Quotable Quote. December 2, 2014. **http://www.goodreads.com/quotes/144768-one-is-always-a-long-way-from-solving-a-problem**.

11. **http://www.nytimes.com/2010/08/13/health/research/13alzheimer.html**

12. A Senate report concluded that waterboarding and other "enhanced" interrogation methods did not produce any important evidence in the search for Osama bin Laden. Klapper, B., "Senate torture report examines hunt for bin Laden," AP News. March 31, 2014.

13. **http://thinkexist.com/quotes/carol_greider/**

14. This is not a null hypothesis, but it is a hypothesis expressing a relationship among natural phenomena. It is not necessary that a hypothesis be expressed as an "if . . . then" statement, only that it can be converted into one. For example, "The reflexes of a person who drives a motor vehicle for five or more hours without a rest period will have deteriorated by 30 percent or more as compared to his or her reflexes after only one to four hours of driving "can be rewritten as "If a person drives a motor vehicle for five or more hours without a rest period, then the person's reflexes will have deteriorated by 30 percent or more as compared with only one to four hours of driving."

15. "Galileo Galilei Quotes," Brainy Quote, September 3, 2009. **http://www.brainyquote.com/quotes/authors/g /galileo_galilei.html**

16. Delbert Charles Miller, *Handbook of Research Design and Social Measurement*, 5th ed. (Newbury Park, CA: Sage Publications, Inc., 1991); John W. Creswell, *Research Design Qualitative and Quantitative Approaches*

(Thousand Oaks, CA: Sage Publications Inc., 1994); Stephen B. Hulley, Steven R. Cummings, Warren S. Browner, Deborah G. Grady, and Thomas B. Newman, *Designing Clinical Research* (Philadelphia, PA: Lippincott Williams & Wilkins, 2001); and Emanuel Mason and William J. Bramble, *Understanding and Conducting Research* (New York: McGraw-Hill, 1989).

17. The "empirical disciplines" as used here refer to the full spectrum of social, behavioral, natural, and physical sciences and all the other areas of study or professional fields, by whatever name, that fundamentally rely on empirical reasoning in the generation of new knowledge.

18. For more on how the peer review process works or should work in science see **http://www.nature.com/ nature/peerreview/debate/index.html**

19. Druyan, A. & Soter, S., *Cosmos: A Spacetime Odyssey* mobile device app issued May 2014, Index, "science."

20. Philip, A. "Dallas Releases 43 from Ebola Quarantine. Officials Plead for Compassion Not Stimga." *Washington Post*. October 20, 2014.

21. "Quotations by author: Hippocrates," The Quotations Page, September 3, 2009. **http://www.quotationspage. com/quotes/Hippocrates**

22. "The Immortals" episode of the FOX Television 2014 series. *Cosmos–A Space Time Odyssey*. May 18, 2014.

23. 2014 *National Climate Assessment*. U.S. Global Change Research Program, Washington, DC.

Chapter 15

24. **http://www.kingsspeech.com/cast.html**

1. FOX's show *Hell's Kitchen* is in its 15th season as we write the third edition.

2. **http://www.collegiatelearningassessment.org/files/ ComputerAssistedScoringofCLA.pdf**

3. **http://www.insidehighered.com/news/2011/02/21/ debate_over_reliability_of_automated_essay_ grading**

4. Since most college courses are organized into disciplines, professional fields, or departments, "academic paper" may still be too broad. You should think about what is required to write an academic paper that fits the writing conventions of the discipline/professional field/ department that sponsors your course.

5. **http://www.collegeboard.com/student/apply/ essayskills/9406.html**. But, if you end up on the home page for the College Board, simply put "write essay" into the search box there.

6. Orwell, G. Essay, "Politics and the English Language," 1946.

7. **http://en.wikiquote.org/wiki/Thomas_Edison**

8. **http://www.aclu.org/blog/free-speech-technology- andliberty/free-speech-and-bart-cell-phone-censorship**

9. Some states and local governments do not supply voter information materials that are this complete. But many do. If you have never seen materials of this kind, you can locate several recent examples on the Internet. For example, here is one from California's 2010 election. **http://voterguide.sos.ca.gov/propositions/19/**

10. **http://www.dartmouth.edu/~writing/materials/faculty/ pedagogies/process.shtml**

11. **http://knol.google.com/k/english-student/how-to- writean-effective-essay/3iocn0q161tw0/1#**

12. Stephen King, *On Writing: A Memoir of the Craft* (New York: Pocket Books, 2000).

13. *Rubric for Evaluating Written Argumentation* © 2012, C. A. Gittens and Measured Reasons LLC. Published by Insight Assessment. Reprinted with permission of the authors and publisher.

14. NPR, August 16, 2011. "Magician Penn Jillette Says 'God, No!' To Religion."

15. **http://www.nypost.com/p/news/national/diet_soda_in_ fat_shocker_ylZ9hr7cn6VA17iXiaLupM**

Chapter 16

1. Academic cheating scandals have plagued college athletics, for example, the University of Minnesota basketball program. See **http://news.minnesota. publicradio.org/features/199903/11_newsroom_ cheating/** and the Florida State University football program, **http://sports.espn.go.com/ncf/news/ story?id=3958292**.

2. Beard, A. and Dalesio, E.P., "Probe: UNC Academic Fraud Was 'Shadow Curriculum'." AP News, October 22, 2014. Stripling, J. "Widespread Nature of Chapel Hill's Academic Fraud Is Laid Bare," *Chronicle of Higher Education*. October 23, 2014.

3. Perez-Pena, R. "Students Disciplined in Harvard Scandal," *New York Times*. February 1, 2013.

4. "Cheating Scandal Snares Hundreds in U. of Central Florida Course." *The Chronicle of Higher Education*, November 9, 2010 and the 2011 update, "UCF reports more instances of academic dishonesty than in years past," **http://chronicle.com/blogs/ticker/cheating- scandal-snares-hundreds-in-u-of-central-florida- course/28200**. For a 2011 follow up, see **http://www. orlandosentinel.com/community/ucf/orl-ucf-academic- dishonesty-100611,0,7358652**.

5. **http://www.collegeotr.com/Wesleyan_University/gmat_ cheating_scandal_starts_a_frenzy_**

6. Mary-Jayne Kay, "Truth and Consequences: A Navy Scandal," CBS News, *48 Hours*. **http://www.cbsnews. com/stories/2002/05/30/48hours/main510629.shtml**.

7. David Epstein, "Cheating Scandal at Virginia," *Inside Higher Ed*, June 30, 2005. **http://www.insidehighered .com/news/2005/06/30/uva**.

8. "Admissions Exam Cheating Scandal Rocks Japan," The Kept-Up Academic Librarian, Steve B, March 1, 2011. **http://keptup.typepad.com/academic/2011/03/ admissions-exam-cheating-scandal-rocks-japan. html**. Yigal Schiefer, The Turko-File, "Turkey: A Cheating Scandal (of the Academic Kind) Grips the Country" May 12, 2011. **http://www.eurasianet.org/ node/63474s**.

9. "The Perfect Score," produced by Katherine Davis. Second segment in the *60 Minutes* episode presented by CBS on January 1, 2012.

10. The 2011. Number 1 overall draft pick and 2010 Heisman Trophy winner is described on the NFL Website as possessing many fine athletic attributes but as having had "several off-the-field issues and his character is in question." **http://www.nfl.com/draft/2011/profiles/cam-newton?id=2495455**. One of the questions raised by FOX Sports was whether he left the University of Florida because he was about to be expelled for multiple incidents of academic dishonesty, something he denies, as reported in a story by Erick Smith, November 10, 2010, in *USA Today*. **http://content.usatoday.com/communities/campusrivalry/post/2010/11/report-cam-newton-left-florida-after-three-charges-of-academic-cheating/1**. The Heisman Trophy is awarded each year by the Heisman Trust. According to its mission statement, "The Heisman Memorial Trophy annually recognizes the outstanding college football player whose performance best exhibits the pursuit of excellence with integrity." Emphasis added **http://www.heisman.com/trust/mission_statement.php**.

11. Various websites offer summaries of studies of academic dishonesty in college. The ETS Research Center's Ad Council Campaign aimed at Discouraging Academic Cheating, "Cheating is a personal foul," on **http://www.glass-castle.com/clients/www-nocheating-org/adcouncil/research/cheatingbackgrounder.html**. See also the On-Line Education Database "8 astonishing stats on academic cheating" at **http://oedb.org/library/features/8-astonishing-stats-on-academic-cheating**.

12. Here and throughout this chapter we rely on the plethora of fine introductory college level ethics textbooks, which are available today. Since this chapter is not intended to be a complete course in ethics, but only a discussion of how to apply critical thinking when thinking about ethical issues, we cannot hope to present contemporary theories of ethics in all the fullness and richness. We recommend the sections on ethics and ethical theories in the Stanford Encyclopedia of Philosophy. The listing of articles online can be found at **http://plato.stanford.edu/search/searcher.py?query=Ethics**.

13. Gittleson, K. "GM Switch Defect Death Toll Rises to 42 People," *BBC News - Business*. December 15, 2014.

14. McGrath, M. "Study shows 'brain doping' is common in amateur sport," BBC News–Science and Environment. January 14, 2014.

15. Perrone, M., "23andMe faces class action lawsuit in California," AP News. February 11, 2014.

16. Lucas, F. "VA Scandal Whistleblower: I Was Suspended for Refusing to Cook the Books on Wait Times," The Blaze. May 19, 2014.

17. Vivek Wadhwa on Ethics, BrainyQuote, May 19, 2014.

18. Each of the eight ethical imperatives here is rooted philosophically in a robust and valuable intellectual tradition. Each reflects wisdom gained through reflection and experience, refined over the centuries, by some of the most insightful members of the human community. None should be trivialized. All apply today. Each is worth serious consideration and study. Strong critical thinking applied to making practical ethical decisions about what to do in a given situation will give due consideration to the implications of each of these important and powerful principles.

19. We use the words *ethical/ethics* and *moral/morality* interchangeably here because these words are used interchangeably in ordinary discourse.

20. P. Facione, T. Attig, D. Scherer, *Ethics and Society* (Millbrae, CA: The California Academic Press, 2001). First edition published as *Values and Society*, Prentice-Hall, Englewood Cliffs, NJ 1978. Second edition as *Ethics and Society* (Englewood Cliffs, NJ: Prentice-Hall, 1990).

21. The return on investment of alternative investments can be compared by holding the time interval constant. This is achieved by measuring the rate of return as a percentage per year.

22. The decision, rendered on June 27, 2011, struck down a California law prohibiting the sale of violent video games. The decision was based on first amendment grounds, violent though they were, the games were seen as a form of protected free speech under the U.S. Constitution. The story was reported widely. Blogs, editorials, and commentaries quickly followed. One source for the basic story is **http://articles.sfgate.com/2011-06-28/news/29711342_1_violent-video-video-games-supreme-court**. Another is **http://www.nytimes.com/2011/06/28/us/28scotus.html**. In the philosophical opinion of the authors of this textbook, freedom of speech is an essential condition for a robust and open democracy.

23. The Dalai Lama: *A Policy of Kindness*, 1990. Goodreads.com. May 19, 2014.

24. Interest-based negotiation is a collaboration aimed at fulfilling the most central interests of both sides fully or at least partially. Interest-based negotiation can be contrasted with position-based negotiation. Negotiating based on the positions each of us takes on a given issue usually demands that one or both of us "give in" or compromise in ways that we feel loss. Position-based negotiation often involves a war of wills and an appetite risking the underlying relationship so one can "win." Interest-based negotiation moves people beyond their initial position or proposal and focuses on their underlying interests. For more on interest-based negotiation see the Thinking Critically box "About Successful Negotiating" in Chapter 4.

25. "Anchor babies" refers to children born in the United States while their parents are in the country illegally. The child's mother may have illegally immigrated to the United States intending that her child, when born, would be a citizen by virtue of the location of its birth.

26. Some interpret the "Golden Rule" cynically. One version is "Do Unto Others Before They Do Unto You" and another is "Those Who Have the Gold Make the Rules." What this tells us about the Golden Rule is that it is insufficient by itself as an ethical guide because it does not supply us with any particular ethical beliefs or core values. A swindler might say, "Hey I agree with the

Golden Rule, I plan to swindle you and if you are smart enough to swindle me, well that's fine too." If your core values are unethical, then the Golden Rule would imply that you are fine with others treating you unethically.

27. Search and watch a video interview with Ameneh Bahrami entitled, "Victim forgives man who disfigured her in acid attack" at BBC Middle East News' Web site.

28. Levintova, H., "Is Giving Food to the Homeless Illegal in Your City Too?" *Mother Jones*. Nov. 13, 2014

29. **http://fusionaut.videosift.com/video/How-To-Brainwash-a-Nation**

30. Lawrence Kohlberg (Oct, 1974). "Education, Moral Development and Faith." *Journal of Moral Education*, 4(1): 5–16; Anne Colby; J. Gibbs, M. Lieberman, and L. Kohlberg. *A Longitudinal Study of Moral Judgment: A Monograph for the Society of Research in Child Development* (Chicago, IL: The University of Chicago Press, 1983).

Chapter 17

31. Consider the simple declarative statement, "Nine billion human beings will inhabit the earth in the year 2050." Given the current population and given current birth and mortality rates and assuming these rates do not change in the future, we can be reasonably confident that this prediction is probably true. And while there is great value for some purposes in differentiating what is true from what might probably be true, the level of logic, which addresses that refinement is beyond the scope of this chapter. The logic of declarative statements at the level described in this chapter functions well in the "timeless" universe of algebra and computer circuitry.

32. Pronounced "till-dah," with the emphasis on the first syllable.

33. Logicians call this the "inclusive" sense of the disjunction. "Inclusive" meaning that both options might be true. But occasionally we use the expression "either   or   " to mean that we must select one or the other of the two options, but not both. For example, "For income tax purposes everyone living in the country is either required to file a tax return or not required to file a tax return, but not both." Or, for example, "Either the Denver Broncos won Super Bowl XLVIII or the Seattle Seahawks won Super Bowl XLVIII." When the option of both being true is excluded, the disjunctive expression is used in what logicians call the "exclusive" sense.

34. The word "interpretation" used in the context of this level of logic can be understood as the assignment of a meaning to each statement letter. There are two ways to create an interpretation at this level of logic. One is to associate a specific simple declarative natural language statement with each statement letter. We have done that in several of the exercises. The other way is to associate a truth value with each statement letter. A truth table shows every possible interpretation of the statement letters used in constructing a given symbolic logic formula. Each row of the table represents one of the possible interpretations.

Credits

Photo Credits

Chapter 1: Page 1 (c): Measured Reasons LLC; 2 (tr): Measured Reasons LLC; 4 (tl): Warner Brothers/Everett Collection; 4 (br): Rex Features/AP Images; 5 (tr): Measured Reasons LLC; 6 (br): Ostill/Shutterstock.com; 6 (tl): Measured Reasons LLC; 7 (bl): Colin D. Young/Shutterstock; 8 (tl): Measured Reasons LLC; 8 (tr): Measured Reasons LLC; 9 (tl): Measured Reasons LLC; 10 (tl): Christy Bowe/Globe Photos/ZUMA Press, Inc/Alamy; 14 (c): Scott Houston/Alamy.

Chapter 2: Page 18 (c): Universal/Everett Collection; 19 (br): SPACE BY NASA/Alamy; 24 (br): Everett Collection; 25 (bl): Melinda Sue Gordon/AP Images; 28 (bl): Everett Collection; 32 (tl): Marc Bryan-Brown/Getty Images; 33 (bl): AFP PHOTO/YOUTUBE/AFP/Getty Images/Newscom; 35 (bl): bikeriderlondon/Shutterstock; 35 (br): i ballet/Alamy.

Chapter 3: Page 39 (c): joefoxphoto/Alamy; 40 (bc): Jaimie Duplass/Shutterstock; 41 (br): Kolett/Shutterstock; 42 (br): ©Monkey Business Images/Shutterstock.com; 47 (tl): stokkete/Fotolia; 47 (br): Dave Granlund; 49 (bl): Mika/Comet/Corbis; 50 (bl): William Perugini/Shutterstock; 53 (br): US Food and Drug Administration FDA; 54 (bl): Gino's Premium Images/Alamy; 57 (tl): Everett Collection/Newscom; 58 (tl): Huntstock/Getty Images; 59 (bl): imagebroker.net/SuperStock; 60 (l): VladisChern/Shutterstock; 60 (c): karam Miri/Shutterstock; 60 (r): Ancient Art & Architecture Collection Ltd/Alamy.

Chapter 4: Page 63 (c): Everett Collection Inc.; 65 (tl): GUSTOIMAGES/Science Photo Library/Alamy; 66 (tl): Colin Underhill/Alamy; 66 (tr): Measured Reasons LLC; 67 (bl): Herb Block Foundation; 67 (tr): Herb Block Foundation; 70 (tr): vbaleha/Fotolia; 71 (br): Gregory Wrona/Alamy; 72 (tc): 20th Century Fox Film Corp/Everett Collection; 74 (c): larry1235/Shutterstock; 75 (bl): wavebreakmedia/Shutterstock; 76 (br): spotmatikphoto/Fotolia; 77 (bc): ikonoklast_hh/Fotolia; 79 (tl): aijohn784/Fotolia; 90 (tr): Measured Reasons LLC.

Chapter 5: Page 88 (c): Golden Pixels LLC/Shutterstock; 96 (tl): J.P. Wilson/Icon SMI; 98 (br): Peter Essick/Aurora Photos/Alamy; 99 (tr): Anatoly Vartanov/Fotolia.

Chapter 6: Page 113 (c): akg-images/Newscom; 114 (bl): Rights Free; 115 (bl): David Woolley/Stockbyte/Getty Images; 115 (br): Alexander Raths/Shutterstock; 118 (tl): Everett Collection; 119 (r): Michael Hitoshi/Digital Vision/Getty Images; 119 (tl): Lisa F. Young/Shutterstock; 119 (c): Marcy Maloy/Digital Vision/Getty Images; 120 (tl): moodboard/Alamy; 120 (br): Columbia/courtesy Everett Collection/Everett Collection; 124 (bl): Susan Montgomery/Alamy; 125 (tr): Jorg Greuel/Photodisc/Jupiter Images; 125 (bl): Dorling Kindersley/Dorling Kindersley, Ltd; 126 (bl): Stuart Jenner/Shutterstock; 128 (bl): White House/AP Images; 129 (tr): Flashon Studio/Shutterstock; 130 (bl): Lioness Media Arts Inc./Shutterstock; 131 (tr): HANDOUT/MCT/Newscom; 133 (tl): World History Archive/Image Asset Management Ltd./Alamy;

133 (br): Julien Behal/AP Photos; 134 (tl): George Thompson/KRT/Newscom.

Chapter 7: Page 138 (c): dotshock/Shutterstock; 140 (tl): Syda Productions/Shutterstock; 140 (br): Andersen Ross/Stockbyte/Getty Images; 141 (br): Jiri Vavricka/Shutterstock; 142 (t): Scott Adams, Inc/United Media/United Feature Syndicate, Inc; 143 (tl): Z.H.CHEN/Shutterstock; 144 (br): Everett Collection; 145 (tr): Domenico Tondini/Alamy; 145 (bl): Stewart Cohen/Blend Images/Getty Images; 146 (br): jennyt/Shutterstock; 149 (tr): Waterlilies, 1908 (oil on canvas), Monet, Claude (1840–1926)/Private Collection/Photo © Christie's Images/The Bridgeman Art Library; 150 (br): Christopher Futcher/Getty Images; 152 (br): Bluster the Bulldog.

Chapter 8: Page 158 (c): HBO/talesfromtheorgantrade.com; 159 (bl): marcorubino/Fotolia; 161 (tl): NASA Goddard Space Flight Center/NASA Images; 162 (cr): Sara Caldwell/The Augusta Chronicle/ZUMAPRESS.com/Newscom; 164 (br): STR/AFP/Getty Images/Newscom; 166 (bl): Paramount Pictures/Photos 12/Alamy; 166 (br): John Parrot/Stocktrek Images, Inc/Alamy; 168 (cr): AF archive/Alamy; 168 (br): Everett Collection; 169 (br): Post Courier/File/AP Images; 171 (tl): John M. Heller/Getty Images Entertainment/Getty Images; 172 (br): Werner Dieterich/Alamy.

Chapter 9: Page 174 (c): Stephen Goodwin/Alamy; 176 (cl): Peter Macdiarmid/Getty Images; 177 (bl): Shane Hansen/Getty Images; 178 (tl): RYAN C. HENRIKSEN/MCT/Newscom; 178 (bl): OJO Images Ltd/Alamy; 178 (tr): Gertan/Shutterstock; 178 (cr): Gert Hochmuth/Shutterstock; 179 (br): Karl Naundorf/Shutterstock; 180 (bl): StonePhotos/Shutterstock; 181 (br): Brand X Pictures/Getty Images; 182 (tl): Ilene MacDonald/Alamy; 183 (br): Rob Byron/Fotolia; 184 (tl): DragonImages/Fotolia; 186 (bl): Salvador Manaois III/Fotolia; 187 (cr): Photos 12/Alamy; 188 (tr): Pearson Education; 189 (cr): Everett Collection.

Chapter 10: Page 193 (c): TDway/Shutterstock; 195 (tl): LAURENTIU GAROFEANU/BARCROFT/Barcroft Media/Landov; 195 (br): Blend Images/Alamy; 197 (bl): Terry Moore/Stocktrek Images, Inc./Alamy; 197 (tr): mertcan/Shutterstock; 198 (tr): Johner Images/Alamy; 199 (tl): Courtesy of Tim Elliot; 200 (tr): studioVin/Shutterstock; 200 (tl): Vanessa Nel/Shutterstock; 201 (c): Dynamic Graphics Group/Jupiter Images; 202 (tr): John Wollwerth/Shutterstock; 203 (br): Africa Studio/Fotolia; 204 (tl): Rita Kochmarjova/Shutterstock; 204 (cl): DAVID FURST/AFP/Getty Images; 204 (c): HARAZ N. GHANBARI/UPI/Landov; 204 (cr): Jim McIsaac/Staff/Getty Images Sport/Getty Images; 204 (tr): AP Photo/Mel Evans; 205 (b): Scott Adams/Universal UClick; 206 (tr): Bas Czerwinski/AP Images; 206 (tl): Courtesy of Kent Dolasky; 207 (tl): The Washington Post/Getty Images; 208 (tr): Hill Street Studios/Blend Images/Alamy; 209 (bl): Kevin Winter/DCNYRE2010/Getty Images; 209 (br): Miami Beach Police Dept/Handout/Reuters; 211 (tr): Steven Lam/Taxi/

Text Credits

critical thinking – Mill to Zinn. Feb. 12, 2014. http://www.procon. org/view.resource.php?resourceID=005439; **32:** Supreme Court of the United States, "Burwell, Secretary of HHS et al. v Hobby Lobby Stores, Inc.; **33:** From Romero, Simon and Shahriari, Sara, "A food's gloabal success creates a quandary at home" *New York Times*, March 20, 2011, p. A6; **37:** Mark Twain; **37:** By permission. From Merriam-Webster's Online, by Merriam-Webster, Inc. (www. Merriam-Webster.com).

Chapter 3: Page 41: "Cochelle, "Dedication of the Heart" found in Lucile Davis, Cesar Chavez *Cesar Chavez: A Photo-illustrated Biography*, Capstone (1998); **41:** Women in America, US Government, the White House, March 2011) http://www.white-house.gov/sites/default/files/rss_viewer/Women_in_America. pdf; **42:** Sylvia Earle, quoted in Cindy Griffin (2014), Invitation to Public Speaking - National Geographic Edition. Cengage Learning; **44:** Arthur W. Chickering and Linda Reisser, *Education and Identity*, 2nd ed. (San Francisco: Jossey-Bass, 1993). Arthur Chickering's model and other approaches are discussed in *Student Development in College: Theory, Research, and Practice* by Nancy J. Evans, Deanna S. Forney, and Florence M. Guido. (San Francisco: Jossey-Bass, John Wiley & Son, 2009); **46:** From The Yogi Book: I really didn't say everything I said! Reprinted by permission of LTD Enterprises, a Berra Family Corporation; **47:** Lyubomirsky, Sonja, *The How of Happiness: A New Approach to Getting the Life You Want* (The Penguin Press, 2007); **48:** Albert Schweitzer; **49:** Lions for Lambs, screenplay by Matthew Michael Carnahan, MGM/United Artists, 2007; **50:** Associated Press, Feb 8, 2014, "Mass college man-in-undies sculpture causes stir."; **51:** Japanese Proverb; **52:** Juvenal: Decimi Junii Juvenalis Saturae XIII, the Satires of Juvenal, edited for the use of schools with notes, introduction and appendices by E. G. Hardy. (London, Macmillan and co., 1886); **53:** Can a Soda Tax Save Us From Ourselves? From *The New York Times*, June 5, 2010 © 2010 *The New York Times*. All rights reserved. Used by permission and protected by the Copyright Laws of the United States. The printing, copying, redistribution, or retransmission of this Content without express written permission is prohibited. www.nytimes.com; **57:** Oprah Winfery; **59:** "Rainn Wilson explores 'life's big questions'" *Salon.com*, December 15, 2012; **61:** Paul Tillich; **62:** Albert Einstein.

Chapter 4: Page 72: My Cousin Vinny, Palo Vista Productions, dir. Jonathan Lynn, writ. Dale Launer, perf. Joe Pesci, Ralph Macchio, and Marisa Tomei. 1992; **74:** First Amendment; **75:** Page 1062, "The Constitution of the United States of America Analysis and Interpretation." U.S. Government Printing Office, Washington DC, 2013. (Includes analysis of cases decided by the Supreme Court of the United States to June 26, 2013.). Prepared by the Congressional Research Service, Library of Congress. Kenneth R. Thomas Editor-In-Chief; **75:** Roger Fisher, William L. Ury, and Bruce Patton, Getting to Yes: Negotiating Agreement Without Giving In (New York: Penguin Books, 1983); **77:** Dawkins, Richard. The God Delusion. Houghton Mifflin Harcourt. (www.hmhco.com) iBooks; **78:** Margaret Wheatley, It's An Interconnected World, Shambhala Sun, April 2002; **79:** California Department of Motor Vehicles, 25 Aug. 2009 http://www.dmv.ca.gov/pubs/vctop/d11/vc23152. htm; **81:** Based on New global index exposes 'modern slavery' worldwide," BBC World News, Oct. 17, 2013; **84:** Tariq Ramadan, The power of counterpower. *Gulf News* September 4, 2012; **85:** Pinker, S. *The Wall Street Journal*, "Why Violence is Vanishing," Sept. 24, 2011; **85:** © 2013, "Today I Will Be," Jerome Jesse Facione. Feb. 25, 2014. http://hellopoetry.com/jerome-facione/; **86:** The National Science Foundation.

Chapter 5: Page 89: "Parents' Guide to Childhood Immunization," Centers for Disease Control and Prevention, 22 June 2009 http://www.cdc.gov/vaccines/pubs/parents-guide/default.htm; **107:** Source: The mapping conventions presented here are drawn from Peter A. Facione and Noreen C. Facione, Thinking and Reasoning in Human Decision Making: The Method of Argument and Heuristic Analysis (Millbrae, CA: The California Academic Press, 2007). That book offers additional conventions that enable the analyst to display the reasoning relationships (logical or statistical inferences) or the heuristic relationships (satisficing, association, anchoring with adjustment, etc.) that connect the reasons and claims; **109:** Source: PBS Web site highlights the May 4, 2010 Frontline broadcast, "College Inc."

Chapter 6: Page 115: "Anonymous online critics must be identified, says court," *BBC News–Technology*. January 13, 2014; **115:** "Yelp admits that a quarter of reviews submitted could be fake," *BBC News–Technology*, September 27, 2013. This story was prompted by a sting operation by the Brooklyn city attorney's office, which set up a fake yogurt shop. Search optimization firms were found to be paying freelance writers to make up fake reviews. These firms sell their services to small businesses to help them be found in Internet searches and thus attract more business. Except this yogurt shop did not exist. See "Fake yogurt shop snares 'astroturf' online reviewers," *BBC—Business*. September 24, 2013. Nineteen firms were fined a total of $350,000; **117:** "Expert," Wikipedia, the Free Encyclopedia, 27 Jul. 2009 http://en.wikipedia.org/wiki/Expertise; **118:** Janet Yellen. The Magazine of the HAAS school of business at the University of California. Berkeley HAAS Fall 2012 from A Force at the Fed" by Russ Mitchell"; **121:** Pope Francis, Inconsistency of Pastors and faithful undermines Church's credibility, News.va 15 April 2013; **122:** Senator Richard Durbin on Sunday, February 23rd, 2014 in an interview on "Fox News Sunday"; **122:** Gov. Paul LePage on Monday, October 14th, 2013 in a speech in Falmouth, Maine; **122:** Hemant Mehta on Tuesday, March 11th, 2014 in a blog post; **122:** Matt Bevin, on Wednesday, February 19th, 2014 in a television ad; **122:** "Ann Coulter, "Democrats to America: We Own the Government!" October 9, 2013; **122:** President Obama on Monday, November 4th, 2013 in a speech to Organizing for Action. White House; **122:** John Boehner on Thursday, March 13th, 2014 in a press conference; **122:** Americans for Prosperity on Monday, March 17th, 2014 in a political ad; **124:** From The Southern Poverty Law Center's Intelligence Report. Reprinted by permission; **124:** Hate Map, Southern Poverty Law Center; **128:** (c) Pearson Education, Inc.: **132:** Secretary of State John Kerry, January 2012. Reported in the Executive Summary of the International Religious Freedom Report for 2012. US Department of State, Bureau of Democracy, Human Rights and Labor; **132:** Aaron Sorkin, "The Newsroom" (pilot), HBO Entertainment, 2012; **132:** Benjamin Edelman, "Red Light States: Who Buys Online Adult Entertainment?" Journal of Economic Perspectives, 23(1) (Winter 2009): 209–220; **132:** Anthony Peckham (screenplay), Invictus, Warner Bros., 2009; **133:** Steven Miller Design Studio, 27 Jul. 2009. http://www.stevenmill-erdesignstudio.com/.

Chapter 7: Page 141: Byrne, Robert, 1988. 1911 Best things anybody ever said (New York: Fawcett Columbine); **142:** Yogi Berra, *You Can Observe A Lot By Watching: What I've Learned About Teamwork From the Yankees and Life*. John Wiley & Sons, 2009; **145:** "National Safety Council Calls for Nationwide Ban on Cell Phone Use While Driving," National Safety Council, 27 Jul. 2009 http://www.nsc.org/news/cellphone_ban.aspx; **155:** Paraphrased from the novel, Rough Country, John Sandford (New York: Putnam's, 2009); **156:** Allen J, Schad M, Oudekerk B, Chango J. What Ever Happened to the "Cool" Kids? Long-Term Sequelae of Early Adolescent Pseudomature Behavior. Child Development. 2014.

Chapter 8: **Page 160:** Sagan, C., Cosmos: A Personal Voyage. Episode 1, "The Shores of the Cosmic Ocean." September 28, 1980; **161:** Aristotle, Metaphysics, 1802, Cambridge, Mass.: Harvard University Press; **167:** Sherlock Holmes -The Sign of Four, Chapter 1: "The Science of Deduction." URL http://www.sherlockholmesquotes.com/Sherlock-Holmes-on-Deduction-and-Deductive-Reasoning.html; **168:** Condensed from Monty Python and the Holy Grail Scene 5: "She's a Witch," 1975.

Chapter 9: **Page 181:** Nurses' Health Study Newsletter Volume 16 (2009); **181:** Liu et al. Pediatrics. 2012; 129(5):e1192–8. Nurses' Health Study Newsletter Volume 20 (2013); **182:** *Little Journeys to the Homes of Great Teachers* by Elbert Hubbard (New York: Roycrafters), 1908; **185:** Sabra, Abdelhamid I. "Ibn al-Haytham | Harvard Magazine Sep-Oct 2003." http://harvardmagazine.com/2003/09/ibn-al-haytham-html; **192:** Real Time with Bill Maher, HBO. July 24, 2009.

Chapter 10: **Page 197:** Croskerry, P. "Audio Interview," *New England Journal of Medicine*, 2013. 368: 2445-2448. June 27, 2013; **207:** MALCOLM X, Quoted in Propaganda Review, Spring 1989; **214:** Based on Zuawski, D., Wicklander, D, et al., *Practical Aspects of Interview and Interrogation*, Second edition. CRC Press: Boca Raton. 2002.

Chapter 11: **Page 222:** The interview was conducted with the woman's informed consent and under a protocol approved by the Human Subjects Research Review Board of a major medical research university. The interview was audiotaped, again with the woman's full knowledge and consent. The interview excerpt and the associated decision map are published in Noreen C. Facione and Peter A. Facione, Thinking and Reasoning in Human Decision Making (San Jose, CA: The California Academic Press, 2007), 108–111. Used with permission; **225:** *A Treasury of Winston Churchill's Wit* By Kay Halle, Cleveland, OH: World Publishing Company 1966 Pg. 308; **226:** Henry Montgomery, "From Cognition to Action: The Search for Dominance in Decision Making," *Process and Structure in Human Decision Making*, Eds. Henry Montgomery and Ola Svenson (Chichester, UK: John Wiley & Sons, 1989) 24; **228:** John Sandford, *Mortal Prey*. New York: G.P. Putnam's Sons, ©2002; **231:** Croskerry, P., Singhai, G., & Mamede, S., "Cognitive debiasing 2: impediments t and strategies for change," BMJ Quality & Safety. First published online August 30, 2013. October 2013, Vol. 22. Supplement 2.

Chapter 12: **Page 240:** Excerpts from Mike Wallace and US Air Force General Brent Scowcrost, *Ethics in America: Under Orders, Under Fire*, (part 1). Copyright © 1989 by Columbia University Seminars on Media and Society; **243:** Osen, L.M., *Women in Mathematics*. Cambridge, MA: MIT Press, 1974, pp. 21–32; **243:** Paraphrased from Cosmos: A Space Time Odyssey. FOX Television. Season 1, Episode 2. "When Knowledge Conquered Fear," March 23, 2014; **244:** T. Franklin, *Crooked Letter, Crooked Letter*, (New York: Harper Perennial, 2010) 251; **245:** Carolyn Lochhead and Carla Marinucci, "Freedom and Fear Are at War," *The San Francisco Chronicle*, 21 Sept. 2001, 1 Sept. 2009 http://www.sfgate.com/cgibin/article.cgi?f=/c/a/2001/09/21/MN48614.DTL; **245:** Allen Newell, *Toward Unified Theories of Cognition*(Cambridge, MA: Harvard University Press, 1990); **246:** Sun Tzu, *The Art of War*. April 29, 2014, http://www.goodreads.com/work/quotes/3200649—s-nz-b-ngf; **251:** Sigmund Freud. *New Introductory Lectures on Psychoanalysis*, trans. and ed. by James Strachey (New York: W.W. Norton, 1965). p. 72.

Chapter 13: **Page 261:** Public document - ruling on the case of M. Kendall Wright, et al. v. State of Arkansas, et al. Circuit Court of Pulaski County, Arkansas. Second Division. Case No. 60CV-13-2662; **264:** "Lutherans Accept Clergy in 'Lifelong' Same-Sex Relationships," CNN.com, 21 Aug. 2009, 2 Sept. 2009. http://www.cnn.com/2009/US/08/21/lutheran.gays/index.htm Copyright © 2009 CNN; **272:** BrainyQuote, Albert Einstein quote. May 9, 2014. http://www.brainyquote.com/quotes/quotes/a/alberteins143096.html; **274:** "Thomas Jefferson Quotes," Brainy Quote, 2 Sept. 2009; **276:** "Galileo Galilei," Wisdom Quotes, 2 Sept. 2009; **276:** Paul's First Letter to the Corinthians, verse 13 (King James Version).

Chapter 14: **Page 285:** Signy, H. Exclusive Interview with Professor Elizabeth Blackburn, Reader's Digest Asia, July 30, 2010; **286:** "Classic Quotes," The Quotations Page, 3 Sept. 2009 http://www.quotationspage.com/quote/24972.html; **286:** "Quotes on Education," Solina Quotes, 3 Sept. 2009 http://isgwww.cs.uni-magdeburg.de/~graham/quotes/sciencefaves.html; **287:** Johns Hopkins Medical Institutions. "A Little Telomerase Isn't Enough: Study Links Length Of Chromosome Ends To A Rare Disease Of Stem Cells." ScienceDaily. 23 December 2005. www.sciencedaily.com/releases/2005/12/051223122747.htm; **289:** "Galileo Galilei Quotes," Brainy Quote, 3 Sept. 2009 http://www.brainyquote.com/quotes/authors/g/galileo_galilei.html; **297:** "Quotations by author: Hippocrates," The Quotations Page, 3 Sept. 2009 http://www.quotationspage.com/quotes/Hippocrates; **297:** The Immortals" episode of the FOX Television 2014 series Cosmos – A Space Time Odyssey, May 18, 2014.

Chapter 15: **Page 312:** http://www.collegeboard.com/student/apply/essayskills/9406.html. But, if you end up on the home page for the College Board, simply put "write essay" into the search box there; **313:** Orwell, G. Essay, "Politics and the English Language," 1946; **313:** http://en.wikiquote.org/wiki/Thomas_Edison; **318:** Gail Gradowski; **320:** Judy A. Bernstein; **322–323:** © 2011 Gittens, C.A., & Measured Reasons LLC. Reprinted with permission of the authors and Measured Reasons LLC. www.measuredreasons.com.

Chapter 16: **Page 331:** Vivek Wadhwa on Ethics, BrainyQuote, May 19, 2014; **338:** Sidney Piburn, *The Dalai Lama, a policy of kindness: An anthology of writings by and about the Dalai Lama*. Ithaca, N.Y., USA: Snow Lion Publications, ©1990.

Index